GENERAL HASTINGS 'PUG' ISMAY

JOHN KISZELY

General Hastings 'Pug' Ismay

Soldier, Statesman, Diplomat
A New Biography

HURST & COMPANY, LONDON

First published in the United Kingdom in 2024 by
C. Hurst & Co. (Publishers) Ltd.,
New Wing, Somerset House, Strand, London, WC2R 1LA
Copyright © John Kiszely, 2024
All rights reserved.

The right of John Kiszely to be identified
as the author of this publication is asserted by him in accordance
with the Copyright, Designs and Patents Act, 1988.

A Cataloguing-in-Publication data record for this book
is available from the British Library.

ISBN: 9781911723202

Printed in the United Kingdom by Bell & Bain Ltd, Glasgow

www.hurstpublishers.com

CONTENTS

Acknowledgements   vii

List of Illustrations   ix

Maps   xi

Abbreviations Used in the Text   xv

Preface   xvii

1. A Child of the Raj: 1887–1914   1

2. Somaliland: 1914–20   13

3. Apprenticeship: 1920–36   25

4. Corridors of Power: 1936–40   43

5. The Fall of France, The Battle of Britain, The Blitz: 1940–41   63

6. Discord and Harmony: 1941   85

7. 'The Trough of the War': 1942   103

8. 'Conference Year': 1943   121

9. 'The Year of Destiny': 1944   139

10. From War to Peace: 1945–46   161

11. Ismay's War   181

12. Partition—Making the Plan: January–June 1947   199

13. Partition—Implementation and Outcome: 221
    June–December 1947

14. Interlude: 1948–52   245

15. Secretary General: 1952–57   267

16. Sunset: 1957–65   293

CONTENTS

17. Epilogue   309

Appendix A: Commandant's Report—Staff College, Quetta, 1922   317
Appendix B: Dieppe   319
Appendix C: 'Rules for the Conduct of NATO'   327
Appendix D: Letter from Eisenhower to Ismay, 14 January 1959   329
Abbreviations Used in the Notes   331
Notes   333
Bibliography   387
Index   405

ACKNOWLEDGEMENTS

There are many people to whom I owe huge thanks for their help in the production of this book.

At the outset I would like to thank Professor Sir Hew Strachan for his encouragement, advice and guidance throughout.

In the course of my four years of full-time research I received much support and a highly efficient service from the staff of all the libraries and archives that I consulted: first and foremost, the Liddell Hart Centre for Military Archives at King's College London, where Ismay's papers are held; if I gave the staff there a pound for every document that I ordered from them (many twice) they would all be rich beyond the dreams of avarice. By the same token, others who would also be considerably better off are the staff of: the Joint Services Staff College library at the Defence Academy, Shrivenham; the National Archives at Kew, London; the Bodleian Library, Oxford; the libraries of All Souls College, Balliol College, Nuffield College and Pembroke College at the University of Oxford; the British Library, London; the Cadbury Research Library at the University of Birmingham; the Churchill Archives at Churchill College, University of Cambridge; the Hartley Library, University of Southampton; the John Rylands Library, University of Manchester; the Imperial War Museum, London; the National Army Museum, London; Royal Military Academy Sandhurst archives; Charterhouse School archives; the NATO Archives, Brussels; the Houghton Library, University of Harvard; the Eisenhower Library, Abilene, Kansas; and the United States Army Heritage and Education Center, Carlisle, Pennsylvania.

I am hugely grateful to the following who read all or part of my manuscript and provided invaluable comment: Air Vice Marshal David Brook, Nigel de Lee, Dr Jonathan Fennell, Dr Rob Johnson, Professor Richard Overy, Professor Jane Ridley, Professor Jamie Shea, Michael Watson, Lt General Sir Barney White-Spunner and Dr Robin Woolven.

ACKNOWLEDGEMENTS

I would like to thank the staff at Hurst, particularly: Michael Dwyer; my managing editor, Mei Jayne Yew; and production director Daisy Leitch. And my thanks to Barbara Taylor for the excellent maps. Others who went out of their way to provide assistance were Christopher Beaumont, Rob Hutton, Philippa McEwan, Allen Packwood, Tom Walker and Professor Mitchell Yockelson.

My thanks also to members of Ismay's family for their assistance: Viscount Allendale; the Hon. Sarah, the late Viscountess Allendale; James Evetts; John Evetts; Jane Finnis; George Harbord-Hamond; the late Hon. Mary Seymour; and Patricia Smyly.

Finally, I am eternally grateful to my wife, Arabella, for her forbearance during the writing of this book, and for her love.

LIST OF ILLUSTRATIONS

1. Ismay with parents and family, 1900. Courtesy of Patricia Smyly.

2. On 'Drummer Boy', 1909. Courtesy of Patricia Smyly.

3. The officers of the 21st Cavalry, 1912. Courtesy of Patricia Smyly.

4. Somaliland. Copyright Michael Runkel/robertharding.

5. Somaliland Camel Corps. National Archives/Spaarnestad Collection/Life. Photographer unknown.

6. Ismay in a group near Shimber Berris, 1915. Courtesy of James Evetts.

7. "A feeling of being trapped in a sideshow…," 1915. Courtesy of James Evetts.

8. Cheltenham polo tournament, 1934. Courtesy of James Evetts.

9. Portrait by Anthony Devas, 1938. Courtesy of James Evetts.

10. With Newall and Dill, 1940. Keystone/Stringer via Getty Images.

11. With the Defence Committee, 1941. © Imperial War Museum (HU 3207).

12. Three days before the fall of Singapore, 1942. Popperfoto via Getty Images.

13. Portrait by Oswald Birley, 1943. Courtesy of Cheltenham Borough Council. Photographed by www.mouseabouttown.co.uk.

14. At the White House, June 1943. © Imperial War Museum (A 17107).

15. With Bracken and Mary Churchill, August 1943. © Imperial War Museum (H 32957).

LIST OF ILLUSTRATIONS

16. With Brooke in Canada, August 1943. © Imperial War Museum (H 31811).

17. Portrait by Augustus John, 1944. Courtesy of George Harbord-Hamond.

18. Chiefs of Staff Committee meeting, April 1945. Jack Esten/Stringer via Getty Images.

19. With Churchill and the Chiefs of Staff, May 1945. © Imperial War Museum (TR 2842).

20. Ismay on VE Day, May 1945. © Imperial War Museum (TR 2839).

21. With Mountbatten, Nehru and Jinnah, June 1947. Keystone-France/Gamma-Rapho via Getty Images.

22. With family at Wormington Grange, 1948. Courtesy of Patricia Smyly.

23. Ismay and Eisenhower, 1951. HQ NATO FRA-4433.

24. The Secretary General, 1952. Photograph by Yousuf Karsh, Camera Press London.

25. Ismay and Darry outside their Paris home, 1953. HQ NATO 00783-11.

26. Ismay and Darry's Christmas card, 1955. Courtesy of Jane Finnis.

27. With grandsons, 1959. Courtesy of James Evetts.

28. With Clementine Churchill, House of Lords, 1965. Evening Standard/Stringer via Getty Images.

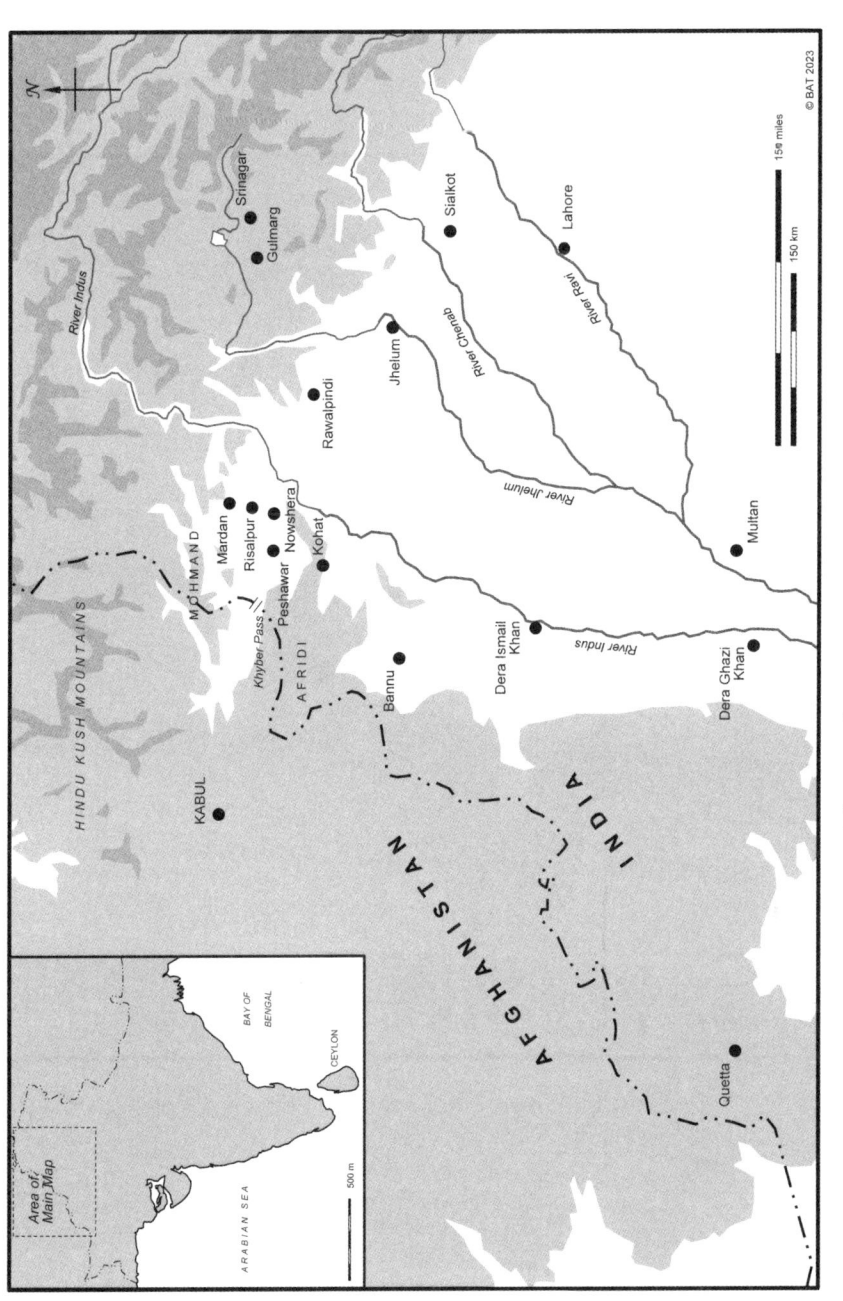

1. The North-West Frontier, 1910

2. Before Partition: British India and the Princely States

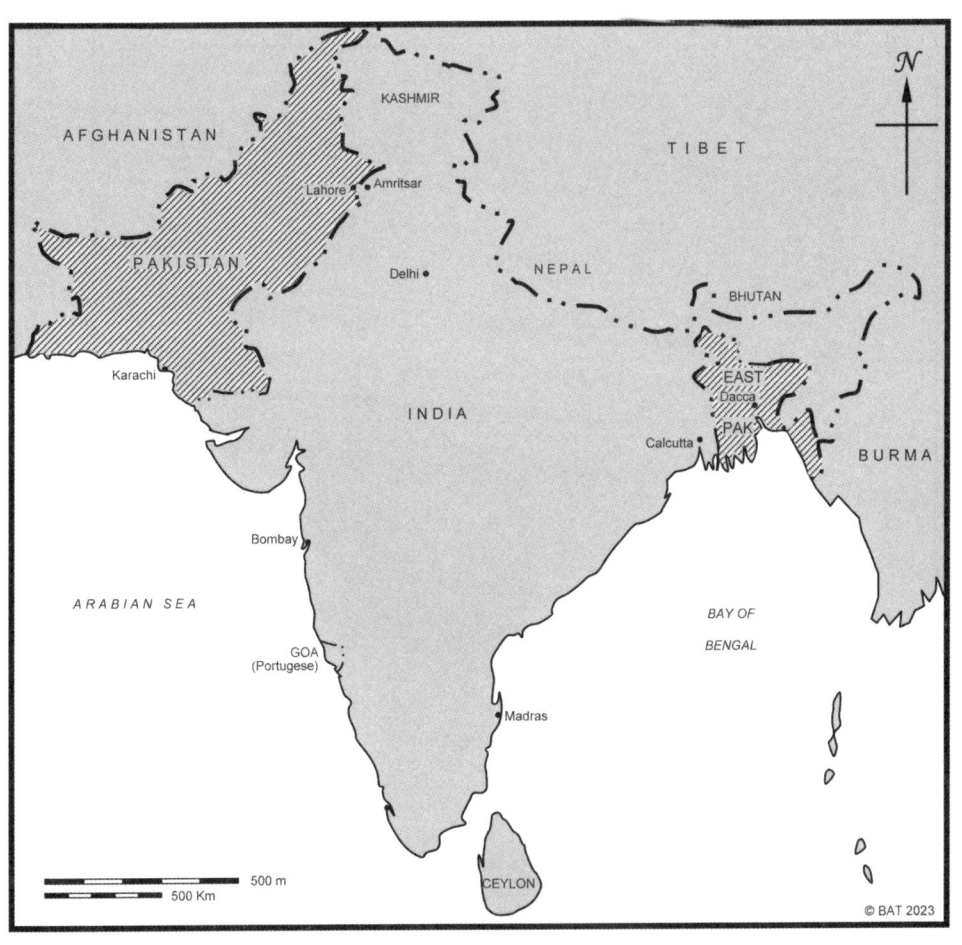

3. After Partition: India and Pakistan

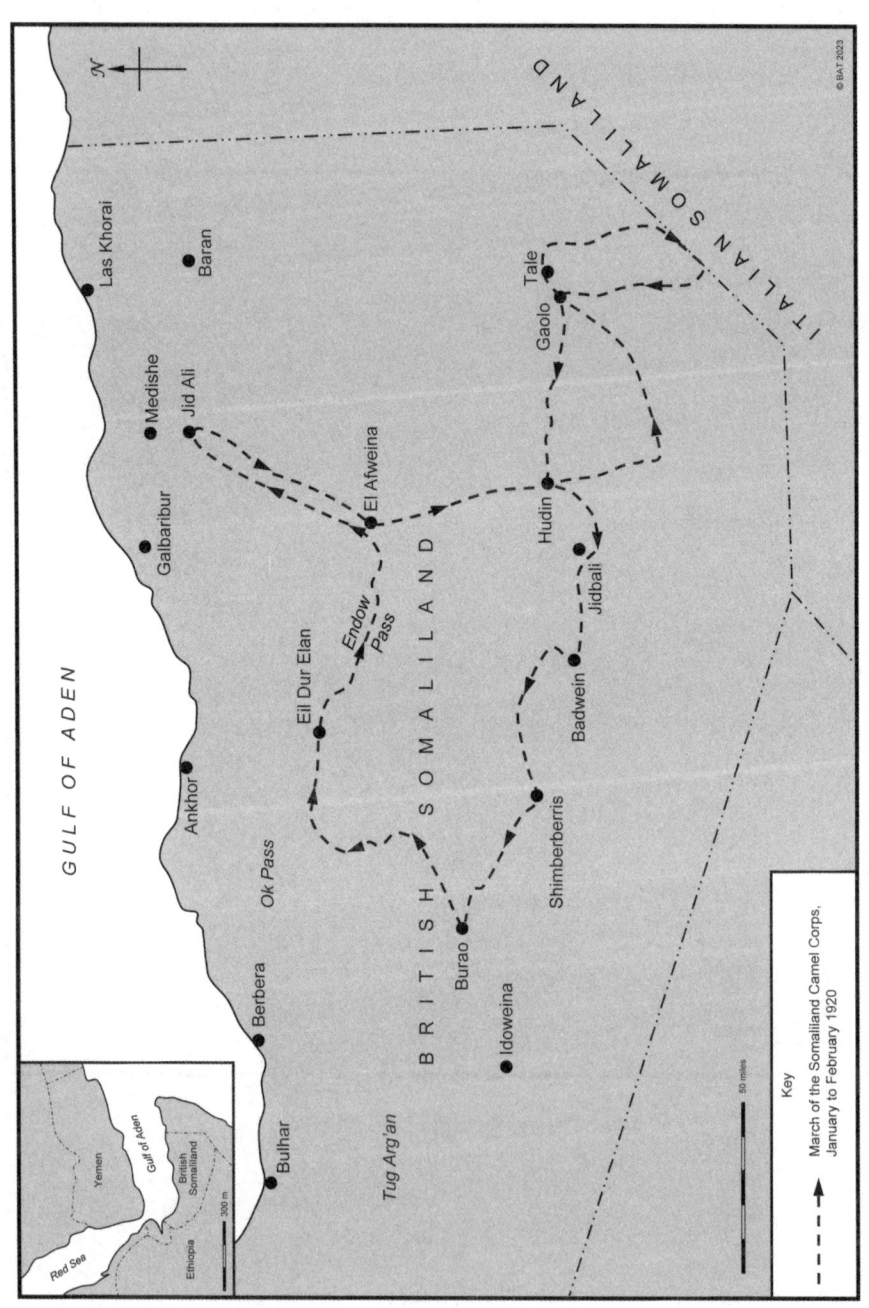

GULF OF ADEN

ITALIAN SOMALILAND

BRITISH SOMALILAND

Las Khorai
Baran
Medishe
Jid Ali
Galbaribur
El Afweina
Tale
Gaolo
Hudin
Endow Pass
Eil Dur Elan
Jidbali
Badwein
Ankhor
Ok Pass
Shimberberris
Berbera
Burao
Idoweina
Tug Arg'an
Bulhar

Gulf of Aden
Yemen
British Somaliland
Red Sea
Ethiopia
300 m

Key

March of the Somaliland Camel Corps,
January to February 1920

50 miles

© BAT 2023

4. British Somaliland

ABBREVIATIONS USED IN THE TEXT

CID: Committee of Imperial Defence

CIGS: Chief of the Imperial General Staff

CinC: Commander-in-Chief

DSO: Distinguished Service Order

EDC: European Defence Council

GCB: Knight Grand Cross of the Order of the Bath

NATO: North Atlantic Treaty Organization

PC: Privy Counsellor

RAF: Royal Air Force

SIS: Secret Intelligence Service

Note: All emphasis shown in quoted text appears in the document quoted.

PREFACE

On 6 April 1982, at the very start of the Anglo-Argentine Falklands conflict, former British Prime Minister Harold Macmillan called on the incumbent Prime Minister Margaret Thatcher to offer advice on the management of the war. 'You will need a Pug Ismay', he told her.[1] Wags have suggested that her first response was 'What is a pugismay?' Although undoubtedly apocryphal, the story illustrates that General 'Pug' Ismay was not exactly a household name at the time, let alone today. Those people who have heard of him will probably have done so because of his wartime connection with Winston Churchill; but few of them would probably be able to specify anything that he, himself, actually did. In the many books about Churchill's wartime leadership Ismay is almost always portrayed as a background figure—part of the furniture—and in documentaries and films sometimes gets a walk-on part but almost never a speaking one.

Yet Ismay was an important figure in twentieth-century British history. In the 1930s, as Deputy Secretary and later Secretary of the Committee of Imperial Defence, he had a key role in the formulation of defence policy, strategy and the preparations for the Second World War. As wartime chief staff officer to Prime Minister Winston Churchill, he became a close confidant and rarely left his side, whether in Britain or abroad at international conferences. He was instrumental in conciliating the sometimes fractious relationship between Churchill and the Service Chiefs of Staff. As chief of staff to the Viceroy, Lord Mountbatten, in India in 1947, he was at the centre of the dramatic events of Partition. When Churchill returned to power in 1951, he appointed Ismay as one of his Cabinet ministers. And from 1952 to 57 Ismay was the first Secretary General of NATO, widely recognised for his contribution to the establishment of Alliance unity and cohesion. He also played a central role in reshaping the higher management of defence in Britain and in the creation of the Ministry of Defence.[2]

Yet accounts, even brief ones, of his life are few and far between. There are just three. Two are short biographies. The first, Ronald Wingate's *Lord Ismay: A Life*, was published in 1970.[3] Wingate was an old friend and wholehearted admirer of Ismay, having worked on his staff for two years during the war. His book is a generous and heartwarming tribute to an old friend who, in his eyes, could do no wrong. Although Wingate had access to Ismay's papers, now held in the archives of King's College London, and had the benefit of numerous conversations with his widow, he did not have access to any of the official wartime documents at the Public Record Office (now the National Archives) since these were withheld under the thirty-year rule. Nor did he have access to NATO's official records. Unfortunately, the book is completely unreferenced and thus unverifiable. The second book is Andrew Sangster's *Pug – Churchill's Chief of Staff*, published in 2023.[4] The book focuses particularly on Ismay's role in the Second World War and his relationship with Churchill. Its author draws heavily on Wingate's biography, the papers at King's College London, the testimony of some of Ismay's wartime contemporaries, and on the third account of Ismay's life: *The Memoirs of Lord Ismay*.

The memoirs, published in 1960, are problematic. Ismay writes with characteristic discretion and self-deprecating modesty, making practically no claims to any personal achievement whatsoever, happy to write rather as Boswell to Churchill's Dr Johnson. But a greater problem is that they were written in the immediate aftermath of the publication of several sensationalist autobiographies and diaries of other wartime generals: in particular, Arthur Bryant's two books—*The Turn of the Tide* and *Triumph in the West*—based on the, at times, vituperative diaries of Field Marshal Lord Alanbrooke, former Chief of the Imperial General Staff.[5] Publication of the diaries appeared to Ismay to be a betrayal of his hero, Churchill, and he was determined that his own memoirs would redress the balance. Moreover, Ismay, who had spent the whole of his career smoothing out fractious relationships, achieving reconciliation and harmony and resolving disputes, carried this approach into his memoirs, sometimes at the expense of the truth. For example, 'The War Cabinet was a band of brothers and… relations between Churchill and his official advisers, both civilian and military, were characterised by mutual understanding, esteem and affection'.[6] Furthermore, a comparison of the early drafts with the published version shows that he edited out anything that could be considered contentious or might give offence to any of his readers. Taking statements in the memoirs at face value can, therefore, be misleading.

The Ismay papers at King's College also need to be treated with caution. Because the collection is voluminous there is a temptation to believe that it is comprehensive. It is not. There are important papers and correspondence elsewhere, for example at the National Archives at Kew, the Churchill Archives at Cambridge, the Imperial War Museum in London, and the NATO archives in Belgium. There are family papers, some of them sensitive, which Ismay's widow chose not to donate to King's College. There is the correspondence with some of his closest confidants which Ismay chose not to include among his papers; these can only be found in the collections of his correspondents. Moreover, some of Ismay's letters in the King's College collection give a false picture of his views or feelings. For example, from time to time during the Second World War he wrote to colleagues deployed overseas, or to influential American friends, with an update on the progress of the war. These tend to be optimistic outlooks, glossing over contentious issues and personal disputes, and often do not replicate the opinions that he was communicating privately to his closest friends, as evidenced in their diaries. Finding out what Ismay really thought about events and people at any one time thus requires much painstaking, detailed research.

There thus is a gap in the historiography for a biography that takes these points into account, that results from greater breadth and depth of research, and that is therefore able to present a fuller picture of its subject. This book sets out to do just that. Drawing on all these sources and many others it tells the story of Ismay's life. Rather than reiterate the narrative of circumstances well told by historians it restricts background to that required to provide the necessary context. It describes the major events and influences that shaped his life as well as those important events in which he was an actor or witness. It analyses the key decisions that he took, the influence that he carried, and the impact that he made. It also aims to assess what Ismay was and what he was not, to provide a portrait of him, and to place him in the context of the history of his time.

The result shows that in all his senior appointments Ismay had an influence out of all proportion to the authority invested in the appointment. His achievements were far greater than he himself ever claimed, and his personality and character were much more complex and nuanced than previous accounts have concluded.

1

A CHILD OF THE RAJ

1887–1914

In many ways Hastings 'Pug' Ismay was a child of the Raj. His roots were in India and in the British governance of it. His mother had been born there, as had all her six siblings and both of her parents. It was her grandfather James Read, a young officer in the British Army, who had arrived from England in 1810. He served briefly on the staff of the Governor of Bengal, Lord Hastings, whom he greatly admired, so much so that he subsequently named one of his sons after him. That son was to join the elite Indian Civil Service, 'a tiny cadre, a little over a thousand strong [which] ruled more than three hundred million Indians: a fifth of the human race'.[1] He started as an assistant commissioner—a district officer—in the Central Provinces. The responsibilities of district officers were extraordinarily wide-ranging:

> Apart from his duties as chief magistrate and revenue officer, the D[istrict] O[fficer] was responsible for law and order and the implementation of new laws; he was in charge of the police, the jail and the law courts, as well as the treasury, the excise and the records, and he had overall responsibility for forests, roads, schools, hospitals, fences, canals and agriculture.[2]

Hastings Read rose to the position of Deputy Commissioner. As such he was a senior figure in the Central Provinces Civil Service, with its responsibilities for the governance of an area roughly the size of the United Kingdom and a population of some eleven million people.

His daughter, Beatrice, fell in love with—and in 1875 at the age of eighteen married—a twenty-seven-year-old junior district officer by the name of Stanley Ismay. Stanley had been born near Dover in Kent where his father, William (a distant cousin of Thomas Henry Ismay, of *Titanic* renown) was a farmer. Following attendance at Bromsgrove School in Worcestershire, one of Britain's oldest 'public' schools,[3] he had at the age of twenty-one passed the highly competitive Indian Civil Service exam and arrived in India in 1871.[4] He was to have a notably successful career in the legal department of the service, being called to the bar of the Inner Temple at the age of thirty-four, and shortly afterwards becoming a judge in the Central Provinces. He worked his way up through the various levels of courts to become the Judicial Commissioner for Central Provinces and a member of the Viceroy's legislative council. He was to be knighted by King George V at the Delhi Durbar of 1911. India was Stanley Ismay's life: he returned to England only three times in the whole of his forty years' service.

Stanley and Beatrice had four children, the youngest a son born in June 1887 at the beautiful Himalayan hill station of Nainital. They named him Hastings. For the first seven years of his life, young Hastings lived with the family in a British cantonment near the town of Jubbulpore where his father worked, although in the hot summer months Beatrice and the children would escape the heat to live in one of the hill stations.

It was not just by birth that the young Hastings was a child of the Raj. He grew up in a family most of whose members were closely involved in its management and dedicated to its purpose. All six of his maternal aunts and uncles had grown up in India. All still lived there.[5] The family was steeped in the self-perceived institutional ethos and values of the Indian Civil Service: a belief, however mistaken, that they represented civilisation and had a moral duty to share this with, or impose it on, what they saw as the benighted people of the sub-continent. They regarded themselves not as oppressors and exploiters of the people of India, but the very opposite: champions of fairness and defenders of the peasantry against those, such as moneylenders and landlords, who would exploit them.[6] At times they saw themselves, however patronising it might seem today, to be 'protecting the Indians from themselves'.[7] Loyalty—to one's country and one's friends—was a matter of honour; duty was a God-given obligation that was taken for granted. David Gilmour offers an interesting insight into their outlook and aspirations: 'District Officers hoped that they deserved to be called "*Ma-Bap*" ("mother and father"), the traditional appellation with which Indians in their district addressed them when seeking assistance, submitting a grievance or begging release from some penalty. Paternalistic feelings were inherent in their office'.[8] Even at a very young age this outlook would not be lost on a child. Nor was it on Ismay, as would become apparent in adulthood in his perception of the British Empire and in the care with which he treated those for whom he held himself responsible.

In 1895, aged eight, he was (like the sons of most British families in India who could afford it) packed off to boarding school in England. He would see India and most of his family again only twice in the next ten years. That he would experience homesickness would only have been natural, but although he rarely wrote or spoke about it subsequently, the degree of that homesickness may be judged by his admission that in later life he experienced quite severe homesickness whenever he was away from his family.[9]

Young Hastings was lucky, however, with what amounted to a surrogate family. One of his mother's sisters, Mabel, and her family lived at Stratford-upon-Avon in Warwickshire. Mabel had married in India an Indian Army officer, Herbert Mullaly. They had four sons and decided that she would live in England while the boys were at boarding school there, to be joined by him when circumstances permitted. It was with Aunt Mabel that Hastings spent all his school holidays.[10] Two of the sons were slightly older than Hastings, two slightly younger. Hastings got on famously with them all and with his aunt. His holidays there were a time of great happiness. His attachment to the family was to contribute all the more to his sadness when three out of the four boys were killed in the First World War.

In September 1900 Hastings started his time at Charterhouse School in Surrey. As another of the oldest-established public schools, Charterhouse had provided the British Empire with many young men to serve as administrators or army officers and it would not have been unusual for boys at the school to have come from far afield to board there. Hastings seems to have enjoyed his time at Charterhouse. In later life he spoke highly of the school and served on its council. As a schoolboy, he was successful without being distinguished. Academically, he was usually in the top third of his class, sometimes in the top quarter,[11] but in a system where renown within the school rested largely on athletic and sporting prowess, he was disadvantaged by being, throughout his schooldays, very small for his age. The pinnacle of his sporting achievement, for example, was playing regularly for his house football team, but not for the school. He recalled his days at Charterhouse with typical modesty. In thanking a school contemporary who wrote many years later to congratulate him on one of his promotions, he replied, 'My school career was so singularly undistinguished that I was unaware that anybody except my special cronies like yourself... had even remembered my name'.[12]

Perhaps the most significant event for him at Charterhouse was one which, in retrospect, he described as 'a turning point, and a very lucky one, in my life'.[13] Based on his academic performance and results, his housemaster and other teachers confidently expected him to gain a senior scholarship.[14] Not only would this achievement relieve his parents of some of the financial burden of school fees, it would also be an important step on the path to fulfil parental ambition for him to go to Cambridge University and enter the Civil Service. However, against expectation he failed to gain the scholarship. His considerable, initial disappointment was mitigated on reflection by the thought that this mishap might allow him to follow his own ambition: to join the army. It took him over a year to pluck up the courage to tell his parents of his intention, and their reaction fell some way short of unbounded enthusiasm. 'My father was particularly upset at the idea of my joining the Indian Cavalry, and never tired of telling the story about the cavalry officer who was so stupid that even his brother officers noticed it'.[15]

In September 1904, shortly following his seventeenth birthday, Hastings left Charterhouse and started the year-long officer training course at the Royal Military College, Sandhurst. He set his heart on joining the Indian cavalry, not least because its officers did not require the considerable private income required in British cavalry regiments. Competition for a place in the Indian Army, however, was fierce: a cadet needed to pass out in the top third of the order of merit to stand a chance of a place. He applied himself to the task with a determination and sense of purpose which was to characterise his military career. His efforts bore fruit. Out of the 150 officer cadets in his intake he came fourth.[16] Surprisingly, bearing in mind his future prowess on horseback, the one subject which let him down was riding, in which he was clearly a beginner.[17] But for his low mark in that subject he would have passed out even higher; not that he would have been anything other than delighted by his actual result. At the age of eighteen Second Lieutenant Ismay left Sandhurst for India. For those familiar with the tall, burly figure that he was to become, it would be a surprise to learn that at this stage he was, in his own words, 'the smallest officer in the Army'.[18]

As was the custom at the time, officers commissioned into the Indian Army first served an apprenticeship with a British battalion in India and

Ismay was posted to the 1st Battalion, The Gloucestershire Regiment based at Ambala in the Punjab, 100 miles north of Delhi. There he was to learn infantry skills. At the end of his year-long attachment, the cavalry regiment which had accepted him had no immediate vacancy so he was sent on further attachments, firstly to spend six months with an Indian Army infantry regiment, the 33rd Punjabis, followed by three months with a British cavalry regiment, the Carabiniers. Unsurprisingly, Ismay found being what he described as 'a bird of passage' for so long immensely frustrating: he was itching to get to his own regiment.[19] But the delay of almost two years would not have been wasted on him. From the three regiments, each very different, he would have been able to compare and contrast their different organisations, leadership styles, morale, discipline and ways of going about business, and in doing so would have learnt much about what makes a good regiment and a good officer. His attachment to the Carabiniers also provided him with the opportunity to brush up his riding skills.

At last it was time for him to join his own regiment, based at Risalpur on the North-West Frontier, just fifty miles south of the Khyber Pass and the border with Afghanistan (see Map 1). His excitement in doing so is palpable from his account, written many years later, of his arrival.

> I had to travel half across India to get there, and arrived at the officers' mess, unkempt and travel-stained, just as dinner was finishing. The scene is indelibly stamped on my memory. Eight or nine of my future brother officers in our magnificent mess kit of dark blue, scarlet and gold, were seated at the table. Behind them stood the waiters in spotless white muslin, with belts of the regimental colours and the regimental crest on their turbans. The table was decorated with two or three bowls of roses and a few pieces of superbly cleaned silver. On the mantelpiece hung a picture of our Royal Colonel, the late Prince Albert Victor, and the heads of tigers, leopards, markhor and ibex looked down from the walls. The assembled company were all strangers to me, but they made me feel at home from the moment I crossed the threshold. As I went happily to sleep that night, I thanked God for parents who had allowed me to choose my own way of life.[20]

Another officer, an exact contemporary of Ismay, had joined the regiment at the same time. His name was Milo Onslow. The two were to become firm friends. The full title of the regiment that they had joined was 21st Prince Albert Victor's Own Cavalry (Daly's Horse). It had a short but distinguished history. Raised in 1849 by Lieutenant Henry Daly, it was one of the five cavalry regiments formed to guard the North-West Frontier and soon became part of the Punjab Frontier Force, nicknamed the 'Piffers'. During the Indian Mutiny of 1857 (also known as the Indian Rebellion of 1857 or the First War of Independence) the regiment had taken part in both the Siege of Delhi and the Relief of Lucknow. During the Second Anglo-Afghan War of 1878–80 it formed part of the Kandahar Field Force and distinguished itself at the narrowly won Battle of Ahmad Khel. Since then it had taken part in numerous border forays and actions, some of them bloody. It was a source of considerable pride to its members that in 1890 Prince Albert Victor, Queen Victoria's eldest grandson, had consented to become the regiment's Royal Colonel. Like many parts of the army, Indian cavalry regiments vied with each other as to their social status, and acquiring a royal colonel as closely related to the monarch would have been considered quite a catch. Although Prince Albert Victor had died the following year the 21st Cavalry continued to bear his name with undiminished pride.

Like most Indian Army regiments the 21st Cavalry was a composite unit: half the soldiers were Hindu and half were Muslim. It was a system that worked well. Ismay was later to write,

> I cannot recall a single case of communal trouble, or even communal prejudice. If, for example, we were called out in aid of the civil power, the men never hesitated to act against their co-religionists with complete impartiality; it seemed as though all else was subordinated to their common devotion to the regiment and their pride in its traditions.[21]

One of the foundations of the Indian Army's exceptional strength was its success in establishing the primary loyalty of its soldiers to the regiment: thus, to bring the regiment into disrepute was the height of shame. The 21st Cavalry was a family regiment, almost literally: a high proportion of its soldiers were related to each other—being fathers, sons, brothers, and cousins. Further characteristics shared with other units of high quality in the Indian Army were a constant striving for excellence in everything it did, underpinned by a strong sense of duty and by unquestioning trust between officers and men.

Just as the Indian Civil Service possessed its own characteristic institutional ethos, so did the officer corps of the Indian Army. Its ethos was similar to that of the British Army, but even more strongly ensconced since the Indian Army lived in cantonments separate from society, and its officers socialised primarily, some almost exclusively, with other officers—of their own regiment and neighbouring ones. Philip Mason, notable biographer (some would say hagiographer) of the Indian Army, described the code of virtues that underpinned this ethos.

> Courage came first and without that nothing else counted… Fear must not be mentioned. Modesty came next to courage… it was an essential ingredient in good form. To boast or show off was the first thing a subaltern must learn he should never do; it was the mark of a bounder. Devotion to duty came next and with it self-denial which again is not always thought of as a military virtue. But it meant self-denial in war, putting duty before life, putting the welfare of the troops under a man's command before his own comfort, putting a wounded comrade before himself.[22]

And just as one of the determining characteristics of the Indian civil servant was paternalism, typified by the expression *ma bap* (mother and father), so it was for the Indian Army officer, and by the same expression.[23]

Ismay's regiment was also infused with what was called the cavalry spirit, defined by Mason as 'dash, elan, swagger, readiness to engage the enemy at once without counting the cost, [and] a touch of added zest and gaiety that came from their irregular ancestry'. This, Mason suggested, was characterised by 'that peculiarly English affectation of achieving excellence without being seen to try very hard and of not being a specialist [together with] an affectation for eccentricity'.[24]

The 21st Cavalry was to be Ismay's home for the next nine years and from the outset he loved the regiment, its ethos and life in it. He quickly learnt the Pushtu language and took every opportunity to communicate with his men. He enjoyed the company of his brother officers, British and Indian. And like most new arrivals in a cavalry officers' mess he was given a nickname, in his case, one that was to stay with him for the rest of his life. His brother officers clearly saw a facial resemblance to a particularly distinctive and affectionate breed of dog—so, 'Pug' it was.

The day's work started early, usually with squadron or regimental training on horseback—a particular favourite for Ismay—followed by activities such as musketry, lectures or administration. His recollection of one event in the daily routine gives an interesting insight into his character and personality. The event was 'Stables'—the officer's inspection of his troop and their horses in the regimental stables.

It was an ideal opportunity for British officers to get to know more about the men and their horses for which they were responsible. As they passed down the line they could talk with each *sawar* [trooper] on every kind of topic. What was the news of his father or uncle or other regimental pensioner in his village? How were the crops going? His horse's coat was staring; why not see what a little boiled linseed oil would do? The day was coming when I knew every man in the regiment by name and the individual characteristics of practically every horse; and a great deal of this information had been acquired at 'Stables' throughout the years.[25]

Most afternoons were free, and for Ismay, now a keen and adept horseman, the opportunities were boundless.

Most of us played polo three days a week, and schooled ponies on other afternoons.[26] In addition there were occasional race meetings at neighbouring stations, and rough shooting for all who wanted it. I could never help thinking, as I drew my admittedly meagre salary at the end of each month, that it was very odd that I should be paid anything at all for doing what I loved doing above all else.[27]

Apart from work, there was the highly active, if intensely hierarchical, social scene of the Risalpur cantonment: elaborate guest nights in the officers' messes, cocktail parties, dinner parties, tennis parties and dances.[28] All of this was not without cost and a subaltern's monthly officers mess bill would have been somewhat in excess of his monthly pay. Ismay had little or no private income and, to make ends meet, trained polo ponies for other players.[29] But life in Risalpur was far from being entirely a matter of sport and socialising; the Punjab Frontier Force was kept at high readiness for its operational role of policing the border and keeping the peace, if necessary by force. From time to time the 21st Cavalry were deployed at short notice for that purpose. Ismay recalled such an occasion. They were called out during dinner one evening to intercept a raiding party from the Mohmand tribe who had crossed the border and were running amok in the border villages. The cavalry rode through the night and were in position by 4 a.m. To their disappointment the raiders did not put in an appearance and at 10 a.m. they returned to barracks. 'That afternoon several of us drove to Mardan [fifteen miles north of Risalpur], the home of the famous Corps of Guides, to play polo: that night there was a dance at Nowshera [ten miles south of Risalpur]: the next day I was due to ride in two steeplechases'.[30] The cavalry spirit was alive and well.

It was to be in Mohmand country a few months later that Ismay, aged just twenty, was to find himself in combat for the first time. The tribe had continued its incursions and violence on an increasing scale and a large punitive expedition was mounted. A force of three brigades of infantry, some mountain guns and the 21st Cavalry was formed to take part in what became known as the Mohmand Expedition of 1908. The deployment was to last for some six weeks and for the cavalry it involved a series of extended, gruelling patrols in the scorching heat, covering long distances in the mountainous country, opposed by parties of well-armed and determined Mohmand fighters holding the hill crests. Some fifty members of the British force were to be killed; Mohmand casualties were estimated to be almost ten times that number.[31]

Ismay's recollection of one incident again gives a further insight into his character and personality. Within the regiment were a number of Indian officers: the link between the dozen or so British officers and the native rank and file. Most had had at least fifteen years' service before gaining their commissions, had spent their lives on the frontier and seen action on numerous occasions. They were key officers of great quality and Ismay admired and respected them accordingly, particularly the senior Indian officer in his own squadron, Dildar Khan.

> He was a beautiful horseman, had a good eye for country, had fought in three campaigns, and did not know the meaning of the word fear... There was no better troop leader in frontier warfare in any army in the world. He often said that he prayed that he would be with me when I had my first baptism of fire; and before long his prayer was granted. We were riding down a broad valley... when a sudden fusillade was opened on us from the crest of the hills. I looked round to see two or three saddles empty, and Dildar Khan gazing into my eyes as though willing me to do the right thing. I was tempted to retire to a knoll which we had just passed, but remembered Dildar Khan's advice that at the beginning of a fight, before the men were warmed up, it was a good rule to go forwards rather than backwards. I therefore led the troop at a gallop to some rising ground about three hundred yards ahead, and ordered dismounted action. The old warrior did not say a word, but looked rather like a proud father who has watched his son kick a goal in his first football match.[32]

Towards the end of May the Mohmands sued for peace and it was with relief, in the increasingly fierce summer heat, that the British forces withdrew to return to their barracks. Throughout the campaign Ismay had driven himself hard—not for the last time in his life, too hard—and scarcely had the troops crossed back over the border when he collapsed with sunstroke. He was carried into the hospital in Peshawar on a stretcher, unconscious. After several days there he returned to the regiment fully recovered and just in time to celebrate his twenty-first birthday. His reflection on the campaign was typical of him: 'The month in Mohmand country had been always uncomfortable, often boring, and sometimes frightening; but I would not have missed it for the world'.[33] The 21st Cavalry's performance had caught the eye of its superior commanders. In his annual report on the regiment the divisional commander, Lieutenant General James Willcocks' comments included, 'An excellent regiment in the field... The discipline shown in "Mohmand" was of a high order. I should like to have the 21st Cavalry with me again on service'.[34]

Just under two years later the regiment was transferred from the North-West Frontier to the rather less spartan cantonment near the town of Jhelum in the Punjab, about 150 miles south-east of Risalpur. Soon after its arrival Ismay was selected, at the remarkably young age of twenty-three, to be the regiment's adjutant: the commanding officer's right-hand man for regimental administration, discipline and recruit training. Part of the reason for his appointment was that the officer originally earmarked for the job had been killed in the Mohmand Expedition; but Ismay's talents and potential had been recognised. In his confidential report for 1909 his commanding officer had written, 'A very promising young officer, zealous and a good horseman, active and popular'. The inspecting officer, a lieutenant general, had added, 'I concur'.[35]

The new job came with considerable responsibilities and a demanding workload, and it caused Ismay to think more seriously about his profession. Hitherto, his ambition had been 'to be a good regimental officer and a first-class polo player'.[36] Now he had wider aspirations and made up his mind to educate himself in his profession. He began to read voraciously. 'My favourites were Gibbon's *Decline and Fall of the Roman Empire*, Henderson's *Stonewall Jackson*, Kipling of all kinds, and Winston Churchill's *River War*. I got so attached to them that I read them again and again, and soon knew long passages by heart.'[37] Such intellectual single-mindedness would have been unusual to the point of eccentricity in the Indian Army, let alone for a twenty-three-year-old lieutenant. It also risked being considered 'bookish' or 'a swot', both derogatory terms of scorn.[38] But Ismay managed to avoid such a reputation, probably, in part, by being wise enough not to quote long passages—or even short ones—of

Decline and Fall of the Roman Empire in the officers' mess, but also because he was genuinely and obviously gregarious, jovial and entertaining. It is interesting to compare Ismay's approach to taking his profession seriously with that of another officer, an exact contemporary serving in India, who had come to a similar conclusion that 'to succeed one must master one's profession'.[39] According to Nigel Hamilton, his biographer, Bernard Montgomery's approach included 'study[ing] the pages of his Field Service Regulations... until he knew it by heart'.[40]

As at Risalpur, Ismay continued to enjoy at Jhelum every opportunity for sport and entertainment that presented itself. This included the social life of the cantonment, getting away for a week to ten days at a time to indulge his passion for polo, playing in tournaments at other military stations, and visiting his parents, now living in retirement at the popular hill station of Ootacamund ('Ooty') south of Mysore (Mysuru). Although entitled to six months' home leave in Britain every three years, Ismay availed himself of the opportunity only once, in 1912, and asserted that he was glad when the holiday was over, preferring his annual two-month-long holidays which he invariably spent in Kashmir, living on a houseboat near Srinagar, with his polo ponies tethered under a nearby tree. In recalling these trips his enthusiasm is obvious:

> When it got too hot at Srinagar, I would migrate, ponies and all, to Gulmarg, a plateau about eight thousand feet above sea-level. The climate was perfect, and the scenery breathtaking. The polo ground was of real English turf, the golf course was the best in the land, and there was a club where we could all meet to settle the affairs of the world. Most of us were very young and all of us were on holiday.[41]

In 1914 Ismay came to the end of his tenure as adjutant. He had made a notable success of the job. He had not always done everything rigidly 'by the book', and he had been enterprising and self-confident enough to adapt regulations to circumstances. One example, of which he was proud, and which would have gained him admiration and respect from his subordinates, was that in the whole of his four years in the job he never gave a recruit a punishment that appeared in official documents. '[Instead], I reported him to his father or brother, and they dealt with him far more effectively than I could have done by giving him the ordinary military punishment of extra drills or confinement to barracks'.[42] His commanding officer's report of him said simply, 'An excellent adjutant and has done me well in every way. Will make a good staff officer. Fitted for promotion when qualified', to which the brigade commander had added, 'First class young officer. Fit for promotion and the Staff College'.[43]

Ismay had been pondering his next move. Although he was deeply in love with his regiment, he was, like many officers of an adventurous spirit, on the lookout for an opportunity for active service and, in his case, an opportunity to save money and have time to read for the Staff College. He had considered various postings, but his mind was made up in the spring of 1914 by a chance encounter with a brother cavalry subaltern, on leave from the British Somaliland Protectorate where he was serving with the Indian Contingent of the King's African Rifles. The Protectorate was beset by an insurgency instigated by someone referred to as the Mad Mullah. A force including a Camel Corps was being raised to defeat him and it needed officers; the list was heavily over-subscribed but there was one vacancy left. The prospect greatly appealed to Ismay. He applied immediately and was accepted.

Shortly afterwards he had sold his polo ponies, paid off his debtors and packed his bags. Tellingly, he was taking preparation for the Staff College seriously: included in his luggage were 'a lot of books, including a treatise on algebra'—a revelation that did not make it past the first draft of his memoirs.[44] By July Ismay was heading for the port of Bombay (Mumbai) and the start of a very different chapter in his life. It was due to be a detachment from his regiment for about two years. Little could he have guessed how it would turn out.

2

SOMALILAND

1914–20

Somaliland had been part of the British Empire since 1885. Following the ejection of the Egyptian administration the previous year, Britain had signed treaties with six of the main tribes and formally established the British Somaliland Protectorate. Situated at the north-east corner of the African continent, on the southern coast of the Gulf of Aden, Somaliland's attraction to Britain was strategic. In particular, Britain wished to deny the main port and capital, Berbera, to other European powers. Italy already had possession of the territory to the south-east; France was in the process of acquiring the area to the north-west. In addition, Britain wanted Somali meat and wheat from the relatively fertile coastal region for its key coaling station at Aden, 150 miles across the Gulf to the north of Berbera. Of less interest to the British was the interior of Somaliland: some 60,000 square miles of sun-scorched, inhospitable scrub, dense bush, rocky hills and mountains reaching 8,000 feet above sea level, interspersed with some grassland which was home to nomadic tribes.

The first years of British rule were relatively peaceful, but all this was to change. In 1895 a deeply religious and highly charismatic leader, Muhammad Abdullah Hassan, aged thirty-nine, returned from the Haj to Mecca, berating the people of Berbera for their decadent living. At first he was met with little support from the people who, according to Douglas Jardine, referred to him as *wadaad wal*—roughly the mullah that is a lunatic—and known to the British press and public as the Mad Mullah.[1] But moving inland he found much greater response from some of the nomadic tribes. In 1899, fervently preaching Jihad, he initiated an active insurgency against the infidel occupiers. Over the next five years the British carried out four separate campaigns against the Mullah and his followers—self-styled 'dervishes'.[2] Each campaign inflicted a heavy defeat on the Mullah but did not destroy him nor dim his ambition. By 1909 he was back, intimidating the tribes in the interior that opposed him and relieving them of the many weapons that the British had unwisely given them to fight him. The British response was to form an armed police force, 150-strong and mounted on camels, to maintain law and order. In August 1913 this wholly inadequate force met with a stunning defeat at the hands of the Mullah, its commander, Richard Corfield, being among those killed.

In Britain the reaction in the press and parliament was one of indignant shock and anger. The government decided to form a new military unit: the Somaliland Camel Corps, 500-strong, and a 400-strong Indian Army contingent, 150 of whom would be mounted on camels and, in effect, be part of the Camel Corps. Recruiting volunteers from the British and Indian Armies began forthwith. In the meantime, the Mullah consolidated his position, established a number of forts up-country and, in March 1914, made his boldest move yet, raiding Berbera itself.

It must have been with inordinate excitement and expectation that Ismay and the other Indian Army officers bound for Somaliland embarked at Bombay towards the end of July 1914. But they were in for a shock. 'Before we reached Aden we received news which turned my hopes to black despair', recalled Ismay. 'War had broken out with Germany'.[3] On arrival at Berbera their first thought was to apply to return to their regiments immediately, but the officers from Britain who had already arrived said that they had tried that and been told to stay where they were. Morale was at a low ebb. As one of the officers, Major Adrian Carton de Wiart—who was to become a lifelong friend of Ismay—put it to him, 'we were going to play village cricket while our friends were playing in test matches'.[4]

It was fortunate that an exceptionally capable, charismatic officer had been selected to command the Camel Corps. Lieutenant Colonel Thomas Astley Cubitt seems to have been universally admired and respected. Ismay described him as 'the beau ideal of a Horse Gunner—a born leader... [with] the stoutest and kindest of hearts, and a remarkable flow of unprintable invective'.[5] He shrewdly appointed Lieutenant Ismay as one of his two staff officers. Cubitt focused the attention of his unit on preparing itself to confront the Mullah. In mid-November, following three months of intensive training, the Camel Corps moved out from its base at

Burao to attack the dervish forts at Shimberberris, about fifty miles to the south-east (see Map 2).

The force dismounted three miles short of the forts and continued on foot up the escarpment on which stood three forts. The leading company, commanded by Carton de Wiart, charged up to the walls of the first fort and tried to gain entry, but without success. Cubitt sent Ismay forward to find out what was happening. He joined Carton de Wiart in a hollow about eighty yards from the fort. Ismay described the scene:

> He had a bandage over his left eye, but I had no idea that he had already lost the sight of it and was in great pain. He said that the riflemen in the gallery were still a menace but that any amount of lead had been pumped into the fort and there could not be many survivors. He proposed that a couple of machine guns should concentrate on the gallery for a full two minutes, and that the five British officers on the spot should then try to rush the door. Everyone thought this was a good idea. The five of us lined up, and two machine guns opened up on the gallery... When the two minutes were up we raced forward in silence. Carton de Wiart, on my right, was immediately hit in the arm and the ear, but did not check his stride. Symons on my left, was the first to reach the door, but a bullet through the head sent him reeling backwards. Lawrence on the left of the line, was hit in the arm. It was clear—so far as anything could be clear in that mêlée—that the gallery was still intact and that the garrison was strong enough to deal with any assault. Hornby and I, who were both unwounded, retrieved Symons' body and retired to cover.[6]

At this point Cubitt arrived, decided to break off the action and ordered a retreat, placing Ismay in command of the rearguard. Ismay fully expected the dervishes to follow up closely, but they did not do so and his party arrived back at camp, 'with scarcely a scratch between the lot of us. We had been on the go for nineteen hours on end, and the tot of whisky which Cubitt gave me when I presented my report was like nectar'.[7] Ismay was lucky to be alive and he knew it.

It was now clear to the attackers that artillery was required to blast a breach in the walls. Cubitt sent for the only cannon in the whole of Somaliland—an ancient seven-pounder, sitting in Burao. With its arrival, three days later, a further assault was made on the forts, this time successfully. But without the explosives necessary to destroy them, and with a number of serious casualties, the Camel Corps now returned to Burao. Cubitt placed Ismay in charge of coordinating a return to

Shimberberris to finish the job. In early February 1915, the Camel Corps, reinforced by two artillery guns, six Maxim machine guns and a pioneer platoon of explosive experts from Aden, duly set out from Burao. They successfully attacked and demolished the three forts as well as three new ones in the valley below, clearing the numerous caves on the hill side. Seventy-two dervishes were killed for the cost of nine men killed and eighteen wounded, five of them British officers.[8] For his part in organising the expedition 'with complete success, this not being easy in a waterless country such as Somaliland in the dry season', Ismay was awarded a Mention in Despatches.[9]

As he was later to recall, the action at Shimberberris 'had taught us that the Somali was a far better soldier than we had been led to expect'. Ismay developed a considerable admiration and fondness for his Somali soldiers, describing them as scallywags, a term he went on to explain. No one, he said, had ever questioned their toughness, powers of endurance or physical courage; but they had earned the reputation of being so excitable as to be hopelessly unreliable. Their detractors, however, had failed to take into account that in the past they had always been put into battle with little or no training, and led by officers whom they did not know.

> Shimberberris was the first occasion on which [the Somali soldier] was given a fair chance, and he took it with both hands. Thereafter he went from strength to strength, and soon established a pronounced moral ascendency over the hitherto dreaded dervish. He never ceased to be vain, volatile and sometimes exasperating; he never ceased to be excitable at the beginning of an action; he never ceased to be a scallywag. But his British officers, during the last years of the Mullah's rebellion, will ever remember him a faithful... and gallant soldier, who was at his best in times of scarcity and hardship.[10]

Ismay clearly struck up a considerable rapport with his soldiers and was happy and proud to describe himself as one of their number. Indeed, the chapter in his memoirs describing his time in Somaliland is entitled 'Scallywag in Africa'.

Following its success at Shimberberris, the Camel Corps had the feeling that it had the Mullah on the run. To build on their success and maintain the momentum a further operation was planned to destroy the Mullah's large fort at Jid Ali in the north-east of the country. But just as the plans were nearing completion came a further blow to morale. With the war going badly on the Western Front, the British government ordered that offensive operations in Somaliland should cease. Ismay, together with all his brother officers, applied to rejoin their regiments; they were all refused. Ismay then persuaded an old friend serving at Gallipoli to take him on the strength of his regiment 'for a few weeks'; Colonel Cubitt acquiesced, but an order was received banning such attachments.[11] Towards the end of 1915 a few officers, including Cubitt, were allowed to leave; Carton de Wiart had already left after the first engagement at Shimberberris (and for which he was awarded the Distinguished Service Order, the DSO).[12]

Letters from former comrades in the Indian Army, some on the Western Front, some fighting the Turks in Mesopotamia, kept Ismay in touch with the wider war.[13] His close friend and most faithful correspondent, Milo Onslow, was serving with the 33rd Cavalry, south of Baghdad. Earlier in 1915 he had written to 'My dear old Pug', giving graphic accounts of cavalry charges, 'an absolute hail of bullets' and divisional-scale attacks, in one of which he had been wounded.[14] Now in March 1916 he was back in India convalescing from a subsequent, more serious wound and reporting on a visit to Ismay's mother in Ootacamund.[15] Although some people might have been relieved to be in a quieter theatre, it was for Ismay a source of constant frustration and jealousy.

Life for the Camel Corps consisted of long periods in camp at their Burao base at a high level of readiness, with occasional no-notice, long-range pursuits—often over 300 miles—of the dervish forces. These were testing operations. 'Time and again it was the same story: difficult terrain for the animals, brackish and sulphurated water debilitating officers and men, inadequate transport, limited rations, intense heat, sometimes blinding sand-storms—but always an elusive enemy with a long start'.[16]

Now the sole staff officer, responsible for administration, operations and intelligence, life became even busier for Ismay. But it was largely unglamorous office work. He appears to have aimed to overcome his frustration by burying himself in his work and doing it to the very best of his ability.[17] He became particularly expert in intelligence, so much so that when, towards the end of 1916, he was allowed to take leave in Britain, he was sent for by the Admiralty to brief Naval Intelligence on the Mullah and the situation in Somaliland. The quality of his report and analysis is probably reflected by the fact that as a young captain he received a personal letter of thanks from the Director of Naval Intelligence, Rear Admiral Reginald Hall.[18] While in England it was announced that Adrian Carton de Wiart had been awarded the Victoria Cross for his action in temporary command of a brigade at the Battle of the Somme, two months earlier. Although happy for his friend's success, Ismay would have been uncomfortably reminded of the comparative backwater in which he was being forced to serve.

Returning to Somaliland, his dejection and frustration deepened, as shown by his letters to his mother. 'How worthless is one's work here, how little it matters… the hopelessness of being stuck here', he wrote in January 1917.[19] 'The fact that one's own regiment—which is practically one's own family—is in the thick of it [in Mesopotamia], makes it even harder to bear with a contented spirit', he wrote three months later.[20] The regiment was indeed in the thick of it, some eighty miles north of Baghdad, as Milo Onslow, still in India, reported to Ismay: '[t]he good old 21st as usual covered themselves in glory', listing some of the awards for gallantry that had been won.[21]

Ismay continued to lobby his friends and contacts to effect an escape from Somaliland, even if it was only a visit to an active war front. One of these contacts was his former commanding officer, Cubitt, now a brigade commander in France. Cubitt replied, 'It is very difficult to get to France on a joy ride—either attached or in any other way, unless you are an M.P. or a munition worker or a *Daily Mail* correspondent'.[22] An attempt by Carton de Wiart to get Ismay an attachment to his brigade in France was similarly thwarted. His own regiment in Mesopotamia tried to get him released from Somaliland, but the Colonial Office vetoed the proposal. In June came recognition of a sort: promulgation of an award to Ismay by the Army Council of an 'honourable entry in his record of service'.[23] But in the context of the Great War this was in the nature of a consolation prize. It also illustrated an irony: the better Ismay did his job, the more indispensable he became and the less his chances of being released. 'My chances of cutting adrift from my present job are less rosy and rather more remote than they ever were', he told his mother the following month.[24] Occasionally his mood was lifted, for example, when given command of a long-range patrol. At the end of July he told his mother, 'I am commanding this stunt—rather fun—very good for me mentally'.[25] But these breaks were few and far between. A month later his despair had returned: 'I'd give my all to chuck it and get to some place that matters'.[26]

In October 1917 any monotony was suddenly interrupted. Reports came in of a dervish force 400–500-strong which had raided the tribes in the mountainous area 130 miles to the north-east of Burao, driving off over 300 camels and 700 sheep and goats. The Camel Corps immediately deployed from Burao and Ismay was placed in command of a flying column of 150 men mounted on ponies to intercept the raiders. They caught up with the dervish rear guard holding two passes through the mountains. Using a levy of friendly tribesmen to create a diversion at the western pass, Ismay led his own force to attack the eastern one, the Endow Pass, and a fierce battle ensued. The main body of the Camel Corps joined them and after five hours' sharp fighting succeeded in clearing the dervishes from their positions. However, with daylight fading it was evident that further advance would have to await the morning. But they had only two days' rations left and were 130 miles from their base at Burao. The pursuit was called off. The operation had inflicted significant casualties on the dervish force: some seventy killed, for the loss of only ten men wounded. In addition, the impact of the action on the morale of both sides had been considerable. It was the cause for celebration when they got back to Burao.

Ismay's sense of elation was to be short-lived. A month later he received news from the 21st Cavalry that Milo Onslow, perhaps his closest friend, who had recently rejoined the regiment north of Baghdad, had been killed in action. For Ismay, this must have been one of the bleakest moments of the war.

In the spring of 1918 Ismay was appointed the acting commanding officer of the Camel Corps. But what might have been an exciting command was stymied by further British government restrictions on offensive activity and an apparent lack of concern in London that the Somaliland Camel Corps was becoming significantly under-resourced and undermanned in key appointments.[27] Despite these restrictions, Ismay succeeded in maintaining the morale of his command, and keeping its focus on defeating the Mullah by every means possible. A series of minor operations constrained the Mullah's activities, wearing down his forces and undermining his support among the nomadic tribes.

When in November the Great War came to an end Ismay argued that now was the time to finish off the Mullah once and for all. The War Office sent out a senior officer, Major General Sir Arthur Hoskins, to assess the situation. Ismay hoped that his own intelligence assessments would convince Hoskins that the Mullah had been so weakened that only a small reinforcement would be required to do the job. He gave him a detailed plan to this effect.[28] Hoskins rejected the plan. Instead Hoskins, who may have expected to command the campaign, recommended a large-scale expedition: a tri-Service force of six warships, a reinforced division including artillery and cavalry, and a flight of RAF bombers. The War Office showed little interest in the plan; the Colonial Office considered the scale of the force unnecessary; and the Chancellor of the Exchequer was clearly horrified at the likely cost. On 24 January 1919 the Cabinet shelved the plan.[29]

While the government in London pondered its options, successful operations continued in Somaliland. In February 1919 the Camel Corps inflicted a significant defeat on the Mullah's forces at the Ok [pronounced 'Occ'] Pass, about sixty miles north of Burao. In April Ismay led a large, mounted column to the same area in a 380-mile pursuit which severely harried the Mullah's force.[30] One month later he produced a major intelligence report that he had been working on for several months. Entitled 'Summary of Intelligence, British Somaliland up to December 1918', it encapsulated in one document all his knowledge, experience and insights gained over four years of research and campaigning in the country.[31] Significantly, it included a detailed historical account of the Mullah with analysis of the culture of his followers and the people of Somaliland. It thus provided its readers with a cultural understanding of the insurgency: something notably lacking in British counter-insurgency campaigns almost a century later.[32] With important decisions pending, its production was timely.

At the Colonial Office and War Office there remained a distinct lack of enthusiasm for further action in Somaliland. This was not, however, the case at the Air Ministry. Air Chief Marshal Sir Hugh Trenchard, the head of the RAF, keen to demonstrate that Service's capabilities, put forward a plan for the Mullah's destruction by the use of air power alone and at a fraction of the expense. The plan involved an air attack on the stronghold which the Mullah had established around the forts in north-east Somaliland. Only a single flight of six aircraft would be required. Ground troops were to be held back and used only if ordered. Trenchard was strongly supported in this plan by the Secretary of State for War and Air, Winston Churchill.[33] After lengthy planning in both London and Berbera, the latter involving Ismay (now a temporary lieutenant colonel), the operation was set for January 1920.

On the fifth of that month Ismay led the Camel Corps on a 250-mile approach march to the area, ready to attack if required. On 21 January the RAF aircraft set off to attack the fort of Medishe. Only one aircraft found the target and released its bombs, but it was enough to cause the Mullah and his men to flee in panic. No one knew where he had gone. Three days later the Air Staff in London gave permission for ground troops to take part in the operation. On 27 January Ismay and the Camel Corps moved up to the second fort at Jid Ali just as RAF aircraft were launching an attack. This time the bombing did not dislodge the enemy. The Camel Corps took up the firefight with the defenders and deployed ready to attack the following morning. During the night, however, the dervishes evacuated the fort.

Two days later came a major development. A deserter revealed that the Mullah and his followers had been hiding in some caves a few miles away and were now heading south. Ismay gave chase. The Camel Corps travelled 150 miles in the first seventy-two hours.[34] The Mullah headed for his fort at Tale, some 200 miles from Jid Ali. When Ismay reached there on the evening of 9 February he found that, following an air attack and ground bombardment, the Mullah and some seventy horsemen had broken out of the fort, heading north. Ismay sent a patrol to track them, but the hard ground and darkness made tracking impossible; the patrol returned a few hours later.[35] It was fortunate that they did so, for when Ismay and the Camel Corps set off at first light in pursuit they soon discovered that the northerly move was a clever diversion. The tracks were now heading south-east. The Mullah and his force were heading towards the border with Italian Somaliland and relative safety.

By the end of the day it was evident that the pace of the pursuit was beginning to tell on the Camel Corps. Many of the animals could no longer keep up and some of the men were suffering from vomiting and diarrhoea as a result of drinking foul water. Ismay decided to continue with 150 of the fittest animals and men and set off again, riding through the night and the following day. They were now very hungry. In a typical Ismay aside, he later recalled that he had the good fortune to discover in his haversack a piece of fat that had fallen out of a sandwich several days previously. 'Unappetising though it looked and smelled, I was about to put it greedily into my mouth when decency compelled me to offer a portion to my adjutant, James Beattie, who was riding alongside. He was as grateful as if I had given him a five course champagne dinner'.[36]

In late afternoon they surprised a group of thirty dervishes and some camp-followers at a watering hole. In the ensuing fight, all the dervishes were killed and the camp-followers taken prisoner. They included four of the Mullah's wives and their children. The next morning, 12 February, Ismay continued the pursuit and caught up with a further small group. Again, the dervish escorts were killed; the prisoners this time included the woman known to be the Mullah's favourite wife. The Mullah himself could not be far off. A scout reported seeing a dozen horsemen several miles away. But few of the camels and ponies could continue. Ismay carried on with twenty pony men, and caught up with the group, but the Mullah was not among them. The trail had run cold. Ismay's men and animals who had been on half rations for several days had now almost run out of food and were sixty miles from the nearest resupply.[37] Later that day he came to the inevitable conclusion. 'Sick at heart, I decided to give up the chase'.[38] Five weeks after they had set out, the Camel Corps began the long trek home.

The march of the Camel Corps from the sea to the southern borders of the Protectorate and back again was, as one historian has commented, 'a magnificent feat of endurance'.[39] It was also a notable military success. No less than sixty of the Mullah's personal following, including seven of his sons, seven other close relatives and four of his close advisers had been killed; his five wives, six of his sons, four of his daughters and two of his sisters had been captured.[40] Other forces had destroyed his forts, killed or captured hundreds of his dervishes and rounded up all his livestock. Security force casualties were only three men killed and nine wounded. Ismay had every right to be proud of his own leadership, determination, skill and stamina. But for him what rankled bitterly was his failure, despite all this effort, to nail his quarry. What he did not know at this stage was that the Mullah and 'dervishism' were effectively at an end: the Mullah was to die of influenza before the year was out.

Although Ismay despised aspects of Mullah Mohammad Abdullah Hassan, not least his ruthless brutality, he nevertheless maintained a professional respect bordering on admiration for him as an opponent throughout his time in Somaliland and after. He never referred to him as the Mad Mullah. In 1919 he wrote that,

> the Mullah's position has demanded military genius, administrative ability, and diplomatic skill. History has shown how effectively he has met these demands... The efficacy of [his] propaganda and of his system of censorship is extraordinary... That his methods have been unspeakable cruel cannot be gainsaid, but on the other hand it cannot be denied that they have been remarkably successful.[41]

It was a characteristically clear-eyed assessment.[42]

Ismay was subsequently to be closely involved in the heated debate which ensued about the role of air power in the Mullah's demise. Lord Trenchard was quick to claim the credit for the Royal Air Force. 'At long last aeroplanes were sent against him and now the Mad Mullah has vanished for ever.'[43] His supporters argued that it had been air power alone that had caused the defeat of the Mullah and that it therefore followed that the RAF could take the leading role in imperial policing. Advocates for the army argued the opposite. The controversy was to be reignited some forty years later with the publication of Andrew Boyle's biography of Trenchard which credited the RAF alone with the Mullah's defeat.[44] In a letter to the *Daily Telegraph* in 1962 Ismay wrote that Boyle 'exaggerates grotesquely' the role of air power in the Mullah's demise. Ismay paid due tribute to the shock action by RAF aircraft that had driven the Mullah and his followers out of the forts at Medishe and Tale. But he underlined the fact that it was the action by ground troops that had finished the job, and thus the importance of joint-Service cooperation.[45]

Significantly, there had been no jealousies or ructions between the army and the RAF in Somaliland at the time.[46] Immediately after the pursuit in February 1920 the RAF commander in Somaliland, Group Captain Robert Gordon, had generously written to him, 'The news from you yesterday was splendid. I congratulate you and your men on one of the most wonderful efforts I have heard of for sheer guts. I hope you… will get over your fatigue and be able to come and tell us the details before you leave the country'.[47] 'Wasn't that topping', Ismay commented to his mother, 'especially from a real silent, hard-bitten fellow'.[48]

In April 1920, two months after the pursuit, Ismay's tour of duty in Somaliland came to an end. It had lasted almost six long years. He had arrived as a twenty-seven-year-old lieutenant and left as a thirty-two-year-old lieutenant colonel (albeit a temporary one). It had been a formative period of his life and one that left its mark on him. His mood on leaving was sombre. 'I was thankful to see the last of the country in which I had been so unhappy.'[49] His frustration and, at times, despair ran deep. It was not just the constant feeling that he was trapped in a sideshow while the main event took place elsewhere: it was also the knowledge, and perhaps a feeling of guilt, that his regiment had been in the thick of it—many of his friends had been killed while he had been in a relatively safe place and survived.

Perhaps even more so was the feeling that his experience of war had been confined to 'scallywag fighting'—what contemporaries might have denigrated as chasing a few dervishes around a desert—and that this was irrelevant to the future of the profession he loved. He would thus be at a severe disadvantage compared with those who had experience of modern warfare, and that almost six years of his life had been wasted. He did not know at this stage that he would be awarded the DSO. Many members of the military might have agreed with his summation. One who was later to give a different opinion was Field Marshal Lord Slim. Reviewing Ismay's memoirs in 1960 and commenting on his experience in the First World War he wrote, 'Yet I have no doubt that this "scallywagging" in Africa, as he calls it, gave him more practice in self-reliance, initiative, and the basic tactics of mobile warfare than most of us got in the vast set-piece battles of trench-warfare on the major fronts. It gave him a fresher and slightly different outlook on affairs from most of his contemporaries'.[50] These were perceptive words.

While Ismay was in Aden on his way home he received a telegram nominating him for a place at the Indian Army Staff College at Quetta. Attendance at one of the staff colleges—Quetta or Camberley—was a major stepping stone for career advancement.[51] Previously, Ismay would have given his eyeteeth for it. 'But the idea of the Staff College appealed to me no longer. I had no experience of modern war; a large number of my best friends had been killed; soldiering could never be the same again; and I was seriously thinking of resigning my commission and trying a new life. I returned a polite refusal to the offer.'[52]

Ismay's psychological state was not good. As he commented ruefully in retrospect, '[r]ecovery from physical fatigue is far quicker than recovery from mental strain'.[53]

On return to Britain, reverting to his substantive rank of captain, he appeared in front of a medical board. According to Ismay, the board diagnosed him as suffering from 'extreme war-weariness', probably a euphemism for mental exhaustion, and gave him twelve months' sick leave.[54] One way or another, it looked as if his military career might, indeed, be nearing its conclusion.

3

APPRENTICESHIP

1920–36

Back in England, on holiday and with no responsibilities, Ismay was soon making up for lost time: seeing friends whom he had not seen for years, making a lot of new ones, and enjoying himself. His depression quickly lifted and it was not long before he had given up any idea of leaving the army. He now informed the War Office that he would, after all, like to take up the offer of a place at the Staff College. He was told that the vacancy had already been filled but that he could sit for the examination for the course which would start in February 1922. He also lobbied influential friends to support a further nomination. His former commanding officer, Cubitt, replied, 'I have sent Lynden Bell [the general responsible for Staff College entrance] a real rouser—I have given you the best chit I know how to write'. Telling Ismay that he would look on it as 'a disaster for the Army' if he did not get to the Staff College, Cubitt admitted, 'on many occasions I simple longed for your help when in France and I also freely expressed this'.[1]

In August 1920 there came a chance meeting which was to change Ismay's life. He returned to Stratford-upon-Avon where he had spent his school holidays. This time he was staying with an old friend from those days, Ellie Lowndes, now married to a neighbour, Spenser Flower. Spenser was a highly accomplished tennis player and about to compete in a local tournament. He invited Ismay to partner him in the doubles. Spenser was also due to play in the mixed doubles, but at the last moment, his partner became ill and he invited as a replacement a young friend, Kathleen (known as Darry) Clegg, who lived not far away. Spenser and his partners won both competitions. For Ismay and Darry it was love at first sight. Within three weeks they were engaged to be married.

Darry's parents had lived in Cheshire where her father, Henry Clegg, had met and married Maude Field, daughter of an American, Joseph Field, whose brother was the founder of Chicago's largest department store. Joseph managed the firm's interests in Britain. In 1904 he bought the couple a forty-acre farm just outside the village of Broadway in Worcestershire. In March 1920 the Cleggs moved from there to Wormington Grange, a large Georgian mansion with a 2,000-acre estate, four miles down the road in Gloucestershire. It was there that they were living in August 1920 with their eighteen-year-old son, Peter, already an officer in the Royal Navy, and Darry, aged twenty-two.

Darry's parents were not in favour of her marrying Ismay. Her mother, in particular, disliked the idea of her daughter being taken off to India—a country that was likely to be injurious to her somewhat delicate health—and was unimpressed that her intended bridegroom had no money nor the prospect of making any. There was, at that stage, no evidence of his military accomplishments; his award of the Distinguish Service Order had yet to be promulgated. It did not help matters that Peter had just returned from a long deployment at sea and was about to deploy on an even longer one.[2] But Ismay and Darry managed to prevail.

The day after the announcement of their engagement Ismay re-appeared before the army medical board for a review. He was able to convince them that not only was his war-weariness a thing of the past but that he had, in fact, never been happier in his life. He was delighted to be passed as fit for immediate service, although less delighted to learn that this meant that he had to return to India forthwith.

The following month Ismay rejoined his regiment at Bannu on the North-West Frontier in time to celebrate his award of the DSO, announced in November.[3] There was no serious fighting on the Frontier while he was at Bannu, just a few occasional brushes with Pashtun tribesmen. Ismay played a great deal of polo and studied assiduously for the 'notoriously difficult' Staff College exam.[4] The exam took place in February 1921. Ismay recalled that he found the papers on the conduct of operations in Europe 'fiendishly difficult' and those on frontier warfare 'absurdly easy' and that these results evened themselves out and allowed him to scrape a pass.[5] Given his military experience, this may not be entirely false modesty; his extensive preparation for the exam was probably not wasted. In April the regiment moved from the Frontier to the more peaceful Rawalpindi. There was one incident there that gives an insight into Ismay's character. He thought that, in terms of social attitudes towards Indians, '[t]hings were moving very slowly after the First World War'.[6] One of his regiment's Indian officers applied for membership of the exclusive Rawalpindi Club and was blackballed, that is to say refused. Ismay considered this iniquitous. He gathered his fellow officers together and said,

> 'Look chaps, we're all resigning from that club tonight, I'm damned if I'll belong to a club where a brother officer is blackballed. And we'll get others [to join us].' I went to see the Glosters… and others… the Gunners… and said, 'Will you all resign?' 'Yes, sure we will'. The Rawalpindi [club] was going to be left without any members… so the blackball was removed.[7]

Ismay's action required moral courage. He would have known that it would make him highly unpopular with some of the older and more influential members of the club; but that had not deterred him.

At the end of April Ismay was allowed to return to Britain to complete his allocation of leave and get married. The wedding took place in August at the village church in Stanton, near Wormington Grange. Darry's mother was, however, unreconciled to her daughter's future. Ismay's family assert that her tears at the wedding were not tears of joy.[8]

Ismay was back in Rawalpindi the following month, this time accompanied by Darry. There was little military activity and his place at the Staff College was assured, so, as he later admitted, he 'devoted more time to polo than to soldiering'.[9] This included five weeks in Delhi taking part in the premier polo tournament of the year. For Darry the time was less pleasurable. She became pregnant soon after arrival and—as her mother had predicted—had a number of health problems, including fever and ear trouble. When the time came for them to move to the Staff College at Quetta in February 1922, Ismay and Darry decided that she should return home to Wormington.

Despite Darry's absence Ismay enjoyed his ten months at Quetta. His initial prospects at the Staff College looked to be somewhat unpromising. He arrived there direct from a whole month playing high-level tournament polo at Delhi with a request to be given two weeks off for the blue-riband Inter-Regimental Tournament later in the year. His indirect approach to the commandant, Major General Louis Vaughan, received a dusty response: 'Any officer who is prepared to sacrifice a fortnight of this vital course in order to play a game—however important—had better not have come here at all'.[10] Despite this inauspicious start to their relationship, Vaughan was to prove one of the most influential forces in Ismay's life.

Louis Vaughan was an Indian Army officer who had served on the staff on the Western Front for the whole of the First World War. Mentioned in despatches no less than nine times, he ended the war as chief of staff to General Sir Julian Byng, Commander Third Army. In 1919 he commanded a division in the Third Anglo-Afghan War before being posted to Quetta as commandant. His troops had nicknamed him 'Father'; so did the students and staff at Quetta. Many years later Ismay wrote an appreciation of Vaughan. He noted that initially the student body, many members of which had considerable wartime experience, some commanding brigades, was not wholly receptive, but 'Father' handled his awkward pupils to perfection. Vaughan gave many of the lectures himself and was renowned for his words of wisdom. Ismay recalled three of his aphorisms in particular. First, was the importance of proportion. 'Learn to distinguish between things that matter and the things that don't matter nearly as much. Never be disturbed by trifles. Force your heart and mind and sinew to concentrate on the big things. Proportion, gentlemen, proportion'. Second was the importance of loyalty: 'loyalty to the cause... to one's friends... to one's commanders and to the Government. The soldier must be absolutely loyal to the statesman [recognising that] war is the instrument of policy... He must not, for example, oppose him or take too unyielding a line on the things that don't matter. On the other hand he must be adamant on the things that really matter'. Third was 'to be ever mindful of the fair name of the staff... Know your job, be human, be helpful, never spare yourself. The staff was made for the Army, not the Army for the staff'.[11] These lessons were to guide Ismay for the whole of his career.

The staff course was intellectually demanding but Ismay was well up to the challenge and worked hard. He valued the time spent mixing with and learning from his fellow students and he took the opportunity to think deeply about his profession. The students were required to write a 15,000-word dissertation during the course; Ismay chose as his topic the relevance of history to a possible future war with special reference to the Middle East. His paper, which survives, shows considerable wisdom and, though not accurate in all its predictions, was nevertheless remarkably prescient. For example, he predicted that future war would be total war, that it would require a coordinated national effort and that it would be essentially a war of movement. And he urged the closest possible cooperation between air and ground forces, while accepting that 'independent action by aircraft will be necessary in order to ensure command of the air'.[12] Not all of these views would have been met with universal military agreement at the time. But his paper met with high praise from Vaughan, who graded it 'excellent', commenting, 'I expected good work from you, and I have got it'.[13]

Ismay, however, was far from being a narrow-minded swot at the Staff College. He enjoyed an active social life, continued to indulge his passion for polo and rode in a number of prestigious jump races at Quetta racecourse. Vaughan's end-of-course confidential report (included in full in Appendix A) was glowing. Among the accolades, he described Ismay's mentality as 'Very quick and alert. Very adaptable. A clear, logical and far-seeing brain with plenty of imagination, and sound, well balanced judgment. Good sense of proportion. Good sense of humour'. His assessment of Ismay's personality included the comment that '[he] inspires confidence, and has a strong influence over others. Essentially a leader of men'. The committee of the Rawalpindi Club would have agreed, albeit some of them grudgingly. Vaughan gave Ismay a very rare 'A' Grade, defined as 'an officer of exceptional merit', and added 'I consider this officer one of the two best, if not the best of the students who have passed through my hands'.[14] Given that this was the fourth course over which 'Father' had presided, this was some tribute.

In March 1923 Ismay was posted to the Indian Army headquarters at Simla (Shimla) in the Himalayas and summer capital of the British Raj. Darry came to join him, leaving behind their nine-month-old daughter, Susan, to be looked after by Darry's mother. The parting must have been heartbreaking, but such arrangements were not unusual at the time: officers' wives were expected to accompany their husbands. Ismay's appointment at the headquarters rejoiced in the impressive title of Deputy Assistant Adjutant and Quartermaster General; in fact, he was one of many majors holding the title in a department concerned with administration and logistics. It was not the most exciting of jobs, but it would have been a good test of his skills as a staff officer and, moreover, of his patience. Ismay did not have a high opinion of the headquarters—'the machine as a whole was impersonal and ponderous'—but, as always, he applied himself fully to the job and made many friendships amongst his colleagues.[15] In particular, he found a meeting of minds with the officer occupying the next-door office, Major Claude Auchinleck, who was to become a close, life-long friend.

Both Ismay and Darry liked Simla.[16] Ismay played a lot of polo; he and Darry got to the final of the mixed doubles in the tennis tournament; and he participated enthusiastically in the local amateur dramatic society. They also enjoyed the company of a wide circle of friends and an active social life. In this they were lucky in that the Viceroy's wife, Lady Reading, was a friend of Darry's mother and, as Darry recorded, 'she [Lady Reading] and Lord Reading were very kind to us'.[17] In a hierarchical, status-conscious environment such as Simla, to be known as a friend of the Viceroy and his wife would have done a young major's standing in the community no harm at all.

During their first year at Simla, however, they faced a setback. Darry's hearing, which had not been perfect, started to deteriorate. Doctors told her that the climate was a major factor. Hitherto, Ismay had anticipated that his future career would be with the Indian Army, but it became clear to him that this was no longer an option. He applied for postings back in Britain, although there were few that attracted him.[18] He was fortunate, however, with another connection in the headquarters—and such connections were influential in the army at the time, just as they were in the rest of society. The commander of the RAF in India, Air Vice Marshal Philip Game, had a house in the village of Broadway and had been a close neighbour of Darry's parents; he had also, like Ismay, attended Charterhouse School.[19] Game took a liking to Ismay and offered to nominate him for a place at the RAF Staff College, located at Andover in Hampshire, starting the following April. Ismay 'jumped at the idea'.[20] Game, however, had been somewhat premature in his offer: the RAF made no provision for an Indian Army officer to attend the course. Luck was again with Ismay: Game was suddenly recalled to London, promoted to become the Air Member for Personnel and used his influence to fix a place for him.[21] In March Ismay and Darry were homeward bound.

The 1924 course at Andover was only the third in the RAF Staff College's existence. A few places on the course were allotted to officers from the other two Services who had attended their own staff colleges. Ismay threw himself energetically into all aspects of the course, showing a willingness to learn all about the RAF and even developing an enthusiasm for flying. 'I made a practice of going down to the tarmac each day and offering myself as ballast'.[22] He also put his thespian talents to good use, playing the leading role in the college play, a racy comedy called 'A Pair of Silk Stockings'.[23] A fellow actor in the play, Jack Slessor, a future Chief of the Air Staff, was one of the many friends Ismay made on the course and one of the many with whom he was later to work during the war. In addition, his year at Andover undoubtedly gave him an understanding of air power far greater than that of most army officers, and an empathy with RAF officers which would not have been lost on his future RAF colleagues. Indeed, one of his wartime staff, Group Captain (later Air Chief Marshal Sir) William Elliot, found his grasp of air power 'astonishing'.[24] There was good reason for Ismay's view in retrospect that, according to Darry, 'that year was one of the most valuable experiences he ever had'.[25] It was also a happy year from a family point of view. Ismay and Darry were able to devote their attention to Susan, to spend weekends and holidays at Wormington with Darry's mother and to ride out with the North Cotswold hunt.

In April 1925 Ismay returned to Simla to complete his tour of duty at army headquarters, but was already thinking ahead to his next job which, for obvious family reasons, he wanted to be in Britain. Again, it was Air Vice Marshal Game who provided the answer. His brother-in-law, Colonel Charles Walker, a pre-war friend of Ismay, was working as assistant secretary at the Committee of Imperial Defence in London, and due to vacate the appointment in December. Game fixed a meeting between them. Walker suggested that Ismay apply for the job. Ismay did so. Shortly afterwards he was summoned for interview with the secretary of the Committee, Sir Maurice Hankey, and, to his delight, was provisionally accepted. He returned to Simla to serve the intervening six months and was back in London in November, ready to start a five-year tour of duty in what was, for him, a very new world.

* * *

Ismay liked to joke that when he was first appointed as an assistant secretary to the Committee of Imperial Defence, commonly known as the CID, he found that 'there were very few even well-informed people who had any idea of the nature of my job; and several of my friends expressed surprise that I should have transferred from the Army to the Criminal Investigation Department'.[26]

The organisation which he joined 'on a cold, dull morning' in December 1925 was an advisory body charged by the government with providing the Cabinet and government departments with advice on both the general principles of defence policy and their detailed application.[27] Situated in Whitehall Gardens, a cul-de-sac off Whitehall, it had been formed in 1904, in the wake of the Boer War, to provide better coordination between the army and the navy. In the decade prior to the First World War its role and responsibilities expanded to include advice to the Cabinet on defence policy, national and imperial strategy and detailed cross-government war preparations. Thus, for the first time in Britain, and in the absence of a Ministry of Defence, it brought together policy and strategy in one organisation. The CID had no formal executive authority—its role remained to coordinate and give advice—but it had great influence: Ismay later estimated that ninety-five per cent of its recommendations were automatically implemented by the government departments concerned.[28] The Prime Minister was its permanent chairman and determined its membership. This comprised ministers, members of the parliamentary opposition parties, Service Chiefs, civil servants, representatives from the Dominions and other experts. The CID could co-opt or call in anyone to join its deliberations; it was thus extremely flexible. With a very small secretariat it transacted its business through a number of subcommittees. Its secretary since 1911 had been Hankey.

Disbanded during the First World War, the CID was reconstituted in 1919. At the same time Hankey was given the additional role of Cabinet secretary. A major development came in 1923 with the establishment of the Chiefs of Staff subcommittee, comprising the heads of the three armed Services: the First Sea Lord, the Chief of the Imperial General Staff, and the Chief of the Air Staff. The Chiefs, as they were known, were charged with 'an individual and collective responsibility for advising on defence policy as a whole'.[29] In Ismay's view, the creation of this subcommittee was 'by far the most significant inter-war development in defence'.[30]

By the time Ismay joined the CID as one of Hankey's four assistant secretaries the number of subcommittees had expanded to about twenty, many of which had several subcommittees of their own.[31] In Ismay's words, 'In effect, though not in name, they constitute an immense and infinitely elastic, combined defence staff'.[32] Each assistant secretary had a group of subjects for which they were responsible and a number of subcommittees of which they were secretary. But their role went way beyond that of arranging the meetings, maintaining the records and drafting reports. They were expected 'to supply the drive, initiate new ideas, and ensure there was no overlap with other committees'.[33] In doing so, they dealt directly with government ministers, generals, admirals and air marshals, rather than going through a chain of command. In particular, they had a close and direct relationship with the chairmen of the committees for which they were responsible. In Ismay's case this included the War

Emergency Legislation Committee, whose chairman and according to Ismay 'an extremely enthusiastic one', was Lord Haldane—Richard Burdon Haldane, the eminent philosopher-statesman.[34]

The CID assistant secretaries were thus people of considerable influence, even if they had no executive power. They did, however, have a huge amount of work, and in the case of new arrival Ismay, a very steep learning curve. But the CID had yet to become the much larger bureaucracy into which it would evolve. For Ismay the contrast with army HQ in India was striking. 'It was like joining a small but highly prosperous family business after working in a mammoth, publicly owned multiple store. I was well content with the change'.[35] Writing to his predecessor Charles Walker in February 1926, he told him with typical modesty, 'I am nothing like in the saddle yet—and doubt whether I'll ever get there—but I'm thoroughly happy and love the job'.[36]

Ismay's first six months at the CID were to be far from typical. The prospect in early 1926 of a general strike resulted in the interruption of normal business and the cessation of almost all long-term planning. Instead, attention focused on contingency planning to keep the country going should the strike materialise. The CID was particularly involved in ways in which the military could help to achieve this. When the strike eventually took place in May 1926, Prime Minister Stanley Baldwin set up a committee to examine whether and how the Territorial Army of reservists could be employed on police duties. Hankey appointed Ismay as its secretary. The committee's chairman was the Chancellor of the Exchequer, Winston Churchill. It was the first occasion that Ismay and Churchill met, although Ismay's name would have been well known to Churchill. As Secretary of State for War and Air from 1919 to 1921, he had been involved in the strategy of the campaign in Somaliland and would have been well aware of the central and dramatic role played in its outcome by Lieutenant Colonel Ismay, DSO. In the management of the general strike Ismay was highly impressed by the way in which Churchill gave leadership to his colleagues, came up with the plan and successfully had it put into immediate operation, using Ismay as an executive aide. Churchill was not to forget the episode, either.

Returning to more normal times, Ismay could now devote himself to the main business of his job. To him fell the responsibility for a highly diverse portfolio of subjects, all of which were part of national or imperial preparation for war. Among the most important of his charges was the Coordination Committee or, to give it its full title, the Committee for

Coordination of Departmental Action on the Outbreak of War. This committee was responsible for ensuring that the plans of all government departments for this eventuality were up to date and coordinated with each other: a vital undertaking and a considerable challenge, particularly when no war was expected, and thus little sense of urgency existed. The master plan was contained in a key document called the Government War Book. Soon after his arrival Ismay considered that the existing War Book was completely outmoded and, with Hankey's blessing, formed a small group to rectify the matter. This work took almost five years, culminating in a new, approved edition in 1930, just before Ismay left the CID.[37] This vital document was one of his crowning achievements of his time there and was to prove its value nine years later.

Ismay's other subcommittees included those for the Defence of India and the Indianisation of the Indian Army—both of which had Churchill as a member and both of which were within Ismay's area of expertise—and those for War Emergency Legislation and Censorship, subjects in which he was quick to become expert. His single biggest responsibility, and the most complex and time-consuming one (it had twelve subcommittees) was the Principal Supply Officers' Committee. It was widely acknowledged to be one of the CID's most important committees. Ismay gives a typically lucid summary of its role. This was 'first to ascertain the sum total of national requirements in a major war in terms of raw materials and productive capacity; secondly, to determine how far these requirements could be met from existing resources; and finally, to make recommendations as to how all these shortages which became apparent could be made good'.[38]

This was, indeed, as he added, 'a tall order'.[39] It was also work potentially critical to national survival. Ismay was quick to identify that one of the greatest obstacles to improving the efficiency and effectiveness of the supply system was the individual Armed Services' resistance to standardisation. To them, standardisation represented interference in their internal affairs and a threat to their independence. To outsiders, their resistance defied common sense and was taken to ludicrous lengths. Ismay later recalled that their objection extended to standardisation of such mundane articles as kitchen utensils, hardware, crockery and blankets.[40] He worked assiduously to achieve improvements to the supply system. Despite his lowly rank, he campaigned for a change of attitude, arguing consistently against 'a peace system under which each Department "does its own shopping"' and supporting moves towards the establishment of a

Ministry of Supply.[41] It would be a further ten years before such a ministry was created.

Ismay's tour of duty at the CID came to an end in October 1930. It had been, as it was to turn out, an invaluable apprenticeship. It had given him his first experience of working at the national-strategic level, and of working with ministers and other politicians. Some things had surprised him. One was his opinion of politicians. 'In the past I had always regarded the politician as a man of few principles and little thought of anything but vote-catching and his own career. After seeing many Ministers in action for five years my views underwent a great change'.[42] Another surprise was the relationship between the Service Chiefs of Staff—not quite the band of brothers that he had imagined:

> [T]he first few years of the Chiefs of Staff [committee] were signalised by the most blazing rows!...I remember sitting at a Chiefs of Staff meeting as a fairly junior major, and feeling that I ought not to be present at such an interchange of abuse. I got up and left the room discreetly.[43]

The uneasy relationship between the Chiefs and their lack of a collegiate approach was, as will be seen, to be a recurring theme for Ismay throughout his career and, indeed, afterwards. On appointment each Chief was given a warrant signed by the Prime Minister which emphasised their collective responsibility for advising on defence policy 'as a whole'.[44] Yet too often the Chiefs, while paying lip service to this mantra, would shamelessly put the interests of their own Service first and foremost, particularly when it came to the allocation of Government funding, even when this resulted in deleterious inter-Service rivalry which was clearly contrary to the interests of defence policy as a whole.[45]

In their almost five years working together Ismay and Hankey had become close colleagues. Both were dedicated to their jobs, highly professional and had a shared outlook on most aspects of policy and strategy. In many aspects of their personalities, however, the two men could hardly be more different. Hankey was something of an ascetic and lived a spartan lifestyle. He was a teetotaler, a virtual non-smoker and a strict dietician. Lawrence Burgis, his private secretary, described him as 'a robot... [with] little or no sense of humour... too intense and taut to be a social success—and he had no "small talk"'.[46] Yet Ismay and Hankey got along well, recognising and appreciating each other's talents and capabilities.

The job had been demanding and Ismay, as he did in every appointment throughout his life, had devoted all his energies to it. He and Darry had been living at their house in Kensington, bought in 1925 with the help of Darry's parents. A second daughter, Sarah, had been born in 1928 and a third, Mary, in 1929. But for Ismay, work remained the first priority. Darry recalled that he had worked over-hard—on return from the office, 'frequently till midnight'—and that they 'did not have much time for social life'.[47] Nevertheless, as their family scrapbook shows, Ismay's work did not stop them going to the theatre from time to time, attending a Buckingham Palace garden party each year or spectating at the Wimbledon tennis championships; nor did it prevent him being a committee member at the Hurlingham Polo Club, participating in polo matches there and at various venues around the country, or from going to watch international rugby and cricket matches.[48] During their years in London, however, Darry had suffered two family tragedies. In 1927 her father had died of a lingering illness, and two years later her beloved brother, Peter, died suddenly of septicaemia.

As a result of his performance at the CID Ismay's talents had been recognised. He had been promoted to the rank of brevet lieutenant colonel and had become something of a marked man in Whitehall. Shortly after his arrival at the CID Burgis took him to lunch with Lord Esher, a progenitor of the CID who was greatly impressed by him and later remarked to Burgis, 'There's your successor to Hankey'.[49] In a farewell letter to Ismay, Hankey wrote, 'Except me, no-one knows better than yourself how far I have relied upon you. Also, no-one knows better than I how reliable you have proved'.[50] He also told Ismay that he would probably be required back at the CID in future. Hankey approached the India Office with a recommendation for an award for him: Commander of the Order of the Indian Empire. But believing that this had been rejected, he then approached the Prime Minister directly for an award of Companion of the Order of the Bath.[51] When the honours list was published on New Year's Day 1931, Ismay's name appeared in it for both awards. Since the rules forbade such a double honour he had to choose between the two and elected to receive the latter award.

But over-work had caught up with Ismay. Yet again he fell prey to exhaustion and once more appeared before a medical board: it placed him on six months, sick leave.[52] His next posting, to which he was greatly looking forward, was due to be back in the Frontier Force in India in command of a regiment; his own regiment had no vacancy so he had been selected to command another one, Sam Browne's Cavalry. But in February 1931, just as he and Darry were on the point of leaving for Florida to complete his recuperation, Hankey sent for him with an offer. He told Ismay that the India Office wished to set up a CID equivalent in Delhi and that the newly appointed Viceroy, Lord Willingdon, wished Ismay to accompany him as his military secretary to arrange the matter.

Ismay's version of this in his memoirs is somewhat different. There he makes no mention of an Indian CID, saying merely that Lord Willingdon offered him the appointment, and that he accepted because the Commander-in-Chief (CinC) India, Field Marshal Sir Philip Chetwode, expressed the wish that he should do so—albeit for a short, two-year tenure. Either way it seems a curious decision of Ismay's. He would have known that this might preclude future command appointments, but he may already have judged that his future was on the staff. Possibly he thought that Darry's health might be adequate for two years in India, but not much longer. Since there was no mention of a CID equivalent once he got to India, it may be that Hankey was stretching a point to keep Ismay from reverting to a uniformed career and thus retain him within the fold of the CID. Whatever the truth, Ismay and Darry embarked for India with the Willingdons in April 1931, leaving the three girls with their grandmother at Wormington. Again, this must have been a heartbreaking separation.

The job that awaited Ismay was in many ways a waste of his talents. The military secretary to the Viceroy was essentially a social secretary with a few additional, but hardly demanding, responsibilities: liaison with the CinC; the Viceroy's security; management of his personal staff and organisation of official functions; and arranging the Viceroy's tours round the country. Ismay, however, seems to have been quite content with his lot, happy to make the most of what amounted to a pleasant break from the unremitting pressure of the previous five years. The Viceroy's security, however, was not to be taken for granted. The anti-British movement was increasingly active and there was often evidence of threats to his life, but there were ample security staff—well practised in their trade—to take care of things. Much of Ismay's time seems to have been spent in arranging the Viceroy's itinerary and accompanying him on his various tours round India, in addition to coordinating and participating in the endless social functions at the palatial residence known as Viceroy's House. There were, however, six aides-de-camp and a large retinue of staff to do the detailed work. The major challenge appears to have been the requirement for constant changing from one smart order of dress to another. As Ismay was to recall, 'I had to spend more time—and money—at my tailor's getting fitted out with all this finery than a young lady would spend at her dressmaker's buying her trousseau'.[53]

Ismay's time in India saw considerable political unrest, but he was reticent about it in his memoirs, merely saying that 'Congress were persistent in their demands that we should quit India, and... Mr Gandhi was a constant thorn in our flesh'.[54] Willingdon went considerably further in his private correspondence, describing Gandhi as 'a slippery little devil', but there is no indication from Ismay's papers as to his personal opinion, either of the political situation or of the personalities involved.[55] What Ismay certainly would have applauded about Willingdon was that, like himself with the Rawalpindi Club, he disapproved of clubs which would not admit Indian nationals. When he found that this was the policy of the Royal Bombay Yacht Club he simply established a rival club in Bombay—the Willingdon Sports Club—the rules for which had no such restrictions.[56]

Ismay had been in India just over a year when he received the sad news that his mother Beatrice, back in England, had died aged seventy-five. Ismay typically made no mention of this in his memoirs, nor is there any reference to the event in any of his papers. It would, though, have been an inordinately sorrowful moment for him. Despite the fact that they had seen little of each other since he left home aged eight, she had been something of a rock for him as his emotional letters from Somaliland, which she had proudly kept, show. His sister, Maude, wrote to him, 'her pride—and belief in you—knew no bounds'.[57]

Darry had returned to Wormington for six months during the summer of 1925.[58] Ostensibly this was because her mother was ill, but it may also have been because the separation from her daughter had become too painful. She returned to Delhi in November in time to hear the welcome news that they would be returning to Britain the following May when Ismay would be taking up a job, on promotion, in military intelligence in the War Office. According to Darry, however, the Willingdons were 'not pleased' that Ismay accepted the posting and there was a brief rupture in relations between them.[59]

In his memoirs Ismay was typically complimentary about the Willingdons. In private he was less so. According to his close friend, Robert Bruce Lockhart, dining with him several years later, Ismay told him that, 'Lady Willingdon was a great woman, but she was ruthless and as egotistical as WSC [Churchill]. It was no use going to Lord Willingdon to complain. He was charming but he just shrugged his shoulders. His attitude was, "I can't interfere; after all, she made me"'.[60] Ismay then related an incident which gives an insight into his own character as well as hers. One morning Lady Willingdon told him to sack one of the Viceroy's ADCs whom, she said, had been rude to her. Having heard both sides of the story Ismay declined to do so. He was then subjected to what he called 'the full blast' and told that he was 'no good... a weakling and afraid of my own staff'. Ismay kept his temper and replied 'very firmly and quietly',

> Your Excellency, I have been very happy here, but if you want to know the truth, I came because the Viceroy asked for me and because I liked you both, but in every way it is a sacrifice on my part. I am not interested in it socially. The financial side means nothing to me and as for my military career it is a definite handicap. So if you are not satisfied, I am quite willing to go.

Ismay added, 'That did it. She melted at once, and the whole thing was settled. There were many other instances and if ever I had lost control everything would have been finished. The experience stood me in a very good stead with Winston'.[61]

In February 1933, shortly before they were due to leave India, Ismay was playing in the final of the major polo tournament and had a serious fall resulting in severe concussion. The very next day Darry received a telegram informing her that her mother had also had a fall, breaking a hip. It was a worrying last few months of the tour. Ismay's injury required several weeks' convalescence and resulted in permanent deafness in one ear, a disability which he was to become adept at concealing. They finally left for Britain at the end of April.

Although Ismay described his job with the Viceroy as largely 'poodle-faking'—empty social pretentiousness and flummery—it was not an entirely wasted two years. It had given him time to draw breath and reflect after an intensive and exhausting five years at the CID. It had taught him patience and diplomacy, and it had allowed him to observe the governance of India from the top. It had also given him the opportunity to meet a wide range of Indian people, including senior rulers, politicians and civil servants. All of this may have seemed unimportant to him at the time, but it was to prove an invaluable part of his apprenticeship for extraordinary jobs that lay well ahead.

* * *

It must have been with unbridled joy that Ismay and Darry arrived back in Britain to be united with their three daughters: Susan, now aged ten; Sarah aged four; and three-year-old Mary. The family returned to their house in Kensington, West London and the girls started at schools there. However, as Mary was later to recall, the hours of work that Ismay kept meant that they saw little of their father during the week, and at weekends he was often away playing polo.[62]

Ismay, now promoted to the rank of full colonel, reported to the Military Intelligence directorate of the War Office in May 1933. His first impressions of the War Office were not favourable: 'It struck me as hidebound, unimaginative, impersonal and over-populated'.[63] His job there was as head of Military Intelligence 2 (MI2)—the branch responsible for intelligence gathering, analysis, evaluation and dissemination for the Middle East, Far East, America, Russia, Poland and the Baltic states: a wide remit.[64] The calibre of officers in military intelligence was high and Ismay paid due tribute to them in his memoirs, noting that every one of the dozen lieutenant colonels and majors who worked for him was to reach the rank of at least major general. Ismay enjoyed intelligence work. Perhaps surprisingly, he visited only one of the countries within his remit—Poland. But in those days, travel time to most of the other countries would have been nigh on prohibitive, certainly for someone with so many competing priorities in their job. His work was highly appreciated by his immediate superior, the Director of Military Operations and Intelligence, Major General John Dill. Shortly after Ismay's departure Dill wrote to him warmly, 'Good luck to you and a thousand thanks for all the help you have given me in the past two and a half years. You have been a joy to work with and in the past few weeks I have missed you badly'.[65]

It was quite early on in his time at the War Office that circumstances in his private life were to change radically. In September 1933 Darry's mother died. She had never fully recovered from her fall earlier in the year and it became clear in July that she only had a short time to live. Her death meant that Darry inherited Wormington Grange and her mother's money. She and Ismay decided to sell the place and they put it on the market. But this was not a good time for such a sale—it being close to the height of the Great Depression—and two years later they withdrew it. They continued to live in London, taking every opportunity to get down to Wormington for weekends and holidays. The inheritance, however, meant that any lingering concerns that Ismay may have had about their financial position were a thing of the past. Not that this altered his lifestyle much, but it gave him a certain security, confidence and independence in that his future was not entirely dependent on his military career and the approval of his superiors. For some other people this might have resulted in them taking things a bit easier and working less hard. Not for Ismay.

In August 1935 he was told by Hankey that he had provisionally mentioned his name to Prime Minister Baldwin, for a new appointment, Deputy Secretary of the CID.[66] Hitherto, the assistant secretaries had reported directly to Hankey; but with the growth in the size of the CID's business and staff, including the number of assistant secretaries, an intermediate level was required in order to relieve Hankey of this increased workload. When the offer was formally made to him the following April, Ismay had pondered the matter but accepted.[67] In his memoirs he says that he did so primarily because he believed that, having been away from troops for fourteen years, it was most improbable that he would be considered for high command. But this was probably not the main reason: the very next day he was offered command of the cavalry brigade on the North-West Frontier of India, an offer he politely declined. More likely is that he knew in his heart something with which he did not wish to burden Darry: with her medical condition, he could not expect her to accompany him to India again and he did not wish to continue in a career that would result in separation from her and the family for what could be long periods of time. Actually, Darry was aware of this conundrum and later admitted to feeling guilty about it.[68] There was an additional factor. As Ismay alludes in his memoirs, with the storm clouds gathering over Europe, he did not wish to find himself again trapped in a sideshow half-way round the world, or, as he put it, 'finding myself on the wrong side of the Suez Canal'.[69]

But it was not an entirely straightforward decision: 'as I signed the letter [of acceptance] I felt a momentary pang at the thought that my days of real soldiering were over. It was like saying good-bye to the dreams of my youth. But reason quickly banished sentiment, and I have never regretted the decision.'[70] The conflict between heart and head, and the reluctant resolution in favour of the latter, were trademark characteristics of Ismay's decision-making throughout his life.

4

CORRIDORS OF POWER

1936–40

For Ismay, returning to the CID in August 1936 'was like coming home—the same chief, the same Civil Service colleagues, the same clerical staff, the same messengers'.[1] His appointment had been given a wide remit—'the general day-to-day supervision and control… of the whole organisation'—and Ismay was somewhat daunted by the challenge that lay ahead.[2] After three years in the War Office intelligence directorate, he was well aware of the growing threat to international peace, Britain and the empire. Germany's openly declared rearmament programme was well advanced and earlier in the year, in defiance of international treaties, Adolf Hitler's troops had reoccupied the Rhineland. In Italy Benito Mussolini's fascist regime was also rearming fast and pursuing an expansionist foreign policy which had included the invasion of Abyssinia, completed in May 1936. Two months later a vicious civil war had broken out in Spain, with one side supported by Russia and the other by Germany and Italy. In the Far East Japan had invaded Manchuria and declared the whole of China to be a Japanese preserve. The briefing papers now presented to him on his arrival underlined the weakness and lack of preparedness of the British armed forces following years of government reluctance to rearm, and the scale of the challenges that lay ahead. He was later to admit that 'the magnitude, complexity and responsibility of the task appalled me. Henceforward all family life would have to take second place'.[3]

Ismay got to work immediately with three initiatives. The first resulted from his concern that the air defence of Great Britain was seriously under-resourced in comparison to other competing demands for air defence, such as that for potential expeditionary forces. Within a month of his return to the CID he wrote a forceful paper on the subject which Hankey forwarded to ministers.[4]

The other two initiatives resulted from Ismay's recent experience in War Office intelligence. The first of these reflected his concern that the newly formed Joint Intelligence Committee was being sidelined in Whitehall. He moved to strengthen its position and in September 1936 persuaded the Chiefs of Staff that, contrary to the advice they were getting from their own staffs, the committee's intelligence reports should be channelled directly to them (the Chiefs), rather than through intermediaries who might adjust the reports to suit their own agendas.[5]

The third initiative resulted from his concern at the lack of an overarching intelligence assessment of potential enemy intentions, together with the preparations required to counter them. He produced his own paper on the subject. In it he anticipated an early bombing campaign on Great Britain on the outbreak of war, and a German naval campaign against the British merchant fleet. He strongly advocated four countermeasures in particular: a higher priority for air defence; maintaining sufficient reserves of food, fuel oil and other necessities; building up RAF Bomber Command with a view to carrying the war into Germany from the outset of hostilities; and preparing a field force to stand alongside the French Army on the outbreak of war, together with plans for its expansion. He was not infallible in his predictions and was later typically self-deprecating about their accuracy. However, his paper—'to which I had laboriously committed my thoughts'—never got further than Hankey's desk. Ismay made light of this in his memoirs, but it was a remarkable rebuff.[6] Ismay's assessment, however, did not chime with Hankey's preconceptions, particularly his firmly held belief that the priority for more resources should be the Royal Navy, and certainly not a field force for deployment to France.

Ismay's relationship with Hankey was increasingly to be characterised by differences of opinion between them. Many of these reflected the fact that Ismay's view of the international situation, and of Hitler in particular, was closer to Churchill's than to Hankey's. He was already a considerable admirer of Churchill and one of his favourite books was Churchill's *World in Crisis*, which told of the events leading up to the outbreak of war in 1914. Indeed, he claimed to know parts of it by heart.[7] Not only did Hankey disagree with Churchill's opinions but he had a considerable antipathy towards him personally, finding his manner 'irritable' and later describing him as 'the most difficult man I ever had to work with'.[8] Ismay had been in favour of a campaign led by Churchill for a coordinating political authority for national defence and had welcomed Prime Minister Baldwin's response: the creation, earlier in 1936, of a Minister for the Coordination of Defence whose responsibilities included political leadership of the CID.

There had been public expectation that the first incumbent would be Churchill—an appointment which Ismay would have welcomed—but Hankey was strongly opposed to this. Ismay may have felt, probably correctly, that Hankey's opinion was a factor in Baldwin's rejection of Churchill for the post. Instead, Baldwin chose a man with no obvious qualification for the job—the Attorney General, Sir Thomas Inskip—who was to prove notably ineffective.[9] According to Ismay, wags described it at the time as '[t]he most remarkable appointment since the Emperor Caligula made his horse a consul'.[10] The fact that he happily quoted this in his memoirs probably indicates that he shared the view.[11] What was more to the point was that, as Ismay acknowledged, the appointment carried with it 'no executive authority whatsoever'. As AJP Taylor put it, Inskip was given 'one room, two secretaries and no powers'.[12]

A further disagreement with Hankey was over the parliamentary delegation, of which Churchill was a leading member, which had met with Baldwin two days before Ismay's arrival to argue for much greater and swifter rearmament. Hankey had been sceptical of some of the arguments and statistics which Churchill had produced at the meeting, but Ismay was sent the evidence by Desmond Morton, head of the Industrial Intelligence Centre, which corroborated Churchill's statements (unsurprisingly, since Morton had covertly supplied them to Churchill in the first place).[13] This conclusive evidence made a deep impression on Ismay, whose job it was to draft the government's response. Three months later Ismay was secretary at the Prime Minister's next meeting with the deputation and witnessed Churchill's long and combative cross-examination of Inskip.[14] Ismay was to have regular contact with Churchill at meetings of the important Air Defence Research Committee of which Churchill was a member and where, in Tim Bouverie's words, 'he was able to make a thorough nuisance of himself'.[15]

Ismay's divergence of opinion with Hankey widened in May 1937 when Baldwin was succeeded as Prime Minister by Neville Chamberlain, his Chancellor of the Exchequer, whose 'overriding objective was to avoid war'[16] and who 'simply could not accept that anyone could positively welcome war'.[17] Hankey 'strongly supported' his policy of appeasement.[18]

Three months earlier the CID, influenced by Chamberlain, had approved a strategic assumption that, despite Mussolini's increasingly bellicose anti-British statements, the continuing brutal suppression of the Abyssinian population and the recently formed Rome-Berlin Axis, 'Italy… need not be regarded as a probable enemy'.[19] Ismay was far from convinced, along with Foreign Minister Anthony Eden and some of his senior officials.[20] Ismay entered into discussions with them, encouraged the production of their paper *The Probability of War with Italy* and arranged for the matter to be addressed in a paper for the Chiefs of Staff which challenged the CID assumption.[21] Hankey was unswayed. Returning from a holiday in Italy in August he was, in the words of Brian Bond, 'firmly convinced that it was in Britain's best interests to appease Mussolini, whose regime he had admired'.[22]

Ismay was again at odds with Hankey in November over the priority which should be given to the expeditionary Field Force to be deployed to France in the event of war. In line with Chamberlain's policy of 'limited liability'[23] the size of the force was restricted to only five divisions (four infantry and one mobile). Hankey now recommended to Inskip removing the funding for the equipping and preparation for the continental commitment of even this small force.[24] Ismay was forthright in his opposition, telling Hankey that in the event of war it would be extremely unlikely for a government to be able to resist the demand for deployment of a Field Force to France and that, therefore, 'it is impossible to wage a national war on a principle of limited liability'.[25] Hankey, who according to his biographer Stephen Roskill had a 'congenital dislike of any commitment on the continent of Europe', was again unmoved and the Cabinet went ahead with downgrading the Field Force to the lowest priority for funding.[26] As Michael Howard observed, '[t]he policy of "limited liability" in continental warfare had now shrunk to one of no liability at all'.[27]

A final disagreement with Hankey came in March 1938 with his precipitate sacking of his private secretary of seventeen years, Lawrence Burgis, a man whom Ismay rated highly. It seems that Hankey wholly overreacted over a trivial matter and later much regretted his decision. In mitigation, Roskill suggests that Hankey was under great strain at the time.[28] Ismay was among the large number of senior CID officials who wrote sympathetic letters to Burgis. He was later to appoint him to a key position on his own staff, where he served throughout the war.

Despite these disagreements, spoken or unspoken, relations remained cordial between Hankey and Ismay and do not appear to have altered Hankey's overall judgement of Ismay's talents and potential. The fact that Ismay was prepared to voice his opinion when it was contrary to that of the man who held his future career in the palm of his hand is an insight into Ismay's character.

Ismay's appointment involved him in a wide range of subjects and highly diverse issues. One issue in the autumn of 1937 concerned a controversy over the development of the Imperial Defence College. The college (now the Royal College of Defence Studies) had been created in 1927 to provide higher education for the most promising senior officers from the British and Dominion armed forces and officials from the Civil Service. A proposal was made—reportedly by Sir John Reith, Director General of the BBC—that attendance at the college should be offered to a limited number of civilian attendees from outside government. The proposal initially received a dusty response both from the commandant of the college and from the Chiefs of Staff. Ismay, however, was enthusiastic and strengthened the wording of the proposal accordingly. Despite winning over the commandant (largely, it has to be said, on the grounds that there were no cost implications), the proposal was again rejected by the Chiefs.[29] It would be another forty-three years before the college opened its doors to non-governmental civilians; their attendance continues to this day to provide a much-valued contribution to the course.

Later in his time as Deputy Secretary Ismay was to take an organisational initiative that was to have critically important consequences for the higher direction of the war. It followed his concern at the government's lack of protected office accommodation in the heart of Whitehall. In 1936 and 1937 two separate committees had considered how government could be continued effectively if central London was subjected to heavy bombing. Their deliberations took many months but both eventually recommended that dispersal either to the suburbs or further afield would be required with, if possible, some hardened accommodation provided in central London. As Nigel de Lee relates in his history of the War Rooms, it was Ismay who in May 1938, concerned at the lack of firm decisions and the need for action, 'used his initiative in anticipation of orders and requirements' and took the matter in hand.[30] Having gained the endorsement of the Chiefs of Staff he persuaded the Treasury to provide some modest funding and tasked the Office of Works with identifying a suitable location. He delegated the further planning and implementation to two of his subordinates: Burgis and Major Leslie Hollis, Royal Marines. At first the plan was for an underground emergency war room in Whitehall to house the Chiefs of Staff and their key support staffs, but this was then expanded to accommodate a small War Cabinet together with its support and communications staffs. Ismay's decision and subsequent drive had come not a moment too soon: the War Rooms—located in the basement of the former New Public Offices in Great George Street—were to become fully operational in August 1939, just one month before the outbreak of war.[31]

Ismay knew that Hankey was due to retire towards the end of 1938 and believed that he had a good chance of taking over from him, a belief encouraged by Hankey. But due to a misunderstanding, Hankey erroneously thought that Ismay would only take on the CID element of the job and not secretaryship of the Cabinet. As a result, in May 1938 he sounded out Major General Henry Pownall, another previous CID assistant secretary. Pownall, however, was a good friend of Ismay and said that he would only accept the job if it was certain that Ismay did not want it. Having clarified the misunderstanding with Ismay, Hankey put Ismay's name forward to Prime Minister Neville Chamberlain.[32]

However, internal Whitehall politics and skulduggery were to come into play. Sir Warren Fisher, Permanent Secretary to the Treasury and Head of the Home Civil Service, and his close colleague Sir Horace Wilson, adviser to the Prime Minister, wanted a civil servant to succeed Hankey in all his appointments. They pressed the case of Edward Bridges, Fisher's deputy at the Treasury, with Ismay to remain as Deputy Secretary of the CID. When Hankey continued to lobby for Ismay, Wilson resorted to what Hankey described as 'trying on a bluff and a blackmail', suggesting to Hankey that if he did not back down, he would not get the directorship of the Suez Canal Company for which he had applied. Hankey remonstrated.[33]

However, confident that the decision would go their way with the Prime Minister, Fisher and Wilson informed Ismay of their recommendation. That evening, deeply despondent, Ismay told Darry who advised him to think it over quietly and do nothing in a hurry. The following night they dined with a close friend near Wormington, Ruby Holland-Martin. Having heard the story, he encouraged Ismay to resign and become a Member of Parliament: a nearby Conservative safe seat was about to fall vacant. On return to London Ismay demanded and got another interview with Fisher. When Fisher confirmed that he would remain as Deputy Secretary, Ismay said that he would resign. Fisher told him that if he did so, it would be the end of his career. Ismay followed Holland-Martin's advice, saying that he had already considered the eventuality and would probably stand for Parliament.[34] As Ismay recounted to Darry, 'there was then a dead silence'.[35] A few days later, Chamberlain made his decision: Bridges to be Cabinet Secretary; Ismay to be Secretary of the CID. Ismay was delighted.[36]

* * *

In early August 1938 Ismay, now a major general (an unusual 'double promotion' which bypassed the rank of brigadier), took over as Secretary of the CID. He was to face a baptism of fire. In March Hitler had annexed Austria and threatened Czechoslovakia. There was now evidence of renewed hostile German intent towards Czechoslovakia. Ismay decided to forego his summer holiday and returned to the office. He became heavily involved in government contingency planning, attending numerous crisis meetings and initiating a series of papers (short title: *CZ*) on defence preparations urgently required.[37] The intelligence assessments became more specific. On 12 September Sir Hugh Sinclair, Chief of the Secret Intelligence Service (SIS, also known as MI6), told Ismay that Hitler intended to attack Czechoslovakia between 24 and 28 September 'and is prepared to support such action by world-wide war if necessary'.[38] Ismay became increasingly concerned at the slow pace of decision-making in defensive preparations, in particular the Government's reluctance to call up the reservist anti-aircraft units responsible for the defence of London, or the fighter squadrons of the Auxiliary Air Force. On 22 September, he voiced his concerns to Inskip, but the minister declined to take action. The following day, however, Ismay returned to the charge and persuaded him to raise the matter with Chamberlain, who had just returned from Germany and the second of his three meetings with Hitler. Chamberlain immediately authorised all Ismay's recommendations. On 30 September Chamberlain held his final meeting with Hitler at Munich at which he agreed to the German occupation of the Czech Sudetenland.

During this period of shuttle diplomacy, Ismay produced an important document for the Prime Minister: 'Note on the question of whether it would be better to fight the Germans now, or to postpone the issue'.[39] In it he focused on Britain's vulnerability to air attack—'the greatest danger to which we are currently exposed'—and the inadequacy of its air defences but pointed out that this was being rapidly rectified. He concluded that 'from the military point of view, time is in our favour, and that, if war with

Germany has to come, it would be better to fight her in say 6–12 months' time, than to accept the present challenge'. It would be a mistake, though, to overestimate the influence of this note; Chamberlain had no intention of going to war. Ismay's advice may, as Richard Overy has suggested, have reassured Chamberlain that 'within twelve months Britain's military position would be quite different'.[40] However, Ismay was later to express the view that at this time 'there was no thought in the Government of waiting until we were better prepared. To avert war, not to postpone it, was the sole object'.[41] Whether Ismay's advice to Chamberlain was well judged is debatable: historians disagree as to whether procrastination was justified. Bouverie for example considers that the strategic advantage lay with the Allies in September 1938 and that Germany more profitably used the so-called 'breathing space' to improve its own warfighting capability.[42]

As an aside, Ismay recalled in his memoirs that he greeted Chamberlain's return from Munich and his declaration of 'peace for our time' with a sense of relief, giving little thought to the price that had been paid or the probability that the reprieve would be temporary.[43] Returning home 'light of heart' he was given a hard time by Darry, who was highly critical of his attitude: 'How could I defend an arrangement which may have saved our own skin for the moment, but which had betrayed a smaller nation?' Although he vigorously defended his support for the Munich agreement he later admitted with typical humility that, 'for ever after I was so ashamed of it that I deliberately put my head in the sand. I refused to allow myself to think about it, still less to discuss it'.[44] This was actually not quite the case. In 1943, with the benefit of hindsight, Ismay was to change completely his opinion of the Munich agreement, declaring that he had been wrong in his advice to Chamberlain and that Britain should indeed have accepted the challenge in September 1938.[45]

Apart from anything else, Britain's response to the crisis had shown just how unprepared the government machinery was to handle such a contingency. The implementation of the state of emergency had been chaotic. While many people preferred to draw a veil over the matter and forget it, Ismay instituted a lessons learned study and produced a comprehensive, single-volume report to ensure that the country would be better prepared next time.[46] It would be less than twelve months before his action was to prove its value.

Once the 1938 Czech crisis and its aftermath had passed, Ismay was able to take a wider view of his job. He instituted a number of changes at the CID, more of emphasis and tone than of policy. First, clearly concerned that his staff might be open to a charge of representing sectional interests or single-Service agendas, he took steps to eradicate such a tendency. 'I told the boys that anyone who failed to be impartial would be ruthlessly sacked', he later wrote, 'because unless we were known to be impartial we would not be trusted, and if we were not trusted we would be useless to the Government and ourselves'.[47] Second, with the division of the Cabinet secretariat and the CID and the need to bring replacements into the latter, Ismay recruited a number of young civil servants from other Whitehall departments on a temporary basis into his organisation. This, as Franklyn Johnson observed, produced 'perhaps more flexible personalities' and improved cooperation from the departments concerned.[48] Third, Ismay saw no reason to follow Hankey's renowned secrecy about the workings of the CID. He happily lectured on the subject to semi-public audiences, such as the Royal United Services Institute.[49]

Ismay now returned to the need for the Field Force, to be deployed to France in the event of war, to be properly equipped. But this was a subject of considerable inter-Service rivalry. According to Brian Bond, Air Chief Marshal Sir Cyril Newall, the Chief of the Air Staff, had 'frequently demonstrated a doctrinaire disbelief in the Field Force's strategic utility while pressing the Air Ministry's case for the bomber as the decisive weapon of war'.[50] In December 1938, at a meeting of the Chiefs of Staff, attended by Newall, Admiral Sir Roger Backhouse (the First Sea Lord), and General Lord Gort (the CIGS), Newall again 'was opposed to equipping any of the Territorial divisions for war because that would open the door to unlimited expansion of land warfare'.[51] Ismay used a ploy which was something of a trademark in any committee of which he was secretary: offering to provide a summary of discussion and using the opportunity to press his own opinion. In this case he made the point that the army might be employed in theatres other than France and Flanders, and that 'wherever it was employed it must be properly equipped'. To what must have been Newall's chagrin, Ismay was immediately and firmly supported by both Backhouse and Gort.[52]

Ismay also worked assiduously to achieve the establishment of a Ministry of Supply, responsible for equipping and provisioning the armed forces: a subject close to his heart since his days as an assistant secretary at the CID. As Deputy Secretary he had again been frustrated by his inability to achieve change, recalling in his memoirs that 'I found it a little difficult to prepare briefs for ministerial speeches based on arguments with which I was in almost total disagreement'.[53] Now, following the Czech crisis, he was convinced that a Ministry of Supply was a clear and immediate necessity. Opposition continued from the individual Armed Services—who wanted to retain responsibility for their own supply and equipment procurement—and from the Prime Minister and other apostles of appeasement. As late as November 1938 the Minister for Air, Sir Kingsley Wood, probably combined both arguments when he asserted that 'we can do little without a Ministry of Supply, but to appoint such a minister would arouse the anger of Germany'.[54] Although there is no direct evidence that Ismay was the catalyst, his minister Inskip, previously an opponent of a Ministry of Supply, had a Damascene conversion in January 1939 and started to argue for it.[55] That may have contributed to Inskip losing his job, but two months later Chamberlain reluctantly approved its creation.[56] It was a cause for only partial celebration for Ismay: the new ministry's remit was restricted to the army and to the supply of items common to all three Services. Nevertheless, it was progress.

A further important deficiency that Ismay addressed was the lack of a capstone in the organisational structure for the higher direction of war which would bring together the British and French governments at the highest level. In February 1939, asked for his recommendation by Inskip's successor, Admiral of the Fleet Lord Chatfield, Ismay proposed a return on the outbreak of hostilities to the establishment of a Supreme War Council similar to that created by Lloyd George in 1917. The Council would consist of the British and French Prime Minsters with whoever they wished to accompany them and would meet from time to time as necessary. The proposal was approved by Chamberlain and by the French government following a visit by Ismay to General Maurice Gamelin, head of the French Army.[57]

Relations between the CID and government ministers were generally good, but in spring 1939 there was one major disruption. Following the German Army's occupation of the whole of Czechoslovakia on 15 March, the government suddenly announced that the size of the Territorial Army would be doubled forthwith and that it was introducing conscription. Neither the CID nor the Chiefs of Staff were consulted, let alone given prior warning. The decision caused considerable confusion and for many months did nothing to improve army capacity or readiness. Ismay was still irritated about the decision when he came to write his memoirs, referring to it as 'extraordinary'.[58]

Over the six years since 1933 the work and size of the CID as an organisation (though not necessarily its efficiency) had increased hugely.

In part this was due to the tendency for all bureaucracies to grow at a great rate and to Hankey's tendency to solve a new problem by creating a new committee to address it; but the increased size and complexity of the CID was also partly due to the increase in the complexity of the subjects for which it was responsible, the need to deal with these subjects in ever greater detail, and a feeling of impending international crisis. For whatever reason the number of participants in its activities, whether as committee and subcommittee members or as temporary attachments, had grown exponentially. In 1933 the number of such participants totalled 405. By November 1936 the comparative number was 532. By the end of 1938 it had reached 876. The number of committee and subcommittee meetings increased in proportion: between March 1934 and March 1935 the number of meetings totalled 237; in 1938 the figure had reached 409.[59] Throughout the spring and summer of 1939, the work rate in the CID intensified still further. As Hollis later recalled, 'we usually worked far into the night and most weekends'.[60] But in early August, with no indication of what was about to happen, Ismay left London for a holiday in Scotland. It was interrupted on 19 August by the arrival of a Cabinet office telegram requesting his immediate return. It was to be his last holiday for six years.

On the day of his return to London news came of the Russo-German non-aggression pact signed in Moscow. In his memoirs Ismay recalled his astonishment. 'Who could have imagined that two gangsters, who had been heaping the vilest abuse on each other for many years, would kiss and make friends overnight?'[61] The procedures for transition to war, so carefully produced by the CID and embodied in the top-secret War Book, were given final scrutiny. Ismay had delegated the key responsibility for the War Book, a subject on which he himself had been the lead officer in his first tour at the CID, to an exceptional officer, Wing Commander Bill Elliot, whom he trusted implicitly. The trust was fully justified. Hollis noted that the War Book had now been produced 'to a high degree of perfection'.[62] In the final weeks of August and the beginning of September, daily War Book meetings were held at which every government department was represented. The process for its adoption was now set in motion. On 31 August Ismay and Bridges put a key paper to the Prime Minister setting out the various systems of higher control which might be adopted and their relative advantages and disadvantages.[63] As they expected, Chamberlain decided to set up a small War Cabinet, as Lloyd George had done in the previous war. The CID was disbanded, and its secretariat merged with that of the Cabinet into a single War Cabinet Secretariat, headed by Bridges.[64] This had two wings, civil and military. Ismay headed the military wing, with the title Deputy Secretary (Military) of the War Cabinet.

On 1 September Hitler invaded Poland. In retrospect it is easy to see the inevitability of what followed, but at the time there was considerable uncertainty—even among those who, like Ismay, might be expected to have had a clear picture—as to the likely course of events and what sort of a war might be being embarked upon. An insight into Ismay's thoughts about this uncertainty and about the prospect of war with Germany is given in a letter he wrote to Darry on the evening of 2 September:

> I know very little more than you do as to what is really happening in Poland, or as to what Hitler is really up to. He hasn't replied to our peremptory warning, but as it was not an ultimatum in the strict sense of the term—we can't fire. I am not for a moment trying to pretend that war is not inevitable, but I cannot believe there is not something going on in Germany which we cannot interpret; and that if we—and the French—stand absolutely firm—it will either be a short war, owing to dissension in Germany itself—or it might not even start at all. The chances of the latter are not less than 1000–1. I am quite certain that whatever may happen, we'll come out on top in the end.[65]

It is difficult to tell whether this apparent optimism was what Ismay genuinely believed or whether it was merely reassurance for his wife. On the one hand, as Overy has asserted, there was a 'growing confidence in 1939 that Franco-British military and economic strength would be equal to the task of defeating Germany in the long run'.[66] And at this stage there was confidence that Britain, and the French, would indeed 'stand absolutely firm'. Yet Ismay will have been aware of the lack of preparedness of Britain's armed forces, particularly that of the army, for the short war that he anticipated and that the government, also aware of this fact, was planning in the event of war to avoid a quick solution and follow what became known as 'the long war strategy'.[67]

On Sunday, 3 September, the day that Britain and France declared war on Germany, Ismay had a surprise visitor to his office in Richmond Terrace. It was Hankey, suggesting that he return and share Ismay's responsibilities with him. According to Burgis, Ismay 'took a poor view of this'.[68] He offered to resign if Hankey wished to take over again, but very sensibly refused to divide the job.[69] Hankey withdrew; his honour and self-esteem, though, were soon to be satisfied: later that day Chamberlain appointed him to his War Cabinet as Minister Without Portfolio.

Ismay settled quickly into his wartime role, but it was not without concerns for him during the seven months of the 'Phoney War'. First, he considered that the system in 10 Downing Street was flawed and deeply unsuited to wartime. Here his main concern related to the role of Sir Horace Wilson, now Permanent Secretary to the Treasury and Head of the Home Civil Service—a close confidant of the Prime Minister—and a figure who was viewed with suspicion and distaste on both sides of the political divide.[70] Ismay later recalled that Chamberlain:

> introduced an innovation by having the most senior and powerful Civil Servant of the day working next door to him and in effect, though not in name, Principal Private Secretary. I can testify from personal experience that this innovation was disastrous, since it led to Mr Chamberlain getting his views on many topics at second hand. Thus, although I was his Chief of Staff in the military sphere, I very rarely had an opportunity of putting technical points to the Prime Minister personally. I nearly always had to see Sir Horace Wilson, who passed on my views, often in garbled fashion. Worse still, if he did not agree with them, he did not pass them on at all.[71]

Ismay made no mention of this in his memoirs, perhaps because Wilson was still alive at the time of writing. He was, however, even more critical of Wilson in a letter to the Earl of Avon (as Anthony Eden became in 1961), referring, with some vitriol, to 'the egregious Horace Wilson... How I suffered from that creature for the first 6 months of the war'.[72]

His second concern was his lack of confidence in Britain's French ally. This resulted from visits to France with the Prime Minister and Ismay's perception that 'our allies were getting more and more despondent as the weeks passed... the soldiers in the trenches were being methodically rotted by the German propaganda campaign... and there seemed to be a grave lack of confidence in the High Command'.[73] On return from one of these trips, Darry remarked to her husband that he 'was looking more exhausted and depressed' than she had ever seen him.[74] Ismay's pessimistic view of the French military capacity was very much a minority one. John ('Jock') Colville, one of the Prime Minister's private secretaries, was to recall that Ismay was 'the only man I ever heard predict, before the enemy attack in May, 1940, that the French Armies would collapse before the German onslaught'.[75]

His trips to France with Chamberlain had revealed a further weakness to Ismay: the lack of coordination between Britain's Armed Services, largely resulting from inter-Service rivalry. Ismay had observed the deleterious effect of such rivalry since his earliest days in the CID. Relations between the Chiefs of Staff—now Newall, Admiral of the Fleet Sir Dudley Pound and General Sir Edmund Ironside—remained inherently tense. In part this resulted from fierce competition for scarce financial resources, but it was also due to fierce disagreements on the control of air power. The army was adamant that, like the Royal Navy, it should have control over all the air assets that supported it; the Royal Air Force saw this, with some justification, as an existential threat. On his visit to France Ismay noted that the British air commander was entirely independent not only from the army commander, General Gort, but also from the French High Command and received his orders from the CinC Bomber Command in Britain. As Ismay put it in his memoirs, '[i]t almost seemed as though the Air Staff would prefer to have their forces under Beelzebub rather than anyone connected with the Army. When one recalls the views which were held by the General Staff on the employment of air power, one can scarcely blame them'.[76]

A further concern, which grew as the months passed by, was a sense that the committee structures and procedures that he had approved were failing. In his draft memoirs, but not in the published version, he made a frank admission:

> I myself was very conscious that, in spite of all the thought that had been given to these matters by the Committee for Imperial Defence in the years between the wars, our machinery was not working as it should; and I was extremely unhappy. I felt that particular blame for the failure attached to myself, because this was a matter in which, by dint of my appointment, I had special responsibility. I recalled all that Lord Hankey had done in the First World War to help the Prime Ministers under whom he had served, and I was ashamed at my ineptitude.[77]

The part of the machinery that was working least well was a new addition to the structure for higher control of the war: the Military Coordination Committee.[78] The War Cabinet had approved its establishment on 2 November 1939 as an interface between the War Cabinet and the Chiefs of Staff Committee to look at long-term or complex defence problems. It consisted of the three Service ministers with Lord Chatfield in the chair, Service Chiefs in attendance and Ismay as secretary. When consulted about the establishment of the committee Ismay and Bridges had favoured the idea but warned that 'it must not cause a delay by constituting an unnecessary link between the Chiefs of Staff and the War Cabinet'.[79] It soon became apparent that the committee not only took up a great deal of time while adding little value, but that it acted as a brake on the speed of decision-making and would be counterproductive when fighting started. The result was immense frustration all round.

But Ismay's greatest concern related to the Allies' drift away from the agreed 'long war strategy' towards seeking a quick win in Scandinavia. The latter idea had originated in the autumn of 1939 with embryonic plans for a small-scale naval intervention to prevent Swedish iron ore, exported through the northern Norwegian port of Narvik, from reaching Germany. But largely due to pressure from Churchill, now First Lord of the Admiralty (political head of the Royal Navy), ambitions and plans had gathered momentum and increased in scope until in January the Cabinet approved a plan for a major Anglo-French land-force expedition to Norway. Lord Halifax's deputy at the Foreign Office, RA ('Rab') Butler, a long-time supporter of appeasement, was one of the ministers strongly opposed to the scheme. His Parliamentary Private Secretary, Henry 'Chips' Channon, noted that 'bizarrely' Ismay was 'backing Rab'.[80]

Ismay's concern, however, was rather different from Butler's. It was one of strategy: in effect, that the ends to be achieved were completely out of balance with the ways and means available. In early February Jock Colville recorded in his diary, 'Personally Ismay can see no point in these risky proposals and thinks we should do better to stick to our original thesis that we can win a drawn-out siege by outstaying Germany'.[81] But few others in Whitehall were as clear-sighted. At one point, on 12 March, the Cabinet approved a plan to send an expeditionary force to assist the Finns in their war against Russia. Newall, chairman of the Chiefs of Staff Committee, raised no objection at the meeting but on leaving it described the plan to colleagues as 'harebrained'.[82] It was aborted the same night when the Finns surrendered; all the British forces for Scandinavia were stood down, some of them disbanded.

Within a fortnight, however, the Cabinet (reacting to French pressure) was again planning expeditions to Norway with little regard for practicalities. Ismay's concern at the lack of consistent strategy was well founded. When a few days later, on 9 April, Germany suddenly invaded Norway and Denmark the British decision making, both political and military, was chaotic. Ismay was, with good reason, particularly critical of the performance of the Chiefs of Staff. At the early-morning crisis meeting immediately following the invasion he noted that not only did none of the three come up with a plan of action but that 'not a single constructive suggestion had been put forward by the time we had to break up the meeting and join the War Cabinet'.[83] But his main criticism of them followed his recurrent theme of the deleterious impact of inter-Service competition and the lack of a joint, tri-Service approach.

> The Chief of the Naval Staff and the Chief of the Imperial General Staff acted with sturdy independence. They appointed their respective commanders without consultation with each other; and worse still, they gave directives to those commanders without harmonising them. Thereafter they continued to issue separate orders to them. Thus confusion was worse compounded. The best that can be said is that we learned, at not too prohibitive a cost, how things should not be done.[84]

In the direction of the campaign Ismay, along with the Joint Planning Staff, consistently made common-sense recommendations but these were frequently overruled or ignored by the Chiefs of Staff and by ministers. If followed, two of these recommendations in particular, both made at the War Cabinet on 9 April, might have altered the course of the campaign. First the recommendation that the focus of action should be the port of Trondheim, halfway up the Norwegian coast, in order to be able to provide vital support to Norwegian forces combating the German consolidation. Instead, the Chiefs—swayed by Churchill—allowed the initial focus to be the port of Narvik despite the fact that it was so far north as to be irrelevant to the action around and south of Trondheim. Second, the War Cabinet prevaricated about authorising the bombing of airfields in Norway and Denmark. During the discussion Ismay passed a note across the Cabinet table to Hankey. 'If we don't go "flat out" against this invasion we will go very near losing this war', he wrote. 'You can't let the Germans consolidate unhampered. If we don't do it now we'll be forced by world opinion to do it later. Better to do it now before they are ready.'[85] Hankey pressed for air action, but only at Oslo—a suggestion easily countered by Newall, who told the meeting that Oslo was out of range of British bombers. The War Cabinet agreed to postpone bombing operations in Norway until further reconnaissance had taken place. By the time the decision was taken to allow bombing, the Germans had established air superiority over Norway.

Ismay much regretted that his advocacy for these policies had been unsuccessful. He sent a note to one of the Joint Planners, Group Captain Slessor, admitting that he had 'completely failed to persuade our elders and betters', adding, 'I only hope that you and your colleagues will appreciate that my failure has been due to incompetence in persuasion and not lack of trying'.[86]

A few days prior to the invasion, Chamberlain had sought to answer criticism of the Military Coordination Committee by dismissing its chairman, Chatfield, and abolishing the appointment of Minister for Coordination of Defence. Ismay had welcomed Chatfield's arrival as Minister in January 1939 in place of Inskip. Following his dismissal Ismay wrote to commiserate, paying tribute to his skilful handling of his appointment under very difficult circumstances. Chatfield's reply shone the spotlight back on Ismay.

> You characteristically omit one factor of overwhelming importance, your own post. I know best of anyone how great that part was, in how many instances it was due to your initiative and creative mind that the step was taken at the crossroads in the right direction, how ably and conscientiously you worked and guided the labour of many into the final machine we were trying to create. I hope the state will realise in full measure what Whitehall owes to you.[87]

In his memoirs Ismay paid considerable tribute to Chatfield for his performance in his ministerial appointment. In commenting on the draft account Ian Jacob, one of Ismay's deputies, demurred, criticising Chatfield—with justification—for taking the job without insisting on the authority to go with it and declaring that he was 'totally ineffective'.[88] Deep down Ismay probably agreed, but his sense of loyalty did not allow him to alter what he had written.

To the surprise of many, Chatfield's replacement as chairman of the Military Coordination Committee was the First Lord of the Admiralty, Churchill. As a long-standing admirer of Churchill, Ismay may have welcomed the appointment, but he was undoubtedly shocked by the result. In his memoirs, he passed over this relatively lightly, saying that the meetings became 'at once more frequent, more controversial and—I may say—more acrimonious!'[89] In private he went much further, telling Colville at the time that Churchill's 'verbosity and restlessness made unnecessary work, prevented real planning and caused friction'.[90] He also told a group of senior officers after the war that, 'we had one awful month in which Mr Churchill was practically Minister of Defence, in addition to being First Lord, and it was hell'.[91] Ismay became so concerned at the level of rancour and ill temper between Churchill and the Chiefs of Staff that at the Chiefs' meeting on 16 April, prior to a meeting to be attended by Churchill, 'he cleared the room... and implored the Chiefs of Staff to exercise the most rigid self-control over themselves and at all costs to keep their tempers. He told them that if there was a row at the meeting, he was afraid of a first class political crisis'.[92] The fact that as merely the secretary of the committee, and two ranks junior to the Chiefs of Staff, he chose to lecture them like naughty schoolboys is as remarkable as their apparent acceptance of it. But his concern, as it was to be throughout the war, was always to see things in context and in proportion and at all costs to keep the show on the road.

It was evident that the pressure of top-level national decision-making and crisis management was taking its toll on ministers and the Chiefs of Staff. In the month of April the War Cabinet met on thirty-one occasions, the Military Coordination Committee twenty-one times and the Chiefs of Staff Committee forty-two. For Ismay, who attended all three groups along with the Chiefs, this made a staggering total of ninety-four meetings.[93] To this total should be added the numerous internal meetings that he held in the Office of the Minister of Defence. But as a study of the period reveals, while others were losing their self-control and showing signs of exhaustion, Ismay managed to remain calm, logical and measured, and his voice remained that of common sense and reason.[94]

At the end of April, Chamberlain summoned Ismay and told him that Churchill was to be given new powers. In future he would have the authority on behalf of the Military Coordinating Committee to give 'guidance and direction' to the Chiefs of Staff Committee. He would additionally be given a central staff to assist him, headed by a senior staff officer who would be an additional member of the Chiefs of Staff Committee. That staff officer, said Chamberlain, would be Ismay. This was the start of what was to be a long and fruitful relationship, but it did not appear that way to Ismay. His admiration for Churchill had survived the recent experiences of management of the Norwegian campaign but when he now reported to him, Churchill made it plain that he wished to use his own trusted companions—such as Oliver Lyttleton, Desmond Morton, Lord Beaverbrook and Professor Frederick Lindemann—as his staff. Remembering the unhappy consequences of the similar coterie of cronies with which Lloyd George had surrounded himself in the previous war—

what had become known as the 'Garden Suburb'—Ismay was bold enough to suggest that his own existing staff could do the job perfectly adequately without the confusion that would result from Churchill's proposal. The relationship looked as if it might be neither long nor fruitful. Churchill told Ismay to put his case in writing and the meeting ended. Ismay went away 'filled with gloom'.[95]

Events, however, intervened. Within nine dramatic days Chamberlain had resigned and Churchill was Prime Minister. On the same day, 10 May, Germany invaded Holland and Belgium.

5

THE FALL OF FRANCE, THE BATTLE OF BRITAIN, THE BLITZ

1940–41

In his memoirs Ismay was to say that he had enthusiastically welcomed Churchill's accession to the premiership on 10 May 1940.[1] This was something of an exaggeration. Colville recalled that the thought of Churchill as Prime Minister:

> sent a cold chill down the spines of the staff at 10 Downing Street... General Ismay had told us in despairing tones of the confusion caused by his enthusiastic irruptions into the peaceful and orderly deliberations of the Military Coordination Committee and the Chiefs of Staff... His verbosity and restlessness made unnecessary work, prevented real planning and caused friction.[2]

Jacob's recollection was similar. 'We in the War Cabinet office were decidedly perturbed.' Knowing of Churchill as 'a cantankerous, headstrong and redoubtable controversialist', and having witnessed 'the outbursts of interfering inquisition that he had unloosed at meetings... we foresaw a stormy future'.[3] Churchill's erratic judgement during the disastrous Norway campaign had been there for all around him to see. As he was later to admit to Ismay with remarkable frankness, 'I certainly bore an exceptional measure of responsibility for the brief and disastrous Norwegian Campaign'.[4] But at the time, whatever Ismay's personal feelings, his sense of duty—as always—came first. Bearing in mind what was to take place, this was fortunate.

Churchill moved swiftly to reorganise the higher direction of the war to suit his purpose. He appointed himself Minister of Defence—an unprecedented post for a Prime Minister—with Ismay as his chief staff officer and, following Ismay's advice, with the military secretariat of the War Cabinet as the Office of the Minister of Defence. Churchill disbanded the Military Coordinating Committee, replacing it with a Defence Committee which he himself chaired. This was to meet either as the Defence Committee (Operations) or, less frequently, as the Defence Committee (Supply). The Chiefs of Staff now reported direct to Churchill in his capacity as Minister of Defence. Ismay thus had four interlocking roles: chief staff officer to the Minister of Defence; head of the Office of the Minister of Defence; Deputy Secretary (Military) of the War Cabinet; and a member of the Chiefs of Staff Committee. As Alex Danchev observed, '[t]he mere specification of his appointments suggests his importance. He embodied the formal and informal links between civil and military authority, between the Minister of Defence and the COS [Chiefs of Staff]'.[5]

Churchill's choice of Ismay to fill these roles was a judicious one. It was based on an appreciation of his professional qualifications and his personality. Having been working in the corridors of power in Whitehall almost continuously since 1926 and having inherited Hankey's mantle at the CID in 1938, there was probably no one better qualified. In the words of David Fraser, 'he knew Whitehall forwards, backwards and sideways'.[6] Furthermore, he had a good working relationship with the important personalities in the key governmental departments and was current with all the issues to do with the direction of the war.

Equally importantly, Churchill recognised that Ismay was someone with whom he could work productively. Although they had lived very different lives, both had quite a lot in common in terms of experience and interests. They had both attended Sandhurst, served as young officers in cavalry regiments and been passionately enthusiastic polo players; both had served in India and were ardent admirers of the Raj; both saw only virtue and glory in the British empire, blind to the faults and evils inherent in imperialism. Both men were autodidacts and voracious readers of British history, especially imperial history. Both had taken part in campaigns against the Mohmand tribes on India's North-West Frontier: Churchill had been attached to the Malakand Field Force some twelve years before Ismay's regiment was to follow almost in its footsteps. Indeed, the 1897 expedition was the subject of Churchill's first book.[7] Both had experience on the battlefield under fire: Churchill famously charging with the cavalry at the Battle of Omdurman in 1898 and then commanding a battalion on the Western Front in 1916. Both had an interest in the Somaliland campaign for which, from 1919 to 1921, Churchill had held political responsibility. Both had a close interest in military intelligence and deception.[8] Both had close American family connections: Churchill's mother was American, as was Darry's mother. Moreover, as has been seen, Churchill and Ismay had worked closely together during the 1926 general strike and their paths had subsequently crossed at various times in the activities of the CID. Although, as a good soldier, Ismay kept his political views to himself, he was (like most army officers of the time) quite obviously a political Conservative by outlook. By temperament both men were sociable, raconteurs and bon viveurs. In short: there were plenty of experiences, interests and reminiscences they could share when the mood took them.

Life for Ismay would eventually settle into something approaching a routine, but there was little routine about the next six, crisis-filled weeks which included the evacuation from Norway and culminated in the fall of France. From the outset Ismay was aware that Churchill was under considerable political pressure at home from those who resented his accession to the premiership and from siren voices suggesting compromise with Germany. He would undoubtedly have heard of the lack of support within Churchill's own party when he addressed the House of Commons for the first time as Prime Minister on 13 May. His famous speech, 'I have nothing to offer but blood, toil, tears and sweat', was received with loud cheering from the Opposition benches, but in silence from Conservative members. When Chamberlain entered, however, they stood up and cheered.[9] Churchill's position as Prime Minister was far from secure and, according to David Reynolds, 'Churchill <u>felt</u> insecure'.[10] This did not, however, deter him from leaving the country. During his first five weeks in office he was to make five visits to France, on each occasion accompanied by Ismay.

Even before their first visit on 16 May—on this occasion accompanied by General Sir John Dill, now Vice CIGS—Ismay was, according to Colville, 'not too happy about the military situation. He says the French are not fighting properly: they are a volatile race and it may take them some time to get into a warlike mood.'[11] But the visitors were in for a shock. As Ismay reminded Churchill after the war, 'From the moment we got out [of the aircraft] at Le Bourget, it was obvious that the situation was far more critical than any of us suspected. The officers who met us said that the Germans were expected in Paris within a few days at most. With the memory of 1914–18 in our minds none of us could believe it'.[12]

In his memoirs Ismay described 'the unmistakable atmosphere of depression' which they found.[13] In private he went further: 'I have never forgotten the complete dejection on the faces of [Prime Minister] Reynaud, [Defence Minister] Daladier and [Army CinC] Gamelin as we entered the room at the Quai d'Orsay. I remember saying to myself, "The French High Command are beaten already"'.[14] Following a French plea for further air reinforcements Churchill told Ismay to telephone to London for Cabinet approval. Fortunately, Ismay had anticipated the need for a telephone conversation. To preserve security, he had arranged for an Indian Army officer to be standing by in his office for such a contingency and they conversed in Hindustani. A couple of hours later the answer (in the affirmative) was passed by the same method. There followed a bizarre coda. Wishing to inform Reynaud in person of the decision, Churchill was told that he had gone home to his apartment. He and Ismay took a car to the address. It was now close on midnight. On arrival, as Ismay later reminded Churchill, 'we found it more or less in darkness, the only sign of life being a lady's fur coat.[15] M Reynaud emerged from his bedroom in his dressing gown and you told him the glad news. You then persuaded him to send for M Daladier, who was duly woken up and brought to the flat to hear the decision of the British Cabinet.'[16] And with that, Churchill and Ismay retired for what remained of the night, Churchill to the British Embassy, Ismay to the Hotel Crillon.

Later that morning they returned to London. Colville recorded in his diary, 'Ismay was very pessimistic and said the French were not merely retreating but were routed. Their nerves were shattered by this armoured warfare and by the German air superiority, and the French government were upended by this sudden shattering of their faith in the invincible French Army'.[17] This proved to be an astute assessment, but at this early stage of the campaign many people in Whitehall—let alone in the remainder of Britain—would have found it hard to believe.

Ismay's focus during this period was not, however, restricted to the crisis across the Channel. The campaign in Norway was still ongoing. He had been hard-headed about the chances of success there. Of the senior officers and government advisers in Whitehall he was the first to articulate what many others were thinking: that what had become a fiasco for the Anglo-French forces deployed there was irretrievable and a dangerous drain on resources. On 25 April he had given his opinion in forthright terms to the Foreign Secretary, Halifax: 'we must get out'.[18] In early May he had thought it might be feasible to retain the strategically important port of Narvik in northern Norway, not least for political reasons, and had argued as such in the Chiefs of Staff Committee. But with the deteriorating situation in France he was convinced that the Allies should evacuate from Norway completely. The deciding factor for him was air support. As he later told one of the protagonists for remaining, were we to retain any troops at Narvik 'there are then bound to be desperate appeals from the Norwegian and French, if not from our own people for fighter protection'[19]. This was sound judgement.

Ismay was also mindful of matters closer to home, demonstrating an ability to learn from past errors and take the necessary action. On 13 May he produced a report, which had been some time in the making, prompted by the intelligence failures which had led to the German surprise attack on Norway. The official historian of the Joint Intelligence Committee describes this as 'an invaluable paper on the nature of the intelligence product' and 'a seminal report'. In it, 'Ismay proposed radical changes to the intelligence process: much faster procedures for getting intelligence to the right people at the right time, at any hour of the day or night, and immediately strengthening the JIC staff in quantity and quality'. Critically, Ismay also recommended 'authorising the JIC to initiate reports into topics of its own choosing—hitherto it was restricted to reporting on topics chosen by the military departments'.[20] The report was immediately accepted and the recommended changes made.

In addition, Ismay acted on his assessment that the French were being routed and the likely consequence: a German invasion of Britain. In his view there was an urgent need for a large network of strongpoints, demolitions and obstacles, and the necessity for the planning and construction of these to begin immediately. He set out his thoughts in a one-page minute to the Prime Minister on 21 May. Bearing in mind the risk of being considered defeatist, Ismay was remarkably frank. He concluded,

I feel very strongly that the grave emergency is already upon us. I suggest-

(a) That a directive to cover the plans and preparations which must now be made should be issued under your authority without delay.
(b) That full powers should be given forthwith to the military authorities to enable them to carry out defensive measures of all kinds without reference to any other authority and without hampering forms of procedure, and to provide them with the necessary labour to supplement the troops.[21]

The War Cabinet agreed to his recommendations the following day and set in train the necessary action.

On 22 May, just five days after their first visit, Ismay again accompanied Churchill to Paris: this time to the French Supreme Headquarters at Vincennes on the outskirts of the city. General Gamelin had been sacked and it was his successor, General Maxime Weygand, who greeted them. Ismay was more impressed by Weygand than he had been by Gamelin and was encouraged by his offensive spirit. But he had severe doubts—which proved to be well founded—about the practicalities of Weygand's plan for a link-up operation between the British Expeditionary Force, now in grave danger of being surrounded, and a new (at least on paper) French Army group. At the British Embassy he confided to the deputy ambassador, Oliver Harvey, that he 'had been through five days of hell over the BEF being cut-off'.[22]

The following day Major General Edward Spears, Churchill's newly appointed liaison officer with his French opposite number, came to Ismay's office to be briefed. Spears, who was bilingual in French and English, had headed the British Military Mission in Paris in the closing years of the First World War and knew many of the leading French politicians and senior military officers. He recorded that Ismay's report of the situation was 'hair-raising'. According to Spears, high-level Anglo-French liaison was proving so bad that Ismay 'was endeavouring to develop his own organisation in an attempt to deal with the problem'. There was no shortage of challenges. He detailed some of these to Spears. 'Pug gave me a grin when he finished', recalled Spears. 'He might have been telling me of the plan for an elaborate paperchase... I walked out, marvelling, as I was never to cease doing throughout the war, at the amazing self-control, balance, good temper and poise of this man.'[23]

With the BEF now heading for the coast, and with Dunkirk already earmarked as the embarkation port for an evacuation, Churchill was increasingly faced with critical decisions, using Ismay both to transmit his orders and as a sounding board. One of the toughest decisions was whether Calais should be evacuated or held. On 24 May he minuted Ismay,

> VCNS [Vice Chief of the Naval Staff] informs me that order [sic] was sent at 2 a.m. to Calais that evacuation was decided in principle, but this is surely madness. The only effect of evacuating Calais would be to transfer the forces now blocking it to Dunkirk. Calais must be held for many reasons, but especially to hold the enemy on its front.

Shortly after, he followed this up in an even more anxious tone, 'I cannot understand the situation around Calais...'.[24] Ismay recalled that when, on 26 May, Churchill made the fateful decision for an evacuation from Dunkirk but for Calais to be held to the end, knowing that this would commit the whole brigade there to death or imprisonment, Churchill said that he felt physically sick.[25]

It was at about this stage in the battle that, according to Hollis, Ismay made an extraordinary proposal to Churchill: that he (Ismay) should parachute into France to join the headquarters of the British Expeditionary Force and fight with them. Even more surprisingly, Hollis claimed that Ismay had gained Churchill's agreement. Hollis tried to talk him out of it; Ismay was not to be dissuaded but agreed to sleep on the matter. The following morning he saw sense and gave up the idea. Hollis certainly believed that Ismay was serious in his proposal and that his mind was made up.[26] If so, it was a wholly rash—if brave—decision and a considerable error of judgement.

Ismay was with Churchill on his next visit to Paris on 31 May. Also in the party were Deputy Prime Minister Clement Attlee and Dill, now CIGS. The meeting of the Supreme War Council gave little grounds for optimism. Ismay's abiding memory of this visit was of:

> a dejected-looking old man in plain clothes [who] shuffled towards me, stretched out his hand and said: 'Pétain'. It was hard to believe that this was the great Marshal of France whose name was associated with the epic of Verdun, and who had done more than anyone else to restore the morale of the French Army after the mutinies of 1917... He now looked senile, uninspiring and defeatist.[27]

Following the visit came further French demands for more support. Spears reported to Ismay that he had had 'a rather difficult interview' with Reynaud who had made what Spears considered to be some improper demands as well as making offensive allegations about Gort. Spears had 'got extremely angry at this', and an argument ensued.[28] While Ismay's sympathy probably lay with Spears he could see that this could all get out of hand. He therefore told Spears to inform Reynaud that all requests for military support should be dealt with by both governments at the highest level.[29] This defused a potential damaging situation, but a few days later Reynaud contacted Churchill urging further air support, particularly fighter aircraft. On 6 June, with the evacuation from Dunkirk now completed, Ismay made his view plain to Colville—as the latter recorded in his diary—telling him, 'We should be insane to send them all our fighters, because if they were lost this country would be beaten in two days, whereas even if France surrenders we shall still win the war—provided our air defences are intact'.[30]

Prior to Churchill's next visit on 11 June, which was to Briare, near Orléans, he told Ismay to 'stay and mind the shop'. But Ismay was determined not to be left behind.

> I got to Hendon well ahead of Churchill and hid behind an aeroplane. As soon as he embarked, I followed close on his heels, and sat in the seat immediately behind him. I felt like a stowaway, and it was a relief when we took off. After we had been flying for about five minutes, Churchill turned round and barked out, 'You're here are you?' There was not much that I could say, so I remained silent. He turned his back on me and continued reading. After a further pause he turned round again and, with an expression of fury, said, 'I knew you'd come'.[31]

Their reception at Briare is well described by Spears: 'It was like walking into a house thinking one was expected, to find one had been invited for the following week. Our presence was not really desired'.[32] Ismay recalled that '[i]n spite of the apparent hopelessness of the situation and of the defeatism around him, [Reynaud] was, as ever, friendly, militant and a bundle of energy. Weygand, on the other hand... seemed to have abandoned all hope, and Marshal Pétain looked more woe-begone than ever.'[33] This was also Ismay's first meeting with Charles de Gaulle. At that time a brigadier general, de Gaulle had been appointed by Reynaud as deputy minister of defence. Although Ismay was later to pay tribute to de Gaulle's inspirational leadership to the French nation, his first impression of the Frenchman was that, 'with all his courage and efficiency, he was frigid, humourless and probably prickly'—an impression that was to change little the more he got to know him.[34]

The conference started with what could have been a major point of disagreement. A bombing raid by British aircraft was due to take place that night against Italian targets near Turin and Genoa. The bombers were to refuel en route near Marseilles. To Churchill's irritation, Reynaud demanded that the operation be called off for fear of retaliation against French targets.[35] Ismay recalled, 'I did a quick calculation. According to my arithmetic, the bombers had already left England, and it was impossible to countermand them.'[36] He explained this to the meeting. Spears recorded that Churchill was 'beaming', while Weygand 'looked at Pug with faint distaste but said nothing'.[37] The story, though, had a less happy ending for Ismay. To his immense irritation he discovered the next morning that after the bombers arrived at the Marseilles airfield, the French had driven farm carts onto the runway to prevent them taking off.[38]

Later in the meeting was the famous exchange between Weygand and Churchill. Weygand urged Britain to commit all of its fighter aircraft to France. Ismay recalled:

> 'Here', he exclaimed, 'is the decisive place. Now is the decisive moment. The British ought not to keep a single fighter in England. They should all be sent to France'... After a pause, and speaking very slowly, Churchill said, 'This is not the decisive point. This is not the decisive moment. The decisive moment will come when Hitler hurls his Luftwaffe against Britain. If we can keep command of the air over our island—that is all I ask—we will win it all back for you.' After another long pause, he continued magnificently, 'Of course if it is best for France in her agony that her Army should capitulate, let there be no hesitation on our account. Whatever happens here, we are resolved to fight on and on for ever and ever and ever.'[39]

Ismay was later to aver that it was '[t]he greatest decision Winston took during the war'.[40]

At the Council's second meeting later that day Reynaud put forward a plan to organise a redoubt in the Brittany peninsular and asked for British Army divisions to be sent there as soon as they could be made available. Churchill agreed to provide them. Ismay was appalled by the prospect of throwing away vital troops on what he considered to be a scheme without 'the ghost of a chance of success'. On arrival back at the airfield for their return flight, he voiced his misgivings to Churchill, suggesting that that they quietly delay the despatch of the divisions. But Churchill roundly rejected this. With an eye on the verdict of posterity, he replied, 'Certainly not. It would look very bad in history if we were to do any such thing'.[41] As Andrew Roberts was to point out, this was poor judgement by Churchill.[42]

Their return flight to Britain was not without event. The pilot spotted a German aircraft beneath them attacking some Allied shipping. But the German airman clearly did not look upwards and would not have known how close he came to possibly changing the course of history. Later, informed of the incident by their pilot, Churchill and Ismay realised that luck had again been with them.

The following day, 13 June, Churchill and Ismay were back on a plane for what was to be their final visit to France, this time to the city of Tours in the Loire valley. Also in the party were Foreign Secretary Lord Halifax; Sir Alexander Cadogan, his permanent secretary; and Lord Beaverbrook. At Tours airfield, pock-marked from the previous night's air raid, Ismay recalled, '[t]here was no sign of life, except for groups of French airmen lounging about in the hangars. They did not know who we were, and cared less'. Ismay persuaded them to loan him a car and the British visitors arrived at the *préfecture* where 'no-one recognised us and we wandered through the dreary building, jostled by swarms of refugees'.[43] At last finding the conference room they were joined by Spears, who tried to judge the mood of the British visitors. 'Ismay, whose expression would, I hoped, give me guidance, looked very stern'.[44] When Reynaud and some of his ministers eventually arrived, the meeting was a short one. It was clear that France was on the point of surrender.

As they motored back to the airport for their return flight Churchill said to Ismay that, 'it seems, we fight alone'.[45] Ismay said that he was glad of it and that 'we'll win the Battle of Britain'. This was possibly the first use of that term. Churchill gave him a long look and said, 'you and I will be dead in three months' time'. Ismay replied, '[q]uite possibly, but we'll have a hell of a good time those last seven days'.[46] On 22 June France signed an armistice with Germany.

For Ismay, the six weeks culminating in the fall of France had been a tumultuous introduction to his new job and, not for the first or last time in his career, a baptism of fire. It was also a seminal period in his relationship with his new chief. They now had a shared experience of extraordinary, sometimes almost surreal circumstances and events, and had come to admire and trust one another. For Churchill, Ismay had passed the test, and the Prime Minister was quick to show his acknowledgement and gratitude: within a fortnight Ismay had been awarded a knighthood. For Ismay, Churchill's courage, fortitude and wisdom were indelibly stamped on his mind. When challenges of a different sort presented themselves later in the war, his memory of those first six weeks, and the debt that he believed that Britain owed to Churchill, sustained and strengthened his loyalty and commitment.

* * *

Although many other challenges continued to occupy Ismay, the end of the campaign in France gave him at least a momentary opportunity to draw breath and consider his appointment in the round.

When Churchill had appointed himself Minister of Defence he had told Ismay, 'we must be very careful not to define our powers too precisely', describing Ismay's role somewhat loosely as 'head of his handling machine'.[47] But Ismay now, quite rightly—and typical of his precise mind—set down what he believed should be his own terms of reference. In a minute of 1 July he advised Churchill that there should be three aspects of his role and that of his staff. First it was to keep Churchill 'in close touch with all important activities of Departments and other bodies concerned with defence' while keeping him informed of 'matters requiring your special attention'. Second it was 'to convey your instructions to those responsible for taking action and to follow matters up to ensure that there is no stagnation'. The third aspect was to coordinate the action of all departments involved in taking such action.[48]

Churchill accepted this advice and subsequently added an important instruction to both Ismay and Bridges: 'Let it be clearly understood that all directives emanating from me are made in writing, or should be immediately afterwards confirmed in writing, and that I do not accept any responsibility for matters relating to national defence, on which I am alleged to have given direction, unless they are recorded in writing'.[49] Equally important was a suggestion later made to Churchill by Ismay that all his directives and questions, and the replies to them, should pass automatically through the Defence Office: 'I should then be in a position to assist in securing the information that you want, and to put it up to you in a convenient form'. Churchill was initially somewhat suspicious of this procedure, annotating Ismay's suggestion in typical style, '[n]o harm in trying. But I like to chew my own food as much as possible'.[50] However, he quickly came round to the idea and it became his standard practice.

It would have been clear to Ismay that Churchill would be working every moment of his waking hours and expect him to do likewise. To execute this, and to keep at bay any further suggestion of a 'Garden Suburb' of cronies, would require a high-grade staff working at peak performance. Ismay had confidence that in the Office of the Minister of Defence he had exactly that. Although there may have been an expectation by some that the minister in question would have a ministry—with an army of military officers and civil servants—the reality was very different. The core staff of the grandly titled Office of the Minister of Defence actually consisted of a tiny secretariat of no more than a dozen staff officers at any one time. Ismay chose to keep it that way and the secretariat was not greatly increased throughout the war. His belief was quite rightly that the most effective and efficient staff organisation was a close-knit team of the absolute minimum number, but of the absolute highest-quality individuals. He had applied this principle at the CID and thus in the military wing of the War Cabinet, and it was these individuals who now formed the core of his staff. Many of them would serve with him for the whole of the war. When staff members left, candidates for their replacement were rigorously screened.

Together with Ismay, two other highly talented individuals comprised the inner core of the staff: his deputy, Leslie ('Jo') Hollis and Ian Jacob. In 1940 Hollis, aged forty-three, was a recently promoted lieutenant colonel in the Royal Marines. He had been working for Ismay at the CID since 1936. An extrovert with a ready sense of humour, he was a popular member of the office. Ian Jacob, three years younger, was a major in the Royal Engineers. His father, Field Marshal Sir Claud Jacob, had retired from active service in 1936. Ian Jacob was a staff officer to his fingertips and a very talented one. Like Ismay, he had passed fourth out of his intake at Sandhurst.[51] Joan Bright, one of Ismay's assistants, remembered him as 'shy and matter of fact... his desk was always tidy, his in-tray systematically emptied and his brain clear and uncluttered'. However, once she got to know him, she described him as 'one of the most delightful characters in the War Cabinet Offices'.[52] Ismay, Hollis and Jacob were to make a formidable team.

In addition to his staff, Ismay was to take responsibility for those he termed his 'foster-children'—small groups for whom no one else claimed parentage.[53] The first such group comprised the dozen-or-so staff of the War Room: the underground situation centre, its walls covered in maps, located beneath the Treasury building in Whitehall. Manned twenty-four hours a day, the War Room was the focal point for the Prime Minister and senior officials seeking the latest information about operations world-wide. The next group to come under Ismay's wing was the very small experimental weapons establishment which Churchill, as soon as he became Prime Minister, brought under his direct control. The group was led by the highly inventive Major Millis Jefferis—a dead ringer for Ian Fleming's 'Q'—who was responsible for creating ingenious devices such as delay-action fuses, 'sticky bombs', booby traps and sabotage devices.[54] Jefferis's group was constantly the object of rival takeover bids which

Ismay was able to thwart.[55] As we shall see, Ismay would acquire a number of other foster-children during the course of the war.

One of his first tasks was to prevent Churchill's cronies—notably Beaverbrook, Bracken, Morton and Lindemann—from becoming his de facto staff. Jacob recalled that they were at first 'like bees round a honeypot' and that Ismay 'had to ensure that the PM received from the military machine rapid and effective service'.[56] He succeeded in doing so and for the most part in ensuring that Churchill used these official channels. He also managed to keep the cronies at arm's length while keeping on friendly terms with them. This he achieved with a mixture of firmness, diplomacy and charm. For example, when Morton tried to bypass him, Ismay wrote to him, 'We will get into a terrible muddle, old friend, if we don't canalise business into the proper channels.'[57]

Potentially the most problematic of Ismay's roles was his membership of the Chiefs of Staff Committee. The challenge was not eased by the fact that Ismay did not have a high opinion of the Chiefs themselves. As we have seen, he was critical of Newall's willingness to be diverted from the 'long war' strategy and by his handling of the Norwegian campaign. And we have also seen that Ismay was critical of Pound and Ironside's 'sturdy independence' in failing to coordinate their plans for the ill-fated Narvik expedition: 'thus was confusion worse compounded'.[58] He had initially welcomed Ironside's appointment, believing that his predecessor, Gort, had been 'a major disaster in the highest councils because his type of mind was quite wrong for the job'.[59] Ironside, he judged, was 'infinitely better in the COS Committee'. However, within a month he considered that Ironside's influence on the cabinet 'had diminished after a good start' and that he had exercised poor judgement in some critical decisions—a state of affairs that would shortly cost him his job.[60]

The day after being appointed a member of the committee on 1 May 1940, Ismay had attended his first meeting. There is no record of the reaction of any of the Chiefs to the imposition on them of their secretary as a member of their august body, but it takes little imagination to hazard a guess that they were neither overjoyed nor overly welcoming. After all, the committee was a committee of the Chiefs of Staff. Ismay was not one: he was a servant of the committee, much their junior, and in the employment of their political master. To them it must have seemed as if their butler had suddenly joined them at the dinner table. He sought to reassure them from the outset by making it clear that he made no claim to the status of a chief of staff, would not sign the minutes of their meetings nor give his views on strategy unless invited to do so. This did not, as he recounted to the members of the Imperial Defence College after the war, 'prevent my arguing my case with individual chiefs of staff in the privacy of their offices'.[61] But he stressed that he did not wish to be consulted about senior officers' appointments, because 'I thought that it would be fatal if the impression got abroad that I was some sort of "eminence gris", intriguing on behalf of my friends'.[62]

During the campaign in France he had shown the Chiefs that he could provide them with useful insights into the Prime Minister's thinking, would give his opinion readily when it was asked for (but not unless) and would not presume to lecture them on the subject of strategy.[63] And he was clear that while reporting the Chiefs' strategic advice to Churchill, he would not inject his own personal view since, in Jacob's words, if the Chiefs 'ever came to think that [he] or his staff were offering strategic advice to the Prime Minister all confidence would have been destroyed'.[64] A similar point was made by Leslie Rowan, one of Churchill's wartime private secretaries, who added that nevertheless, Ismay's contribution 'might all have gone wrong had he not said at a crucial moment what he really believed, though it was not to the liking of Churchill'.[65] An early example of this was Churchill's strong desire in late 1940 to appoint as chairman of the Chiefs of Staff Committee his great friend, Admiral of the Fleet Sir Roger Keyes, the sixty-eight-year-old hero of the 1918 Zeebrugge raid and now Director of Combined Operations. In Colville's opinion Keyes was 'long past his prime', which as Alex Danchev commented, was 'a considerable understatement'.[66] Ismay certainly shared this view of Keyes who, as he later recalled, had 'drifted around Whitehall and Westminster saying that the Chiefs of Staff were a bunch of lily-livered so-and-so's'.[67] He sided firmly with the Chiefs in dissuading Churchill from appointing him.

Having witnessed Churchill as chairman of the Military Coordination Committee, Ismay would have sensed that perhaps the greatest task facing him would be that of maintaining a productive working relationship between the Prime Minister and the Chiefs of Staff. As he was later to explain,

> [I saw] the primary purpose of my job as being the link between the Prime Minister and the Fighting Chiefs. That is to say, I had to interpret the one to the other... I conceived it to be my job not only to make the Statesmen and soldiers trust me, but almost more important, to make them trust

each other—and certainly to prevent them quarrelling. A large-sized oil can was often needed.[68]

That need for the oil can was set to increase as the war progressed.

The combination of Ismay's roles amounted to a considerable challenge, not least in terms of hours of work. He would normally leave his house at Lowndes Square, Knightsbridge, shortly after 8 a.m. to be in his office by 8.30 a.m. to read the overnight reports and prepare the necessary briefs for the Prime Minister. At around 9.30 a.m. he would see Churchill, usually in bed, and leave with the minutes which he had dictated either late at night or earlier that morning.[69] He would then return to his office to set in train the necessary action before attending the Chiefs of Staff Committee meeting, usually held at 10.30 a.m. This was immediately followed at 11.30 a.m. by the daily meeting of the War Cabinet, of which he was the Deputy Secretary. Depending on the agenda and the mood of the Prime Minister the meeting would normally last between one and two hours. Sometimes he would then be asked to remain behind by Churchill to discuss aspects of the meeting. Ismay would usually manage to escape the office for lunch at his club—initially the United Services Club but, finding himself constantly being lobbied by other members, he moved to the less military atmosphere of White's.

When Churchill retired to bed for his customary afternoon nap, Ismay would usually be attending meetings or holding them with his staff or visitors, in between which he would catch up with paperwork in his office. From late afternoon to dinner time, this might be interrupted by a summons from the Prime Minister to come for discussions or by the arrival of notes (often a flurry of notes) from him requiring 'Action This Day'. Ismay habitually dined at his club or as a guest elsewhere, but this was usually a hurried meal to allow him to return in time for a further meeting with Churchill, a duty occasionally delegated to Hollis or Jacob. If Churchill was working alone—and if he was alone he was almost always working—Ismay joined him. In his memoirs Ismay typically understates his role here:

> I was under no illusion about the value of my contribution to the war during these sessions. Occasionally I could give him information which he wanted, or receive his instructions on this or that question. Occasionally I could persuade him to tone down a harsh minute or telegram, or postpone its despatch until he had had time for further reflection, or for the facts to be checked. But as a rule the most that I could hope was that

the mere fact of my presence and my unspoken desire to help, gave him a grain of support.[70]

These sessions rarely ended before 1 a.m., often much later.[71] If Ismay pointedly looked at his watch, Churchill's usual reaction was 'that I could go to bed if liked, but he was going to do his duty'.[72] By the time Ismay got home, this often left him only four or five hours sleep before the routine started all over again. The pattern would be broken if Churchill went on visits, whether in London or around the country; Ismay was usually in attendance, often the only accompaniment apart from the driver, private detective and a private secretary.

Work of some sort continued for Ismay and the secretariat at weekends. Only very rarely could he escape to Wormington where the family was based. He was often bidden for weekends at the Prime Minister's country residence at Chequers. In the latter half of 1940, for example, he was there for all or part of half the weekends. A typical weekend guest list might include a few Churchill family members, a minister, one or more senior Service officers, a few of Churchill's close friends and advisers (such as Professor Lindemann or Max Beaverbrook), and a private secretary. For Churchill and thus for Ismay, these weekends were a continuation of work rather than an escape from it, albeit in a different and more relaxed environment and sometimes with a film show after dinner. But discussions usually went on well beyond midnight.

An upcoming speech by the Prime Minister was a time of particularly high pressure for Churchill and those around him.[73] He personally composed all his speeches, dictating them to one of his shorthand-typists before distributing the semi-final draft for comment. Ismay was responsible for fact-checking; and knowing Churchill's tendency to leave speech preparation to the last moment had a team of assistants standing by to work fast against the clock to provide the necessary comment. Although Ismay was proud of the fact that the team never failed to meet the deadline he also admitted that 'there were some hairbreadth escapes'.[74]

All of this added up to a formidable and continuous workload for Ismay. Describing his job in July 1940 to a former brother-officer he wrote, with humour but also some feeling, 'Do you remember the poor little donkeys that one used to see in India, staggering under loads that they could not bear, but nevertheless adorned with a string of bright-coloured beads? I feel just like one!'[75]

* * *

As it turned out, time for reflection was in short supply for Ismay. In the immediate aftermath of the fall of France his attention was quickly focused on two challenges. The first was the imminent threat of invasion, a subject now preoccupying Churchill. Within a week of the French–German armistice, signed on 22 June, Ismay was writing to Hollis, 'It seems to me essential to instil into the civilian population a thoroughly offensive spirit and a determination to attack the enemy by every means in their power, even after he may have succeeded in occupying some of our territory'. He set down the capabilities that needed to be developed—intelligence, sabotage and assassination—as well as the organisation, coordination and training which would be required, using the Irish resistance movement in the early 1920s as a possible example.[76] He was certainly not the first person to advocate the involvement of the civilian population in 'home defence' (the War Office had instigated a system of Local Defence Volunteers a month earlier), but his advocacy would have helped concentrate minds. The same day he persuaded the Chiefs of Staff that coastal defences would be improved by moving more divisions forward, thereby reducing the length of coastline to be held by each and allowing these divisions to keep a divisional reserve within striking distance of any landing.[77] A week later he recommended to Churchill that the area of trenches being dug across potential landing grounds should be extended out to a radius of 10 miles using local volunteer labour. Churchill gave immediate approval.[78]

In addition, Ismay moved to address the threat closer to home. In mid-May a plan for the defence of Whitehall had been produced. It involved a number of checkpoints and sandbagged machinegun emplacements, with each building having its own independent guard force: the Admiralty had Marines; the War Office, Grenadiers; the Air Ministry had Airmen; some other departments used Local Defence Volunteers. But there was no coordination between these groups, many of whom prided themselves in their independence, and no central plan for the active defence of the area. Ismay now gave firm direction to establish a central command structure under the aegis of the CinC Home Forces.[79] He also addressed the vulnerability of Chequers to enemy bombing and attack by parachute forces, establishing a permanent guard force of a company of 150 Guardsmen with four anti-aircraft Bofors guns, and proposing camouflage measures to disguise the property from the air.[80]

At the same time his attention was focused on the second and very different challenge. During the frenetic crisis management that had characterised Churchill's first six weeks in office Ismay had had a chance to observe the system for the higher direction of the war in action. It would have been clear to him that some changes were required, particularly in War Cabinet procedures. A Prime Ministerial directive on 27 June—according to Allen Packwood, written 'almost certainly with the help of Ismay'—addressed the matter. War Cabinet meetings were streamlined by the production of written daily intelligence summaries, replacing the time-consuming oral briefings given by the Chiefs of Staff; a rota system for attendance at weekends was introduced; and the attendance of additional ministers was regularised.[81] Subsequently, the requirement for government departments to action War Cabinet instructions promptly was also tightened. Together, these changes added up to a significant increase in the effectiveness of the machinery of government. As Hollis was later to recall, 'the days of mere "coordination" were over for good and all. We were now going to get direction, leadership, action—with a snap in it!'[82]

Just a week later came the War Cabinet's decision—subsequently a subject of much contention among historians—to destroy the French fleet at Mers-el-Kébir in French Algeria to prevent it falling into German hands.[83] As Ismay later admitted, he was not initially in favour of the decision, partly on ethical grounds and partly on practical grounds (it might lead to a declaration of war by the Vichy government), but also because it offended his sense of chivalry. 'To kick a man when he is down is unattractive at any time' he wrote, 'but when that man is a friend who has already suffered grievously, it seems almost to border on infamy'. However, after due consideration and much soul-searching he overcame these scruples. 'In the end... I was completely convinced that we had no option', but added that when the order was drafted to the British admiral who was to carry out the action, 'all who were present could not but feel sad and, in a sense, guilty'.[84] The action took place on 3 July with the loss of almost 1,300 French servicemen.

Looking ahead at the wider prospects for the war, Ismay was apprehensive about the immediate future. He told the American military attaché Brigadier General Raymond Lee, with remarkable frankness, that 'the fate of our Western civilization rests on the shoulders of the British Navy and about five thousand pink-cheeked young pilots'.[85] He also reported that the government was 'greatly worried by the disposition of the French fleet, the bulk of which is in French colonial harbours'.[86] However, within a fortnight and just after the action at Mers-el-Kébir, his spirits were much higher. Having been entertained to dinner by Ismay and Darry on 7 July, Lee recorded in his journal that 'Pug is all optimism and hope now, when just two weeks ago he was anxious, strained, and wishing that Hitler might be going east. The British, freed of French shackles, are now taking the offensive'.[87] Within one month this optimism was to be severely tested when the Luftwaffe started their attacks on RAF Fighter Command bases, a campaign that was to last for almost four months and become known as the Battle of Britain.

Ismay often accompanied Churchill on his visits to RAF stations at this time. Perhaps the most memorable for him was on 16 August to Uxbridge, home of Fighter Command's 11 Group, responsible for the aerial defence of London and the south-east of England.[88] Ismay recorded in his memoirs:

There had been heavy fighting throughout the afternoon; and at one moment every single squadron in the Group was engaged; there was nothing in reserve, and the map table showed new waves of attackers crossing the coast. I felt sick with fear. As the evening closed in and the fighting died down, we left by car for Chequers. Churchill's first words were: 'Don't speak to me; I have never been so moved.' After about five minutes he leaned forward and said, 'Never in the field of human conflict has so much been owed by so many to so few.' The words burned into my brain and I repeated them to my wife when I got home.[89]

Churchill was to immortalise these words in a speech to the House of Commons four days later.

By late August the Luftwaffe had begun to transfer its main effort from attempting to crush Fighter Command to carrying out heavy raids on British cities. What became known as the Blitz started in earnest on 7 September and lasted until May 1941. It initially concentrated on London. Ismay accompanied Churchill on many of his frequent visits to bomb-damaged areas and it was on Ismay's first-hand accounts that many of the historical accounts of Churchill's most famous words during these visits were based.

The first of these visits was to the London docks, immediately following the initial heavy attack; it was later estimated that some 650 German bombers had killed 448 civilians and injured another 1,337.[90] Ismay was surprised and shocked at the scale of destruction,

much more devastating than I had imagined it would be. Fires were still raging all over the place, some of the larger buildings were mere skeletons, and many of the smaller houses had been reduced to piles of rubbish. The sight of tiny paper Union Jacks which had been planted on two or three of these pathetic heaps brought a lump to one's throat.

Ismay was also much moved by the population's reaction to Churchill. At one air-raid shelter which had received a direct hit, killing about forty people and wounding many more, Ismay thought that the people might be resentful against the authorities responsible for their protection. But as soon as Churchill got out of the car, he was mobbed by the crowd, with shouts of 'Good old Winnie. We thought you'd come and see us. We can take it. Give it 'em back.' Churchill broke down in tears and Ismay heard a voice say, 'you see, he really cares; he's crying'.[91] The visit continued on foot and it was evening before they left. By this time the Luftwaffe had returned to the brightly lit target area and as the car navigated the partially blocked streets a shower of incendiary bombs—target indicators for the bombers—fell just in front of them. 'Churchill, feigning innocence, asked what they were', recalled Ismay. 'I replied that they were incendiaries, and that we were evidently in the middle of the bull's eye!'[92] They were lucky to escape unharmed.

On subsequent visits to bombed cities and towns, Ismay continued to be struck by people's reaction to Churchill. Particularly memorable was their visit to Bristol. They travelled by a special train which stopped for the night just outside the city, but close enough to witness a major air raid. The following day they visited the stricken areas, but there was no lack of resolution among the people there. At one of the rest centres, Ismay recalled, 'there was a poor old woman who had lost all her belongings sobbing her heart out'. But as soon as Churchill entered, 'she took her handkerchief from her eyes and waved it madly shouting "Hooray, hooray"'.[93]

By mid-September 1940 the threat of the obliteration of central London, followed by invasion, was so serious that on Saturday 14 September Churchill tasked Ismay and Bridges as a matter of urgency to produce a plan 'by Sunday night' for the evacuation of key elements of government from Whitehall to a fortified underground site, codenamed 'Paddock', earmarked for this contingency at Dollis Hill in north-west London.[94] This they had already done: the comprehensive plan was on Churchill's desk the next day. It was not a moment too soon. Two days later the Luftwaffe launched a major raid on central London. Ismay, along with the Chiefs of Staff, were led out of the War Rooms by Churchill to watch the bombing. Some of the bombs fell just the other side of

Green Park, a few hundred yards away.[95] The following weekend Ismay accompanied Churchill on an inspection of the Dollis Hill site and the War Cabinet held a trial evacuation there later that month. The site was never used, but in December Ismay and his staff moved from the highly vulnerable Richmond Terrace to the more secure New Cabinet Offices in Great George Street, off Parliament Square.

September had also seen the failed assault by a Free French force, supported by British ships and aircraft, on the strategic port of Dakar in French West Africa (modern Senegal) held by the Vichy French. Ismay was closely involved in the inquiry, ordered by Churchill, into what was rapidly referred to as 'a fiasco'. The failure was being attributed variously to the leakage of information into what was meant to be a highly secret operation and to poor intelligence provided by SIS. Sir Stuart Menzies, SIS chief, was quick to blame the former together with the fact that SIS had not been specifically tasked to provide information on Dakar. In contributing to the report Ismay was critical of SIS and 'effectively accused Menzies of being disingenuous'. But he was most concerned with ensuring that all intelligence agencies and staff were proactive in coordination, emphasising that it was their job 'to keep in touch with plans of likely or pending operations, and to take steps to get information in relation to them without specific orders'.[96] It was an important lesson that was to be well learnt; it was also probably fortunate that Ismay's personal remarks about Menzies were not passed on to him. Indeed, Ismay managed to achieve his aim with SIS while maintaining good relations with Menzies, discussing the matter with him and concluding that 'if at any time he felt that he was not kept sufficiently in touch with events, he should not hesitate to let us know'.[97]

For Ismay, 1940 had seen a transformation of his job, his career and his life. His experiences in Britain and in France would remain vivid in his memory. In particular, seeing at first hand the highly emotional public reaction to Churchill's visits—and, indeed, his similar reaction in return—made a deep and lasting impression on Ismay. These visits, like those to France earlier in 1940, served to strengthen both his admiration for Churchill and the bond between them.

The seriousness of the situation did not, however, prevent Ismay from ending the year in some style. On New Year's Eve he was partying in the underground Cabinet War Rooms. Coville recalled that 'General Ismay plied Tommy Thompson [Churchill's aide de camp] and me with brandy and regaled us with stories of the field of battle, and then proceeded upstairs to drink to the New Year in champagne'.[98]

6

DISCORD AND HARMONY

1941

Being in such close contact with both the Prime Minister and the Chiefs of Staff, Ismay was well aware in late 1940 that the relationship between them, tense from the outset, was going downhill fast. Churchill's impatience—his constant, almost obsessive search for ways to get at the enemy and his endless flow of ideas for doing so—met with the caution and circumspection of the Chiefs and their staffs, whose task it was to balance the ends to be achieved against the ways and means available. Churchill had already made his frustration known in June, minuting Ismay,

> How wonderful it would be if the Germans could be made to wonder where they were going to be struck next instead of forcing us to try and wall in the Island and roof it over. An effort must be made to shake off the mental and moral prostration to the will and initiative of the enemy from which we suffer.[1]

Churchill's frustration was particularly directed at the CIGS General Sir John Dill and the War Office staff. He believed that Dill was overcautious and lacked an aggressive spirit and, according to Ian Jacob, that the War Office was 'hidebound, devoid of imagination, extravagant of manpower and above all slow'.[2] Indeed, Ismay believed that 'the main reason for Winston pushing all these impossible offensives was to try and eradicate the defensive attitude of mind of the War Office'.[3] For his part, Dill thought Churchill dangerously impulsive.

Several issues had arisen in late 1940 which contributed to discord between Churchill and the CIGS. One of these was Churchill's decision in late August to appropriate the Chiefs' Joint Planning Sub Committee to work directly under his orders with immediate effect and become part of Ismay's Office of the Minister of Defence. This was a considerable blow to the Chiefs: the Joint Planners were their staff, working at full capacity analysing proposals and embryonic plans. Dill may have wondered if Ismay himself had a hand in this decision, particularly as Churchill went on to direct that 'they may initiate plans of their own after reference to General Ismay'.[4] The Prime Minister may or may not have consulted Ismay but the initiative was certainly his own, following his frustration that the Joint Planners seemed consistently to find faults with his proposals and represented what he called 'the whole machinery of negation'.[5] Dill tried to enlist the support of his fellow Chiefs for a formal objection, but having failed to do so went ahead on his own, and in forthright terms.[6] Ismay will have had some sympathy with Dill's point of view—he later tried unsuccessfully to persuade Churchill to reverse his decision—but equally he would undoubtedly have wished that Dill had expressed himself in a less confrontational way. [7]

Ismay was also concerned about the relationship between Churchill and General Sir Archibald Wavell, CinC Middle East. From the moment he became Prime Minister, Churchill had urged him to take the offensive. Wavell had replied that his force was not yet ready. Recalled to London in August, he presented his case to Churchill, who was unimpressed by Wavell's taciturn response to his questions and by his lack of 'mental vigour and resolve to overcome obstacles'.[8] Ismay was aware of Churchill's lack of confidence in the CinC and that he was considering sacking him. Secretary for War Anthony Eden and Dill threatened simultaneous resignation in Wavell's support. This was shaping up to be a major political crisis. Ismay was present at Chequers that weekend along with Wavell and was on the point of counselling him about his relationship with Churchill. A year or two later he probably would have done so, 'But I felt that I did not know him well enough and was too junior; so I blurted it out to John Shearer [Wavell's staff officer] in the hope that he would pass it on'.[9]

Similarly, Ismay considered that Dill handled Churchill unskilfully but again did not feel he had a close enough relationship with the CIGS to broach the subject with him, probably correctly. According to the Director of Military Intelligence, Brigadier Frederick Beaumont-Nesbitt, Dill 'did not receive suggestions from Pug very well'.[10] Ismay shared Churchill's opinion that Dill was overcautious and also his view of the War Office, going back to the mid-1930s when he worked there when '[i]t struck me as hidebound, unimaginative, impersonal and over-populated'[11]. In 1940 he still held a disparaging view of it: Leo Amery, lunching with him in

September, noted that 'he has no use for the War Office'[12] and three months later Colville recorded that he referred to it as 'that House of Shame.'[13] Ismay's view was unchanged when he came to write his memoirs—an early draft included a sub-chapter heading 'War Office Idiocy'.[14]

At the end of October 1940, as Wavell was finalising his plans to attack the Italians in the Western Desert, an additional factor presented itself: Italy invaded Greece. Churchill immediately and publicly pledged support for the Greeks and instructed the Chiefs of Staff to make plans accordingly. They, however, were highly dubious about this new, unresourced commitment. Ismay agreed. Colville recorded in his diary, 'Ismay says there is nothing we can do on a sufficiently large scale to save the Greeks and the COS [Chiefs of Staff] seem unenthusiastic about the PM's determination to throw considerable forces into the fray even at the expense of weakening Egypt'.[15] To Churchill, the Chiefs' reaction merely served to confirm the need for him to spur them further into action.

When, in November, Wavell eventually announced his plan for an offensive, Churchill urged that its scope should be greatly expanded. The Chiefs, Dill in particular, counselled caution. Churchill's irritation increased into anger. He goaded Dill, describing him to his face as 'the dead hand of inanition' and disparaged the army to him.[16] Dill was deeply hurt by this. He returned to the War Office from a late-night session with Churchill on 4 December saying to Director of Military Operations Major General John Kennedy, 'I cannot tell you how angry the Prime Minister has made me. What he said about the army tonight I can never forgive. He complained he could get nothing done by the Army... He asked me to wait and have a drink with him after the meeting, but I refused'[17]. In a letter after the war to John Connell, Wavell's biographer, Ismay was critical of Dill's reaction:

> The one thing that was necessary and, indeed, that Winston preferred, was someone to stand up to him, instead of which Dill looked, and was, bitterly hurt. If, for example, Winston made rude remarks about the courage of the British Army in my presence, I either disregarded it or I laughed or I referred him to the magnificent tributes that he paid them in his various writings, and was told that I was being irrelevant. Dill, on the other hand, was cut to the quick that anyone should insult his beloved army and vowed that he would never serve with him again, which of course was silly.[18]

Ismay was not being entirely fair to Dill here. As Daniel Todman has pointed out, 'Dill infuriated Churchill, not only because he stood up to him and told him what he couldn't do, but also because he responded to Churchill, goading him with carefully argued written papers rather than by shouting back in the prime minister's face'.[19] And, as Alex Danchev commented, Dill 'did lack ready repartee'—something of a prerequisite to a good relationship with Churchill, but not a skill that could be easily acquired.[20]

Even after Wavell's long-awaited offensive, which began on 9 December 1940 and resulted in a run of victories—culminating in the decisive defeat of the Italian Army at Beda Fomm on 5 February 1941— Churchill's relationship with Dill did not improve. Churchill had made it plain to the Chiefs that 'supporting Greece must have priority after the western flank of Egypt has been made secure' and this now appeared to be the case.[21] Churchill urged the immediate transfer of troops from Egypt to Greece. On the evening of 11 February Dill told him, 'all the troops in Egypt are fully employed and... none are available for Greece'. This provoked a furious response, as Dill related to Kennedy:

> The Prime Minster lost his temper with me. I could see the blood coming up his great neck and his eyes begin to flash. He said, 'What you need out there is a Court Martial and a firing squad. Wavell has 300,000 men,' etc etc. I should have said, 'Whom do you want to shoot exactly?' But I did not think of it till afterwards.[22]

Although Churchill's relationship with the other two Chiefs—Pound and Air Chief Marshal Sir Charles ('Peter') Portal who had succeeded Newall in October 1940—had not degenerated to this level, it was nevertheless one that could be tense and confrontational. On occasions it called for all Ismay's skills as an intermediary. One such occasion was on Sunday, 20 April 1941. Ismay, at home in Gloucestershire, was awakened by a call from Churchill summoning him to Ditchley Park in Oxfordshire where he was weekending. On arrival, Churchill told him that tank reinforcements were urgently required by Wavell and that the Chiefs of Staff should meet that very day to agree delivery by fast convoy through the Mediterranean 'at all costs'.[23] Ismay summoned the Chiefs to London from their weekend retreats and convened a meeting that afternoon. 'They did not seem too well pleased at having their one day of rest interrupted', he recalled, 'and at first they showed little enthusiasm for the Prime Minister's proposals. It was argued that the despatch of a large number of tanks would dangerously weaken Home Forces, and that their passage direct through the Mediterranean would involve unwarrantable risks. By the time we adjourned for dinner, no decision had been reached'.[24]

Ismay would have been well aware of the confrontation and possible constitutional consequences that would ensue if Churchill's direction was thwarted, and he would have worked hard to avoid that outcome. There is no record of what exactly was said by whom over dinner. The minutes of the subsequent meeting, which lasted until after midnight, are carefully worded. But as Ismay recorded with some relief, the outcome was that 'they agreed to recommend that... the risks were acceptable'.[25] The convoy—Operation Tiger—arrived by the middle of May with the loss of only one ship.

The Chiefs' grudging agreement to Tiger, however, foreshadowed a further clash with the Prime Minister. Churchill was increasingly suspicious that they did not wholeheartedly support his commitment to the campaign in the Middle East. Ismay was present at Chequers the following weekend when Churchill's suspicions were dramatically confirmed. A fellow guest, Kennedy, was asked by Churchill during dinner for his views on the situation in Egypt. His reply included a statement that 'the Germans might attack at such scale that we would be unable to provide adequate forces for its defence'. This provoked a response similar to that which Churchill had given Dill two months previously. As Kennedy recalled, 'Churchill flushed at this, and lost his temper. His eyes flashed and he shouted, "Wavell has 400,000 men. If they lose Egypt, blood will flow. I will have firing parties and shoot the generals"'. Kennedy unwisely went on to say that Wavell had a plan for withdrawal from Egypt should it be forced upon him, but that this would not spell ultimate defeat for Great Britain. 'At this he fairly exploded. "This comes as a flash of lightening to me," he exclaimed. "I never heard such ideas... It is pure defeatism to speak as you have done".'[26] There were some situations that even Ismay could not finesse and this was one of them. Kennedy, though, may have resented the fact that he did not attempt to do so.

Two days later, a clearly still irate Churchill issued a directive emphasising that 'the loss of the Middle East and Egypt would be a disaster of the first magnitude to Great Britain, second only to successful invasion and final conquest', adding pointedly that, '[i]t is to be impressed on all ranks, especially the highest, that the life and honour of Great Britain depends upon the successful defence of Egypt'.[27] The Chiefs responded, agreeing that the loss of Egypt would be 'a disaster of the first magnitude' but disputing that 'the life of Great Britain depends on the successful defence of Egypt'.[28] Perhaps at Kennedy's suggestion, Dill chose to preempt this with his own paper stating with remarkable bluntness, '[t]he loss of Egypt... would not end the war. A successful invasion alone spells our final defeat. It is the United Kingdom therefore and not Egypt that is vital... If need be, we must cut our losses in places that are not vital before it is too late'.[29] Although the logic was indisputable, the inference of the last sentence was in the circumstances a bombshell. Ismay recorded that Churchill, having read it, was 'shaken to the core'.[30] Ismay's own view of the document was unequivocal, even twenty years later describing it with considerable hyperbole as 'the most extraordinary document that has ever seen the light of day. Put yourself in the Prime Minister's place', he wrote to Connell, 'and ask yourself whether you would have confidence in the strategical advice of a man who put his signature to that document'.[31] If Churchill had lost confidence in the CIGS, so had Ismay.

The internal pressures on the Prime Minister and Chiefs of Staff alike over this period should be seen within the context of the external ones, not least of which was the ongoing Battle of the Atlantic. On 20 March Churchill had told the War Cabinet, 'I'm not afraid of invasion. I'm less afraid of the Balkans—but—I'm anxious about the Atlantic'.[32] Indeed, one month later Ismay emphasised to the American military attaché Raymond Lee 'the importance of the Battle of the Atlantic over every other phase of war', and that 'available reserves of foreign shipping are beginning to fail'.[33] These external pressures were set to increase during May and June 1941. The humiliating evacuation of Greece, completed on 30 April, was closely followed by a pro-German revolution in Iraq which seized most of the country (although only for about a month). On 24 May the battlecruiser HMS *Hood,* at one time the largest warship in the world, was sunk by the German battleship *Bismarck*; there were only three survivors from its crew of 1,400. As he went to bed the following night at Chequers, Churchill remarked wearily to Ismay and Colville that 'the past three days had been the worst yet'.[34] A week later came the fall of Crete. Churchill now came under considerable political pressure and suffered a slump in popularity. The pressure on Ismay was also beginning to tell. On 11 June Lockhart, at that time Director General of the Political Warfare Executive, found him 'a tired and ill-looking man... not at all impressive [with] few clear ideas about anything'.[35]

A lot was now riding on Wavell's new major offensive in the desert— Operation Battleaxe—for which Churchill had inordinately high expectations. When the operation, which took place 15–17 June, resulted in abject failure he moved swiftly to take (and be seen to take) decisive action. Within four days he had sacked Wavell, exchanging him with the CinC India General Sir Claude Auchinleck who had impressed him as the commander in Iraq. As Ismay reminded Churchill many years later, 'I can see you now, holding out both your hands as though you had a fishing rod in each of them, and you said: "I feel that I have got a tired fish on this rod, and a very lively one on the other"'.[36] Ismay was to pay fulsome tribute to Wavell in his memoirs, but in private at the time was highly critical of him. Following dinner with Ismay in January 1942, Lockhart wrote in his diary,

> Pug Ismay was very interesting about Wavell's appointment [as CinC India] which he did not think was a good one. Wavell, he said, was a lucky general and luck counted for something. But every decision he had made in this war had been wrong. He had not wanted to advance into Libya against the Italians, had raised every objection, had finally to be pushed in, and then agreed only to make a raid. The success which came was therefore not his. He was also pushed into Iraq against his will. Here again success. The one decision he could and should have made was about denuding Libya, or rather Cyrenaica, for the Greek show. He could have said, 'If I have to do this for political reasons, I shall obey orders, but I must emphasise the risks in Cyrenaica'. Here, on the contrary, he gave a clear opinion that the Germans would not be able to do anything in time before the hot weather.[37]

To what extent, if any, Ismay may have influenced Churchill in his replacement of Wavell with Auchinleck is hard to judge. But it would have been surprising if at some time during the long watches of the night Churchill had not at least shared with Ismay his concerns about Wavell and, in considering possible successors, if Ismay had not at least dropped a hint to Churchill about the talents of his old friend Claude.

Churchill's hope that Wavell's replacement would have a higher appetite for risk was quickly to result in disappointment. From the outset Auchinleck made it plain that he was not to be rushed into a major offensive before he considered that his forces were sufficiently prepared, and that this was unlikely to be the case for at least four or five months. At the end of July Churchill summoned Auchinleck to London to discuss the matter. Although in his memoirs Ismay says that the visit went 'extremely well' and that Churchill was 'impressed by the strength of character, professional competence and freshness of mind of the new Commander-in-Chief', that is not how Auchinleck perceived it.[38] He told his wife that at the meeting of the Defence Committee on 1 August he had been 'put through it properly by the PM and some others', describing the day as 'awful'.[39]

Despite what he says in his memoirs, Ismay clearly sensed that all was not well in Auchinleck's relationship with the Prime Minister, because at Chequers that weekend, where both were guests, he had a long talk with Auchinleck explaining Churchill's idiosyncrasies and advising him how best to deal with them. Later that month in a letter to Auchinleck, he proffered further advice. After referring to 'that stormy meeting', he urged Auchinleck 'most earnestly to write him [Churchill] a long and private letter telling him your hopes and fears more fully and more freely than is possible in a telegram or even in an official letter'. He reiterated that 'the main point is—do write him long personal chatty letters occasionally'.[40] It was advice that Auchinleck followed, probably unfortunately because as Connell later pointed out to Ismay 'the more Winston was told, the more he wanted to know, and the more he believed that he could exercise day-to-day control'. This prompted endless, time-consuming and distracting requests for details and justification, which was to contribute to a degenerating relationship between Churchill and Auchinleck.[41]

It was not just with Auchinleck that Churchill was frustrated. 'Everywhere he turned [he] found himself frustrated', wrote Taylor Downing, adding perceptively '[a]nd from frustration came irritation, exhaustion and anger'.[42] This extended to the Chiefs of Staff and boiled over at a late-night meeting chaired by Churchill on 3 September. Churchill urged an offensive 'somewhere on the Continent' in early 1942, offering as an example northern Norway, and was angered by the Chiefs' lack of enthusiasm. He lectured them on 'the urgency and importance of early offensive action' and demanded that the matter 'be tackled with determination and vision'.[43] After the meeting, according to Colville, he 'expressed himself forcibly about the pusillanimity and negative attitude shown by our military advisers. "And you are one of the worst", he said to the indignant Pug Ismay'.[44] Churchill's remark will not have been intended as such, but it was actually a considerable compliment to Ismay's moral courage, good judgement and professionalism.

The Prime Minister's frustration with his strategic advisers was about to escalate into another potential resignation crisis. The following month he threatened to sack Air Marshal Arthur Tedder, Air CinC Middle East, who had produced an assessment supporting Auchinleck's decision to delay his offensive. Portal; his deputy, Air Marshal Sir Wilfrid Freeman; and, according to Portal's biographer, Denis Richards—possibly even the Secretary of State for Air, Sir Archibald Sinclair—contemplated simultaneous resignation.[45] Ismay will undoubtedly have been aware of the situation and its potential; he was also an admirer of Tedder. It is likely that he will have done his best to defuse the situation, but there is no evidence as to whether action on his part influenced Churchill's subsequent withdrawal of the threat.

In the summer of 1941 there had been a small addition to Ismay's responsibilities which was to have an impact out of all proportion to its size. On 17 June Churchill formally tasked Ismay with setting up a room in the Cabinet offices, 'by 1 July at the latest', where visiting commanders-in-chief could brief themselves on the overall strategic picture.[46] As the prime point of contact with them, Ismay may himself have been behind the idea, but he never attempted to claim any credit for it. The person he chose to create and manage this 'Special Information Centre' was a thirty-one-year-old member of his staff, Joan Bright. Prior to joining Ismay's office in December 1940 Bright had worked in the War Office, firstly as personal assistant to the head of a secretive intelligence branch and then for the head of the branch responsible for commando raids. Ismay recognised her talents and promoted her from secretarial duties to be, in effect if not in title, his office manager. She was a highly capable organiser and a highly personable character. She was later to date the author Ian Fleming and was thought to be one of the models for his creation of James Bond's Miss Moneypenny.[47] The Special Information Centre provided the necessary top-secret documents and maps and was much used and valued by the very senior officers for whom it was intended.

While Ismay's primary preoccupation had been the more immediate challenges facing the Prime Minister and preserving the peace between him and the Chiefs of Staff, a further (and more agreeable) matter had increasingly been gaining his attention: establishing cordial personal relations with Americans in London. He was of course well aware of the priority which Churchill gave to the trans-Atlantic relationship and the necessity of engaging the United States as an active ally. In the summer of 1940, however, Churchill had been decidedly circumspect about aspects of the relationship. When it was suggested that Britain should share its anti-submarine and radar secrets with the United States, he had confided his objections to Ismay, minuting him,

> Are we going to throw all our secrets into the American lap and see what they give us in exchange? If so, I am against it. It would be very much better to go slow, as we have more to give than they. If an exchange is to be arranged, I should like to carry it out piece by piece, i.e., if we give them our Asdics, they give us their Norden bomb-sight; if we give them our RDF [Radio Direction Finding equipment], they give us their highly developed short-wave gadgets.
>
> Generally speaking, I am not in a hurry to give our secrets until the United States is much nearer to the war than she is now. I expect that anything given to the United States Services, in which there are necessarily so many Germans, goes pretty quickly to Berlin in time of peace.[48]

In his reply the following day Ismay sought to reassure Churchill, pointing out that Britain's ambassador in Washington, Lord Lothian, had been strongly urging that an early exchange of information would be to Britain's advantage and that in Britain the three Service departments, particularly the RAF, were strongly in favour. He reminded Churchill that he had recently approved a general exchange of information and that a technical mission was being set up to go to the United States for that very purpose.[49] At a meeting the same evening with representatives of the Service departments, the Foreign Office and the Ministries of Supply and Aircraft Production, Churchill confirmed that the exchange should go ahead.

Now, in 1941, Churchill was unrestrained in his enthusiasm for closer relations with the United States. In support of this objective Ismay took every opportunity to establish personal friendships with Americans in London. But if there was an element of duty in it, it was for Ismay a most pleasurable duty. He liked Americans and they liked him. It certainly helped that Darry was half-American and that unlike most Britons at the time the Ismays readily welcomed American officials into their home. One of Ismay's first American wartime contacts had been the military attaché, Brigadier General Raymond Lee, whom he had got to know in London before the war. On the day Britain declared war on Germany, Lee, a firm Anglophile, had telegraphed Ismay from Washington with the far from neutral message, 'Let the British move up; God bless your arms'.[50] From the moment of Lee's return as attaché in June 1940, the two of them met regularly both in the office and socially. A frequent subject of their discussions was ways of improving Anglo-American cooperation, information exchange and intelligence sharing, clearly with a view to a time when the trans-Atlantic relationship would be a more active one.

It was through Lee that Ismay played a role (albeit a supporting one) in the establishment of initial staff talks between the British and American militaries. The Royal Navy and United States Navy had been conducting highly secret conversations about strategy, in particular strategy in the Far East, for some time but in November 1940 Ismay had expressed his enthusiasm to Lee for sending to Washington a delegation of staff officers to begin discussions on wider cooperation.[51] Lee advised waiting for some intimation from Washington welcoming such an approach, but the intimation was not long in coming.[52] In January 1941 a small tri-Service delegation of senior British officers was sent in great secrecy to Washington for formal discussions with senior American military representatives. Their cover was as 'Military Advisers to the British Supply Council'.[53] The delegation remained there for two months and reached informal agreement on a number of significant policy issues: most significantly 'that Germany was the primary threat to the security of both countries, that the defeat of Germany and Italy was the priority and that a purely defensive deterrent policy should be maintained against Japan'.[54] Three months after the delegation's return a permanent Joint Staff Mission was established in Washington. By November this numbered some 200 military personnel. As Danchev observed, '[t]his was in itself the mark of considerable progress towards "combination"'.[55] When America entered the war, much of the preparatory, detailed groundwork in creating a functioning military alliance had already been completed and the Combined Chiefs of Staff Committee could immediately be set up.[56]

During late 1940 Lee had introduced to Ismay a number of senior American colleagues, including Major General James Chaney and Rear Admiral Robert Ghormley, both of whom Ismay would work closely with later in the war. When the new American ambassador, John 'Gil' Winant, arrived in March 1941 to replace the Anglophobe Joseph Kennedy, Ismay was one of the first senior Britons whom he invited to brief him. Their meeting lasted a full two hours.[57] Ismay also established a close relationship from the outset with Roosevelt's two special envoys to Britain, described by Reynolds as 'the two pre-eminent transatlantic go-betweens'.[58]

The first was Harry Hopkins. On his arrival in January 1941, Hopkins was immediately whisked off by an enthusiastic Churchill to join him visiting the fleet at Scapa Flow, off the north coast of Scotland. Ismay, who was accompanying them, noticed that the frail Hopkins was not a happy man on the pitching deck of a destroyer in the bitter cold and driving rain and took it upon himself to look after him. After Ismay had lent him an extra sweater and his own fur-lined flying boots, Hopkins cheered up; he did not forget the incident at subsequent meetings. Ismay much admired Hopkins as a 'fanatical fighter for freedom' and a great supporter of Britain, but also as a person: 'a human, lovable character with a delightful, if somewhat waspish sense of humour'.[59]

The other special envoy was Averell Harriman, the President's coordinator of the Lend-Lease programme by which the United States supplied Britain with arms and other defence materiel. He and Ismay were fellow guests at Chequers on four occasions during the summer of 1941 and immediately struck up a rapport. Ismay was to pay a warm tribute to Harriman and his commitment to the Lend-Lease programme. 'No-one could have done the job more sympathetically or effectively... He proved a staunch friend to us throughout the war, but we owe him a special debt of gratitude for all that he did for us in our time of greatest need.'[60] Following their meetings at Chequers, their paths would cross again sooner than either of them could have anticipated.

Anglo-American cooperation took a major step forward in August 1941 with the first wartime meeting between Churchill and Roosevelt. It took place at Placentia Bay, Newfoundland. The major outcome was the Joint Declaration, which was to become known as the Atlantic Charter. Ismay had been left behind 'to mind the shop' but the outcome did not quite match his expectation.[61] 'Personally, I cannot help being a little disappointed', he wrote to Auchineck, '...I had hoped that America would take a more definite and more dramatic step towards full participation. We'll never get a third of the production for which we have the potential until they are in the fight'.[62]

A lesser-known outcome from the Newfoundland meeting—one that would involve Ismay almost immediately—was a joint initiative to develop relations between the Western Allies and Russia. Following Germany's invasion of Russia in June 1941, both Churchill and Roosevelt had been trying to establish a relationship with Stalin but found little reciprocal enthusiasm. In July Hopkins had flown from Britain to Moscow to meet Stalin and had subsequently reported to the joint meeting at Newfoundland. Churchill and Roosevelt decided to send an Anglo-American mission to Moscow the following month to develop relations and discuss plans for military cooperation and the provision of material support. Each delegation would contain about five members, civilian and military. The British delegation was headed by Beaverbrook, now Minister of Supply, with Ismay as senior military representative. Their American counterparts were Harriman and Chaney.

The delegations held several meetings in London, were received at Buckingham Palace by the King and Queen, and on 22 September set off from Scapa Flow for Archangel on HMS *London*. From there they flew in a Russian plane to Moscow. Their initial reception was, recorded Ismay, 'correct if somewhat frigid'.[63] The atmosphere did not improve subsequently, with Stalin much dissatisfied by what was on offer from the Western Allies. In a letter to be handed by Beaverbrook to Stalin, Churchill had written, 'General Ismay, who is my personal representative on the Chiefs of Staff Committee and is thoroughly acquainted with the whole field of our military policy, is authorised to study with your commanders any plans for practical cooperation which may suggest themselves'.[64] But Beaverbrook and Harriman decided, despite Ismay's protest, that no information should be given to the Russians on current operations.[65] Unsurprisingly, the Russians reciprocated. As a result, as Ismay recalled, '[i]t became obvious that the Soviet generals were not authorised to give information of any kind, and that to try to do business with them was a waste of time'. It was at a farewell banquet at the Kremlin that Ismay first came into contact with Stalin. 'He moved stealthily like a wild animal in search of prey, and his eyes were shrewd and full of cunning', wrote Ismay, also recalling that '[a]s he entered the room, every Russian froze into silence, and the hunted look in the eyes of the Generals showed all too plainly the constant fear in which they lived. It was nauseating to see brave men reduced to such abject servility'.[66]

During the banquet Stalin taunted Beaverbrook about the apparent lack of action in opening a second front. 'What is the good of having an army if it doesn't fight?', he said, 'An army which does not fight will lose its spirit'. At this, Harriman recalled, Ismay stepped in,

> to explain to Stalin that the British army in fact was fighting hard in the Middle East but that an early invasion of France was out of the question. Patiently, Ismay went over the troop figures, and Stalin listened. But he was not persuaded. The British must realize, he said, that they could no longer depend upon their sea power. They would have to build their army and learn to fight, or they would be defeated'.

Harriman considered it 'a supremely tactless remark'.[67]

Ismay's disagreeable exchange with Stalin coloured his view of the remainder of the evening: 'The banquet dragged on until the early hours of the morning. There was too much food, too much vodka, too many speeches, and too much artificial bonhomie'.[68]

Ismay was unimpressed by much of what he saw in Moscow. On his return he told Leo Amery that while he found the Russians 'surprisingly efficient on the mechanical side... [they were] without any kind of higher war direction. All their counter-attacks though very spirited have been purely local and they have none of the power of movement for concentration of the Germans'.[69] He made perceptive observations, too, about the people he met and saw, and 'came away with a firm conviction that the Russian Army and people were going to fight to the bitter end and that Moscow would hold out'. When on return there was speculation as to whether the Germans would be in Moscow by Christmas, Dill estimated the odds at five to four on, and Churchill at even money. Ismay, however, wagered ten to one against.[70] Sadly for him, it appears that no money changed hands.

Ismay liked to tell a story—almost certainly apocryphal—about the visit, but a story that so amused Churchill that he repeated it in *The Second World War*.

> His [Ismay's] orderly, a Royal Marine, was shown the sights of Moscow by one of the Intourist guides. 'This', said the Russian, 'is the Eden Hotel, formerly the Ribbentrop Hotel. Here is Churchill Street, formerly Hitler Street. Here is the Beaverbrook railway station, formerly Goering railway station. Will you have a cigarette, comrade?'. The Marine replied, "Thank you, comrade, formerly bastard!'[71]

In early October Ismay acquired a further addition to what he called his foster-children: individuals and groups for whom there was no obvious parent.[72] This was the group of deception planners who were to have a critical role to play in Allied victory. Hitherto deception had been the responsibility of a War Office committee, the Inter-Service Security Board. But its remit had been largely defensive, 'concealing our own intentions'.[73] Now there was a proposal that deception should take a much more proactive role: 'persuading the enemy to make a calculated false move of which we could take operational advantage'.[74] The leading proponent of this wider remit was Colonel Dudley Clarke, the highly talented deception planner at Headquarters, Middle East in

Cairo. Clarke was summoned back to London—he believed as a result of prompting by his former boss, Wavell—to present the case for the greater centralisation of strategic deception planning.[75] Clarke arrived in London on 18 September, attended meetings of various committees involved in deception and appeared before the Chiefs of Staff Committee on 7 and 9 October.

In his autobiography, Ronald Wingate (a major on Ismay's staff at the time) recounts that he was tasked (he does not say by whom) to prepare a brief for the Chiefs, prior to the meetings, in favour of Clarke's proposal for the setting up of a central organisation for the planning and coordination of strategic deception.[76] At Clarke's final appearance on 9 October, the Chiefs gave their approval. They tasked the head of the Future Operational Planning Section of the Joint Planning Staff, Colonel Oliver Stanley, with taking on the additional responsibility.[77] The deception planners would later be given the deliberately vague cover name of the London Controlling Section.[78]

Although Ismay was not present at either of the Chiefs' meetings and was absent in Moscow from 28 September to 3 October, there is reason to suppose that he played a major role in this decision.[79] But since he makes no claim to it or even mention of it in his memoirs or papers, it is—like so much in pinning down Ismay's achievements—a case of assembling small pieces of evidence to find his fingerprints and determine his involvement. First, in his biography of Ismay, Wingate credits him with the formation of the London Controlling Section. He states it was 'Ismay's own creation, and for which he made himself personally responsible', but he does not elaborate or present any evidence.[80]

Second, there is reason to suppose that Ismay was Clarke's contact in London, that the two met when he visited and that they discussed his mission. Indeed he may have been the contact whom Wavell prompted to invite Clarke back to London. Wavell was himself in London in early September and called in at Ismay's Special Information Centre.[81] Moreover, Clarke and Ismay had met each other several times before the war and Ismay's assistant Joan Bright (whose office was two doors down from Ismay's) had worked directly for Clarke in the War Office in 1940.[82] Given all of that, it would have been strange if Ismay and Clarke had not met when he visited London and if Ismay had not played a role as an intermediary.

Third, after creation of the section it was certainly the case that Ismay was something of a father figure to its members. He occasionally gave direction to the Controlling Officer, showed close interest in all of the section's work and actively represented its interests.[83] And it was to him that they turned when they needed support with a plan, intervening with other agencies or finding extra office space. There is therefore much evidence, albeit mostly circumstantial, that points towards his close involvement in the creation of the London Controlling Section.

In December 1941 a change took place in the Chiefs of Staff Committee, and one that Ismay may have considered long overdue. Churchill finally replaced Dill—or 'Dilly-Dally' as he had unkindly come to refer to him—as CIGS.[84] Despite successes in Libya, where an offensive by the Desert Army had relieved the long-standing siege of the key port of Tobruk, their relationship had degenerated even from the low point that it had reached in April and May. To be fair to Dill, he had given his all to the job but was exhausted—not only by Churchill but also by having to care at the same time for his wife through her long, terminal illness.[85] On the return journey from Moscow Beaverbrook had told Ismay that 'he considered it was high time that Winston got rid of Dill'.[86] Alex Danchev is probably correct in suggesting that 'Beaverbrook and possibly Ismay influenced him [Churchill] against Dill', although there is no hard evidence of Ismay's part in this.[87] To be sure, Brigadier Vivian Dykes who worked for Ismay and later for Dill recorded (and deprecated) Ismay's 'dislike' of Dill.[88] And as has been seen, Ismay believed that Dill was overcautious and did not handle Churchill well. He had probably concluded that the relationship was non-viable. General Sir Alan Brooke, whom Churchill appointed as Dill's successor, was an admirer of Dill but he too recognised that '[t]hey were entirely different characters, and types that could never have worked harmoniously together'.[89] According to Ismay, Brooke was not Churchill's first choice as successor to Dill, instead favouring the Vice CIGS, Lieutenant General Sir Archibald Nye.[90]

Brooke's own relationship with Churchill would not be exactly the epitome of harmony but, as Andrew Roberts points out, nor was it 'one of constant friction and mutual irritation': the rows and clashes were 'not a very regular occurrence'.[91] What Brooke's diary gives us is graphic (if one-sided) evidence of the relationship between the Chiefs of Staff and the Prime Minister, and thus of the scale of the challenge facing Ismay as the self-appointed 'man with the oil can'. In his first week as CIGS, Brooke attended a late-night meeting of the Chiefs of Staff Committee with the Prime Minister in the chair. Churchill proposed gifting tanks and aircraft to Stalin; the Chiefs were unenthusiastic.

This produced the most awful outburst of temper, we were told we did nothing but obstruct his intentions, we had no ideas of our own, and whenever he produced ideas we produced nothing but objections etc etc! Attlee pacified him once, but he broke out again, then Anthony Eden soothed him temporarily, but to no avail. Finally, he looked at his papers for some 5 minutes, then slammed them together, closed the meeting and walked out of the room![92]

Churchill's mood cannot have been improved by the fact that earlier in the day he had witnessed a fragmentation of his parliamentary support when thirty-five Labour members of parliament, a fifth of the parliamentary party, voted against the government. The following evening, over dinner with Kennedy at the Carlton Grill, Ismay told him that Churchill was 'tired and irritable and difficult'. Kennedy observed in his diary that, 'Winston seems to suck the vitality out of his entourage like a leech. Ismay looks very tired and unwell.'[93] What Brooke and Kennedy may not have been aware of, but Ismay almost certainly would have been, was that on top of the many other pressures on Churchill he had had to explain just a few days previously to Clementine that her twenty-three-year-old nephew, Esmond Romilly, serving with the Canadian Air Force, was 'missing believed killed' from a bombing mission over Germany.

Four days later, on 7 December, squabbles between the Chiefs and Churchill were eclipsed by a momentous event: the Japanese attack at Pearl Harbor. Ismay was dining at a restaurant that evening when a waiter told him of the BBC announcement. He recalled that,

My first reaction was stunned surprise. It had never occurred to anyone in London, nor I believe in Washington, that such a thing was possible. My next reaction was thankfulness, for of course I had no idea of the grievous injury which the American Fleet had suffered. Indeed, had I not been in a public place, I would have shouted for joy. How I wished that I could have been with the Prime Minister [who was away at Chequers] at that moment![94]

Ismay admitted that more sober judgments followed the reports of the casualty figures at Pearl Harbor and the news over the next three days that Hong Kong had been invaded and that the British battleships *Prince of Wales* and *Repulse* had been sunk off the east coast of Malaya.

Within a week of Pearl Harbor, Hitler had declared war on the United States, 'a strategic misjudgement of fatal proportions', and Churchill was en route to Washington.[95] Ismay was again left behind to mind the shop, this time with Brooke. It would be the last Anglo-American wartime conference that Ismay would miss. Much responsibility fell on his shoulders during Churchill's absence, particularly as it lasted for a full five weeks— at the time an unprecedentedly long period of absence for a British Prime Minister in time of war. Two major decisions emerged from the Washington conference. First, Roosevelt and Churchill formally agreed that the defeat of Germany should be the Allies' primary objective, with Japan being contained until that was achieved. Second, and close to Ismay's heart, was the President's decision to set up a Chiefs of Staff organisation on the British model together with a joint agreement to establish a Combined Chiefs of Staff Committee, an idea which had grown out of the success of the Joint Staff Mission. Churchill decided that Dill would remain in Washington as head of the Mission and as his personal liaison officer with the President. The Combined Chiefs of Staff Committee quickly became a central feature of the alliance. Ismay was later to say that 'when history comes to be written, the verdict will be that the decision [to establish it] had a greater effect than any other single decision that was taken by the High Commands or in the field'.[96] As someone who had been an early protagonist of the Joint Staff Mission and who would be closely involved in the Committee's development, his was not an unbiased judgement— but not a wildly inaccurate one either.[97]

7

'THE TROUGH OF THE WAR'

1942

Ismay's optimism at the start of 1942 was to be short-lived. On 19 January, two days after Churchill's return from his trans-Atlantic visit, Ismay reported for his morning meeting with the Prime Minister and found him in 'a towering rage'. Churchill thrust a telegram into his hands. It was from Wavell, now CinC India, reporting that Singapore's defences contained a critical flaw: all the heavy guns were sited to repel a sea-borne attack; there were no fixed defences to prevent an attack from the north, across the narrow and shallow Johore Straits which linked Singapore with Malaya. Ismay recalled. 'I could scarcely believe my eyes'. Churchill was forthright in his challenge: 'You were with the Committee of Imperial Defence for several years before the war broke out. You must have known the position. Why did you not warn me?'[1] It was a good question.

In his memoirs, Ismay's unspoken response was that, 'the Committee of Imperial Defence had concerned themselves solely with the installation of heavy guns at Singapore to meet sea-borne attack, and with the period for which the fortress must be prepared to hold out until relief came, and it had been taken for granted that the commanders on the spot would see to the local defences against land attack from the north'.[2] All of this is true, but it does not tell the whole story, nor does it absolve Ismay from some share of responsibility. In the draft of his memoirs he made a candid admission: 'I had always visualized that Singapore was a self-contained fortress'.[3] This was a common error at the time: Singapore was often referred to, both in the press and in official documents (including those of the Chiefs of Staff), as 'the fortress', even though this conjured up a highly misleading picture.[4] Ian Jacob, to whom Ismay had sent a copy of his draft memoirs, commented on Ismay's admission, 'Had you really? I never had... The COS [Chiefs of Staff] had always said that Singapore was untenable if the mainland was lost'.[5] Clearly embarrassed, Ismay removed his admission from further drafts.

Ismay's mistaken assumption is puzzling. Singapore was not unknown to him. When he had been a colonel in the intelligence directorate of the War Office from 1933 to 1936 his remit included the Far East. In November 1938 when he was Secretary of the CID, the CIGS, Lord Gort, had warned the Committee that 'a land attack from the north is now considered to be the chief danger [to Singapore]'.[6] In August and September 1940 Ismay was present at several meetings of the Chiefs of Staff when the subject of Singapore's vulnerabilities and the need for reinforcement were discussed.[7] Indeed, he had intervened at one of these meetings (at which Churchill had declared that 'the threat to Singapore had been overrated') to argue for an increase in the size of the garrison 'as much as possible'.[8] And he was present at a Chiefs' meeting in December 1941 at which the urgent need for reinforcement for Burma and Malaya was discussed, and after which Brooke wrote in his diary, 'Personally, I do not feel there is much hope of saving Singapore'.[9] Ismay may have been influenced in his ignorance by the CinC Far East Command, Air Chief Marshal Sir Robert Brooke-Popham. From October 1940 to October 1941 Brooke-Popham sent Ismay detailed monthly reports on the challenges facing him, but not one of these reports mentions any concern about the vulnerability of Singapore's defences to an attack from the north.[10]

The powerful and fatal image of a fortress endured in Ismay's mind as it did in Churchill's, and doubtless the mind of many others. Churchill was later to admit that, 'It had never entered my head that no circle of detached forts of a permanent character protected the rear of the famous fortress... I cannot understand how it was I did not know of this... My advisers ought to have known and I ought to have been told, and I ought to have asked'.[11] It is certainly surprising that when Churchill was making light of the threat to Singapore, as he was frequently doing both before and during the war,[12] that none of the Chiefs of Staff nor ministers (such as Lord Hankey) who might have been expected to know better had suspected that he might be labouring under a false assumption about the security of 'the fortress' and raised the matter with him. It was certainly a belated lesson—and one that endures to this day—in the constant need to challenge strategic assumptions.

For the four weeks from 19 January the probability of defeat in Singapore hung like a cloud over Churchill. He clashed with the Chiefs of Staff over the policy for its defence; faced a potentially troubling House of Commons vote of confidence (which in the event he won easily, though with many abstentions); and received further criticism in the press following another major defeat for the Desert Army at the hands of General Erwin Rommel, with Tobruk again under siege. The pressure on the Prime Minister was reflected—as was to be the case throughout the war—by pressure on Ismay. This was compounded by pressure associated with the development of the trans-Atlantic alliance, following the Prime Minister's meeting with the President at the turn of the year. In February Ismay confided to Auchinleck, 'I must admit to having felt the burden far, far heavier during the last six weeks than at any previous juncture of the war. There are now so many fronts to be considered: so many competing priorities to be assessed: so many people to be brought into consultation. It is very nice to have allies, but they add immensely to the already sufficiently complicated business of the conduct of total war.'[13]

Things were not about to get better. Within a fortnight came the humiliating 'Channel Dash' by the German battle cruisers, *Scharnhorst*, *Gneisenau* and *Prinz Eugen*, escaping from Brittany into the North Sea. It was but a prelude to the far greater humiliation three days later of the fall of Singapore with the loss of 130,000 troops—described by Churchill in his memoirs as 'the worst disaster and largest capitulation in British history'.[14] Particularly galling were indications that the defenders 'had little fight left in them'.[15] With further criticism in Parliament and the press, now of a personal nature, and a radio broadcast to which '[t]he overall response… was at best lukewarm', Churchill badly needed a military success—and quickly.[16] For this he looked to the Western Desert, but in the absence of any plans for immediate action his frustration focused on what he perceived as the inertia of the CinC Middle East, Auchinleck.

The deteriorating relationship between the two men became a serious concern for Ismay. On 27 February, despite prodding by Churchill for a major offensive, Auchinleck informed the Prime Minister that such action would not be possible before June. Churchill drafted what Brooke ominously described as a 'bad wire' to Auchinleck, 'pouring abuse on him for not attacking sooner' and 'trying to force him to attack at an earlier date than is thought advisable'.[17] In a lengthy meeting Ismay worked with the Chiefs of Staff to amend the draft in a manner that would be acceptable to the Prime Minister.[18] Late that night a reluctant Churchill accepted their redraft, but subsequently summoned Auchinleck to London 'for consultation'.[19] Auchinleck's reply was forthright, 'Am certain that I cannot repeat NOT leave MIDEAST in present circumstances'.[20] Ismay, alarmed at this impasse, sought to find a solution. In a letter which gives a remarkable insight into his view of Churchill, his empathy with Auchinleck and indeed his own character, he wrote to his old friend,

I have been thinking of you so much these last few weeks, and wishing above all else that I could have a heart to heart talk with you. The written word is such a poor substitute for the spoken—but I must try.

The outstanding point is that though the PM is <u>at present</u> at cross purposes—and even loggerheads—with you, this is a purely temporary phase of a relationship which is marked by mutual esteem, and I might almost say affection.

You cannot judge the PM by ordinary standards: he is not in the least like anyone that you or I have ever met. He is a mass of contradictions. He is either on the crest of a wave, or in the trough: either highly laudatory, or bitterly condemnatory; either in an angelic temper or a hell of a rage; when he isn't fast asleep he's a volcano. There are no half measures in his make-up. He is a child of nature with moods as variable as an April day, and he apparently sees no difference between harsh words spoken to a friend, and forgotten within the hour under the influence of friendly argument, and the same harsh words telegraphed to a friend thousands of miles away—with no opportunity for 'making it up'...

Before you came home last time, your refusal to attack before you were ready was grudgingly admired as a sign of strength, but harshly criticized nevertheless. You came home—you had it all out in the open: the clouds of misunderstanding were dispelled: and you went back in a blaze of goodwill and confidence. Your ears would have burned, if you had known all the nice things that were said about you...

And now let me state my own case. I think I can lay claim to having been called every name under the sun during the last six months—except perhaps a coward; but I know perfectly well in the midst of these storms that they mean exactly nothing, and that before the sun goes down, I shall be summoned to an intimate and delightfully friendly talk—to 'make it up'.

One more point. You are both indispensable, the PM as the only possible national leader: and you as a universally admired Commander of perhaps the most important force we have. And so you have <u>got</u> to make it up.

This leads me to the only possible conclusion. You must do what you did with such happy results last time, YOU MUST COME HOME. I know how hard it is for you to leave your Command at this juncture, but nothing matters so much as the removal of the wall of misunderstanding which has grown up between you two. I know that at heart, the PM thinks the world of you, but he will never confess this, even to himself, until you have got together again and had the whole thing out.

I know that you are a selfless person, who cares only for the Cause: and I am writing in this strain, old friend, not because I admire you, and am so fond of you—but for that same Cause...

Before you burn this letter, will you wire in the following sense: 'Reluctant as I am to leave my post at present, I regard it as even more important that I should come home at once for consultation. I will start as soon as I have your approval.'[21]

The letter, however, did not change Auchinleck's mind. He did not return home. In Connell's words, 'it was a calamitous error of judgment'.[22]

While Ismay's mind had been taken up by the need to mediate between Churchill and Auchinleck there had been a development closer to home. In March Ismay had been joined on the Chiefs of Staff Committee by another senior officer who, like himself, was not a Chief of Staff. In October 1941 Churchill had appointed Commodore Lord Louis Mountbatten as Adviser on Combined Operations in the place of Admiral Keyes. On 4 March 1942 Churchill elevated Mountbatten's appointment from that of Adviser to that of Chief of Combined Operations; promoted him to hold the ranks of vice admiral, lieutenant general and air marshal; and gave him a seat as a full member of the Chiefs of Staff Committee. If the Chiefs had had limited enthusiasm about Ismay joining their committee in 1940, it was nothing compared with their resentment—or at least that of Pound and Brooke—towards Mountbatten. The fact that he was a young, dashing, decorated, glamorous, unconventional officer with royal connections (he was second cousin to the King) and an obvious talent for self-publicity may have impressed Churchill, but it cut no ice with the Chiefs of Staff: least of all with Pound, being twenty-three years and until recently four ranks his senior. The disdain of Brooke and Pound for Mountbatten and his opinions was unconcealed.

Ismay, however, did not share this adverse view of Mountbatten. As someone whose seat at the table was also manifestly below the salt, he probably empathised with Mountbatten. He certainly made an effort to put him at ease. Mountbatten recalled that the first night he attended a Defence Committee meeting Ismay said to him, 'Don't be nervous. This is the best evening show in London—it's much better than the Palladium'.[23] Ismay was to be increasingly impressed by Mountbatten's energy and drive, and by the transformation that he achieved in the Combined Operations organisation, much of it in the face of opposition from the three Services: the Chiefs appeared to oppose on principle all proposals for combined operations. Ismay readily provided Mountbatten with help, support and friendship. Their careers were to cross in unexpected ways in the future.

Ismay was now planning the imminent visit of a high-level US delegation to be led by Hopkins and the Chief of the Army, General George Marshall. On 8 April 1942 the visitors arrived. They were given a warm welcome: their itinerary including attendance at a meeting of the Defence Committee, dinner at Number 10 (at which King George was also a guest) and a weekend at Chequers, all of which Ismay attended. Cordial personal relationships were established. But it quickly became apparent to the British that the two nations' strategies were at cross-purposes. The Americans were pushing for an early cross-Channel attack. This was a most unwelcome prospect for the British who believed that such a move would be dangerously premature, but who nevertheless wanted a rapid build-up of American forces in Britain, not least to discourage German invasion. But the British did not openly state their disagreement with the American strategy and the visitors left under the impression that their proposal had been accepted. This was to lead to bitter recrimination and accusations of perfidy when the British later announced their absolute opposition to the American plan. As Ismay was later to write in his memoirs, with characteristic tact, 'perhaps it would have obviated future misunderstandings if the British had expressed their views more frankly'.[24] In an interview with Forrest Pogue in the same year that the memoirs were published he was to be much franker and more illuminating about the underlying reasons for the British reluctance to commit to a precipitate cross-Channel assault:

> I think we could have come clean, much cleaner, than we did, and said, 'We are frankly horrified because of what we have been through in our lifetime… We, who survived, had got that into our minds, never again, you see. We are not going into this until it is a cast-iron certainty'.[25]

One of the visitors was Marshall's aide Lieutenant Colonel Al Wedemeyer, later in the war to rise to the rank of three-star general, who was an acerbic commentator aware of his own reputation for being anti-British.[26] In his memoirs, he produced pen pictures of his hosts, including a candid one of Ismay.

At first blush, Sir Hastings Ismay appeared to be what we in America would call a 'smoothie'. He had a talent for ingratiating himself, and he obviously enjoyed the aura which surrounded his position of proximity to Prime Minister Churchill. I thought that he was insincere—a man without real convictions and incapable of reaching sound conclusions. Sir Hastings seemed cast in the role of Mr Fix-It, of spreading oil on troubled waters, of alleviating difficult solutions for the PM and for all of the senior officials in their relations with one another.

I was right about Sir Hastings' penchant for smoothing over difficulties for his colleagues in the British Government. But I was totally wrong and did him grave injustice in my initial impression that he was superficial. As I got to know him better, I learned that he made use of his charming personality, even to the extent of resorting to double-talk or flattery, but invariably when it served a constructive purpose. My final opinion of the man was that he would never stoop to duplicity when the chips were down. Further he had moral courage and could exercise it when the occasion demanded.[27]

The two men established a close friendship which lasted the war and after. Ismay was one of the few senior British officers whom Wedemeyer liked and respected. Ismay reciprocated these feelings, later telling Harriman, '[h]e is one of the most capable officers I have ever met, and an extremely nice one too'.[28]

It was at about this time that Ismay was involved in a controversy about Churchill's working practices and methods in running the war. In a House of Lords debate both Hankey and Chatfield had been highly critical of the prevalence of late-night committee meetings chaired by the Prime Minister, and the resulting strain on all concerned.[29] In a letter to Hankey commissioned by Churchill, Ismay refuted these accusations, saying that in the previous six months no more than nineteen such meetings had taken place, thus only about three per month—a seemingly reasonable figure in time of war.[30] This, however, was a somewhat selective use of evidence. As Hankey pointed out in his response, leaving aside weekends and periods when the Prime Minister was abroad the rate was one late meeting every four or five nights—and this did not include informal meetings, nor the staff work that extended after the meetings.[31]

Although Ismay was working long hours under considerable pressure he nevertheless found time for occasional relaxation. It was rare that time allowed for visits to Wormington Grange, although he was there at the end of April for the wedding of his eldest daughter, nineteen-year-old Susan, to Captain Neville Chance. The house had become a residential nursery for children under the age of two evacuated from London, together with thirty staff. Some rooms were retained by the family and Darry based herself there with the three girls, coming to stay with Ismay in London from time to time. Their house in Knightsbridge had more than a touch of luxury to it, with a live-in Belgian couple: Félicien the butler and Marie the cook. When Ismay was alone in London he often entertained there, including his colleagues at work. He also patronised smart London restaurants, dining in some style. Major General Kennedy was one of the guests at a dinner given by him in May 1942 at Wilton's oyster bar in Jermyn Street, recalling,

> a red-letter day... but for gastronomic rather than historic reasons... We had sherry, Chablis, prawns, turtle soup, lobsters from Oban (which were collected off the Scotch express every morning), cheese and coffee. As he paid the bill, Pug remarked that eating was almost the only pastime busy people could have, and that it was a good idea to concentrate on it. [32]

Ismay's reputation as a bon viveur was well earned.

There were also weekends at Chequers and occasionally at Churchill's home, Chartwell, in Kent. One of Churchill's secretaries, John Peck, was present at Chartwell on one such occasion and witnessed a memorable exchange between Churchill and Ismay as they watched the geese on the Chartwell lake.

> One goose he [Churchill] was particularly attached to because if he stood on the terrace and bellowed across the valley a call approximately translated 'Ah-wah-wah', the goose would reply with a distant 'Honk honk'. Churchill believed that he was the only person whom his faithful goose would answer... The PM's first act was to demonstrate his exclusive dialogue with his pet goose.

Ismay decided to try his luck and followed suit. Peck continued,

> To my frozen horror—for the outcome was predictable—the goose replied, 'Honk honk'. The Prime Minister was not only put out: he was genuinely grieved by the perfidy of the goose. [33]

In May there was a significant development in the deception organisation—the London Controlling Section—for which Ismay was at least in part responsible. The section's Controlling Officer Oliver Stanley announced his intention to resign: his wife was terminally ill, and this had unsurprisingly affected his energy and enthusiasm for the job. On 20 May he informed Ismay that his successor would be Lieutenant Colonel Johnny Bevan, recently appointed as his deputy and an officer with a background in intelligence, counter-intelligence and deception. Bevan, he told Ismay, 'had very special qualifications for the work'.[34] The next day a telegram came from Wavell to the Prime Minister, urging 'a policy of bold imaginative [centrally controlled] deception worked between London, Washington and Commanders in the field.'[35] This was at least in part implied criticism that the central organisation he had helped to create (through Dudley Clarke) in October 1941 had not fulfilled its full potential. Churchill would undoubtedly have discussed Wavell's telegram with Ismay. The following day it was circulated to the Defence Committee. The result was a paper, drafted by the Joint Planning Staff and Bevan, setting out the arrangements for what was now formally to be known as the London Controlling Section. This included a directive to the Controlling Officer under which he was now authorised to report direct to the Chiefs of Staff.[36] The Chiefs agreed the paper on 21 June.[37]

The new formal arrangement did not, however, achieve immediate and universal acceptance of the section in Whitehall, nor end the need for it to have a father figure like Ismay to smooth its path. For example, its most junior member Flying Officer Dennis Wheatley, already a well-known novelist, recalled that meetings with senior staff in the War Office 'proved definitely hostile... some of them took no pains to hide their view that this new-fangled business of strategic deception was a crack-brained idea upon which there was no justification for wasting the time of busy men like themselves', adding that, 'selling deception to most senior officers [was] extremely uphill work'.[38]

On 17 June 1942, together with Brooke, Ismay accompanied the Prime Minister on his second visit to Washington DC for an Allied conference. As Ismay was to recall, on many long-distance flights with Churchill it was his fate to lie in a bomb rack or sit on a bucket-seat. But for this twenty-six-hour journey they flew in a luxury Boeing flying boat with full-length bunks and easy chairs. Brooke recorded that Churchill was 'in tremendous form and enjoying himself like a schoolboy!'[39] To Ismay's amusement, when they were about four hours from Washington Churchill looked at his watch and announced, 'It's eight o'clock... where's dinner?' Explanations that it was only 4.30 p.m. by sun time and that he was due to dine at the British Embassy on arrival were summarily dismissed. Churchill made it clear that he did not go by sun time: 'I go by tummy time, and I want my dinner'.[40] So they all had dinner, and a second one on arrival.

The following day Churchill travelled to New York to stay with the President. Ismay and Brooke remained in Washington to meet with the American Chiefs of Staff. It was the first occasion that Ismay had seen all three American Chiefs together. He had met General Marshall in London in April and had been impressed by his obvious integrity and competence, describing him as 'a big man in every sense of the word'.[41] The US Army Air Force chief was General Henry 'Hap' Arnold who, Ismay recorded, was to prove 'a staunch and generous friend'. The third member, Admiral Ernest King, was rather different. Ismay described him as 'tough as nails... blunt and stand-offish, almost to the point of rudeness [and] at the start, intolerant and suspicious of all things British, especially the Royal Navy'. But as Ismay also observed, 'he was almost equally intolerant and suspicious of the American Army'.[42] And, it seems, of civilians: it was said of him that he believed that they 'should be told nothing of the war until it ended, and then only who had won'.[43] The American Chiefs were much less cohesive than their British counterparts and it was often King who was out of step.

On this occasion, however, the American Chiefs were in relative agreement with each other and with Brooke and Ismay. The meeting agreed that priority should be given to cross-Channel operations and that an invasion of North Africa should not be undertaken in the present situation. This, however, met with a problem. When Brooke briefed Churchill on the agreement the following morning Churchill became 'very upset'.[44] Unbeknown to Brooke, he had given Roosevelt a paper the previous day arguing almost exactly the opposite. At the subsequent meeting of the Chiefs with the President and Prime Minister at the White House there followed what the official historian described as 'animated discussions'.[45] According to Wedemeyer, '[d]espite Ismay's tactful mollifying efforts, the meeting was quite acrimonious'.[46] It was left to Ismay to record what agreement had been reached. What he produced was a carefully drafted statement designed to satisfy all parties. It appeared to give priority to cross-Channel operations but concluded that 'if, on the other hand, detailed examination shows that, despite all efforts, success is improbable, we must be ready with an alternative'. The alternative specified was of course Churchill's North African operation. It was as Andrew Roberts described, 'a veritable masterpiece of misleading prose', but with minor amendment, it achieved the agreement of all those present.[47]

Later in the afternoon the whole visit was overshadowed by a momentous announcement. Ismay recalled that he was with Churchill, Roosevelt and Brooke in the Oval Office 'when a secretary came in with a telegram. Roosevelt read it and passed it without a word to Churchill. It announced the fall of Tobruk. This was a hideous and totally unexpected shock, and for the first time in my life I saw the Prime Minister wince'. Ismay left the room to seek further details and returned with another telegram confirming the report. He handed it to Churchill.

> For a moment no-one spoke. The silence was broken by President Roosevelt. In six monosyllables he epitomised his sympathy with Churchill, his determination to do his utmost to sustain him, and his recognition that we were all in the same boat. 'What can we do to help?'[48]

Before they returned to Britain, Ismay accompanied Churchill on a visit to US Army troops training at Fort Jackson, South Carolina. The training included a brigade of young soldiers carrying out a field-firing exercise with live ammunition. Churchill asked Ismay what he thought of the training. Ismay replied that 'the organisation was wonderful and the enthusiasm admirable, but that to put those divisions against the Germans in their present state of training would be murder'. Churchill's immediate rejoinder was that 'they were grand material and that they would learn extraordinarily quickly'; but on reflection he suggested to his hosts, Marshall and Secretary of War Henry Stimson, that the training period should be extended to two years.[49]

Ismay's first visit to the United States had been most worthwhile. It had given him invaluable insights into the highest level of American decision making, allowed him to build on old friendships and establish new ones, and had enhanced his reputation with highly important and influential policy makers. Among those who were struck by his talents was Marshall, who wrote to him after the visit, 'I am relieved to know that you made a safe return, and I want you to know that I considered it a great opportunity for us to have you here, and that you personally made an important contribution to our problems.'[50] In Washington Ismay had also met someone who was to become one of his closest and most trusted friends: a recently promoted major general, Dwight Eisenhower. Within a week, Eisenhower would be in London as the newly appointed commanding general of US troops in Britain.

For Ismay the ten days away had been his longest absence from his office since the outbreak of the war, and a welcome break. As he told

Spears, '[t]he trip to America had been the greatest fun, but ruined by the news from Tobruk'.[51] But almost immediately on return the old pressures resumed. With the Desert Army now in full retreat towards El Alamein, only 40 miles from Alexandria, the Prime Minister faced a vote of censure in the House of Commons, which he won by a wide margin. Two days later, however, came the news of the destruction of Convoy PQ 17 en route to Archangel. In addition, the planned raid on Dieppe was called off at the last moment. Unsurprisingly, Churchill was in ill humour and ministers in Cabinet were rounding on the military in what Brooke described as 'a dreadful exhibition of amateur strategy... [in] a most depressing and lamentable meeting'.[52] In the Foreign Office Oliver Harvey, Principal Private Secretary to Eden, described the Chiefs of Staff in his diary as 'a menace... [who] seek to interfere in policy... we suspect Ismay as an obstructionist who fans the PM's dislikes'.[53] On 11 July Ismay spent the morning trying without success to persuade Churchill to moderate what Brooke called 'a most unpleasant wire' to Auchinleck.[54] Ismay was depressed with the overall situation, telling a close friend 'I feel that we are in the trough of the war at present, with Germany making her supreme effort to finish the business this year'.[55]

On 18 July Hopkins, Marshall and King paid a week-long visit to London, under instruction from the President to reach immediate agreement on plans for strategic action in late 1942 and 1943. The daily meetings of the Combined Chiefs of Staff, all of which were attended by Ismay, were characterised by forthright, brusque, sometimes ill-tempered argument. The American proposal for an immediate cross Channel action was unanimously rejected by the War Cabinet and the unfortunate Ismay instructed to break the news to Marshall. Tempers were getting frayed. At a subsequent meeting there was a clash involving Ismay and Brigadier General Walter Bedell Smith, American secretary of the Combined Chiefs of Staff Committee. Marshall had objected to Ismay's minute taking and insisted that Smith and Dykes produce the official record. Ismay then 'raised procedural issues' during the meeting and Smith, according to his biographer, 'rose up in anger'.[56]

This was an unfortunate 'rift', as Ismay later referred to it, because just two months later Smith was to return to London as Eisenhower's chief of staff.[57] But when he did so Ismay was quick to mend fences and establish a friendship with him which was to endure throughout the war and after. Smith was well known for his volatile temper, but Ismay took it in his stride. In his memoirs he painted a fond and remarkably life-like cameo of him.

> Bedell Smith had a face like a bulldog and many of the characteristics of that attractive breed. He was a master of his profession—businesslike, decisive and self-confident. In spite of a not too strong constitution, his hours of work were prodigious. He was the perfect complement to Eisenhower, to whom he was the soul of loyalty and devotion. He had a quick and direct temper, which he was wont to vent on friend and foe alike. But the storm generally blew over and left not a vestige of ill-feeling.[58]

The pug and the bulldog were to get along just fine.

On 2 August, Churchill left Britain with Brooke to visit the Desert Army and thence to Moscow for a meeting with Stalin. Ismay, to his disappointment, was again asked to remain behind. The focus of his immediate attention was detailed discussion with Eisenhower about the organisation and planning of Operation Torch—the proposed Anglo-American invasion of North Africa—which Eisenhower would command. The operation had been approved by Roosevelt, for the only time in the war invoking his position as CinC to overrule his military advisers and, as Eisenhower would have known, there was an ongoing rearguard action in Washington to get the decision reversed.[59]

On the evening of 7 August Ismay dined with Harold Nicolson, telling him that despite working sixteen hours a day for eight years he still loved the job. He said of Churchill, '[w]hen things are going well, he is good; when things are going badly, he is superb; but when things are going half-well, he is "hell on earth"'. He also spoke of Churchill's veneration for the House of Commons. One day he had found Churchill exasperated about having to prepare a parliamentary speech. Ismay had said to him, 'But why don't you tell them to go to hell?' Churchill had rounded on him, 'You should not say things like that; I am the servant of the House'.[60]

The following day Ismay received the Prime Minister's signal from Cairo informing the War Cabinet of his decision to dismiss Auchinleck.[61] Although Ismay was to tell Auchinleck that he was 'dumfounded' by the news, he wrote in his draft memoirs (subsequently redacted) that he was 'not altogether surprised'.[62] He had seen at close hand the level to which relations between Churchill and Auchinleck had descended. He had also questioned Auchinleck's judgement (as did Brooke) about some of his senior appointments, for example cautioning him about taking Major

General Thomas Corbett as his chief of staff: 'but he had clearly made up his mind'.[63] Ismay would have been saddened, though, that evening by the denigration of Auchinleck in the War Cabinet and Defence Committee, and the opposition of certain ministers—in particular Secretary for War Sir James ('PJ') Grigg—to Churchill's proposal to offer him a further appointment on the grounds that 'he would not have the confidence of his troops'.[64] As to Auchinleck's replacement, Ismay approved of Churchill's choice of General Sir Harold Alexander as CinC, although rather less so the subsequent appointment of Lieutenant General Bernard Montgomery to command the Eighth Army.

Alexander had previously been assigned to Eisenhower as his deputy, planning Operation Torch. On the day of Eisenhower's appointment as Supreme Allied Commander for the North African theatre, Ismay had gone to his headquarters to explain to him that Alexander was being transferred to the Middle East and that he would be replaced by Montgomery. Montgomery had arrived the next day, but the following morning Ismay was back to explain to the bemused Eisenhower that Montgomery, too, would be leaving, immediately. Understandably, Eisenhower asked Ismay, 'Are the British really taking "Torch" seriously?'[65]

It was while Churchill was in Cairo, returning from Moscow, that the disastrous amphibious raid on the German-occupied port of Dieppe in Northern France took place. Subsequently there was a major controversy as to who if anyone authorised the raid, and whether there was a cover-up. Allegations were made that Ismay was implicated in this. The issue is addressed in Appendix B.

On 27 August, just two days after Churchill's return from Moscow and Cairo, Ismay found himself having to mediate, this time between the Chiefs of Staff over the strategy for Operation Torch. The Chiefs were in sharp disagreement with each other on the subject. Brooke admitted that at their meeting the previous evening he was 'rather rude to all members of the COS, including poor old Dudley Pound', whom he described as 'maddening and long past retirement'.[66] The following morning, according to Michael Howard, it was only due to 'second thoughts, the intervention of General Ismay and the need to present an agreed view to the Prime Minister, with whom they met at 11 a.m.' that the Chiefs were able to reach agreement.[67]

At the beginning of September Ismay suffered what he himself described as 'a temporary breakdown'.[68] This was serious enough to cause him to be absent from his office for three weeks. What exactly the symptoms and diagnosis were would remain unclear, but it is likely that he was suffering from mental and physical exhaustion. He later told Spears that he had been 'on the sick list (nothing much wrong, just over tired)'[69] and told Auchinleck on 23 September that he was 'now back at work with batteries completely recharged'.[70] It seems that, not for the first time in his life, he had simply been driving himself too hard. But, as on previous occasions (in April 1920 and November 1930), he bounced back to full energy with apparently no lasting damage.

On the day of Ismay's return the War Cabinet considered Churchill's pet project: an expedition to clear the Germans out of northern Norway, a proposition which filled the Chiefs with horror—or as Churchill put it, of which 'on the whole they took a rather unfavourable view'.[71] According to Brooke, Churchill reacted to their resistance by again bemoaning that 'everyone did nothing but produce difficulties.'[72] Ismay also found himself having to reconcile further inter-Service disputes between the Chiefs, in particular on the subject of the command and control of air forces supporting land operations. Having earlier in the war seen how quickly disputes on this subject could get out of hand, he wasted no time in producing an acceptable, compromise solution: this mirrored the system successfully used in the Western Desert whereby all air forces were placed under the command of an Air CinC operating alongside the Army CinC.[73]

With two key operations upcoming—the desert offensive at El Alamein and the Anglo-American landing in north-west Africa (Operation Torch)—plus the questionable viability of the Murmansk convoys following the destruction of convoy PQ 17, the months of September and October were a tense time for Churchill and those around him. Churchill later described them as 'the two most anxious months of the war'.[74] The mood was swiftly to change in early November with Montgomery's victory at El Alamein. During the battle, however, Churchill had become agitated following a report from Alexander that it could take about a week before progress could be expected and that a redeployment was taking place. At a meeting of the Defence Committee he urged that a signal be sent, spurring Alexander to further action. A draft seemingly written by Churchill and expressing his concern and thinly veiled criticism of the commanders remains amongst his papers. The telegram that was actually sent to Alexander on 29 October adopted a very different tone.

> The Defence Committee congratulate you on the resolute and successful manner in which you and General Montgomery have opened the decisive

battle which is now proceeding. They feel that the general situation justified all the risks and sacrifices involved in its relentless prosecution. We assure you that you will be supported whatever the cost, in all the measures which you are taking to shake the life out of Rommel's army and make this a fight to the finish.[75]

In Michael Howard's words, it 'bears signs of General Ismay's emollient drafting'.[76] It is certainly typical of other redrafts that Ismay made during the war.

Following the successful conclusion of Alamein, attention in London turned to Operation Torch. The Anglo-American negotiations and discussions over the operation had allowed Ismay to develop his friendship with Eisenhower. Ismay would have been aware that many senior officers, notably Brooke, held Eisenhower in disdain as a mere staff officer 'who had never even commanded a battalion in action'.[77] He would also have been aware that Eisenhower himself could not have failed to pick up this feeling towards him. Ismay, however, liked Eisenhower as a person, recognised his talents and potential, and saw him as someone who needed and deserved every support. 'The more I see of him, the more I admire him', he wrote to Hopkins, 'and the more certain I am that he is going to make a very great contribution to our common effort'.[78] Following the July visit of the American Chiefs of Staff Ismay met Eisenhower frequently, both formally and informally, as well as corresponding regularly with him. Within weeks they were on 'Dear Pug' / 'Dear Ike' terms and Ismay invited him to stay at Wormington for a weekend in August. 'I cannot tell you how much I appreciated your cordial invitation', Eisenhower replied, 'There is nothing I would rather do than spend the weekend with you and your family', before explaining regretfully that he was required to be on call twenty-four hours a day in London.[79]

Their developing friendship helped avert a formal clash between Eisenhower and the British Chiefs of Staff. In early October the Chiefs endorsed a War Office directive to General Sir Kenneth Anderson, commander of the British First Army for Operation Torch, giving him the right of appeal to the War Office if he considered that an order from Eisenhower 'might imperil any British troops in the Allied Force, even though they may not be under your direct command'. Eisenhower strongly objected to both the spirit and letter of the order, but according to Howard, 'very wisely raised the matter not with the Chiefs of Staff directly but with that master of discretion and common-sense... Ismay'.[80]

As a result, Ismay represented the issue to the Chiefs and the directive was redrafted to meet Eisenhower's objections. 'The difference between the two drafts', Howard commented, 'was the difference between two world wars—almost between two historical epochs'.[81] While Eisenhower was delighted, the War Office was not and would have resented Ismay's intervention.

Eisenhower left Britain in November to command the Torch landings in Morocco and Algeria. Initially successful, the operation quickly became bogged down and as its commander, Eisenhower came under criticism. Ismay was quick to bolster Eisenhower's self-confidence, congratulating him on 'the brilliant start' of the operation and adding, 'Your handling of the whole business, both military and political, fills me (and I imagine everyone else in England) with unbounded confidence'.[82] The criticism, though, rapidly increased to the extent that Eisenhower's aide, Captain Harry Butcher, recorded 'The boss's head is in the noose. If anything more goes wrong, he's had it'.[83] Eisenhower's reply to Ismay showed warm appreciation of his support; he also commented with remarkable, frankness on the lack of progress, '[it] is heart-breaking, but I manage to keep my chin up and kicking everybody forward as hard as I know how'.[84]

The year ended on a somewhat sour note in the Chiefs of Staff Committee. In late October there had been a sharp disagreement between Portal and Pound over the relative priority of the bomber offensive and the anti-submarine campaign—Pound had threatened Churchill with his resignation over the issue.[85] Now, three days before Christmas, there was what Brooke described as 'a very heated discussion lasting about an hour' on the subject of Mountbatten's role and charter as Chief of Combined Operations. Mountbatten himself was not present. There was a suggestion that he should command the naval forces for the invasion of France. According to Brooke, 'Portal and Pug Ismay were supporting him, and Dudley Pound and I were dead against it on the grounds that his job is one of an advisor and not of a commander. We finally shook the other two and went a long way toward making the point'.[86] Since the invasion was not planned to take place for some time, the argument was somewhat academic, but the altercation illustrated the strength of feeling that existed amongst the Chiefs and the fact that Ismay was prepared to enter the lists on Mountbatten's behalf.

Ismay described 1942 as 'a year of extraordinary contrasts'.[87] It had seen a run of abject Allied defeats and failures, most of them British: Singapore, Hong Kong, the loss of the *Prince of Wales* and *Repulse*, Convoy PQ 17, the escape of the *Scharnhorst* and *Gneisenau*, Dieppe, defeats in the Western Desert and in Burma, the continuing advance of the German Army in Russia. But the year had closed with some notable successes: Alamein, the American naval victory at Midway, the Torch landings in North Africa and the unfolding defeat of the Germans at Stalingrad. In addition, Bomber Command 'were now strong enough to launch a thousand aircraft against Germany on a single night and the US Air forces were almost ready to join in the massive destruction by daylight bombing'.[88] In Britain public confidence in the higher direction of the war during the year had dipped to an unprecedentedly low level and the pressures on Churchill had been constant.[89] As Downing has suggested, if 1940 was Churchill's finest hour, 1942 was his 'darkest hour'.[90] Perhaps unsurprisingly, the tensions between him and the Chiefs of Staff and pressure on his own staff had reached an unprecedentedly high level. For Ismay, trying to maintain a constructive relationship between Prime Minister and Chiefs while at the same time keeping on top of all his other responsibilities had been severely challenging. It was a challenge, however, that he had met, even though it had at one point resulted in his temporary breakdown. In addition, he had actively contributed towards strengthening the Anglo-American relationship. He had been right in identifying the year as being in the trough of the war, but by its end would have been justified in a certain optimism about the future.

8

'CONFERENCE YEAR'

1943

For Ismay 1943 was to be a very different year, not least because he was to spend almost half of it abroad. It was, in his words, 'Conference Year'—a total of seven international conferences, all of which he was to attend.[1] He was responsible for administrative aspects of most of the conferences as well as being an active participant, both as a member of the Chiefs of Staff Committee and as Churchill's personal staff officer. Ismay was keen to disabuse those who imagined that these events might be something of a holiday for him. 'I can assure you that… these Conferences were no picnic', he told an audience after the war, 'personally, I was out on my feet at the end of practically every one of them'.[2]

It is not the purpose here to give comprehensive accounts or analyses of these conferences. This is well covered elsewhere, most notably by Andrew Roberts in *Masters and Commanders*. Here we will focus on Ismay's experience and observations of the events.

The first conference was an Anglo-American meeting at Casablanca, Morocco, in January. Its purpose was to agree future joint policy and strategy for the war. The journey to get there was a bizarre adventure in itself. In order to preserve secrecy Ismay, like all senior British attendees, was ordered to travel by car to a late-night rendezvous at a village some eighty miles west of London where he would receive further instructions. Arriving at the village Ismay found—predictably—a traffic jam, but he was eventually directed to a nearby RAF airfield. There he was briefed on action to be taken in the event of sundry emergencies, strapped into a parachute harness and invited to board a waiting, 'crudely adapted' Liberator bomber.[3] After a long and sleepless flight lying in a bomb rack, he arrived at Casablanca airfield on the morning of 13 January where, when the aircraft doors were opened, the party was greeted by Churchill, disguised as a RAF air commodore, with the cry, '[n]ow tumble out, you young fellows, and get on parade'.[4] Ismay was amused by Churchill's attempt at deception, remarking wryly, '[a]ny fool can see that is an air commodore disguised as the Prime Minister'.[5] As so often at these conferences, Churchill was at times in something approaching a holiday mood. Arriving a few days later, Harold Macmillan, Minister Resident in the Mediterranean, noted 'I have never seen him in better form. He ate and drank enormously all the time, settled huge problems, played bagatelle and bezique by the hour and generally enjoyed himself'.[6]

The prospects for the conference were somewhat less rosy. As was often to be the case at the Anglo-American wartime conferences the two sides arrived with very different and firmly held ideas about future strategy. The Americans continued to favour an Allied cross-channel invasion of continental Europe as soon as possible; the British believed that is was necessary first to weaken Germany through a peripheral strategy, especially through operations in the Mediterranean. Having just returned from a visit to Washington in December, Bedell Smith, referring to Churchill's enthusiasm for a campaign in the Mediterranean, had warned Ismay 'I must tell you that I found our people rather cold towards the major exploitation from this area which so interests the Prime Minister'. He went on to emphasise the urgent necessity for an agreed Anglo-American strategy before concluding, 'Unless our great men sit down and reach a definite decision as to whether we exploit the Mediterranean area, push a campaign in the Pacific and Burma, or build up in the UK for "Roundup" [the cross-Channel invasion of Europe], we shall continue to flounder and will be unable to pull together'.[7] Just before departing for Casablanca Ismay had replied, 'We have pretty well cleared our own minds on the "definite decision" to which you refer… and I hope and pray that general agreement may be reached within the next fortnight. Personally, I shall continue to feel miserable until this is done'.[8]

For the Casablanca conference Ismay had arranged for a large number of staff officers to be present, well prepared with position papers on subjects that might crop up. With Mountbatten's help he had also arranged for a ship to be present as an administration and communications hub. HMS *Bulolo* was a 6,000-ton converted liner, with an operations room and enough communications equipment to keep the delegation permanently in touch with London. The large staff and ship were to prove their value, so much so that the American delegation with a small staff and very limited communications felt outmanoeuvred. It was, as Macmillan noted, a significant 'advantage over the Americans'—and a disadvantage that they took pains to avoid at future conferences.[9]

The Combined Chiefs' first plenary meeting was no cause for optimism. 'At the outset', observed Ismay, 'there seemed to be an atmosphere of veiled antipathy and mistrust'.[10] As predicted, the main difference of opinion centred on strategic priorities, with sharply conflicting views. Ismay considered that the American Chiefs 'were united in suspecting that the underlying motive of the British proposals to continue operations in the Mediterranean was to postpone the cross-Channel assault for as long as possible, if not prevent it altogether'.[11] Over the next nine days some tough negotiations took place. Diary entries by Brooke included 'a very long and laborious day', 'another hard day', and 'a desperate day! We are further from obtaining agreement than we ever were'.[12] Part of the problem at these conferences was that Brooke's style—quick-thinking, fast-talking, certain of his own rectitude and often unable to conceal his disdain for those who disagreed with him—grated with the Americans. According to Danchev, 'He never recanted the view that the CCS [Combined Chiefs of Staff] should have been based in London, not Washington, possibly migrating later when the Americans had learned something of war'.[13] An additional factor that caused American irritation was that the British were far quicker in analysing and adapting to new circumstances or changing plans, thanks to the large team of key staff officers that Ismay had brought along.

As with all Anglo-American strategic disputes at which he was present, it was Dill who brought harmony and achieved compromise and agreement. Having been a critic of Dill as CIGS, Ismay was fulsome in his praise of him in his role as 'an invaluable intermediary' with the Americans.[14] (And not just in public, telling Spears, 'we owe a deep debt of gratitude to Dill for his work in Washington'.[15]) But Ismay himself played a significant supporting role, constantly working to achieve harmony and build friendships, based on the foundations that he had already laid. For example, when at one point the two staffs were 'at complete loggerheads' and a deadline was approaching, Dill suggested that Ismay and Slessor (now Assistant Chief of the Air Staff), should together produce a paper for the Combined Chiefs' approval.[16] They withdrew to another room and rapidly did so. And, as always, what happened outside the conference room was almost as important as what happened inside it. Ismay commented to Spears,

It was very satisfying to argue vehemently and frankly round the Council table all morning and then to lunch together in intimate parties at small tables; so different from those ghastly official meals that are usually associated with Allied gatherings. I certainly felt that it would be impossible for any two nations to get closer together in their outlook and their ideas than the Americans and ourselves.[17]

This was of course a Panglossian view, as Ismay's post-conference reports, even to his close friends, tended to be. But it was all part of his self-perceived mission to keep Anglo-American relations as harmonious as possible whatever the merits of the arguments on either side. In his memoirs, he also chose to skate over a major disagreement which emerged among the British Chiefs on the relative merits of Sicily and Sardinia as the next objective in the in the Mediterranean.[18] Having agreed on Sicily before the conference, they were now presented at a late-night meeting with a paper by the Joint Planners arguing for Sardinia. According to Brooke, a protagonist for Sicily, Mountbatten was supporting the Joint Planners: 'Peter Portal and Pug Ismay were beginning to waver and dear old Dudley Pound was, as usual, asleep, and with no views either way!' Brooke had 'a hammer and tongs battle to keep the team together and to stop it from wavering' but eventually, at midnight, achieved agreement.[19]

In addition, Ismay had considerable doubts about perhaps the most significant—and certainly the most controversial—policy decision to emerge from the conference: that of unconditional surrender. This was announced, much to Churchill's surprise, by Roosevelt at the press conference on the final day. As Churchill was later to write, 'General Ismay, who knew exactly how my mind was working from day to day, and was also present at all the discussions of the Chiefs of Staff when the communiqué was prepared, was also surprised'.[20] But it was the substance rather than the presentation that concerned Ismay. As he confided to Newall, now Governor-General of New Zealand, 'I am not sure myself whether it is a very wise formula'.[21] He retained this view in his memoirs, writing that he did not believe that it 'served any good purpose', but adding that he doubted 'whether it made any material difference to the length of hostilities'.[22] The wisdom of the unconditional surrender announcement has been much debated by historians. It may be that, as Thomas Mahnken has asserted, 'unconditional surrender was part of the glue that held the alliance together', but it did not look that way when it was first announced.[23]

From Casablanca Ismay flew to Algiers on his own initiative to visit Eisenhower. Churchill had been mildly surprised when Ismay told him of his intention to do so and, much to Ismay's amusement, told him not to 'loll about' there.[24] One of the main outcomes of the Casablanca conference had been a decision to pursue a Mediterranean strategy, with Sicily as the first objective—a decision that had required some persuasion by the British in the face of American reluctance. Ismay wanted to brief Eisenhower at first hand about this and to convince him that the operation was both feasible and in the best interests of the Alliance, and that the Prime Minister and British Chiefs of Staff had full confidence in him. It takes little imagination to see that this would have been much appreciated by Eisenhower and that it would have strengthened the relationship between him and Ismay. When in late May 1943 King George awarded Eisenhower the Knight Grand Cross of the Order of the Bath, Ismay immediately wrote offering his congratulations. Eisenhower replied, 'I scarcely know how to thank you for your generous and thoughtful note', and, referring to the backing and support that Ismay had given him, continued, 'In all this I have always counted with complete confidence on you—you know that'.[25]

On his return from Algiers on 7 February Ismay was immediately back at full stretch. His deputies, Hollis and Jacob, were both off sick and would remain so for a month. On 16 February Churchill contracted pneumonia, was incapacitated for a week, and spent a further three weeks convalescing at Chequers. The following month it was Ismay's turn; he was bedridden for five days with influenza, possibly exacerbated by exhaustion.[26]

No sooner was he back at work than planning started for the next Anglo-American conference, to be held over a fortnight in mid-May in Washington. Ismay was again to be responsible for the British side of the planning and administration. The preparation for the conference was intensive and continued as Churchill and the large delegation of about seventy travelled west on the liner *Queen Mary*: so much so that Ismay's only escape on-deck in the entire voyage was for a fire drill. As at Casablanca, the British and American Chiefs of Staff approached the conference with strongly held and diametrically opposed views on a number of strategic issues. At the very first plenary meeting, Ismay recalled, 'there was an unmistakable atmosphere of tension'.[27] The American Chiefs, highly suspicious, with good reason, that the British still wished to postpone cross-Channel operations in favour of a Mediterranean offensive, were determined that they would not allow themselves to be outmanoeuvred and misled as they believed that they had been at Casablanca. The result was 'what is regarded as one of the most ill-tempered and rancorous of all the wartime summits', with arguments at meetings of the Combined Chiefs at times so bitter that junior staffs were asked to leave the room.[28] Ismay was relieved that a weekend away at the restored colonial town of Williamsburg had been arranged for the Combined Chiefs; he described it as 'a memorable interlude in a fortnight of hard slogging'.[29]

In summing up the conference in his memoirs Ismay claimed that despite the acrimonious official discussions, 'personal relationships between the British and Americans were all that could be desired'.[30] This was something of an exaggeration although certainly true of his own relationships. One that developed strongly during the conference was with Admiral William Leahy, whom Roosevelt had brought back from retirement to be his chief of staff and chairman of the Joint Chiefs. This was the first Anglo-American conference that Leahy had attended and therefore the first occasion that he had met the British Chiefs. 'General Sir Hastings Ismay became my favourite', he later wrote, paying tribute to Ismay's grasp of both the military and political aspects of the issues under discussion. 'By his sympathetic understanding of our common war problems [he] quickly acquired my acceptance of him as a friend whose advice was always available to me.'[31]

Some historians have suggested that Leahy's and Ismay's roles were analogous, not least because in his memoirs Leahy suggested that '[Ismay's] position closely paralleled my own' and Ismay told Churchill when advising him on his memoirs that Leahy was 'more like an opposite number to me than anyone else'.[32] But when he came to draft his own memoirs Ismay acknowledged that, 'In point of fact, the similarity was more apparent than real'.[33] Leahy, unlike Ismay, was chairman of the Joint Chiefs of Staff but was not in charge of their secretariat. The extent of the dissimilarity became apparent in Phillips O'Brien's 2019 biography of Leahy, which established that (unlike Ismay) he was very much a direct and formal strategic adviser to his political master. The book also shows that Leahy paid the penalty in his sometimes-fractious relations with the individual Service Chiefs of Staff—a disadvantage that Ismay avoided.[34]

Immediately following the conference, Churchill decided that he would visit Eisenhower at Algiers, taking Brooke, Ismay and—with the President's permission—Marshall with him. It took them two and a half days to get there, flying via Newfoundland and Gibraltar. Ismay was exhausted and slept for the entire Atlantic crossing, unawakened even when the plane was struck by lightning. At Algiers discussion centred on Operation Husky—the planned invasion of Sicily, due to take place in July—and subsequent operations. After three meetings of hard negotiation considering these subsequent operations, Churchill succeeded in persuading the Americans, including a sceptic Marshall, that a contingency plan should be prepared for the invasion of the Italian mainland.[35] But there was time and opportunity for relaxation, including a tour of the battlefields near Tunis, a visit to Carthage and a swim in the sea. 'Everyone was happy', recorded Ismay.[36] Churchill was to assert in his memoirs that he had 'no more pleasant memory of the war than the eight days in Algiers and Tunis'.[37]

Shortly after returning from Algiers Ismay found that Joan Bright, his keeper of the Special Information Centre (the briefing room for visiting commanders-in-chief) had been made homeless by a German bomb on her flat in Curzon Street. He decided to offer her temporary accommodation in his Lowndes Square flat. Bright was careful in her book to say that 'Lady Ismay suggested that I should move into their flat', adding, 'I did—and remained there for three and a half years'.[38] Bright had become something of an institution in the office of the War Cabinet since her arrival in December 1940. She was highly efficient, charming and personable. She had established the reputation of the Special Information Centre not only as an essential port of call, but also a haven where a visiting senior officer could relax and unwind. Several, notably Wavell, found her to be not only a fount of knowledge but even more importantly a sympathetic ear and source of advice. In addition, she had proven her mettle in the challenging role as administrator for the overseas conferences. Ismay clearly regarded her highly and liked her personally, hence his invitation. She would become a close confidante of his. Nevertheless, it was an unusual arrangement, particularly as Darry was often away from London, and since it was well known amongst his staff (indeed the two travelled into work together in his chauffeur-driven car) it must have set tongues wagging in the office and beyond.

On 9 July, Operation Husky was successfully launched. Ismay had a very personal interest in it. A key part of Husky was the deception plan: Operation Mincemeat. This involved the British dumping into the sea off Spain a dead body, dressed as an officer, carrying papers suggesting that the invasion of Sicily was merely a feint, with the main attack being made in Greece and Sardinia. The group with overall responsibility for the deception plan was the London Controlling Section. As is not uncommon in the intelligence community, tensions arose between different agencies—in this case between the Section and the group where the idea for Mincemeat had originated, the Twenty Committee. This became a 'titanic personality clash' between the head of the London Controlling Section, Lieutenant Colonel Johnny Bevan, and the Twenty Committee member responsible for detailed implementation of Mincemeat, Lieutenant Commander Ewen Montagu.[39] The dispute did not escape Ismay's notice. While a strong supporter of Bevan he clearly managed to achieve a workable compromise because when Montagu in 1953 published an account of the operation under the title *The Man Who Never Was*, he invited Ismay to write the foreword, singling him out for warm personal thanks 'for his help in 1942 and 1943'.[40]

According to Ronald Wingate, Ismay played a significant role in the approval of Mincemeat: 'without his... advocacy, the Chiefs of Staff would never have allowed this plan to go through'.[41] Although he may have had no formal role in the approval process for deception plans, Ismay used his influence from time to time, as on this occasion. He was not initially convinced about Mincemeat; in his foreword to Montagu's book he admitted that, 'I was, I confess, a little dubious whether it would work'.[42] The Chiefs approved the plan on 14 April. With timing tight, Ismay fixed for Bevan to brief Churchill the very next morning and, following his direction that Eisenhower's agreement be sought, obtained it two days later.[43] Although there is no mention in official documents or accounts of Mincemeat of Ismay's involvement with the plan, he would have watched its implementation with bated breath and taken due pride in the success of his foster-children.

With Husky underway, but no firm plans beyond it yet to be agreed by the British and Americans, it became clear to the Allies that another high-level conference was required to settle the matter. They agreed in mid-July that this event would take place in Quebec the following month. Ismay and his staff again set about planning the arrangements for the British delegation. The conference, like its predecessors, was to be characterised by some heated arguments over strategy between the British and American Chiefs of Staff. It was, however, also characterised by some equally heated arguments among the British delegation, particularly between Brooke and Churchill. As the intermediary between them it was preventing these from occurring or escalating that was to preoccupy Ismay.

Part of the reason for these arguments were strongly held differences of opinion over policy, for example strategy in the Far East: a dispute which was to continue well into the following year. But part of the reason was that both Churchill and the Chiefs were suffering from exhaustion, and tempers were short. In the week before they embarked on the *Queen Mary* the pace of work had been even higher than usual. For example, Churchill had held War Cabinet meetings that were late-night even by his standards: one of these ended at 2.30 a.m., another at 4 a.m.[44] In addition, Churchill had confided to Ismay that he was increasingly finding the composition of his speeches 'a terrible strain' and he was due to make an important broadcast in Quebec.[45]

The crossing was again far from being a relaxed pleasure cruise. 'Throughout the voyage we worked unceasingly', recorded Ismay.[46] Brooke had what he described as 'a hammer and tongs' argument with Churchill over command arrangements in South-East Asia, and Clementine Churchill, who had embarked 'in a state of profound physical and nervous exhaustion', was 'still jaded and fatigued' at the end of the voyage.[47] On arrival in Quebec on 10 August Ian Jacob noted that Churchill was 'too exhausted to work'.[48] There is no mention of Ismay's state on arrival, probably because if he, too, was exhausted he successfully disguised the fact.

In Quebec the relationship between Brooke and Churchill was soured early on by Churchill's decision, communicated to Roosevelt and then to Brooke, that the commander of the invasion of Western Europe (Operation Overlord) should be an American and not a British general. The Prime Minister had previously told Brooke on several occasions that he would be the commander, and the decision came to the CIGS as 'a crashing blow'.[49] For most of the conference Brooke remained in a dark mood. Several bitter arguments between him and Churchill took place, including one where Churchill shook his fist in Brooke's face.[50]

The initial relationship between the two delegations also left something to be desired. In their history of the Chiefs of Staff Committee, William Jackson and Edwin Brammall wrote, 'Both sides approached [it] in an exasperated mood verging on outright distrust of each other'.[51] The American Chiefs were again dubious of the British commitment to Operation Overlord and wary of being hoodwinked by ambiguous drafting. The British Chiefs—'haunted by memories of the Somme and mindful of Dunkirk, Greece, Singapore and other disasters in 1940–42'—wished to avoid being hustled into agreeing a precipitate date for the operation.[52] The American Chiefs tabled a paper at the opening plenary which their British opposite numbers considered to be 'quite unacceptable'[53]. The meeting went into closed session. A 'frank discussion' took place but no agreement was reached.[54] Further heated discussions, on Overlord and other strategic issues, took place in closed session the following day. There is no evidence of Ismay's role in the reconciliation that was to take place, but judging by his efforts at other conferences he would have been as active outside the conference chamber as Dill was within it to maintain a constructive atmosphere, establish good personal relationships and move discussion towards agreement. By the final plenary session on 24 August agreement had been reached with compromises made by both sides. The conference had followed a familiar pattern. Ismay later summed it up succinctly in a letter to Newall, 'Here again we started badly, but ended up all right.'[55]

As always at the end of overseas conferences Ismay held a staff party—much appreciated, especially by the junior members and secretaries—on this occasion taking them to a memorable picnic at the spectacular Montmorency Falls, seven miles outside Quebec City.[56] Next day the British delegation departed but Ismay remained, accompanying the Churchill family on a five-day break at a fishing lodge in the Laurentian mountains. It was, however, by no means a complete break from work for Ismay, with long evenings including one listening to Churchillian reminiscences until 3.45 a.m.[57] From there the party went by train to Washington, arriving on 1 September and staying at the White House before accompanying Roosevelt for an overnight stay at his home at Hyde Park, New York. During the visit the Allied landing at Salerno took place and on the return train journey up to Halifax Ismay had the greatest difficulty restraining Churchill from flying to Salerno, only succeeding by shrewdly enlisting the help of Clementine Churchill.[58] The rail journey was nearly memorable for another reason. Twenty-year-old Mary Churchill recalled that, having descended to the platform at one station to stretch their legs, 'Pug Ismay and I and a few others nearly got caught out… and had to make a dash to jump back on the moving train'.[59]

The voyage back to Britain on the battleship *Renown* was also memorable. Mary later recalled that after dinner on the first evening at sea, 'Pug, Papa, John [Martin, private secretary] and I (in duffle coat) paced the Quarter Deck doing Cavalry drill! Papa was in the highest spirits'.[60] Churchill would have been less amused three nights later had he been told that Mary, standing on the quarterdeck with one of the young officers, was, to the horror of onlookers including Ismay, very nearly swept overboard by a large wave. But Ismay, to her eternal gratitude, kept silent about the incident. On return he presented Mary, who was a lieutenant in a

London-based air defence battery, with a cigarette case for her twenty-first birthday addressed to 'My Favourite Subaltern'. Her letter of thanks was addressed to 'My Favourite General'.[61]

Churchill arrived back on the evening of 20 September invigorated and the following afternoon was on his feet in the House of Commons delivering a well-received speech which, excluding the break for lunch, lasted two and a half hours. Ismay, too, was quickly back to business, finding the time the same day to write congratulating the American commander at Salerno, the Anglophobic General Mark Clark, 'knowing that you would pull it off if anyone could. And you have done so'.[62] The letter would have been appreciated: Clark was not popular with the British Chiefs—Brooke described him as 'very ambitious and unscrupulous'—and he had come under criticism for his handling of the battle.[63] Clark was to express his gratitude to Ismay the following year for again providing reassurance when Clark suspected that confidence in him was being undermined.[64]

A few days later came confirmation of the favourable impression that Ismay had made at Quebec. Colonel Henry Willis-O'Connor (the comptroller at Government House, Ottawa) wrote to Sir Alan Lascelles (the King's private secretary) telling him how impressed he had been by Ismay, and commenting 'Don't you think he would make an excellent Governor-General?' Lascelles relayed this to Ismay, adding 'Well, what about it?'[65] Ismay's reply is unrecorded, but he would undoubtedly have felt deeply honoured to be sounded out for the appointment. It was certainly recognition of the increasing admiration and respect in which he was held.

One of the decisions from the Quebec conference was for an immediate, joint meeting of American, British and Russian foreign ministers as a prelude to a meeting of heads of government. The Russians insisted that the venue be Moscow. The British Foreign Secretary, Anthony Eden, arranged for Ismay to accompany him in order to brief the Russians on the military plans agreed at Quebec for a second front in Europe in 1944. So less than three weeks after returning from Quebec, Ismay was en route to Moscow, this time by air, via Cairo and Teheran.

In Cairo they were briefed on the situation in the desert and took the opportunity to visit the troops there. Then it was on to Teheran to meet up with the American delegation, led by Secretary of State Cordell Hull, and discuss their joint approach to the dialogue with the Russians. They reached Moscow on 18 October and were pleasantly surprised to be greeted at the airport by the Russian foreign minister, Vyacheslav

Molotov. Ismay noticed 'a very different atmosphere' from his previous visit.[66] It was clear at the first plenary meeting that the sole agenda item proposed by the Russians concerned the timing and manner of the Anglo-American invasion of France. The following day Ismay gave the conference an hour-long presentation on the decisions from the Quebec conference and plans for Operation Overlord and was closely cross-examined on them by Molotov. But Ismay's openness in answering the questions was particularly well received by the Russians and later attracted the plaudits of both Eden and the American ambassador, Harriman.[67] That evening Molotov and a number of senior Russian ministers paid the unusual compliment of agreeing to dine at the British embassy. Next day Ismay received the even more unusual compliment of an invitation from Marshal Aleksandr Vasilevsky to join him on a tour of the Russian front line but, to his disappointment, the week-long tour was vetoed by Churchill, who needed him back in London.[68] On their final evening in Moscow both delegations were entertained to a dinner hosted by Stalin at the Kremlin. There were the inevitable and interminable toasts. Sitting next to Marshal Kliment Voroshilov, Ismay noted, '[a]s I suspected, he was filling his glass with lime juice part of the time. I did not play fair either. Did not get home till 3 a.m.'[69]

The conference and the reception given to the delegations had exceeded Ismay's expectations, as he explained in a letter to Mark Clark. After offering him his 'warmest congratulations' and telling him that he had heard 'the nicest things said of your leadership', Ismay wrote:

> The Moscow conference was surprisingly a great success. We thought we were in for a rough ride on the military side but from the moment we arrived at the airport it was quite evident that a totally different spirit prevailed from that which had met us when I accompanied the Beaverbrook-Harriman mission in 1941. These first impressions were confirmed when we got round the conference table.[70]

As a result of the visit Ismay changed his view of the Russians, and not just his view of them as wartime allies. 'For the first time I was optimistic about our post-war relations with Russia', he recorded.[71] He would retain this rose-tinted view for a surprisingly long time.

The Moscow trip had also changed Ismay's opinion of Eden. Although in his memoirs he says that he 'had always liked and admired him', his admiration had not always been fulsome: in May 1941 he had described him to a friend as, 'Nice fellow, but a lightweight'.[72] In Moscow, however,

Ismay was much impressed by Eden, and the admiration was mutual. Eden wrote to Churchill, 'I must put on record how deeply in debt I am to Ismay. He helped us at every stage in Moscow... and played chief part in inducing the suspicious Bruin to have faith in our intentions. Thank you so much for his help'.[73]

Ismay's trip to Moscow may also have served as welcome relief for him from the tensions and acrimony of Whitehall. Just before he left for Moscow Churchill was reported by his staff as being 'tired and bad tempered',[74] and at one point 'seemed distressed and said that he felt "almost like chucking it in"'.[75] Brooke had what he called a 'pitched battle' with him and, while Ismay was in Moscow, confessed to 'a desperate feeling of failure, incompetency and incapacity to carry this burden any longer!', later commenting, 'I am inclined to think that I cannot have been very far off a nervous breakdown at the time.'[76] There was discord, too, among the Chiefs of Staff when things 'took a nasty turn' with an argument between Portal and the new First Sea Lord, Admiral Sir Andrew Cunningham, when 'neither would give in'.[77]

Ismay was back in London for only four days before it was time to set off with Churchill for the next conferences in Cairo and Teheran.[78] Travelling in HMS *Renown* they stopped at Malta where Churchill stayed with the governor, Lord Gort. Churchill, unwell and confined to bed, found Gort's strict adherence to the rationing rules somewhat testing. When Ismay visited him Churchill pleaded, 'If you are going back to our lovely ship do get them to send me a pound of butter'.[79] Arriving in Cairo on 21 November for bilateral discussions with the Americans prior to meeting the Russians at Teheran, both Churchill and Ismay were surprised and irritated not only to find a Chinese delegation with Generalissimo and Madame Chiang Kai-Shek already ensconced there at American invitation, but that Roosevelt had 'promised Chiang that the Allies would carry out a major amphibious operation in Burma in 1944'.[80] The agenda was hastily reorganised to give priority to south-east Asian affairs, with meetings dominated by both the Generalissimo and his wife. Ismay appeared still to be irritated when he reported to Admiral Sir James Somerville, CinC Eastern Fleet, two months later, 'CKS struck me as knowing damn little about the war, and Madame, in spite of her acute mind, even less. However, we managed to get rid of them after two or three days craziness, though with what promises I do not know. All that I hoped... was that none of them would have to be redeemed'.[81]

The bilateral meetings of the American and British Chiefs of Staff, now under considerable time pressure, were even less satisfactory. Following the pattern of previous conferences, it was not long before major differences of opinion surfaced and the atmosphere became acrimonious. The first altercation was between Brooke and Admiral King, a spat described with relish by the highly Anglophobic Lieutenant General Joseph 'Vinegar Joe' Stilwell: 'Brooke got nasty and King got good and sore. King almost climbed over the table at Brooke. God he was mad. I wish he had socked him.'[82] Three days later Brooke had what he described as 'the father and mother of a row' with Marshall which required an off-the-record meeting to resolve.[83] Ismay will have done his best to preserve a cordial and constructive atmosphere, but he was choosing his words very carefully when he later described the Cairo conference as having been a great success 'in the long run'.[84]

On 27 November the delegations flew on to Teheran, but at the end of the following morning the British and Americans were still not agreed on the main points for discussion with the Russians, with whom they were due to meet in a plenary session later that afternoon. In Joan Bright's opinion,

> [t]he fact that a meeting took place at all that day was in no small measure due to General Ismay. Quietly and unostentatiously he worked to reconcile the independent attitudes of the Americans and British, smoothing over their failure, either in Cairo or during the... [first] morning in Teheran, to have reached prior agreement on the line they wished to take when confronted by the Russians.[85]

According to Bright, Ismay later told her that it was at the Teheran conference that he thought that Brooke 'came to realise that [his] behind-the-scenes role had its uses and that he was not just a courtier-in-waiting beside Churchill's throne'.[86]

The opening plenary was the first time Roosevelt, Churchill and Stalin had met together. Ismay watched the Russian leader carefully.

> Stalin would have made a fine poker player. His expression was as inscrutable as the Sphinx and it was impossible to know what he was thinking about. He did not speak much, but his interventions made in a quiet voice and without any gestures, were direct and decided. Sometimes they were so abrupt as to be rude. He left no doubt in anyone's mind that he was master in his own house... My outstanding expression of Stalin

was that he was completely devoid of the milk of human-kindness. I was thankful that I was neither his enemy nor dependent upon his friendship.[87]

After the meeting, Roosevelt made it plain that he wanted to see Stalin alone—a move that predictably was much resented by the British. Ismay, seeking to head off trouble, privately warned Harriman that—as the latter termed it—'storm signals were flying in the British legation' and Harriman walked over to see for himself 'whether there was any need to calm the waters'.[88] Ismay's concern was to prove well founded: it became apparent that Roosevelt had come to Teheran intent on establishing his own special relationship with Stalin at the expense of Churchill. In his memoirs Ismay, ever diplomatic, described the President at Teheran as 'at his best throughout the Conference—wise, conciliatory and paternal'.[89] In reality Roosevelt spent much of the time teasing Churchill in Stalin's presence to the point of humiliation and making common cause with Stalin against Churchill's proposals and opinions 'in an effort to "charm" the Soviet leader and illustrate that he did not face any Anglo-American bloc'.[90] Roosevelt succeeded on both counts but the experience 'made Churchill acutely aware of his waning influence in relation to both the United States and the Soviet Union'.[91]

But despite these fissures the conference proceeded with at least superficial harmony and reached agreement on, amongst other things, the May 1944 date for Operation Overlord and a supporting operation in the south of France. For Stalin, the latter operation achieved keeping the Anglo-American forces well away from the Balkans, for which he had his own post-war plans. It was only subsequently, Ismay considered, that the Western Allies realised that they had been outmanoeuvred.[92] Ismay disliked Stalin but he had a sneaking admiration for the way that he moved business forward at meetings, later telling Somerville, 'Whenever there was any disposition to shirk the issue by referring a problem to a sub-committee he said: "What for? What are we here for?"'[93]

The conference ended with a large dinner held by Churchill at the British Legation to celebrate his sixty-ninth birthday. Roosevelt and Stalin were the principal guests. 'The speeches started directly we sat down and continued almost without interruption until we got up', Ismay noted wearily, adding, 'It is a great advantage on these occasions to be too unimportant to be required to get to one's feet'.[94]

As planned, the American and British delegations left Teheran to return to Cairo on 2 December to take stock of the conference with the

Russians and settle outstanding matters of strategy. But the two Western Allies were soon in dispute with each other. As Ismay told Somerville,

> [h]aving got back to Cairo, things were quite hopeless. Our friends advocated doing marvels in all parts of the world: while we took the line of first things first, and protested against any resources of any kind that were required to beat the Boche being diverted at this juncture against the Yellow Man.[95]

The specific issue was the relative priority of the major amphibious operation in the Pacific, promised by the Americans to Chiang Kai-Shek, and the upcoming Anzio operation favoured by the British. Brooke admitted to having been 'unnecessarily bitter' with the American Chiefs and noted that Churchill was also 'not in a good temper'.[96] Brooke persuaded Churchill to intervene personally with Roosevelt: he did so but the President was unmoved. At the conclusion of the military discussions Ismay urged Churchill to have one last attempt. This time Churchill succeeded. As he reported to Ismay, quoting the Book of Proverbs, 'He that ruleth his spirit is greater than he that taketh a city'.[97]

Later the same day, 5 December, Ismay was taken ill with what he called in his memoirs 'an acute attack of bronchitis'.[98] This description, however, was something of a euphemism. He was holding a meeting with his staff when they noticed worrying symptoms. Lieutenant Colonel George Mallaby remembered, 'a session of doubt and perplexity with General Ismay who suddenly seemed finished, breathless, almost inanimate.'[99] That evening Hollis went to his room: 'I was horrified to see how ill he looked. He was in fact suffering from complete exhaustion. He had worked on average for anything up to eighteen hours in each twenty-four for the previous three years'.[100] Doctors were summoned and arrangements made for Ismay to travel back to Britain three days later, on HMS *London*. On arrival he was taken home to Wormington where he remained convalescing until early January. He was not the only casualty of the second Cairo conference. One week after Ismay was struck down, Churchill arrived in Tunis to visit Eisenhower and was taken seriously ill with what was eventually diagnosed as pneumonia and atrial fibrillation (irregular heartbeat).[101] He was to remain in North Africa, convalescing at Marrakesh for over a month, only returning to Britain on 17 January.

Conference Year had followed a punishing schedule. Ismay calculated that he had spent twenty-four weeks out of England and flown over 40,000 miles. Each conference had taken weeks of preparation, and each had included moments of crisis that had placed demands on his skills and stamina. That each had ended with considerable agreement and with relationships still intact was in no small part due to his efforts.

A contributing factor in preserving those relationships had been the trust and friendship between Ismay and Eisenhower which had developed over the year. Having visited him in Algiers in February and again with Churchill in May, Ismay had dined with Eisenhower on his return to London the following month and maintained contact with him during the campaign in Sicily. Eisenhower's was an influential voice in Washington at a time when there was considerable anti-British feeling in America and suspicion over what was seen as British duplicity and imperial motives in strategy—what Colville later referred to as 'the American obsession with colonialism [which] almost led to a breakdown'.[102] According to Mark Stoler, 'So widespread and intense was the hostility against Britain within the services that it aroused the concern of both Marshall and Eisenhower', prompting Eisenhower to warn a colleague in the Pentagon, 'one of the constant sources of danger to us in this war is the temptation to regard as our first enemy the partner that must work with us in defeating the real enemy'.[103] Ismay was probably one of the few Britons whom Eisenhower may have felt he knew well enough to share at least some of these concerns, and it would be surprising if on at least one occasion when they were alone together he had not done so. Their relationship was to prove even more important in the year ahead.

9

'THE YEAR OF DESTINY'

1944

When Ismay returned to his office on 2 January 1944 he noted that he had been in it for only one month in the last six, and only four days in the last three months.[1] Whether this was said with regret or relief is hard to judge, perhaps a bit of both. If some things had changed, much had remained the same, and not least his workload. The following Friday he dined with Alan Lascelles who noted in his diary that Ismay was 'up to his eyes in work, under trilateral bombardment from Winston in Morocco, the Chiefs of Staff in Whitehall, and the American ditto in Washington; they seem to find it difficult to agree on future plans'. Knowing that Ismay had been seriously ill and opining that the series of strenuous conferences had 'nearly killed him', Lascelles added, 'he seems to have recovered and was most amusingly reminiscent'.[2]

Ismay's skills as peacemaker were required almost immediately. Within two days of the Prime Minister's return on 17 January—and following a series of long, argumentative meetings—Brooke was venting his frustration in his diary, 'My God how tired I am of working for him! I had not realized how awful it is until I suddenly found myself thrown into it again after a rest!'[3] One unspoken source of tension for both Brooke and Churchill was the impending landing at Anzio, just a few days away, and for which both men felt great personal responsibility. Brooke confided in his diary, 'I feel a special responsibility for it... it may fail'.[4] Churchill, with the spectre of Gallipoli never far from his mind, later commented that Anzio was 'my worst moment in the war. I had most to do with it. I didn't want two Suvla Bays in one lifetime'.[5] In the event, their fears proved groundless. The landings commenced on 22 January and achieved complete surprise. The exploitation of success, however, was to prove worryingly sluggish.

There were two further disputes which now made demands on Ismay's time and energy. The first was a spat between Mountbatten, now Supreme Allied Commander South East Asia, and his senior naval subordinate Somerville. Both lobbied Ismay in a series of letters with their complaints against the other. Mountbatten complained about Somerville's generally uncooperative attitude, including 'his refusal to let me go on board any ships or visit any Naval Establishments'.[6] Somerville compared Mountbatten with the egotistical American supreme commander General Douglas MacArthur, complaining that Mountbatten was 'out-MacArthuring MacArthur to a degree which I thought was impossible' and deprecating the enormous staff that he had created at his headquarters.[7] Ismay, who was friends with both men, found himself in a difficult position, particularly as he was aware of the ill feeling caused by the proliferation of Mountbatten's staff. Indeed, he had urged Somerville to 'stop Dickie collecting staff in this crazy way. I have implored him not to make the same mistake as he made as C[hief] C[ombined] O[perations] (where incidentally he did a damn fine job)'.[8] But he set about soothing the relationship between the two men and succeeded in dissuading Mountbatten, who was 'demanding a showdown' with the Chiefs of Staff.[9]

The second dispute concerned the relationship between the British and American Joint Staff Planners in Washington. Bedell Smith came to see Ismay with a complaint about the matter. Ismay relayed to the secretary of the British Mission in Washington, Brigadier Harold Redman, that there was 'undoubtedly a feeling at American Headquarters here that perhaps the Combined Staff Planners at the present time are not working together with that sympathy and understanding which should be characteristic of them'.[10] Although Redman roundly rejected the charge, there were no further complaints about the relationship.

In many ways these disputes were tedious and time-consuming distractions from the major and more immediate issues confronting Ismay, but it was characteristic of him both that supplicants tended to come to him for solution of their disputes and that he invariably gave these his time and attention, thus preventing their escalation. In doing so he provided a singularly valuable service.

In spring 1944 there were several momentous events competing for the attention of those responsible for the higher direction of the war: notably the exploitation of the landings at Anzio, the subsequent prolonged battle for Monte Cassino, and the bombing campaign over Germany. But as Ismay pointed out in his memoirs these were dwarfed by the upcoming operation which could decide the outcome of the war and 'thoughts of [which] dominated all our minds': Operation Overlord. For Ismay, 1944 would 'always live in my memory as the year of destiny'.[11] The nagging fear of possible failure was to add to the pressure on all those responsible for its planning and to the tensions between them, right up to the event itself in June. But for Churchill there was also the growing realisation that his power and influence—and that of Britain—on the international stage was waning, with a resulting feeling of impotence, irritability and ill temper. Coping with this became a major challenge for all around him.

The issue which was to dominate strategic discussion throughout the spring and early summer of 1944 and cause the most acrimonious disagreements was not, however, Overlord—but the subject that had raised its head en route to Quebec the previous summer: strategy for the war against Japan. It was to lead to what Andrew Roberts identified as 'the lowest point in relations between Churchill and the Chiefs of Staff in the Second World War' and cause Ismay unceasing concern.[12] The Chiefs believed strongly that this strategy should be focused on land, sea and air operations in support of the Americans—and under American command—in the Pacific. Churchill believed equally strongly that British forces should instead be committed across the Bay of Bengal against Sumatra, Malaya, Singapore and Japanese communications with Burma— thus retrieving lost property and regaining imperial prestige.[13] The Chiefs rejected outright what Churchill called his 'Bay of Bengal Strategy' as a waste of military resources. Churchill was adamant, accusing the Chiefs of having taken decisions behind his back while he was convalescing in Marrakesh 'without in any way endeavouring to ascertain and carry the views of the civil power under which they are serving'.[14] The Chiefs contemplated resignation. With Churchill's threat to escalate the issue to War Cabinet level, the deadlock was shaping up to be a constitutional crisis.

This was exactly the type of situation that Ismay dreaded. On 4 March he intervened to mediate. He wrote to the Prime Minister, warning him of the possibility of resignations, which 'would be little short of catastrophic at this juncture', and suggesting that he 'take the line that the issue cannot be decided on military grounds alone and that... political considerations must be overriding... I cannot but think that the Chiefs of Staff would accept this decision with complete loyalty'.[15] He followed this eminently

141

sensible suggestion with a proposal, which Churchill accepted, for a meeting of the Defence Committee the following week to pursue this line and resolve the issue. When the meeting was held, however, with Churchill accompanied by Cabinet ministers Attlee, Eden, Lyttleton and Leathers, debate quickly descended into heated argument over the relative merits of detailed strategies. Brooke recorded that he 'went at it hard arguing with the PM and 4 Cabinet Ministers' for two and a half hours, noting that Cunningham was 'so wild with rage that he hardly dared let himself speak!!'[16] No resolution was reached. As David Reynolds perceptively observed, '[t]he clash between Churchill and the Chiefs of Staff involved more than strategy. It was a contest of wills between opinionated men whose mutual patience had almost snapped under the incessant strain of war'.[17] Ten days later Churchill issued a ruling, addressed to each Chief individually, directing that the Bay of Bengal Strategy was to be followed. This the Chiefs flatly rejected, again contemplating resignation.[18]

The argument continued through March and April with neither side prepare to give ground. Ismay now championed a compromise 'Middle Strategy' which combined parts of the Chiefs' Pacific Strategy with elements of Churchill's Bay of Bengal Strategy. Under this proposal, no British resources would be allocated to the American operations. In commenting on what he referred to as the 'middle course', he told Pownall, in some exasperation,

> I am using what little influence I have to persuade the COS that anything is better than the present uncertainty. It would be far better to agree some plan even though it may not the best and to push it forward unitedly and wholeheartedly, than to go on doing what we are at the moment. When history comes to be written I believe that the waffling that there has been for nearly nine months over the basic question of our strategy in the Far East will be one of the black spots in the record of the British Higher Direction of War, which has, on the whole, has been pretty good.[19]

Both Churchill and the Chiefs of Staff agreed that the Middle Strategy should be subjected to detailed analysis. The resulting lengthy process took much of the immediate heat out of the confrontation even if it did not bring the argument to a conclusion. Subjects of more immediate concern—not least the imminent Operation Overlord—came to dominate the strategic agenda and relations between Churchill and the Chiefs never descended to quite such a low level again.

During these disputes relations between Churchill and Brooke had come close to fracture. Joan Bright was later to recall what Ismay had told her about it.

> Brooke in the company of other ministers was far more rude to the PM than he had any right to be—and WSC was shocked. He broke up the meeting and said to Ismay 'I have decided to get rid of Brooke. He hates me. You can see the hate in his eyes'. Ismay [replied], 'I think that he behaved very badly at the meeting but he is under a terrific strain. He is bone honest and whatever else his views may be, he doesn't hate you'. Ismay left then to see Brooke and said 'The PM is frightfully upset and says you hate him'. Whereupon Brooke said 'I don't hate: I adore him tremendously; I do love him; but the day that I say that I agree with him when I don't, is the day he must get rid of me because I am no use to him any more'. Asked if these words could be repeated to the PM he said 'Yes'. Ismay went back and told WSC what had been said and his eyes filled with tears: 'Dear Brooke…'[20]

The argument between Churchill and the Chiefs in March and April acted as an unhappy backdrop to ongoing operational events and strategic developments, few of which were being crowned with success. 'We are going through testing times here', wrote Ismay to Pownall, 'everything seems to be going wrong lately'. He cited the situation at the Anzio bridgehead, relations with the Russians ('the "bear" is being more grumpy than usual'), the fate of Poland, and the build-up of German air assets in Northern France. 'I am glad', he added, 'that the general feeling in this country that all was over bar the shouting is beginning to evaporate… I cannot see the faintest sign of a crack in the German military machine'.[21] But as well as focusing on current challenges, Ismay was as usual thinking well ahead. He shared with Pownall a wider strategic issue:

> Superimposed on all the worries about how to win the war in the shortest possible time, are the worries about how to win the peace, and thereafter how to organize the British Commonwealth, Europe and the world. Committees considering the various aspects have sprung up like mushrooms but the problems are so nebulous and complicated as to be insoluble. Moreover, as far as the fighting services are concerned, all the better brains are required to deal with our immediate affairs and the postwar problems have perforce to be left to lesser lights who are long past their best![22]

It is evident that Ismay's efforts and achievements during this difficult period were appreciated by the Prime Minister. On 19 May he was promoted to the rank of full general. Although he may have considered this of less importance than he might have done in more normal times, he would undoubtedly have valued the show of confidence in him. He would also have appreciated the large dinner party thrown in his honour by his close colleagues and office staff at Claridges hotel on 25 May. According to Lawrence Burgis, '[t]he champagne and brandy flowed freely… we were all glad to be able to pay tribute to a man who not only had made such an important contribution to the winning of the war, but was respected and loved by all, of either high or low degree, with whom he came into contact'.[23]

The tribute was clearly written subsequently because at the time of the event, just two weeks before D-Day, victory was no foregone conclusion. Indeed, there was without doubt considerable apprehension amongst all those responsible for the higher direction of the war. Ismay had remained close to the planning for Overlord, including the weekly briefings given since January 1944 to Churchill by Eisenhower. He had also played a direct role in the coordination of deception planning for the operation, providing support and guidance to the London Controlling Section.[24] A key element of the section's deception plan, codenamed Bodyguard, was to persuade the Germans that the landings in Normandy would be a diversion for the main landings which would take place in the Pas de Calais.[25] The plan—in Overy's words, 'a work of artistic mendacity'— had been hatched during the late autumn of 1943.[26] Ismay's support included (as it had for deception planning for the invasion of Sicily) the coordination of plans with allies, with other government departments and with commanders-in-chief, as well as personally briefing the Prime Minister on the progress of planning. For example, he coordinated the Bodyguard plans with Eisenhower and Montgomery, arranged for the Controlling Officer Bevan to visit Moscow to brief the Russians, and kept Churchill continually informed of developments.[27] And although formally the London Controlling Section reported to the Chiefs of Staff through the Directors of Plans, in practice Bevan submitted many of the section's plans to the Chiefs through Ismay.[28]

Ismay also assisted in the development of a subsidiary part of Bodyguard, designed to persuade the Germans in late May that no Allied invasion was imminent.[29] To this end an actor with a close resemblance to Montgomery—the most prominent of the Allied commanders—was sent on a high-profile visit to Gibraltar. There, as anticipated, German agents reported his presence. The ruse was later made into the book and film, *I Was Monty's Double*.[30]

In early January—when Churchill was still in Marrakesh—Ismay, on behalf of the Deception Planners, had sought to persuade the Prime Minister to authorise travel restrictions from 1 February into the areas along the south coast where troops for Overlord would be concentrating. This was especially important in south-east England where, according to the deception plan, American forces were meant to be massing for the main assault on the Pas de Calais. Churchill did not share the pressing need for secrecy. He replied that he was not in favour of a visitors' ban, particularly at such an early date, summing up his objection in typically Churchillian style, '[w]e must beware of handing out irksome for irksome's sake'.[31] However, he allowed the matter to be referred to the War Cabinet. This delayed, but did not prevent, approval of the restrictions.

As D-Day approached, Ismay recalled, 'the days passed too slowly and yet too fast. Too slowly because of our impatience to start; too fast because of the haunting fear that all would not be ready in time'.[32] Part of the challenge for him was dealing with Churchill's close and personal involvement in the direction of the Overlord plans, including some bizarre proposals, such as that for a '"reverse Dunkirk"... with small [civilian] boats landing infantry to follow up and supplement proper assault troops after beaches had been cleared'.[33] The Prime Minister had a further, more covert scheme in mind. Following the presentation of the final plans on 15 May Churchill had confided to Ismay that he himself intended to accompany the invasion force in one of the bombardment cruisers. Ismay was horrified and attempted to dissuade Churchill, not least on the grounds that he would be out of communication at a time when critical decisions might be required, '[b]ut my objections were abruptly silenced by the whispered promise that, if I kept my mouth shut, he would take me with him'.[34] Resisting this temptation, Ismay went to see Lascelles at Buckingham Palace, only to find that Churchill had already briefed the King, who also had tried and failed to dissuade him. He was shown into the presence of the King, who wrote in his diary that Ismay 'was very upset by the P.M.'s attitude'. The following day the King recorded, 'Ismay sent me a message early to say that the P.M. was wavering & hoped I would send him another message imploring him not to go on the expedition'.[35] The King did so, and an exasperated Churchill agreed with as good grace as he could muster.[36] Fortunately for Ismay his part in the plot remained a secret until after the war.

On 2 June, three days prior to D-Day, Ismay was one of a very small group accompanying Churchill on the Prime Minister's special train to Southampton to visit Eisenhower's headquarters and the embarking troops. Parked in a siding at a nearby village, with only one telephone line, the train was a far-from-ideal war headquarters and Ismay was subject to a high level of aggravation and pressure.

> The next morning everybody seemed to be on edge, and there was chaos. The Prime Minister wanted to talk to all and sundry at one and the same moment—to the President in the White House, to Eden at the Foreign Office, and to the Chiefs of Staff in Whitehall. When the inevitable delay occurred, he was full of complaints. When I suggested in desperation that it might be better to get back to civilisation my head was bitten off. Were we not next-door to Eisenhower and at the very centre of affairs?[37]

That afternoon he accompanied Churchill to watch the embarkation and was highly impressed by the mood and bearing of the troops. In a sideswipe in his memoirs which will have infuriated one of his readers, he sought to put the record straight as to where he believed the credit for this lay, 'Paget [General Sir Bernard Paget, Montgomery's predecessor as commander of 21st Army Group] had forged a magnificent weapon and Montgomery had imparted the final polish'.[38]

During dinner that evening he took a telephone call from Bedell Smith: the weather forecast was bad and it looked as if the landings would need to be postponed; a decision would be taken at 4 a.m. Ismay 'repeated this grim message to the assembled company, and no one made any comment'.[39] Late into the night, in a highly personal letter reflecting the pressure he felt under, Ismay wrote to Joan Bright.

> This is the longest railway journey I've ever undertaken. I am just going to bed but am being called at 4.30 a.m. to take a very immediate and vital telephone call... we've just had a sledgehammer blow... It's hell here—impossible to get a moment to oneself, and ONE telephone, very inefficiently staffed, in a van 4ft x 3ft occupied by three people... Master is in the bath all the time. Today has been bloody... I have such a lot to tell you. God bless you, darling. I am so humbly and dearly grateful for all your loving help and support. Tonight is the worst of the war from the "decision" point of view... Much love, Pug.

At 4.45 a.m. on 4 June Smith telephoned with the news that Overlord was to be postponed for twenty-four hours. Ismay added a postscript to his letter:

> I was woken for work at 4.45, 5.15 and 6 a.m. The worst—or almost the worst—has happened. Anyway, we're in a hell of a mess, but we'll get out all serene if we keep our heads on our shoulders. I'm doing my best to get master back to London tonight. We are hopelessly out of touch here; and there are vital decisions to take which can only be properly taken if we get round a table and assemble all the relevant facts and arguments. How I've hated the last 48 hours! Much love.[40]

After several days of what Ismay later described as 'the most exquisite hell I have ever had', Churchill and the party returned to London that afternoon 'in an agony of uncertainty', and the Prime Minister held a meeting of the War Cabinet that evening.[41]

The letter belies the image of the totally unflappable Ismay. It also shows just how close was his relationship with Joan Bright, raising the question as to whether that relationship was more than platonic. They had been sharing a house for over a year and were to do so for another two years. Ismay's wife was an infrequent visitor. Bright was certainly a close confidante of his and he was obviously very fond of her. But there is no other evidence to suggest that their relationship was more than platonic, or that Ismay's relationship with his wife had in any way deteriorated. Furthermore, Bright was to remain a friend of the whole Ismay family after the war and indeed of Darry after Ismay's death.

Ismay had not been optimistic about the prospect for the Normandy landing, a week after it admitting to an American friend, Lew Douglas, that '[w]e got the beach defences at about one-tenth of the cost that I had anticipated'.[42] In his memoirs Ismay depicts the post-Overlord atmosphere in Whitehall as an aura of relief and the release of pent-up tension, with accounts of a dinner held by Churchill at Downing Street for the King and the visiting American Chiefs of Staff, and of the King's visit to the troops in Normandy, accompanied by Ismay. In fact, anxiety remained, with uncertainty as to how long the Germans would remain deceived into believing that the main invasion would occur in the Pas de Calais. For several days it appeared that the deception was holding. But one night about a fortnight after D-Day Bevan appeared at Ismay's office with the alarming news that General von Rundstedt had given orders for his troops near the Pas de Calais to move to the Normandy bridgehead.

Bevan proposed to Ismay that a message should immediately be passed to Hitler by German agents in British hands confirming that the main attack was coming in the Pas de Calais. He pointed out, though, that this was bound to compromise the agents concerned. Without delaying to consult the Chiefs of Staff or Churchill, Ismay gave him the go ahead.[43] In doing so he took considerable responsibility on his own shoulders, but it was sound judgement. The deception continued to be successful. The incident was still highly secret when Ismay reminded Churchill of it in 1951.

In the wake of the post-Overlord euphoria, life for Ismay quickly returned to a familiar pattern as old tensions returned and new ones surfaced. The arrival of the US Chiefs of Staff on 9 June heralded discussions on future strategy, differences of opinion and argument. The Americans pressed for advancing the date for Operation Anvil, the landing in Southern France agreed at the Teheran conference. Churchill and the British Chiefs objected: the operation would require troops transferred from Italy where General Alexander needed them to continue his drive northwards up the Po Valley towards Austria and Trieste. Roosevelt and Churchill exchanged strongly worded letters on the subject, 'far more acrimonious than anything which had previously passed between them'.[44] Churchill felt so passionately about the subject that he drafted a message to Roosevelt threatening resignation if Anvil went ahead.[45] In an attempt to defuse the situation Ismay enlisted the support of Brooke to reach some sort of compromise. At a late night meeting on 30 June the Chiefs persuaded Churchill to withdraw his threat and as Brooke noted, 'left Winston and Pug drafting a telegram'.[46] Ismay's drafting skills were much required at this time. Just five days later, Lascelles went to see him and 'found him busy trying to tone down a decidedly petulant telegram which the PM wishes to send to FDR [Roosevelt]'.[47] Indeed, according to Andrew Roberts, '[m]any of the more ill-tempered telegrams that followed were not published in his [Churchill's] memoirs, and there were many others which Ismay persuaded him not to send and which were then destroyed'.[48]

A further tension which had certainly grown with Overlord was the British government's relationship with General de Gaulle. Ismay had many dealings with de Gaulle during the war but later described him in private as, 'most difficult. Thought he was Jeanne d'Arc and Louis Quatorze. Used to come in to me and demand to be on COS [the Chiefs of Staff Committee]. I said what about Canada, and Australia, and New Zealand, and Holland, and Belgium, and Denmark, and Norway. Then the only place we could have a meeting is in [the] Albert Hall'.[49] On the eve of D-Day, de Gaulle had refused Churchill's request to broadcast to the French people. De Gaulle later accused Churchill of being 'a gangster'; Churchill accused him of 'treason at the height of battle'.[50] However de Gaulle relented and on the evening of 6 June made the speech—an impassioned and much praised one. Ismay was among a small group sitting with Churchill listening to it on the radio. Churchill, overcome with emotion, started to cry. But noticing Ismay staring at him snorted, 'You great tub of lard! Have you no sentiment?'[51]

In his memoirs Ismay was typically diplomatic about de Gaulle, giving a generous tribute to his many qualities. De Gaulle was of course President of France at the time he was writing (and Ismay the recently retired Secretary General of NATO). But in the summer of 1944 Ismay was less complimentary, telling the government's former representative in the Middle East, Richard Casey, 'We are having the most awful trouble with de Gaulle. You, having had some of his tantrums, will sympathise'.[52] In July Edward Spears told Ismay, 'if we allow de Gaulle to dominate France, as he certainly will if he is given half a chance, the France that will emerge will not, I believe, be either very friendly or very useful to us'.[53] Ismay replied, 'I myself entirely agree with your views towards... de Gaulle. That he is no friend of ours, I feel very certain, whatever his protestations'.[54] The following month, according to Lockhart, Ismay told him that if he were Eisenhower, he 'would kick de Gaulle out of France'.[55] The Churchill/de Gaulle relationship at this time is a rare example of Ismay not even attempting to bring about reconciliation.

If relations between Churchill and both Roosevelt and de Gaulle had reached their respective nadirs, relations between him and the Chiefs of Staff and ministers were in danger of following suit. On 3 July, in a War Cabinet meeting which lasted from 5.30 p.m. to 9.15 p.m., Brooke recorded that Churchill was 'in one of his worst maudlin moods [and] wasted hours'.[56] Three days later at a late night meeting of the Defence Committee, called to address strategy in the Far East, he was, according to Brooke, 'in a maudlin, bad tempered, drunken mood, ready to take offence at anything, suspicious of everybody and in vindictive mood against the Americans...' When the Chiefs repeated their argument in support of the American position, the three ministers present (Attlee, Eden and Lyttleton) sided with the Chiefs. 'This', according to Brooke, 'infuriated him more than ever and he became ruder and ruder'.

Churchill then started to criticise Montgomery; Brooke 'lost my temper and started one of the heaviest thunderstorms that we had!'[57] Eden summed up the event as 'a really ghastly Defence Committee meeting… altogether a deplorable evening which wouldn't have happened a year ago'.[58] Ismay's opinion can only be guessed at, but it would almost certainly have been one of embarrassment and deep disquiet. That he attempted to defuse such disputes and placate Churchill is indicated by an entry in Kennedy's diary later that month. '[Churchill] said to Ismay the other day that he (Churchill) was not now combative enough, and he accused him of being "a bromide" in trying to get settlements and agreements. He told Ismay that his job was to prod him and help him make rows and oppose his advisers, or words to that effect'.[59]

On 20 July Ismay accompanied Churchill on a four-day visit to the troops in Normandy. It was a welcome break for the Prime Minister from the disputes and arguments in London and as usual on such visits Churchill was in good form. He inspected Mulberry harbours, visited army units, conferred with Montgomery, and flew with the RAF commander to visit Allied airfields where he talked to air and ground crews. On Eisenhower's instructions, and to Churchill's irritation, the Prime Minister was kept well away from the front line. Ismay and Churchill's aide, Commander Tommy Thompson, took the opportunity to carry out their own tour of the battle area. According to Thompson, when they rejoined the Prime Minister they were taken to task for having managed to get closer to the front line than he had.[60]

It was not long after their return to London that relations between Churchill and the Chiefs hit another rocky patch. Following a conference on 9 August the Chiefs complained amongst themselves that Churchill had tricked them by suddenly producing the paper for discussion at the last moment. Ismay revealed that the paper had been available half an hour earlier, but Churchill had given orders that it was not to be circulated before the meeting. Cunningham was sharply critical of Churchill in his diary that same night, accusing him of having a 'crooked mind'.[61] Brooke had written in his diary the previous night, 'I am at my wits end and can't go on much longer!'[62] Two days later, according to Cunningham, Ismay told the Chiefs in a closed session that Churchill 'was just raving last night and absolutely unbalanced. He cannot get over not having had his own way over [Operation] "Anvil"'. 'To my surprise', recorded Cunningham, 'it was Portal who suggested that we must have a showdown with him before long if he went on as he is now. I have long thought it'.[63] It would have been to Ismay's relief, if not his suggestion, that the Chiefs decided to postpone the issue for twenty-four hours to let matters cool off. By this time Churchill was en route for a fortnight's visit to British troops in Italy.

Ismay took the opportunity of Churchill's absence to visit Eisenhower at his advanced command post, recently established near Bayeux in Normandy. Following dinner and an overnight stay at Eisenhower's lodging at Tournières, he was briefed at the Allied Expeditionary Force headquarters the next day. Ismay came away impressed and full of optimism. On his return he reported to Lascelles, who recorded in his diary:

> Ismay cannot see how the Germans can get their army, in any shape as a fighting force, out of the jam in which it now is. He did not seem disturbed about Anglo-American relations—there have been stories of Eisenhower and Bedell Smith having fallen out with Monty. Ismay takes a sane and broad-minded view of the Americans—they have won their spurs, and the days are past when we could treat them as green and untried soldiers; in fact, he went as far as to say that we might well have something to learn from them, and that maybe we have been a bit too 'staff collegey.'[64]

Ismay's view of the American military had certainly changed since his June 1943 visit to US Army troops training in South Carolina.

When Churchill returned from Italy on 29 August planning was well advanced for a further Anglo-American conference in the second week of September, again to be held in Quebec. Churchill was still suffering from a bout of pneumonia that he had picked up on his travels and may have been short of patience. On the day of his return, he took issue with Ismay on a relatively trivial matter. Both governments had agreed in principle to limit staff numbers at the conference, although both would have known that neither would comply very strictly. When Ismay informed Churchill that the British would take twenty-five staff members, Churchill wrote, '[t]here can be no question of taking 25 staff officers to the conference. 15 is the number agreed upon. The expression "only 14 more" means in fact more than double... Have a list prepared showing the titles of all the officers you propose to take'.[65] This entirely impractical parsimony could not have failed to irritate Ismay, and it foreshadowed a more serious decline in their relationship.

The party travelled to Quebec on the liner *Queen Mary*. For Churchill, the Chiefs of Staff and Ismay it was not a happy voyage. Ismay alluded (but no more) to this in his memoirs: 'Mr Churchill had not yet recovered from his illness, but instead of having a rest, he insisted on working harder than ever. Large doses of M and B [antibiotics] wrought miracles with his pneumonia but had not improved his temper, and although the sea was calm, some of us had a rough passage'.[66] As the voyage progressed the tempers of all on board were not improved by 'Gulf Stream weather... very hot, sticky and cloudy like the equator', remembered Colville.[67] For Churchill, Gulf Stream weather combined badly with the antibiotic drugs he was taking and according to Colville, '[t]he PM was... highly irascible'.[68] There followed a series of bitterly acrimonious meetings with the Chiefs of Staff where according to Brooke, Churchill 'repudiated everything he had agreed to up to date... [and] was quite impossible to argue with'.[69] Cunningham recorded that on 8 September Churchill 'was in his worst mood. Accusing the COS of ganging up against him and keeping papers from him & so on'.[70] For Ismay, whose 'days were spent either at the conference table or in the Prime Minister's cabin', there was no escape.[71] The pressures and frustrations not only of the voyage but of the past five years poured out in an emotional and revealing letter he wrote to Darry the following day.

> 'Things' have been just about as difficult, and delicate, as they have ever been. Whatever job the post-war years have in store for me, nothing will induce me to continue to be a go-between, and a mirror of other people's opinions, or to be vested with a certain amount of authority but no <u>executive</u> responsibility. It has been a <u>very</u> hard five years; and the hardest part has been the necessity of keeping my 'place' and my temper, and the prohibition against forming <u>my own</u> view, and fighting <u>my own</u> battles.[72]

Further acrimonious conferences with the Chiefs continued, with Churchill, according to Brooke, 'in a most unpleasant mood'. But on arrival in Quebec Churchill met with them 'all smiles and friendliness for a change', causing Brooke to comment, '[h]ow quickly he changes. An April day's moods would be put to shame by him!'[73] The following day was to illustrate the point. Colville noted, 'After dinner, the PM saw Ismay, who is in trouble about strategic matters in SE Asia Command'.[74] The exact subject is unknown but Churchill must have been at his most vituperative. Ismay's secretary, Betty Green, was awaiting Ismay's return from the meeting. 'He came back more upset than I had ever seen him before, and said, "I can't take any more of this. I've told the Prime Minister I'm going to resign. I can't stand any more. I'm going to write my resignation letter now"'.[75] The next morning Brooke '[f]ound him very upset, having had a ghastly time on previous evening with Winston!…Winston had accused us all to Ismay of purposely concealing changes of plan from him to keep him in the dark. That we were all against him, and heaven knows what not!' Ismay asked Brooke whether he should send the letter. 'I told him this decision must rest with him', wrote Brooke, 'but that I agreed it would probably bring Winston to his senses'.[76]

Ismay described what happened next in a further letter to Darry:

> Master has been extraordinarily difficult—so much so that after consulting the COS privately, I wrote yesterday offering to resign. He dealt with it in typical fashion; handed it back to me saying: 'don't write me this sort of rubbish, dear Pug: we are going to the end—together—you and I. I'm sorry if I get angry, but you must admit I have cause'. I replied that he had abundant cause, but why vent it all on me! And why give me the feeling that I could do nothing right. He denied this: said he had every confidence in me, and was much dependent on my industry, tact and judgment. So that is that! He was really rather sweet.[77]

If Ismay's hope had indeed been to 'bring Winston to his senses' and effect a change in his behaviour, his action seems to have had little effect. The very next day the Chiefs met with Churchill at what Brooke called 'a frightful interview… with Winston in one of his worst tempers'.[78] Nor did Churchill immediately moderate his treatment of Ismay. Three days later (on 18 September) Ismay was confiding to Darry in some emotional turmoil, 'Master has been more difficult than it's possible to say, He is at his most intolerable—and I feel that I can't go on. It just drains me out mentally and spiritually. Like a bloodsucker'.[79]

In later life Ismay gave a rather different account of his resignation. Recounting the circumstances to Eden in 1964, he explained that after the fractious voyage on the *Queen Mary* the Chiefs decided that they were all going to submit their resignation. In order to prevent this, Ismay claimed, 'I therefore stepped into the breach by saying that I would resign and that even if Winston accepted my resignation no-one had heard of Ismay and it wouldn't matter very much'. He added that, 'Winston suspected me for some time of having ganged up with the Chiefs of Staff but he was distinctly less rough with them from that time onwards'.[80] Ismay's letters to Darry, however, indicate that this account does not provide the full story, in particular giving no indication of the personal nature of the dispute, nor of just how fragile Ismay's mental state had become and how close he was to breakdown.

Although the Quebec conference witnessed some aggressive clashes between the two sets of Chiefs—Admiral King again being well to the fore—Brooke summed up the whole event in his diary: '[t]hings have gone well on the whole in spite of Winston's unbearable moods'. He later added,

> The fact that dear old patient Pug had at last reached the end of his tether and could stand Winston's moods no longer is some indication of what we had been through. Of course, poor old Pug always got the worst of it, but he was always so patient, and made so many allowances for Winston's whims, that I felt it would take a climax to make him hand in his papers.[81]

The return voyage lasted five days and seems to have been the very antithesis of the troubled outward voyage, and something of a catharsis for all who had been under such pressure en route and at Quebec. With the successful conference behind him the Prime Minister was relaxed and affable: by lunch on the first day (attended by Ismay) Churchill was, according to Colville, 'in the best of humour and form'[82] Little work was done. The whole voyage was, said Ismay, 'a delightful relaxation', recalling that '[i]t was the first voyage throughout the war on which I had been able to find time for a daily promenade on deck'.[83] He threw a cocktail party in his suite and attended a staff party hosted by Clementine Churchill, 'enjoyed enormously' by Churchill's secretary, Marian Holmes, 'particularly being entertained by... dear General Ismay'.[84] The storm had passed.

Ismay was off again on 7 October, just twelve days after their return, along with Eden and Brooke to accompany Churchill on a visit to Moscow. Roosevelt, unable to attend due to the US presidential elections, was represented by Harriman. This was Ismay's third visit to Moscow and he noted that the welcome was warmer than it had been the previous year and that 'the atmosphere of goodwill continued throughout the visit'.[85] Practically the first event was a sumptuous luncheon hosted by Stalin. Judging by his past comments on formal Russian banquets, Ismay is likely to have regretted that it lasted from 2.30 to 6.15 p.m. and even more that since his health was specifically proposed by Stalin, he had to make a reply.

Although Ismay attended two of Churchill's and Harriman's evening meetings with Stalin and Molotov, he was not present during the discussions on the division of post-war Europe or those on the political future of Poland over which the Russians were immutable. On one of these evenings he took fourteen members of the delegation to the opera at the invitation of their hosts. Sitting in a box which seated twelve, he was put out to hear that his two sergeants who were allocated front-row seats in the stalls had been told that 'other ranks' [non-officers] were not allowed in the stalls. Ismay's solution was simple: two brigadiers in the box immediately exchanged seats with the sergeants.[86] This was the highlight of the evening for Ismay. Being tone-deaf, he was soon asleep.[87]

Since the official programme included two further musical evenings—another opera and a ballet—plus a further banquet, and since many of the main meetings were late-night affairs, Ismay may have been looking forward to the day of departure and disappointed when it was postponed by twenty-four hours. The departure itself was a major ceremonial affair. At the aerodrome they were honoured by the presence of Stalin himself, with guard of honour, bands and national anthems. Furthermore, on boarding their aircraft they discovered that their Russian hosts had loaded it with two large crates of vodka and caviar. On return to London these welcome delicacies were duly divided up amongst the party. Ismay distributed his share of caviar in small jars to a number of his staff and friends, but recalled,

> A few days later we had an unpleasant surprise. An agitated Foreign Office official telephoned to say that the Soviet Ambassador in London was anxious about the non-arrival of a consignment of caviar and vodka which had been loaded in our plane at Moscow and was intended for the forthcoming celebration of Russia's National Day at the Soviet Embassy.

An abject apology was accompanied by the offer to make up for this embarrassing faux pas by 'a handsome present of Scotch whisky'.[88]

On a more serious note, Stalin's warm welcome, the atmosphere of goodwill, the banquets, concerts, glad-handing and bonhomie were of course not without their purpose. Despite having suffered major setbacks such as the failure to secure the future of the Polish people, the British delegation—Ismay included—returned having been dangerously charmed by Stalin. Ismay wrote to Casey the following month, 'I confess that after three visits to Moscow, I am no nearer understanding the Russians than I was at the beginning of the war; but I believe that they want to be friends with us, and I think that unless we and the Americans acquire and retain their friendship, there is little hope for the peace of the world'.[89] It could have been Chamberlain talking about Germany in 1938.

A fortnight after their return came news of Dill's death in Washington. Ismay's admiration for Dill as Churchill's representative with the American Chiefs of Staff had continued to grow ever since he was appointed in December 1941. He had seen at first hand Dill's skill and impact at numerous conferences and knew of the high regard in which he was held in Washington. He would also have appreciated how hard he would be to replace. What he probably did not know was that his own name was being mentioned as a possible successor. For, as Halifax informed Churchill, Marshall had approached him with the suggestion. Ismay had made a most favourable impression at the Anglo-American conferences and was widely respected both in Washington and with senior American officers in Europe. He was also in Churchill's inner circle. As Halifax told Churchill, '[His] close contact with you and knowledge of your thought would, in Marshall's view, be of great value to the partnership between us'.[90] If Churchill was tiring of Ismay as his chief staff officer, here was the perfect opportunity to move him. But, as Halifax had predicted to Marshall, Churchill was not prepared to lose Ismay. Instead, he appointed General Sir Henry Maitland Wilson, Supreme Allied Commander Mediterranean, to succeed Dill. Wilson, however, never came close to matching Dill's skill or influence.[91] In Roberts' view, 'the rows that later developed would not have been avoided had Dill survived or Ismay succeeded, but their intensity might have been lessened in either case'.[92]

At the beginning of November, Ismay accompanied Churchill on a four-day visit to France, including the Armistice Day parade in Paris. For both men the visit will have brought to mind their journeys together to France in May and June 1940, and their bond of friendship with each other. The parade was to be an emotional moment. Ismay told a friend, '[t]he march of the troops from the Arc de Triomphe down the Champs Elysees was one of the most moving scenes I have ever witnessed. The PM was in floods of tears from start to finish, and I confess that I cried unashamedly when the Guards contingent came past to the tune of the British Grenadiers'.[93] Ismay had mixed memories of the visit. 'Paris was bitterly cold and the hotel in which we stayed was like a mausoleum— no heating, no fires, no baths'. His further observations were even less charitable. 'The French seemed dazed. It will take some time for them to get rid of their inferiority complex which was born of their surrender in 1940 and nourished by their subsequent suppression.'[94]

By early December Ismay had lost the sense of optimism that he had expressed in late summer about the progress of the war. 'I confess that

I cannot escape a sense of disappointment', he told Casey. 'Things were going so fast in August and September that I had good hopes that coherent opposition in Europe would cease by the end of the year. Nor was I the only one, by a long chalk, who indulged in these daydreams. Alas they have not come true…' He went on to cite the lack of progress on the Western Front, Italy and Burma, the 'unpleasant commitment in Greece' (where British troops were aiding a counterinsurgency), 'the possibility of trouble in Palestine', and the prospects in China. Against this, though, he admitted that 'there is a great deal to be thankful for on the credit side'—noting the German losses on the Western Front, the prospects of a Russian winter offensive and the potential effects of the winter bombing campaign on German production, particularly that of oil.[95]

Ismay also commented to Casey on the challenges on the home front, in particular the effect of the 'doodle-bug and the rocket' (the V1 and V2 weapons). In the weeks following the first V1 weapons hitting London in June Ismay considered that it 'seemed to have a greater effect on public morale than the authentic blitz had done'.[96] The threat was also serious enough to cause Cabinet meetings to again be held in the underground Cabinet War Rooms. By December, although far fewer V1s were penetrating the air defences, V2s were now in use and those that fell in London were causing considerable destruction. Ismay's view of the V1 and V2, however, was that,

> [a]s weapons of war against a brave people they are futile, but they are damned unpleasant nevertheless. The British people have stood up to them as one knew they would, but there is going to be an awful lot of suffering this winter unless superhuman efforts are made to get roofs over their heads. They have, so far as one can judge, taken the disappointment of having to fight through a sixth winter magnificently.[97]

On 12 December, along with the Chiefs of Staff, Ismay was a guest at a dinner at Downing Street, given by the Prime Minister for Eisenhower who was making a brief visit from his headquarters in France. At some stage in the evening Eisenhower spoke about his own personal post-war plans which, according to the editor of the Eisenhower papers, were 'to devote [himself] to the cause of post-war Anglo-American unity'.[98] It provoked an interesting and revealing exchange of correspondence between him and Ismay who wrote to him the following day,

I was intensely interested in, and impressed by all you said about the Cause to which you propose to devote the afternoon and evening of your days, because, in a very much smaller way, I have been thinking on precisely the same lines myself. I am ready to leave the public service the moment they are ready to let me go, but I am doubtful whether, in this particular cause, and in this country, I might not be able to serve the Cause better by staying in harness than by doffing it. Anyhow, at this stage, all I want you to know is that I have a very keen desire to put my hand to your plough and that I will pull it with all my strength when the time comes.[99]

Eisenhower replied,

I fear that the other evening I got a bit loquacious in talking about my post-war personal plans... The fact is that it is something that lies so closely to my heart that when I begin talking about it I cannot help letting my blood pressure rise a bit. In any event, I would be completely helpless without the aid of you and others like you, who believe the same way.[100]

The relationship, already close, between the two was set to become even closer.

Eisenhower would have had little time to consider the matter further. The same day that he wrote the letter—16 December—the Germans started their Ardennes offensive, catching the Allies totally by surprise. Even as the scale of the attack and the danger it posed became evident, Churchill remained surprisingly detached from the unfolding events, preoccupied by the political and security crisis in Greece. Indeed, he flew to Athens on Christmas Eve to attempt to influence the situation there. Ismay, though, remained focused on events on the Western Front, aware of the ongoing dispute between Eisenhower and Montgomery and sensitive to the pressure under which Eisenhower was operating. On 30 December he wrote an 'entirely private' letter to Bedell Smith, 'wondering whether and in what way we here can help you'. In particular Ismay looked ahead to the major operation that would be required to cross the Rhine in the face of German opposition, offering 'anything and everything from the resources of this country that human ingenuity and effort can provide'. A handwritten postscript added, 'May 1945 be a great and victorious year for you, old friend; and may it bring you all the good things that you desire and deserve'.[101] The letter was a small gesture of friendship and support, but it would have been hugely appreciated by both Smith and Eisenhower.

For Ismay 1944 had been the most demanding and exhausting year of the war. As an indication of the workload, the number of meetings of the Chiefs of Staff Committee alone numbered 414; and the number of meeting papers ('memoranda') totalled 1,063.[102] At the start of the year Ismay had been recovering from breakdown and had come close to another one during it. But at the year's end, although he was less optimistic than he had been about a swift outcome in Europe, his sense of duty and his determination to give his best and meet whatever challenges 1945 might bring were undiminished.

10

FROM WAR TO PEACE

1945–46

In December 1944 Churchill, Roosevelt and Stalin had agreed that a further Allied conference was now required and that it should take place in the first week of February at Yalta in the Crimea. As for the previous conference at Teheran, there would be a prior Anglo-American conference, this time held in Malta. Eisenhower was due to attend the latter but decided that he could not leave his command and sent Smith to represent him. According to Wingate, on arrival in Malta on 29 January, Ismay was informed that Smith, who had repaired to bed with ulcers, 'had announced that, if the British intended to insert a Ground Force Commander under Eisenhower, then both Eisenhower and Smith would resign'.[1] Stopping only to collect a bottle of champagne, Ismay hurried round to Smith's bedroom to reassure him that the British had full confidence in Eisenhower.[2] If Smith was reassured, it was only temporarily; two nights later he suddenly confronted Brooke on the subject, losing his temper.[3] Brooke, according to Ian Jacob, 'was stunned'.[4]

The subject of Eisenhower's competence and Montgomery's proposal for a narrow-front thrust on Berlin arose at the Combined Chiefs of Staff's meeting the following day. Ismay recalled that 'the altercation which ensued was vehement and at times acrimonious'.[5] Admiral King 'launched a bitter invective against Brooke'.[6] Then, Marshall cleared the room of staff and according to Cunningham, 'let off a tirade… [and] said some pretty straight things about Montgomery, allowing personal feelings to enter into things'.[7] Brooke leapt to his defence, refusing to do anything more than 'note' Eisenhower's plan. Although the British Chiefs of Staff appeared united on this point, they were not; Cunningham later commented that both he and Portal would have preferred to 'note with agreement', a seemingly pedantic but actually significant difference.[8] The atmosphere at the meeting would have troubled Ismay and it is likely that he shared his disquiet with Churchill. When Eisenhower's plan came up for political endorsement at the next day's meeting, chaired by the President and the Prime Minister, Churchill raised no objection to it and the plan was approved. Afterwards Ismay reassured him, 'General Eisenhower's intentions are more or less exactly what you and the Chiefs of Staff would have them to be'.[9] For Ismay 'more or less' was good enough if it meant keeping the show on the road.

On 3 February the two delegations flew to Sevastapol, and thence by car over the mountains to Yalta. As usual at these conferences Ismay's responsibilities included the transport and administrative arrangements for the British delegation. On this occasion he arranged with the Admiralty and Ministry of War Transport to commission the Cunard liner, *Franconia*, as the British communications centre. And, as in the past, he delegated the administration of the British contingent to the highly capable and versatile Joan Bright. Ismay, along with the Prime Minister and all the senior British delegates, were housed in the Vorontzov Palace. The palace was not, however, to everyone's taste. Cadogan described it as 'a big house of indescribable ugliness—a sort of Gothic Balmoral—with all the furnishings of an almost terrifying hideosity'.[10] It had been Field Marshal von Manstein's headquarters during the German occupation but ransacked when the Germans left. All the furniture, as well as the cutlery, crockery, food and wine, had recently been imported from Moscow. So, too, had the domestic staff. Ismay recalled,

> Two of the waiters who had looked after me at the Hotel Nationale [in Moscow, the previous year] were standing in the entrance hall when I arrived, and I felt hurt that they gave me no sign of recognition. But they made amends as soon as they were out of sight of their masters. They conducted me to my bedroom, dropped on their knees, kissed my hand and went out without a word.[11]

The week-long conference itself focused on political issues, notably the future of eastern Europe (especially Poland) and the establishment of the United Nations Organization. Military strategy was largely absent from the agenda. As Ismay described it in his memoirs,

> At all previous conferences, the military element had been the prima donna, occupying the centre of the stage. At Yalta we hung about in

the wings waiting for calls that never came. Hitherto my difficulty at conferences had been to find the time to do all the work which fell to my lot. At Yalta, my difficulty was to find sufficient work to occupy my time.[12]

This was not quite what he felt at the time. His enthusiasm for overseas conferences was clearly on the wane because towards the end of the week at Yalta he complained to Darry, 'it's terribly difficult here. No office, no pens, no ink—and no privacy. I am tired of people! Also there has been a fairly consistent pressure of work together with the hanging about that always goes with bad organisation—or rather lack of organisation'.[13]

Nevertheless, meetings with the Soviet military took place and Ismay noted, '[i]t was the first time that we were allowed to have discussions alone with representatives of the Russian High Command who have had practical war experience. Hitherto, either Stalin or Molotov have always been present'.[14] He also noted that, 'the difference between the way they treat us now and the way they treated us in 1941 is remarkable. One is now free to walk wherever one likes without being shadowed, and the ordinary Russian in the street is only too ready to come up and have a friendly talk, instead of passing by in stony silence'.[15] Ismay, though, may have been naive in assuming that those only too ready to come up and have a friendly talk were ordinary Russians.

There was a ceaseless round of lavish Soviet hospitality, with no expense spared on either quality or quantity. The social programme included what for Ismay was the highlight of the week: a post-conference visit to the Balaclava 1854 battlefield. And Churchill, he reported to Darry, was in good temper. However, like others, Ismay was shocked and saddened by Roosevelt's state of health: later describing him, somewhat brutally, to Lascelles as 'more than half gaga'.[16] At the end of the conference Churchill made a last-minute decision to fly to Athens before returning to London via Alexandria. Ismay made the most of the circumstances: 'All this time I was living in clover on the *Franconia*. I had been moved into the suite which had been specially prepared for Mr Churchill. The sea was calm; the weather was lovely; and I had no work to do. I was sorry to leave the ship in Malta and fly to London'.[17]

In his memoirs, Ismay summed up the Yalta conference as: 'From the gastronomical point of view, it was enjoyable: from the social point of view, successful: from the military point of view, unnecessary: and from the political point of view depressing'.[18] The political aspect to which he was referring was of course the complete failure to safeguard the democratic future of the countries of Eastern Europe, particularly Poland. But at the time he was, like many others, pleased with the overall outcome at Yalta. Writing to Mountbatten a week after returning he commented that the conference had been 'a great success not so much because of the formal conclusions that had been reached, but because of the spirit of frank co-operation which characterised all the discussions'.[19] However, many years later he reflected, with typical humility,

> Looking back on those days, I suppose that we ought to have seen the red light when Stalin insisted that for Russia, Poland was a question not only of honour but of security, or, in other words, that it was thought to be a matter of life and death for the Soviet [Union] that Poland should be under the Communist yoke. But perhaps we were all deceived by the spirit of exuberant bonhomie which had prevailed throughout the Conference; or perhaps we preferred not to look unpleasant facts in the face.[20]

For Ismay the spring of 1945 was probably the least stressful period of the war. News from the Western Front continued to be good, and the end was in sight. 'The Prime Minister is in splendid shape', he told Casey, 'far better, in fact, than he was this time last year'.[21] This view, as so often in Ismay's reports, was considerably overstated. Churchill was certainly in better humour than twelve months previously—at the time of the long, acrimonious dispute about strategy in the Far East—but he was in less splendid shape in other ways. For example, as Andrew Roberts noted, 'he was certainly starting to ramble on in Cabinet meetings, some of which were now taking up to four and a half hours', which must have tested even the ultra-patient Ismay.[22]

By the beginning of March Allied troops had broken through the Siegfried line and Ismay, together with Brooke, accompanied Churchill on a three-day visit to the Western Front. They based themselves on Eisenhower's train and spent much of the time visiting British formations and units as guests of Montgomery. On the final day they visited Eisenhower's headquarters and on return Churchill sent him 'warmest congratulations on the great victory won by the Allied armies under your command'.[23] Ismay remained in London when, a fortnight later, the Prime Minister visited Montgomery at Venlo, on the Rhine. Churchill crossed to the far side of the river, 'got as near as he could to being under the fire of the enemy', and, according to Ismay, 'enjoyed every minute of it'.[24]

Over this period Ismay was to be involved in what was to be one of Churchill's final wartime eruptions, on this occasion directed at both the Americans and the Chiefs of Staff. It resulted from a signal that Eisenhower sent direct to Stalin on 28 March informing him of his decision to concentrate his efforts in central and southern Germany and not to mount a thrust towards Berlin. Eisenhower was supposed to conduct such dealings through the Combined Chiefs of Staff. To do so direct to Stalin was unprecedented and unwise, particularly as his message had a highly political implication: that the Soviet Union could be assured that the Western Allies would not be competing with them for the German capital. Churchill, who had not given up hope of beating the Russians to Berlin, was understandably furious. If past experience is anything to go by, Ismay will have been busy attempting to tone down the flurry of messages that came from Churchill's hand, to both Roosevelt and Eisenhower.

However, when Churchill's messages elicited less response than he had hoped for (at this stage Roosevelt had only a few days to live), his frustration and ire became directed at Eisenhower's deputy Tedder (never a Churchill favourite) who, Eisenhower assured him, had been 'freely consulted [and] was in agreement' with the message to Stalin.[25] Churchill wrote to the Chiefs of Staff, through Ismay, decrying Tedder as 'an utter cypher... [of] no professional standing in a military sense'.[26] Brooke considered it 'one of the worst minutes I have ever seen. I can only believe that he must have been quite tight when he dictated it'.[27] The Chiefs leapt to Tedder's defence, but Churchill steadfastly refused to withdraw his accusations. It was left to Ismay, an admirer of Tedder, to minute Churchill with typical tact and advise him that the Chiefs 'regret that you have decided that this exchange of minutes must be left on record'.[28] It was not until December 1945 that Churchill, no longer Prime Minister, relented and asked Ismay to destroy the minutes in question.[29]

Ismay was in bed asleep when, in the early hours of 7 May, Eisenhower telephoned him with the news that the Germans had signed the surrender document. Darry, beside him, heard what was said and, as Ismay recalled, 'her eyes filled with tears. I too felt a lump in my throat, and could scarcely voice my congratulations'. This momentous scene of high emotion rapidly descended into farce. Having put the telephone down and got back into bed it occurred to Ismay that Eisenhower expected him to inform the Prime Minister of the German surrender. He tried to telephone Downing Street, but the operator had not properly disconnected the previous call and the line was dead. 'There was nothing for it but collect some coppers, put on a dressing gown, and go to the public call-box a hundred yards down the road.'[30] The excursion was wasted: when he got through to

165

the Number 10 switchboard he was told that Churchill had already been informed and had gone back to bed.

Later that day Ismay was present at a hastily arranged lunch given by the Prime Minister for the Chiefs of Staff at which Churchill toasted the three as 'the architects of victory'. Tellingly, none of them chose to return the compliment. In his memoirs, Ismay passed this off with apparent lightness: 'I hoped that they would raise their glasses to the chief who had been the master planner; but perhaps they were too moved to trust their voices.'[31] The heavy irony, and the shock and sadness that lay beneath it, would not have been lost on those who knew of the relationship and the depth of feeling that it had generated.

The following day—designated Victory in Europe Day—Ismay was at Buckingham Palace with the Chiefs of Staff. After the formal photographs the King joked that there should be a photograph of himself, Ismay and Bridges as the only people present who had kept their jobs throughout the war. Sadly, if it was ever taken, the photograph does not survive. That evening the Ismays threw a party at their flat. The eclectic guest list included Lewis Douglas (one of Ismay's closest American friends), the Dowager Lady Reading (founder of the Women's Voluntary Services), the whole of Ismay's personal staff from the office, the head porter from the block of flats and Ismay's long-serving Belgian butler, Felicien. 'After supper the whole party walked arm-in-arm to Buckingham Palace and mingled with the crowds'.[32]

One of Ismay's first acts as the German surrender became imminent had been to write a warm message of support and congratulations to Eisenhower, telling him 'how eternally grateful I am to you for having saved my hearth and home, and my country'.[33] Having recently had a somewhat rocky relationship with the British Prime Minister and Chiefs of Staff, Eisenhower clearly appreciated this gesture. His letter of thanks included, 'I want you to know that there is no one whose high opinion I value more; you have been a staunch friend and a great help ever since I met you, more than three years ago. I will always be indebted to you and so will both our countries'.[34] Bedell Smith wrote in the same vein, apologising for the many times he had called on Ismay for support, adding, 'but usually you were the only one to whom we could turn, and you never failed us'.[35]

While Britain continued to celebrate victory in Europe, Churchill was deeply concerned about the Soviet domination of eastern Europe, in particular Poland. Within a week of VE day, he astounded the Chiefs of Staff by commissioning a feasibility study into what amounted to war with Russia: an Anglo-American offensive to drive Russian troops back to the Soviet Union and gain 'a square deal for Poland'.[36] The date for opening of hostilities was to be 1 July. The offensive was appropriately codenamed—it is not clear by whom—Operation Unthinkable. Brooke probably summed up the Chiefs' reaction to the proposal in his diary, declaring that 'the idea is of course fantastic and the chances of success quite impossible'.[37] Ismay's reaction is unrecorded but it is highly probable that he shared Brooke's view and may have been alarmed about Churchill's mental state. As Reynolds points out, 'That Churchill could entertain such an amazing idea… surely reveals his total exhaustion after five years of war leadership'.[38] The Chiefs' succinct, top-secret report unsurprisingly concluded that 'it would be beyond our power to win a quick but limited success and we should be committed to a protracted war against heavy odds'.[39] In forwarding the report to Churchill and bypassing the usual channels, Ismay added pointedly 'They felt that the less was put on paper on this subject the better'.[40] Churchill accepted the report and focused the attention of the planners on defensive measures to counter the Soviet threat to the British Isles and Western Europe.[41]

With a General Election now called for 5 July, Churchill was busy electioneering and Ismay had more time to himself. He was able to spend a long weekend—his first for several years—at Wormington with his family and to go and stay with Smith at the Allied headquarters near Frankfurt. The latter visit was nearly aborted. Due to a misunderstanding, Smith believed that Ismay had dealt behind his back over an emotive issue. Smith, again in hospital with ulcers, immediately telephoned Ismay, lost his temper, roundly abused him and declared their friendship at an end.[42] The next day, having ascertained the facts, Ismay wrote to him. 'I was so flabbergasted by your blitz yesterday afternoon', the letter began, before setting out the facts in detail. It concluded, '[t]he very last thing that entered my mind was to do anything behind your back, or unworthy of the trust that you have always given me. Anyway, my own conscience is crystal clear, and I refuse to believe that you meant a single word of what you said yesterday afternoon'. Then, in a handwritten postscript, so typical of him, he added,

> I must add, Bedell, that I required 4 aspirins, 3 gins and a bottle of port to recover from your onslaught! Seriously, though, I do hope that your stay in hospital will be short, and that I shall find you in good shape & good heart when I come over to pay you a visit. As ever, Pug.[43]

Smith made a fulsome apology; the visit took place a few weeks later. The friendship was healed.

A further Anglo/American/Russian conference, with the British participation again to be organised by Ismay's staff, was scheduled to take place in mid-July at Potsdam and there was much work for him back in the office. Lockhart called on him there on 20 June and considered him 'in terrific form', but saying that Churchill was 'very depressed and disliked the whole election business. He was therefore being very difficult, and in consequence Pug's life was intolerable… He, Pug, thought it a damned shame that all this trouble should be foisted on the old gentleman who had really won this war, when there was another still to finish'.[44]

Ismay's 'terrific form' may have been only temporary, because at the beginning of July he wrote to an old school-friend, Burgon Bickersteth,

> I always anticipated disappointment and disillusionment when Germany collapsed, and I therefore feel that it is somewhat unreasonable of me to have been so depressed for the last two months. The PM said to me on VE Day or just after, 'When the eagles are silent the parrots begin to chatter. When the war of the giants is over, the squabbles of the pygmies begin'. It has proved devastatingly true.[45]

The election took place on 5 July but declaration of the result was not due until three weeks later in order to allow for Service votes to be counted. After the vote Ismay was in low spirits, concerned about the effect of all the electioneering on Churchill's health and pessimistic about the election result. On the eve of the Potsdam conference, he told Lockhart, 'I'd give a fortune not to be going'. Lockhart commented, 'Pug, I think, feels the decline of the PM almost personally, I thought him in a more depressed mood than I had ever seen him before'.[46]

Ismay flew to Berlin on 14 July. The conference was scheduled to last fourteen days—the longest by far of the series—with a break of three days in the middle to allow for the British politicians (Churchill, Deputy Prime Minster Attlee, and Foreign Secretary Eden) to return to London for the election result. Ismay's initial lack of enthusiasm seems to have remained with him throughout, perhaps due to the overfamiliar conference routine mixed with further foreboding at the election result, but undoubtedly exacerbated by fatigue. It was the peripheral aspects of the conference, rather than the agenda, that provided interest for him. Meeting President Truman was clearly one highlight: 'he gave the impression of being decisive, intensely human, and full of common sense, but he had as yet little time to get into the whole picture'.[47]

A conversation during a Joint Chiefs' meeting with the American Air Force chief, General 'Hap' Arnold, was another memorable moment. Ismay whispered to Arnold that the Japanese would collapse long before the invasion of their homeland. Arnold bet him two dollars they would last out the year. In the event, the Japanese surrendered in mid-August. 'Shortly afterwards', recalled Ismay, 'I received a novel form of paper-weight—two silver coins mounted on a block of polished walnut wood. It was inscribed: "To Pug Ismay from Hap Arnold. Thank God I can pay this now"'. For Ismay it was 'one of my most cherished mementoes of the war'.[48] A further memorable moment was at the formal banquet when, to Ismay's amazement and delight, Admiral King, with whom Ismay had not always seen eye to eye, proposed his health 'in very flattering terms'. As Ismay was to recall, 'I was as proud as a subaltern getting his first mention in despatches'.[49]

But perhaps Ismay's most dramatic recollection of the conference was an afternoon visit to Berlin. Immediately following it he wrote to Richard Casey that he had never dreamt:

> that an immense city like this could be so completely devastated. It is the abomination of dissolution if ever there was one. And though they brought it on themselves, I confess to feeling immensely sorry for the droves of Germans, particularly the very old and very young, wandering aimlessly about the roads, dragging the remnants of their possessions in hand-carts, wheelbarrows, perambulators or a couple of boards on wheels. They seem to be quite dazed and not to know whether they are coming or going.[50]

On 25 July Ismay accompanied Churchill and his ministers on their return flight to London. The next day came the election result. Two days later Ismay was accompanying Prime Minister Attlee to Potsdam. Ismay remained at the airport to greet the new Foreign Secretary, Ernest Bevin. Ismay was an admirer of Bevin and recalled that, on arrival, practically his first words to him were 'I'm not going to have Britain barged about'.[51] For Ismay, though, the remaining five days of the conference were not happy ones. He wrote to Darry, 'I'm feeling thoroughly rotten—headache in addition to cold—and in a foul temper'.[52] The same day he wrote to Eden, 'This place is full of ghosts. It's hard not to cry sometimes'.[53]

Despite the revised perceptions of the Russians epitomised by Operation Unthinkable, Ismay appears to have (as at Yalta) been bamboozled by the Russians at Potsdam. On return, according to Lascelles, he was 'convinced that they are feverishly anxious to keep in well with us'.[54] The Russians were undoubtedly feverishly anxious to convince the Western Allies that they wished to keep in well with them—and in Ismay's case appear to have succeeded. Unless Lascelles had misreported the conversation it is difficult to see Ismay's judgement in the matter as being anything other than naive.

The same day Ismay confided to Lockhart that 'he was really a tired and sick man, and the doctors had told him he must have a long rest before doing more work. Now he felt it a matter of honour to stay on with the new people for a few months at any rate. He would take a month's leave and then carry on until the end of the year'.[55] The war had indeed taken its toll on Ismay's health. His youngest daughter Mary, aged sixteen in 1945, later remarked, 'Quite interesting looking at pictures of my father before the war—a young slim man. By the end of the war he was a tired, old man. It was very noticeable'.[56]

Ismay now went to say goodbye to Churchill. It must have been a sad occasion. 'His farewell remark to me was typical', recounted Ismay: '"Anyway, we've had a damned good gallop for five and a half years"'.[57] In Churchill's resignation honours list, two months later, Ismay was created a Companion of Honour. This was a most unusual award for a serving soldier, and many people must have considered it rather less than Ismay deserved—the three Chiefs of Staff had been granted peerages. But Ismay declared himself deeply honoured and hugely grateful. 'I was delighted to have the CH', he told Wavell, 'because it is obviously Winston's personal idea. It is a rather overwhelming award'.[58] It may also have reflected Churchill's wit in paying tribute to the person who throughout the war had, indeed, been his companion of honour.

Ismay also knew that a further honour awaited him. A fortnight previously Lascelles had written to tell him,

> I should like you to know that when you finally leave your well-worn chair, it is the intention of your Sovereign to supplement this mark of recognition of yr [sic] great service to the State by giving you the GCVO [Knight Grand Cross of the Royal Victorian Order] in gratitude for yr no less signal service to him personally.[59]

Leaving aside the remarkable irregularity of this breach of confidentiality, the letter poses the question of what exactly had been Ismay's signal service to the monarch personally. The evidence available is limited, but it is clear from correspondence between Ismay and Lascelles and from Lascelles's diary that Ismay was his point of contact in Whitehall, kept him briefed on events and developments, and from time to time visited Buckingham Palace to brief the King in person. These briefings may have included confidential matters such as Churchill's relations with Roosevelt and with the Chiefs of Staff. An example is the June 1944 issue about Churchill's intention to accompany the D-Day fleet. Clearly the King considered that Ismay had played an important role as a mediator and gone out of his way to serve the interests of the crown. Further details may emerge if and when the Lascelles diaries become available to the public. To what extent Churchill knew about the briefings is not known.

At Attlee's suggestion Ismay now took a holiday—his first for six years. At the beginning of September, he and Darry departed on vacation to the United States. It was to last seven weeks. They travelled on the *Queen Mary* along with 15,000 American servicemen returning home. Ismay recalled that the Americans were 'packed like sardines', some of them sleeping on deck, but all of them in good heart and seemingly not caring about the discomfort. He remembered, 'the welcome that they received from the moment the *Queen Mary* passed the Statue of Liberty had to be seen, and heard, to be believed'.[60] In America Ismay and Darry spent their time in Chicago, Washington, South Carolina and New York. According to Ismay they were 'almost killed by kindness. It was fun to meet many of my war comrades and to have carefree talks about past quarrels with each other as well as with the enemy'.[61] Having so many of her own American friends and relations to visit, Darry may have been spared the fun of these carefree talks.

On return from America, joking that he was 'feeling ten years younger and more disinclined for work than I ever have been', Ismay was back in the office serving his new master.[62] Some people may have thought that for Ismay, Churchill was irreplaceable and that he would find it impossible to give to Attlee the loyalty and commitment that he had given to his predecessor. This would, however, have been to underestimate Ismay's huge sense of duty. The closeness of his personal relationship with Churchill and the admiration in which he held him despite all the vicissitudes of the wartime years did not for a moment prevent him from giving his wholehearted service and support to his successor. Ismay's loyalty was to the office of Prime Minister, whoever the incumbent. This was made easier for him by the fact that he and Attlee had had the chance to get to know—and respect—each other well over the five years that Attlee had been Deputy Prime Minister and a member of the War Cabinet. Indeed, Ismay seems to have shared the view of Attlee as 'a decent Englishman who had somehow strayed into the wrong party'.[63] Ismay had also got to know and respect Ernest Bevin. After Potsdam he had told Wavell, 'I have a considerable regard for both of them [Attlee and Bevin]. They both love their country just as much as you and I do, though they may express it rather differently. As it turned out, they were both excellent at the council table'.[64]

The subject that came to occupy much of Ismay's time in the latter part of 1945 and into 1946, and in which he was to play a highly influential role, was the future organisation of national defence at the highest levels. Should there be a return to the pre-war structure and the CID? Should the Chiefs of Staff Committee be reorganised? Should there again be a Minister for the Coordination of Defence? What other options should be examined? Ismay had been considering such questions throughout the war. Back in 1942 he had discussed the structure of the Chiefs of Staff Committee with Leo Amery, who had strong views on 'the futility of three chiefs of staff with no one in charge of them'. Amery recalled that Ismay 'strongly took the view that a superior chief of staff would be a fifth wheel on the coach and that the present arrangements were perfect'.[65] In early May 1944 Ismay delivered to Churchill a paper, probably drafted initially by Jacob, entitled 'Our Defence Organisation After the War'.[66] The paper clearly reflects the frustrations which both men were experiencing with the existing system, in particular with Service ministries 'dedicated to the interests of the Services they administered', and thus the need for centralisation in the higher direction of defence planning and management.[67]

> The whole purport of this memo is that the increasing independence of the three Services, and the need for reviewing defence policy as a whole make it necessary that a Minister of Defence should be charged with responsibility for
>
> a. The Preparation of strategic plans,
> b. The apportionment of effort between the three Services and also for
> c. Directing the planning of our industrial war potential.

They recommended that either the Prime Minister or an appointed deputy should hold the appointment of Minister of Defence, and that the Service ministers should be restricted to the provision and administration of forces. They looked ahead to a full-blown Ministry of Defence but advised that this should follow 'natural evolution'. More controversially they suggested that some other organisations such as the Special Operations Executive and SIS 'might profitably be brought into the orbit of a Minister of Defence'.[68]

These were far-reaching proposals and although not all were to survive the test of time, many were to do so and form the basis of later major changes in the higher organisation of defence. That Ismay and Jacob produced them at a time of such challenge in war planning is remarkable. But the fact that they delivered their memorandum to the Prime Minister just one month before D-Day was unfortunate. Perhaps unsurprisingly, Churchill directed that the paper should be printed but shelved. He 'did not... find it possible to carry the matter further during the stress of war'.[69]

It was not until the conclusion of the war in Europe and the replacement of Churchill by Attlee that the subject of defence reform was resurrected. By that time Ismay's ideas had developed further. In August 1945, after a meeting with him, Lockhart reported that 'Pug... developed at length his favourite theme of a co-ordinated defence system for the future. He wanted not only co-ordination but amalgamation. For instance, one intelligence corps for the three Services, one medical corps. It was so easy on paper, so difficult in practice owing to vested interests'.[70]

Shortly after, on Ismay's advice and endorsed by Bridges, Attlee tasked a small group to examine the future organisation of defence and make recommendations.[71] The group—Ismay, Bridges and Jacob—made their first recommendations in November and completed their report in February 1946.[72] Further work continued for the next six months and resulted in a White Paper, 'Central Organisation of Defence'.[73] The paper considered but rejected a number of radical changes, such as: an all-powerful Minister of Defence heading a ministry which absorbed the three Service departments; a combined tri-Service General Staff; and an independent chairman of the Chiefs of Staff. Instead its proposals included: replacing the old CID with a single Defence Committee of the Cabinet, chaired by the Prime Minister; the appointment of a separate Minister of Defence with executive authority, albeit with very limited powers over the three Services; and the establishment of a Ministry of Defence, but one which comprised only a small central staff and allowed the continuation of the single-Service departments, each with its own Secretary of State. The report was thus relatively conservative in its recommendations and has been criticised as such.[74] It reflected, perhaps overly much, the fact that its authors—none more so than Ismay—had been intimately involved in making the existing defence organisation work well. But as the White Paper stressed, 'the new plans were but a stage in the process of steady evolution of the central organisation for defence', or as Attlee called it, 'a jumping-off place for the future'.[75] In October the 'Ministry of Defence Act', based on the White Paper, was approved in Parliament by a substantial majority.[76]

Ismay's expertise and his leading role in the production of the report were recognised by a request in May 1946 from the United States government for advice on the future American defence organisation. In shaping their own central organisation of defence during the war, senior American ministers and military officers had looked closely at the British system. Roosevelt had told Churchill that what he needed was 'an Ismay machine'.[77] And George Marshall had taken the opportunity of a flight from Northern Ireland to Gibraltar in July 1943 with Ismay to get him to explain the organisation and processes of the pre-war CID as well as those of the War Cabinet, and its committees and secretariat. Subsequently Ismay had sent him a paper on the subject.[78] This in turn informed the US government's 1945 Eberstadt Report, *Unification of the War and Navy Departments*. In July 1946 Ismay visited Washington at the invitation of Secretary of the Navy (subsequently Secretary of Defense) James Forrestal, to discuss the matter. Forrestal had a second meeting with Ismay when he visited London later that month.[79]

One theme that Ismay pursued in his discussions with American interlocutors was that of post-war Anglo-American defence cooperation in the face of a potential Soviet threat. In the course of 1945 he had developed his thinking on this subject and he took the opportunity of a congratulatory letter in December to Eisenhower on his appointment as Chief of Staff of the Army to pitch his view about the continuation of the Combined Chiefs of Staff.

> Personally, I feel sure that something of the kind (though in what precise form, and with what precise duties, would require careful consideration) is almost essential, not only for our two countries, but also for the peace of the world at large. If your armed forces and ours had more or less the

same equipment, more or less the same doctrine, more or less the same organisation—AND NO SECRETS of any kind between them—they would at once contribute a hard core of resistance to any breach of the peace. Thereafter, any other nation that was worthy and willing could join 'the Club'.[80]

It was the germ of an idea that foreshadowed the establishment of the NATO alliance.

For some time, though, Ismay had been tiring of his job and considering his options. But he was being selective. In early December 1945 Attlee had offered him a prestigious appointment in the Far East. Ismay described this to Lockhart as 'a super-governor or Minister of State whose writ would run from India to Hong Kong and who would report direct to the Cabinet'. The job, he said, had been offered to Portal and to him, but they had both refused. 'Portal was tired, and he, Pug, felt that after six years of slavery in the War Cabinet offices it was not fair to his family to go to the tropics'.[81]

Ismay amplified this in his reply to Atlee:

In the first place, my daughters are just the wrong age to accompany me to that distant and unsuitable part of the world. We have no relations in whose charge we would care to leave them, my wife would therefore have to spend most of the time in England. Having grievously neglected my family for the last 9 years, I shrink from the prospect of being separated from them for another four years—or more.

Secondly, I honestly doubt whether <u>at the present time</u> I have the energy, drive and above all crusading spirit to tackle this new and vital job…[82]

Within a fortnight, he had also come to a decision about his current appointment, confiding in Eisenhower,

I have—strictly between you and me—told the Prime Minister (a) that I should like to be relieved of this wearing job as soon as possible. (I took it on for five years, and I have been doing it for nine.) (b) that I am not particularly anxious to be given any further <u>official</u> employment, but that I am prepared to do anything, whether at home or abroad, for which I have the necessary crusading spirit. Attlee was extremely nice about it, but has asked me to stay on a bit and help to settle them in.[83]

It almost goes without saying that despite his obvious weariness, Ismay deferred to Attlee's request. Nevertheless, a month later, in January 1946, he was telling Lockhart that 'he would like some other job—preferably something connected with Anglo-American co-operation'. Lockhart told him that he had suggested him several times to Sir Orme Sargent, then about to take over as Permanent Secretary at the Foreign Office, as ambassador to Washington.[84]

In January 1946 Eisenhower's wartime aide, Captain Harry Butcher, published his highly indiscreet diaries under the title *My Three Years with Eisenhower*. Eisenhower, now Chief of the Army Staff in Washington, wrote to Ismay to confide his 'deep regret that it was ever written' and to criticise Butcher's incessant focus on disagreements and disputes: '[m]omentary exhibitions of temper... and every difference of strategic and tactical conception are all played up. On the other hand, there is not running through the book that continuous thread, repeated over and over again, of the miracle of international and inter-service cooperation which was soul and source of victory'. Eisenhower ended philosophically, 'Oh Well...'[85]. In his reply Ismay emphatically shared Eisenhower's condemnation of the published diaries and assured him of his continued support and friendship.

In May Ismay received a letter from the Prime Minister which will have surprised and delighted him. Attlee was clearly of the opinion that Churchill's award to Ismay of a Companionship of Honour the previous year did not fully recognise his wartime contribution. On 21 May he wrote to Ismay,

> The forthcoming Honours List is the final Victory List and it would not be complete if it did not contain your name. I think you know how highly all have valued your untiring service, selfless devotion to duty and wise advice. It is, therefore, my intention that your outstanding contribution in the war should be recognised by the submission of your name to the King for appointment as Knight Grand Cross of the Bath (Military Division).[86]

The King who, as we have seen, intended to award Ismay his personal gift of the GCVO, clearly decided that the State's recognition was more appropriate. Already a KCB (Knight Commander of the Order of the Bath), Ismay would have hugely appreciated this advancement to GCB. It was obviously seen as well deserved by the many people who wrote to congratulate him, perhaps none more so than Brooke (now Lord Alanbrooke):

> What we should have done without your help & all your invaluable advice I hardly like to think of! I always marvel how you survived peevish remarks

from the COS at one end and abuse from Winston at the other, whilst endeavouring to smooth and iron out our path for us. You certainly played a very great part in the running of the war, and the country owes you a great debt... Personally, I shall always feel deeply indebted to you for all your wonderful friendly help and assistance... With <u>deep</u> gratitude, Brookie.[87]

The spring and early summer of 1946 had seen wholesale changes in the membership of the Chiefs of Staff Committee. Portal had been replaced in January by Tedder. Cunningham was replaced in May by his namesake (but no relation) John Cunningham. Now in June Brooke was replaced by Montgomery. Ismay will have been sorry to say farewell to the wartime team that had been together since 1943. The new incumbents could hardly be described as a team. Montgomery 'hated Tedder and did not trust the cleverness of Cunningham'.[88] The feeling was mutual. In one meeting, Mallaby recalled seeing, 'all three of them caught in a short spell of hatred and spite which they could not break'.[89] Although not an ardent admirer of Montgomery, Ismay would nevertheless have done his best to keep the show on the road. With the newcomers he was less reluctant to make his voice heard in the Chiefs' meetings. In August he spoke on a subject on which he felt increasingly strongly: his perception—in the wake of Churchill's 'iron curtain' speech at Fulton, Missouri, five months earlier—that the government was underestimating the Soviet threat. He gave his view that the Russians held the initiative in the Middle East and were 'fomenting mischief' against British interests. He believed that 'we were at present adopting a somewhat negative attitude in the face of continental Russian provocation'. The Chiefs agreed with his proposal to task the Joint Intelligence Committee with addressing the issue and making recommendations.[90] This action resulted in a major government initiative involving Military Intelligence, SIS and the Foreign Office.[91]

When, later the same month, Eisenhower informed Ismay of his intention to make a private visit to Britain and his wish to attend an informal meeting of the Chiefs of Staff, Ismay steered the discussion in the direction he wished by providing an aide-mémoire for his colleagues.[92] Eisenhower had already decided that he would seek an opportunity to discuss a joint Anglo-American approach to the Soviet threat. The meeting was a highly secret one. It was not even categorised as a meeting: merely lunch at the American embassy. There was no agenda and no minutes. Ismay produced a record of the meeting which he copied to Eisenhower and which shows that the subject discussed was a joint approach to a possible war with the Soviet Union.[93]

From the spring of 1946 Ismay and Churchill had been seeing each other frequently. In early April 1946 Ismay had met with Churchill who was seeking his assistance in the writing of his memoirs. He was setting up a small team, which became known as 'the Syndicate', to help with research and advice. The other principal members were William Deakin, his pre-war research assistant, and Henry Pownall. They were later to be joined by a naval officer, Commodore Gordon Allen. Ismay's job would be to assist with his recollections of events when he was at Churchill's side, and to keep an overall watching brief on what was being written.[94] Ismay had accepted, no doubt honoured and pleased to be invited. But, knowing his former boss as well as he did, he may also have had an inkling that this could develop into something more than a minor commitment. A month later he had sent Churchill his dictated recollections of their visits to France in 1940. In June he was dining and staying the night at Chartwell and found himself elected as a member of The Other Club: Churchill's small, highly exclusive dining club of 'those with whom it is agreeable to dine'.[95] On 2 October he was again at Chartwell when the verdicts of the Nuremberg trials were announced. Ismay recalled that Churchill said to him, 'It shows… that if you get into a war, it is supremely important to win it. You and I would be in a pretty pickle if we had lost'. In his memoirs Ismay added wryly, 'He certainly would have been'.[96]

By November Ismay and Churchill were corresponding weekly and by December by return of post. A grateful Churchill was thanking him warmly for his contributions and asking him to 'please remind me of things that occur to you. It is a great help to have one's memory jogged'.[97] Ismay reported to Churchill that 'Pownall and I have had a preliminary talk about the first draft of your Book… [attaching notes that] show you how we have allocated the work between ourselves'.[98] Such a close relationship between Ismay and the Leader of the Opposition while he was at the same time chief staff officer to the Prime Minister[99] would have been seen by some as highly irregular, unsound and a conflict of interest. But it would have been completely contrary to Ismay's ingrained integrity if he had entered into any gossip or betrayed the confidence of either man.

In early December Ismay received a letter from the Prime Minister informing him that his name would be appearing in the New Year's Honours list with yet another award: a barony. Having been awarded the GCB in June this would have come as a huge surprise to him: receiving two such major awards within six months of each other was, and is, highly unusual. Attlee's appreciation of Ismay's work will have been a factor but despite the fact that Ismay's political sympathies were not with the Labour party, a far greater one is likely to have been his potential contribution as a member of the House of Lords. Ismay was typically modest in his replies to the large number of congratulatory letters and telegrams that he received. In this, the final month of his appointment and of his military service, he could be forgiven had he taken his foot off the accelerator, but that was not his style. Right to the end he was working at full stretch, ensuring that his successor, Hollis, had the best handover possible.

11

ISMAY'S WAR

Ismay was now at the end of his six and a half years as chief staff officer to the Prime Minister.[1] For just over five of those years Britain had been at war, Churchill had been Prime Minister and Ismay had been almost literally at his right hand. What was Ismay's contribution to Churchill's success as Prime Minister and to the Allied victory?

The contribution was wide-ranging, with some of the most important aspects more obvious than others. One of the less obvious was the pre-war role that Ismay had played as Deputy Secretary, then Secretary, of the CID in guiding national strategy in the immediate pre-war years and in preparing the government administration for transition to war: for example, in preparation of the War Book and the construction of the underground War Rooms. Less obvious also, at least to outsiders, was that he was instrumental in designing and managing the 'handling machine' that converted the Prime Minister's decisions into action. Its critical importance in complementing one of Churchill's weaknesses was graphically described after the war by Ian Jacob.

> In my opinion the lack of administrative understanding displayed by Mr Churchill would hardly have been counterbalanced by the other qualities he possessed, if it had not been quickly harnessed to a most effective machine, which was ready at his hand without his knowing it. It was in achieving this that General Ismay made what I regard as his greatest contribution to the winning of the war.[2]

In the words of Ronald Lewin, 'the new High Command structure... proved to be the most efficient central system for running a war ever evolved, either by Britain or any other country. Ismay rather than Churchill was its architect'.[3] In Lawrence Burgis's view it was preventing Churchill from 'jettisoning our organisation which had been built up over the years and replacing it with some contraption of his own' that was 'a notable contribution to eventual victory... To his everlasting credit Pug Ismay fought this revolutionary idea tooth and nail. What is more, he won'.[4] In fact, the outcome was only a partial victory. Churchill infiltrated a number of his 'garden suburb' cronies to advisory appointments: Lindemann, Morton and Bracken each with their own office near his; Lyttleton, with a watching brief over the Ministry of Supply; and Duncan Sandys similarly over home defence. Churchill did, though, consult Ismay before doing so.[5]

Ismay was largely responsible for the steady development throughout the war of the machinery for its higher direction. This development was not the onward march of unnecessary bureaucracy, but the effective response to new circumstances and needs. The extent of the development was only really apparent in retrospect. At the outbreak of the war the Chiefs of Staff Committee had two sub-committees: Joint Planning and Joint Intelligence. By the war's end, the number of these sub-committees had necessarily increased to cover other subjects of vital importance to the conduct of the war and the transition to peace.[6]

Ismay's contribution to Churchill's direction of the war was largely dictated by the idiosyncratic way in which the Prime Minister ran the war and by his relationship with the Chiefs of Staff. Churchill 'believed that strategy needed to be tested by argument'.[7] He would put forward a constant flow of ideas—some brilliant, some impractical, some counter productive—and subject any opposition to them to intense cross-examination using his powerful forensic skills. 'All I wanted was compliance with my wishes after reasonable discussion', he wrote, not entirely in jest.[8] If the opposition wilted, he got his way. If his professional advisers decisively out-argued him, it was he who gave way, albeit reluctantly and sometimes in ill humour—but he would not overrule them. Given the right personalities and circumstances it was a perfectly workable system. But it was essentially confrontational; and in circumstances of very high stakes, emotive issues and big egos it carried a high risk of catastrophic failure—for example, a constitutional crisis or the resignation of the Chiefs of Staff.

An essential element in such a system was thus someone to prevent that failure, or at least to lower the risk. But it required a person with a special talent as a facilitator and mediator, someone who was trusted and respected by all parties and someone who could handle the constant pressure and abuse that was inherent in the role. It also required someone who could manage Churchill's increasing belief that anyone opposing his ideas was opposing not just his ideas, but him personally. Ismay proved to be a match for that demanding job specification. As he was to tell Brooke after the war,

> Often and often I had the feeling that I ought—somehow—to save the COS from more of the unnecessary aggravating, and sometimes humiliating burdens that were thrust upon their already overloaded shoulders. But I found that if I tried to apply the brake too hard and too often, I merely made matters worse. The trouble was that our beloved Chief regarded any disagreement with his view as a personal affront: he never understood that if you—and I in a more lowly field—had started saying we agreed with him when we didn't, we would have been of no more use to him. And so throughout those long years, I had to try and run with the hare, and hunt with the hounds—an ignominious and scarcely honest performance.[9]

If it had not been Ismay in the role, it is difficult to identify an alternative: possibly Hollis, or later Jacob, although both lacked Ismay's experience, his contacts within Whitehall and his personal affinity with Churchill; possibly Pownall who nearly got the job of Secretary of the CID in place of Ismay, but became Gort's chief of staff in the British Expeditionary Force. Ismay described him as 'one of the best brains of my vintage in the Army, courageous, competent and cool as a cucumber'.[10]

Ismay also became adept at handling Churchill, knowing when and how to counter a proposal, when to let it go forward—possibly with a bit of rewording—or when to divert Churchill's attention with a more pressing matter. This did not always work, and sometimes resulted in abuse being heaped on Ismay. Occasionally when Churchill drafted an insulting note to someone and Ismay tried to dissuade him, suggesting that there was no point in angering people, Churchill would shout 'Appeaser!' at him.[11] On other occasions when Ismay opposed one of his proposals, Churchill would retort, 'You have grown fat in honours from your country and now you betray her' or 'All you want to do is draw your pay, eat your rations and sleep'.[12] But for the most part these insults were delivered with a twinkle in the eye and received in good part. Sometimes, the mood was darker, as when Churchill angrily accused him of being 'a bromide'.[13] And sometimes the criticisms were bitter and wounding, for example on the voyage to Quebec in July 1944, prior to Ismay's tendered resignation. Ismay was far from alone in being the object of Churchill's periodic ill temper. Indeed, many of his staff who left records of their service with him mention angry Churchillian outbursts, albeit that he seldom failed to make it up with them later.[14] Ismay mentioned this only once—to Darry after the tendered resignation—but what he clearly understood and made allowances for was that, as Richard Toye identified, 'these outbursts... in part were a way of venting emotion at a time of great stress, and he was usually persuaded to see reason'.[15]

The source of much of the stress on Churchill, and in turn on Ismay, was the Prime Minister's relationship with the Chiefs of Staff. As Ismay related to Lockhart, 'Often he would send for me after he had read a COS comment on his own proposals. He would storm, curse me, saying: "What the hell is this?" Accuse me of aiding and abetting the COS. Crumple up the paper and throw it on the floor, in front of his stenographer. I never picked it up'.[16] Frequently the insults were coming from both directions. As Brendan Bracken reminded Ismay after the war, 'When the boss was in a bad temper with the brass hats you were greeted with a rolling salutation, "You are nothing but a lackey of the Chiefs of Staff". What a life you had, Pug, because the COS were equally saying that you were Winston's Man Friday'.[17] Ismay's relationships with the Chiefs of Staff could indeed be tense. He was later to comment, 'I had an idea that during the war [they] hated my guts'.[18]

Ismay was probably overstating here what was in all likelihood, at its worst, only a very occasional feeling. As we have seen, when he first joined their committee the Chiefs may have resented his imposition on them and viewed him with some suspicion. They may also have begrudged the fact that on occasions he was privy to some of the most secret intelligence to which they were excluded, such as some Enigma decrypts[19] and, until November 1944, details of the development of the atom bomb.[20] And it may be that, at first, they questioned Ismay's utility: as we have also seen, Ismay considered that it was not until the Teheran conference in November 1943 that Brooke came fully to value his role and contribution. But in general, his relationship with the three Chiefs who were in post for the longest wartime period (Brooke, Pound and Portal) was one of mutual respect and trust. Brooke had joined the committee in December 1941 and become chairman six months later. Ismay held him in high regard. In his memoirs he was unequivocal, recalling that in his eighteen years' service in Whitehall he had worked with eight different CIGSs and declared that, 'I would unhesitatingly say that Brooke was the best of them all'.[21] In private, though, he was more candid—and remarkably perceptive:

The Americans at first did not take to Brooke, due to his direct and positive approach to common problems, and his ill-concealed contempt for 'theoretical' soldiers—he spoke fast and abruptly, like a machine-gun, and they could not understand him. Later they came to trust him completely and recognised in him the 'complete master' of his profession...

In all his dealings with the Chiefs of Staff and the Combined Chiefs of Staff Brooke was frank to the point of brutality. He held back nothing—there was no finesse, no bluff. At times he could be extremely obstinate. Impatient, peppery, quick tempered, celtic, he was deep down very kind hearted—consequently he suffered such remorse afterwards for his hasty words...

As CIGS [he] was very fierce and frank in argument with Mr Churchill. He was in fact apt to be more abrupt with him in public than was proper. While he admired Mr Churchill's courage and drive, he had an ill-concealed contempt for his ignorance of the mechanics of war.[22]

What Ismay thought of Pound is harder to determine. In his memoirs he leapt to Pound's defence against the accusations of many that he regularly fell asleep in meetings, and paid tribute to his technical skills as First Sea Lord: 'He was a master of his profession, a sailor to the very depth of his being. There seemed to be nothing that he did not know about the Navy and the Seven Seas', adding that 'he was a brave, generous character, and a willing work horse if ever there was one'.[23] But, perhaps tellingly, he makes no comment on Pound's contribution—or lack of it—to wider strategy. Ismay's high regard and admiration for Portal, however, is unmistakable.[24] According to Portal's biographer, when asked who he considered to have been the greatest commander on the British side in the war Ismay answered, 'Peter Portal—*quite easily*'.[25]

These remarks were of course made many years after the war and there were undoubtedly moments during it when, as Bracken suggests, Ismay came under considerable, simultaneous pressure from the Prime Minister and the Chiefs. Indeed, given that this was the case, it is perhaps surprising that Ismay did not crack or resign. As we have seen, there were times when he came close to doing both. His tendered resignation at Quebec in 1944, rejected by Churchill, was perhaps the closest. But his breakdown in August 1942 and the exhaustion which prevented his return to work in December 1943 were also critical moments. There were others. Burgis, who saw things at first hand, commented after the war,

[He] must have been tough to stand up to what he did until 1945. Fantastic hours, often from 8.30 one morning until 3 the next. Constant travelling; meetings, meetings, meetings and, most exhausting of all, the go-between the COS and the PM. Often Churchill lost his temper with Ismay and I know there were moments when he felt he had reached the end of his tether, for, driving himself hard, the PM never realised the mental and physical strain to which he subjected his subordinates.[26]

John Connell points to a source of Ismay's resilience and stamina. 'There was that in Ismay's physique and temperament', he wrote, 'which permitted him to bear his load with an apparent debonair ease, with wit and zest'.[27] Ismay's unwavering sense of duty and almost superhuman patience were also key contributors. But a further factor was his success in surrounding himself with a strong and close-knit team. His selection and management of his subordinates and staff was masterly. As has been mentioned, he restricted his staff to the smallest possible number, but of the highest-grade individuals. He had confidence in them and delegated accordingly. His two closest subordinates were united in their appreciation of him as a boss. Hollis described him as 'an easy man to work for and with… He had the happiest knack of delegating responsibility to his subordinates without in any way failing to retain the final responsibility in his own hands. We went through some pretty awkward times together and always he showed the highest qualities of leadership and devotion to duty… His example was indeed inspiring'.[28] For Jacob, Ismay was:

a true decentraliser. That is to say he never allowed the usual feeling of protocol to stand in the way of speed and efficiency of work. He never insisted that everything destined for the Chiefs of Staff or the Prime Minister must pass through him. Hollis and I could deal directly with anyone, so there were no bottlenecks… Such an arrangement would have been impossible with a man who had not the faculty of inspiring his assistants with his spirit and the unselfishness to waive all questions of personal status. His position never suffered.[29]

It was not just his immediate subordinates who held Ismay in admiration, respect and affection. George Mallaby remembered him as:

a cheerful friendly man, a lover of good living, anxious always and in all circumstances to feel that 'all is for the best in the best of all possible worlds', agreeable and smiling to all and sundry, warm and affectionate, not in the least degree ingratiating but determined to promote harmony, to make sure that there [was] no unnecessary grit in the machine.[30]

Mallaby recalled an incident that illustrates Ismay's style. One day, hurrying down a passage in the War Cabinet office, he met Ismay, who told him,

'You are suspended from duty.' For a moment I had an uncomfortable feeling, a hasty recapitulation of culpable negligence, but he was smiling, his pug-like wrinkles upward-turning, his eyes merry. 'What do you mean, sir?' I asked. 'The Prime Minister', he said, 'has seen a report by one of the staffs to which he has taken great exception. It should never have been written, let alone circulated, and he has decreed that the whole of the Military Secretariat of the War Cabinet from me downwards should be immediately suspended from duty while the culprits are discovered and suitably chastised.' He was laughing cheerfully and I felt a surge of true admiration for the sense and balance of this man. He knew just when things were really serious and just when they were exasperatingly silly. 'I am glad', he went on, 'that you are taking your suspension in the right spirit,' and with that we parted happily.[31]

General Vaughan's homily at Quetta on the subject of proportion had not gone amiss.

A significant part of Ismay's success as an intermediary was the importance he attached to presentation of the case to each party and the care he took in it. He was to emphasise this in a lecture to an audience of senior officers after the war. 'The soldier', he said—although it has a wider application—'must take the greatest trouble and consideration in the presentation of his case. This is the outstanding lesson that I have learned in the last twenty years—the presentation of the case and the timing thereof. It is from faulty presentation that so many misunderstandings and quarrels arise'.[32] Ismay's skill in presentation, developed over his career and particularly in Whitehall, was exceptional.

Ismay was adept, too, at ensuring a good relationship with all the agencies with whom he worked, in particular between the military and civilian members of the Prime Minister's staff—especially between himself and Cabinet Secretary Bridges. This was not a foregone conclusion. Close relationships between a Prime Minister's most senior military and civilian advisers have not always been the case in Whitehall and were notably absent during the days of Chamberlain, Hankey and Wilson. Nor were Ismay and Bridges obvious soulmates. Betty Green, who saw the two together on many occasions, described them as completely opposite in temperament and personality. Bridges was 'very much an intellectual, quiet, shy… and remote… they didn't <u>really</u> understand one another ever… [but] I think they got on well together… it would have been difficult not to with Ismay'.[33] The relationship 'was one of mutual respect and forbearance', recalled Joan Bright, '… and there was no shadow of disloyalty or intrigue between them'.[34] 'In all those five strenuous years relations between the military and civil sides of the PM's office could not have been better', wrote John Martin. 'In fact we were really one team.'[35]

Ismay made it his business to maintain cordial relations with the other members of what Churchill called his 'secret circle' and with his coterie of cronies. This was not always easy. In the case of Bendan Bracken, Ismay was 'alarmed at his apparent inability to keep his mouth shut' from the very start: the public announcement of the sinking of the French fleet at Mers-el-Kébir in 1940 had to be made precipitately because he had 'blabbed the news at a dinner party'.[36] Ismay remarked that no one could ever know if Bracken was talking the truth, because '[he] would never admit to anyone that he did not know every secret of the P.M.'s'.[37] Yet the two of them had an easy-going relationship with good-humoured banter, Ismay happy to recount the occasion when Bracken told him, 'Shut up, you chutney-eating general!'[38]

With Lindemann, Ismay recorded in his memoirs that the Prof was 'as obstinate as a mule… seemed to have a poor opinion of the intellect of everyone with the exception of Lord Birkenhead, Mr Churchill and Professor Lindemann; and a special contempt for the bureaucrat and all his ways'.[39] But if Ismay and Lindemann did not always agree, they remained friends and kept in touch after the war, with Ismay being Lindemann's guest at his Oxford college and Lindemann a weekend guest at Wormington. Beaverbrook was clearly harder work for Ismay. Although he was polite about him in his memoirs and paid tribute to Beaverbrook's work as Minister of Supply, he told Lockhart, following his return from the 1941 Moscow trip, that 'Max had scored a great personal success with Stalin… but one thing he knew nothing about was strategy'.[40] He later told Lockhart that Beaverbrook was 'very tiresome over the second front, demanding it violently at a time when we had neither ships nor men, nor the armaments'.[41] Ismay had little to do with him after the war and resented the personal criticisms of Mountbatten which appeared from time to time in the columns of Beaverbrook's *Daily Express*.

With the Churchill family, Ismay was popular and highly regarded as a firm friend and ally. He had a strong (and mutual) admiration for Clementine with whom he developed a close, lifelong friendship. 'She knew precisely how to handle him', he told her biographer.[42] 'If the Prime Minister... was too naughty, she could look after him and stop him as no one else could'.[43] (Ismay, himself, was no mean performer at this task: Bracken used to refer to him as 'Winston's nannie'.[44]) Ismay also considered her a very sound and astute judge of character, and a rather better one than Churchill.[45] Summing up her influence on her husband he wrote, 'Without her, the history of Winston Churchill and of the world would have been a different story'.[46] Ismay was also a firm admirer of Mary Churchill, but less so of her brother. Following a wide-ranging conversation in March 1946 Lockhart recorded in his diary that Ismay had been 'Very down on Randolph. Dislikes him both drunk and sober'.[47]

Turning to specific areas in which Ismay made noteworthy contributions during the war, his contribution in the field of strategic deception and specifically to the effectiveness of the London Controlling Section has often been underestimated. Easily overlooked, too, is his initiative in May and June 1940 in contingency planning for Home Defence in the event of German invasion. Similarly, his interventions in 1940 which resulted in the radical improvement of intelligence handling have been largely forgotten. Here he was also instrumental in securing the services of the talented chairman of the Joint Intelligence Committee, Victor Cavendish-Bentinck. In late 1941 Cavendish-Bentinck had something of a crisis of confidence and suggested to Ismay that he should be replaced as chairman by someone more senior. Ismay, who had a high regard for him, would not hear of it and told him to 'soldier on'.[48] Cavendish-Bentinck did so with success, continued to be promoted in the Foreign Office throughout the war and was awarded the CMG (Companionship of the Order of St Michael and St George). He was later to write, 'Pug Ismay was a remarkable man. Highly intelligent, kindly but very firm, very clever in dealing with the PM and others. He was the prop and mainstay of the War Cabinet organisation'.[49]

Prop and mainstay he may have been, but did Ismay play a major role as a strategic adviser to Churchill? He did not set out to carry out such a role and was always quick to deny that he played any part in the formulation of strategic policy. As was noted earlier, had the Chiefs believed that he was giving the Prime Minister separate strategic advice their confidence in him would have been undermined. Many years after the war Leslie Rowan recounted an anecdote that illustrates this. Soon after he became Prime Minister, Churchill asked Ismay for his own personal view on a piece of advice proffered by the Chiefs of Staff. Ismay had replied that if Churchill wanted him to be of value 'then you will never ask me that question again'.[50] And according to Rowan, Churchill never did so. This is undoubtedly the story that Ismay would have liked to propagate, and the source of the anecdote would almost certainly have been Ismay himself.[51] But it is hard to believe that in total privacy Churchill never sought Ismay's opinion on a matter of strategy and, that if he did so, that Ismay never gave it.

Similarly, Ismay was at pains to declare (for example to the Chiefs of Staff when he joined their committee in 1940) that he would not give advice to Churchill on senior officers' appointments.[52] Even after the war he kept up this façade, and previous biographers have taken him at his word, Sangster adding that he was 'always refusing an opinion to Churchill's annoyance'.[53] But there is evidence of him having given such advice. For example, in 1940, along with the Chiefs of Staff, he dissuaded Churchill from appointing Keyes as chairman of the Chiefs Committee; in late May 1943 he told Churchill that Wavell 'had aged and was not up to the east Asia Command'; and two months later he supported Churchill's proposal to appoint Mountbatten as Supreme Allied Commander South East Asia.[54] Indeed, since Churchill clearly trusted his opinion and Ismay always wished to be helpful to him, it would be surprising if in private he invariably and stubbornly refused to express an opinion.

The extent of Ismay's influence in Churchill's decisions can only be guessed at. During the war he spent more time alone with Churchill than anyone else outside the Churchill family. As has been seen, he would make a point of joining Churchill when he was working alone in the evenings and late into the night. What was said between them is unreported. Churchill trusted him to be a true confidant and (sadly for the biographer), a true confidant he was—never betraying that trust in any way, even in private. The only glimpse of their conversations comes from the shorthand typists who occasionally were present, taking dictation. One of these, Elizabeth Nel, who described Ismay as the Prime Minister's 'constant adviser on military affairs', remembered that, '[i]n the evenings Mr Churchill would often sit in the office, beside the cheerful fire, and talk to General Ismay about the most dreadful secrets of the war—Future Operations! Mostly they would use code-names'.[55] Another, Patrick Kinna, recalled of Churchill and Ismay, 'Oh yes, they were very, very close... and Winston used to listen to him very, very carefully'.[56]

Not only is it therefore difficult to assess Ismay's influence on Churchill, Ismay's discretion makes it equally hard to gauge his opinion of Churchill's views or policies on some of the key decisions of the war such as the strategic bombing campaign, the Battle of the Atlantic, or the use of the atomic bomb—let alone Churchill's opinions of the key personalities with whom he interacted.

One of the pillars of Ismay's success in his role was his firm view of the relationship which he believed should exist between the political leaders and their military advisers. His view would be shared by many more members of the military today than would have been the case before and during the Second World War. He lived by the maxim that he had learnt from General Vaughan at Quetta expressed in his Staff College dissertation:

> It is essential that the statesman and the soldier should be in the closest touch with each other, and that they should work together frankly, openly and loyally... The soldier, for his part, must... realise that war is the instrument of policy, and therefore, that, if any subservience is necessary, he is subservient to the statesman.[57]

He also understood—rather more clearly than some of his contemporaries—the importance of recognising that military strategy is but one strand of grand strategy, and in doing so referred to Field Marshal Sir William Robertson, CIGS 1916–18:

> Now that war is an affair of whole nations, it is as Wully Robertson said many years ago, not nearly so much a matter for soldiers and sailors as soldiers and sailors sometimes appear to think. The commanders in the field have to be rigidly controlled by the Government at home, duly advised by the Chiefs of Staff, since it is by no means only military considerations that have to be taken into account. There are political, economic, industrial and home front matters which can only be brought into proper focus by the Government itself.[58]

A further key element of Ismay's success in his role was his awareness that, as he put it himself, 'it should be carried out by a man relatively obscure and not desirous of power'.[59] He was genuinely and obviously devoid of ambition other than to do his job to the best of his ability, and he was adept at keeping himself in the background. Indeed, for a man almost constantly at Churchill's side, the wartime photographs which include him are remarkably few in number. When his publisher asked for some,

Ismay replied, 'I am afraid these are in short supply, as I took great pains to avoid publicity during the war years'.[60]

Finally, one of Ismay's greatest contributions in his wartime role was that of helping to cement the Anglo-American partnership. As has been seen, he developed warm friendships with a number of Americans in the early years of the war, particularly when he sensed that Churchill set great store by achieving a strong and active trans-Atlantic alliance. Eisenhower was later to remark that given Ismay's immensely powerful position, '[it] was fortunate... that he was devoted to the principle of Allied unity and that his personality was such as to win the confidence and friendship of his American associates'.[61] His relationship with Eisenhower was particularly close and was to remain so for the rest of their lives: the lifetime correspondence between them totals no less than 140 letters.[62] But he made it his business to develop and sustain friendships with many other influential Americans, including Marshall, Hopkins, Harriman, and Bedell Smith, and especially with (at that time) Anglophobes such as Clark, Wedemeyer and King. At the Anglo-American wartime conferences he was, in the words of one of Marshall's biographers Ed Cray, 'often the genial broker in arguments between Yanks and Brits'.[63] Marshall told Forrest Pogue, 'He straightened things out for us time after time. I was fond of him'.[64] Indeed, Ismay was second only to Dill in achieving conciliation and harmony between the two sets of Chiefs.

Critics of Ismay in his wartime role are notable by their remarkably small number. Indeed, one has to search hard to find them. Two of these were peripheral members of Churchill's inner circle who resented Ismay's closeness to the Prime Minister, notably Churchill's doctor Sir Charles Wilson (later Lord Moran), who Colville recalled, 'was the only man I ever heard speak ill of Ismay'.[65] Rowan agreed: 'I think Moran stands alone in belittling him'.[66] Moran suggested to Rowan that Ismay 'passed on only what was agreeable to Churchill' and told Lockhart that, 'all this story of his being a buffer between Winston and the Chiefs of Staff is quite untrue'.[67] In a diary entry at the time of the 1943 Quebec conference Moran observed of Pug, with palpable jealousy, that 'he thinks like a politician—he never does anything without a purpose—he has a remarkable knowledge of human nature and his influence is increasing, as the drip of water in time makes its mark on stone'.[68] The other inner-circle critic was Desmond Morton who told the author RW Thompson sniffily, 'Pug never had a first-class brain in my opinion'.[69] The antipathy was mutual. According to Lockhart, 'Pug [was] very anti-Desmond'.[70] There was also mutual antipathy between Ismay and 'Chips' Channon, Member of Parliament, socialite and notorious snob. Channon, who believed that Ismay had 'made mischief' about him with Churchill, dismissed him as 'scarcely a social figure and knows nobody except the Butlers. I have always found him tiresome and hostile'—a comment that says rather more about Channon than it does about Ismay.[71]

More substantial criticisms of Ismay came from the War Office. The acerbic Sir Percy Grigg told the official historian, JRM Butler, that 'Both Dill and Brooke used to speak to me pretty contemptuously of his contribution'.[72] Kennedy, too, was critical. He quoted Ismay as telling him in April 1941 that 'if the PM came in and said he'd like to wipe his boots on me I'd lie down & let him do it'.[73] The following month Kennedy told Hankey,

> Ismay is completely bemused by the PM and doctors their [the Chiefs of Staff] reports so as to make them acceptable to the PM to the point of emasculating them. They do not trust him (Ismay) and will not circulate Memoranda lest he should show them to the PM before they are discussed. He interferes too much in strategy, and they cannot help feeling that he may report what they say to the PM.[74]

This conversation with Hankey may have been influenced by the fact that it took place at the height of the dispute between Dill and Churchill in May 1941, and just a few days after Kennedy's fractious argument with Churchill at Chequers at which Kennedy may have resented the fact that Ismay did not step in to offer him any support. In his memoirs, Kennedy damned Ismay with faint praise. 'We were indeed fortunate to have Ismay to take so much of the initial shock of the Prime Minister's impact on the Staffs', he wrote.

> He never claimed that he influenced Churchill to any extent, and probably he did not. No man with the inclination and capacity to deal seriously with Churchill could have retained Ismay's post for long. He was always charmingly frank in admitting that his chief function was to act as whipping boy, and as a person to whom Churchill could blow off steam at all hours of the night and day. We all felt that we would not have his job for anything in the world. He was, in his own right, one of the most remarkable men of the war.[75]

In addition, Kennedy's predecessor as Director of Military Operations Major General Richard Dewing believed that by accepting membership of the Chiefs of Staff Committee in May 1940, 'Pug had betrayed the C.O.S in unforgivable manner'.[76] All of these criticisms are indicative of a feeling amongst some at the War Office that Ismay not only lacked loyalty to the army and the War Office but that he was on occasions actively hostile to their interests. As we have seen, Ismay did not think highly of the War Office and probably would have seen no reason why he should put its interests above those of the other services or of the three Armed Services as a whole.

A more valid question might be whether Ismay could or should have done more to restrain what was one of Churchill's most deleterious habits: that of attempting to micromanage military operations. Some historians, for example Eliot Cohen, have applauded Churchill's constant questioning, probing and spurring of his senior deployed commanders.[77] There is plenty of evidence, though, that such activity was on many occasions taken to such an extreme as to be counterproductive, preoccupying those commanders to the detriment of their focus on operations. Ismay, having never been a senior deployed commander, may not have appreciated this, or more likely believed that this was a Churchillian obsession that he could not cure or even much restrain—not worth his while trying. What he would not do is to tell Churchill that he agreed with him if he did not do so. He vowed as much at the start of their relationship. On one occasion when they had an argument and Ismay obstinately stuck to his opinion he told Churchill of his vow. Ismay recalled that, 'His reaction was characteristic. "You should forget these outmoded Staff College shibboleths". This with, simulated ferocity, betrayed by an endearing twinkle, indicated that the argument was closed—for the time being.'[78]

What of Ismay's candid opinion of Churchill? His opinion changed from time to time during the war. Had he committed his thoughts and emotions to a diary at the end of each day (like Brooke), there would undoubtedly have been occasions when his criticisms would have been similarly vitriolic. But moments of frustration apart, the overall respect, admiration and affection which he had for Churchill sustained from 1940 through to the end of the war and beyond. He had witnessed Churchill's extraordinary leadership in the dark days of 1940 and 1941 and firmly believed that without that leadership Britain would probably have lost the war. As he wrote to Lord Chandos (formerly Oliver Lyttleton) many years later, 'It was not the British people who held the fort alone for nearly two years against the powers of darkness but Winston Churchill'.[79]

Ismay was not, however, blind to Churchill's weaknesses and some of his criticisms even make the pages of his memoirs, slipped in between fulsome tributes. For example,

> [h]is knowledge of military history was encyclopaedic, and his grasp of the broad sweep of strategy was unrivalled. At the same time, he did not fully realise the extent to which mechanisation had complicated administrative arrangements and revolutionised the problems of time and space; and he never ceased to cry-out against the inordinate 'tail' which modern armies required.[80]

More often Ismay pulls his punches in his memoirs. For example, in his draft memoirs he acknowledges Churchill's 'interference' with detailed operations.[81] But in the published version this is replaced by justification of Churchill's motives for intervening, such as 'imparting to the commanders his own "impetuous, adventurous and defying character"'.[82] Ismay believed that Churchill could rise to the occasion of major world events and crises but was far less good at more mundane challenges: as he put it to Colville, Churchill 'can be counted on to score a hundred in a Test Match but is no good at village cricket'.[83]

Since Churchill issued all his directions in writing, and almost all of them through the Office of the Minister of Defence, Ismay was constantly bombarded with pieces of paper from the Prime Minister, many of them carrying the famous 'Action This Day' tag. These varied from statements of policy and grand strategy to communications with Roosevelt, questions to be relayed to the Chiefs of Staff and directives to commanders-in-chief around the world. Interspersed with these were wild ideas, questions on low-level tactical matters and seeming trivia which must have tested even Ismay's legendary patience.

As to Churchill as a strategist, Ismay differentiated between, on the one hand, military and campaign strategy—'which practically merges into tactics'—and, on the other hand, what he called 'the overall strategy for the conduct of the war', in other words, grand strategy.[84] Reflecting on Churchill's wartime leadership, he commented to Eisenhower in 1951 that Churchill had had 'an unrivalled knowledge of the broad strategy of the war and that in the political-military field he was the outstanding expert of our day—indeed of any day. At the same time, he was, and is, completely ignorant of the mechanics of modern war and of logistics'.[85] When the time came to draft his memoirs Ismay wrote, 'I have no hesitation in expressing the view that Churchill knew more about waging total war than all his military advisers put together'.[86] But the fact that this did not appear in the published version may indicate that, on reflection, he did indeed have a hesitation about expressing such a controversial view in public. Furthermore, he did not choose to share in his memoirs (or elsewhere) his assessment of the quality and consistency of Churchill's strategic judgement—a highly contentious subject among historians, but one to which Ismay may have simply closed his mind.

In summary, Ismay's war had been one of unremitting hard slogging and pressure. In some ways this was far from exceptional: war—particularly one of the scale, intensity and circumstances of the Second World War—places wholly extraordinary demands on the mind and body of all those responsible for its higher direction. And in Britain, arguably, nowhere were these demands greater than on the person ultimately responsible for that direction—Churchill—not least due to the highly centralised, personal way in which he conducted business and drove himself. Ismay was well aware of, and alluded to, the great pressure on Churchill and its effect—for example telling Auchinleck, '[t]he PM gets terribly worried at times... and terribly impatient'.[87] Unsurprisingly, the pressure contributed to great stress and strain on those around him, for all of whom it was only one of the sources of stress and strain in their lives. Few can have been under greater pressure than Ismay. Indeed, in Ronald Lewin's view he 'endured strains more continuous than any battle-commander and sometimes equally intense. Not even Sir Alan Brooke... was so exposed to the exigencies and exhaustion of intimate work with Churchill by day and by night'.[88]

If in the absence of evidence, the extent of Ismay's influence on Churchill's decision-making can only be guessed at, what is clear is that he had become an instrumental and indispensable part of Churchill's machinery of government. In his foreword to Ismay's memoirs Churchill wrote that 'we became hand in glove and much more'.[89] Just how much more was indicated by Colville when he wrote that it was Ismay 'to whom Churchill owed more, and admitted that he owed more, than to anybody else, military or civilian, in the whole of the war'.[90]

A large part of this perceived debt was the role that Ismay had played as an intermediary and emollient between Churchill and the Chiefs of Staff, in achieving compromise and workable solutions where none looked possible and thus in preventing disputes from becoming catastrophic ruptures. In short, it was Ismay's most significant wartime achievement. He was, as Max Hastings described him, 'a superb diplomat'.[91] The higher direction of the First World War was frequently characterised by the acrimonious conflict between statesmen ('Frock Coats') and generals ('Brass Hats'). In his volume of the official history of the Second World War, John Ehrman drew attention to this before paying a singular tribute to Ismay. 'If the "Frocks" and "Hats" of the First World War do not reappear in the vocabulary of the Second', he wrote, 'a not inconsiderable part of the credit must be given to him'.[92]

This should not, though, blind us to those facets of Ismay's war that leave him open him to criticism: his lack of support for Wavell over the Bengal famine, his ignorance of the weaknesses of 'Fortress Singapore', and his part in the failure to ensure formal approval of the Dieppe raid are notable examples. But appreciation of his contribution was not restricted to Churchill. Perhaps the most significant tribute to Ismay's wartime role was the fact that the signal honours he received—the GCB and the barony—were not awarded on the recommendation of Churchill, whom he had served for five long years of wartime and with whom he had had a famously close relationship. They were awarded on the recommendation of Attlee, whom he had served for just eighteen months, and almost solely during peacetime, but who had witnessed at close quarters Ismay's wartime contribution. Few of those who had also witnessed that contribution would have disputed Attlee's recommendation.

12

PARTITION—MAKING THE PLAN

JANUARY–JUNE 1947

In December 1946, his retirement date fast approaching, Ismay was looking forward to paying a three-month visit, accompanied by Darry, to Australia and New Zealand at the invitation of their governments. The week before Christmas was full of farewell engagements. The 19 December, his last day in office,[1] was particularly busy. He was due to make a farewell speech to his staff before attending a dinner given in his honour by Attlee and to be attended by Churchill. A last-minute addition to his programme for the day was a request for a meeting from Mountbatten, who was back in England, having completed his tour of duty as Supreme Allied Commander South East Asia six months earlier. There was no indication of what Mountbatten wanted so urgently to discuss but Ismay agreed to see him. It was a meeting which would lead to a momentous change in his life.

Mountbatten duly appeared at Ismay's office in the late afternoon. He told Ismay that the previous evening he had been summoned by Attlee with the invitation to take over from Wavell as Viceroy of India. He was here, he said, to ask Ismay's advice as to whether he should accept. In his memoirs Ismay recorded that his first reaction was that 'it was one of the most delicate and perhaps distasteful assignments imaginable, but that it was difficult to see how he could refuse'. He told Mountbatten that he would think about it further and give him a considered opinion the next day. However, as Ismay recalled in his memoirs,

> [d]irectly he left me I wondered whether I ought not at least offer to accompany him. The idea of emerging from my newfound retirement and getting involved in the last chapter of the story of British rule in India was

singularly unattractive. On the other hand I owed so much to India that it was my bounden duty to lend a hand, if I was wanted.[2]

He consulted Darry, 'whose sense of duty has always been more highly developed than my own. [She] had no doubts whatsoever'. The following morning he offered Mountbatten his services 'as a chief of staff or general factotum', but made no attempt to disguise his feelings about the prospects, telling his fellow polo player that, 'We would be "going out to the last chukka twelve goals down"'. Mountbatten immediately accepted the offer.

It has been suggested that Ismay was, himself, considered for the appointment of Viceroy. Sangster makes the claim, citing Andrew Lownie.[3] Lownie in turn cites Shahid Hamid, Auchinleck's military assistant.[4] But Hamid offered no source and his claim is dubious: there is no separate corroboration, and some historians have warned that his testimony is not always to be trusted.[5]

Ismay's given reason for offering his services as Mountbatten's chief of staff ('I owed so much to India') invites some examination. For a start, the India to which he was clearly referring was the Raj—British rule in India—a concept to which he felt intensely loyal and an experience which he had cherished from childhood. But in addition, his offer was a highly personal one to Dickie Mountbatten, a friend and colleague in his hour of need. The relationship between the two men had grown steadily over the four years since Mountbatten, as Chief of Combined Operations, had been given a seat on the Chiefs of Staff Committee somewhat analogous to Ismay's. Ismay was often the first person to whom Mountbatten turned for advice, particularly career advice.[6] As Ismay reminded him in May 1946,

It seems a long time ago since you crashed into my room at Quebec [August, 1943] and told me the Prime Minister had offered you the job of Supreme Commander [South East Asia]. 'I feel as though I have been pole-axed' was your opening gambit. I remember too that I was not very encouraging and that the most I could say in reply to your request for a frank opinion was that if I had to have a bet on this particular race, I'd sooner back you than anyone else in the world. Thus for once in my life, I tipped a winner![7]

When Mountbatten had deployed to the Far East Ismay made a point of (as with other deployed, senior commanders) keeping him in touch with strategic developments, but in his case also as a friend. A month after D-Day, and mindful of Mountbatten's role in developing combined operations, he wrote to congratulate him for his part in the successful operation. 'If anyone had told us two years ago that we could throw ashore a million men, two hundred thousand vehicles and three-quarters of a million tons of stores, across open beaches, in none too favourable weather, in thirty days, we would have dubbed him mad. So that's a great feather in your cap, Dickie.'[8] Mountbatten purred with pleasure; but equally he would take without offence criticism, sometimes expressed in pretty plain language, from him.[9] Nor was Ismay oblivious to Mountbatten's limitations. Although he made no criticism of Mountbatten in his memoirs he recalled in private that Brooke 'used to get infuriated when [Mountbatten] put forward "half-baked" ideas at inappropriate times'.[10]

Mountbatten lobbied Ismay shamelessly to attempt to influence high-level decisions in his favour.[11] Undoubtedly, it was Ismay's position and ability to achieve the latter that provided one of his main attractions to Mountbatten. For Ismay's part, he admired Mountbatten's energy, dynamism and charisma, and sympathised with him in his battles with the older and more traditional senior officers of his Service. He also genuinely liked him as a person. And he may not have been completely unconscious of Mountbatten's very close connection with the royal family—a connection to which Mountbatten himself was constantly alluding. Indeed, Attlee's letter informing him of his imminent elevation to the peerage will have come as no surprise to Ismay. Mountbatten had told him almost a month earlier that he had heard about it from none other than the King himself, making it 'one of the happiest days of my life'.[12]

Mountbatten's choice of Ismay as his chief of staff was widely welcomed in Britain by those who had witnessed Ismay's, and Mountbatten's, performance during and immediately after the war.[13] Many thought that he had been specially selected by Attlee to act as a brake on Mountbatten's perceived impetuosity. Others gave credit to Mountbatten for his wise choice. 'My opinion of your new boss has gone up', wrote Lascelles to Ismay on 5 January. 'I know that you, throughout the war, never hesitated to hit him over the head, hard and often, whenever he deserved it, and it is greatly to his credit that the first person he should ask to help him now, is yourself'.[14] Many agreed that Mountbatten needed a close adviser with a deep knowledge of India, and this may have been at the back of Ismay's mind when he made his offer to Mountbatten.

Much had changed in India, however, since Ismay last served there in 1933. Firstly, the constitutional position had altered markedly with the implementation in April 1937 of the Government of India Act. Although the act did not specifically mention the British handover of power, many in India saw it as an acknowledged milestone in that process. The act took a major step towards democracy, introducing a federal system with substantial power devolved to the provinces, including that for law and order. It increased the number of those eligible to vote from six million to almost thirty-five million. It also, rather less democratically, included in the constitution the Princely States. There were over 500 of these, ranging from Hyderabad—roughly the size of Italy and with a population of some sixteen million—to small tracts of land with populations of under a hundred. Together they comprised over one third of the territory of India and a quarter of its population.[15] Although not fully autonomous, the princes held extensive powers within their states and under the system of paramountcy had a direct relationship with the British crown, exercised through the Viceroy. Following their display of loyalty to the British during the 1857 mutiny, Queen Victoria had pledged 'We shall respect the rights, dignity and honour of Native Princes as our own'.[16] The princes had been notably stalwart supporters of the imperial war effort in 1939, some raising their own regiments at a time when much of India was showing its opposition to any involvement.

A further change on the political landscape in the years following Ismay's departure from India in 1933 had been the increased antipathy between the Muslims on the one hand and the Hindus and Sikhs on the other. Both Jawaharlal Nehru's Congress Party and Muhammad Ali Jinnah's Muslim League were committed to the ending of the British Raj, but the Muslim League was increasingly gaining popular support for the division of India on religious lines and the creation of a separate Muslim state. Relations between the two parties and between the communities which they represented were becoming increasingly antagonistic, visceral and violent.

In the provincial elections of 1939 Congress celebrated a notable victory, winning almost fifty per cent of the seats in the provincial assembly and forming the government in seven of the eleven Indian provinces. By contrast the Muslim League performed badly, failing to win outright victories in any of the remaining provinces. It emerged deeply suspicious of the potential for Hindu domination of the political agenda. Further internal political ructions in India had followed the declaration of war in 1939. The Viceroy, the Marquess of Linlithgow, without consulting any of the Indian political leaders, informed them that India had declared war on Germany. The Congress Party demanded a guarantee of total independence. Linlithgow responded only with the offer of discussions on Dominion status—independence within the Commonwealth—at some unspecified date in the future. All the Congress ministers resigned. The two provinces controlled by the Muslim League, however, offered support for the war effort and a third province, the Punjab, controlled by the Punjab Unionist Party followed suit.[17] The British had continued its policy of divide and rule. As Alex von Tunzelmann commented, '[it] had worked exceptionally well. Both sides now hated each other even more than they hated the British'.[18] This steadily increasing state of affairs, and the latent danger it represented, was probably not apparent at the time to many observers in London.

In March 1942, with the surrender of Singapore, the war had arrived on India's doorstep. Wishing to buy greater Indian support for the war effort and at the same time placate anti-imperialist sentiment in both the United States and the Labour party, Churchill sent one of his ministers, Sir Stafford Cripps, to India with the offer of full Dominion status at the end of the war. This was famously dismissed by Mohandas Gandhi as 'a post-dated cheque drawn on a failing bank'.[19] Cripps's negotiations to accommodate Congress and the Muslim League led to both parties condemning the proposals as a sell-out to the other. His mission failed to achieve any agreement. Raised expectations in India were dashed. Congress immediately launched a 'Quit India' civil disobedience campaign which has been described as 'the most serious threat to British rule since the 1857 revolt'.[20] The British contained the threat, largely by brutal suppression of violent demonstrations and by jailing most of the Congress leaders and thousands of other activists around the country. But the need to do so further undermined British confidence in the long-term prospects of the Raj.

The most momentous event in India during the war, and the most damning indictment of British rule, was the famine which occurred in Bengal from late 1942 to 1944. Estimates of the number of deaths vary between two million and nearly five million out of a population of sixty million. The major cause of the famine was not so much a catastrophic failure of crop as a catastrophic failure of distribution, administration and management. The provincial governor blamed the Viceroy; the Viceroy blamed the provincial governor. It was only when Wavell took over as Viceroy in October 1943 that decisive action in Bengal took place. Wavell also made his case forcefully to London and in February 1944 enlisted

Ismay's support. Stressing that the famine crisis was far from over and the next year could see 'incalculable effects in loss of human life', Wavell urged Ismay to 'impress on the Prime Minister that this is a really serious matter, and is the whole keystone of the present situation in India... please do use your influence with the P.M. about this'.[21] Ismay replied, somewhat lamely,

> I have not been present at the meetings on the food situation in India, but I have seen all the telegrams between you and H.M.G [His Majesty's Government] on the subject. I get the strong impression that the inability of H.M.G. to give you anything like adequate help is not due to lack of sympathy but lack of resources. This is poor consolation for you, and I can imagine how anxious and vexed you are about it all. I wish I could help.[22]

It was not the answer that Wavell wanted and it begs a number of questions. Had Ismay attempted to lobby Churchill but did not want to tell Wavell that he had received a dusty response? Or did Ismay consider Wavell's request a low priority or not worth an argument with Churchill? If it was either of the latter, it would have been a failure of moral courage of which Ismay, on reflection, would not have been proud. By 13 June his view had changed, telling his friend Richard Casey who had just taken over as governor of Bengal, 'Personally, I feel that we <u>must</u>, if necessary, curtail military operations rather than have another famine'.[23] Or was this, one week after D-Day, merely telling the governor of Bengal what he wanted to hear?

With the election of a Labour government in July 1945 came the impetus for a rapid move towards British withdrawal from, and self-government in, India. In March 1946 Attlee sent a three-man Cabinet mission, again led by Cripps, to India to negotiate a way ahead. What became known as the Cabinet Mission Plan proposed a federal India, with considerable powers devolved to provinces and groups of provinces. Cripps gained Jinnah's support for the plan but Nehru prevaricated and then rejected it.

The year 1946 saw further outbreaks of unrest in India. There was a spate of strikes across the country and a number of 'mutinies' (albeit isolated) by Servicemen, some of them British, upset by the slow pace of demobilisation. In January 1946 members of the RAF in Karachi refused to obey orders and demanded to be sent home. Their action spread across India and into the Indian Navy. In February sailors at Bombay went on strike, some of them opening fire on troops sent to disarm them. In May naval mutineers in Karachi turned their ship's gun on an army barracks.[24] Later that month police in Bihar mutinied. All of this caused disquiet in India—and in London.

In August serious inter-communal violence erupted in Calcutta (Kolkata) in what became known as the Great Calcutta Killings. The official figure put the number of those murdered during the three days of mayhem at 4,000, with some estimates over double this figure. Estimates of those injured vary between 10,000 and 100,000. As shocking as the scale of casualties was the grotesque brutality involved. This was to become commonplace. The violence spread to other parts of India, with official figures of casualties in Bihar province well exceeding those in Calcutta. The violence also took on a new form. As Ian Talbot and Gurharpal Singh chillingly observed, 'The violence from August 1946 onwards differed from earlier episodes in that it contained dimensions of "ethnic cleansing"'.[25]

In early December Attlee summoned Wavell, Nehru and Jinnah to London for urgent consultation. Little agreement of any kind was reached and after three days of argument Nehru left abruptly to return to India. Wavell told the Cabinet that if the political parties in India could not reach agreement in the Constituent Assembly on a plan for the handover of power 'we should not be able to enforce British rule in India beyond 31st March 1948'.[26] He also presented Attlee with what he called his Breakdown Plan—which he privately referred to as Operation Madhouse—in the event of a complete breakdown of law and order. It envisaged 'the withdrawal of the British, province by province, beginning with women and children, then civilians then the army'.[27]

Attlee had been concerned for some time that Wavell was tired and due for replacement. What he had now heard from him confirmed in his mind that the time for this was fast approaching. By 18 December he had also come to the conclusion that the replacement should be Mountbatten, in many ways the very antithesis of Wavell. He did not, however, inform Wavell of his decision to remove him until 31 January.[28]

* * *

Following his meeting with Mountbatten on 19 December and Mountbatten's grateful acceptance of his offer to accompany him, Ismay—though now retired from the army—had much business to attend to. Sworn to secrecy, he may have had some difficulty in explaining his change of plans, such as the cancellation of his trip to Australia and New Zealand.

On 1 January 1947 his peerage was announced in the New Year's Honours List. Congratulations poured in. Amongst those he may have valued most were the continued tributes from Hankey—'nothing can adequately repay the debt your country owes you'[29]—and a touching note from Attlee's wife, Violet: 'At the breakfast table this morning Alison (the youngest) said, "Dear old Pug!"—neatly expressing the opinion of us all'.[30]

Ten days later he was the overnight guest of Churchill at Chartwell. He was there together with other members of the advisory group, Bill Deakin and Henry Pownall, to discuss Churchill's book, *The Second World War*. It is likely that Ismay will have taken Churchill into his confidence about his forthcoming appointment in India, and therefore this may have been the occasion to which he later referred in a letter to Mountbatten.

> Winston, when he first heard I was going, said: 'You are very foolish. You will get nothing out of this'. I was very angry, and replied: 'You don't imagine I have agreed to go in order to get something for myself. If I had been offered £100,000 and a step in the peerage as an inducement, I should have said, "Go to hell"'.[31]

On 14 January he was a guest of Lindemann, now Lord Cherwell, at a gaudy (college feast) at Oxford; and the following morning had a farewell audience with the King at Buckingham Palace.[32] On 5 February he was formally introduced to the House of Lords—his sponsors were Lord Chatfield and Lord Tedder—where he sat as a crossbencher (not aligned to any political party). Prior to departure for India, he was also frequently consulted by Mountbatten, who had yet to give his formal acceptance to Attlee of the appointment of Viceroy. Mountbatten was shrewd enough to stipulate conditions for doing so and sought Ismay's opinion on the subject. One of these was the offer by Cripps to accompany Mountbatten to India—an offer most unwelcome to Mountbatten and one that he needed little encouragement to reject. More substantial was Ismay's advice that Mountbatten's terms of reference should include a commitment to keep India within the Commonwealth. This was a subject on which Ismay felt strongly. In August the previous year he had told the Chiefs of Staff that he thought that 'neither [the Prime Minister] nor the Cabinet were fully aware of what the likely repercussions were from the military point of view if India chose to stand out from the Commonwealth'.[33] The Chiefs had agreed—and Ismay had written on their behalf to Attlee—that 'it was as nearly vital as anything could be that India remained within the Commonwealth', direction which the Defence Committee had repeated to the India Office.[34] Mountbatten's terms of reference were duly amended to include the point.[35]

Ismay also felt strongly about the need for full compensation for members of the Indian Civil Service who would be losing their jobs. Dispute over who would foot the bill for this threatened to leave the civil servants involved with much reduced compensation. Ismay persuaded Mountbatten to take up their cause. In his memoirs Ismay recalled with obvious satisfaction that that his recommendations were approved, 'lock, stock and barrel'.[36] His draft memoirs included the added comment, 'If any other decision had been recorded, I would have had to withdraw my offer to go to India and I am fairly sure that Mountbatten would have done the same'.[37] According to Wingate, it was Ismay making this clear to Bridges that swayed the Cabinet decision in favour of full compensation.[38]

Mountbatten also consulted Ismay on the extent of the powers which he should seek from Attlee. According to Mountbatten this included the 'plenipotentiary powers' which he liked to claim he had been given. The phrase does not appear in any of the contemporary documents, and Mountbatten may have been exaggerating somewhat. When, many years later, he was questioned on the absence of any evidence of such powers Mountbatten responded, '[i]t is quite true that I only mentioned this to Pug Ismay and he strongly advised that I should not mention it to anybody else at all'. Ismay was no longer alive to corroborate or dispute the assertion. As Mountbatten's biographer Philip Ziegler points out, Mountbatten may have had wider discretion to act than previous Viceroys but he never exercised his powers without referral back to London.[39]

A further subject of consultation was the personal staff that Mountbatten wished to accompany him. Some were officers who had been with him in the Far East. Others were known to Ismay, notably Sir Eric Miéville who had served alongside him as private secretary to Viceroy Willingdon. Throughout the war Miéville had been assistant private secretary to King George. As such he would have been known to Mountbatten, but Ismay would certainly have been a strong supporter of his, given his experience. Lastly, Cripps had advised that Wavell's private secretary, George Abell, had alienated Nehru and should be replaced. Having made enquiries Ismay considered that this interference was unwarranted and advised Mountbatten accordingly. Abell was retained and proved to be a key player.[40]

There is no evidence, however, of Ismay's input, if any, to Mountbatten's most significant (and successful) demand of Attlee: that a firm date should be established by which time Britain would have transferred power, and that that date should be 1 June 1948. But it is highly unlikely that Mountbatten would not have discussed this with him, or at least mentioned it to him. And in his memoirs Ismay wrote that 'before I left England I [thought that] fifteen months was far too short a time in which to complete arrangements for the transfer of power'.[41] This may therefore have been an issue on which the two men agreed to differ.

In February and March Ismay contributed to a number of policy meetings in Whitehall on the subject of India. On 11 February he accompanied Mountbatten to Downing Street to discuss with Attlee Mountbatten's letter of appointment and the draft announcement of it. Sufficient agreement was reached for Mountbatten to formally accept his appointment and for a statement announcing it and Ismay's appointment to be published the following week. On 11 March at a meeting at the India Office he argued forcibly (and successfully) against an attempt to water down the commitment to keep India within the Commonwealth. Two days later, together with Mountbatten and Miéville, he attended a meeting of the Cabinet's India Committee, chaired by Attlee, which agreed amongst other things to the inclusion in Mountbatten's directive of the goal of Commonwealth membership for India.[42] Lastly, on 18 March, the eve of departure, he accompanied Mountbatten to a meeting of ministers and the Chiefs of Staff to discuss the Chiefs' concern about defence arrangements after the transfer of power. He warned the meeting that if in six months' time it became apparent that power could not be handed over to a unified India, the armed forces would need to be divided, and that it would be difficult to prevent word of this from getting out.[43] It pointed towards what was about to become a key issue.

Given Ismay's previous service and upbringing in India many of those attending meetings with him in Whitehall may have bowed to his experience and knowledge of the country. Not all did so. He was with Mountbatten at a meeting with a brilliant scientist—he would receive the Nobel Prize for Physics the following year—who had just returned from a visit to Delhi. Patrick Blackett had met Nehru several months previously in London, was already something of a confidant of his, and spent much time with him during his visit. Blackett considered that Ismay was a Colonel Blimp,[44] reporting to his friend Cripps on 11 March that at the meeting Ismay had 'produced more Blimpisms than I have heard from anyone for ages. He did not seem to me to have a clue as to the real situation in India'.[45] It is easy to dismiss Blackett's comments on the grounds of his limited experience of India, the limited breadth of his contacts there and the fact that he and Ismay had little if anything in common; but at least Blackett's first-hand experience of India was fresh, and some fourteen years fresher than was Ismay's.

All of these various meetings, and the preparation for them, had left little opportunity for Ismay to spend time and relax with his family. For them it was a situation with which they had become familiar. Darry and the three daughters—Susan, now aged twenty-four; Sarah, eighteen; and Mary, seventeen—may have been expecting at last to see him at home at Wormington. But it was not to be. Sarah and Susan elected to join their father in New Delhi once he had settled in. Darry would join them later in the year if the situation allowed.

Ismay left London for India on 19 March together with Miéville and his aide-de-camp, John Lascelles, the son of Ismay's friend Sir Alan Lascelles, and arrived in Delhi via Cairo and Karachi three days later. At the airport to greet him was his old friend Claude Auchinleck, CinC of the Indian Army. Just how out of touch Ismay had become with changing attitudes since he last lived in India is illustrated by his anecdote of the meeting.

> We arrived at Delhi in the boiling heat of an Indian afternoon… I was astonished to see he was wearing a beret. Having been brought up in the belief that anyone who failed to wear a pith helmet while the Indian sun was still in the sky was a lunatic. I blurted out, 'Have you gone mad, Claude? Where is your topee?' He replied that, on the contrary, we had all been mad for a hundred years or more to wear such an uncomfortable and un-necessary form of head-gear.[46]

Ismay and Miéville drove to the villa they were to share, situated in the grounds of Viceroy's House. There Ismay found many of the domestic staff who had been with him fourteen years previously. But there was also to be a reunion which tells us much about Ismay's character and values, and about what India meant to him.

> In addition to the house staff, I found Pensioner Abdul Rahman Khan, who had joined the 21st Cavalry as a recruit about the same time as I had done. He had been my orderly on and off for about a quarter of a century, and for some years I had been paying him a small monthly allowance to supplement his meagre pension. Just before leaving home, my Bank Manager told me that Abdul Rahman Khan had not drawn his money for the last two months, and I feared that he was ill or even

dead. But his explanation was simple. He had heard on the radio several weeks previously that I was coming out to India, but no date had been mentioned. He had therefore taken a train for Delhi the next day, in order to make sure of being on the spot when I arrived; and he had been there ever since.[47]

Later the same day Mountbatten and his wife, Edwina, arrived. Typical of Mountbatten's work ethic, he spent the evening in conferences which went on till midnight. The first subject was an update on the security situation. In the preceding three weeks there had been prolonged inter-communal violence in the Punjab. Estimates put the number of those killed at between 7,000 and 8,000; about 40,000 people, mainly Sikhs, had fled their homes. In the past week serious inter-communal violence had returned to the streets of Calcutta with pitched battles between Hindu and Muslim gangs. Communal tensions in Bihar and in Delhi itself were escalating. Mountbatten and Ismay were coming face to face with the chilling prospect of a widespread, immediate breakdown of law and order. As Ismay told Darry in a letter just three days later, 'The situation is everywhere electric, and I get the feeling that the mine may go up at any moment... There is very little anti-British feeling, but the inter-communal hatred is a devouring flame'.[48]

Having believed before he left England that fifteen months was far too short a time for the transfer of power, it was less than three weeks before he was convinced that, 'far from being too short, it was too long'.[49] He recalled an event which stimulated this change of mind. He attended a dinner party at which a Congress minister was sitting on his right and a Muslim League minister on his left. 'Throughout the meal both of these cultured men, who normally had impeccable manners, spoke to me unceasingly and in loud voices about the iniquities of the opposing community'. It contributed to 'the realisation that communal bitterness had grown to incredible proportions since I was last in India'.[50]

Mountbatten's energy knew few bounds and he immediately started a frenetic daily schedule of consultations and meetings from early in the morning to late at night. Central to the management of business at Viceroy's House were the Viceroy's daily staff meetings. The staff concerned were an inner circle of his closest staff members. Along with Ismay (now titled Chief of the Viceroy's Staff), the core members of this group were Miéville (Principal Secretary), Abell (Private Secretary), Captain Ronnie Brockman, Royal Navy (Personal Secretary), Alan Campbell-

Johnson (Press Attaché) and Lieutenant Colonel Vernon Erskine Crum (Conference Secretary)—the latter three, talented young staff officers who had served Mountbatten in Headquarters South East Asia Command. The group met each morning with Mountbatten to review events of the past twenty-four hours, look ahead to forthcoming events and consider future policy. In pursuit of the latter, Mountbatten very much used the group as a sounding board for ideas.[51] In the words of John Christie, a staff member and occasional attender, 'Ideas popped out of His Excellency's head like rabbits out of a warren, and it was the duty of his staff to catch them, and return the wilder ones to their holes before they had run too far'.[52] Having been Churchill's chief staff officer Ismay was not totally unfamiliar with the situation, and it was to him that the group often turned when the most intractable problems presented themselves.

In the week after their arrival, Calcutta had descended even further towards anarchy, rioting in Bombay resulted in gun battles between police and rioters, and in Bihar the police mutinied. It quickly became clear that they needed to stem the tide of violence. The analogy that came to Ismay's mind was that,

> we are on a ship which contains a large quantity of highly inflammable, highly explosive and highly destructive material. The ship is on fire, but the fire has not reached the magazines. We MUST put the fire out very soon, or at least check it. Thereafter we have to get up steam and sail the ship to port—a British port if possible.[53]

He was also clear that speed of decision was the prerequisite. He wrote to Darry on 28 March, 'If we do not make up our minds on what we are going to do within the next two months or so, there will be pandemonium. If we do, there may be pandemonium'.[54] Mountbatten, too, recognised the need for swift action. Three days later he reported to Attlee, 'The whole country is in a most unsettled state… the only conclusion that I have been able to come to is that unless I act quickly I may well find the real beginning of a civil war on my hands'.[55]

On 31 March, just a week after his arrival in India, Ismay paid a three-day visit to the Punjab and North-West Frontier Province to see the situation for himself and confer with the governors, Sir Evan Jenkins and Sir Olaf Caroe. He was under no illusions about the seriousness of the situation that he found there. He wrote to Darry from Government House, Peshawar, on 2 April,

Both the Punjab and this N.W.F.P. are in turmoil, and on the verge of civil war. The former is the worse for the moment; but if things go wrong here, really wrong, the tribes will come down, and then the fat will be properly in the fire... [In Punjab] I had about four hours talk with the Governor (Jenkins)... I left Lahore at crack of dawn and was here by 10.30 a.m. It is now 5 p.m. and I've been in conference with the governor (Caroe) all the time except for a break for lunch.

The situation in both provinces is about as hectic as it can be; and in the existing state of emotionalism, it is very difficult to see what should be done. There is <u>no</u> good answer to either problem; so the only thing to do is to find the answer that is least bad.

At the end of the letter Ismay added a rare insight into his inner feelings, 'I am terribly homesick at times, darling, and I miss you dreadfully. I long for your letters and news'.[56]

On his return to Delhi, Ismay held separate meetings with Gandhi, Nehru and Jinnah partly to establish relations with them, but specifically to sound them out—as had Mountbatten—about future policy. Gandhi he described to Darry as 'very old and at times he really doesn't make much sense, but his influence is still immense'. Nehru struck him as 'very tired mentally and physically and... subject to "emotion" to an alarming degree. But he has courage and statesmanship of a sort'.[57] His longest meeting was with Jinnah, reporting to the staff meeting the following morning with obvious distaste that 'the dominating feature in Mr Jinnah's mental structure was his loathing and contempt of the Hindus. He apparently thought that all Hindus were sub-human creatures with whom it was impossible for the Muslims to live'.[58] Mountbatten was equally disparaging, describing Jinnah as 'a psychopathic case'.[59] The meetings did little to clarify viable ways ahead.

It was not just the bitterness of inter-communal relations that lay behind Ismay's doubts that the Raj could function effectively for much longer. To him its approaching demise was becoming its own undoing, and in two areas in particular. First, he quickly 'got the impression that the whole administrative machine was running down'. A high number of British officials in the Indian Civil Service had already returned home.[60]

The few... still in service were at the end of their tether. They had been subjected to unceasing calumny. Everything that went wrong was ascribed to their incompetence, sloth or wickedness... They had not had much support from England and they had no guarantee about their future... they had received no refreshment by new recruitment since the outbreak of the war, were now a mere handful, and there were not nearly enough Indian Civil Servants of sufficient experience and responsibility to fill the gaps.[61]

Secondly, the approaching transfer of power was seriously undermining the integrity of the police force and its ability to deal with the inter-communal violence.

> In the past there had been a splendid police force to deal with disturbance of this kind, but they had ceased to be reliable from the moment that our impending departure from India had been announced. Until then, the Indian policeman had seldom hesitated to act against his co-religionists. He knew that if he did his duty, he would be supported by higher authority, and that if he failed to do so he would get into trouble. But soon the British would no longer have the power either to reward or punish; and it was only natural that the policeman should not be willing to compromise himself with his new masters.[62]

Ismay cited a further major reason for the need for action. The Interim Government of India, set up by the British in September 1946 to assist the transition to independence, consisted of nine members from the Congress Party and five from the Muslim League. They could agree on little. In early April 1947 Nehru declared that the Muslim members should be dismissed on the grounds that they were making effective government impossible. He threatened that if they were not dismissed, he and all his Congress colleagues would resign. He knew that this would be unacceptable to the Viceroy. As Ismay commented, 'He was not bluffing. There was no need to bluff. They held all the aces'.[63]

All of this contributed to his radically changed view about the period of fifteen months in which to complete arrangements for the transfer of power. And it underlined the urgency for decisions and action. As he told Darry on 6 April,

> [w]e are still running around like squirrels in a cage and certainly nowhere nearer a solution than when we arrived. But of one thing I am clear and that is that the decision must be taken within the next six weeks. Every moment that is delayed means a further drift apart, and the greater possibility of a general conflagration.[64]

One of the many things that stood in the way of a speedy solution was the question of the future of the Indian Army. As soon as his appointment was announced, Ismay knew that Auchinleck might feel that his own position as the Viceroy's military adviser was about to be compromised: Mountbatten was bringing a general with him as an adviser, even if that general was an old friend of his. Ismay was right. Auchinleck's adjutant general, Lieutenant General Sir Reginald Savory, noted in his diary on 2 March, 'Saw Chief. In bad humour, due I think to an announcement in "The Statesman" this morning that Ismay is coming as military adviser to Mountbatten. The Auk said, "You and I, Reg, are rapidly being put into an impossible position"'.[65] Ismay had written to reassure Auchineck on 20 February (the letter had clearly not arrived by 2 March), 'I am not going to be his military adviser in any sense of the word... I will not trespass on your preserves'.[66]

On arrival Ismay had renewed his friendship with Auchinleck but they had differences of opinion. On his second evening in Delhi he went to Auchinleck's house and had a long conversation with him. 'He was a little depressed and more than a little depressing', Ismay told Darry. 'I do not at present see eye to eye with him on the wider strategic issues. I hope to convert him.'[67] But whereas Auchinleck and Ismay could disagree amicably, this was not the case between Auchinleck and Mountbatten. They had clashed previously when Mountbatten was Supreme Allied Commander South East Asia. Thus, Ismay was again required to be 'the man with the oil can'. Within a week of Mountbatten's arrival, Auchinleck had told him that 'it would take from five to ten years satisfactorily to divide the Indian army'.[68] This was not what the Viceroy wanted to hear. But when he arrived in India, Mountbatten knew little about the Indian Army. For example, it required Ismay to point out to him a very basic fact: that 'there was not in the Indian Army a single wholly Muslim unit, whereas there were numbers of units which consisted wholly of personnel of other communities'.[69] Mountbatten, however, was already looking to divide the Indian armed forces on communal lines, and recalling previous differences of opinion with Auchinleck found him 'more difficult to deal with than I can remember at any time since October 1943'.[70]

The plan for the transfer of power was produced in a rush by an overworked staff. On 8 April Ismay later started drafting it with the aim of submitting an outline for the conference of provincial governors just one week later. He proposed to Mountbatten the target date for the completion of firm proposals as the week of 8–15 May when, he suggested, the Viceroy should take the plan to London for approval. Mountbatten's response was that 'these dates appeared highly optimistic to him'.[71] Mountbatten's ideas were still evolving. His two most favoured alternatives were what he called Plan Union—essentially similar to Cripps' Cabinet Mission Plan—and Plan Balkan, which accepted a partition, leaving to each province and by implication each Princely State the choice of its own future.[72] This was generous to the Princely States and would prove highly contentious, but Ismay was in general an admirer of them and of their contribution to the war effort. He respected both their constitutional position and the pledge that Queen Victoria had made to them in 1858. He also knew a number of the princes personally: he had met them during his time with Lord Willingdon, had shot duck with the Maharajah of Nawanagar in 1933 and played polo at Cheltenham with the Maharajah of Kashmir in 1935.[73]

Bearing in mind that the Cabinet Mission Plan with its offer of Dominion status had previously been roundly rejected, Mountbatten now asked Ismay to develop Plan Balkan. With the help of Vappala Pangunni ('VP') Menon, the senior Indian in the Indian Civil Service and Reforms Commissioner on the Viceroy's staff, he produced a completed draft which he handed to Mountbatten on 14 April. Mountbatten approved it and—not wishing to leave India at such a critical time—asked Ismay to go to London on his behalf to present the proposals to the Cabinet. The Viceroy gave the governors' conference a summary of the plan, describing it as 'one of the plans under consideration' although he unwisely continued to refer to it as 'Plan Balkan' despite acknowledging that 'the "Balkanisation of India... [went] against everything that Congress stood for'.[74] Thereafter, 'Balkan' was quietly dropped as the plan's title.

In the days after the conference Ismay and the staff continued to revise the plan. He also took the opportunity to meet with Jinnah and sound him out about the possible division of Bengal and the Punjab, both of which provinces had a narrow Muslim majority. Jinnah was stoical about the prospect, commenting 'Better a moth-eaten Pakistan than no Pakistan at all'.[75] To Ismay's immense frustration, however, Mountbatten kept changing his mind about the plan. On 24 April, Campbell-Johnson noted in his diary, 'We held long drafting meetings with Ismay today, hammering out the Plan',[76] The same day Ismay wrote to Darry,

> I myself am having a hard and very worrying time. We simply must make up our minds very soon about how we are going to transfer power in June '48; and then we've got to draft the announcement... and finally we have to prepare a plan of action to implement whatever policy we may be decided upon. We have made almost innumerable drafts under

all these head[ing]s, but it is impossible to get Dickie to go through them methodically. He's a grand chap in a thousand ways, but precision of thought is not his strong suit.[77]

The next day he delivered the final version to Mountbatten. His covering note contained a dire warning that the British authority in India was 'in the process of liquidation [and that] if we then stick to the last date and the last hour, we shall probably find the country in turmoil, and a measure of responsibility for this state of affairs will be attributed to H.M.G.' It went on to advocate transfer of power taking place 'earlier than 1948', although just how much earlier was left unsaid.[78] This was to become a critical judgement.

Ismay intended to brief both Jinnah and Nehru on the plan, but due to a bout of 'Delhi belly' this task was carried out by Miéville. He reported that although Jinnah 'did not react favourably' to the plan, neither did he reject it.[79] Nehru, he said was in general agreement with it.[80] Ismay left Delhi for London on 2 May. On arrival he went to brief the Cabinet's India and Burma Committee, chaired by Attlee. Ismay underlined the bitterness of communal feeling in India which had 'become an obsession with both Hindus and Moslems' but emphasised that both parties had acquiesced to the plan. He warned the committee that the plan had been leaked to the press and that the parties were now trying to stir up opposition to it: a decision should therefore be taken without delay. The committee agreed the plan subject to some minor amendments, mostly concerned with its presentation.[81] Including and approving these changes delayed the response to Delhi by four days, but on 10 May the revised plan was sent to the Viceroy, who was at Simla with a number of Indian political leaders, for his comments.

Not anticipating anything adverse, Ismay was on the point of packing his bags the following day when a telegram arrived that was to shock both him and the British Cabinet. Mountbatten reported that Nehru, to whom he had shown the revised plan, had objected strongly to it and repudiated his support for it. This, said Mountbatten, had come to him as 'a bombshell'; rapid redrafting, he said, would now take place.[82] It would need to. Without the support of Congress the plan was dead in the water. Miéville gave an indication of the sense of crisis at Simla when he telegraphed Ismay, 'We are naturally a bit rattled by Nehru's *volte face*'.[83] Ismay replied, 'So are we'.[84] Indeed, he was in some difficulty trying to explain to the government how this *volte-face* had come about. 'Bewildered and out of touch', he recommended to Attlee that either he return to India to be briefed or that Miéville should be sent to replace him or that Mountbatten himself should come to London.[85] Attlee, understandably irritated, chose the latter.

What Ismay did not appreciate at this stage was that 'Plan Balkan' and its presentation contained considerable flaws. One clue was in the name, which was still used by some as its title. It is not clear how thoroughly Miéville had briefed Nehru on the plan, but Nehru claimed that he had been shown only part of it. He said that he had been horrified when he subsequently read the whole document, recognising that, as he told Mountbatten, 'India was being Balkanised'—thus that India would become ungovernable.[86] Furthermore, Ismay had advised Mountbatten to make no mention of Dominionhood in the plan, since with Dominion status his own powers would become purely advisory with no control for example over the armed forces. Yet Nehru, previously an opponent of Dominionhood for India, now looked on the grant of Dominion status as a positive advantage since it was likely to bring forward the date of transfer of power—a key determinant for him. The argument for Dominionhood had been made to Ismay by VP Menon, who had disagreed with Plan Balkan despite assisting in its drafting.[87] But Ismay had already advised Mountbatten against the grant of Dominion status and was somewhat wary of Menon: from the outset he had not included him in the staff meeting group, having been advised by Abell that he was too close to senior Congress officials and therefore not to be trusted.[88] Although Menon may have been leaking information he had a major contribution to make to deliberations, as was shown when he was admitted to the group's membership from 10 May.

Summoned by Attlee, Mountbatten duly arrived in London on 19 May with a new version of the plan amended to meet Nehru's demands. For example, it now accepted the grant of Dominion status and that this should take place 'as soon as possible'. It also—critically—excluded the option for provinces or parts of provinces to remain independent, 'since this might encourage the princes to adopt a separatist policy'.[89] In general, Mountbatten was sympathetic to the princes but he did not allow his sympathy to get in the way of pragmatism. The Cabinet immediately approved this plan in its entirety. Mountbatten emphasised that the transfer of power should be brought forward to 'not later than the early autumn of 1947'.[90] Attlee did not demur. He declared that 'it was essential for practical reasons that the interim period between the announcement and the actual transfer of power on the basis of Dominion status should be reduced to the minimum'.[91] An important consideration was whether the Conservative opposition party would back or impede the necessary change of legislation, but it was ascertained that Churchill was prepared to back it. Ismay had met him at a dinner of The Other Club on 8 May and no doubt used the opportunity to brief him and gain his support.[92] At any rate, when Churchill received Mountbatten a fortnight later he agreed not to oppose the legislation when it was presented.

Following their final meeting with the India and Burma Committee on 28 May Ismay and Mountbatten hurried back to Delhi. 'A long flight with Mountbatten was an experience which I was careful not to repeat', wrote Ismay, '[t]he idea of a reasonable degree of comfort never entered his head. Speed was all that mattered'.[93] There was, however, much work to be done in a short space of time. Mountbatten had called a conference of the main political leaders for 2 and 3 June to present the plan to them and gain their support: no mean challenge. Ismay recalled, 'I woke up on 2 June feeling rather like I had done on the various D-Days during the war; but on this occasion I had less confidence in the result'.[94]

He was present later that morning when around the table with the Viceroy sat Nehru and Jinnah, each with two of their colleagues, and the Sikh leader Baldev Singh. The plan that was now handed out proposed amongst other things that by the end of the year British India would be divided into two Dominions within the British Commonwealth: India and Pakistan, the latter consisting of East and West Pakistan. The provinces of Punjab and Bengal would be partitioned between India and Pakistan. And a boundary commission would determine the exact dividing line between the Dominions. Over the next two days Mountbatten displayed all his notable presentational skills and succeeded in winning the support of those present, including their agreement to broadcast that support on the radio. To their considerable surprise he informed them that it was his intention that Partition would take place 'not later than 15th August 1947'.[95] Bearing in mind that he was something of a conjurer—indeed, a proud member of the conjurers' Magic Circle—it was like pulling a rabbit out of a hat.

Mountbatten later maintained that the 15 August date came to him by inspiration and that 'even my own staff was horrified and kept saying "It can't be done! It can't be done!"'[96] This begs the question as to whether Ismay was among their number or whether he readily agreed to it. Bearing in mind the scale of the task it would be a surprise if he acquiesced without some serious discussion. In his memoirs Ismay says that it was while Mountbatten was in London that 'he proposed that 15 August should be the appointed day for the transfer of power' and that '[t]he Cabinet agreed'.[97] It would appear that he was mistaken about this: there is no mention whatsoever of this significant proposal in the minutes of either the Cabinet or of its India and Burma Committee. In his memoirs he made only slight criticism of the decision, noting that it 'meant that there were just over ten weeks in which to create two entirely new administrative machines and divide all the assets and liabilities of the old India between the two Dominions'.[98] There is, however, no mention of discussion with Mountbatten over the date.

It is inconceivable that the Viceroy would have produced the paper announcing the date of partition without discussing it with his chief of staff and although there is no hard evidence of Ismay's reaction there is a possible indication of it contained in a letter to Darry written on 2 June: 'Dickie doesn't object to me speaking my mind, even when it is working directly opposite to his; so even a heated argument leaves no ill-will'.[99] It is possible therefore that Ismay may have argued for a postponement, even a short one of a few weeks, against a date which left such a short period for implementation. It is puzzling as to what else could have been the subject of the 'heated argument'. Yuvraj Krishan amongst others has concluded that the 15 August date was 'a bargain' that the Viceroy had struck with Nehru 'to secure India's accession to the British Commonwealth'. If so this may have been the decisive factor in any argument between Mountbatten and Ismay, although Mountbatten must have considered that he held a very weak hand not to hold out with Nehru for a date even a month later.[100] But the plan had been approved, and now the date had been fixed.

In summary, soon after their arrival on 22 March both Ismay and Mountbatten had recognised that the transfer of power was required well before June 1948 and that quick decisions were required to enable this to happen. Far from being a brake on Mountbatten, Ismay had been ahead of him in seeking quick decisions—arguably too quick—which would achieve the formulation of the plan and its approval, and a transfer date earlier than 1948. But having achieved it Mountbatten had pitched, with or without Ismay's advice, for a transfer date which as events were to show left insufficient time for the necessary preparation. It is easy to see this in retrospect, but it was not impossible to see it at the time. One constraint (self-imposed) on Mountbatten's judgement, and that of his staff, was the phenomenal work rate that he chose to follow. At the beginning of May, six weeks into the job, he told his daughter Patricia that his working day had been averaging seventeen hours and that 'I'm just about worn out'.[101] In that period alone, in addition to his other work, he had conducted no less than 133 interviews, almost all of them with political leaders.[102] He expected his staff to show the same dedication to their work, and Ismay led by example. At the age of sixty this was not conducive to good health. When he came to leave India he was to confess that 'six months with Lord Mountbatten had exhausted him more than six years with Winston Churchill'.[103] Perhaps the limit of Ismay's influence was that, as with Churchill, he could not change Mountbatten. But, as with Churchill, he could use his influence to make him more effective. Either way, the decision had been made. It was now time for implementation.

13

PARTITION—IMPLEMENTATION AND OUTCOME

JUNE–DECEMBER 1947

Following the announcement of the date for the transfer of power, Ismay had been speculating to Darry about when she might come out to India and when he would return. A lot depended, he told her, on whether Mountbatten became Governor General of both Dominions or just one. If it was the latter, 'he would not require—or be able to justify—a high powered staff like the present one; in which case I should be free at the end of August. Personally I should <u>love</u> this, but wouldn't like to go at any price, if it meant leaving the job half done'.[1] As always with Ismay, duty came first.

At this stage, duty must have seemed quite daunting to him. Many members of the Viceroy's staff doubted the practicality of the truncated timing.[2] The fact that they had not been in any way consulted would also have contributed to lower their morale. Ismay's task was to convince them that the task was challenging but achievable. He amused Campbell-Johnson by telling him that, 'every morning when I get up I say to myself "Patience and Proportion"'.[3] With echoes of General Vaughan at Quetta, it was of course a message to his staff. Ismay's first priority was to create a structure and mechanism which would manage the process and drive it forward. A key element of this was a steering committee although, predictably, Congress and Muslim League leaders could not agree on its composition or role. After much persuasion by Mountbatten and Ismay it was agreed at a meeting on 5 June. Also agreed at the meeting was that the Boundary Commission, which would decide on and delineate the boundaries between the two states, would report direct to the Viceroy. In addition both sides agreed that the armed forces of both Dominions would temporarily remain under central command of a Supreme Commander, initially Auchinleck, reporting to a Joint Defence Council chaired by the former Viceroy.

But perhaps the biggest challenge was effecting the reorganisation of the army into two separate entities by 15 August. Mountbatten had told Auchinleck on 3 June that the army must be divided before independence, 'a development that outraged many senior British officers'.[4] Ismay, too, felt strongly about the matter. In his memoirs he described the division of the army on ethnic lines as, 'the problem that caused many of us the greatest grief'.[5] Privately he went much further, calling it 'the biggest crime and the biggest headache'.[6] The statement reflects, of course, not only the practical difficulty involved but also Ismay's deep, sentimental attachment to the Indian Army and a belief that he owed his loyalty to it. This was more than just nostalgia. As Connell asserted, 'Auchinleck and the surviving cadre of British officers wanted to preserve that Army, not as an instrument of some devious policy of British imperialism, not as a museum piece, not even as an end in itself, but to hand it on, strong and unimpaired to their successors'.[7] Initially Ismay thought, optimistically, that both sides might have allowed the army to remain undivided, 'but Jinnah would have none of this', he recalled. 'I spent many weary hours impressing on him that an army was a single entity.'[8]

Where Ismay differed from Auchinleck, however, was that while his heart told him that it would be a crime to divide the thing of beauty that was the Indian Army, his head told him that political reality required its reorganisation on ethnic lines forthwith. That reality was brought home to him on 20 June at a meeting with Liaquat Ali Khan, General Secretary of the Muslim League. As Ismay reported to Mountbatten, 'I emphasised to him over and over again that unless there was to be chaos, the whole Army must be under a single central administration'. Liaquat, however, was unmoved and delivered an ultimatum. Either the army was divided, with Pakistan being given its own army on the spot and under its own control, or he and Jinnah would not take over the reins of government in Pakistan. Ismay concluded his report to Mountbatten, 'whatever the military position, political considerations demand that these movements should be put through as a matter of the greatest urgency'.[9] An additional concern was the perceived need to keep in place the British officers of the Indian Army. Auchinleck had written to Ismay on 11 June, 'I cannot stress too strongly my conviction that the success of any plan for the division of the Indian Armed Forces depends on the willing co-operation of the British officers now serving with them, the great majority of whom it will be essential to retain during the process of reconstruction'.[10] Here Ismay was at one with Auchinleck. But Mountbatten did not see this as a priority for action and just over half of those British officers opted out of service on 15 August.[11]

The pressure of work continued unabated, seven days a week, and in un-air-conditioned offices at a time of year when the government would normally have long since left the sweltering heat of Delhi for the relative cool of the summer capital at Simla.[12] Much of Ismay's time was spent in meetings, both with his own staff and with visitors and Indian politicians, either together with Mountbatten or separately. A procedure which he and Mountbatten often adopted was for Ismay to hold a meeting with visitors after Mountbatten and then compare notes.[13] What exactly happened in Mountbatten's meetings is hard to determine since the Viceroy kept a close hand on history by often holding his meetings without staff present, then giving his meetings secretary, Erskine Crum, a verbal résumé afterwards.[14] Ismay considered, probably rightly, that Nehru used emotional pressure on Mountbatten. He told Darry that Nehru 'flies into an ungovernable rage at the slightest provocation. He might easily resign and the effect of his doing so is quite unpredictable. Nevertheless... there are limits to "appeasement"'.[15] In the same letter he made several interesting observations of his boss: first, that Mountbatten was 'absolutely whacked and scarcely making any sense' when he left for a visit to Kashmir on 18 June, but that 'he comes again very quickly'; secondly, that 'I've never met anyone in my life who has greater need of firm wheel brakes'. He also spoke, tellingly, of the pressures on himself: '[e]ven in the worst days of the war I never felt the burden of responsibility weigh so heavily'.[16]

On return from Kashmir, Mountbatten hosted a visit by Montgomery, the CIGS. Ismay told Darry,

> Monty is here. He and Dickie together are a scream. They both concentrate on their own 'ego' and on their own personal views and achievements, and so discussion becomes a bit confused. Between them they have got the only problem that they've tackled into a real tangle and I must spend my morning unravelling it.[17]

In addition, as Ismay may have anticipated, Montgomery used the opportunity to disparage Auchinleck to Mountbatten—the antipathy between the two generals dating back to the Western Desert in 1942. Montgomery's latest intervention put further distance between the Viceroy and his CinC.

223

With India and Pakistan about to be granted Dominion status, Mountbatten assumed that he would be invited to be the first Governor General of both India and Pakistan. Nehru had made him the offer in May but by late June Jinnah had yet to do so. Ismay 'pressed him on several occasions, but he always stalled'.[18] Eventually, on 2 July, Jinnah told Mountbatten that he intended that he himself would be the Governor General of Pakistan. In his memoirs Ismay wrote, with some restraint, that 'This unexpected turn of events was a blow'.[19] At the time and in private he went a lot further, describing it as 'a bombshell [and] a terrible shock to us all'.[20] It certainly resulted in a blow to his morale and a rare bout of pessimism. That evening he confided to Joan Bright,

> How I long to get away from it all! But how glad I am that I came and had a go—even if it all ends in failure. The next three or four days are going to be <u>critical</u>. Even if we were dealing with people who had a glimmering of tolerance and fair play and administrative expertise the task would be Herculean. As it is, I wonder whether it can possibly be achieved.[21]

Mountbatten had serious doubts, encouraged by Edwina, about staying on as Governor General of just one of the Dominions. Ismay was convinced that he should do so and sought to persuade him accordingly. Still undecided, Mountbatten sent him back to London to obtain the government's advice and direction.

Accompanied by Miéville and two junior staff members, Christie and Campbell-Johnson, Ismay left Delhi on 5 July, arriving two days later. Campbell-Johnson noted with approval,

> Ismay had taken great pains over our itinerary, and so arranged that at our various landing points—Karachi, Habbaniya [Iraq], Malta—we landed in good time for dinner and left at a comfortable hour in the morning. He said the journey back to India with Mountbatten in May had been an ordeal he would never undergo again. In an effort to beat the clock, all they had succeeded in doing was playing havoc with everyone's digestion.[22]

In the series of meetings which followed, Ismay was supposed to be impartially seeking advice but, as he later admitted (though not in his memoirs), he 'put the case' for Mountbatten to accept the governor-generalship of India.[23] The first meeting was with the Prime Minister. 'After an hour's talk', Attlee was persuaded that Mountbatten should become Governor General of India, and the Cabinet came round to this view when it met later that evening.[24] The following day Ismay met a number of

Opposition leaders—Churchill was absent, sick—and received a similar response from them. Churchill's own endorsement would be important, so Ismay travelled down to Chartwell to discuss the matter with him. In his private account Ismay admitted 'anticipating difficulty' convincing him, 'but I was quite wrong. Winston had no doubt that Dickie must remain'. 'The symmetry at the summit does not matter', Churchill told him, 'What matters is that Dickie's guiding hand should be there during the difficult days ahead'.[25] Ismay, 'much relieved' according to Campbell-Johnson, returned to London to convey the message to Mountbatten.[26] That evening Ismay was at Buckingham Palace where the King 'at once made it clear to me that he also wished Dickie to stay'.[27] Thus, the matter was settled. Christie was full of admiration, writing in his diary, 'This was Ismay's day and it is worth recording his achievement... He was deadbeat at the end... but he had scored resounding successes all along the line & the whole day was a major victory'.[28]

Ismay left London on 19 July. He would have been well satisfied with the outcome of his various meetings but he was realistic about the overall situation, telling Campbell-Johnson on the plane back to India that 'he felt that we were "over Becher's Brook first time round", and no more than that'.[29] During the flight Ismay expanded on his unease about the future.

> I was worried when I was in England at the prevalence that everything was over bar the shouting. Personally I feel that we are nothing like out of the wood yet. There is much explosive material lying about and it remains to see whether it can be prevented from going off. I am, for example, extremely worried about the Sikhs. They imagine that they are going to get a far more favourable boundary than, so far as I judge, the Boundary Commission can possibly award them... it may be a very unpleasant business [in Kashmir]. The truth is that both sides are in a panic, and people do sillier things when they are frightened than they do under the stress of any other emotion. Then there is the North West Frontier... [30]

Ismay's concern about the North-West Frontier was not about internal, inter-communal violence but about the external threat—a concern that the Chiefs of Staff had expressed at a meeting which he had attended on 9 July. 'The position there is probably weaker than it has ever been', Ismay noted, '[i]f India had grasped the elementary fact that the North West Frontier is just as much their frontier as Pakistan's, I should be less disturbed. But as it is, I doubt that they will come to this way of thinking, except after bitter experience'.[31]

While Ismay had been away the security situation had again deteriorated. 'Calcutta had passed beyond gangster methods', recalled the GOC Eastern Command, Lieutenant General Sir Francis Tuker, '[i]t was in the grip of anarchy'.[32] Elsewhere tensions were increasing and violence escalating, particularly in the Punjab. Anticipating serious trouble there after the transfer of power, the Partition Council requested Auchinleck form a security force for the Punjab.[33] On 17 July the Council approved his proposal for what was to be called the Punjab Boundary Force: a mixed, composite formation that was largely British officered and based on the 4th Indian Division which would report direct to the Joint Defence Council. But this was very much last-minute planning: the commander, Major General Pete Rees, was given just nine days to get the Force operational.

On Ismay's return on 21 July he expressed reservations to Mountbatten about the Force's small size of around 15,000 men. His concerns were shared, not least by the Punjab governor Jenkins, and in mid-August Mountbatten agreed to a reinforcement of six extra battalions to increase the total strength (including headquarters and logisticians) to some 23,000.[34] This may have looked good on paper but, in the circumstances that were to arise, it was a totally inadequate force to keep the peace in an area the size of Ireland with a population of fourteen million people living in 18,000 villages and with a largely ineffective police force.[35] Available but excluded from the force were some 30,000 British troops based in India.

Having consulted Auchinleck, Mountbatten had recommended to London that British troops should not be used to intervene in inter-communal violence, largely on the grounds that they would seen as partisan—although 'in emergency, they might be used to save British, or even European lives'.[36] Following endorsement from London, Auchinleck issued an order which included authorisation for their deployment for the protection of British lives, but 'NOT... to protect Indian subjects'.[37] In forwarding the document to Mountbatten, Ismay did not demur: 'It is very hard to cater for all eventualities', he wrote, 'but these orders look as good as they can be'.[38] Also unused were some 35,000 Gurkhas. The inclusion of both British and Gurkha units would thus have more than doubled the size of the Punjab Boundary Force. The decision to exclude British and Gurkha troops gives substance to the judgement of historians like Yasmin Khan who contend that from the moment the Partition bill was rushed through Parliament, 'It is difficult to avoid the damning conclusion that, in the minds of British policy-makers, the duty to protect the lives of South Asians had already ended'.[39]

Ismay's absence had also seen the arrival of Sir Cyril Radcliffe, the man selected by the British government to head the Boundary Commission. Radcliffe was a London barrister whose main qualifications for the job were that he was willing to undertake it and that he was an uncontroversial figure, acceptable to all the main political parties in India. It was accepted that he had no knowledge whatsoever of the Indian sub-continent and, indeed, this was considered by some to be a positive advantage. He had arrived on 8 July, leaving him just five weeks to carry out his work and present his report defining the boundary between India and Pakistan. The other members of his commission were two Hindu and two Muslim judges, both of whom—unbeknown to Radcliffe but unsurprising to anyone who knew anything about India—were sharing the commission's secrets with their political leaders. In order to be seen to be impartial and uninfluenced by anyone, Radcliffe eschewed business or social contact and lived alone with his private secretary, Christopher Beaumont, in a bungalow in the grounds of Viceroy's House. Shortly after Ismay returned, however, he persuaded Radcliffe to break his purdah and come to dine, along with Beaumont and Christie.[40]

Ismay's own future had been the subject of much discussion during his absence. Looking beyond the transfer of power, Mountbatten had canvassed opinion separately from both Jinnah and Nehru about 'whether they thought any useful purpose would be served by keeping Lord Ismay on my staff'. Jinnah 'became excited and enthusiastic and said that [he] considered it absolutely essential that Lord Ismay should stay'.[41] Nehru 'warmly welcomed the suggestion'.[42] Since Mountbatten had been trying to persuade Ismay to remain and wanted more ammunition for further persuasion, it may be that his question was not as innocent as it sounded: Mountbatten likely anticipated their answers. Either way, it was a tribute to Ismay that both sides held him in such high regard.

As the date for transfer of power neared, tensions in and around Viceroy's House reached fever pitch. On 7 August an exasperated Ismay told Darry,

> The last 2 days have been pretty good Hell. Both Dickie and Edwina are dead tired and nervy. They can be right across each other. So that in addition to my other troubles, I have been doing peace-maker and general sedative, at the request of both of them. It's very wearing for them and for

me… I've had a long argument with Dickie about when I leave, but I have refused to budge from the position that I go at the end of the year unless it is obvious by November that I still have a real job of vital work to do.[43]

Two days later he wrote to Bright presciently, 'We are, I believe, on the verge of much bad trouble in the Punjab. There is certain to be fire, and there may easily be conflagration which will spread throughout India'.[44]

A significant contributor to the tension was the imminent submission of Radcliffe's report and his map which would show the boundary between India and Pakistan. The potential for outcry and large-scale violence following the publication of his findings was obvious. Mountbatten directed that the results of the report and the announcement would remain secret until 16 August—the day after the Independence Day ceremonies and celebrations—in order to avoid upsetting 'good Indo-British relations on the day of the transfer of power'.[45] He had also made it clear from the outset that he would in no way seek to influence Radcliffe's work.

The findings of the Radcliffe Report became, and remain, a highly controversial aspect of the partition of India. In 1948 serious accusations were made, which Mountbatten always denied, that he had after all used his influence to persuade Radcliffe to make a last-minute alteration to his report. There were also suggestions that Ismay had been complicit in this. The alteration related to the district of Ferozepur (Firozpur) in the Punjab. It had a Muslim-majority population and was strategically highly significant: not only was a major arsenal located there but the area contained the headworks of the waters on which large areas of lower-lying land were dependent. It was therefore highly coveted by the future leaders of both India and Pakistan. Radcliffe awarded the area to India. The accusations—made initially by the Pakistani government—were that in the first week in August Radcliffe had awarded Ferozepur to Pakistan in his draft report, but that pressure from Mountbatten caused him to reverse his decision.

It was alleged that in response to a request by the Punjab governor Sir Evan Jenkins for a provisional draft of Radcliffe's boundary map, George Abell had sent him one on 8 August with the comment, 'There will not be any great change from this boundary'.[46] The provisional draft had shown Ferozepur awarded to Pakistan. What caused Radcliffe to change his mind? Further indication came from Christie's diary entry for 9 August observing that Abell had told him, 'H[is] E[xcellency] is in a tired flap & is having to be strenuously dissuaded from asking Radcliffe to alter his award'.[47] For many years historians tended to dismiss the accusations.[48] But more direct evidence came in 1989 with an account by Christopher Beaumont. In it he stated that on 12 August Radcliffe was invited to lunch at Ismay's house but, unusually, told to come without his secretary. That same evening Jenkins was informed that Ferozepur would now be awarded to India. Beaumont believed that Nehru had told Mountbatten that 'to give Ferozepore [sic] to Pakistan would result in civil war between India and Pakistan' and that at the lunch Radcliffe had been 'without doubt persuaded by Ismay and Mountbatten' to make his amendment.[49]

In his book, *Eminent Churchillians*, Andrew Roberts provides a detailed account of the lengths to which Mountbatten subsequently went both to distance himself from Radcliffe's amendment and to influence Ismay's recollection of events surrounding it.[50] In letters to Ismay in 1948 Mountbatten admitted that they discussed details of the award at the 12 August lunch but not that any pressure was put on Radcliffe. In one of his letters (which, significantly, he asked Ismay to burn), Mountbatten wrote, 'I think I went as far as to say that provided he was really satisfied that the overall decision, both East and West, was absolutely fair to both communities, then I trusted that any generosity to Pakistan should be given more in Bengal than the Punjab since there was no Sikh problem in Bengal'. Ismay annotated the margin of this passage in ink, 'I do NOT remember this!', and in his reply told Mountbatten, '[m]y recollection of events is very different from yours'.[51]

In summary, though, it is clear that Ismay was present at the lunch, indeed that he facilitated the occasion, and to that extent was complicit in Mountbatten's subterfuge. It is also clear that Mountbatten (with or without Ismay's support) successfully persuaded Radcliffe to alter his award—although, in the opinion of Radcliffe's biographer, 'he could not have been persuaded against his better judgment'.[52] What is less clear is Mountbatten's motive for his intervention. If it was to ingratiate himself with the leaders of the country to which he was about to become Governor General he is rightly open to condemnation. But he is less easily censured if—as Ismay may have believed and as Beaumont has suggested—it was a genuine belief that in doing so he was averting civil war and was thus faced with a considerable moral dilemma.[53] Ismay never thereafter referred to the alleged alteration of Radcliffe's report. He never gave Mountbatten the slightest support in his efforts to distance himself from the subject, but neither did he ever contradict Mountbatten's account.[54]

In the days leading up to the transfer of power Ismay was involved in a further imbroglio, this time concerning the future of the Princely States. Nehru, determined that the States should be compelled to accede to one or other Dominion, had attempted to force Mountbatten's hand by threatening that he would 'encourage rebellion in all States that go against us'.[55] Mountbatten duly pressurised the Nizam of Hyderabad, telling him to accede or face ruin. The Nizam's constitutional adviser, the eminent London lawyer Sir Walter Monckton, accused Mountbatten of blackmail. In early August Mountbatten, undaunted, threatened to remove all British troops from Hyderabad. Ismay, together with Abell, intervened and succeeded in persuading the Viceroy to drop the idea. This did not prevent Monckton indulging in a bit of blackmail of his own, threatening Ismay on 10 August that he had already drafted letters, now in London, which would be despatched to leading members of the Conservative opposition party 'if improper pressure on Hyderabad was not relieved'.[56] By this time, however, according to Ziegler, Mountbatten had succeeded in persuading Nehru to postpone further negotiations for two months.

Right up to 15 August there was unsurprisingly no shortage of urgent matters to be addressed and last-minute decisions to be taken by Ismay and his staff. But on the eve of Independence Day his mind seems to have been elsewhere, perhaps as a form of escapism. Writing to Darry on 14 August he seemed more interested in the Jersey cattle herd back at Wormington, somewhat bizarrely asking for details of individual cows by name: for example, 'Erica—date of calving... Scarlet Penny—total milk to date... Elizabeth and Princess—date of last calf.'[57] This may have been pure escapism or perhaps he was already sickening, because in the early hours of the following morning he went down with dysentery. He was later to say that this came as a 'providential dispensation', sparing him the formalities and celebrations of Independence Day.[58]

In his memoirs Ismay says that immediately following Independence Day he had 'a deep foreboding about the immediate future'.[59] But in a letter to Darry just a week later he had told her, '[t]he 15th was a wonderful success... In fact, we've jolly nearly pulled off a miracle. If only the Punjab Boundary situation would settle down, we'd be very nearly home'.[60] His report is curiously detached from reality: already by this time there were major incidences of horrific violence, and not just in the Punjab.

On 25 August he left Delhi for Srinagar and a fortnight's recuperation in Kashmir, taking his elder daughter Susan with him. His mood was still optimistic—almost euphoric. He penned an effusive note to Mountbatten, now in Simla,

> I still can't believe you have pulled it off. It's the greatest personal triumph for you and Edwina of modern times… I confess that I had not much hope that you'd do the trick when I volunteered for the team; but I was absolutely positive that NO ONE ELSE IN THE WORLD could do it.[61]

Within five days his mood had darkened. On 30 August he wrote to Joan Bright,

> I'm going through a bad patch of homesickness. It's partly this foul dysentery—from which I have never completely recovered—and partly reaction after 15th August. Without detracting from the sheer miracle which Dickie performed, things are still very much touch and go out here. The Punjab situation is really bad, and the balloon may go up at any moment. Provided that the Indian army—or rather the two armies—continue to do their duty, all will come right in the end; but they are being subjected to an almost intolerable strain.[62]

One of the purposes of Ismay's visit to Srinagar was Mountbatten's wish that he persuade the ruler, Maharajah Hari Singh, to hold an immediate referendum as to whether his people wished to accede to India or Pakistan. 'But each time that I broached the question', recalled Ismay, 'the Maharajah changed the subject. Did I remember our polo match at Cheltenham in 1935? He had a colt which he thought might win the Indian Derby! Whenever I tried to talk serious business, he abruptly left me for another guest'.[63] Ismay was to reproach himself all his life for not having brought the Maharajah to a decision.[64] The consequences were to be tragic.

His stay in Kashmir was cut short. On 5 September he returned to Srinagar from a trip up-country to find the Viceroy's plane waiting to take him back to Delhi. Massacres were taking place in the Punjab. He was also given the news that his daughter Sarah and her fiancée Wentworth ('Wenty') Beaumont, one of the Viceroy's aides-de-camp, had personal experience of one closer to home. The train carrying them back from Simla stopped at a station about twenty miles from Delhi. Waiting there was a Hindu mob who proceeded to drag all the Muslim passengers from the train and butcher them. Beaumont hid his Muslim servant under the seat. When two Hindus entered and demanded to search the compartment, they were dissuaded by Beaumont's resolute refusal and by the sight of he and Sarah, both flourishing revolvers. The servant was the only Muslim on the train to reach Delhi alive.[65]

On Ismay's return he found:

> the situation already critical in the extreme and over the next five or six days it got progressively worse. Moslems were being systematically hunted down and killed. Thousands were herded into camps, where the conditions defied description... the dead lay rotting in the streets... the hospitals were choked with the dying and wounded... arson and looting were widespread.[66]

He was deeply shocked by the two camps he visited, describing them to Sir Terence Shone, the British High Commissioner, as 'Belsen without the gas chambers'.[67] At one of the camps—crowded with men, women and children—snipers in buildings overlooking the site 'were amusing themselves firing occasional shots into the midst of them'.[68] Ismay was also briefed about the continuing large-scale violence which had been taking place elsewhere: both in India and Pakistan, especially Calcutta and in the Punjab respectively. There the scale of violence had been so large and fierce that the Punjab Boundary Force was simply unable to cope. There had also been numerous instances of the breakdown of discipline in 'mixed' units. The Force had been disbanded the previous week. Ismay told Shone that British officers serving in the Indian forces were getting 'browned off' and that some, even senior ones, were handing in their resignation. He had it 'on good authority' that the same was also happening in Pakistan.[69] A major humanitarian catastrophe was unfolding with widespread slaughter and panic resulting in mass refugee movement.

Paucity of information was a major challenge, as Ismay told Sir George Cunningham, Governor of the North-West Frontier Province. 'The information that we get about the situation in the Punjab is so scanty, so distorted and generally so late that it is impossible to say what is likely to happen.'[70] Ismay, probably rightly, attributed the breakdown of the intelligence system to the fact that many experienced British intelligence officers had left India at the time of the transfer of power.[71] At one point, Ismay overflew the Sikh and Muslim refugee columns in the Punjab—'a spectacle that I can only describe as appalling'—noting the difference between the Sikh and Muslim columns moving in opposite directions. The Sikhs appeared well organised, seemingly with 'all their goods and chattels with them—bullock carts, ponies, cattle, sheep, household effects... The Moslem refugees were a very sorry contrast. They seemed to have little or nothing with them in the way of property, and they just struggled sorrowfully along the road like a lot of tired ants'.[72]

Ismay devoted much time to meeting with Indian and Pakistan leaders to persuade them to show leadership and defuse the situation. Having met with Nehru in Delhi he flew to Karachi on 12 September and over a period of three days spent a total of eleven hours in discussion with Jinnah 'to persuade [him] that the Government here were doing their damnedest to cope with the disorder and to look after the Moslems, and to explain the avalanche that has swept over Delhi and rendered their task almost superhuman'.[73] He told him that Nehru was making huge personal efforts to stem the violence and had seen him 'charge into a rioting Hindu mob and slap the faces of the ringleaders… [with] no thought whatsoever for his personal safety'.[74] Ismay felt that he had at least 'done something towards convincing Jinnah of the true state of affairs'.[75]

Ismay was increasingly despondent. On 12 September he had told Darry, 'there is a possibility and more than possibility that orderly government may collapse, and that we may have to return home with all our work destroyed, and leaving behind anarchy and misery and meaningless slaughter'.[76] Four days later he was even more dejected, writing, 'our mission was so very nearly a success; it is sad that it has ended up such a grim and total failure'.[77] On 20 September he confided to Joan Bright,

> In your last you said that I was having a bloody time. You are right, dear. It is just as hectic, twice as anxious and far more heartbreaking than anything during the last war. The mortal hate and bitterness and the suffering will endure for a generation at least; but we are hanging on like grim death to prevent the whole country sliding into chaos and anarchy.[78]

Ismay also concluded that there was now only a limited contribution that he, himself, could make. With Partition, his job had changed fundamentally. Having been chief of staff to the Viceroy, whose executive responsibility and authority extended across the whole of the Raj, he was now chief of staff to the Governor General of just one its two successor Dominions, with almost no executive responsibility or authority. There was no longer a role for most of the additional staff that Mountbatten had brought with him—indeed, two of the senior members, Miéville and Abell, had already departed. Ismay had told Mountbatten that he would be leaving in November unless it was clear that he had a proper job of work to do, and it was becoming increasingly clear to him that he did not. He had a further, more fundamental reason to wish to leave. Since childhood he had spent his life wedded to the basic principle of impartiality in Indian affairs. Unlike Mountbatten he was now distinctly uncomfortable in a role that challenged that principle. In mid-September he explained this to Mountbatten in the letter tendering his resignation,

> Having regard to my background and my lifelong friendship with Indians of all creeds and classes, I could not possibly regard myself as owing allegiance to one side rather than the other, I always have been, and I shall always continue to be strictly impartial. There is, of course no need for me to advertise my impartiality, but I would not be prepared to take any steps to conceal it. On that fundamental point I could not yield an inch.[79]

He went on to point out that since Mountbatten considered that, as Governor General, he felt allegiance to India, 'we have thus reached the hopelessly anomalous position of having a Governor General who must think and act in one way, and a Principal Adviser who thinks and acts in another'. He therefore asked Mountbatten to release him 'as soon as you possibly can' but qualified this, typically, 'I should not dream of quitting in the middle of a "battle", unless you wished me to, but it looks to me either the position will soon become one of uneasy equilibrium, or that it will go completely wrong'. The date he suggested was 'about 15 October'. Mountbatten's reply is unrecorded but judging by subsequent correspondence, he accepted Ismay's request in principle although deferring any decision about a specific date.

A case of the uneasy equilibrium, if not of things going completely wrong, came within a few days with Nehru's insistence that Auchinleck should be dismissed and the Supreme Headquarters disbanded. For some time Nehru had considered—or so he said—that Auchinleck was biased, demanding that he be sacked immediately. Predictably, Jinnah also now accused Auchinleck of bias. Montgomery had already given his unsolicited opinion to the Viceroy: '[i]t is my view that Auchinleck's usefulness in India is finished'.[80] Mountbatten, who had in any case lost patience with his CinC, acquiesced to all this pressure and wrote to Auchinleck on 26 September, enclosing a draft letter of resignation for him to sign.[81] At first Ismay was 'very unhappy' about this, but eventually came round to accepting it. He wrote a long letter of commiseration to Auchinleck, suggesting that Mountbatten's proposal was probably the least worst option, but expressing his own deep sense of frustration. 'I feel as strongly as I have ever felt anything in my life', he wrote, 'that you in a big way, and

I in a much smaller way, are now in a completely impossible position, by reason of our lack of power'. He concluded, 'If you decide to go, let's go together. I haven't yet tied Dickie down to a definite date'.[82] Auchinleck agreed to leave at the end of November. Although their departure was not coordinated, Ismay was to leave on almost exactly the same date.

For Ismay the crisis management during September had been particularly challenging and exhausting. 'Personally, I cannot remember having been harder worked or more worried at any time of the war', he told Cunningham on 30 September.[83] Some of this pressure, though, resulted from Ismay's inability to say 'No' to Churchill. Extraordinarily at this time, Churchill had been sending drafts of his memoirs, asking for Ismay's comments. Even more extraordinarily Ismay had obliged.[84]

At the end of September, with the chaotic scenes continuing in both India and Pakistan (covered with varying degrees of accuracy in the British press) and much speculation about the future, Mountbatten considered that the British government should be briefed at first hand and asked Ismay to do so on his behalf. To ensure that he would be completely up to date, Ismay met with Nehru on 2 October (the day before he departed) and flew via Karachi for discussions with Jinnah lasting two hours. On arrival in London on 6 October he went straight to Downing Street for a private meeting with Attlee. After delivering his report, Attlee asked him 'whether we had taken the wrong course or rushed things'. Ismay replied that he felt quite sure in his own mind that 'we had no option left but to do what we had done, and that as for rushing things too much, we would probably have been in a worse mess than we are now if we had delayed matters, with the essential difference that we would be responsible for clearing up the mess without any means of doing so'.[85] That evening he dined alone with Churchill who, he told Mountbatten, was 'very tired but not too critical'.[86]

On 8 October Ismay briefed the Chiefs of Staff Committee. His report was candid and unvarnished, telling them that 'the hatred and revenge would not die down for a generation or more', and that 'the best that could be hoped for on a short term view was an uneasy truce, which would almost certainly be disturbed by isolated incidents, riots due to famine and, above all, guerrilla warfare on the Punjab boundary'.[87] General Savory, who was present, thought that Ismay was not in very good form: 'he did not speak with much conviction or confidence this afternoon and seemed depressed this morning. I think he must have had a rough passage with Winston last night'.[88] Savory may not have been very wide of the mark.

Despite what Ismay had told Mountbatten, Churchill would probably have been highly critical of the whole partition business and Mountbatten in particular. Ismay would also have been irritated at the Chiefs' meeting, as was Savory, by Montgomery being 'unnecessarily rude about the Auk' and 'clearly delighted' that Mountbatten was removing him.[89] Ismay also shared with Savory—as he may have done with Churchill—his view that Mountbatten was no longer being impartial 'and felt that he [Mountbatten] had to back India as their Governor General', whereas his own role was to be impartial. Savory concluded that, '[a]ll does not appear to be plain sailing between Mountbatten and Ismay'.[90]

Ismay seems to have been in no hurry to return to Delhi, remaining in England for a further fortnight. He left London on 25 October in a mood of some optimism: 'there was reason to hope that the storm might have spent itself and that the two Dominions would soon settle down together, at least in guarded neutrality if not in brotherly love'.[91] His hope would not last long. In the three days that he took to reach Delhi a major crisis erupted in the Princely State of Kashmir. An armed mob about 5,000 strong crossed the border from Pakistan heading for the capital Srinagar, slaughtering Hindus as they went. The Maharajah declared the accession of Kashmir to India and fled the capital. When Ismay arrived back in Delhi at 1.30 a.m. on 28 October he was handed the latest news, including the telegram from Nehru to Attlee informing him that Indian troops had been flown to Kashmir. The potential for this escalating into full-scale war was obvious. 'I was absolutely horrified', recalled Ismay, 'and got on to the telephone at once to Dickie'. Ismay was forthright, telling Mountbatten bluntly that, 'it seemed to me that he and the Government of India had now put the cat amongst the pigeons', adding that, 'world opinion would judge them very harshly'. Mountbatten, he recalled, 'was very distressed and wanted to come round at once'.[92] Ismay, however, told him that since it was now past 2 a.m. they should meet at eight o'clock in the morning.

From that meeting onwards, managing the Kashmiri crisis was to be the focus—almost the single focus—of Ismay's attention for the whole of his remaining month in India. Together with Mountbatten he met with Nehru and accepted an invitation from Jinnah for the three of them to fly to Lahore for a meeting on 1 November. However, the night prior to their departure Nehru—under pressure from his Cabinet not to attend—cried off pleading illness, so Mountbatten and Ismay went without him to meet Jinnah. 'We had a 3½ hour meeting with him', Ismay told Darry, 'but did not get very far. It is a fantastic and maddening situation'.[93] Jinnah

1. Ismay (standing, right) with his parents and family in India, 1900.

2. Ismay on his favourite horse, 'Drummer Boy', 1909.

3. The officers of the 21st Cavalry, Jhelum, Punjab, 1912 (Ismay standing, centre).

4. Somaliland desert.

5. Somaliland Camel Corps.

6. Ismay (front row, left) with Lt Col Cubitt (rear row, left) and other officers,
near Shimber Berris, 1915.

7. 'A feeling of being trapped in a sideshow…', Somaliland, 1915.

8. Ismay's team, winners of the Cheltenham polo tournament, 1934.

9. Portrait by Anthony Devas, 1938.

10. Ismay (right) crossing Whitehall with Air Chief Marshal Sir Cyril Newall and General Sir John Dill, May 1940.

11. Ismay with the Defence Committee, 1941. Seated, left to right: Beaverbrook, Attlee, Churchill, Eden, Alexander; standing, left to right: Portal, Pound, Sinclair, Margesson, Dill, Ismay, Hollis.

12. A worried man. Ismay, February 1942—three days before the fall of Singapore.

13. Portrait by Oswald Birley, 1943.

14. Ismay with Churchill, Roosevelt and the Combined Chiefs of Staff at the White House, June 1943. Standing, left to right: Dill, Ismay, Portal, Brooke, Pound, Leahy, Marshall, King, McNarney. Seated: Churchill and Roosevelt.

15. With Brendan Bracken and Mary Churchill on a train, Canada, August 1943.

16. In deep discussion with Brooke, Canada, August 1943.

17. Portrait by Augustus John, 1944.

18. Meeting of the Chiefs of Staff Committee, April 1945. Left to right: Hollis, Cunningham, Brooke, Portal, Ismay.

19. Churchill with the Chiefs of Staff, VE Day, May 1945, Hollis and Ismay standing.

20. A delighted Ismay. VE Day.

21. A historic moment: the Partition plan agreed, 3 June 1947. Left to right: Nehru, Ismay, Mountbatten, Jinnah.

22. Ismay and family at Wormington Grange, 1948. Left to right: Darry, Sarah Beaumont, Kay Rodman, Patricia Chance, Susan Chance, Ismay, Mary Ismay, Wentworth Beaumont.

23. Old friends. Eisenhower and Ismay at Supreme Headquarters Allied Powers Europe, Paris, 1951.

24. The Secretary General, 1952.

25. Ismay and Darry outside their Paris home, 1953.

26. Ismay and Darry's Christmas card, 1955.

27. Ismay with his grandsons (and 'Gemmie'), 1959. Left to right: Mark Henry Beaumont, James Evetts, Charles Beaumont, Wentworth Beaumont, John Evetts.

28. Ismay (with Lord Norman Brook) sponsors Clementine Churchill for her introduction at the House of Lords, June 1965.

'was at his most obstinate and on his highest horse'[94]—blaming it all on India, denying any Pakistani involvement and refusing to go to Delhi to meet with Nehru.[95] Ismay believed that the fighting could be stopped if only the political leaders on both sides would meet, but as he told Darry, exasperated, 'neither will go to meet the other—for fear of losing face… the sheer mistrust and hatred between the high-ups on each side is far greater than it was when I left England a month ago… Very depressing'.[96]

It was typical of Ismay that in the midst of dealing with the demands of high-level policy and state affairs he was also concerned for those for whom he felt a responsibility. His old servant, Abdur Rahman, was now living in Kashmir in an area at the centre of the troubles. On 8 November Ismay sent a truck to pick him and his family up and bring them back to Delhi to stay with him. The next day another old retainer and refugee, Mahfuz Ali Khan, appeared on his doorstep. Ismay immediately accepted him and his thirty-five family members, finding temporary accommodation for them within the Governor General's compound.[97] A week later the Indian ADC of the Governor of East Bengal appeared at Ismay's office, frantic for help. His family were neighbours of Abdul Rahman. When Ismay asked him 'Why come to me?', he replied that all Muslim soldiers all over India regarded Ismay as their hope. As a distraught Ismay told Darry, 'It's so damnable to be in that position and to have no power.'[98] It was also an indication that although Ismay considered himself to be completely impartial, that was not how he was universally viewed.

By 11 November—on the eve of Mountbatten's fortnight absence in Britain for the wedding of his nephew, Philip, to Princess Elizabeth— Ismay was again feeling the pressure and was letting off steam to Darry. 'Things are so bad they can scarcely get worse without busting altogether. Edwina has been dreadfully tiresome lately. There have been daily scenes about Dickie's decision to go home for the wedding.' Ismay, however, supported the decision:

> Personally I think it's advisable on every count. It's good for the Govt of India because it will show them that they can do without him. It's good for Pakistan because it will show them that he is not—as they charge— the Supreme Commander of the Kashmir offensive: and it's good for Dickie himself as he badly needs a rest.[99]

Mountbatten's absence, though, meant that the mantle of responsibility for the continuing crisis management rested well and truly on Ismay's shoulders. He was indefatigable in his efforts to ameliorate relations between the two Dominions, in particular through bringing the two sides together at the summit. On 18 November he spent two hours with Nehru urging him to go to Lahore to meet with Pakistani Prime Minister Liaquat Ali Khan. Ismay told High Commissioner Shone that 'Nehru thought that a meeting was desirable in principle [but that] there was no real hurry', surmising that Nehru believed 'that the longer the discussion with Liaquat was deferred the stronger would be India's position'.[100] But Ismay persevered and the following week the meeting took place in Delhi. Invited to join them to hear the outcome, he was heartened 'by the friendly and realistic way in which they were tackling the problem. It seemed to me that they were genuinely determined not only to break the deadlock about Kashmir, but also to remove the causes of friction between the two Dominions'. Ismay was 'delighted and relieved' when Nehru undertook to go to Lahore the following week to continue the discussion.[101] Writing in early December, Campbell-Johnson considered that, 'One of Ismay's most important contributions to peace was the part he played both in early November and during the "cordial" talks between Liaquat and Nehru in Delhi only last week'.[102] The 'man with the oil can' had not lost his touch.

While in London, Mountbatten had made a speech at India House which sought to put a favourable gloss on the situation, saying that 'only' 100,000 people had died in the violence following Partition.[103] When he heard about this Ismay was incandescent. 'I was horrified at Dickie's speech—making light of the situation out here', he told Darry,

> It seems to me immaterial whether one hundred thousand or a million have actually died, or whether 3% of the country is in turmoil. The crucial facts are that there is human misery on a colossal scale around me—and millions are bereaved, destitute and homeless and worst of all desperately anxious and almost hopeless about their future.[104]

He remained in a somewhat recalcitrant mood, telling Darry on 24 November, 'Dickie arrives tonight. I've a hunch he will try to persuade me to postpone my departure: but I won't. I've reached the stage when I couldn't stand a single extra minute'.[105] There is no record of whether Ismay's hunch was correct, but in his final letter to Darry from India were further signs that he was tiring of Mountbatten:

> He has come back full of the wonderful reception that he got from all quarters in England and of the overwhelming congratulations he got on

his work here. He is such a confirmed optimist, and so prone to believe what he wants to believe that I take it all with a slight pinch of salt.[106]

Ismay's last few days in India were spent bidding farewell. He held final meetings in Delhi with Nehru, with other leading politicians, and with Gandhi; and personally thanked all his colleagues and staff. He also flew to Peshawar and Rawalpindi for an emotional farewell with his regiment. There was a final interview with Mountbatten. Ismay later recalled that on going into his study he noticed on Mountbatten's desk a typed list of recommendations for awards for the Declaration of Independence honours list, with what appeared to be Ismay's name at the top, recommended for the highest award—a Knight Grand Cross of the Order of the Indian Empire. He asked Mountbatten if that was the case. When Mountbatten confirmed this, Ismay chided him, 'Dickie, you should have known better... Nothing on earth would induce me to accept an honour for the most painful and distasteful episode in my career. I must ask you to delete my name at once'.[107] Mountbatten protested but acceded.

On 30 November Ismay travelled to Bombay, spent three nights with the Governor and departed by ship on 4 December. While in Bombay he wrote a farewell letter to Mountbatten. It is a remarkable document. It reads not as a subordinate writing to his erstwhile boss, but as a father counselling his youthful, headstrong son. After expressing warm thanks and paying tribute to Mountbatten's skills and talents Ismay goes on to give firm—and wise—advice. His first point was to urge Mountbatten not to stay in India beyond April 1948; this, he said, would not be good for India or for Mountbatten. He then became more specific.

> My second point is that you should gradually assume more and more the role of the Constitutional Governor General. Start absenting yourself from the meetings of the Defence Committee, and finally drop out altogether—save for very exceptional circumstances. Even when you preside, take things a bit easier; sit back and let the Committee ventilate all their views before you sum up. You are the best chairman of a committee—except for Neville Chamberlain—with whom I have ever worked: but you are so eager, so anxious to get clear cut decisions, so amazingly quick in the uptake, that you are sometimes apt to be impetuous in your summing up, and, worse still, not to give every member of the team an innings. Bradman wins matches by making a hundred or so himself on every occasion: but if the tail-enders don't get a knock now and then, the Australians will have a poor side when Bradman retires!

Finally—to complete this catalogue of crime!—I suggest that you do your utmost to order your arrangements well ahead and then to stick to your programme as closely as possible. Thus, and only thus, can you keep your staff confident and happy. Uncertainty is always demoralising. Forgive me, Dickie, for pointing out these very insignificant shortcomings so frankly. They are a drop compared to your ocean of virtues: courage, industry, drive, vigilance and magnetism.[108]

The letter says much about Mountbatten, and even more about Ismay. The moment of departure from India was an emotional one for him. He later confessed that as his ship left Bombay, he could not bear to watch the shore fading out of view and went to his cabin, 'to be alone with my memories'.

I thought of the two million British graves that dotted the land, and of the devoted service that many generations of my countrymen had given to it... Would these forefathers of ours think that all their work and sacrifice had been wasted and their trust betrayed by those who came after them? Or would they regard the renunciation of power as a fitting ending to the story of British rule in India?[109]

During the voyage he wrote a retrospective, analysing the key decisions of the past eight months. He asked himself three questions, two of which echoed questions that Attlee had put to him at their October meeting. First: 'Was the 3rd June Plan the best that could be evolved in the circumstances then existing?' His conclusion was that, in the circumstances pertaining at the time, it was not only the best but the only possible course open. Many historians have, of course, disagreed. Ismay's conclusion also sidesteps the fact that his plan—Plan Balkan—was not the plan adopted. It had had as we have seen a number of significant flaws, several of which could have been avoided if he had brought VP Menon into his confidence. Some of these flaws resulted from his overzealous loyalty to the Princely States.

Ismay's second self-question was, 'Was the transfer of power too rushed?' It is doubtful if there is a single history of Partition that has not addressed this question and few that have concluded that it was not too rushed.[110] Ismay's answer was that it needed to be rushed and to follow the timeline that it did for two reasons: first because Congress would not have agreed to an extension of the Interim Government by 'even a single month'; second because 'we had with deliberate purpose over a period of years weakened our capacity to govern until the position was reached that we had no effective voice in the matter'. He was subsequently to make clear that he believed that the British capacity to govern and maintain law and order had been weakened to the extent that any delay to the transfer would have resulted in greater bloodshed rather than less. 'We had lost the power to punish and reward, and it was time for us to go'.[111] He was also to say that although at the time he was confident that within the period given for Partition the army would 'stand firm', he did not on reflection believe that this would have been the case had Partition been postponed. 'I don't believe the Army would have stayed if we had hung on any longer. If the Army had gone wrong, if the Army had started shooting, there's just no limit to what the casualties might have been. It would have been a holocaust which one just can't imagine'.[112]

His final question was 'Could the tragedy in the Punjab have been averted or at least mitigated?' In the partial answer which remains on file, Ismay expressed the belief that 'once the impartial British Raj had been removed, no soldier or policeman felt that he would have the support of the civil power if he acted against his own kith and kin'.[113] He amplified this in a speech in June 1948. The disturbances were foreseen, he said, and prior to the transfer of power the Punjab Boundary Force was formed and concentrated in the areas of most likely violence. At the time he had expressed reservations about the size of the force, but the reason he gave here for its failure was that the discipline of the troops—a force of mixed religions, under command of a British general and composite staff—broke down. 'It was difficult to believe that within the space of three weeks, the ingrained mutual trust of a lifetime—indeed of many lifetimes—would be dissipated. But this, alas, is what happened. No units would operate against their co-religionists, however brutally they were behaving. The flames spread far and wide'.[114] In private he was even more specific. Commenting on Mountbatten's assertion in his final Viceroy's Report that the small size of the Punjab Boundary Force was the major factor in the force's failure, he wrote 'the principal reason for the massacres in the Punjab [and Delhi] was not that the number of troops was inadequate, but that the troops failed to do their duty... bereft of [their] British officers'.[115] While there were certainly instances of breakdown of discipline—and Mountbatten had previously admitted this—it is difficult to argue that the small size of the force was not also a major factor.[116]

It is noteworthy that in this paper, and in other reflections, there was a theme to Ismay's explanation of the chaos following the transfer of power, and one that remains contentious, particularly among historians from the sub-continent. This theme was that the Raj came apart at the seams with the exodus of the British personnel, civilian and military, who led the institutions that held it together. Thus, as we have seen, the Indian Civil Service was from the end of the Second World War short of British recruits and losing its experienced British members to early retirement. British police officers, the backbone of the police force, were similarly leaving in large numbers. The intelligence system broke down for the same reason. The army, too, faced with the splitting up of regiments and division between the two Dominions, was experiencing unprecedented levels of resignations of its British officers after partition. The Punjab Frontier Force was a microcosm of the army as a whole. His conclusion was that the morale and effectiveness of all these critical institutions had depended on British leadership, without which they ceased to function effectively. Unsurprisingly this opened him to accusations of having a patronising and imperialist attitude, typical of the Raj itself.

It is debatable as to whether Ismay, in his valedictory retrospective, was looking back at his experience over the past eight months to make sense of it in his own mind; or whether he was preparing his case for the questions—or indeed accusations—that he knew he would need to answer on his return. Perhaps a bit of both. He was not, however, to change radically the answers he set down in his account during the rest of his life. Nor was he to divert from his view that his eight months in India were among the unhappiest of his life. But he was fortified by the belief that he had done his duty and done it to the best of his ability, and therefore could hold his head high. For Ismay, that was always the test by which he judged himself.

Judgements of Ismay's performance as Mountbatten's chief of staff vary. Mosley in *The Last Days of the British Raj* was highly critical of him. 'His instinct was to do the job quickly—and damn the consequences. It hardly surprised him when the Indians, released from the benevolent control of the British, reverted to type and began to kill each other. He was too sick at heart at the end of the Indian Empire to have any desire to stop it'.[117] However, Mosley produced no evidence to back his accusation and this alleged mixture of recklessness and apathy are singularly out of character for Ismay. A further accusation came in the 2017 film about Partition, *Viceroy's House*. In it Ismay is depicted as the sinister arch-villain: an agent of Churchill, manipulating Mountbatten towards Partition in order to preserve Britain's strategic position vis-à-vis Russia through the creation of Pakistan. When Mountbatten discovers this, in the film, he turns on Ismay in fury:

Mountbatten: 'You've used me—and my family'.

Ismay: 'You came here to serve your King and country. And you've done so admirably. I hear they're promoting you from viscount to earl'.

Mountbatten: 'What about the people whose lives have been destroyed by this?'

Ismay. 'That is unfortunate. Nobody foresaw...'

Mountbatten: 'Blood is on your hands for this.'

Ismay: 'But Dickie, it's your name on the plan. It'll always be known as the Mountbatten Plan.'[118]

There is no evidence to suggest that this highly entertaining depiction is even loosely based on fact; nor is there anything in the subsequent friendship between Ismay and Mountbatten which would indicate that they ever had such a relationship or such a confrontation.

There are a number of criticisms, though, that can be levelled in retrospect against Ismay during his time as Mountbatten's chief of staff: his failure to achieve any delay in the timing of Partition; his sentimental attachment to the Princely States; his acquiescence in the alteration of the Radcliffe boundary report; his failure to include VP Menon amongst the inner group of advisers; and his initial reluctance to contemplate the division of his beloved Indian Army. But there is much on the credit side of the balance sheet, for example: his level-headed advice to the Viceroy and the British government; the relationship he built with the political leaders on both sides of the religious divide; his damage limitation efforts in the Kashmir situation in November; and, throughout his time in India, his masterly management of the Viceroy's staff. Observers drew attention to his influence on affairs. Christie noted, 'The lord needs George [Abell] or Ismay to steady him', and later, 'Ismay is back today. This is reassuring; one is never quite sure of Mountbatten's political judgment'.[119] On his return to London, Cyril Radcliffe told Lockhart that, 'all went well when Pug was there and decidedly badly when he wasn't'.[120] Perhaps Lewin best summed up this aspect of Ismay's role: 'Trusted by all parties, by his calmness and accumulated wisdom he balanced the mercurial energy of Mountbatten'.[121]

Ismay was later to say, 'I anticipated an unhappy time and I certainly had it'.[122] Olaf Caroe, who knew him well, paid tribute to his performance in his role but added, 'Yet at the end he felt he had failed; for him, as so for so many of us, the departure was a personal tragedy'.[123] A large part of Ismay's unhappiness was undoubtedly, as he explained to Caroe's wife Kitty, 'What a nightmare it was to see the things we gave our life to— broken'.[124] Yet Ismay was to maintain that he had no regrets about his decision to accompany Mountbatten. 'If I had the decision to make again, I would do the same thing'.[125]

While Ismay was returning to Britain consideration was being given in London as to a successor to Mountbatten, who was expected to leave the following year. The Secretary of State for Dominion Affairs, Viscount Addison, wrote to Attlee, 'We should look for… a man of the highest ability and authority that we can find', before naming Ismay as his choice.[126] It is not known whether Ismay was ever offered the appointment: if he was, he would have felt honoured to be asked, but it is not difficult to guess what his answer would have been.

14

INTERLUDE

1948–52

Ismay arrived back in Britain on 20 December looking forward to a long holiday with the family at Wormington and the retirement which he had had to postpone exactly one year previously. Among the many letters of welcome on his return was one from Churchill: 'I am so glad you are out of that terrible business. It hurts me so much that I cannot read about it any more'.[1] But Ismay's holiday lasted just a week. Shortly after Christmas Attlee contacted him with a request. The Indian government had referred the Kashmir situation to the United Nations for resolution: would Ismay be prepared to accompany Secretary of State for Commonwealth Relations Philip Noel-Baker to New York the following week for the hearing? In the same circumstances many other people might have politely or even impolitely declined, or accepted only with reluctance. Ismay, however, positively relished the prospect. 'I jumped at the chance', he recalled. 'If only this quarrel could be settled, India and Pakistan would become good friends instead of bitter enemies, and the unity of the sub-continent would be virtually restored'.[2]

On 3 January he embarked on the liner *Queen Elizabeth* for America. His task within the delegation was both to advise Noel-Baker and to act as a mediator between the Indian and Pakistani delegations. He had long meetings with the leaders of each delegation in turn. But he was not optimistic about progress. As he told Darry, 'Goodness knows whether we will be able to bring them together as each of them is positive that their own side is 100 per cent (not 99½ per cent) right and that the other side is 100 per cent (not 99½ per cent) wrong!'[3] Ismay's scepticism was well founded. To his immense frustration the proceeding ended with nothing to show for the efforts at reconciliation. Before he left New York, however, his spirits were lifted by a dinner invitation from General Marshall, now Secretary of State, who sent his own plane to bring Ismay to Washington. Guests included Eisenhower, Wedemeyer, Forrestal, Douglas, Harriman, Generals Collins and Spaatz, and Admiral Stark. 'It was', recalled Ismay, 'a red-letter evening'.[4]

He was back in England at the end of January and just ten days before his daughter Sarah's wedding to Wenty Beaumont. Since the wedding was in the local church and the reception at Wormington Grange, his part in its organisation was somewhat belated, but the family may have come to expect that matters of state might take precedence. They may also have been surprised to see speculation in the newspapers that he might be the next British ambassador in Washington: according to the Peterborough column in the *Daily Telegraph,* 'recently his candidature... was seriously discussed by the Cabinet'.[5] They may also not have known that he had been sounded out by his friend Richard Casey, now Australia's Minister for External Affairs, as a potential Governor of the State of Victoria; Ismay had turned it down, citing work commitments.[6]

Ismay now divided his time between Wormington and his house in Lowndes Square in London. In addition to his work assisting Churchill with his book he had taken on a number of appointments, including chairmanship of the National Institute for the Blind and directorships of London-based companies (Lloyds Bank and the Commercial Union Assurance Company were two). He also planned to play an active role in the House of Lords, contributing to debates on defence matters. None of this prevented him from resuming his notably active social life and his many friendships. One which meant much to him was that with Auchinleck, who was now living in London but had been very much keeping a low profile. Their friendship was close enough for Auchinleck to unburden himself to Ismay, which he did in a letter that awaited him on his return from America. 'I think you knew how I felt—or knew something of what I felt—when I left India', Auchinleck wrote, 'I wanted to be shot of it all and to get away from any contacts which could bring it all before me again—all the crookedness and dishonesty and manoeuvring—you know it all so well!! That is passing now...'[7]

Ismay was also in demand as a lecturer and speaker on the subject of his experiences and current affairs. He was choosy about which he accepted and tended to be very discreet in what he said. He also tended to give a sanitised account which, as was to be the case with his memoirs, sometimes allowed propaganda to trump history. This was true even when speaking to audiences where he might have been expected to be frank: for example, the senior officers of the Imperial Defence College. Speaking to them about the Chiefs of Staff Committee, he asserted, 'I can safely say that during the two or three years before the war the Chiefs... worked together in complete harmony'.[8] As numerous historians have since shown, this was stretching the truth. For instance Brian Bond, harking back to a notorious example, asserted that 'In the summer of 1939 personal relations among the COS were as bad as in the Beatty-Trenchard era'.[9]

In March 1948 Ismay was again approached to provide a public service. Summoned by the Prime Minister to Downing Street, Ismay feared that he was about to be asked to take up some role overseas again; but Attlee had something completely different in mind. He explained that the Cabinet had decided to commemorate the centenary of the 1851 Great Exhibition with exhibitions and concerts to be held simultaneously in London and throughout the United Kingdom. It was to be called the Festival of Britain. To organise this an executive committee had been formed and this committee would report to a supervisory Festival Council. Attlee asked Ismay to chair the council. Ismay was surprised that the choice had fallen on someone like himself who was 'a complete ignoramus about science and somewhat of a Philistine about the arts'; but he was 'so relieved at not being asked to go abroad again that [he] accepted at once'.[10] Actually, Attlee's choice was a canny one. As a Labour Party initiative, the festival, if popular and successful, had the potential to win much political capital for the Labour Party. Attlee expected criticism of the scheme from Churchill but knew that Churchill would be much less likely to cause trouble if Ismay was in charge.[11] According to Paul Wright, the festival's chief of public relations, when the Conservative press started to campaign against the festival Ismay went to see Churchill and pleaded its case. 'Churchill was reported as saying, "All right, Pug, you old fool, you can have your damned festival" and called off the hounds.'[12]

For the next three years the festival was to be a major commitment in Ismay's life because, like every task he agreed to undertake, he devoted his wholehearted energy and commitment to it from the moment he agreed to do it until it was completed. Although the festival was three years distant, initial planning was already well under way. Ismay's first engagement was to chair the inaugural meeting of the council on 31 May, a meeting addressed by Princess Elizabeth in her capacity as President of the Royal Society of Arts. The council, appointed by the minister responsible for the festival, Herbert Morrison, was unlike anything Ismay had chaired before. Its membership included politicians of all persuasions but also luminaries of the arts such as John Gielgud, Malcolm Sargent, TS Eliot, AP Herbert and Noel Coward. Council meetings certainly had the potential to be entertaining. Ismay enjoyed his role, made easier by his confidence in the Director General of the festival, Gerald Barry, former editor of the national daily newspaper the *News Chronicle*.

The council was mainly advisory, but certain key decisions were referred to it. One of the most important was the location for the flagship events which were to be held in London. A number of options were put forward but the one that Ismay favoured—and which the council agreed—was to situate it on a 30-acre, heavily bomb-damaged site across the River Thames from the Houses of Parliament. This was to be called the South Bank. Work started soon after on clearing the site and building what was to become the leading concert hall in Britain, the Royal Festival Hall. In addition to his role in the council Ismay saw one of his other main roles as promoting the festival, and he immediately worked with the Lord Mayor of London, Sir George Aylwen, to convene a major promotional event in the capital for the leaders of cities and towns around the country. The Lord Mayor invited almost every mayor or local council chairman in the United Kingdom to the event at the Guildhall which Ismay and Barry addressed. In the coming months Ismay also travelled around the United Kingdom, stimulating interest in and commitment to the festival.

A further role increasingly fell to Ismay. As interest in the festival and enthusiasm for it grew, so did the number of organisations involved in its planning and development. Apart from the government these included the London County Council, the Arts Council of Great Britain, the Council of Industrial Design and the National Film Institute, as well as many organisations outside London. Unsurprisingly, not all of these bodies had a shared vision of the festival or agreed as to how the available funds should be allocated. Ismay took on a role familiar to him: mediating between them and preventing differences of opinion from becoming damaging disputes. An early example concerned the character and purpose of the festival. Originally the government had accepted the proposal that the festival should be, like the 1851 Great Exhibition, an international event. In 1948, however, the Cabinet decided to change this to a purely national event (not even including Commonwealth countries), promoting British science, technology, industrial design and arts, but also an event to lift the British people's spirits after the war and be, in Barry's words, 'a tonic to the nation'.[13] Not everyone agreed with this, particularly with the exclusion of the Commonwealth. The Conservative Party, for example, opposed the change. The Beaverbrook press continued its hostility.

The commitment which was to take up even more of Ismay's time than the festival, however, was assisting Churchill in researching and writing his memoirs, *The Second World War*. Having received Ismay's assistance in 1946 and on occasions pursued him while he was in India for comments on drafts, Churchill had no compunction in doing so frequently now that he was back in England. He sent every draft, revised draft, and galley proof to him for comment. Ismay was as conscientious and patient in this task as he had been with Churchill during the war, consistently providing detailed comments and offering advice which Churchill almost invariably accepted.

As David Reynolds has pointed out, Ismay was one of a small group of advisers—'the Syndicate'—whose contributions can be seen, often almost verbatim, in the text of the book.[14] For example, Churchill's account of his five visits to France in May and June 1940 are closely based on the fifteen pages of notes supplied by Ismay.[15] There are numerous instances of Churchill drawing heavily on Ismay's drafts, and several of him incorporating complete paragraphs virtually unchanged—such as the account of their visit to Briare in June 1940.[16] Similarly, Ismay supplied many of the most famous anecdotes of Churchill visiting bomb-damaged areas during the Blitz.[17] 'These moving passages', observed Reynolds, 'though elaborated in Churchill's own words, originated entirely from Ismay'.[18] A further task that fell to him was correcting errors and rectifying omissions, such as (to Ismay's amazement) the lack of any mention of the setting up of the Combined Chiefs of Staff organisation.[19] In addition, as Reynolds notes, Ismay supplied the basic narrative for each of Churchill's meetings with the Americans in 1942–43.[20]

Ismay was also influential in Churchill's treatment of a number of the controversies addressed in the book. One of these was Churchill's account of the 1942 Dieppe Raid (discussed in Appendix B). Another was the 1941 Greek campaign. In April 1948, two books had recently been published— one by Major General Sir Francis de Guingand, one by Professor Cyril Falls—repeating the charge that Churchill had cajoled Wavell into agreeing to send troops from the Western Desert to Greece, resulting in defeat in the desert and an embarrassing evacuation from Greece.[21] Churchill told Ismay that he had read the relevant parts of these books, and that they 'contain many challenges to our work based on ignorance or impudence, or both?'[22] Ismay considered that Churchill's draft chapter on the campaign was not nearly robust enough in his own defence. He told Churchill that 'it was the men on the spot, both statesmen and soldiers [Foreign Secretary Eden, Dill and Wavell] who pressed vehemently for intervention in Greece', and that their recommendation made it 'almost impossible for the Cabinet to pull out'.[23]

This was true, but Ismay was being somewhat selective in his presentation of evidence. Since the Italian invasion of Greece the preceding October, and especially since the British victory at Beda Fomm on 5 February 1941, it had been Churchill who had been pressing vehemently for intervention in Greece and the Chiefs of Staff and Wavell who had been dubious about the prospect. But there was suddenly a reversal of roles. On 20 February when Eden and Dill were with Wavell in Cairo, about to visit Athens, Churchill—clearly mindful of the debacle in Norway in 1940—suddenly telegraphed to Eden, 'Do not consider yourselves obligated to a Greek enterprise if in your hearts you feel it will only be another Norwegian fiasco'.[24] But this crossed with a telegram from Eden, no doubt influenced firstly by Churchill's underlying intent, and secondly by Dill who had according to PJ Grigg been 'worn down into acquiescence'.[25] Eden concluded, 'it is of course a gamble... no-one can give a guarantee of success... the risks are great but there is a chance of success', adding, crucially, 'this attempt to help Greece should be made'.[26] At the time, according to Jacob, 'when he and Ismay heard this they were extremely doubtful'.[27] But Churchill wasted no time in securing the agreement of the Chiefs of Staff and War Cabinet and directed Eden, 'Full steam ahead'.[28] The confusion was to continue. On 4 March Eden duly signed an agreement with the Greek government but the following day reported a 'changed and disturbing situation and an atmosphere quite different from our last visit'. But the signed agreement 'presented the War Cabinet with virtually a fait accompli', and was not reversed.[29] In 1948, however, Churchill was reassured by what Ismay had told him, and 'heavily reworked' his draft accordingly.[30]

Ismay also influenced Churchill in his portrayal of a number of individuals in his memoirs. One of these was the former Cabinet Secretary Bridges of whom Ismay was a considerable admirer, rather more so than was Churchill. Unlike Ismay, Bridges did not establish a close personal relationship with Churchill and was, for example, never invited to become a member of The Other Club—always a touchstone of such matters. Ismay persuaded Churchill to pay tribute to Bridges in his memoirs and when Churchill indicated that he might do so he wrote again, giving further encouragement while at the same time suggesting to Churchill that it was his idea in the first place. 'You have said very nice things about Hollis, Jacob and myself, and I am so pleased that you have it in mind to do likewise for Bridges'.[31] Churchill duly obliged.[32] Similarly, Ismay persuaded Churchill to omit his highly critical comment that Auchinleck's decision to postpone the Operation Crusader offensive in 1941 'constituted one of the major disasters of the war'.[33] On other occasions Ismay could be less charitable—and surprisingly forthright. He took issue with Churchill's comment that his 'great friend' Admiral Keyes would have made a good First Sea Lord:

> I am quite sure that it would have been disastrous if Admiral Keyes had been First Sea Lord. As matter of fact, his ambition was to be First Lord and First Sea Lord at the same time, and to hold much the same position as Kitchener did for the first year of the First World War. Is it not therefore a mistake to say that he could have filled the office of First Sea Lord with distinction?[34]

Again, Churchill bowed to his advice.

One of the most significant of the amendments resulting from Ismay's advice was Churchill's portrayal of Halifax in the summer of 1940. In a draft of Volume 2 of the *Second World War,* Churchill had written that at a meeting in May 1940 attended by Halifax, Attlee and Chamberlain with French Prime Minister Reynaud, Halifax, in contrast to the other attendees, 'showed himself willing to go a long way' in seeking the cooperation of Mussolini to mediate with Germany. Ismay commented to Churchill that 'this might be taken to mean that Halifax was all for appeasement'. As he told Churchill, he had recently checked with Halifax, who had used 'words to the effect that "I did not believe that anything could be done to buy off Italy, but I did not like to be too unsympathetic to Reynaud in his distress"'.[35] Ismay commented, 'I feel sure that Halifax would be hurt by any inference that he was not as tough <u>during the war</u> as the rest of them'.[36] Churchill duly omitted his criticism of Halifax. That he did so is remarkable since, as he knew better than most, Halifax was indeed not as tough as the rest of them when it came to resisting compromise attempts through Mussolini. That for Ismay the most important consideration was not hurting Halifax's feelings is equally remarkable, but it was not out of character for Ismay.

A further wartime memoir published in 1948 was Eisenhower's *Crusade in Europe*. A review appeared in *The Sunday Times*, clearly written by an admirer of Montgomery, which was waspishly critical of Eisenhower's generalship. Ismay wrote to Eisenhower the same day, '[t]o say that I am disgusted with it is putting it mildly. I am so mad that I cannot think or dictate straight'.[37] The following week Ismay's review of the book was published in the *Daily Telegraph*. It occupied practically a whole page and robustly refuted the accusations made in *The Sunday Times* review while paying tribute to 'a grand fighter, a great American and a sincere, generous-hearted friend of Great Britain'.[38] Among the many who complimented Ismay on his review while criticising that in *The Sunday Times* was Lascelles, at Buckingham Palace, who described the article as 'a gross mis-representation... and a very mischievous article'.[39] The following week Lascelles added, 'You could say [to Eisenhower] that there is no-one in this house who did not think *The Sunday Times* article damnable'—a broad hint that this included the King's personal opinion, and a message Ismay was happy to pass on.[40] Ismay also rallied others to express public criticism of the article: Cunningham and Brooke being amongst those who did so. Eisenhower was understandably grateful: 'Last Monday morning I think was practically a post-war low point for me', he confided, '...your letter meant so much to me'.[41]

Ismay was to suffer ill health again in 1949. Although his commitments were nothing compared to those under which he had laboured during the war years and in India, he nevertheless succeeded in overworking. In March 1949 he was ordered 'three weeks rest' by his doctors.[42] He was in hospital again in May for ten days having a sinus operation, followed by three weeks, convalescence at home. He returned to London on 7 June but was far from fully recovered; ten days later he was replying to Pownall's enquiry about his health, 'I'm going on all right, but get terribly tired and rather depressed. Apparently the doctors expect one to go very slowly for six months or so after a mauling of this kind'.[43] He was fit enough, though, by August to travel to northern Italy to spend 'a very nice ten days' as the guest of Churchill and Clementine.[44] They stayed firstly at Gardone, on Lake Garda, and then at Carezza in the Dolomites. Since Churchill's research assistant Bill Deakin and two secretaries were also there it was something of a working holiday, focusing on Volume 4 of Churchill's memoirs. But Churchill was in relaxed mood. Ismay reported that '[h]e did a lot of painting each day and we did a lot of work on his book each night'.[45]

At the same time that Ismay was busying himself with Churchill's memoirs and the Festival of Britain, he had not entirely shaken the dust of India from his boots. Before Mountbatten returned to Britain in June 1948, he continued to correspond frequently with Ismay. The main subject of his letters was the reverberations of the Radcliffe award, discussed earlier. Mountbatten also wrote to him seeking career guidance. That he turned to Ismay for such advice says much about the closeness of their relationship and the respect in which he held him. Mountbatten may also have calculated that Ismay was well placed to influence opinion formers and decision makers who might have a say in his career, and in particular his next appointment. He was particularly concerned that those at the top of the Royal Navy had not fully recognised his obvious talents and potential. 'John Cunningham is second only to Andrew Cunningham in his desire to do me down', Mountbatten told Ismay. In the Mediterranean Fleet (one of his options), 'there were enough tireless busybodies about to cause mischief... the one way my enemies could wreck my career would be to cause trouble between the Senior Flag Officers and myself'.[46]

Ismay replied sympathetically, before concluding, '[m]y final advice to you is that you should do whatever you think best, both on public as well as private grounds. I have not the slightest doubt that you will be First Sea Lord, whichever course you take'.[47] His prediction was, of course, spot on. A few months later Mountbatten wrote to Ismay complaining about 'grossly unfair attacks' on him in the Beaverbrook press about his time as Viceroy, asking Ismay to get 'Master' to intervene with Beaverbrook. Knowing what Churchill currently thought about Mountbatten, Ismay offered sympathy but told Mountbatten, 'I feel it would be a mistake to be asking a favour from that quarter'. He also pointed out to him that he was open to criticism from several angles about his time in India, adding with considerable candour, 'there are people who consider that after Partition you were not as unbiased as you should have been'.[48] Mountbatten replied, 'As usual, I entirely agree with your advice'.[49]

In addition, there was a particular issue from Ismay's days in India which resurfaced. One of the aspects of Partition that still rankled with him was what he considered to be the shabby treatment of the Princely States, most of which had succumbed to pressure to join one or other of the two Dominions. One State which had managed to remain independent had been Hyderabad, but from the moment of Partition Nehru had been coercing the Nizam—unsuccessfully—to accede to India. In September 1948 Nehru ordered an invasion of Hyderabad and within a week had annexed the state to India. Ismay wrote to Attlee to express his anger. 'This is the last straw and I am most unhappy and humiliated', he told Attlee. He wished, he said, to avoid saying or doing anything that might be:

> embarrassing to HMG [His Majesty's Government]. And I particularly hate the idea of saying or doing anything that would be at all embarrassing to you yourself... On the other hand I feel very strongly in this matter that it would be moral cowardice on my part if I did not take any opportunity that may arise of expressing my view.[50]

The implication was clear. Ismay was warning Attlee that he was about to go public. This would undoubtedly be embarrassing, and not just for the Prime Minister. Attlee was, as ever, adept at handling Ismay. He immediately sent a handwritten letter, advising him that '[i]n the circumstances I should not think a condemnatory statement from you would be useful... but If you should care to come round I should be delighted to show you the reports and discuss the present position'.[51] Ismay took up the offer but having again stated his case to Attlee, allowed the matter to drop.

There was one further matter from India that troubled Ismay. It emerged that, due to an administrative oversight, there were junior grades in certain parts of the Indian Civil Service—such as the police, railway and central secretariat—for whom neither India nor Britain accepted full pension liability. Ismay felt some responsibility for the oversight and saw it as his duty to fight on their behalf. He joined forces with Wavell, Mountbatten and others to get the British government to accept its responsibility for these people. His maiden speech in the House of Lords in April 1948 was on the subject, urging the government to recognise its 'moral obligation towards them'.[52] But the issue lingered on into 1949 without resolution. He continued campaigning and returned to the charge in the House in July 1949, this time with success.[53] The matter was resolved in the employees' favour.

In the closing months of 1949 Ismay was able to spend more time with the family at Wormington. His elder daughter Susan, who had been divorced from her first husband for several years, became engaged to a young officer in the Royal Scots Fusiliers, Mike Evetts: the son of a friend of Ismay's, Lieutenant General Sir John Evetts. Susan and Mike were married at Wormington in December. Through the winter Ismay devoted much effort and interest to his estate, and in particular to his prize herd of Jersey cattle. He told a friend, with considerable pride, that he had 'the second highest milk yield for Jerseys in England', while lamenting that 'I lost no less than five cows this year, including two Gold Medallists'.[54]

In late 1949 the pace of work on Churchill's memoirs significantly increased. With a General Election expected in early 1950, Churchill was keen to finish the book as quickly as possible. Drafts for comment, together with requests for a speedy response, appeared through Ismay's letterbox with alarming frequency. The size of contribution requested also increased, from a few sentences or paragraphs to whole chunks of text, for example 'a thousand words on Tube Alloys [codename for the atomic bomb]'.[55] This particular request caused Ismay some perplexity and he had to turn for assistance to Cherwell. As the election approached, Ismay was also concerned that Churchill was allowing party-political matters to colour his narrative. An example was the treatment in these drafts of Sir Stafford Cripps, Chancellor of the Exchequer, a notable critic of Churchill and in turn the object of some disparaging remarks in one of the draft chapters. Ismay expressed his concern about this to Churchill's assistant, Dennis Kelly, telling him that, 'we should not be making political capital out of those great days when we all worked together'.[56] Kelly shared these concerns and passed them on to Churchill. The offending references were removed.

In the immediate post-war years Ismay had become increasingly concerned about the Soviet threat to Western Europe. He welcomed the formation of the Western Union following the Treaty of Brussels in March 1948, but saw it very much as a stepping stone to the development of a larger defensive organisation incorporating the United States. He was, therefore highly supportive of moves to establish the North Atlantic Treaty, signed in April 1949, and the creation of the organisation—NATO — that resulted from it. 'I feel in my heart of hearts', he had written to Eisenhower the previous summer, 'that, provided we do not give way to appeasement in any shape or form, the dire catastrophe will be avoided'.[57]

His concern for international security continued into 1950 and intensified in June with the Soviet-backed invasion of South Korea by North Korea. In a defence debate in the House of Lords the following month he questioned whether the United Nations had the necessary command and control structure to be effective 'at this critical time', suggesting that 'without it there will be hesitations, confusions, delay, uninformed public opinion and a deadly waste of blood and treasure'. He even went so far as to suggest that the wartime Anglo-American Combined Chiefs of Staff, suitably augmented, might be given the responsibility for the supreme direction of the UN's military affairs, 'at any rate for the next few critical months'.[58] He also suggested that the Prime Minister and the Chiefs of Staff with other ministers and representatives should go to Washington 'at a very early date and confer with our friends there.'[59] In a further defence debate in September, with British troops now joining the American forces in Korea, he believed that his urgings were bearing fruit with the announcement that the British Chiefs of Staff were about to go to Washington for joint staff talks.[60]

Ismay's focus on international security became a preoccupation following China's entry into the Korean War on 19 October and the American response to it. There were calls in Washington for the declaration of a state of National Emergency. On 30 November President Truman told reporters that the use of the atomic bomb was under 'active consideration'.[61] In Britain, too, speculation was rife as to where the crisis might lead. A full confrontation between the United States and the Soviet Union looked to some like a distinct possibility. Ismay now seriously questioned whether during this international crisis the Festival of Britain, due to commence in early May, should go ahead. He was not alone. A number of British national newspapers, particularly Beaverbrook's *Daily Express* and *Sunday Express,* had always been critical of the event, as had some members of the Conservative Party, including Churchill. After long deliberation Ismay concluded that the festival should be postponed or at the least curtailed. His advice went unheeded. On 6 December he wrote to Morrison tendering his resignation as Chairman of the Festival Council. His letter concluded,

> It has, of course, always been recognised from the outset that the international situation might deteriorate to an extent which made it impossible to go forward with the Festival in its entirety. I had hoped against hope that we might get a respite until after 1951, but alas, this hope has now been shattered; and it is my personal conviction that to continue to insist on having the Festival in its entirety would not only be wrong in itself, but could not but be misunderstood in this country and still more in America. I feel this so very fervently that I must, with the greatest regret, ask you to accept my resignation...

He went on say that he would be prepared to remain as chairman 'if Parliament should make a categorical decision that, despite the gravity of the situation, the festival should go forward... [or] if it were decided that the festival should be entirely re-cast by the postponement of such features as the South Bank Exhibition, the Battersea Gardens and the Travelling Exhibitions, and possibly by modifying such other features as would be inappropriate'.[62]

Morrison saw Ismay the next evening and, as Ismay told Lord Salisbury four days later, 'was sympathetic and friendly' but 'he did not agree that the festival should be postponed or curtailed. The British people needed and deserved a "jolly". It was sure to be an outstanding success... I got the feeling that he thought I had lost my nerve—or been keeping bad company!' Ismay agreed to postpone his decision until the Prime Minister returned from America 'and possibly until towards the end of the month'. He added that he sincerely hoped that if the Opposition decided to take up the issue, 'they will do so by way of talks behind the scenes with the PM. It would be a thousand pities if it came to be regarded as a party issue'.[63]

Throughout December Ismay continued to brood over the international situation and the wisdom of holding the festival. In doing so he was drawing parallels in his mind between the current international situation and that in the early days of 1940. On Christmas Day he wrote to his friend Lew Douglas, recently retired American ambassador in London, 'a state of war exists between the free world and the Dictator States. You may call it "phoney war" or "twilight war", or whatever you will: but it is undeniably WAR nevertheless'.[64]

In January 1951 Ismay wrote twice to Attlee on the subject, lastly on 17 January, emphasising his 'burning conviction' that it would be wrong to go ahead with the festival in its entirety 'at a time that our country is at the present time confronted with the gravest peril in all its long history'.[65] Attlee was faced with potential embarrassment over Ismay's intended resignation, but knew the way round it. Within two days Ismay had received a letter from Lascelles telling him that 'His Majesty... very much hoped that I would continue at my post'.[66] As Attlee will have predicted, Ismay immediately withdrew his resignation.

This whole episode begs several questions. First, was there good reason to cancel, postpone or reduce the scale of the festival? The answer is simple. The festival took place as planned, and there were no recriminations from across the Atlantic and no evidence that the Russians questioned the seriousness with which the United Kingdom took the Soviet threat; nor were voices raised in the United States in protest against the British indulging themselves in a festival. In that sense, it was a miscalculation and a rare misjudgement by Ismay. Second, was his decision to resign based entirely on his own deep conviction, or was he influenced and used by the government's political opponents? Here it is less easy to judge. There is no hard evidence that this was the case. But Ismay's resignation would have suited the Conservative Party's opposition to the festival and Ismay had been in contact with Salisbury, leader of the Conservative peers in the House of Lords. Indeed, Ismay thanked him for his 'support and wise counsel'. Conceivably it was Salisbury's idea for Ismay to demand a parliamentary vote. The Conservative party did not, however, try to make political capital out of the issue. In fact, the story of Ismay's action did not emerge, and he kept the matter very much to himself. Darry respected his reticence and possibly his embarrassment; after his death the correspondence relating to the episode was not amongst that gifted to King's College London.

That Ismay was sincere in his conviction about the gravity of the Soviet threat is substantiated by his contribution to the defence debate in the House of Lords the following month. In an impassioned and much reported speech—which, one newspaper commented, 'rose above the somewhat niggling mediocrity that had so far characterised the two-day... debate'[67]—he reiterated his view that Britain was 'confronted with the gravest peril in our history'. This could be averted or overcome, he said, 'provided that the free people are resolute, vigilant and, above all, united, and provided that we put an end to wishful thinking and reluctance to face facts'. The penalty for not doing so, he warned, was that localised wars such as those taking place in Korea and Indo-China could 'at any time, by accident or miscalculation, or by deliberate intent, flare up into a world conflagration, a Third World War'.[68] Ismay followed this up with interviews published in national newspapers and a full-page article in the *Daily Telegraph* arguing passionately for the establishment of a supreme council of peace-loving nations with worldwide authority. He urged the British government to take a lead in setting this up.[69]

There was of course a certain incongruity about the author of these sobering public warnings of impending Armageddon now leading the 'jolly' that the nation needed and deserved. But he devoted all his energy to the task, determined to make the festival the greatest possible success. On 3 May he and Darry were present at a packed St Paul's Cathedral for the service that marked its official opening, and that evening received the King and Queen at the Royal Festival Hall for the inaugural concert. The latter occasion was particularly memorable for him because he and Darry, along with the Lord and Lady Mayoress and Gerald Barry and his wife, were stuck in the lift for the first forty minutes of the concert—

thus providing him with an anecdote which he never tired of including in his speeches for years after. Throughout the summer Ismay and Darry travelled the length and breadth of the country, attending festival events of every kind. The closing ceremony took place on 30 September.

Judgements about the success of the festival varied. As one author observed, the government had ensured that the festival carried 'an unuttered, yet unmistakable, message that the Labour Party, in office since 1945, was the force behind Britain's recovery, as well as its guiding light for the future'.[70] Predictably, therefore, the Tory press were generally unimpressed. 'It may be likened to a moderately successful party', sniffed the *Daily Telegraph*, 'but one held on the wrong day and at far too great a cost'.[71] Most commentators both at the time and since have been more complimentary. Over ten million people had visited the main London exhibitions and the Travelling Land Exhibition had attracted almost 900,000 visitors. Its legacy included development of the South Bank site into the South Bank Centre, which along with the Royal Festival Hall was to include the Queen Elizabeth Hall, the Purcell Room, the National Theatre, and the National Film Theatre. In addition to its material legacy, it inspired a renewed interest in the arts all over the United Kingdom and received international acclaim. Accounts of the Festival agree that, in the words of Paul Rennie, 'Ismay did a very effective job in persuading everyone to work as a team'.[72] He could be well pleased with the outcome and could now look forward at last to the long holiday that had been denied to him for so long. He was, however, in for another surprise.

On 25 October 1951 a General Election took place. Churchill and the Conservative Party won with a small majority of seventeen seats. The following night Ismay was asleep in bed at his Lowndes Square house when he was telephoned by Churchill who asked him to come and see him immediately. Not knowing what to expect, Ismay dressed rapidly and hurried round to Churchill's house at Hyde Park Gate. Without preamble, Churchill told him that he wanted him to be Secretary of State for Commonwealth Relations. Ismay's astonishment can only be guessed at. In his memoirs he only hints at his reaction: '[o]fficials do not usually make good Cabinet Ministers, and there was no reason why I should be an exception to this rule. But I was overjoyed at the prospect of serving under Churchill again'.[73] It is likely, though, that he questioned the decision. According to Jock Colville, Churchill inveigled him, 'against [his] own better judgment' to accept the appointment.[74] If so it was not the first, nor would it be the last, time that Churchill succeeded in doing so. Ismay was to find that Churchill's new Cabinet was 'like an Old Boys reunion, full of his wartime comrades'.[75] Familiar faces around the table included Lord Cherwell, Lord Leathers, Lord Woolton, and Oliver Lyttleton. They were to be joined at the end of February by Field Marshal the Earl Alexander as Minister of Defence, on completion of his term of office as Governor General of Canada.

By the afternoon following Ismay's interview with Churchill he was already at work in the Commonwealth Relations Office. Although much of his previous experience gave him advantage in his new appointment, he had been away from Whitehall for five years, had no knowledge of current issues of Commonwealth relations, and had much to learn about his new trade as a politician: he had never even sat on the Conservative benches in the House of Lords. Nevertheless, as he told Spears, he received 'over 600 letters and telegrams' of congratulations on his appointment.[76] Now in his sixty-fifth year and not in the best of health, he faced a considerable challenge and found that '[t]he work of my new post proved to be heavier, and the hours longer, than I had anticipated'. This was exacerbated by the fact that in Alexander's temporary absence, Churchill had appointed himself Minister of Defence and Ismay found himself reprising his former role, 'frequently summoned... "after hours" for consultation' on defence matters.[77]

Towards the end of 1951 defence matters came to dominate Ismay's work. He was called upon to accompany Churchill on an extended visit to the United States and Canada. Since the large entourage which embarked on the *Queen Mary* on 30 December included many who had made similar journeys together during the war (including Eden, Cherwell, Norman Brook, Moran, Colville, Rowan and Mallaby) there must have been a considerable atmosphere of *déjà vu*. Indeed, Churchill's purpose was to re-establish the warm personal relationships which underpinned the wartime atmosphere of partnership. But as Mallaby recalled, 'It was not to be. The Americans were hospitable, as they always are, and some useful and successful negotiations took place, but there were different names and different powers and different influences'.[78] After an absence of almost three weeks, Ismay flew back to London ahead of the remainder of the party to host a dinner of Dominion High Commissioners and Finance Ministers.

The following month Churchill deputed to Ismay the role of Acting Minister of Defence to accompany Foreign Secretary Eden to a meeting of NATO's governing body, the North Atlantic Council, in Lisbon. This required Ismay to travel there on 19 February. It presented a problem.

The wedding of his youngest daughter Mary was due to take place that day. She recalled that when her father announced at breakfast one day that he would not be able to attend her wedding, her mother 'went off like a whistle'.[79] Ismay backed down, although he had to leave for the airport immediately after the service, 'discarding my wedding garments en route'.[80]

The North Atlantic Council consisted of the Foreign Secretaries of the fourteen NATO member states. The chairmanship rotated through the Council members. The Council met two or three times a year in the capital of one of the member states and was periodically also attended by Defence and Finance Ministers, accompanied by a large number of officials. Immediately subordinate to the Council was a Council of Deputies which was collocated with a small secretariat in London. There were also several sub-committees, for example a Defence Committee and a Finance Committee, which had grown in number since NATO's formation in 1949. But by 1952 it had become clear that the complexity of an organisation the size of NATO demanded a fundamental rethink and reset of its management structure.

Apart from attending the main meeting of the Council itself, Ismay was closeted with the other Defence Ministers discussing ways of improving NATO's common infrastructure and integrated command arrangements. This was complicated enough but gaining agreement on how the £150 million improvement programme would be financed was, said Ismay, like 'getting blood out of a stone'.[81] After sixteen hours of tortuous negotiation, agreement was finally reached. The foreign ministers had no easier a time. The Council chairman, Canadian foreign minister Lester Pearson, recalled that 'the 1952 meeting... was a particularly difficult [one] in respect of defence planning upon which Britain and the US [Eden and his American opposite number, Dean Acheson] found themselves in some strong disagreement [resulting in] a vigorous post-prandial verbal battle'.[82] Ismay wrote to Darry, 'All well here, but I've loathed nearly every minute of it. Apart from the fact that one has had to wallow in tons of paper and listen to hours of verbiage, it's so humiliating to be poor <u>as a nation</u>—and a novel experience for me at any rate'.[83] Even in his memoirs he was prepared to admit that he felt 'like a fish out of water' and that he told an American colleague, '[t]his is the first that I have seen of NATO, and thank heaven it's the last'.[84] Little did he know what was about to follow.

One of the Council's decisions had been to appoint a Secretary General to head a strengthened staff secretariat which would take on the responsibilities of NATO's various civilian agencies and assist the Council in broadening its activities and responsibilities. It was agreed that the secretariat's headquarters should move from London to Paris. It was also unofficially agreed that the first Secretary General should be British. The British government's first choice as its candidate for the appointment was Sir Oliver Franks, the British ambassador in Washington, but he declined. Churchill and Eden quickly agreed that Ismay's name should be put forward. It was to be an inspired choice.

The proposal was well received by NATO members, nowhere more so than the United States. There, an influential voice in the consultation process was that of Averell Harriman. He expressed the view that 'Lord Ismay had basically sound judgements… was never bewildered by difficult situations that developed… was absolutely straight and had an excellent sense of the relative importance of things…' He reiterated that 'Ismay had an excellent sense of balance as between political, military and economic considerations [and]… thought that the appointment would give NATO a lift'.[85]

Ismay recalled that the approach to him was made in bizarre circumstances. Eden was ill in bed when, in the second week in March, he asked Ismay to call on him as soon as possible. On his arrival Eden told him straight away that NATO member governments were unanimous that he should be appointed Secretary General. Ismay declined. The more Eden tried to persuade him to accept, the more obdurate Ismay became. Eden telephoned the Prime Minister, who hurried to join them. Churchill was at his most persuasive, underlining the importance of NATO to world peace, appealing to Ismay's sense of duty and indicating that his tenure need be no more than two years. 'My arguments were demolished one by one', wrote Ismay, 'and there was nothing for it but to surrender'.[86]

When the appointment was made public on 13 March it was warmly welcomed. The political correspondent of the *Daily Telegraph* wrote of 'an appointment cordially applauded… the choice could not have been bettered'.[87] The leading article in *The Times* referred to Ismay's 'good sense, personal modesty, and tact of the kind which makes men forget that they represent different nations'. And enumerating the challenges that faced the new Secretary General, it continued, '[i]f anyone can overcome these difficulties… it should be Lord Ismay, whose personality, training and experience all fit him for the work'.[88] Among the many letters of congratulation was one from Eisenhower, since April 1951 NATO's Supreme Allied Commander Europe. Ismay had kept up a correspondence with him since the war and indeed had spent a weekend with him in Paris in the first month of his new appointment. Eisenhower wrote now, 'Partners once more! It will be great!!!'[89]

On 25 March 1952 Ismay handed over to Salisbury as Secretary of State for Commonwealth Relations. He had been in the job for only five months and for much of that time had been involved with matters outwith his appointment. But how did he look back on his tenure, and how should it be judged? Ostensibly he was 'very sad to leave', as he told the *Daily Telegraph* on 20 March [90] And four days later he told a friend how sorry he was to be leaving 'this delightful office'.[91] But that was not what he told his family. 'He hated that job—hated it, hated it', his daughter Mary recalled. 'It just wasn't him.'[92] Although it is easy to understand that the role of politician 'just wasn't him', what was it about the job that caused such intense hatred? The answer almost certainly lies in the one contentious issue with which he had to deal during his tenure: that of Seretse Khama. The case tells us much about Ismay.

Born in 1921 in the Bechuanaland Protectorate (modern day Botswana), Seretse Khama was the son of the paramount chief of the Bamangwato tribe. At the age of four, on the death of his father, he had been proclaimed paramount chief with his uncle Tshekede as regent. After attending schools in South Africa he had come to Britain in 1945, attended Balliol College Oxford and enrolled as a trainee barrister at the Inner Temple, London. In 1948 he had married a white British woman, Ruth Williams. The inter-racial marriage met with a furore in Bechuanaland's neighbour, South Africa. South Africa had just elected the ultra-racist National Party on the platform of apartheid—racial separation—and one of its first pieces of legislation had been an outright ban on mixed marriages. The South African government had demanded that the British government remove Seretse as paramount chief.

This had put the Attlee administration into a quandary. Britain was heavily dependent on South African gold and uranium, and Bechuanaland was completely open to South African military incursion; but the British government could not be seen to be bowing to racist South African pressure. The solution had seemed simple: commission an enquiry to declare that Seretse was not a fit person to be paramount chief. Unhappily for the government the enquiry had reported that Seretse was, after all, a fit person 'but for this unfortunate marriage' which prevented good relations with Bechuanaland's racist and potentially aggressive neighbour.[93] The report was duly suppressed for thirty years. In 1950

Seretse and his wife had been tricked into returning to Britain where they were placed under exile from Bechuanaland, to be reviewed after five years. Meanwhile Bechuanaland was subject to direct rule from London. The case had attracted dramatic coverage in British newspapers and the Khamas received widespread and vociferous public support.

This was the poisoned chalice that Ismay inherited in October 1951. His natural sympathy lay with Seretse and his wife, but realpolitik dictated that wider issues had to take precedence. As he explained to the House of Lords in March 1952, he knew on taking office that one option was to do nothing: to let the remaining three and a half years of the ban run their course. 'There was no sort of pressure, no hint, from any quarter that I should do otherwise—except from my own conscience', he told the House. 'I am thankful that I resisted the temptation to take the line of least resistance. Had I done so, I should have looked back upon my short period in office with shame'.[94] The course that he actually took in November 1951 was to recommend to the Cabinet that, 'after an appropriate interval' an announcement should be made excluding Seretse from chieftainship of the tribe and residence in the territory, not just for five years, but permanently.[95]

In doing so Ismay had been heavily influenced by the senior civil servants in the Commonwealth Relations Office, in particular the Permanent Secretary, Sir Percivale Liesching. An architect of the original ban, Liesching now believed that relations with South Africa required the removal of any doubt about Seretse's possible return as chieftain. His briefing documents to the incoming Secretary of State painted the picture that decisive action was required forthwith.[96] Ismay may have believed that 'there was no sort of pressure, no hint from any quarter—except my own conscience', but he seems to have missed the covert pressure from his own senior adviser. Liesching will certainly have been delighted that the Cabinet endorsed Ismay's recommendation, although for tactical reasons it decided that 'this would not... be announced for the time being'.[97]

Ismay's absence from his office—advising Churchill on defence matters, accompanying him to Washington, and attending the NATO conference in Lisbon—meant that he was something of a part-time Secretary of State for Commonwealth Relations, and all the more reliant on his advisers: particularly in surprisingly complex matters such as the intricacies of Bamangwato affairs. He was, though, genuinely concerned about Seretse and Ruth, both of whom he had made a point of meeting soon after he took office. Early in 1952 he had unwisely, with or without

Liesching's encouragement, persuaded the Colonial Office to find Seretse a job in Jamaica and put the offer to him on 14 March at a meeting also attended by his nominated successor, Salisbury. Seretse turned down Ismay's offer but, unsurprisingly, it was not long before accusations of attempted bribery were made.

Salisbury was a much cannier political operator and got straight to the heart of the problem as he saw it. Referring to Seretse Khama, he advised Churchill just before taking over that, 'we are bound to have this row sooner or later, and if we leave it for three and a half years… we are likely to have to take the same decision on the very eve of a General Election here, which will be even more embarrassing'.[98] As the new Secretary of State he was in the chair at a further meeting attended by Ismay with Seretse on 26 March, and very much dominated proceedings. However, when Seretse announced that he was prepared to give up his claim to the chieftainship if he was permitted to take part in the political life of his tribe, Ismay intervened to say that this completely altered the situation and should be considered. However, Salisbury clearly did not wish to pursue this and after a short adjournment announced that 'renunciation but retention of full political liberty was unacceptable'.[99] The next day the government announced its decision that Seretse would never be recognised as chief and was to be permanently excluded from the Reserve.[100]

Ismay's final involvement in the Seretse Khama affair was his attendance at the House of Lords emergency debate on the subject on Saturday 31 March. He spoke of the 'melancholy and distasteful legacy' he had inherited and the difficult options that had faced him. He justified his decision to ban Seretse largely on the grounds that it is 'the welfare of the tribe that must be paramount, though individuals may suffer'. At the same time he also expressed his personal concern for Seretse, defending his offer to him of a secure job in Jamaica against accusations of bribery largely on the grounds that 'it would have been cruel and callous and un-Christian' not to help him find a purposeful and happy life until a time came when he could return home as a private citizen.[101] There were, however, few members of the House who expressed any support for Ismay or who were anything other than highly critical of the government's decision. The debate was a sad postscript to Ismay's short tenure of his ministerial appointment.

Ismay made no mention whatsoever in his memoirs of the Seretse Khama affair. It was clearly a subject of which he was neither proud nor happy. He had lived and worked with politicians for much of his career, but he was not himself a natural politician—he was notably lacking in guile, cunning and cynicism. At times he was positively naive—for example, offering Seretse what was bound to be described as a bribe—and he found it hard to compromise his integrity, scruples and compassion with the necessary political pragmatism.[102] The contrast with Salisbury in this respect is notable. It is perhaps surprising that Churchill brought Ismay into his Cabinet in the first place, although his appointment of Alexander as Defence Secretary proved to be even less happy. For all Ismay's protestations about his appointment to NATO, it provided an honourable way out for him and one which he may have looked back on with some relief.

15

SECRETARY GENERAL

1952–57

Following his address to the House of Lords on 31 March things now started to move very quickly for Ismay. The inaugural ceremony for his induction as Secretary General took place at Belgrave Square, London, on 4 April. He used the press conference to say that he was a reformed sceptic in his attitude to NATO. He had, he said, previously considered that 'there was too much talk and too little action; too much harness and too little horse', but that having attended a Council meeting in Lisbon in February, 'I realised what splendid progress had been made; and I made no secret of my conversion when I returned to London'.[1] This was, of course, not quite the case but it showed a talent for capturing the headlines with a neat turn of phrase.

Finally, before Ismay left London Churchill gave a farewell lunch party for him at Number 10. It was a memorable event, not least for a Churchillian quip that interrupted Ismay's speech. Ismay was saying how much he regretted leaving his beloved herd of Jersey cows in Gloucestershire when Churchill interjected, 'Quite easy. Milk the cows in the morning. Fly to Paris and milk the Americans in the afternoon'. Lascelles, who recorded this in his diary, added somewhat nervously, 'I don't think there were any Americans in the room'.[2]

The following week Ismay and Darry arrived in Paris. Since he had been nominated as Secretary General only one month previously and had only ceased involvement with his ministerial appointment a fortnight ago, Ismay had had practically no time to think about, let alone to prepare for, the move or the job. And since the role, structure and location of the new headquarters had only been approved in February, logistic arrangements for its offices and for the accommodation for its staff had been hastily made and were far from complete. An interim home for the headquarters was found in temporary buildings at the Palais de Chaillot, across the Seine from the Eiffel Tower. Temporary accommodation for the Secretary General and his wife was arranged in the rather more salubrious Hotel Bristol, in Rue du Faubourg St Honoré.

Ismay's tenure as Secretary General is well documented, both in NATO records and in a number of books, notably two by Robert S Jordan, *Political Leadership in NATO:A Study in International Diplomacy*, and *The NATO International Staff/Secretariat 1952-1957*, both of which had the benefit of author interviews with Ismay.[3] In addition there is the semi-official history, *NATO, The First Five Years: 1949-1954*, of which Ismay himself was author.[4]

Ismay started work immediately. In addition to heading the International Staff/Secretariat, the Secretary General was also Vice Chairman of the North Atlantic Council. The two roles were closely intertwined. The most significant decision made at the Lisbon meeting had been that the Council would now exist in permanent session, replacing the Deputies with more senior Permanent Representatives of ambassadorial status with the authority to act on their Ministers' behalf. Although Ismay placed no formal pre-conditions on his acceptance of his own post, he had let it be known that firstly, in the absence of the chairman, he expected to chair the bi-annual ministerial-level Council meetings; and secondly that he expected to have freedom of action in his dealings with the Council, 'including the right to initiate business and the right of direct access to member governments'.[5] In addition, he obtained formal recognition that he had freedom of choice in the senior appointments of his staff. These measures contributed greatly to establishing the authority and effectiveness of the Secretary General and his centrality in Council affairs. On the first occasion that the Council chairman was not present for a ministerial meeting there was some suggestion that another Minister take the chair, but Ismay succeeded in arguing that as vice chairman this was his role, thus establishing an important precedent.

Ismay's initial challenge was the practical one of establishing a private office and staff for himself as well as setting up the International Staff and wider Secretariat. He arrived with his personal secretary, Betty Green, who had been with him during the war, in India in 1947 and at the Commonwealth Relations Office. He found that his private office consisted of just two people: a British Foreign Office official, Peter Scott, who had also worked for him in India, and a French official from the Quai d'Orsay, Gilles de Boisgelin. Clearly, he needed to act quickly to create an effective staff and secretariat. Before doing so he set down some principles for himself as a guide. These would not be surprising to anyone who knew how he liked to work. First, he wanted to keep his staff small. He had achieved this in the Office of the Minister of Defence in the war by only accepting top-quality individuals. In his new job this would have been harder: he had to rely on the recommendations of people he did not know and to share the appointments around the member nations, ensuring that the smaller nations were not 'squeezed out'.[6] Next he wanted the Council, the International Staff/Secretariat and the delegations to work as a single team. This, too, would have been much easier said than done in a multinational environment. In addition, he wanted to establish and maintain close relationships with other international organisations—in particular the Organisation for European Economic Cooperation, not least for the evaluation of the economic and financial implications of NATO's programme for member states.[7]

The existing secretariat was a small, international group containing some talented officials from NATO member nations. Among them was Captain Richard Coleridge, Royal Navy,[8] who had been a member of Ismay's wartime staff in Whitehall before serving in the Joint Staff Mission in Washington and after the war with the United Nations headquarters in New York. Ismay knew and trusted Coleridge; he gave him the title of Executive Secretary to the Secretary General and used him as his chief of staff. Ismay was also responsible for the work of the Council's twelve committees. These covered subjects such as Infrastructure, Emergency Planning, and Civil Organisation in Wartime. Bearing in mind the breadth and depth of these subjects and the multinational dimension, the integration of these committees and additional working groups was a complex business. Ismay, though, quickly arrived at a suitable organisational structure. At his first press conference just four days after arrival, he announced his proposal to appoint a Deputy Secretary General and three Assistant Secretary Generals, each heading a section—political, economic and production—and pledged to keep the staff as small as possible.[9] He dismissed a question about whether he would seek the Council's endorsement for his personal staff appointments with typical brio: 'You might as well get fourteen people to choose your wife for you'.[10]

While Ismay moved quickly and decisively to address the administrative challenges facing him, he moved more circumspectly in addressing the political challenges, recognising that his own authority was strictly limited: he later joked to Lester Pearson over dinner that he 'had more authority as a first subaltern in the British army than as Secretary General of NATO'.[11] He would also have been aware that some member nations were more enthusiastic than others about the new appointment of the Secretary General and, indeed, about him personally. Some European nations, for example, were suspicious of a Briton occupying the post. And at the outset some 'unkind and ill-informed persons', as a *Daily Telegraph* journalist put it, 'talked of a job having been found "for another dead-beat general"', adding that, '[m]any members of the world's press were frankly hostile'.[12]

Ismay had to tread carefully and use all of the skills of tact and diplomacy that had served him so well in the past. He knew that he had to win his critics over. He went about this in a number of ways. He immediately set out to reassure the member nations and their representatives at NATO headquarters that he did not consider himself to be a figure of authority within the Alliance. He described himself modestly as the 'servant' of the Council and declared, 'I cannot speak or issue instructions on my own authority. I can only speak in the name of the Council and on the authority of the Council'.[13] Soon after he arrived he embarked on a series of visits to capitals to introduce himself and listen—and be seen to be listening—to member governments' opinions of NATO and their aspirations for its future. On return from a 'very enjoyable and very hectic, but, I believe very successful tour of Denmark and Norway', he told Spears, '[t]he more I can get to meet the Ministers of the fourteen Governments whom I am trying to serve, the better'.[14] His easy-going personality, modesty and charm quickly won him friends. In Paris he went to equal lengths to establish good relations with the Permanent Representatives and the Secretariat.

For Ismay, bringing individuals together socially was a key element in achieving cooperation and creating a team spirit. This had been difficult to achieve at the Hotel Bristol. Ismay had asked the French government to find him a permanent residence, but after waiting in vain for eight months he and Darry found a suitable house in central Paris where they could entertain. Number 10, Villa Säid, was situated in a cul-de-sac off the Avenue Foch. Although it had only two spare bedrooms it had large public rooms which could seat about thirty guests for dinner. Ismay and Darry were to put the 'Villa Säid', as it became known, to good use in NATO's interests. They brought their butler, 'Albert' Hodges, from Wormington and followed an exhausting schedule of official entertainment: cocktail

270

parties, almost weekly, for between fifty and 100 guests; frequent lunches and dinner parties; hosting visiting royalty or ministers overnight; and numerous events for major conferences. Darry recalled that in the three weeks before Christmas each year, they held lunch and dinner parties almost every day for a week; a cocktail party for 150; hosted the Council chairman and his wife for the duration of the conference; and the Headquarters NATO Christmas party at the Palais de Chaillot for no less than 1,100 guests. In addition, throughout the year they were expected to attend many external social events as guests. Unsurprisingly, as Darry recalled, 'there were times when the household and all of us were almost out with fatigue'.[15]

Ismay was also aware that he might be perceived as a far from impartial agent of the British government, advancing British interests within the Alliance. He adopted a typically disarming approach to such perceptions, openly admitting at his first press conference that when he left London to take up his new post Churchill's parting remarks to him had been, '[n]ow that you are going to serve fourteen different countries, I hope that you will not consider it absolutely essential to put Great Britain absolutely last on every possible occasion'.[16] He was also careful to be seen to distance himself from close contact with British ministers. For an official visit the following year he planned to travel across the Atlantic on the liner *Queen Elizabeth,* but when he found out that Foreign Secretary Eden and his advisers would be travelling on the same ship he switched to another liner.[17]

From the outset, Ismay ensured that the atmosphere within the Council was congenial and cooperative. Since unanimity was required for all Council decisions, this was a wise move. With all the Permanent Representatives apart from the British having been ministers in their own governments, the fact that he himself had also been one gave him, he believed, equivalent status in their eyes.[18] In Council meetings, whether of Permanent Representatives, who met around twice a week, or at the biannual ministerial meetings, he deliberately did not attempt in any way to dominate proceedings. Rather than push his own ideas and agenda he gently steered discussion, and in summing up emphasised points of agreement. Indeed, he rarely interjected his own view unless invited to do so.[19] He also frequently held informal meetings of Permanent Representatives, with no staff present, 'no agenda, no record, no commitments and therefore no formal decisions'. These meetings, preceded by lunch at Villa Säid, were, said Ismay, 'characterised by the utmost frankness'.[20] Many issues which might have proved contentious and disruptive at a formal meeting were thus identified early and steps were taken to resolve them.

Ismay's efforts to increase cohesion within the Alliance were applied at all levels. Nearest to home he acted to bring the Council and the International/Staff Secretariat closer together. Having his Executive Secretary Coleridge as secretary of the Council was a useful first step. He also believed that the military and civilian leadership of the Alliance would benefit from a closer mutual understanding. In addition to NATO's military committee, on which sat representatives from each member state, was its executive body the Standing Group based in Washington and comprising representatives of the Chiefs of Staff of the nations known as NATO's 'Big Three': the United States, the United Kingdom and France. A tendency had developed for the Standing Group to act somewhat independently from its parent body, and thus from the Council. Establishing closer relations with the Group was to prove an ongoing challenge for Ismay.

In his relations with NATO's European military headquarters, just down the road at Versailles, he was helped at the outset by the fact that Eisenhower was still the Supreme Allied Commander Europe. The two had kept in close touch since the war. Within the past year alone Ismay had visited Eisenhower in Paris and given a dinner party (attended by, amongst others, Churchill, Portal and Cunningham) for him in London; Eisenhower had offered Ismay the use of his Scottish *pied-à-terre*—the top floor of Culzean Castle in Ayrshire—for a holiday.[21] However, only two months after Ismay's arrival Eisenhower left to return to the United States to run for the presidency. Ismay was keen to ensure not only that his successor, who would undoubtedly be an American, would be acceptable to all NATO members but that they would feel that they had been consulted over his selection and not just presented with a fait accompli. He therefore personally spoke to each of the Permanent Representatives in turn to ensure that there would be no difficulties over the prospective nominee, General Matthew Ridgway. As a result, Ridgway's appointment was unanimously endorsed and welcomed. Ismay told the *New York Times* foreign correspondent Cyrus Sulzberger, off the record, that the British War Office was particularly pleased with his selection because 'the war office is still dominated by "stuffed shirts" who emphasise the need of command experience'. Ismay gave his opinion that 'this is quite unnecessary for the job', explaining that while a divisional commander needed such experience, the leader of an Allied coalition did not. 'If such had been the case', he told Sulzberger, 'Eisenhower would never have commanded [Operation] Torch'.[22] Ismay's comments on the need for command experience had merit. They also showed that his disdain for the War Office was undimmed by time.

Although Ismay did not know Ridgway well he went out of his way to ensure that the relationship between Secretary General and Supreme Allied Commander remained cordial and that the civilian and military sides of the Alliance in Europe were brought closer together. For example, he took the Council to visit the Supreme Headquarters and instituted the custom of the Permanent Representatives being invited to visit major NATO exercises.

Ismay also recognised that NATO as an organisation needed to sell itself internationally. He raised the Information Services branch to the level of a division reporting directly to him and set out, himself, to fill the role of NATO's front man. He inaugurated a bi-weekly press conference at NATO headquarters and made a point of appearing at presentations given for groups of influential visitors. On his many visits around NATO countries, he always took the opportunity to give interviews and press conferences. In 1952 alone he made no less than thirty-two speeches and broadcasts.[23] His first public speech in Britain, in September, addressing delegates from NATO member countries, epitomised his message. 'Soviet expansion, intransigence and aggression showed that there were two worlds: the slave world behind the Iron Curtain and the world of free men', he said. 'The democracies were confronted by even greater perils than those surmounted in the war... The storm might break at any time... One of the first tasks was to crusade against ignorance and apathy'. It was a powerful message and, the *Daily Telegraph* reported, 'Lord Ismay scored a notable success with this address'.[24]

Ismay was well placed to enlist some high-priced help in his crusade. A few days later he wrote to Churchill, telling him that NATO needed 'a boost, and that this should come from you'. He continued,

> If therefore you could see your way to proclaiming your steadfast belief in all that NATO stands for and is doing, it would have far more effect than all the speeches of all of us put together and all the efforts of all the public relations staff in the fourteen countries. And I confess it would be a great help to a Secretary General who is not having too easy a ride.[25]

Churchill duly obliged in a high-profile speech at the Lord Mayor's Banquet on 10 November.

A further consistent theme in Ismay's speeches was NATO unity. Speaking in Rome in October he said that the unity of NATO's nations was more important than anything else: it was 'the real answer to the threat of aggression and is what potential enemies fear and want to destroy more than anything else'. The nations had to guard against propagandists' efforts to split this unity because 'nations cannot afford to stand alone and be picked off one by one'.[26]

Many of the political challenges that were to confront Ismay in his time as Secretary General had Alliance unity at their root. The first of these came just one month after he took over. In early May the United States, the United Kingdom and France agreed to a proposal by Stalin that they should meet to resolve issues of international security. The other NATO members asked that the Council should be consulted before the Big Three adopted a position on any policy changes; they were not pleased when told that they would only be retrospectively informed of the discussions and decisions. There was further disquiet at the next Council meeting in July, with the Big Three appearing to brush off criticism of them. Ismay 'expressed his unhappiness with the discussion' and after the meeting took steps to conciliate the two sides.[27]

The result was a change of attitude on the part of all three nations, particularly the United States, but it was not to be the last time that a lack of consultation on the part of the Big Three was to threaten Alliance cohesion. Just two months later a lack of consultation came close to resulting in crisis. In late September NATO carried out a large-scale naval manoeuvre—Exercise Mainbrace—close to Soviet territorial waters in the Barents Sea. The Soviet Union complained of a warlike act, but NATO headquarters and the Council were unaware that the exercise was even taking place: the Standing Group had not seen a requirement to inform them. Unsurprisingly, Ismay was not amused by this. The following month he convened and chaired a joint meeting of the Council and the Standing Group, gaining agreement that in future the Council would be consulted prior to all large-scale military manoeuvres.[28]

One of the most important political challenges facing NATO—and thus Ismay—in 1952 resulted from the related issues of the participation of West Germany in Western defence and the plan for a European army. In October 1950 France had put forward a plan for a supra-national European army under a European minister of defence. By the time that Ismay arrived as Secretary General both the United States and the United Kingdom supported the proposal as a way of bringing West Germany into the Western defence community. One month after his arrival the six members of the European Community signed the Treaty of Paris, establishing a European Defence Community (EDC). Once ratified, this would bring West Germany and its armed forces into European defences without allowing it full membership of NATO—the latter firmly opposed by the French.

Ismay viewed the creation of the EDC as a pragmatic means of achieving West German involvement, and from the start had made it clear that 'the sooner the EDC treaty was ratified the happier he would be'.[29] He was to work hard behind the scenes to achieve it. Much of the opposition to ratification was, perversely, coming from its proposers, the French; political opinion in France was sharply divided on the subject. Although Ismay was far too diplomatic and discreet to let his irritation be known, he was less so in private. When Edward Spears sent him an advance copy of his book, *Prelude to Dunkirk*, Ismay replied, '[o]ur friends here have been behaving as irresponsibly as they did in the days of your story; and they are just as inclined today, as they were then, to put the blame on everyone except themselves'.[30]

At the same time as Ismay was dealing with these major political issues he and his staff were preparing his annual review for the December 1952 ministerial-level Council meeting. The provision of such a review had been agreed by the Council at Lisbon. Some nations might have been hoping that it would be a box-ticking exercise, largely confined to generalities. Ismay, however, was determined that it should be a substantial instrument in the development of the Alliance by assessing NATO's progress in achieving its agreed targets, setting 'force goals' for the coming years and making recommendations. Considering the level of detail required and the fact that the review was unprecedented, this would have been a significant task for a single nation; coordinating it across fourteen nations was no mean undertaking. Indeed it would be surprising if, at times, Ismay did not wonder whether he had been wise to attempt it. But the review was duly completed on time and formed the basis of remarkably productive discussions at the December Council meeting. Also remarkable is that, as Ismay himself pointed out, all the member nations were prepared to submit their defence efforts and budgets to the scrutiny of all other members.[31] The NATO annual review continued to be—and remains to this day—the major instrument in the development of the Alliance, thus fulfilling the role for it that Ismay intended.

Following the Council meeting Ismay and Darry returned to Wormington for the Christmas holiday with the family. Unfortunately, he was confined to his bed with flu for much of the time and did not return to Paris until mid-January. His first trip abroad in 1953 was to be in early March—a visit to Ottawa before moving on to Washington for his first meeting with the newly elected President Eisenhower. Two things would happen before he did so which would dominate the agenda of these visits. The first was Eisenhower's decision, taken shortly after taking office in January, to honour his election pledge to make substantial cuts to American defence spending. This was obviously unwelcome, though not entirely unexpected, news at NATO headquarters and the cause of some alarm and confusion within the Alliance. Other NATO governments, including Canada, found themselves in difficulty at home justifying their own commitments to make substantial increases to defence spending, made at the Lisbon conference the previous year. The second event, on 5 March 1953, the day before Ismay's arrival in Ottawa, was the death of Stalin.

In the discussions in Canada and the United States it would still be too early for anything more than speculation about the impact for NATO of the latter event, but the Canadian government expressed their concern to Ismay about the American defence cuts. The cuts would have been a touchy subject in Washington too, but apart from expressing regret, there was little to be gained by further discussion of what was now an established fact. Ismay met the President at the White House on 12 March. There is no record of their discussion, but it was probably a frank one between two people who implicitly trusted each other. The following day Ismay and his staff had a formal meeting with US officials and, amongst other things, gained agreement to closer ties between the Standing Group and the NATO Council.[32] Less successful was his proposal for Western nations to coordinate their efforts against the growing worldwide communist threat.[33] That evening the President threw a party at the White House in Ismay's honour. In a personal letter of thanks to Eisenhower the next day, Ismay confided, 'I confess I am finding my present job the most difficult, and perhaps the most lonely, that I have ever attempted. Quite honestly, if I did not enjoy the support and friendship of your people in Paris, I would have wilted under the strain'.[34] It was a rare glimpse of the closeness of the relationship between the two men.

Ismay was back in Paris when Stalin's successors announced their clever and much publicised 'Declaration of Peaceful Intent'. This succeeded—as had Stalin's peace initiative the previous year—in severely undermining public support for NATO and creating a feeling, as Ismay put it, that 'NATO was going downhill'.[35] The Council's spring ministerial meeting that April in Paris was an unhappy one, with talk of American cutbacks as 'a return to isolationism' and 'the end of NATO'.[36] Despite Ismay's best efforts, the Council agreed to abandon the expenditure goals agreed the previous year in Lisbon. NATO was facing something of an existential crisis.

The situation was not helped the following month when the United States, the United Kingdom and France decided to hold a three-power summit in Bermuda. To other NATO members this looked like the Big Three again setting out to make decisions about the Alliance behind closed doors without consulting them. A number of Permanent Representatives raised their dissatisfaction privately with Ismay; he had considerable sympathy with them and, no doubt, considerable irritation that his efforts to achieve close consultation between the Big Three and the Council were not achieving the desired results. A row about consultation and the general state of the Alliance surfaced at a meeting of representatives in June with, according to John Milloy, 'an outpouring of pent-up frustration' by various Council members.[37] Ismay openly shared many of these frustrations and announced that he would produce a paper forthwith addressing the areas, including consultation, where he believed NATO was falling short.

Ismay's paper was a sobering assessment of NATO's position and it showed real leadership within the Alliance. While underlining that the threat from the Soviet Union had not lessened in any way despite its protestations of peaceful intent, Ismay expressed his concern about reductions in member states' defence budgets and about calls for further relaxation of defence efforts, concluding that 'NATO is losing momentum'. Of particular concern, he said, was the failure to secure a West German contribution to the defence of Western Europe, with the prospect of ratification of the EDC seeming to be 'further off than ever'. His conclusion to his fellow Council members was that 'we must revitalise NATO'.[38] He gave a number of examples of steps that should be taken to achieve this, including extending the duration of the North Atlantic Treaty to fifty years. Many of his suggestions—including the last—were taken up and approved by the Council, and the paper was to provide an important backdrop to the Bermuda meeting.

Ismay's publicly stated support for the EDC concept belied his real opinion. In a private conversation with Sulzberger he gave his view that the European army was 'a crackpot idea' and that he was personally opposed to the EDC, but that 'we must not let arguments on this subject divide us', because that would be playing into Russian hands. What he said he wanted, and had wanted for five years, was German rearmament and a German contribution to NATO, but with restrictions on German manufacture of armaments. According to Sulzberger, he also confided his 'perpetual nightmare… the thought of a rearmed, independent Germany tying itself up with Russia and using its organising ability and energy together with Russia's vast manpower and fighting ability'.[39] These were, to put it mildly, highly sensitive views to be telling a journalist, even in confidence, but Ismay trusted Sulzberger—arguably with good reason, although it was coincidence that publication of his diaries came in 1970, five years after Ismay's death.

That summer Ridgway was succeeded as Supreme Allied Commander Europe, after only fifteen months in the job, by General Al Gruenther who had been chief of staff to both Ridgway and Eisenhower. As an admirer of Gruenther, Ismay was delighted with the selection. He had first met him when Gruenther was Eisenhower's deputy chief of staff in London ten years earlier. Nicknamed 'the brain', he was, at the age of fifty-three, the youngest four-star general in American history; he was also an expert bridge player who had written books on the game. Ismay invited him and his wife to stay at Wormington during August. Although unable to accept, Gruenther would have been delighted to have been asked. The invitation certainly served to strengthen the relationship between them. It was one which would develop even further: evidenced by frequent correspondence, sharing their thoughts and concerns, with Gruenther's letters sometimes beginning, tongue in cheek, with 'My Lord and Master'; sometimes, 'Pug, my pal'.[40] When Gruenther was convalescing after an illness in October 1955 Ismay and Darry offered him and his wife the use of Wormington Grange.[41]

During their 1953 summer holiday in England, Ismay and Darry were guests at Chequers where Churchill was recuperating following a stroke. Churchill's illness had caused the postponement of the Bermuda summit to December. As part of the efforts on the part of the Big Three to be seen to be engaging in greater consultation with the NATO Council, they invited Ismay to attend part of the summit. Ismay's contacts at the highest level with both the British and American governments meant that he was well placed to press NATO's case to good effect. Addressing the meeting of foreign ministers on 7 December, he stressed the great progress that had been made in the Alliance in the build-up of forces, standardisation in training and procedures, and in the integrated command structure; but he was also unequivocal in expressing his concern that, despite this progress, force levels and military budgets were still inadequate.[42] His four days in Bermuda included numerous formal high-level meetings but also—less formally—a lunch party with Churchill, breakfast with the President, and an impromptu dinner party given for him by the Downing Street staff. But he was not greatly enamoured by the conference itself, telling Sulzberger that he did not think it was useful, calling it vague and inconclusive, and according to Sulzberger summing it up in forthright terms: 'This meeting is a sod'.[43]

His breakfast meeting with Eisenhower, however, was an important event. It lasted a full hour-and-a-half and for most of it they were alone. Despite being classified as top secret, Ismay's record of the meeting survives among his private papers. Their conversation was focused on the subject of the EDC. The President was 'deeply upset' by the French government's failure to achieve ratification of the EDC treaty and its attempts to gain concessions from the US and UK governments as a pre-requisite for the agreement of the French parliament. Congress, said Eisenhower, 'regarded the failure to ratify the treaty as a failure of Western Europe, and particularly France, and to set their house in order, and they [the United States] would not continue to maintain indefinitely their present massive support, both in cash and in kind, for the defence of Europe'. There was a further factor. Eisenhower wanted to amend the McMahon Act which prohibited the exchange of nuclear information, but he said that 'there was not the slightest hope of getting this through Congress unless EDC was ratified'. In his judgement the EDC was not only the best, but also the only hope of a solution to the problem of a West German contribution 'without which NATO would fall down'. Eisenhower urged that the Council pass 'a very strong resolution' at its next meeting underlining the vital importance of early ratification.[44]

For the next eight months finding ways of achieving EDC ratification became Ismay's major preoccupation. Serious divisions in French public and political opinion proved the stumbling block and eventually, on 29 August 1954, France formally rejected the EDC treaty outright. Ismay was closely involved in the frenetic activity that followed. The British government immediately convened a conference of the nine Brussels Treaty signatories which met in London at the end of September. Britain, the US and France agreed to the ending of the occupation of West Germany but with Allied forces remaining by invitation of the newly formed Federal Republic of Germany. Among the Conference's other agreements were

West Germany's accession to full NATO membership and the creation of the Western European Union. The conference then transferred to Paris for the completion of the work and the integration of all the agreements. It was here that Ismay played a leading role. The work was completed in remarkably short order, and announcements made on 23 October.

For Ismay, resolution of the issue of West German membership represented a culmination of his appointment, but he was already considering leaving the job. The two-year tenure, which Churchill had indicated (but, cleverly, not specified) on his appointment, was due to terminate in April 1954 and he wished to inform the Council in good time for it to find his replacement. But, as he told Lascelles in September, he had informed Churchill of this when he was staying at Chequers the previous month and Churchill had talked him out of it. He had therefore decided to postpone his departure but added, 'I certainly do not want to stay for more than a year from now at most'.[45] Rumours that he was about to announce his departure started to circulate and in December he found it necessary to issue a statement declaring that these rumours were 'quite untrue and without foundation'.[46] His wish to leave in the following year was not to be fulfilled. In November 1954 he was once more talking of imminent retirement and was once more persuaded to stay. Possibly, Churchill may again have had a word with him. Possibly some NATO members, notably the United States, exerted their influence at a high level. Certainly, a number of people went out of their way to express to him their pleasure when he announced that he was remaining for a further two years. In a hand-written note the following month, US Secretary of State John Foster Dulles wrote, 'Let me say how delighted I was that you will remain as secretary general until 1956. This is a good Christmas present for NATO'.[47]

How much persuasion was required is debatable. Although the pressure of the job had been continuous and he looked forward to spending more time at Wormington, Ismay undoubtedly derived satisfaction and fulfilment from his work. There were also numerous plus sides to life in Paris. Darry thoroughly enjoyed it and was a tireless hostess at the many social events at Villa Säid. They both had made a large number of French friends and friends within the diplomatic community. They could both indulge their passion for horse racing. Ismay was a member of the Jockey Club and they were regular attenders at all the racecourses round Paris, with a member's box at Saint-Cloud. Ismay, dressed in his suit and grey bowler hat, was a familiar sight at the racecourses: 'Papa OTAN, avec son melon'.[48] All three daughters and their children were regular visitors to Paris. Ismay and Darry lived life to the full. Indeed, sometimes too much so. As Darry related, 'Pug's salary was not large. He had a generous entertaining allowance—but there were times when we were broke'.[49]

Following the decision to accept West Germany into the Alliance, there remained the many detailed practical issues of integrating the country into NATO and these would occupy Ismay and his staff right the way through to the formal accession in May 1955. He was less enthusiastic about the newly formed Western European Union, and strongly opposed to it having a military arm which might rival NATO. But bearing in mind the need to keep all member governments onside he was careful in his wording. 'It is most undesirable', he said in November 1954, 'that the ideal of a European Community should weaken the ideal of an Atlantic Community', urging that 'NATO and the WEU must be complementary to each other, and not in competition with each other'.[50]

More prosaically, during the closing months of 1954 Ismay had gone out of his way to assist in the career advancement of Mountbatten, now CinC Mediterranean Fleet. In August he had received a letter from Edwina, applying her considerable charm in seeking his support for her husband's appointment as First Sea Lord:

> I am sure you will be able to help, dear Pug. It would be heartbreaking if Dickie's remarkable personality and outstanding ability were to be wasted in these next vital [double underlined] years in a backwater... Dear Pug, thank you for all your sweetness and friendship and for your unfailing support to us both in times of crisis.[51]

Ten days later she was asking him to get Prime Minister Churchill's support. 'If [he] turns out to be "sticky"... I wish you [double underlined] could have a word with [him] as he is always so full of confidence in your judgement'.[52] Knowing the improbability of help from that quarter, it is highly unlikely that Ismay wasted his time doing so. But he did write to his former colleague Andrew Cunningham championing Mountbatten's cause and asking him to lobby the First Sea Lord James Thomas.[53] Cunningham did so.[54] Within a week of Ismay's letter came the announcement that Mountbatten would indeed be the next First Sea Lord. Whether Ismay's intervention so late in the day played any part in the decision is questionable. But judging by their effusive letters of thanks, both Mountbatten and Edwina believed it had done so.[55]

Also towards the end of 1954, Ismay was commissioned by the BBC to compere a full-length television documentary about the life of Churchill. It was an uncritical tribute with which Ismay was delighted to be associated. He retained amongst his papers the review of which he would have been most proud: a letter from Colville. 'It was superb last night and quite the superbest [sic] element was the compere', Colville wrote. 'I watched with the PM... who was stirred and moved deeply... I was glad that I had given him a pocket handkerchief as a birthday present'.[56]

Early in 1955 came the publication of Ismay's book, *NATO, The First Five Years*—a semi-official account of the Alliance in the period 1949–54. He readily acknowledged that, following his initial direction, the real work in drafting this large volume had been done by his staff and that he had completed the final writing. He had wisely submitted the book in draft to Council members and incorporated their comments. It is clearly and unsurprisingly a work of propaganda, painting NATO in the most favourable light and focusing on its benefits and achievements. As such, it conveyed an important message at the time of its publication—not least that over its first five years NATO had developed out of all recognition and was here to stay. The book remains an important source document. Its production was something of a triumph for Ismay and one of which he remained quietly proud long after he retired.

With the previous twelve months having been dominated by the EDC saga, Ismay was keen to take back the initiative and move the agenda on. One of his early intentions on assuming his appointment had been to steer thinking towards widening the scope of the alliance and developing its non-military role and activities such as economic collaboration.[57] In addition, he had looked towards NATO becoming involved in international affairs outside the North Atlantic area, in February 1953 declaring, 'we cannot do our business except on a global basis'.[58] As a start he had hoped to develop a link between NATO and the Australia, New Zealand, United States ANZUS Pacific pact, formed in April 1952. In April 1954 he had told Sulzberger of his aspiration that NATO might one day 'just become a piece of an overall world alliance which would include ANZUS, Middle East defence areas, and so on; NATO would merely be the biggest piece'.[59] Now, in early 1955, it seemed to him that the concept of widening the scope of the Alliance should be re-visited. He was not alone in believing this. A number of representatives subscribed to the idea, notably Paul-Henri Spaak, the Belgian foreign minister, who, at the spring Ministerial meeting in May, called for 'some type of "Atlantic Commonwealth"'.[60]

Sadly, Ismay was unable to be present to add his impetus to the discussion: a serious attack of bronchitis caused him to cancel all his engagements for a fortnight. He also missed the subsequent visit to the United States and Canada which he had arranged for all the Permanent Representatives.

Two months later in July 1955 the United States, the United Kingdom and France held a summit meeting with the Russians in Geneva. Ismay would have been pleased that his efforts to get the Big Three to consult the other NATO members prior to major events such as this had borne fruit: representatives of the Big Three gave a presentation to the Council well in advance of the summit and a special meeting of foreign ministers was held on the eve of it. Although the summit was widely considered at the time to be a success, its main effect was unfortunate: the creation of what became known as 'the spirit of Geneva'—an atmosphere of optimism about the international security situation which was largely based on wishful thinking and led to a questioning of the necessity for the Alliance. Ismay was persuasive in countering member nations' inclination to reduce their contributions to NATO. For example, when American Treasury Secretary Hubert Humphrey arrived in Paris in September with the intention of announcing such cuts it was, according to British Ambassador Gladwyn Jebb, Ismay's intervention that caused him to reconsider. As Jebb told British Foreign Secretary Harold Macmillan, Humphrey had been 'profoundly impressed' by Ismay's argument, 'and the cuts have now been shelved for the time being'.[61]

Ismay will have had the opportunity to share his misgivings about 'the spirit of Geneva' with Churchill when a guest at Chartwell in August. By October Eisenhower, too, was expressing concern that there was 'now a feeling growing abroad that NATO may be unnecessary'.[62] Ismay redoubled his efforts to counter this feeling with a number of press interviews and broadcasts. Jordan recounted,

> A story [he] liked to tell to underscore the continuing requirement for NATO concerned a road outside a mountain village which passed a precipice with a sheer drop of 300 feet. The road at this point was so dangerous that the villagers had a wall built. Some years later a traveller returning to the village found that the wall had crumbled. He was told: 'It was unnecessary. There were no accidents.'[63]

It was memorable illustrations such as this that captured the imagination of his listeners and readers.

At the start of 1956, his last full year as Secretary General—and now formally Chairman of the North Atlantic Council—his stock had reached new heights. *The New York Times* noted that 'Ismay has emerged… as the real successor to General Eisenhower as the supreme figurehead and symbol of the Western Alliance'.[64] The year ahead, however, was to prove the most challenging one for Ismay. It did not start well. In early March he told Churchill, now retired, '[e]verything seems in a mess at the moment and I feel we have lost the initiative'.[65] Things were about to go further downhill with a series of crises. The first of these had been brewing throughout the previous year. It concerned Cyprus, at the time a British colony, and the subject of a long-standing and bitter dispute between Greece and Turkey—both NATO members. Ismay strove to keep relations cordial between the Greek and Turkish ambassadors and succeeded in doing so. In March 1956 with the dispute in danger of boiling over, he called a meeting of the Council and proposed that NATO engage diplomatically to resolve matters between the two nations. The proposal became a contentious issue: both Turkey and the United Kingdom opposed it; Greece insisted on Cypriot self-determination. The proposal got no further and Ismay was forced to drop the issue.[66]

Ismay was becoming exhausted, telling Churchill 'I have been working longer hours since I got back to Paris than at any time since the war: and the worst of it is, every problem seems more insoluble than the last… and I am getting despondent'.[67] He was now talking openly about his wish to retire. Responding to suggestions that he was about to resign he replied, 'I have never made any secret of my own opinion that, in the interests of NATO, the time is fast approaching for me to make way for a younger, fitter person, sometime in the next year or so. But I have never fixed on a definite date, and I have not resigned'.[68] Part of the strain was undoubtedly due to the wearing business of countering anti-NATO opinion including, much to Ismay's irritation, in the United Kingdom. For example, a *Daily Express* opinion column in June 1956 advocated reducing both the British garrison in West Germany and support for the Alliance: 'The NATO pact is too far gone to be revived. Britain should stop trying to put strength into this relic and concentrate on putting strength into herself. Bring the troops home and relieve the strain on the country's economy'.[69]

The next crisis was just round the corner. On 26 July Egypt's president, Gamal Abdel Nasser, nationalised the Suez Canal. At the time the implications of this, and the subsequent action by Britain and France, were far from certain. Ismay and Darry set off on their usual summer holiday at Wormington and had the Gruenthers to stay. But Ismay cut short his holiday and returned to Paris. Word had come from Washington that Eisenhower favoured consultation within the Alliance and believed that any intervention, if necessary, should be carried out 'in the name of NATO'. Eden, now Prime Minister, also favoured taking the discussion to NATO. Ismay made preparations accordingly. However during August United States policy changed completely, now opposing NATO involvement. Ismay returned to England and while he was there Eden asked him to call. 'Anthony gave me half an hour yesterday morning', Ismay told Churchill, 'and put me fully into the picture; and I then had a long talk with [Foreign Secretary] Selwyn Lloyd'.[70] What exactly was said at these meetings is unrecorded, but Ismay will have come away aware of the gravity of the situation and of the military plans being considered by the British government.

As the crisis deepened, an unwelcome distraction for Ismay appeared in the form of a speech given in London on 10 October by Montgomery, now NATO's Deputy Supreme Allied Commander Europe, in which he declared that rather than ask for political clearance before authorising nuclear release, 'I would use the nuclear weapons first and ask afterwards'.[71] This raised a flurry of protests in political circles and newspaper headlines, and not just in the United Kingdom. It was left to Ismay to deal with the perceived challenge to the principle of political control of the military. He succeeded, at least in part, in calming disquiet with a statement that, 'Everyone realizes that the use of the A-bomb is a political decision. No commander could take it without consulting his government'.[72] But the statement raised further awkward questions about what exactly were the controls and procedures within NATO for nuclear release, a subject that had yet to be fully addressed within the Alliance.

The distraction did not last long. On 31 October Israel bombed Egypt. British and French military intentions were in little doubt. At the Council meeting that day the British representative Sir Christopher Steel recorded, 'the feeling of the council ran strongly against us and the atmosphere was bad. Lord Ismay, who was visibly dejected, said that in his view NATO faced the greatest threat to its solidarity since the signing of the Treaty'.[73] Ismay was right. The Alliance was badly split with emotions running high on all sides. The reluctance of the United Kingdom, France or the United States to discuss the issue in Council served to demonstrate the degree to which NATO was being sidelined. The sense of crisis was heightened on 4 November: as British and French troops were deploying to Suez, the Soviet Army invaded Hungary to crush an uprising.

The bitter divisions over Suez were to deepen during November, with Ismay increasingly unhappy. Wingate states that Ismay felt that Eisenhower's 'outspoken condemnation of Britain seemed to him at the time to be a betrayal of the friendship and loyalties forged during and after the war'.[74] No source is given but it was almost certainly Darry. Ismay's view was irrational and highly emotional. (It is difficult to agree with Sangster that it was because he was 'rooted in Britain' and it was 'a touch of unadulterated nationalism'.[75]) Again according to Wingate, when Ismay heard that the United States had for a second time voted against the United Kingdom at the United Nations he expressed the intention to resign immediately 'but Darry persuaded him to grin and bear it'.[76] He was clearly deeply distressed by the potential for a catastrophic fracture of the Alliance. On 27 November he telephoned the President of the United States 'in a "desperate", tearful mood', saying that NATO might be 'broken up'.[77] It would appear that Ismay was close to breakdown.

But he quickly recovered his rationality and composure. He devoted his efforts to damage limitation, and to keeping the Suez dispute in perspective by drawing attention to the continuing Soviet threat as witnessed by the brutal action in Hungary.[78] Eisenhower and Secretary of State Dulles also worked quickly to heal wounds. Eisenhower let it be known that he wanted the crisis 'washed off the slate as soon as possible';[79] and Dulles, arriving at the ministerial Council meeting on 9 December, declared that 'we will have to prove that although we differ in some matters, we remain united in vital matters... It is our firm purpose to find the way to bury past discords'.[80] Considering the level to which relationships between the United States and the French and British had sunk, the meeting was remarkably free of argument, let alone rancour. As Dulles reported to the President, 'no serious fireworks and... every evidence that ranks will be closed'.[81] Ismay had worked hard to ensure that that was the case. 'The man with the oil can' had been well placed.

Although the Suez crisis dominated the ministerial meeting it did not totally eclipse a substantial, positive development for the Alliance. Ismay's efforts to extend NATO cooperation in non-military fields had been rewarded earlier in the year by the Council's decision to appoint a committee to examine the subject and produce recommendations. Known as the Committee of Three (or, more colloquially, the Three Wise Men) and comprising the foreign ministers of Canada, Italy and Norway, it reported at the December meeting with far reaching recommendations which widened the areas of cooperation, strengthened internal solidarity and cohesion, and established NATO as a political as well as military alliance. Although not all of the recommendations were fully implemented, the report is seen to this day to have had 'a resounding impact on the development of NATO'.[82]

On the last day of the ministerial meeting Ismay submitted his formal resignation to the President of the Council, to be effective from the end of April 1957.[83] Typically, he was generous in his reference to his successor, the Belgian foreign secretary Paul-Henri Spaak, 'with his infinitely greater experience than I possess'.[84] Council members were unanimous in their warm tributes to Ismay. 'Seldom have such kind words flowed at NATO as on the subject of Lord Ismay yesterday', read one press report which declared that he had become 'the most popular foreigner in Paris'.[85] Ismay had given no reason for his resignation but the following month, in a remarkably frank letter to one of his close colleagues who had written to congratulate him on his five years of service to NATO, he confided, 'I am not retiring for purely selfish reasons but because I sincerely believe that I have just about exhausted my energy, imagination and patience and that it is quite time for the Organisation to have a fresh brain and a fresh hand at the helm'.[86]

Jordan is probably correct in saying that in early 1957, with his departure only three months away and his successor already nominated, Ismay 'no longer commanded the full authority of his position'.[87] In any case, he now focused on preparation for his handover. He had planned to pay farewell visits to all fifteen capitals but having been 'pretty bad with bronchitis for a fortnight at Christmas' his doctors advised no more than five.[88] Rather than make invidious choices, he made no visits. He did, however, manage a few days away in early March with Darry in Monte Carlo during which they dined with Churchill who was staying nearby.

There was one major ceremonial commitment left: the three-day state visit to Paris of Her Majesty the Queen, accompanied by Prince Philip, which took place 8–11 April. Ismay and Darry were involved at almost every stage of the visit with a hectic programme of ceremonial parades, banquets, official receptions and—as Darry later recalled— 'an unforgettable boat procession down the Seine at night with all the bridges and famous buildings floodlit'.[89] The trip was also unforgettable for another reason. On disembarking, and unbeknown to Ismay, his row of medals fell from his chest as he climbed into his car. It was only after they had driven off that he and Darry realised what had happened. They raced back to the spot and found the medals in the gutter.[90]

There was a memorable moment, too, for Ismay's fourteen-year-old granddaughter Patricia who was staying with them at the time of the royal visit. A guest at one of the banquets was Mountbatten, who was visiting Paris at the time. He came to change at Villa Säid. Patricia remembered seeing him coming down the stairs in knee breeches and a tailcoat, 'looking like an actor from a Ruritanian comedy—covered in medals and decorations, sashes over both shoulders, something round his neck'. She recalled her grandfather and Lord Salisbury, who was also visiting, 'walking round him, saying, "what's this, Dickie?… what's that?… the order of the pink elephant?" or something'. To her great amusement, her grandfather eventually said to Mountbatten, 'Really, Dickie, you wear things on your chest I wouldn't put on my arse!' Mountbatten evidently took it in good part (although not without the faintest hint of irritation), replying, 'Ah Pug, you will have your little joke'.[91]

A week after the visit came the announcement of the Queen's appointment of Ismay as a Knight of the Garter—a singular and prestigious honour which he would not have expected, but one which meant a great deal to him. He admitted to Mountbatten that when the Queen's private secretary Michael Adeane had first told him, he had 'dissolved into tears'.[92] Among the many letters and messages of congratulations, one which may have moved him more than most was a telegram from Chartwell which read simply, 'Congratulations and my love, dear Pug. Clemmie'.[93]

Ismay's last month in Paris was largely taken up by a series of farewell lunches and dinners given in his honour by hosts varying from the President of France, the British Ambassador and the Supreme Allied Commander Europe, to the Paris branches of the British Legion and the St George's Society. A highlight was the dinner given by the Permanent Representatives at the Eiffel Tower, with the Palais de Chaillot illuminated in the background. These events were not entirely relaxed and carefree for Ismay: at all of them he was required to make speeches.

Ismay chaired his last Council meeting on the afternoon of 13 May and the following morning he and Darry departed from Paris. He recalled his feelings in his memoirs with remarkable frankness,

> Towards the end, I found myself longing to get home. But when the time came, my wife and I were utterly miserable. The Council had been like a family, and the staff like our children… when it came to leaving Paris, we could hide our feelings no longer. As I passed slowly down the ranks of the French Guard of Honour at the airport, I felt that the *poilus* must

have been astonished to see a British general with tears pouring down his face.[94]

He was not the only one overcome by emotion. A large number of his colleagues and staff were there. One of them wrote, '[t]hose of who were present at Orly airport to bid him goodbye when he left NATO will never forget the scene in which we were all in tears'.[95]

How successful was Ismay as Secretary General?

His five-year tenure as NATO's first holder of the appointment was a formative one for the Alliance and fundamental to its successful development. His period in office was characterised—as has that of most Secretary Generals—by continual crises or potential crises of varying magnitude requiring a flexible, pragmatic response and much political acumen. He was most unusual as Secretary General in that he was not, as all his successors bar one have been, a career politician.[96] Indeed, he had been a politician for barely five months. But 'he viewed his role as being first and foremost of a political nature' and had sufficient experience of politics at the highest level to be well capable of mastering that role.[97] He was wise enough to move circumspectly. He did not, as some of his successors did, devote his energies to driving forward political initiatives of his own. In Ryan Hendrickson's words, 'he was not a policy entrepreneur who pushed his own agenda onto the member states'.[98] That is not to say that he was devoid of policy initiatives; he was not. But he was careful only to take forward those that met with consensus among Council members. He quietly dropped other ideas, such as mediation in Cyprus and coordination of anti-communism world-wide, which were met with a lack of enthusiasm from within the Alliance. His crisis management skills were of a high order, and widely recognised as such. As in his wartime role as Churchill's chief staff officer, keeping the show on the road was his top priority.

Instead of driving forward political initiatives Ismay focused on strengthening the foundations of NATO, both organisationally and politically, and establishing the authority of the post of Secretary General. This proved to be a shrewd and wise choice. Jamie Shea, former Deputy Assistant Secretary General, has observed that the Council's decision in 1952 to restructure NATO's headquarters and establish the post of Secretary General 'finally put the "O" into NATO'.[99] A large part of the credit for putting this into practice belongs to Ismay. The foundations of NATO were also greatly fortified by Ismay's constant focus on strengthening the unity of the Alliance, and on achieving fuller foreign policy consultation between member nations—a theme he chose to emphasise in his 'parting message' to them entitled 'Rules for the Conduct of NATO' (see Appendix C).[100] He was also notably successful in representing to the larger nations the views of the smaller ones.[101]

Ismay established cohesion amongst NATO members by focusing attention on what he saw as the primary purpose of the Alliance. His message was constant: 'The business—the paramount, the permanent, the all-absorbing business—of NATO is to avoid war'.[102] And he was equally clear as to how this was to be achieved: 'If we are prepared for battle, we will not be called upon to engage in it'.[103]

There were, inevitably, areas where Ismay failed to achieve the degree of success which he set out to attain. The complete cohesion and unity he would have liked to bequeath to his successor was stymied by the Suez crisis. The degree of authority which governments were prepared to delegate to their Permanent Representatives was, in many cases, less than that for which he had hoped. And despite his efforts and the report of the Committee of Three, NATO's non-military role had not expanded as much as he wished. He may also have been aware of the developing French discontent which would lead to France's withdrawal from NATO's integrated military structure ten years later. But given the situation he found on his arrival and the circumstances in which he operated, his five-year tenure as Secretary General can be judged to have been highly successful.

That success owed much to Ismay's warmth of personality, his modesty, and to all his skills as mediator, conciliator and facilitator that had proved his making throughout his career. In addition his style of quiet, unobtrusive diplomacy behind the scenes was offset by his notable presentational skills in public. Also notable was the respect and affection in which he was held, both within his headquarters and within the wider Alliance.

His contribution and legacy as Secretary General is well summed up by Jordan:

> Lord Ismay's greatest contribution was the creation of an international climate in which political decisions could be taken by the Council with the least friction. In the political realm, his role was one of 'playing-down'—finding the common denominator among varied and sometimes conflicting interests. In the realms of public relations and administration, his role was one of 'playing-up'—pouring content into such general

conceptions as 'Atlantic Community', 'equitable sharing of the defence burden', and 'an Alliance for Peace'. Great quantities of tact, patience, determination, and optimism were required to overcome the temptations towards frustration, cynicism, and discouragement. Lord Ismay was the servant of the council and the leader of the International Staff/Secretariat in the highest sense of both functions. He created the habit of working together and bequeathed it as a precious legacy to his successors.[104]

It is both a tribute to Ismay and his legacy that most of his successors have, consciously or unconsciously, chosen to emulate the model and style that he established and which stood him in such good stead during his tenure.

* * *

Finally, for many people Ismay as Secretary General is best known for the much quoted aphorism that '[t]he primary purpose of NATO is to keep the Russians out, the Americans in and the Germans down'. It may come as a disappointment to many that there is no evidence that he ever wrote or uttered the words. The quotation appears to have originated in Peter Hennessy's 1989 book, *Whitehall*. 'According to MOD legend', Hennessy wrote, 'Ismay produced this unforgettable job description while explaining NATO's functions to a private meeting of Conservative backbenchers in 1949'.[105] This is highly debatable. There is no reason why he should have addressed a meeting on the subject of NATO in 1949 (long before his association with the Alliance) and no record of him having done so. The catalogue of his speeches as Secretary General, however, shows that in June 1956 he spoke on the subject at the Junior Carlton Club, many of whose members were Conservative backbenchers, but the text of his speech does not include the remark.[106] It is of course possible that he made it during subsequent discussion, but given its undiplomatic tone it is highly unlikely that he, as Secretary General, would have done so unless quoting a third party. Furthermore, none of the attendees at the meeting or anyone else has ever borne witness to hearing the 'unforgettable' quotation at first hand. Nor is there mention of the remark in any of his private papers. Nevertheless, since the publication of Hennessy's book, it appears that no new book, journal or academic paper about the early years of NATO is complete without quoting the aphorism and attributing it to Ismay.

16

SUNSET

1957–65

When Ismay retired from NATO in May 1957, a month short of his seventieth birthday, he was undoubtedly exhausted. But any hopes that he may have had for immediate rest were—as so often in his life—to be overtaken by events. First there were the immediate commitments in the month following his return: the reports to be made in person to the Prime Minister and Foreign Secretary, receiving an honorary doctorate from the University of Cambridge and preparations for his investiture as a Knight of the Garter on 17 June. Then, just one week after the Garter ceremony, he was in hospital for a fortnight suffering from what the Press were told was 'sinus trouble', but which Ismay privately referred to as exhaustion.[1] After less than a month at home he was again in hospital, this time for three weeks, and again in September—each time with a severe infection of the lungs.[2] What Ismay had almost certainly contracted over the years—exacerbated by a lifetime of heavy smoking—was chronic obstructive pulmonary disease. This debilitating illness took its toll and he was never fully to recover his former strength and vitality.

Ismay was already overcommitted. He had taken up a number of business appointments on leaving NATO, rejoining the boards of Commercial Union Assurance and the paper manufacturers Portals Ltd, both of which he had relinquished when he became a government minister; and he had joined the board of Ashanti Goldfields, the chairman of which was his old friend, Spears. He also had a large number of charitable commitments: President of the Royal National Institute for the Blind; President of the English Speaking Union; Chairman of the Governors of Cheltenham Ladies College; a governor of Charterhouse and Sedbergh schools;[3] a trustee of the Shakespeare Memorial Theatre at nearby Stratford-upon-Avon; and President of the Gloucestershire Branch of the British Legion. In addition, he was a Deputy Lieutenant for the county of Gloucestershire. Nevertheless, he was about to take on two further roles: the vice presidencies of the Institute of Directors and of the United Service Corps.

At the same time, he was embarking on his memoirs. He had been approached with offers from prospective publishers as early as May 1956 but had given them non-committal replies. He clearly had it in mind to write his memoirs once he retired, and from that time he was quietly collecting documentary material. He was further prompted in February 1957 on receiving a prepublication copy of Sir Arthur Bryant's book, *The Turn of the Tide*, based on Alanbrooke's diaries. In his wartime diary entries Alanbrooke had vented his frustration with highly disparaging remarks about Churchill. Ismay was horrified. He considered the publication of such diaries a breach of confidence and a betrayal of Churchill. He was also irate that Bryant appeared to magnify Alanbrooke's contribution to victory at the expense of Churchill's, making him out to be 'the strategic genius of the war'.[4] Above all, he was concerned that Churchill would feel hurt by the book.[5] He declined an invitation from the editor of the *Daily Telegraph*, Colin Coote, to write a review of it, telling him that,

> Much as I love and admire Brookie, I myself am convinced that Winston was out by himself not only in the political, but also in the military field so far as the broad sweep of strategy was concerned. The Chiefs of Staff, headed by Brookie, with their excellent technical qualifications in their respective spheres, were magnificent watch-dogs who ensured that his conceptions were militarily practicable and desirable and that the necessary resources were available. No military project was ever undertaken without their full agreement ... [But] there was no one—not even Brookie—within lengths and lengths and lengths of Winston![6]

This was more than somewhat overstated but Coote's subsequent editorial included many of Ismay's reservations.[7]

A few days later Ismay wrote an emotionally charged letter to Churchill about the book, expressing amazement that Alanbrooke had given Bryant carte blanche with his diaries and that 'a historian of Bryant's reputation could have produced anything so unbalanced and cheap'. He continued,

> In his attempt to build Brookie into a Marlborough and Napoleon combined, he has merely succeeded in doing him grievous injustice. He has made him a self-centred, smug, ungenerous and whining character,

who believed that he, and he alone—with occasional assistance from the Almighty—was responsible for everything that went right, and that everyone except himself were to blame for everything that went wrong.

Those who know Brookie and admire him for many of his qualities will recognise Bryant's picture as a most unfair caricature, but the historian of the future may take it seriously.[8]

Ismay's remarks were, for him, unusually emotive and unbalanced. He also wrote to both Bryant and Brooke with forthright criticisms of the book.[9] The need—as he saw it—to put the record straight became a major motivation in writing his own memoirs. Another book will have added to this impulse, and for the same reasons. Later in 1957 Kennedy, the wartime director of military operations at the War Office, produced his memoirs, *The Business of War*. This, too, was highly critical of Churchill, highly supportive of Dill and Brooke, and at times somewhat unflattering to Ismay.

Over the next two years writing his memoirs was to become practically a full-time activity for Ismay. He set about it with typical thoroughness: amassing a wealth of detailed material, using his own copious private papers, and fact-checking frequently with former colleagues such as Bridges, Hollis, Jacob and Colville. He also brought to Wormington a shorthand typist—Jo Sturdee, one of Churchill's former secretaries— to whom he dictated almost the whole book. He produced a number of drafts, all of which remain among his papers, and the unfortunate Sturdee had to cope with deciphering his inexecrable handwriting in the many amendments. In a reaction against the Alanbrooke diaries, Ismay was determined that his memoirs would, above all else, be discreet. 'I need hardly say', he told Mountbatten, 'that my Memoirs will not, like some others, raise any controversial points or betray any confidences'.[10] He was also clear from the outset that the memoirs would reflect his unalloyed admiration of Churchill. They would not, though, claim that Churchill was perfect: 'My immediate object is to tell the story of Winston at war', he wrote to Spears, '...Many of the stories about Winston may appear too trivial for inclusion. They are intended to illustrate various facets of that extraordinary man, including his waywardness, humanity and childishness... I shall be accused of making him out a superman, but that is exactly what he is'.[11]

Ismay's work on his memoirs was interrupted in the spring of 1958 by a further government reappraisal of Britain's higher defence management. Three years earlier Prime Minister Eden had called for a report on the subject and his defence secretary, Selwyn Lloyd, had sought Ismay's advice. A particularly contentious issue was the proposed appointment of a chairman of the Chiefs of Staff Committee, additional to the three Service Chiefs—something strenuously opposed by many senior serving and retired officers. Ismay, however, had supported the move, provided that the chairman worked through existing staffs and did not impair the responsibility of the Service Chiefs as military advisers to the government.[12] His advice had been followed.

In 1957 Eden's successor, Macmillan, launched a more extensive and urgent inquiry through his defence secretary, Duncan Sandys. Within three months Sandys had produced a far-reaching White Paper which proposed (amongst other things) abolishing National Service, substituting nuclear weapons for conventional forces and making swingeing cuts to the defence budget.[13] These proposals were strongly opposed by the Chiefs of Staff and by numerous politicians of all parties. By early 1958 it looked as if deadlock had been reached. In late March Mountbatten, now First Sea Lord, wrote to Ismay informing him of the impasse and telling him that he had had 'a brainwave... urging Norman Brook [the Cabinet Secretary]... that the PM should call you in to advise'. As usual with Mountbatten there was a personal agenda, and he pressed Ismay with the idea of a Chief of the Defence Staff: an appointment that, if offered to him, 'I felt it my duty to say that I would accept'.[14]

Whether or not as a result of Mountbatten's prompting, Macmillan invited Ismay to Downing Street in April and showed him Sandys' proposals. There were, as Ismay recalled, 'two or three features with which I emphatically disagreed'.[15] 'I told him my views... with brutal frankness', he told Slessor.[16] One of the features which Ismay and other opponents of Sandys' proposals most strongly opposed was that for a powerful Defence Minister and central staff with immense power but no responsibility for implementation. They characterised this as an 'OKW, recalling Hitler's *Oberkommando der Wehrmacht* (Supreme Command of the Armed Forces) which they believed had played a large part in German defeat. 'Anything in the nature of an OKW would be a retrograde step', Ismay told Coote.[17] Michael Howard was later to point out that such an analogy was 'curiously inept', resulting from a false reading of the role of OKW in German failure.[18] Nevertheless, when the government produced a further White Paper at the end of July 1958 many of Sandys' proposals had been significantly watered down: the Service ministers still retained the real power and the newly titled Chief of the Defence Staff lacked much authority or even an executive staff.[19] Mountbatten, who assumed the appointment a year later, may thus have regretted involving Ismay in the process. It would not be long, however, before Ismay was to have a further and even greater opportunity to influence the higher organisation of the nation's defences.

In early October 1958, however, Ismay was again in hospital, this time with pneumonia. Remembering how ill he had felt the previous winter, he and Darry accepted the invitation from her cousin Ronald Tree to spend the winter at his villa in Barbados. They sailed for the West Indies in November but Ismay had another bout of pneumonia on board the ship and told Norman Brook that he 'arrived feeling more like a worm than a man'.[20] They remained in Barbados for the whole of the winter, returning in March, though with Ismay not fully recovered from further bouts of pneumonia.

While they were in Barbados Montgomery's memoirs were published.[21] These contained some highly disparaging remarks about Eisenhower. As soon as he had read the book Ismay wrote a letter of support to Eisenhower, saying that he 'deplored' the book. Of Montgomery he wrote, 'I had always hoped he would go down in history as one of the great captains of war and his less attractive personal qualities would be forgotten. But alas he has now insured by his own hand that posterity will know all about him'.[22] In his reply five days later, marked 'Personal and Confidential', Eisenhower, still President of the United States, did not hold back his feelings. The letter shows not only his deep resentment of Montgomery but also the depth of the relationship between Eisenhower and Ismay and the degree of trust that existed between them. The full text of the letter is in Appendix D. Later in the year Ismay continued the correspondence with a letter that no doubt made Eisenhower chuckle. 'If only someone would muzzle, or better still chloroform Monty', Ismay wrote, 'I should be spared the constant danger of high blood pressure. I have come to the conclusion that his love of publicity is a disease, like alcoholism or taking drugs, and that it sends him equally mad'.[23] In public, however, Eisenhower was at pains to demonstrate that he bore no grudge against Montgomery. For example, on a visit to the United Kingdom in September, he included him in a dinner party (also attended by Ismay) at the American ambassador's residence.

Eisenhower's correspondence with Ismay was not purely reminiscences and social chit-chat. For example, he consulted Ismay prior to a state visit he was to make to India and Pakistan in January 1960. For the President of the United States to be seeking such advice from a foreign national was highly unusual, but Eisenhower knew he could trust Ismay's discretion as well as his judgement. Ismay duly provided him with advice about the Indo-Pakistan relationship, including insights into the personalities that he would meet. One of his observations about Indian Prime Minister Nehru was that 'being a Kashmiri Brahman [he] had a blind spot where Kashmir was concerned, and that had it not been so, the problem could have been settled in half an hour'.[24] 'I can't tell you how much I valued your letter',[25] Eisenhower wrote on return from his visit. Eisenhower's respect for Ismay was such that he advised his publishers to get Ismay to write the foreword to the reprint of his book, *Crusade in Europe*.[26]

In Barbados Ismay had continued to work on his memoirs, now with the working title of 'Giving Thanks Always', and continued to do so on his return.[27] He was highly irritated by the publication in October 1959 of Bryant's second volume of Alanbrooke's war diaries.[28] 'I thought [it] much worse than the first', he wrote to his friend Bill Elliot. 'A breach of confidence... Since I am very fond of Brooke it makes me sad to see how much he has been exploited.'[29] Ismay was also not best pleased that Bryant had included Brooke's references to Ismay's proffered resignation at the Quebec Conference in September 1944. Ostensibly his concern was again the hurt this would cause Churchill, but perhaps he was also concerned that his action might be seen as a lack of robustness or loyalty on his part. He felt strongly enough about it to demand from the publishers, Collins, that the references be removed from *The Sunday Times* serialisation of the diaries and from the forthcoming American edition.[30] Collins acquiesced and Ismay received an apologetic letter from a 'very distressed' Alanbrooke.[31]

Ismay's memoirs were published in September 1960. Churchill, who had written the foreword, presided at a dinner at the Dorchester Hotel in London to mark the book launch and 'insisted on the proceedings lasting far into the early hours of the morning'.[32] The twenty guests were all Ismay's former colleagues of various levels from either the war or from his time in India. A silver framed copy of their signatures was to occupy pride of place in his study at Wormington. The book was serialised in the *Daily Telegraph* and was an instant bestseller.[33] On the day of the first serialisation, some newsagents in London complained that they had run out of copies of the paper by 9 a.m.[34]

The book was widely reviewed in national newspapers in the United Kingdom and around the world. Most reviewers were highly complimentary, focusing on the Second World War years: 'the best account that I have read of what major things happened and why they happened', wrote Slim in *The Observer*; 'no better picture of the war as seen from London' read the review in *The Guardian*; 'must reading for Americans today' read that in the *New York Herald Tribune*.[35] Reviewers hoping for sensational revelations were to be disappointed: 'pages of good-natured cliché', wrote John Raymond in *The Sunday Times*; 'adds very little to the history of the war... seems rather simple and dull', wrote Hugh Trevor-Roper in *The Listener*; 'inclined to be stodgy', commented the *Daily Express* reviewer.[36]

With the passage of time the memoirs can be seen in a clearer perspective, especially in Ismay's coverage of the wartime years. Having spent the war almost entirely in Whitehall and—on his rare forays outside it, whether at home or abroad—almost always at Churchill's side, his view was unsurprisingly very Whitehall-centric and Churchill-focused. In September 1940 Colville had written in his diary that 'his admiration [for Churchill]... knows no bounds', and not much had changed when Ismay came to write his memoirs.[37] He sent Churchill all the final drafts of the book and appears to have been writing throughout with him in mind as the primary reader. He makes very few comments about him that could be considered to be serious criticisms, and any such criticisms are diplomatically worded with considerable (almost laughable) understatement; for example, 'He was perhaps too impatient and self-willed to be an ideal chairman in the generally accepted sense'.[38] Not once does he express disagreement with any of Churchill's strategic decisions or his misjudgements of character, such as his early judgement of Stalin.[39] Nor is there any mention of those occasions when Churchill, visiting local communities during the Blitz, received a less-than-rapturous welcome.

As a result the memoirs reproduce a stereotype which is sometimes closer to myth than to reality. For example, he views the war very much as a 'people's war' in which the nation came together, united behind Churchill and remained so—a perception which historians have increasingly challenged. As Jonathan Fennell has suggested, such views have contributed to a 'mythologised version' of the war.[40] And although there is allusion in his memoirs to some of the emotional pressures on Churchill, Ismay avoids mention of pressures which might have embarrassed Churchill even though they provide insight into his mind. For example, there is no mention of Ismay's view, expressed elsewhere, that the Dardanelles experience '"had the most tremendous impact on him, an impact that people never realised" and one that lasted in the back of his mind even after he became Prime Minister'.[41]

In addition, as mentioned earlier, Ismay wrote his memoirs with the same diplomacy that he exercised throughout his career and was at pains not to cause offence of any sort to anybody. His assessments of colleagues were invariably complimentary and, taken at face value, can lead to the conclusion that he 'always managed to see the best side of other commanders'.[42] He certainly did so in his memoirs and in public but this was often at odds with what he said about them in private. To give just two examples: Ismay was unbounded in his praise for Mountbatten in his memoirs; but in private he was critical of aspects of his character and performance. For instance, as we have seen, he deprecated his lack of impartiality between India and Pakistan and his downplaying of the casualty numbers of Partition; Ismay also observed candidly that 'there's an undue amount of ego in his Cosmos, and tact is not exactly his strong suit'.[43] Second, he was equally fulsome in his memoirs about General George Marshall. But following a trans-Atlantic flight with Ismay in 1953 Sulzberger recorded in his diary that, 'Pug thought Marshall was a very bad strategist. He had old-fashioned ideas of always wanting to get straight at the enemy regardless of the over-all strategic requirements'.[44]

The memoirs therefore need to be treated with due circumspection as a historical source. They were, though, a considerable financial success. Heinemann organised a promotional lecture tour for Ismay, both in the United Kingdom and in the United States. To his immense annoyance he had to curtail the American tour due to illness and prior to the dinner due to be given in his honour by Eisenhower at the White House.[45] Over the course of the next few months, book sales were to earn Ismay a substantial sum of money: according to his daughter Mary, he was able to pass on £5,000 (around £115,000 at 2023 prices) to each of his three daughters.[46]

From now on he was to spend almost all his time in the country, only occasionally venturing to London. At Wormington he was feeling 'a bit of a crock these days', confined for much of the winter to 'living the life of a hermit in my study'.[47] Although he was able to give more attention to the estate his ill health meant that even when the weather improved, he required a vehicle to move even a short distance.

He still had his business and charitable commitments, the latter now including a fund for impoverished senior Polish officers in the United Kingdom who were unable to return to their homeland. Since the start of the Second World War Ismay had remained 'a firm friend of the

Poles', particularly since the Yalta Conference at which in retrospect he considered the Western Allies had badly let down Poland.[48] In 1958 he had been approached by Count Stefan Zamoyski, a Polish exile living in Britain, about the plight of these officers. He had then jointly, with Field Marshal Alexander, signed a letter to the *Daily Telegraph* highlighting their plight and persuaded other senior figures, civilian and military, to support their cause. In 1961 he was instrumental in launching the Polish Senior Officers Appeal, along with the other signatories: Prime Minister Macmillan, Alexander, Cunningham, Portal, and Lord Astor.[49]

A further campaign that Ismay supported was that for the award of a medal for Bomber Command. Tucked away in his memoirs is a paragraph complaining about the inadequate recognition that the Command had received. Accepting that controversy remained over the ethics of area bombing, Ismay argued that 'no one can question the valour, efficiency and team-work that they brought to their task, or deny the ordeals they faced night after night, week after week, month after month [which] seemed too frightful for flesh and blood to endure'.[50] Here there was veiled criticism of Churchill who had opposed the award. Indeed, there is indication that the subject may have been something of a bone of contention between them. He told Spears that he thought that Churchill had been 'unnecessarily obstructive' over the matter. 'I never understood', he wrote, 'why he resisted a special medal for Bomber Command... Their casualties were something of the order of the PBI [poor bloody infantry] in World War I and yet Winston wouldn't give them a special flag.[51] He could be maddening, couldn't he?'[52]

At the start of 1962, after yet another bout of pneumonia, Ismay, who was still a heavy smoker of unfiltered cigarettes (State Express 555 was now his preferred choice) was persuaded to give up smoking and Darry banned smoking in his presence.[53] Ismay admitted to Spears, 'I'm afraid that I've just got to face the fact that I must live the life of a semi-invalid for the rest of my days'.[54] Being a semi-invalid did not, however, prevent Ismay from starting new initiatives, even ones that he knew were going to cause him much work. The first of these was prompted by the publication in late 1961 of the book *The Last Days of the British Raj*, by Leonard Mosley. The author, a former journalist, produced what one reviewer aptly described as 'journalese under the guise of history': a racy, sensational account of Partition with no confusion about who the villain was.[55] According to Mosley, Mountbatten made numerous avoidable blunders and recklessly rushed through Partition in order to be 'back in the Navy by June 1948, just as he had always insisted he must be'.[56] Some saw in the book the hand of the virulently anti-Mountbatten Beaverbrook, for whom Mosley had once worked. As seen earlier, Ismay was also depicted unflatteringly.

In March 1962 Ismay wrote to Mountbatten, now Chief of the Defence Staff, urging newspaper articles to be written refuting Mosley's allegations and setting the record straight. Mountbatten's response was to propose that a book should be commissioned about the transfer of power, suggesting a number of possible authors.

Over the next fourteen months a flurry of correspondence took place between Ismay and several authors including Alan Moorehead, Peter Fleming, Cecil Woodham-Smith, Penderel Moon, and Desmond Young— all of whom, for various reasons, declined. In September 1963, after lengthy negotiations, HV Hodson—former Fellow of All Souls College, Oxford and recently retired assistant editor of *The Sunday Times*—finally accepted. His book *The Great Divide* was far from journalistic, but it was also a semi-official account with almost no criticism of either Mountbatten or Ismay.[57]

By the late autumn of 1962 Ismay was again afflicted by what he now called 'the beastly bug', and by the end of the year was not only regretting not being in the West Indies but also finding family Christmas to be rather trying.[58] 'This very cold weather doesn't suit my bellows, and I sometimes wonder if I was wise to refuse to go to Barbados', he wrote to Bill Elliot on 28 December. 'The house is at present overflowing with grandchildren. Six of them and a fiancé, so I've taken to the library and locked myself in'.[59]

Just four days later, on New Year's Day 1963, he received a call from Mountbatten which was to result in what was to be his final service to the State. Mountbatten, now in his fourth year as Chief of the Defence Staff, explained that he had sent a paper to the Prime Minister with far-reaching proposals for the higher organisation of Defence. Macmillan and his Defence Minister Peter Thorneycroft had called for the proposals to be reviewed by 'someone of outstanding national stature' and had agreed that Ismay and Ian Jacob should together be invited to carry out this task.[60] Ismay protested that he was now out of date with the subject and in ill health, but Mountbatten persuaded him that his name 'would carry so much more weight in the Service Ministries', and that Jacob could do all the legwork in London.[61] This was followed by a formal request from Thorneycroft and a letter from Jacob hoping that Ismay would accept. Somewhat reluctantly, he agreed to do so: the call of duty was too strong, although what the government really wanted of course, even more than Ismay's input to the report, was his name on the cover.

With a deadline of six weeks to produce their report, Ismay and Jacob faced an intense challenge. As Ismay was the first to admit, Jacob performed the lion's share of the work: carrying out interviews in London, producing drafts for Ismay's comments, and coming down to Wormington for face-to-face discussions.[62] They worked together as harmoniously as they had done in the war and, indeed, in the production of the 1946 report on the higher organisation of defence. In their work on the 1963 report they agreed about most things but not everything, although their disagreements were mostly differences of emphasis.

From the start Ismay's focus was on having a revitalised Defence Committee and immediately merging the three Service departments into a single Ministry of Defence ('My every instinct cries out that this is the time to do it').[63] He believed that a Chief of the Defence Staff was essential, but not the all-powerful one that Mountbatten proposed, instead retaining the Service boards, with the right of the Service Chiefs, should they disagree with the Chief of the Defence Staff's advice, to have direct access to the Prime Minister.[64] He also continued, as he had done in previous reviews, to set his face against anything resembling Hitler's OKW. Ismay's opposition to the creation of an effective—and much needed—central staff was instrumental in preventing its adoption in the report.

One of the obstacles to achieving a consensus was the acrimonious nature of the relationship between the Service Chiefs and Mountbatten who, as Jacob observed, 'seems to be universally mistrusted'.[65] The Chief of the Air Staff, Marshal of the Royal Air Force Sir Thomas Pike, probably articulated the essence of their view of the need for change in Defence when, alluding to Mountbatten, he wrote succinctly 'What is wrong is the driver, not the car'.[66] The Chiefs' views seemed to be representative of those of most retired senior officers and a number of politicians. Ismay and Jacob were old hands at the game of effecting change in Defence organisation and were essentially pragmatic in their approach. They were well aware of the emotive issues at stake and realised that if they wanted their recommendations to be implemented, there was a limit as to just how radical or controversial they could be.

What became known as the Ismay–Jacob Report was presented on 23 February 1963.[67] Of the three options considered, it chose the middle path: the amalgamation of the Ministry of Defence, Admiralty, War Office and Air Ministry, and their collocation in a single building with a Secretary of State for Defence presiding over three junior Service ministers. Under this option, the central staff would be strengthened somewhat but the Chiefs of Staff would remain as professional heads of their Services and retain their corporate responsibilities. There would also be a 'general list' of all senior officers who would have titles common to the three Services and who would wear the same insignia and uniform. At a higher level, the Defence Committee would be revitalised and become the Defence and Overseas Policy Committee. Ismay and Jacob saw all of this as a step towards the third option: 'a completely integrated, functionally-organised Ministry of Defence with the three Services retaining their identity in units and formations while being fused together in their higher organisation'.[68]

The resulting White Paper which Thorneycroft presented to Parliament and was approved in July 1963 followed the Ismay–Jacob proposals, as Michael Howard noted, 'very closely indeed'.[69] It was to be described twenty years later by the House of Commons Defence Select Committee as 'the most fundamental change in the organisation of Defence in modern times'.[70] Despite Ismay's reservations about taking on the assignment and his limited contribution to the hard graft of producing the report, he had again played a central role in shaping the nation's higher direction of its defence.

Producing the report had interrupted work on a further task that Ismay had set himself. Like his previous initiative in the 1960s this one also concerned authorship of a book, this time a biography of his old friend Carton de Wiart. Ismay had clearly had such a biography in mind for some years, to be partly authored by himself. In 1960 he had produced several pages of notes as the basis for a chapter on Carton de Wiart in Somaliland in 1914. In August 1962 he was approached by a friend of Carton de Wiart's—Hugh Molyneux, Earl of Sefton—suggesting that Ismay write the biography. Ismay began to sound out various friends who had served with Carton de Wiart, starting with General Sir Richard O'Connor who had been a prisoner-of-war in Italy with him in 1942–43. 'Adrian was an inspiration to me personally', wrote Ismay, 'and I should like to think that his story would inspire those that come after me'.[71] O'Connor heartily approved the idea and agreed to write a chapter on their time there. Ismay wanted an editor who would undertake the main coordination work and gained the approval of the publishers, Constable, to go ahead and find one. Ismay approached several potential editors, including Peter Fleming, Dennis Kelly and Alistair Horne, but without success. In February 1964 an offer by a lesser-known author, Bryan Lewis, was accepted by

Constable and then retracted. The project foundered, though not for want of effort: it had lasted two years and involved Ismay in an exchange of correspondence of over 130 letters.[72]

From mid-1963 Ismay was to be continually beset by episodes of ill health. Much to his regret he was unable to attend Carton de Wiart's funeral in June. But between these episodes he was in comparably good health and good humour, attending local agricultural shows with his prize cows. His grandson James Evetts, then aged ten, fondly recalls Ismay's sense of humour at the local Evesham show of which he was president. Ismay got into conversation with a group of young undergraduate friends of his granddaughter and showed them how to crack a hard-boiled egg on his forehead, challenging one of them to follow suit. However, he purposely gave the unfortunate man a raw egg—with predictable results. Ismay was 'falling about all over the place in mirth, false teeth going in all directions'. Fortunately, the undergraduates also saw the funny side of it.[73]

In August, however, he was in St Bartholomew's hospital in London and remained ill at home for several months afterwards. In November Clementine Churchill wrote to him, 'I am so grieved that you are ill and feel so wretched'.[74] Thereafter, increasingly housebound, he spent more time reading and reminiscing with his close friends, mostly his wartime colleagues. Among the most frequent correspondents was Eisenhower who continued to confide his inner thoughts to Ismay. In early 1962, a year into his retirement from the presidency of the United States, he had shared with Ismay his sadness at the death of Bedell Smith and his high respect for the abilities of Al Gruenther ('Frankly, I wish it were possible under existing circumstances to push him for President of this country').[75] In the summer of 1963 he was seeking Ismay's perspective on the political situation in the United Kingdom and the United States. With an American election imminent Eisenhower admitted that he was wearying of many aspects of politics but that nevertheless, 'I am so bitterly opposed to the domestic and economic policies espoused by the current administration that I am very much afraid that I will be getting deeper and deeper into the coming battle'.[76] In September he was sharing with Ismay his opinion of Prime Minister Macmillan: 'doing a good job... Harold does not panic!' He went on to pay Ismay a considerable and sincere tribute.

> No others stand out as you do in the combined qualities of judgement, common sense, dedication, selflessness, understanding and moral courage. I realize that a male Anglo-Saxon rarely indulges in the embarrassing habit

of expressing feelings of admiration to another; but I've so long believed that you were not only the greatest of modern British soldiers and at the same time the least recognized that I wanted to put my sentiments in the written record. The difficulty was that you were so valuable to Winston in the tense years of the war that he would not let you go to one of the big command positions you so well deserved, and I don't blame him![77]

In November Ismay was in London for what was to be his last attendance at an Other Club dinner. Later that month he was ill again with bronchitis and by March 1964, 'convalescing slowly—but oh so slowly'.[78] In the summer, hearing that Churchill's health was now declining rapidly, Ismay was driven to Chartwell on 5 June to pay what he must have known was his farewell visit. On arrival he said to Churchill that, it being Derby Day, they would watch the race together on BBC television, '[b]ut alas, I couldn't make him understand what the Derby was, or what the BBC was'.[79] Back at home that evening Ismay watched a documentary commemorating the twentieth anniversary of D-Day. As he related to Eisenhower, he was enjoying the programme until Montgomery appeared on the screen, 'raving like a demented creature and reviling your strategical conception of the operations opposite Caen'. Ismay 'switched him off... but not before I had almost succumbed to blood pressure and... given vent to a flow of language from the barrack room'. Ismay contrasted the programme with another the following night which featured Eisenhower in which the only person he did not mention was himself. 'Characteristic', commented Ismay.[80]

When Churchill died on 24 January 1965, Ismay was one of the escort pallbearers at his funeral. He was far from well, having just recovered from a bad attack of bronchitis, but determined to carry out the duty even if it killed him—which it nearly did. Fellow members of the congregation noted that he was struggling. In reply to a subsequent letter from Lascelles expressing concern, he admitted, 'I only just made it'.[81] It was a cold winter's day, which adversely affected his breathing. He nearly faltered on the steps of St Paul's Cathedral and had to sit down behind a pillar to rest on the way out. On return to Wormington he was confined to bed, recovering only two months later. He was, however, able to attend the Garter Ceremony at Windsor in June and to be present in the House of Lords the following week as one of the two sponsors of Clementine Churchill on her introduction to the House as Baroness Spencer-Churchill of Chartwell. It was the last time he was to see her. Their relationship had developed into a close one. He had seen her regularly and frequently throughout the war: at the Churchills' flat when he came to brief Churchill, for weekends at Chequers, at other social engagements and on overseas trips to conferences. As has been seen, they trusted each other completely and, on occasions, conspired to prevent Churchill from misbehaving. After the war he had been a guest at Chartwell and had joined them on overseas holidays. She had been a guest at Wormington, on one occasion staying for a week. Touchingly, when she considered putting the Chartwell kitchen garden on a commercial basis the first person she turned to for advice was Ismay—very much behind her husband's back.[82] Market gardening was not actually one of Ismay's strong suits but, true to form, he knew the right people to ask.[83]

Attending Clementine's introduction to the House of Lords was to be the last time that Ismay left Wormington. Thereafter, until near the end, he and Darry continued to entertain their friends and he remained the cheerful and amusing raconteur that they remembered. But he was 'going downhill fast'.[84] He had increasing trouble with his breathing, frequently required oxygen, and found even climbing stairs difficult. His grandson John Evetts remembers as a teenager watching him climbing laboriously up the main staircase at Wormington Grange and having to sit in a chair that had been placed in an alcove, half-way up, in order to rest and take oxygen before continuing.[85] In early December his health suddenly deteriorated, and it was clear that the end was approaching. He died at home on the night of 17 December.

Ismay's funeral was held in the Wormington church on 21 December. That his death was not unexpected was shown by the fact that the memorial service at St George's Chapel, Windsor—a formal event requiring considerable notice and preparation—was held the very next day. The Queen and other members of the royal family were represented at the service and the large congregation included government ministers, representatives of numerous embassies and high commissions, many senior officers from all three Services and a host of former colleagues and personal friends. Mountbatten read the lesson. Obituaries in the national newspapers to General Lord Ismay KG, GCB, CH, DSO, PC, DL all paid fulsome tribute to his wartime role and his contribution to the successful development of NATO.

17

EPILOGUE

Ismay's life was a remarkable one. It had been a life of distinguished service to his country, and his achievements in four of his appointments (at the CID, with Churchill in the war, with Mountbatten in India, and as NATO's first Secretary General) were of historic significance. Throughout his life he had been held in respect, admiration and with affection not only by colleagues but by almost everyone with whom he came in contact. What was the essence of his personality? How was his character moulded?

Throughout his life Ismay demonstrated certain characteristics in large measure, most obviously a sense of duty and service, honour, loyalty and patriotism. As has been suggested, the root of these characteristics can be found in his upbringing in India in a family steeped in the self-perceived institutional ethos of the Indian Civil Service and the British Raj, even where this ethos was at odds with reality. His patriotism, however, never strayed into outright nationalism. But he remained for the whole of his life an unashamed imperialist in the sense that he never questioned what he perceived to be the unalloyed beneficence of the British Empire and Commonwealth. *Time* magazine once described Churchill as 'An imperialist of the Rudyard Kipling school';[1] the epithet could equally, perhaps more appropriately, be applied to Ismay, who did not share Churchill's more extreme views of empire but who was a devotee of Kipling and his works.[2]

From an early age he developed a determination to succeed at whatever he was doing. Brought up to believe that hard work was a prerequisite for success, he showed from his schooldays onwards a capacity for single-mindedly applying himself to his work. On occasions he took this to extremes, driving himself to exhaustion and breakdown: for example, in Somaliland, at the CID, and while working for Churchill.

Ismay was blessed with considerable intelligence and, as he demonstrated throughout his career, was very much a 'thinking soldier', although—like most successful army officers of his time—he was always keen to downplay his intellectual attributes. (Hollis recalled once asking him what languages he spoke; to which the answer was, 'parade ground'.[3]) In addition, throughout his life he demonstrated considerable emotional intelligence, showing a self-awareness together with an instinctive perception of the emotional needs of other people, as well an ability to handle interpersonal relationships with skill and empathy. He also possessed—and became renowned for—his common sense, good judgement and wisdom. Whether it was commanding the Camel Corps in Somaliland, operating in the CID, performing his wartime role in London, acting as chief of staff in India, or in his capacity as secretary general of NATO, he could analyse facts or a situation quickly and draw logical and clear-eyed conclusions when others were allowing emotion to colour their judgement and skew their decisions. He also became renowned for those qualities noted by Carton de Wiart in Somaliland: 'his thoroughness, soundness and utter dependability'.[4] In India Campbell-Johnson, who got to know Ismay well, remarked perceptively that '[h]e has the Roman virtue of *acquinimitas* [sic]', that is, equanimity: calmness and composure, especially under stress.[5]

This is not to say that he never succumbed to stress or emotion, or that his judgement was faultless. He was sometimes pushed to the edge and over it by the pressure on him from all sides, and as has been seen he came close to resignation and breakdown. Occasionally he was overcome by emotion, for example at the time of the Suez Crisis. There were also occasions when he was over-hasty in decision-making. His precipitate arrival at Plan Balkan—the plan he took back to London in May 1947 —was one such occasion. His intention to parachute into France in May 1940 was, if it was serious, an obvious misjudgment. And, as we have seen, his handling of the approval process for the Dieppe Raid in 1942, of the Radcliffe Award in August 1947 and his threatened resignation from the council of the Festival of Britain in 1950 open him to further criticism.

Among Ismay's most notable attributes was his considerable intuition. His wartime colleague Ian Jacob noted his 'remarkable perception—a kind of sixth sense—which foresaw the likely course of events and of men's actions'.[6] Joan Bright noted something similar, linking it to judgement of character. He had 'a psychic perception of men's foibles', she wrote, 'and, more often than not, a sure discernment of their true motives'.[7] There were, however, occasions when he showed a certain naivety. Lacking cunning and guile, he sometimes failed to recognise these traits in others, and this contributed to his limitations as a politician. His dealings with the Seretse Khama case as Secretary of State for Commonwealth Relations provides an illustration. He was also overtrusting in some of his dealings with politicians at the time of Partition in India.

Other notable defining characteristics were his sense of duty and of loyalty. It was these that consistently drove his decisions and actions. A sense of duty was deeply ingrained in him, and he always put duty before personal considerations and wishes. Colville described him as 'the most conscientious slave of duty'.[8] Loyalty was a matter of honour; the idea of letting down a friend was abhorrent to him. One of the clearest examples of his sense of duty and interpretation of loyalty was the loyalty that he gave to the appointment of Prime Minister rather than to the incumbent. Although he was personally devoted to Churchill, and greatly saddened by his political defeat, he gave to the new Prime Minister the same wholehearted commitment and loyalty, both in public and private.

Yet he sometimes took his sense of duty and loyalty to extremes. For example, his sense of duty was somewhat narrowly defined. For him, duty to his country or to his job always took priority over any duty to his family, although this was not always without a pang of conscience. In the case of loyalty, although he was a man of great integrity, he sometimes allowed loyalty to a friend to trump all other considerations. His relationship with Mountbatten was a case in point; that with Churchill, especially in the advice that he gave to Churchill during the writing of his memoirs and the portrayal of him in his own memoirs was, less obviously, another.

Ismay possessed several other attributes that contributed notably to his success throughout his career. The first was courage. It was not so much physical courage—although he demonstrated this both as a subaltern in the 1908 Mohmand expedition and, later, on several occasions in Somaliland—as moral courage. He had shown moral courage as a major in India, taking on the management of the Rawalpindi Club over their rejection for membership of an Indian officer, and later in standing up to Lady Willingdon in her attempt to sack an aide-de-camp. But it was in telling Churchill what Ismay believed he needed to hear, even when he knew that a Churchillian explosion would probably result, that Ismay displayed a high (and necessary) level of moral courage. It could be argued that he did not do this often enough, but it was sometimes wiser and ultimately more successful to circumvent the issue by deferral or re-presentation of the case. It was also to Ismay's advantage in speaking his mind that, after Darry's inheritance of Wormington, his livelihood did not depend on his military career nor on the patronage or approval of his superiors.

A further, related attribute was Ismay's high level of tact and diplomacy. This he demonstrated not just in his capacity as Churchill's chief staff officer but in all his other senior appointments, not least at NATO. Finding common ground between disputants and achieving conciliation was part of his nature. Even in his memoirs he preferred to follow this path, often as noted earlier at the expense of objectivity. Mention must also be made of a characteristic that Ismay appeared to have had in unlimited quantities: patience. In a life during which the time he spent in committee could be measured not in hundreds of hours but in thousands, there are no suggestions of him ever raising his voice, let alone losing his temper, inside or outside committee.[9] He was also noted for his insistence on high standards. Hollis told Bright, 'Whether in food or drink, work or people, Pug just isn't interested in anything but the best'.[10]

At the same time Ismay possessed a warm, outgoing personality and was respected and well liked by his staff whether in Whitehall, India or at NATO. This was as much the case with junior subordinates and secretarial staff as with more senior staff officers, and it reflected Ismay's genuine respect for them and gratitude for their work. When his young assistant, twenty-eight year-old Lieutenant Commander Ian McEwan, Royal Naval Volunteer Reserve, left in 1945, Ismay inscribed his farewell present, 'For Ian McEwan who has been my guide, philosopher and friend for over three years… with my most grateful thanks'.[11] Another of his junior wartime subordinates, Captain Wendy Wallace, wrote to him after she left: 'I often wondered what it was that made our office such a happy place, but now I know the answer. Many great men must be admired and respected by their staffs, but there can be few who are really loved as you are by us all… it will be as "our general" that I shall remember you'.[12] This affection was shared by other staff with whom Ismay dealt. Kathleen Hill, one of Churchill's secretaries, wrote to him on his retirement from his wartime role, 'I should like to tell you what you may perhaps already know, that in my small circle at No 10 during the War, there was no one— after the Master—for whom we had greater respect and affection, whose fine character we admired more'.[13] Another of Churchill's secretaries, Elizabeth Nel, described Ismay as 'a charming person, always full of fun, and far more approachable than most British officers', recalling that at Chequers, 'sometimes before dinner he would bring glasses of sherry into the office for the personal staff... somehow, having to drink it hastily without being caught at it made it all the more delicious'.[14]

Bright noted 'his fatherly concern about subordinates... lift-men, messengers, shorthand typists, clerks, junior officers, cleaners—all felt free to speak to him and be sure of a hearing, a reaction, a joke, or an enquiry about their families'.[15] Betty Green recalled that late one evening during the war as she was rushing to catch her bus home Ismay was 'standing at the doorway of the office, talking to the security guard with his spectacles on and looking at this chap's photographs of his family'. As she commented, 'not many busy, tired men who'd had a very long and busy day would have done that. He was so interested in everybody—it didn't matter what rank, grade or anything you were'.[16]

Ismay was ahead of his time in his attitude to the employment of women. At a time when female staff in government offices were generally employed only as shorthand typists, he was prepared to employ them on their merits. Thus Betty Green, though a graduate of the University of London, was initially employed in the Cabinet Office as a shorthand typist. But Ismay recognised her talents and promoted her to be one of his executive assistants.[17] Joan Bright, too, was promoted to be in charge of the Special Information Centre and to have executive authority as an international conference administrator. She described him as 'a great supporter of women workers', interested only in an employee's ability to perform to a high standard.[18]

Ismay thoroughly enjoyed life beyond the workplace. A highly sociable character with a wide circle of friends, he was a bon viveur who enjoyed good company. He was a natural raconteur with a ready sense of humour. Jacob recalled, 'he had a most infectious laugh, and gave one the feeling that life was hitched up a peg or two by his presence'.[19] Many of his friends and colleagues remarked on his modesty, humility and charm. A talented sportsman, he excelled at polo and tennis; his prowess as a bridge player was well known. At heart, Ismay was a countryman. He loved to be at his home in rural Gloucestershire, managing his estate, taking inordinate pride in his prize herd of Jersey cattle and enjoying country pursuits: horse racing was a passion, and he was also a keen shot.

Despite his tendency to put the demands of state above family responsibilities, his family life was stable and happy. His marriage to Darry was a close one and a meeting of minds. When they were apart—for instance when he was at Quetta in 1922, in India in 1947, or attending overseas conferences with Churchill—he would write to her frequently, sometimes daily, confiding his innermost thoughts and emotions.[20] When they were together he would seek (and usually take) her advice, for example over important career decisions. On occasions she prevented him from taking over-hasty decisions (such as precipitate resignation during the Suez Crisis), and she never allowed him to take himself too seriously: as Bright noted, 'her sense of the ridiculous kept him well below the line at which many men become pompous'.[21]

Ismay, however, was aware of the fact—and not without a feeling of guilt—that he had generally put his family as second priority. In his speech at the farewell dinner given in his honour by Attlee on 19 December 1946 he paid heartfelt tribute to Darry. 'She, like many other women, has had a much worse time than I have had, but she never faltered. Her care sustained and supported me through all the critical war years: her patience amazed me: her unselfishness shamed me: and her courage inspired me'.[22] He was, though, a somewhat distant father, certainly as far as his youngest daughter Mary was concerned. She recalled that, from the age of four to eight, when living with her parents in London, she saw little of him because he was either at work or away at weekends playing polo. And during the war when she was living with her sisters at Wormington he only visited occasionally, and then was either in his study, working, or out round the farm. 'He wasn't a very close father, if you see what I mean.'[23]

Outwardly, Ismay presented an image to the world of a robust, calm, confident, imperturbable extrovert. The image, however, somewhat belied the reality. He succumbed to severe ill health many times in his life, the more so as he grew older, suffering from bronchitis and other lung problems—largely the result of being a heavy smoker and spending his life alongside other heavy smokers in smoke-filled rooms. There were also numerous incidences of severe physical and mental exhaustion which resulted from overwork. In 1945 Bright noted the toll that the war years had taken on him. 'He was, as always, outwardly calm and cheerful, but we knew that, in fact, the loosening of the threads of his intensely concentrated and selfless service was making room for the fatigue which he had never acknowledged was there, as one long year had followed another.'[24] As someone who knew Ismay particularly well, she was well placed to comment. As to the image of the imperturbable extrovert, Ismay admitted to Wavell during the war that he had 'many hours of fright, suspense and sleepless anxiety'.[25] And at times he was close to mental breakdown: at Cairo in December 1943, at Quebec in September 1944, and at NATO during the 1956 Suez Crisis. Bright observed that, '[b]eneath the broad shoulders and the seeming imperturbability lay a sensitive and humble spirit'.[26] He was, she said, 'apparently simple, inwardly complex'.[27] Betty Green, having served with him throughout the war and later in India and Paris, also knew Ismay well and provides a further insight into his character.

> He had a slight feminine streak which seems rather odd because he was a very attractive man to women... he said to me once during the war, 'There's some evenings when I go home', because his wife was for long periods down in the country with the children, he said, 'I don't want to go to my club and talk to men, I want to talk to a woman'... he understood women very well.[28]

During his time in London, when Darry was often down at Wormington, the woman to whom he spoke most was his lodger and confidante Bright. She was a perceptive observer, although in the case of Ismay—for whom she had great admiration and affection—a far from unbiased one. But her observations, which include criticisms as well as compliments, ring true. For example she wrote of him, 'he had little patience with fools, was obstinate, and, at times, pig-headed, but he was supreme in his field'.[29] But for all that, she would probably have agreed— as would many others—with Ian Jacob's astute summary of Ismay: 'In the very best sense of the word, he was a gentleman'.[30]

Yet there is a paradox about Ismay. He had, as has been seen, numerous personal qualities in large measure; but he had few, if any of them, to an extraordinary degree. In fact, there was much about Ismay that was quite ordinary. But his performance in a succession of highly challenging jobs was far from ordinary and the sum total of his lifetime achievements was quite extraordinary. Perhaps the explanation lies in the combination of all his talents and the fact that this combination was exceptionally well suited to the circumstances in which he found himself.

What, then, is Ismay's legacy? Perhaps rather less acknowledged than it should be. In 1948 Eisenhower commented that, 'his name may be forgotten; but the contribution he made to winning the war was equal to [that] of many whose names became household words'.[31] Since that time, though, the opening of archives and the publication of other primary source material have resulted in historians giving greater recognition of his role and contribution. His performance as Churchill's chief staff officer is rightly recognised as a case study in the establishment and maintenance of good civil–military relations, and of the effective translation of government policy into action in time of war or crisis ('You will need a Pug Ismay'[32]). His achievements as the first Secretary General of NATO in laying many of the foundations on which the Alliance was built are recognised by historians of the subject, although less so more widely. Even less well-known but equally deserving of recognition are his contribution as Secretary of the CID, not least in the meticulous preparations for the transition from peace to war which worked so effectively in 1939, and his post-war role in the creation and development of the Ministry of Defence.

A further important legacy his career offers is as a role model for Service officers in his marked ability to rise above single-Service chauvinism and act in the interests of defence as a whole, to view defence within the context of national and international interests, and to act as an exemplar in politico-military cooperation: as he said, '[a]fter all, there can be nothing more essential to the successful conduct of war than that statesmen and soldiers should work together in the fullest understanding, sympathy and mutual respect'.[33] This is easy to say but, history would suggest, rather harder to achieve in practice. Perhaps his greatest legacy, though, is the example he showed of a life of duty and service, of achievement on behalf of his country and the free world, and the humanity and modesty with which he lived that life.

APPENDIX A

COMMANDANT'S REPORT
STAFF COLLEGE, QUETTA, 1922

CONFIDENTIAL REPORT ON MAJOR HL ISMAY[1]

'Employment for which best suited: Any branch.

Ability: Exceptionally good.

Professional Knowledge: Very good, all round.

Character: A fine open character, eminently straightforward, honest, loyal and trustworthy. Determination very good. Initiative marked. Self reliant. Inclined by nature to be impulsive, but has a good hold over himself.

Personality: Unusually marked and attractive. Very good manners. Human, sympathetic and helpful. Inspires confidence, and has a strong influence over others. Essentially a leader of men.

Mentality: Very quick and alert. Very adaptable. A clear logical and far-seeing brain with plenty of imagination, and sound well balanced judgment. Good sense of proportion. Good sense of humour.

Tact—Excellent. Power of expression—Excellent. Logic—Very good. Energy—Excellent. Horizon—Unusually broad. Habits—Normal. Physique—Very good. Recreation—Very good. A fine rider and polo player. Social qualifications—Normal. Very popular. Other points—Unusually well educated with a wide range of reading.

I consider this officer to be one of the two best, if not the best of the students who have passed through my hands. His work has been maintained consistently at the highest level. He is a very capable officer of a very fine stamp who will be a distinct asset to the Empire. He will make a most efficient staff officer or commander, and with greater experience, should rise high.'

(Signed. Louis Vaughan, Major General)

Grade A: An officer of exceptional merit

APPENDIX B

DIEPPE

The Dieppe raid—Operation Jubilee—was carried out in the early hours of 19 August 1942. It was a disaster. Of the 6,086 men, mostly Canadians, who landed at Dieppe, 3,625 (about sixty per cent) were lost—killed, wounded or taken prisoner. The RAF lost sixty-three men and 106 aircraft; the Royal Navy lost 523 men, a destroyer and thirty-three landing craft.

The raid was planned and mounted by Vice Admiral Lord Louis Mountbatten, Chief of Combined Operations. There were clearly serious flaws in the tactical plans and their implementation. A major controversy concerning the operation—and the one which involved Ismay—surrounds whether Operation Jubilee was authorised, if so by whom, and whether there was a cover-up at the time and/or after the war of where the responsibility lay. Several historians of the Dieppe raid have alleged or implied that Ismay obfuscated Churchill's enquiry into this aspect of the raid, failed to tell him the whole truth and/or abetted Mountbatten in the latter's cover-up of his responsibility.[1]

Much about the authorisation of Operation Jubilee remains obscure. What is clear is that there is no written evidence that the raid was categorically authorised by the Chiefs of Staff, the Defence Committee, the War Cabinet or the Prime Minister. It is also clear that after the disastrous operation Mountbatten went to considerable lengths to distance himself from responsibility for its failure and claimed that it had indeed been authorised.

Since June 1940 Churchill had urged '"butcher and bolt" operations... [as part of] a vigorous, enterprising and ceaseless offensive against the whole German-occupied coastline'.[2] A number of cross-Channel amphibious raids took place in 1942. The first two were small small-scale affairs on French coastal targets at Bruneval (in February) and St Nazaire (in March). Mountbatten now proposed a much larger raid, this time on

319

the Normandy port of Dieppe. Originally code named Operation Rutter, it was approved, somewhat grudgingly, by the Chiefs of Staff on 13 May. The Chiefs directed that the plan for Rutter was to be refined by Mountbatten and his Combined Operations Headquarters—the coordinating and supplying agency—along with the three force commanders, one from each Service, who would command the operation. Also involved in the planning were the headquarters of the individual Service commands which were providing assets for the operations: the Royal Navy's Portsmouth Command, the RAF's Fighter and Bomber Commands and the army's Home Command. The latter's representative on the planning group was its south-east area commander, Major General Bernard Montgomery.[3]

The raid was scheduled to take place in early July, but it was called off twice: the first time because rehearsals had been shambolic, the second time due to bad weather. Many people, such as Montgomery, were delighted to see it aborted: the tactical plan was controversial; preparations had been most unsatisfactory, and the self-confidence of the troops was questionable. He recommended that the operation should now be cancelled 'for all time'.[4] Indeed, there was opposition at a senior level within Mountbatten's own headquarters to any resurrection of the operation.[5] Mountbatten, however, informed the Chiefs of Staff on 6 July that that after various minor alterations had been made to the plan the operation would be remounted. The Chiefs 'approved the revised plan for Operation Rutter to take place at a date reported to the Chiefs of Staff... and agreed should Operation Rutter not take place as now proposed, the Force should be dispersed and the Chief of Combined Operations should consider re-mounting it at a later date'.[6] Mountbatten pressed ahead with planning for remounting the operation under a new codename: Operation Jubilee. The operation was discussed by the Chiefs on 20 July and they agreed the appointment of a new naval force commander.

One week later Mountbatten proposed, and the Chiefs approved, a revised and highly significant procedure for the mounting of raids such as Jubilee. Hitherto, he had required the Chiefs' authority for two key decisions: first, approval of both the outline plan and the appointment of the force commanders before detailed plans were made and the required forces trained and mobilised; and second, approval of the final plan prior to the launch of the operation.[7] Now he was no longer required to submit the final plan; he himself had the authority to launch the operation, subject to the approval of the local naval CinC. As Peter Henshaw has pointed out, '[i]n accepting the new procedure... the Committee, knowingly or otherwise, divested itself of any further responsibility for Jubilee'.[8] However, even though their authority was no longer required, the Chiefs will undoubtedly have expected to be kept informed of developments in the planning of such a major operation.

Mountbatten cloaked the whole planning process in the utmost secrecy and took the 'need to know' principle to absurd lengths. For example, although he copied the preliminary Combined Plan to (at least) two of the three Service headquarters,[9] he withheld information from other people who certainly needed to know, such as the Service intelligence chiefs, the Inter-Service Security Board and even his own deputy.[10] He subsequently claimed that the reason for this was operational security, 'following special instructions from the Chiefs of Staff'; but he almost certainly feared, probably with good reason, that if these other people knew of his plans they would probably seek to have the operation cancelled.[11] Henshaw suggests that it was for this purpose that both Ismay and Hollis abetted Mountbatten by helping him to limit the number of individuals and organisations who knew about Jubilee.[12] He produces no evidence to support this somewhat far-fetched accusation. An additional factor in Mountbatten's subterfuge may have been that, as Villa points out, he 'liked seeing himself as something of a rulebreaker', well aware of Churchill's admiration for 'buccaneers and swashbucklers'.[13]

It is important to view Operation Jubilee in context. Shining the spotlight on it can obscure the fact that for many of those in Whitehall not directly involved in its planning and preparation there were, in the weeks leading up to its launch on 19 August, a number of high-priority operational and political issues demanding their attention—a fact often overlooked by those carrying out Jubilee post-mortems. From the start of the month of July a major battle had been taking place at El Alamein, ending when Rommel called off his attack on 27 July.[14] From 18 to 25 July the Combined Chiefs of Staff (the Americans represented by Hopkins, Marshall and King) had been in session in London, with heated discussions on future Allied operations. For Churchill, following the Americans' departure, two subjects vied for his attention: preparation for his upcoming meeting in Moscow with Stalin, given added focus by the clamour for a Second Front of a 60,000-strong demonstration in Trafalgar Square;[15] and his distinct unease at the Desert Army's continued lack of decisive success, exacerbated by Auchinleck's apparent procrastination over a counterattack.[16]

In the fortnight following Churchill's departure for Cairo and Moscow on 2 August three new subjects competed for attention in Whitehall: the reorganisation of senior appointments following Churchill's sacking of Auchinleck and other officers in the Western Desert; the start of intense planning for the Allied campaign in North Africa—Operation Torch (Ismay holding no less than four meetings with the nominated commander, Eisenhower); and a high-risk operation of great strategic importance. This was Operation Pedestal—the resupply convoy to Malta on which the island's continuing defence depended. As Max Hastings has pointed out, the convoy was 'the largest fleet that the Royal Navy had committed to action since Jutland in 1916'; it set out on 3 August and battled its way through the Mediterranean, arriving on 15 August.[17] The day before his departure Churchill had briefed the War Cabinet on a critical upcoming operation, but it was Pedestal, not Jubilee.[18] He did not return until 24 August. While he was away Ismay and his staff dealt with the coordination of all these activities, together with the flurry of telegrams which emanated from the Prime Minister and demanded priority attention. Jubilee was far from being the only show in town.

When Jubilee was launched the operation came as a complete surprise to a number of people who might have expected to be informed about it—most notably Lieutenant General Sir Archibald Nye, Brooke's deputy who was standing in for the CIGS, accompanying Churchill. Ismay recalled 'the fury of Nye, who had no idea that the operation was on until reports started to flow in from the scene of the action'.[19]

In the aftermath of the raid many of those involved, particularly Mountbatten, sought to put a brave face on it. In the weeks and months that followed, however, there was an increasing number of people voicing criticisms. These came to the ear of the Prime Minister. On 21 December he minuted Ismay,

> Although for many reasons everyone was concerned to make this business look as good as possible, the time has now come when I must be informed more precisely about the military plans. Who made them? Who approved them? What was General Montgomery's part? Did the General Staff check the plans? At what point was VCIGS informed (in CIGS's absence)?... You should first collect through the Defence Office the ascertainable facts about this, and I will then consider whether there should be a more formal inquiry and what form it should take.[20]

Ismay immediately passed this to Mountbatten, adding, 'Treat this as... private, not to be shown even to your staff.[21] Was this, as Villa suggests, evidence of some sort of collusion between them? Possibly. But it is more likely that Ismay sought confidential information and did not want Mountbatten to think that he was going behind his back.

Ismay's reply to Churchill, informed by Mountbatten's comments, was somewhat evasive and avoided the issue of whether the final plans were approved by the War Office or the Chiefs of Staff. Instead he pointed the finger at Montgomery whom, he said, 'was the senior Army officer concerned with the Raid from about the end of April onwards'; this was not entirely true: Montgomery had been replaced on Mountbatten's planning group in early July, after Rutter had been called off. Ismay's answer to the question about the VCIGS was minimalist: 'VCIGS was not specially informed of the operation'.[22] These answers were hardly comprehensive or encouraging to further enquiry, but were they designed to mislead Churchill? At this stage the answer was far from clear. Villa writes that 'Churchill let his enquiry drop despite the evidently unsatisfactory nature of Ismay's replies'.[23]

And there the matter rested until 1950 when Churchill was writing his memoirs, assisted by a small group of advisers which included Ismay. Coming to 1942 and Dieppe, Churchill contacted Ismay seeking further information about the operation and the authorisation for it. In particular, he may have wished to ascertain what evidence existed of his own part in the process; indeed, another historian, David O'Keefe, has suggested that, 'he deliberately tried to distance himself from the disastrous Dieppe Raid'.[24] Churchill wrote to one of his other advisers, Lieutenant General Sir Henry Pownall, 'I think I had already started for Cairo and Moscow when the decision to renew the operation was taken. Certainly I heard about it and did not oppose it'.[25] To be sure, Churchill would have had good reason to welcome the decision; the abandonment of Rutter would, in Robin Neilland's words, have 'sent him naked to the Moscow conference table'.[26] Ismay undertook to search for the answers but attempted to discourage Churchill from giving the subject major coverage in his memoirs, observing that, 'it was not one of our most creditable ventures, because the underlying object was never sufficiently closely defined, nor, as far as I can remember was the chain of responsibility... I do not believe we deserved success'.[27] In July, following lengthy research, he reported to Churchill that there were considerable gaps in the records, this time suggesting to him that the section in his memoirs about Dieppe was 'redundant because the military story has been told so fully and accurately in other publications' and that 'it could be briefly disposed of in three paragraphs'.[28]

This did not satisfy Churchill because a few days later he wrote to Ismay,

> I can see nothing in the papers I now have from you... which explains who took the decision to <u>revive</u> the attack after it had been abandoned and Montgomery had cleared out... Surely the decision could not have been taken without the Chiefs of Staff being informed. If so, why did they not bring it to my attention, observing I did not leave England till July 30 or 31? This is the crux of the story. Did the Chiefs of Staff or the Defence Committee or the War Cabinet ever consider the matter of revival... or was it all pushed through by Dickie Mountbatten on his own without reference to higher authority?[29]

A fortnight later, having both conducted a search of the relevant Cabinet documents and consulted Mountbatten, Ismay—'now very flustered', according to Reynolds—reported to Churchill that it appeared that 'in the vital interests of secrecy, nothing had been put on paper'.[30] He suggested to Churchill that he 'must have approved the operation in principle' because in a telegram to Ismay from Cairo on 17 August 1942, two days before the operation, he had used the new code name for the operation—Jubilee—rather than Rutter.[31] However, Villa asserts that '[w]hat Ismay did not tell Churchill was that in the same file there was another telegram from Churchill in Moscow inquiring into the status of Rutter and that Ismay had cabled back informing him of the new code name and giving him possible dates'.[32] Firstly, the other telegram (and Ismay's reply) were on different files which Ismay may or may not have consulted.[33] But in any case, this was something of a red herring by Villa, overlooking the fact that by asking, 'What is the position on the renewal of Operation Rutter?' Churchill was tacitly acknowledging that he knew that the operation had not been cancelled, only postponed.[34] Nevertheless, Villa implies that Ismay's reply was conspiracy to deceive rather than error.

Churchill had, indeed, known that the Dieppe operation was about to take place. On Saturday, 15 August at a meeting in the Kremlin he had personally briefed Stalin about it. 'In order to make Germany anxious about an attack from across the channel, there will be a more serious raid in August', he said. 'It will be a reconnaissance in force. Some 80,000 men with 50 tanks will be landed. They will stay a night and a day, kill as many Germans as possible and take prisoners. They will then withdraw'.[35]

On 1 September 1950 Churchill produced a draft of the section in his memoirs on Dieppe. Mountbatten, to whom he copied the draft, objected strongly to much of it and sent ten pages of comments to Churchill with his own redraft of the section. This included a statement saying that he had discussed the remounting personally with Churchill and that the Chiefs of Staff had given verbal approval. Churchill told Ismay that he accepted this redraft, adding, '[t]there is no doubt that I had several conferences about all this, though I must say I cannot remember the details'.[36] Ismay, to whom Mountbatten had also sent a copy, wrote to Churchill, supporting Mountbatten's redraft as 'substantially correct' although acknowledging 'with shame' that he had no recollection of Mountbatten's discussion with Churchill on the subject of remounting the raid. He also said that he thought that Churchill would 'drastically revise' Mountbatten's redraft.[37] But Churchill did not do so. After five months of a copious exchange of detailed correspondence on the subject, and now under his publisher's pressure to produce the goods, Churchill, in Reynold's words, 'simply nodded through Mountbatten's re-write'.[38] This included the statement that after the Chiefs of Staff had given their approval (for Operation Jubilee), 'I personally went through the plans with the CIGS, Admiral Mountbatten, and the Naval Force Commander'.[39] It is most unlikely that Churchill would have included this statement if he did not believe it to be true—a point which Reynolds and Villa do not address.[40]

Nevertheless, during the course of Churchill's enquiries into the authorisation of Operation Jubilee, both in 1942 and 1950, Ismay had been, at best, uncomfortable about the spotlight being shone on the subject, and had tried to minimise Churchill's coverage of it in his memoirs. He had also been less than totally objective in his advice to Churchill, giving Mountbatten the benefit of considerable doubt and seeming to shield him from public criticism. Why?

The authorisation process for the raid on Dieppe had demonstrated, amongst other things, serious flaws in the design and implementation of procedures for the authorisation of major operations. The procedural loopholes and absence of written authority (and thus of an audit trail) smacked of sloppiness and amateurism. There had clearly been a lack of oversight of the development of the operation from the moment that Rutter was cancelled right up to the launch of Jubilee. Responsibility for this state of affairs lay in large part with the Office of the Minister of

Defence—the machine responsible for the coordination of such matters—and with the Chiefs of Staff Committee. The head of that Office and a member of that Committee was Ismay. Moreover, during the absence of the Prime Minister from 2 August it was clearly Ismay's duty to keep a watchful eye on his behalf over all his defence responsibilities, particularly the development of a major, high-risk operation such as Jubilee. Some of the competing priorities had resulted in it getting much less attention than it deserved.

None of this will have escaped Ismay's attention and it may have caused him embarrassment, both in the immediate aftermath of the operation and eight years later when Churchill was drafting his memoirs. He may also have recognised that a number of people involved in the authorisation for Jubilee, notably Mountbatten but also others, including Churchill himself and the Chiefs of Staff, could also be embarrassed by their part, or lack of it, in the decision-making process. He certainly attempted to discourage Churchill from dealing at length with the Dieppe raid in his memoirs, but it is far from clear that he set out to deceive him. Indeed, it would have been most out of character for him to have done so. On the other hand, although there is no evidence that Ismay consciously 'abetted' Mountbatten in his deception,[41] it is hard to avoid the conclusion that he allowed his perceived loyalty to his old friend and former close colleague to colour his advice to Churchill during the latter's enquiries, both during and after the war. Notably, Ismay makes no mention whatsoever of the Dieppe raid in his own memoirs.

It is unlikely to be a coincidence that at the end of August 1942, a fortnight after Jubilee and one week after Churchill's return from Cairo, Ismay suffered what he himself privately admitted was a 'temporary breakdown'. It was serious enough for him to be absent from work for no less than three weeks before returning 'with batteries completely recharged'.[42] Certainly the strain of his workload and of the unfolding events surrounding Operation Jubilee will have contributed to this breakdown. The extent to which that strain was already affecting his capacity and judgement prior to Jubilee or his memory of events after it is a matter of speculation.

APPENDIX C

'RULES FOR THE CONDUCT OF NATO'

A speech given by Ismay at the dinner of the English Speaking Union, 4 June 1957.[1]

'It is the privilege of the old retainer to speak his mind to his masters. So, greatly daring, I am going to address this parting message to them. It is called "Rules for the Conduct of NATO".

Rule Number One. Do not forget that although the alliance was born of fear, and security had to be given first priority, it is not merely a military alliance of the old-fashioned sort. If it is to survive it must be strong, not only militarily, but politically and morally. It is therefore imperative that the partners should keep in the closest touch with each other on all matters, great and small which affect the Alliance. This means that none of you should take action, or reach firm decisions on such matters, without consulting your allies or, at the very least, without keeping them fully informed. As I have explained, effective machinery for the purpose exists; there is therefore no excuse.

Rule Number Two. It is a cardinal sin for one of the members to do anything which might disturb or even seriously weaken the Alliance. At the same time, there are bound to be quarrels in the best regulated families. If, therefore, you find yourselves at loggerheads with one of your partners, pause for a moment to reflect that you and he are fundamentally like-minded people, dedicated to the principles of democracy, individual liberty, and the rule of law. This being so, you can even question his judgment, but you ought not to question his motives. That is the thought that should govern your conduct towards the quarrel. The main thing is to settle it as quickly as possible. Let not the sun go down upon your wrath. If you can settle it between yourselves without involving your other friends, so much the better. Above all, if there is any dirty NATO linen to be washed, do not wash it in public.

Rule Number Three. Never relax your vigilance, unless it is absolutely certain that the danger has passed. Remember the recent past. The Soviet has always hated NATO: they have always tried to disrupt it. When they found that blustering and threatening were no use… they substituted the grin for the growl, smooth words for rough, goodwill visits all over the world for isolation within the walls of the Kremlin… The brutality with which [the Hungarian] revolt was crushed showed the men of the Kremlin in their true colours. They out-Stalined Stalin. The lesson should not be forgotten.

Rule Number Four. Do not forget that the North Atlantic Treaty is not only a solemn obligation, but also an insurance—a collective insurance—against measureless catastrophe. An individual may decide for reasons of economy not to insure his property for its full value. If it is lost he at least recovers some of its value, but nations who economize in the premiums which they pay for their security, and thereafter become the victims of overwhelming aggression, recover nothing.

Rule Number Five. Do not forget that the world in which we live is now a small place, and that there may be developments outside the NATO area which may exercise a permanent influence on the security of that area. NATO must therefore always have an agreed policy for dealing with such developments as they occur, and must pursue that policy resolutely.

All that I have tried to say can be summed up very simply. NATO must behave like a family, all of whose members are engaged in the same business—the business of preserving the peace and of making the world a safer and a happier and a kinder place for all peoples. We have only to be vigilant, resolute and, above all, united; we have only to be true to ourselves and to each other. And all will be well.'

APPENDIX D

LETTER FROM EISENHOWER TO ISMAY, 14 JANUARY 1959

<u>PERSONAL AND CONFIDENTIAL</u>

Dear Pug,

...So far as Monty's book is concerned, my opinion is probably so much lower than yours that I would not like to express it, even in a letter. As a matter of fact, I think that, regardless of how he might have conducted and expressed himself during the post war years, he would scarcely stand much chance of going down in history as one of the great British captains. Alexander was much abler. He was also modest.

I recall the impatience with which we waited for any northern movement of Montgomery's out of the Catania Plain and the long unnecessary wait before he stepped across the Massena Strait. Do you remember the great promises that he made during the planning of OVERLORD about moving quickly to the southward beyond Caen and Bayeux to get ground fit for airfields, and his post-war assertions that such a movement was never included in his plan? Next consider his preposterous proposal to drive on a single pencil-line thrust straight at Berlin, and later his failure even to make good his effort for a lodgement across the Rhine, and this after I had promised and given him everything he requested until that particular operation was completed.

I cannot forget his readiness to belittle associates in those critical moments when the cooperation of all of us was needed. So, I personally believe that, on his record, historians could never be tempted to gild his status too heavily, even if his memoirs had not reflected traits far from admirable.

On the other hand, so far as Brookie is concerned, I think that while he possibly made an error in publishing a diary that reflected the anxious doubts and frustrations of a wartime experience, yet he was always honest, quick and generous. That image of him will never be destroyed in my mind. I believe that just about a year ago I wrote you what he said to me on March twenty-fourth of 1945, just as we had, for the third time, crossed the Rhine. I felt then, and still do, that in those comments was evidence of bigness.

With all my heart I applaud your idea of telling your story without consciously throwing grenades or even bricks. During the years that publishers in this country were trying to get me to write a war memoir (this started in 1943) the negative argument I always advanced was that I had no intention of trying to make a profit out of criticism of others— their personalities or their judgments. I told the publishers that I would never write anything sensational in the hope that the sale of books would be helped. It was only after two publishers assured me that they would never urge or argue that I do anything more than tell the plain unvarnished truth about the war as I saw it and experienced it that I finally agreed to make the attempt at writing. You can imagine, therefore, my satisfaction when, in the event, the book had a far greater sale in this country than any other book on the war. The publishers actually made a profit out of it, even though they had paid me handsomely.

You have a long and rich experience that gives assurance that your book will contain much that will be both interesting and helpful. I hope that it will not be too long delayed in its distribution.

With warm greetings to your charming Lady and, of course, all the best to yourself.

As ever,

Ike

PS. Because I have never before, to my knowledge, put on paper or spoken publicly in a disparaging fashion about any other public figure— particularly if he was an old comrade-in-arms—I hope that you will understand why I am marking this letter personal and confidential.[1]

ABBREVIATIONS USED IN THE NOTES

BL: British Library, London
CAC: Churchill Archives Centre, Churchill College, University of Cambridge
Cadbury: Cadbury Research Library, University of Birmingham
COS: Chiefs of Staff Committee
Hartley: Hartley Library, University of Southampton
IDC: Imperial Defence College
IWM: Imperial War Museum, London
JRL: John Rylands Library, University of Manchester
LHC: Liddell Hart Centre for Military Archives, King's College London
NAM: National Army Museum, London
TNA: The National Archives of the United Kingdom, Kew, London
USAH&EC: United States Army Heritage and Education Center, Carlisle, Pennsylvania

NOTES

PREFACE

1.   Charles Moore, *Margaret Thatcher: The Authorised Biography, vol. 1: Not for Turning* (London, Allen Lane, 2013), 680.

2   Indeed, he has been described as its "chief architect". Franklyn Johnson, *Defence by Ministry. The British Ministry of Defence 1944-1974* (London, Duckworth, 1980), 67.

3.   Sir Ronald Wingate, *Lord Ismay: A Biography* (London, Hutchinson, 1970).

4.   Andrew Sangster, *'Pug' – Churchill's Chief of Staff. The Life of General Hastings Ismay KG GCB DSO PC, 1887-1965* (Barnsley, Pen & Sword Military, 2023).

5.   Arthur Bryant, *The Turn of the Tide, 1939-1943, A Study Based on the Diaries and Autobiographical Notes of Field Marshal The Viscount Alanbrooke* (London, Collins, 1957), and *Triumph in the West, 1943-1946* (London, Collins, 1959).

6.   Hastings Ismay, *The Memoirs of General the Lord Ismay KG, PC, GCB, CH, DSO* (London, Heinemann, 1960), 167. The statement has been accepted unquestioningly by at least one historian: Maxwell Schoenfeld, *The War Ministry of Winston Churchill* (Iowa, Iowa State University Press, 1972), 68.

1.   A CHILD OF THE RAJ

1.   Clive Dewey, *Anglo-Indian Attitudes. The Mind of the Indian Civil Service* (London, The Hambledon Press, 1993), 3.

2.   David Gilmour, *The British in India. Three Centuries of Ambition and Experience* (London, Penguin Books, 2019), 162.

3.   That is to say private, fee-paying schools.

4.   According to Wingate, 'the family tradition avers' that William Ismay had lost all his fortune in "gaming" [gambling]' (Wingate, *Lord Ismay*, 1). Sangster states that it was Stanley Ismay who did so, but offers no evidence (Sangster, *Pug*, 3). It is likely that the former account is closer to the truth.

5.   Such multi-generational 'Anglo–Indian' families were far from rare in India at that time. Bernard Porter, *The Absent-Minded Imperialists: Empire, Society and Culture in Britain* (Oxford, Oxford University Press, 2006), 42.

6.   David Gilmour, *The Ruling Caste. Imperial Lives in the Victorian Raj* (London, Pimlico, 2007), xiv; Lawrence James, *Raj. The Making and Unmaking of British India* (London, Abacus, 1997), 308.

7. Allen Greenberger, *The British Image of India: A Study in the Literature* of *Imperialism, 1880-1960* (Oxford, Oxford University Press, 1969), 22.

8. Gilmour, *British in India,* 167. But as Robin Moore observed, 'The ICS has been variously described as a *corps d'elite*, Platonic guardians of the mission, and a body of self-serving careerists preoccupied with their official status'. Robin Moore, 'Imperial India 1858-1914', in Andrew Porter (ed.), *The Oxford History of the British Empire, vol. 3. The Nineteenth Century* (Oxford, Oxford University Press, 1999), 429. For a more critical view of the ethos of the Indian Civil Service and 'the myth of enlightened despotism', see Shashi Tharoor, *Inglorious Empire. What the British Did to India* (London, Hurst Publishers, 2017).

9. See for example Ismay to Darry Ismay, 25 March 1947, LHC, Ismay Papers [hereafter Ismay] 3/8/1; Ismay to Joan Bright, 30 August 1947, IWM, Bright Astley Papers, 20514; and Ismay, *Memoirs,* 177.

10. Mrs Mullaly became Lady Mullaly in 1917 when her husband was knighted.

11. Gerald Davies (housemaster) to Stanley Ismay, 15 December 1900, LHC, Ismay 1/1/2; Charterhouse School Records, Verites House 1900–05.

12. Ismay to Lancelot Allen, 3 July 1943, LHC, Ismay 5/1.

13. Ismay to Brian Young (Headmaster, Charterhouse School), 24 September 1956, LHC, Ismay 1/14/29.

14. Davies to Beatrice Ismay 15 December 1902 and 15 October 1903, LHC, Ismay 1/1/3 and 1/1/4.

15. Ismay, *Memoirs,* 4.

16. Royal Military College Sandhurst Records for 1905, Royal Military Academy Sandhurst Archives.

17. Ibid.

18. Ismay, *Memoirs,* 4.

19. Ibid., 5.

20. Ibid., 5–6.

21. Ibid., 8.

22. Philip Mason, *A Matter of Honour: An Account of the Indian Army, Its Officers and Men* (London, Jonathan Cape, 1974), 366.

23. Moore, 'Imperial India', in Porter (ed.), *Oxford History of the British Empire,* 428.

24. Mason, *Matter of Honour*, 379.

25. Ismay, *Memoirs*, 10.

26. For the significance of team games in the British imperial ethos and the role of polo as 'the characteristic imperial sport' see JA Morgan, '"The Grit of Our Forefathers". Invented Traditions, Propaganda and Imperialism', in John MacKenzie, *Imperialism and Popular Culture* (Manchester, Manchester University Press, 1986), 120–1, and John Mackenzie, *A Cultural History of the British Empire* (New Haven, Yale University Press, 2022), 102.

27. Ismay, *Memoirs*, 11–12.

28. Gilmour, *Ruling Caste*, 77.

29. Betty Green, IWM, Oral History 13029, Reel 2.

30. Ismay, *Memoirs,* 12.

31. Although few, if any, of those who took part in the Mohmand campaign or similar cross-border raids would have stopped at the time to question the ethics of their actions, it is perhaps surprising that Ismay's account of the campaign in his memoirs does not give even a passing nod to the fact that these operations were largely an exercise in deterrence through brutal punishment—burning villages, killing livestock, destroying crops and shooting those who resisted.

32. Ismay, *Memoirs*, 9.

33. Ibid., 14. Ismay's somewhat romantic account illustrates historian John MacKenzie's view of imperial soldiering that, 'The officers of the imperial forces certainly saw these wars a chivalric, virtually sporting events, brief and intense bouts of dragon-slaying. The campaigns were always expected to be over in a matter of weeks and invariably led to a feverish scramble on the part of the officers to get to the scene of the conflict, as to a sporting event'. John MacKenzie, *Popular Imperialism and the Military, 1850-1950* (Manchester, Manchester University Press, 1992), 9.

34. Review Report of the 21ˢᵗ Cavalry, 1908-09, BL, IOR/L/MIL/7/17017.

35. Ibid.

36. Ismay, *Memoirs*, 15.

37. Ibid., 16.

38. Mason, *A Matter of Honour*, 364; Richard Hart Sinnreich, 'The Influence of Culture on the Victorian British Army', in Peter Mansoor and Williamson Murray (eds.), *The Culture of Military Organizations* (Cambridge, Cambridge University Press, 2019), 169.

39. Bernard Montgomery, quoted by Nigel Hamilton, *Monty. The Making of a General. 1887-1942* (London, Hamish Hamilton, 1981), 53.

40. Hamilton, *Monty*, 53.

41. Ismay, *Memoirs*, 17.

42. Speech to the Pakistan Society, 1 July 1958, LHC, Ismay 1/7/36.

43. Annual Review on 21ˢᵗ Cavalry 1913, BL, IOR/L/MIL/7/17022.

44. Ismay, Draft Memoirs, 2, LHC, Ismay 1/15/5/5.

2.   SOMALILAND

1. Douglas Jardine, *The Mad Mullah of Somaliland* (London, H Jenkins, 1923), 53.

2. Ibid., 42.

3. Ismay, *Memoirs*, 19.

4. Ismay's script for a 1964 television documentary about Carton de Wiart, LHC, Ismay, 4/5/132.

5. Ismay, *Memoirs*, 24.

6. Ibid., 25–6.

7. Ibid., 26.

8. Malcolm Page, *King's African Rifles. A History* (Barnsley, Pen & Sword, 2011), 21.

9. *London Gazette* 19690/7633 and TNA, WO 106/272.

10. Ismay, *Memoirs*, 27.

11. Ibid., 36.

12. 'Appointed a Companion of the Distinguished Service Order'.
13. LHC, Ismay 1/1/13–19.
14. Onslow to Ismay, 5 February and 19 June 1915, LHC, Ismay 4/25/1 & 2.
15. Onslow to Ismay, 28 March 1916, LHC, Ismay 4/25/3.
16. Jardine, *Mad Mullah*, 251.
17. Ismay to Beatrice Ismay, 28 January 1917, LHC, Ismay 1/2/7.
18. Hall to Ismay, 21 December 1916, LHC, Ismay 1/1/17.
19. Ismay to Beatrice Ismay, 19 January 1917, LHC, Ismay 1/2/6.
20. Ibid., 9 April 1917, LHC, Ismay 1/2/16.
21. Onslow to Ismay, 24 May 1917, LHC, Ismay 4/25/5.
22. Cubitt to Ismay, 7 September 1916, LHC, Ismay 5/3.
23. Commissioner's Order Number 84, 2 June 2017, LHC, Ismay 3/1/1.
24. Ismay to Beatrice Ismay, 11 July 1917, LHC, Ismay 1/2/27.
25. Ibid., 30 July 1917, LHC, Ismay 1/2/31.
26. Ibid., 14 August 1917, LHC, Ismay 1/2/29.
27. Ismay to Col Jardine, 7 February 1919, LHC, Ismay 3/1/9.
28. 'Outline of a Plan to Defeat the Mullah', January 1919, LHC, Ismay 3/1/8.
29. Ray Beachey, *The Warrior Mullah. The Horn Aflame 1892-1920* (London, Bellew Publishing, 1990), 124–5; Cabinet Minutes, 24 January 1919, TNA, CAB 23/9/6.
30. 'Digest of History of the Somaliland Camel Corps', TNA, WO 106/272.
31. Dated 21 May 19, LHC, Ismay 3/1/20. See also Ismay's intelligence notebook, 'The Campaign Against the Mullah', TNA, WO 106/23.
32. For example, the campaigns in Iraq and Afghanistan.
33. Roy Irons, *Churchill and the Mad Mullah of Somaliland. Betrayal and Redemption 1899-1921* (Barnsley, Pen & Sword, 2013), 193–6.
34. Jardine, *Mad Mullah*, 271.
35. Ismay to Officer Commanding Somaliland Field Force, 11 February 1920, LHC, Ismay 3/1/59.
36. Ismay, *Memoirs,* 33.
37. Ismay's report to the Officer Commanding Somaliland Field Force, 10 March 1920, LHC, Ismay 3/1/96.
38. Ismay, *Memoirs*, 34.
39. Jardine, *Mad Mullah*, 277.
40. Despatch of GF Archer, Governor and CinC Somaliland Protectorate, *London Gazette*, No. 32107, 29 October 1920.
41. 'Lecture on Somaliland', 1919, TNA, CAB 127/1.
42. The prominent statue of Mohammad Abdullah Hassan in Mogadishu, capital of Somalia, is testimony to the respect in which he is held today as a heroic pioneer of Somali independence.
43. Quoted by CN French, letter to *The Times* 16 April 1930, LHC, Ismay 3/1/85.
44. Andrew Boyle, *Trenchard* (London, Collins, 1962), 369.
45. *Daily Telegraph,* 15 April 1962.
46. Despatch of Group Captain R Gordon, Commander Z Unit, RAF, *London Gazette*, No. 32116, 8 November 1920.

47. Ismay to Beatrice Ismay, 6 March 1920, LHC, Ismay 1/2/40.

48. Ibid.

49. Ismay, *Memoirs*, 35.

50. Slim, *The Observer*, 25 September 1960.

51. In 1919 and 1920 selection for the staff colleges was based purely on nomination by the military members of the Army Council, rather than by an entrance examination. Iain Farquharson, '"The Staff College Candidates Are Not Right Yet". The Importance of Nomination to British Army Staff College Entry, 1919-1939', in *British Journal for Military History*, 8/3 (November 2022), 108–27.

52. Ismay, *Memoirs*, 36.

53. Ibid., 35.

54. Ibid., 37.

3.   APPRENTICESHIP

1.   Cubitt to Ismay, 23 June 1920, LHC, Ismay 5/3.

2.   Darry Ismay, untitled manuscript notes (hereafter MSS), Ismay Family Papers.

3.   LHC, Ismay 3/1/76.

4.   Mark Frost, 'The British and Indian Staff Colleges in the Interwar Years', in Robert Engen et al. (eds.), *Military Education and the British Empire 1815-1949* (Vancouver, The University of British Columbia Press, 2018), 156.

5.   Ismay, *Memoirs*, 38.

6.   Ismay interviewed by HV Hodson 25 August 1965, BL, Sound Archives C940/16.

7.   Ibid.

8.   Author interview with Mary Seymour. Kintbury, 30 January 2020; author interview with Patricia Smyly, Little Buckland, 20 July 2020.

9.   Ismay, *Memoirs*, 39.

10. Ismay to Chapman Houston, 28 October 1947, 'Recollections about Major General Vaughan, Commandant Quetta, 1919-1923', LHC, Ismay 5/22.

11. Ibid.

12. LHC, Ismay 3/2/10.

13. Ibid.

14. Confidential Report by Commandant, Quetta, LHC, Ismay 1/1/22.

15. Ismay, *Memoirs*, 40.

16. Darry Ismay, MSS notes, Ismay Family Papers.

17. Ibid.

18. Ismay to Mrs Clegg, 3 June 1923, Ismay Family Papers.

19. Later Air Chief Marshal Sir Philip Game GCB, GCVO, GBE, KCMG, DSO; Governor of New South Wales 1930–1935; Commissioner of the Metropolitan Police 1935–45; Winner of the Royal United Services Institute's 1910 Chesney Gold Medal essay competition.

20. Ismay, *Memoirs*, 41

21. Game to Director of Staff Duties, 24 January 1924, TNA, AIR 2/251/ 480808/24.

22. Ismay, *Memoirs,* 41.

23. Ismay family scrapbook, 1924, in the possession of James Evetts.
24. Elliot, in BBC Radio 4 documentary, *Thinking Soldier: Lord Ismay* (British Library, Sound Archives, 6 June 1970), P526R.
25. Darry Ismay, MSS notes, Ismay Family Papers.
26. Franklyn Johnson, *Defence by Committee. The British Committee of Imperial Defence 1855-1959* (Oxford, Oxford University Press, 1960), Foreword.
27. Ismay, *Memoirs*, 43.
28. Ismay, 'The Machinery of the Committee of Imperial Defence', *Journal of the Royal United Services Institute*, 84/534 (May, 1939), 243.
29. *Report of the Committee of Imperial Defence*. Cmd 2029 (London, HMSO, 1923); WGF Jackson and Lord Bramall, *The Chiefs. The Story of the United Kingdom Chiefs of Staff* (London, Brasseys, 1992), 129.
30. Quoted in Johnson, *Defence by Committee*, 210.
31. By 1926 the number of attached or co-opted members of the CID's committees totalled some 430 individuals (Ismay, 'The Organisation and Functions of the CID', LHC, Ismay 3/4/3).
32. Ismay, 'The Machinery of the Committee of Imperial Defence', *Journal of the Royal United Services Institute*, 84/534 (May, 1939), 251.
33. Ismay, *Memoirs*, 53.
34. Ibid.
35. Ibid., 45.
36. Ismay to Walker, 10 February 1926, Bodleian Library Special Collections, Papers of Colonel Charles William Walker, MSS. Afr. S. 717.
37. Johnson, *Defence by Committee*, 268.
38. Ismay, *Memoirs*, 53–4.
39. Ibid.
40. Ibid., 54.
41. Ismay, Lecture on the Principal Supply Officers Committee (audience unknown), 19 January 1929, TNA, CAB 127/6.
42. Ismay, *Memoirs*, 63.
43. Ismay, Lecture to IDC, October 1949, LHC, Ismay 3/4/12.
44. Ismay, *Memoirs*, 51.
45. A state of affairs not totally unknown to this day.
46. Burgis, 'The Memoirs of Lawrence Burgis' (unpublished), CAC, Burgis Papers, BRGS 1/1.
47. Darry Ismay, MSS notes, Ismay Family Papers.
48. Family scrapbook in the possession of James Evetts.
49. Burgis, 'Memoirs', CAC, Burgis Papers, BRGS 1/1, 41–2.
50. Emphasis in original. Hankey to Ismay, 27 November 1930, quoted in SW Roskill, *Hankey, Man of Secrets, vol. 2, 1919–31* (London, Collins, 1974), 531.
51. Hankey to Ismay, 27 November 1930, quoted in Roskill, *Hankey, vol. 2*, 531.
52. Darry Ismay, MSS notes, Ismay Family Papers.
53. Ismay, *Memoirs*, 66.
54. Ibid., 67.

55. Willingdon to Viscount Ratendone, 23 August 1931, George Bergstrom, 'Lord Willingdon in India 1932-1936. A Study of an Imperial Administrator' (University of Oxford, DPhil Thesis, 1978, unpublished), 120.

56. Gilmour, *British in India*, 402.

57. Maud Ismay to Ismay, undated, LHC, Ismay 1/1/55.

58. 'Summary of Lord Ismay's Letters to Lady Ismay', Ismay Family Papers.

59. Darry Ismay, MSS notes, Ismay Family Papers.

60. Lockhart diary, 21 March 1946, Kenneth Young (ed.), *The Diaries of Sir Robert Bruce Lockhart, vol. 2, 1939-1965* (London, Macmillan, 1973), 534. Note should be taken of Michael Hughes's opinion that, 'his writings cannot always be relied on for factual accuracy'. Michael Hughes, 'Lockhart, Sir Robert Hamilton Bruce' (2010), *Oxford Dictionary of National Biography* (Oxford, Oxford University Press), accessed 3 May 2021.

61. Lockhart diary, 21 March 1946, Young, *Diaries,* 534.

62. Author interview with Mary Seymour, 30 January 2020.

63. Ismay, *Memoirs*, 68.

64. Ismay, Lecture to the Staff College, 1935, TNA, CAB 127/7.

65. Dill to Ismay, 28 August 1936, LHC, Ismay 5/4.

66. Ismay to Major General Twiss, 21 August 1935, LHC, Ismay 1/1/32.

67. According to Basil Liddell Hart, his own appointment 'as [Hankey's] deputy for defence had been urged at several times from 1932 onwards'. *The Memoirs of Captain Liddell Hart, vol. 1* (London, Cassell, 1965), 324.

68. Darry Ismay, MSS, Ismay Family Papers.

69. Ismay, *Memoirs,* 69–70.

70. Ibid.

4. CORRIDORS OF POWER

1. Ismay, *Memoirs*, 76.

2. SW Roskill, *Hankey, Man of Secrets, vol. 3, 1931-1963* (London, Collins, 1974), 205.

3. Ismay, *Memoirs*, 77.

4. Brian Bond, *British Military Policy between the Two World Wars* (Oxford, Clarendon Press, 1980), 264.

5. Michael Goodman, *The Official History of the Joint Intelligence Committee* (Abingdon, Routledge, 2014), 21–2.

6. Ismay, *Memoirs*, 85.

7. Ibid., 77; later demonstrating that he could do so, Colville diary, 1 September 1940, John Colville, *The Fringes of Power: Downing Street Diaries 1939-1955* (London, Hodder and Stoughton, 1985), 237.

8. Hankey to Inskip and Baldwin, 1 March 1937, quoted by Roskill, *Hankey, vol. 3,* 260; Hankey to Ismay, undated but probably April 1961, LHC, Ismay 4/16/18.

9. Historians are divided on this assessment. For example, Johnson maintained that Inskip's tenure 'was generally marked by procrastination, uncertainty and complacency' (Johnson, *Defence by Committee*, 274). However, in Roskill's view,

'[Inskip's] accomplishments as a minister have been unfairly disparaged' (Roskill, *Hankey, vol. 3,* 207). Similarly, see Tim Bouverie, *Appeasing Hitler. Chamberlain, Churchill and the Road to War* (London, Penguin Random House, 2019), 97.

10. Ismay, *Memoirs*, 74–75.

11. Unlike Hankey, who later wrote that he 'liked Inskip immensely' and that they had worked together 'like twin brothers'. Hankey to his son, Robin, 3 April 1938 and 24 May 1938, quoted in Roskill, *Hankey, vol. 3*, 319 and 358.

12. Ismay, *Memoirs*, 109; AJP Taylor, *English History 1914-1945* (Oxford, Clarendon Press, 1965), 390.

13. Ismay *Memoirs,* 78; Morton to Ismay, 25 August 1936, CAB 21/437; Martin Gilbert, *Winston S Churchill, vol. 5*, *The Prophet of Truth, 1922-1939* (London, Heinemann, 1997), 560.

14. Record of Discussion, 23 November 1936, TNA, PREM 1/193.

15. Bouverie, *Appeasing Hitler,* 100.

16. Richard Overy, *The Road to War* (London, Vintage Books, 2009), 107.

17. David French, *Deterrence, Coercion and Appeasement: British Grand Strategy, 1919-1940* (Oxford, Oxford University Press, 2022), 383.

18. John Naylor, 'Hankey, Maurice Pascal Alers, first Baron Hankey' (2004), *Oxford Dictionary of National Biography* (Oxford, Oxford University Press), https://www-oxforddnb-com.ezproxy-prd.bodleian.ox.ac.uk/10.1093/ref:odnb/9780198614128.001.0001/odnb-9780198614128-e-33683?rskey=ytPdu5&result=2, accessed 22 January 2021.

19. CID 288th meeting, 11 February 1937, TNA, CAB 2/6; Ismay to Hankey, 11 June 1937, TNA, CAB 21/558.

20. GC Peden, *Churchill, Chamberlain and Appeasement* (Cambridge, Cambridge University Press, 2022), 158.

21. Ismay to O'Malley 27 May 1937, TNA, CAB 21/558 f259; Ismay to Hankey, 11 June 1937, TNA, CAB 21/558; JPS paper, 'Mediterranean and Middle East Appreciation', 22 June 1937, TNA, CAB 55/10/7, and 26 July 1937, CAB 53/32/6; Howard Welch, 'The Origins and Development of the Chiefs of Staff Sub-Committee of the Committee of Imperial Defence 1923-1939', PhD thesis (unpublished), 1973, University of London, 169–83. http://ethos.bl.uk/OrderDetails.do?uin=uk.bl.ethos.289189 accessed 15 December 2022.

22. Bond, *British Military Policy*, 266; Hankey was firmly in Chamberlain's and Inskip's camp in the dispute with the Foreign Office, telling Inskip, 'The P.M. asked me to do anything I could to help him with the F.O. over Italy… I have been working on Van [Sir Robert Vansittart, Permanent Secretary, Foreign Office]'. Hankey to Inskip, 2 November 1937, TNA, CAB 21/558. See also Roskill, *Hankey, Man of Secrets, vol. 3*, 270.

23. At one point Chamberlain 'claimed that he was not suggesting that Britain would be able to fight the next war "upon the principle of limited liability". But that was exactly what he was doing'. French, *Deterrence, Coercion and Appeasement*, 377.

24. Hankey, 'The Cost of Defence', memorandum 23 November 1937, quoted in JP Harris, 'The War Office and Rearmament 1935-39', PhD thesis (unpublished),

1983, Kings College London, 112, http://ethos.bl.uk/OrderDetails.do?uin=uk. bl.ethos.289189 accessed 15 December 2022.

25. Ismay to Hankey, 1 December 1937, TNA, CAB 21/510.

26. Roskill, *Hankey, vol. 3*, 284 and 320; Hankey abandoned his objection to the continental commitment only after Hitler's 'Anschluss' of Austria in March 1938, Ibid., 313; Norman Gibbs, *Grand Strategy, vol. 1, Rearmament Policy* (London HMSO, 1976), 468–9.

27. Michael Howard, *The Continental Commitment* (London, The Ashfield Press, 1989), 127.

28. Roskill, *Hankey, vol. 3*, 315–17.

29. Frost, 'The British and Indian Staff Colleges' in Delaney, *Military Education*, 203-4..

30. Nigel de Lee, 'History of the Cabinet War Rooms' (unpublished), IWM, LBY 86/2038; See also Richard Holmes, *Churchill's Bunker. The Secret Headquarters at the Heart of Britain's Victory* (London, Profile Books, 2009), 23.

31. Holmes, *Churchill's Bunker*, 35.

32. Roskill, *Hankey, vol. 3*, 352–7.

33. Hankey diary, 16 May 1938, CAC, Hankey Papers, HNKY 1/8.

34. 'Lady Ismay's Description of Important Events', Ismay Family Papers.

35. Ibid.

36. Roskill, *Hankey, vol. 3,* 357.

37. CID Paper 1473-B, 14 October 1938, TNA, CAB 4/28.

38. Sinclair to Ismay, 12 September 1938, Keith Jeffery, *MI6: The History of the Secret Intelligence Service 1909-1949* (London, Bloomsbury, 2010), 304.

39. Dated 20 September 1938, TNA, CAB 21/544; SW Roskill, *Hankey, vol. 3,* 380.

40. Overy, *Road to War*, 121.

41. Colville diary, 22 October 1940, Colville, *Fringes of Power*, 273.

42. Bouverie, *Appeasing Hitler*, 295–6. See also Howard, *The Continental Commitment*, 123.

43. Andrew Roberts, *Churchill. Walking with Destiny* (London, Allen Lane, 2018), 434.

44. Ismay, *Memoirs*, 92.

45. Lascelles diary, 30 September 1943, Duff Hart Davis (ed.), *King's Counsellor. Abdication and War: The Diaries of Sir Alan Lascelles* (London, Weidenfeld & Nicholson, 2006), 167; Ismay, *Memoirs*, 92.

46. 'Measures Taken in Connection with the Czechoslovak Crisis', 14 October 1938, TNA, CAB 16/189, and CAB 4/28.

47. Ismay to Salmon, 2 December 1963, LHC, Ismay 5/19.

48. Johnson, *Defence by Committee*, 266–7.

49. Ismay, 'The Machinery of the Committee of Imperial Defence', *Journal of the Royal United Services Institute*, 84/534 (May, 1939), 241–57.

50. Bond, *British Military Policy,* 241.

51. Ibid., 295.

52. COS Minutes, 21 December 1938, TNA, CAB 53/10/3.

53. Ismay, *Memoirs*, 84.

54. Nicolson diary, 14 November 1938, Nigel Nicolson, *Harold Nicolson. Diaries and Letters. 1930-1939* (London, Collins, 1966), 381.

55. CID 345th Minutes of Meeting, 26 January 1939, TNA, CAB 2/8.

56. Adrian Phillips, *Fighting Churchill, Appeasing Hitler. How a British Civil Servant Helped Cause the Second World War* (London, Biteback, 2019), 235–7.

57. Ismay, *Memoirs*, 87.

58. Ibid., 93.

59. Johnson, *Defence by Committee,* 253–4.

60. Leslie Hollis, 'Random Reminiscences', IWM, Hollis Papers, IWM/2773, 38.

61. Ismay, *Memoirs*, 97.

62. Hollis, 'Random Reminiscences', 38.

63. Ismay to JRM Butler, 17 June 1954, TNA, CAB 140/83.

64. Ismay, Lecture to IDC, October 1949, LHC, Ismay 3/4/12.

65. Ismay to Darry Ismay, 2 September 1939, Wingate, *Lord Ismay*, 39.

66. Richard Overy, *Blood and Ruins. The Great Imperial War 1931-1945* (London, Allen Lane, 2021), 68. Similarly, David Edgerton, *Britain's War Machine* (London, Allen Lane, 2012), 11.

67. Talbot Imlay, *Facing the Second World War: Strategy, Politics, and Economics in Britain and France, 1938-1940* (Oxford, Oxford University Press, 2003), 100.

68. Burgis, CAC, Burgis Papers, BRGS 1/1, 38.

69. Roskill, *Hankey, vol. 3,* 412.

70. Paul Addison, *The Road to 1945. British Politics and the Second World War* (London, Jonathan Cape, 1994), 60, 65 & 110.

71. Ismay to HM Patel, 12 August 1947, LHC, Ismay 3/7/67.

72. Ismay to Avon, 7 September 1962, Cadbury, Papers of the Earl of Avon, AP 23/41/2

73. Ismay, *Memoirs*, 106.

74. Ibid.

75. John Colville, *Footprints in Time* (London, Century, 1985), 92.

76. Ismay, *Memoirs,* 104.

77 Ismay, Draft Memoirs, 6, LHC, Ismay 1/15/1.

78. Full title: The Standing Ministerial Committee on Military Coordination.

79. Bridges to Chatfield, 12 October 1939, TNA, CAB 21/1342; Patrick Cosgrave, *Churchill at War* (London, Collins, 1974), 68.

80. Channon diary, 12 January 1940, Simon Heffer (ed.), *Henry 'Chips' Channon. The Diaries, vol. 2, 1938-1943* (London, Hutchinson, 2021), 237.

81. Colville diary, 2 February 1940, Colville, *Fringes of Power,* 79–80.

82. John Kennedy, *The Business of War; The War Narrative of Major-General Sir John Kennedy* (London, Hutchinson, 1957), 48–9.

83. Ismay, *Memoirs*, 120.

84. Ibid., 111.

85. Emphasis in original. Roskill, *Hankey, vol. 3,* 458. In his diary Colville recalled that 'During the Cabinet "Pug" Ismay came out and said that as far as he could see the Cabinet were proposing the only thing that could lose us the war: namely <u>not</u> to

take vigorous action' (emphasis in original, Colville, *Fringes of Power,* 98). Sangster quotes this, stating that Ismay made the statement <u>at</u> the meeting, rather than, as almost certainly happened, coming out <u>from</u> the meeting and making the remark to those waiting in the next room (Sangster, *Pug,* 37).

86. Ismay to Slessor, 21 April 1940, TNA, AIR 75/9. See also John Kiszely, *Anatomy of a Campaign. The British Fiasco in Norway 1940* (Cambridge, Cambridge University Press, 2017), 117–21.

87. Emphasis in original. Chatfield to Ismay, 10 April 1940, LHC, Ismay 5/3.

88. Jacob to Ismay, 24 January 1959, LHC, Ismay 1/14/69.

89. Ismay, *Memoirs,* 111.

90. John Colville in John Wheeler-Bennett (ed.), *Action This Day. Working With Churchill* (London, Macmillan, 1968), 48.

91. Lecture to IDC, 2 November 1950, CAC, Randolph Churchill Papers, RDCH, 4/23.

92. Edward Bridges, Meeting Note, 25 April 1940, TNA, PREM 1/404.

93. Albeit that he did not attend every meeting of each group.

94. See Kiszely, *Anatomy of a Campaign,* 39, 43, 63, 65, 74, 103, 153, 159, 167, 211, 215, and 235.

95. Ismay, *Memoirs,* 114.

5. THE FALL OF FRANCE, THE BATTLE OF BRITAIN, THE BLITZ

1. Ismay, *Memoirs,* 116.

2. Colville, in Wheeler-Bennett, *Action This Day,* 48.

3. Ian Jacob, 'His Finest Hour', *The Atlantic,* 215/3 (March 1965), 81; similar in Jacob to Ismay, 24 January 1959, LHC, Ismay 1/14/69.

4. Churchill to Ismay, 26 May 1946, TNA, CAB 127/50.

5. Alex Danchev, 'The Central Direction of the War 1940–41', in John Sweetman (ed.), *Sword and Mace. Twentieth Century Civil–Military Relations in Britain* (London, Brasseys, 1986), 59.

6. David Fraser, *Alanbrooke* (London, Collins, 1982), 208.

7. Winston Churchill, *The Story of the Malakand Field Force* (London, Thomas Nelson & Sons, 1916).

8. Warren Dockter, 'Learning Lessons. Lieutenant Churchill and Miliary Intelligence', in Allen Packwood (ed.), *The Cambridge Companion to Winston Churchill* (Cambridge, Cambridge University Press, 2023), 49–50.

9. Daniel Todman, *Britain's War. Into Battle 1937-1941* (London, Penguin Books, 2017), 320.

10. Emphasis in original, David Reynolds, *From World War to Cold War: Churchill, Roosevelt, and the International History of the 1940s* (Oxford, Oxford University Press, 2006), 76; and David Reynolds, 'Churchill and the Decision to Fight on in 1940: Right Policy, Wrong Reasons', in FH Hinsley and Richard Langhorne (eds.), *Diplomacy and Intelligence During the Second World War* (Cambridge, Cambridge University Press, 1985), 149.

11. Colville diary, 15 May 1940, Colville, *Fringes of Power*, 131.
12. Ismay to Churchill, 20 May 1946, LHC, Ismay 2/3/2; Martin Gilbert, *Winston S Churchill, vol. 6, Finest Hour 1939-1941* (London, Heinemann, 1983), 349.
13. Ismay, *Memoirs*, 126.
14. Ismay to Churchill, 20 May 1946, LHC, Ismay 2/3/2.
15. A pointed reference to the fact that Reynaud had an Anglophobic mistress, the Comtesse de Portes, whom Churchill thoroughly disliked.
16. Ismay to Churchill, 20 May 1946, LHC, Ismay 2/3/2.
17. Colville, *Fringe of Power*, 133.
18. Cadogan diary, 25 April 1940, David Dilks (ed.), *The Diaries of Sir Alexander Cadogan, 1938-1945* (London, Cassell, 1971), 273.
19. Ismay to Rear Admiral WS Chalmers, 30 May 1940, LHC, Ismay 5/3.
20. Goodman, *Official History*, 74–5.
21. Annex to War Cabinet Conclusions, 22 May 1940, TNA, CAB 65/7/28.
22. Harvey diary, 22 May 1940, John Harvey (ed.), *The Diplomatic Diaries of Oliver Harvey, 1937-1940* (London, Collins, 1970), 365.
23. Edward Spears, *Assignment to Catastrophe, vol. 1, Prelude to Dunkirk, July 1939-May 1940* (London, Heinemann, 1954), 159–60.
24. Churchill to Ismay, 24 May 1940, Martin Gilbert, *The Churchill Documents, vol. 15, Never Surrender, May-December 1940* (Hillsdale, Hillsdale College Press, 2011), 138.
25. Ismay, *Memoirs*, 131.
26. James Leasor, *War at the Top; Based on the Experiences of General Sir Leslie Hollis* (London, Michael Joseph, 1959), 94–6.
27. Ismay, *Memoirs*, 133.
28. Spears to Ismay, 2 June 1940, CAC, Spears Papers, SPRS 8/11.
29. Ismay to Spears, 3 June 1940, TNA, CAB 21/1282.
30. Colville diary, 6 June 1940, Colville, *Fringes of Power*, 150.
31. Ismay, *Memoirs*, 137.
32. Edward Spears, *Assignment to Catastrophe, vol. 2, The Fall of France, June 1940* (London, Heinemann, 1954), 138.
33. Ismay, *Memoirs*, 138
34. Ibid.
35. In Churchill's draft for *The Second World War, vol. 2, Their Finest Hour* (London, Penguin Books, 2005) he wrote that the French 'requested us' not to carry out the mission. Ismay commented to Churchill that '"requested us" is too mild. The French Government were absolutely adamant that we should take no offensive action of any kind'. Ismay to Churchill, 16 Feb 47, LHC, Ismay 2/3/36D. Churchill chose to omit all reference to this interchange.
36. Ismay, *Memoirs*, 139.
37. Edward Spears, *Fall of France*, 140.
38. Ismay, *Memoirs,* 140.
39. Ibid.
40. Ismay to Spears, 30 July 1946, CAC, Spears Papers, SPRS 7/13,
41. Ismay, *Memoirs,* 142.

42. Roberts, *Walking with Destiny,* 555.

43. Ismay, *Memoirs*, 143–4.

44. Spears, *Fall of France*, 199.

45. Historians are divided as to whether Britain was, indeed, alone. Those who, like David Edgerton, assert that 'Britain was not "alone" between June 1940 and June 1941; nor did it believe itself to be', citing the existence of 'the mighty British Empire' (Edgerton, *Britain's War Machine*, 47) can claim Ismay's support for their argument. In his memoirs he made an almost identical assertion, adding that when a worried Darry asked him for his candid opinion of Britain's chances of survival his answer was 'Three to one on', denying that he was just 'whistling to keep up her courage' (Ismay, *Memoirs*, 154 and 153). He would no doubt have revised the odds just two months later during the Battle of Britain.

46. Ismay, interview with Robert Sherwood, 11 July 1946, Sherwood Papers, Houghton Library, University of Harvard, MSS Am 1947/1891.

47. Ismay to Churchill, 30 May 1946, Gilbert, *Finest Hour,* 322; Ismay, *Memoirs*, 168.

48. Ismay to Churchill, 1 July 1940, Gilbert, *Finest Hour* 323.

49. Churchill to Bridges, Ismay and Dill, 19 July 1940, TNA, CAB 120/9.

50. Ismay to Churchill, 15 November 1940, TNA, CAB 120/9.

51. John Shortal, *Code Name Arcadia: The First Wartime Conference of Churchill and Roosevelt* (College Station, Texas A&M University Press, 2021), 40. Jacob was to become Director General of the BBC from 1952 to 1959.

52. Joan Bright Astley, *The Inner Circle: A View of War at the Top* (London, Hutchinson, 1971), 88.

53. Ismay, *Memoirs*, 171.

54. Stuart Macrae, *Winston Churchill's Toyshop. The Inside Story of Military Intelligence (Research)* (Stroud, Amberley, 2012), 53.

55. Ibid., 90; Giles Milton, *Churchill's Ministry of Ungentlemanly Warfare. The Mavericks who Plotted Hitler's Defeat* (London, John Murray, 2017), 84.

56. Ian Jacob in Wheeler-Bennett, *Action This Day*, 164.

57. Ismay to Morton, 23 June 1940, LHC, Ismay 5/12.

58. Ismay, *Memoirs*, 111.

59. Kennedy diary, 29 September 1939, LHC, Kennedy Papers 4/2. A view with which many historians have concurred; see, for example, Hew Strachan, *The Politics of the British Army* (Oxford, Clarendon, 1997), 153; Nick Smart, *British Strategy and Politics during the Phony War. Before the Balloon Went Up* (Westport, Praeger, 2003), 60.

60. Kennedy diary, 29 September 1939, LHC, Kennedy Papers 4/2.

61. Lecture to IDC, November 1956, LHC, Ismay 3/4/15.

62. Lecture to IDC, 1949, LHC, Ismay 3/4/12.

63. Ibid.

64. Ian Jacob, in Wheeler-Bennett, *Action This Day*, 167.

65. Leslie Rowan, in Wheeler Bennett, *Action This Day*, 24.

66. Colville, in Wheeler Bennett, *Action This Day*, 63; Danchev, 'Central Direction', in Sweetman, *Sword and Mace*, 62.

67. Ismay to Robin Bousfield, 15 November 1962, LHC, Ismay 4/24/84.

68. Lecture to the IDC, November 1956, LHC, Ismay 3/4/15.

69. Jacob, CAC, Jacob Papers, JACB 4/7, 50.

70. Ismay, *Memoirs,* 175.

71. Marian Holmes, 'Diary of Marian (nee Holmes) Walker Spicer' (unpublished), 1, 2, 3, 4 et al.; Patrick Kinna in Cita Stelzer, *Working with Winston. The Unsung Women behind Britain's Greatest Statesman* (London, Head of Zeus, 2019), 79; Grace Hamblin, Ibid., 28; Forrest Pogue, interview with Ismay 17 December 1946, US Army Heritage and Education Center, Carlisle Barracks, Pennsylvania., Pogue Papers; Hollis, 'Random Reminiscences', IWM, Hollis Papers, 47.

72. Ismay, *Memoirs,* 175.

73. Richard Toye, *The Roar of the Lion. The Untold Story of Churchill's World War II Speeches* (Oxford, Oxford University Press, 2013), 50, 112.

74. Ismay, *Memoirs,* 169.

75. Ismay to JMG Taylor, 17 July 1940, LHC, Ismay 5/19.

76. Ismay to Hollis, 26 June 1940, TNA, CAB 21/1476.

77. COS Minutes, 26 June 1940, TNA, CAB 79/5/21 and COS Memo 27 June, CAB 66/9/16.

78. 1 July 1940, Gilbert, *Finest Hour,* 623.

79. Nigel de Lee, 'History of the Cabinet War Rooms' (unpublished), IWM, LBY 86/2038, 54–55.

80. Gilbert, *Finest Hour,* 691–2; Ismay to General Venning, 8 August 1940, WO 199/303; Ismay to P Allen, Ministry of Home Security, 29 August 1940, TNA, PREM 14/33.

81. Allen Packwood, *How Churchill Waged War. The Most Challenging Decisions of the Second World War* (London, Frontline Books, 2019), 55.

82. Leslie Hollis, *One Marine's Tale* (London, Deutsch, 1956), 67.

83. The Cabinet decision followed the French rejection of an ultimatum to remove the fleet to the French West Indies, to scuttle the ships or to face the use of force to prevent them falling into enemy hands.

84. Ismay, *Memoirs*, 148–9.

85. Lee diary, 26 June 1940, James Leutze, *The London Observer: The Journal of General Raymond E Lee, 1940-1941* (Boston, Little Brown, 1971), 17.

86. Brigadier General Miles to Chief of Staff, War Department, 27 June 1940, 'Paraphrased messages from the Military Attache', US War Dept G-2/2657–234, 50, Records of the War Dept, Gen and Special Staffs (Record Group 165, Entry 65), US National Archives and Records Administration.

87. Lee diary, 7 July 1940, Leutze, *London Observer*, 13.

88. In response to a query from Ismay about the exact date, Air Chief Marshal Sir Dermot Boyle told him, 'It is more than likely that 16 August 1940 was the day'. Boyle to Ismay, 3 October 1956, LHC, Ismay 1/14/19.

89. Ismay, *Memoirs*, 179–80. A slightly different version is given in Rupert Hart-Davis, *Halfway to Heaven: Concluding Memoirs of a Literary Life* (Stroud, Sutton, 1998), 41.

90. Victoria Taylor, 'Churchill and the Bombing Campaign', in Packwood, *Cambridge Companion*, 325.

91. Ismay, *Memoirs*, 183–4.

92. Ibid., 184.

93. Ismay to Churchill, 28 November 1946, LHC, Ismay 2/3/21.

94. Churchill to Ismay and Bridges, 14 September 1940, Gilbert, *Never Surrender*, 810.

95. FW Winterbotham, *The Ultra Secret* (London, Weidenfeld and Nicholson, 1974), 58.

96. Jeffery, *MI6*, 348–9.

97. Ibid., 350.

98. Colville diary, 31 December 1940, Colville, *Fringes of Power,* 325.

6. DISCORD AND HARMONY

1. Churchill to Ismay, 4 June 1940, Gilbert, *Finest Hour*, 460.

2. Ian Jacob, 'Churchill as War Leader', in [no author cited] *Churchill by His Contemporaries: An Observer Appreciation* (London, Hodder and Stoughton, 1965), 74.

3. Ismay to John Connell, 13 September 1961, LHC, Ismay 4/9/39.

4. Churchill to Ismay and Bridges, 24 August 1940, TNA, PREM 3/119/10.

5. George Mallaby to Jacob, 31 January 1968, CAC, Jacob Papers, JACB 4/8.

6. Dill to Churchill, 28 August 1940, TNA, PREM 3/119/10.

7. Ismay to Churchill, 13 June 1942, TNA, CAB 121/232. On 13 June 1942 Ismay minuted Churchill, 'May I with respect point out that the Chiefs of Staff have a rule that papers by the Joint Planning Committee go to no one except the Chiefs of Staff themselves until, or unless, they have been approved by them'. Churchill wrote on the minute dismissively, 'No. They are serving under me'. TNA, CAB 121/232.

8. Churchill to Eden, Packwood, *How Churchill Waged War*, 65, citing CAC, Churchill Papers, CHAR 20/2/42–43.

9. Ismay to Connell, 21 August 1961, quoted in Victoria Schofield, *Wavell. Soldier and Statesman* (London, John Murray, 2006), 151.

10. Lee diary, 7 January 1941, Leutze, *London Observer*, 208.

11. Ismay, *Memoirs*, 68.

12. Amery diary, 18 September 1940, John Barnes and David Nicholson (eds.), *Empire at Bay. The Leo Amery Diaries, vol. 2, 1929-1945* (London, Hutchinson, 1988), 642.

13. Colville diary, 13 December 1940, Colville, *Fringes of Power,* 312.

14. 'Notebook for Memoirs', LHC, Ismay 1/12.

15. Colville diary, 3 November 1940, Colville, *Fringes of Power*, 286.

16. Kennedy, *Business of War*, 60.

17. Ibid., 63.

18. Ismay to Connell, 13 September 1961, LHC, Ismay 4/9/39.

19. Todman, *Into Battle*, 425–6.

20. Danchev, 'Central Direction', in Sweetman, *Sword and Mace*, 67.

21. Churchill to COS, 6 January 1941, Winston Churchill, *The Second World War, vol. 3, The Grand Alliance* (London, Cassell, 1950), 9.

22. Kennedy, *Business of War*, 75; Alex Danchev, '"Dilly-Dally", or Having the Last Word: Field Marshal Sir John Dill and Prime Minister Winston Churchill', *Journal of Contemporary History*, 22/1 (January 1987), 21–44.

23. Annex 1 to COS Minutes, 21 April 1941, TNA, CAB 79/86/2 (1).

24. Ismay, *Memoirs*, 203.

25. Ibid.

26. Kennedy, *Business of War*, 105–6.

27. Prime Minister's Directive, 28 April 1941, JRM Butler, *Grand Strategy, vol. 2, September 1939-June 1941* (London, HMSO, 1956), 576.

28. Minute by the Chiefs of Staff, 7 May 1941, Butler, *Grand Strategy, vol. 2*, 578–80.

29. 'The Relation of the Middle East to the Security of the United Kingdom', 6 May 1941, TNA, WO 216/5.

30. Danchev, 'Dilly-Dally', *Journal of Contemporary History*, 22/1 (January 1987), 28. The bitter exchange between Churchill and Dill was to continue for a further fortnight: see Churchill to Dill, 13 May 1941; Dill to Churchill, CIGS/PM/119, undated but probably 20 May 1941; both in TNA, CAB 216/5.

31. Ismay to Connell, 13 September 1961, LHC, Ismay 4/9/39.

32. Gilbert, *Finest Hour*, 1040.

33. Brigadier General Miles to the Chief of Staff, War Department, 23 April 1941, 'British Estimate of the Situation', US War Dept G-2/2657–298, Records of the War Dept, Gen and Special Staffs (Record Group 165, Entry 65), US National Archives and Record Administration.

34. Colville diary, 25 May 1941, Colville, *Fringes of Power*, 391.

35. Lockhart diary, 11 June 1941, Young, *Diaries,* 102.

36. Ismay to Churchill, 2 February 1949, LHC, Ismay 2/3/138.

37. Lockhart diary, 6 January 1942, Young, *Diaries*, 134.

38. Ismay, *Memoirs*, 269.

39. John Connell, *Auchinleck. A Biography of Field Marshal Sir Claude Auchinleck* (London, Cassell, 1959), 267.

40. Ismay to Auchinleck, 28 August 1941, JRL, Auchinleck Papers, AUC/303.

41. Connell to Ismay, 6 October 1954, LHC, Ismay 4/9/34.

42. Taylor Downing, *1942. Britain at the Brink* (London, Little Brown, 2022), 154.

43. COS Minutes, 3 September 1941, TNA, CAB 79/14/10.

44. Colville diary, 3 September 1941, Colville, *Fringes of Power*, 436.

45. Denis Richards, *Portal of Hungerford. The Life of Marshal of the Royal Air Force, Viscount Portal of Hungerford, KG, GCB, OM, DSO, MC* (London, Heinemann, 1977), 235–7.

46. Martin Gilbert, *The Churchill Documents, vol. 16, The Ever-Widening War. 1941* (Hillsdale, Hillsdale College Press, 2011), 814.

47. Joan Bright Astley's obituary, *The Independent,* 28 January 2009.

48. Churchill to Ismay, 17 July 1940, TNA, PREM 3/475/1.

49. Ismay to Churchill, 18 July 1940, TNA, PREM 3/475/1.

50. Ismay, *Memoirs*, 212.

51. Greg Kennedy, *Anglo-American Strategic Relations and the Far East 1933-1939. Imperial Crossroads* (London, Routledge, 2011), 262 and 267. Lee diary, 30 November 1940, Leutze, *London Observer,* 147.

52. Lee diary, 30 November 1940, Leutze, *London Observer,* 147.

53. Alex Danchev, *Establishing the Anglo-American Alliance. The Second World War Diaries of Brigadier Vivian Dykes* (London, Brassey's, 1990), 10.

54. David Reynolds, *The Creation of the Anglo-American Alliance 1937–1941: A Study in Competitive Co-operation* (London, Europa Publications, 1981), 184; Ismay, *Memoirs,* 217.

55. That is to say combined planning and operations. Danchev, *Very Special Relationship,* 20.

56. Ismay interview with Sherwood, 11 July 1946, Robert E Sherwood Papers, Houghton Library, University of Harvard.

57. Lee diary, 21 May 1941, Leutze, *London Observer,* 284.

58. Reynolds, *Anglo-American Alliance,* 181.

59. Ismay, *Memoirs,* 214.

60. Ibid., 219. Ismay's typically warm tribute fosters the myth about Lend-Lease which, as he will have been well aware, 'was far from being an act of disinterested American generosity as later propaganda suggested'. Brian Bond, *Britain's Two World Wars Against Germany. Myth, Memory and the Distortion of Hindsight* (Cambridge, Cambridge University Press, 2014), 172.

61. Ismay, *Memoirs,* 221.

62. Ismay to Auchinleck, 28 August 1941, JRL, Auchinleck Papers, AUC/303.

63. Ismay, *Memoirs,* 230.

64. Ibid., 228.

65. Ismay to Churchill, 7 September 1949, LHC, Ismay 2/3/171.

66. Ismay, *Memoirs,* 233.

67. Averell Harriman and Elie Abel, *Special Envoy to Churchill and Stalin 1941-1946* (London, Hutchinson, 1976), 101.

68. Ismay, *Memoirs,* 233–4.

69. Amery diary, 27 October 1941, Barnes and Nicholson (eds.), *Empire at Bay,* 740.

70. Ismay, *Memoirs,* 234–5.

71. Churchill, *Grand Alliance,* 416.

72. Ismay, *Memoirs,* 171.

73. Dudley Clarke, quoted in Thaddeus Holt, *The Deceivers: Allied Military Deception in the Second World War* (London, Weidenfeld & Nicholson, 2004), 41.

74. Ibid.

75. Dudley Clarke to Peter Fleming, 1 June 1971, IWM, Clarke Papers, IWM 8080.

76. Ronald Wingate, *Not in the Limelight* (London, Hutchinson, 1959), 189–90.

77. Oliver Stanley MP, former Secretary of State for War, personally selected by Churchill for the appointment of Head of the Future Operational Planning Section. Churchill to Ismay, 22 December 1940, Churchill, *Their Finest Hour,* 625–6.

78. 'Historical Record of Deception in the War Against Germany and Italy', TNA, CAB 154/100.

79. COS Minutes, 7 and 9 October 1941, TNA, CAB 79/14/44 and CAB 79/14/48.

80. Wingate, *Lord Ismay,* 77–8.

81. Schofield, *Wavell,* 218–19.

82. Astley, *Inner Circle,* 67.

83. For example, in February 1943 Ismay directed the Controlling Officer to 'put over a threat of an attack on Norway and start "soft pedalling" threats of attacks elsewhere'. Ewen Montagu, 'Naval Intelligence in the Second World War, vol. 2, Deception,' TNA, ADM 223/794.

84. Ismay to Churchill, 10 November 1949, LHC, Ismay 2/3/188.

85. She died on 23 December 1941.

86. Brooke diary, 22 November 1940, Alex Danchev and Daniel Todman (eds.), *War Diaries, 1939-1945. Field Marshal Lord Alanbrooke* (London, Weidenfeld & Nicholson, 2002), 124.

87. Danchev, 'Dilly-Dally', *Journal of Contemporary History*, 22/1 (January 1987), 23.

88. Ibid., 31.

89. Brooke diary, 20 October 1941, Danchev, *War Diaries*, 192.

90. Marion Long, Notes on Interview with Ismay, March 1957, LHC, Alanbrooke Papers, 11/7.

91. Andrew Roberts, *Masters and Commanders. The Military Geniuses Who Led the West to Victory in World War II* (London, Penguin, 2009), 113.

92. Brooke diary, 4 December 1941, Danchev, *War Diaries*, 207.

93. Kennedy diary, 5 December 1941, LHC, Kennedy, 4/2.

94. Ismay, *Memoirs*, 241.

95. Overy, *Blood and Ruins*, 168.

96. Ismay, Lecture to the IDC, 1946, LHC, Ismay 3/4/11.

97. See for example Daniel Todman, *Britain's War. A New World, 1942-1947* (London, Penguin Books, 2021) 45.

7.   'THE TROUGH OF THE WAR'

1. Ismay, *Memoirs*, 247.

2. Ibid.

3. Ismay, Draft Memoirs, 89, LHC, Ismay 1/15/1.

4. For example, Dill's paper of 4 May 1941, TNA, WO 216/5.

5. Jacob to Ismay, 24 January 1959, LHC, Ismay 1/14/69.

6. Gort's covering letter dated 15 November 1938 to CID paper 480-C, TNA, CAB 5/9.

7. COS paper 'The Situation in the Far East in the Event of Japanese Intervention Against Us', COS (40) 592 dated 31 July (and revised 15 August) 1940, TNA, CAB 80/15/1.

8. COS Minutes, 19 September 1940, TNA, CAB 79/6/67.

9. COS Minutes 17 December 1941, TNA, CAB 79/16/25 & CAB 79/16/26; Brooke diary, 17 December 1941, Danchev, *War Diaries*, 212.

10. LHC, Brooke-Popham Papers, 6/2, 'Correspondence with Ismay'.

11. Winston Churchill, *The Second World War, vol. 4, The Hinge of Fate* (London, Cassell, 1951), 43.

12. See for example Churchill to Dill, 13 May 1941, TNA, WO 216/5.

13. Ismay to Auchinleck, 1 February 1942, JRL, Auchinleck Papers, AUC/679,

14. Churchill, *Hinge of Fate*, 81.

15. Jonathan Fennell, *Fighting the People's War. The British and Commonwealth Armies and the Second World War* (Cambridge, Cambridge University Press, 2019), 207.

16. Toye, *Roar of the Lion,* 130.

17. Brooke diary, 2 March 1942, Danchev, *War Diaries*, 235

18. Ibid.

19. Churchill to Auchinleck, 7 March 1942, Connell, *Auchinleck*, 464.

20. Emphasis in original, Auchinleck to Prime Minister, 9 March 1942, Timothy Bowman, *The Military Papers of Field Marshal Sir Claude Auchinleck: vol. 1, 1940-42* (Woodbridge, Boydell Press, 2021), 363.

21. Emphasis in original, Ismay to Auchinleck, 3 April 1942, JRL, Auchinleck Papers, AUC/774, courtesy of the University of Manchester.

22. Connell, *Auchinleck. A Biography of General Sir Claude Auchinleck* (London, Cassell, 1959), 466.

23. John Terraine, *The Life and Times of Lord Mountbatten* (London, Arrow Books, 1980), 90. The Palladium: a London theatre popular for its entertaining variety shows.

24. Ismay, *Memoirs*, 249.

25. Pogue interview with Ismay, 18 October 1960, Forrest Pogue, *George C Marshall: Ordeal and Hope, 1939-1942* (New York, Viking Press, 1966), 320.

26. Albert Wedemeyer, *Wedemeyer Reports!* (New York, Holt, 1958), 254. Wedemeyer stoutly denied being anti-British, just 'pro-American'. Ibid., 83.

27. Ibid., 108.

28. Ismay to Harriman, 17 March 1944, LHC, Ismay 4/17/4.

29. 25 March 1942, *Hansard*, House of Lords, vol. 122, cols. 441–7 and 463–7.

30. Ismay to Hankey, 31 March 1942, CAC, Churchill Papers, CHUR 4/34.

31. Hankey (no addressee specified), 9 April 1942, Ibid.

32. 11 May 1942, Kennedy, *Business of War*, 231. At a time of strict rationing it was, of course, only the most fortunate people, busy or otherwise, who had access to such gastronomic delights.

33. John Peck, *Dublin From Downing Street*, (Dublin, Gill and Macmillan, 1978), 71.

34. Stanley to Ismay, 20 May 1942, TNA, CAB 121/105; Holt, *Deceivers*, 186.

35. Wavell to Churchill, 21 May 1942, TNA, CAB 120/769.

36. 'Directive to Controlling Officer', TNA, CAB 121/105; Michael Howard, *Strategic Deception in the Second World War* (London, Pimlico, 1992), 243.

37. COS Minutes, 21 June 1942, TNA, CAB 79/21/7.

38. Dennis Wheatley, *The Deception Planners: My Secret War* (London, Hutchinson, 1980), 39 and 42.

39. Brooke diary, 18 June 1942, Danchev, *War Diaries*, 266.

40. Ismay, *Memoirs*, 251.

41. Ibid.

42. Ibid., 253.

43. Quoted by Holmes, *Churchill's Bunker*, 58.

44. Brooke diary, 21 June 1942, Danchev, *War Diaries*, 268.

45. JMA Gwyer and JRM Butler, *Grand Strategy, vol. 3, June 1941-August 1942* (London, HMSO, 1956), 627.

46. Wedemeyer, *Wedemeyer Reports!*, 156.

47. Roberts, *Masters and Commanders*, 202.

48. In his memoirs Ismay states incorrectly that this episode took place that morning. Ismay, *Memoirs*, 254–5.

49. Ismay to Churchill, 8 February 1949, LHC, Ismay 2/3/137; Raymond Callahan, *Churchill and His Generals* (Kansas, University of Kansas, 2007), 107.

50. Marshall to Ismay, 30 June 1942, LHC, Ismay 4/22/1.

51. Ismay to Spears, 21 July 1942, LHC, Ismay 4/31/2.

52. Brooke diary, 7 July 1942, Danchev, *War Diaries*, 277.

53. Harvey diary, 7 July 1942, John Harvey (ed.), *The War Diaries of Oliver Harvey, 1941-1945* (London, Collins, 1978), 138.

54. Brooke diary, 11 July 1942, Danchev, *War Diaries*, 279.

55. Ismay to Gordon Grimsdale, 15 July 1942, LHC, Ismay 4/14/2.

56. Daniel Crosswell, *Beetle. The Life of General Walter Bedell Smith* (Lexington, University Press of Kentucky, 2010), 274.

57. Ismay, draft of memoirs, LHC, Ismay 1/15/3/A/2.

58. Ismay, *Memoirs*, 262.

59. Overy, *Blood and Ruins*, 247; Roberts, *Masters and Commanders*, 269.

60. Nicolson diary, 7 August 1942, Nigel Nicolson (ed.), *Harold Nicolson. Diaries and Letters. 1939-1945* (London, Collins, 1966), 238.

61. Ismay to Auchinleck, 23 September 1942, JRL, Auchinleck Papers, AUC/1007.

62. Ismay, Draft Memoirs, LHC, Ismay 1/15/3A/2.

63. Ibid., 32; Brooke, Notes by Marion Long, LHC, Alanbrooke Papers, 11/7.

64. WC Confidential Annex, 7 August 1942, TNA, CAB 65/31/11 and 'Secretary's Rough Notes' of Defence Committee meeting, 7 August 1942, CAC, Burgis Papers, BRGS 2/12.

65. Churchill, *Hinge of Fate*, 420.

66. Brooke diary, 26 August 1942, Danchev, *War Diaries*, 315.

67. Michael Howard, *Grand Strategy, vol. 4, August 1941-September 1943* (London, HMSO, 1972), 125.

68. Ismay to Auchinleck, 23 September 1942, JRL, Auchinleck Papers, AUC/1007.

69. Ismay to Spears, 4 October 1942, CAC, Spears Papers, SPRS 1/180.

70. Ismay to Auchinleck, 23 September 1942, JRL, Auchinleck Papers, AUC/1007.

71. War Cabinet Conclusions, 21 September 1942, TNA, CAB 65/21/3.

72. Brooke diary, 24 September 1942, Danchev, *War Diaries,* 324.

73. Ismay to Churchill, 6 October 1942, TNA, CAB 120/10.

74. Lord Moran, *Churchill at War*, 85, quoted by Roberts, *Masters and Commanders*, 286.

75. Howard, *Grand Strategy*, 68.

76. Ibid.

77. Brooke diary, afternote to 24 November 1942, Danchev, *War Diaries*, 343.

78. Ismay to Hopkins, 1 July 1942, LHC, Ismay 4/18/12.

79. Eisenhower to Ismay, 19 August 1942, LHC, Ismay 4/12/1.

80. Howard, *Grand Strategy,* 114–15; Eisenhower to Ismay, 10 October 1942, Alfred

Chandler (ed.), *The Papers of Dwight David Eisenhower, vol. 1* (Baltimore, Johns Hopkins University Press, 1970), 602–4.

81. Ibid. Ismay glosses over this incident in his memoirs, Ismay, *Memoirs*, 264.

82. Ismay to Eisenhower, 18 November 1942, LHC, Ismay 4/12/2.

83. Norman Gelb, *Ike and Monty: Generals at War* (London, Constable, 1994), 191.

84. Eisenhower to Ismay, 16 December 1942, Alfred Chandler (ed.), *Papers of Dwight David Eisenhower, vol. 2* (Baltimore, Johns Hopkins University Press, 1970), 847.

85. Brian Farrell, *The Basis and Making of British Grand Strategy, 1940-1945: Was There a Plan?* (Lewiston, Lampeter, 1998), 423–4.

86. Brooke diary, 22 December 1942, Danchev, *War Diaries*, 350.

87. Ismay, *Memoirs*, 279.

88. Ibid., 280.

89. Downing, *Britain at the Brink*, 356.

90. Ibid., 18.

8.   'CONFERENCE YEAR'

1.   Ismay, *Memoirs*, 283.

2.   Lecture to the IDC, 1946, LHC, Ismay 3/4/11.

3.   Ismay, *Memoirs*, 285.

4.   Kennedy, *Business of War*, 280.

5.   Harriman, *Special Envoy*, 180.

6.   Harold Macmillan, *War Diaries, The Mediterranean 1943-1945* (London, Macmillan, 1984), 9.

7.   Smith to Ismay, 15 December 1942, LHC, Ismay 4/29/1.

8.   Ismay to Smith, 7 January 1943, LHC, Ismay 4/29/3.

9.   Harold Macmillan, *The Blast of War* (London, Macmillan, 1967), 242.

10. Ismay, *Memoirs*, 285.

11. Ibid., 286.

12. Brooke diary, 14, 15 and 17 January 1942, Danchev, *War Diaries*, 358, 359 and 361.

13. Danchev, *Very Special Relationship*, 65.

14. Ismay, *Memoirs*, 286.

15. Ismay to Spears, 8 February 1943, LHC, Ismay 4/31/7.

16. Slessor, 'Conduct of the War in 1943', TNA, AIR 75/11.

17. Ismay to Spears, 8 February 1943, LHC, Ismay 4/31/7.

18. Ismay, *Memoirs*, 287.

19. Brooke diary, 21 January 1943, Danchev, *War Diaries*, 365–6.

20. Churchill, *Hinge of Fate*, 615.

21. Ismay to Newall, 28 January 1944, LHC, Ismay 5/14.

22. Ismay, *Memoirs*, 290.

23. Thomas Mahnken, 'US Grand Strategy, 1939–1945', in John Ferris and Evan Mawdsley, *The Cambridge History of the Second World War, vol. 1, Fighting the War* (Cambridge, Cambridge University Press, 2015), 209.

24. Ismay, *Memoirs*, 289. See also Packwood, *How Churchill Waged War*, 157–81.

25. Eisenhower to Ismay, 3 June 1943, Chandler, *Eisenhower Papers, vol.* 2, 1166.

26. Ismay to Eisenhower, 13 April 1943, LHC, Ismay 4/12/5.

27. Ismay, *Memoirs*, 296.

28. Roberts, *Masters and Commanders*, 376; Ismay, *Memoirs*, 298.

29. Ismay, *Memoirs*, 299.

30. Ibid.

31. William Leahy, *I Was There. The Personal Story of the Chief of Staff to Presidents Roosevelt and Truman, Based on His Notes and Diaries Made at the Time* (London, Victor Gollancz, 1950), 163.

32. Ibid.; Ismay to Churchill, 11 September 1951, LHC, Ismay 2/3/293; John Ehrman, *Grand Strategy, vol, 6, October 1944-August 1945* (London, HMSO, 1956), 340–1.

33. Ismay, Draft Memoirs, LHC, Ismay, 1/15/3b.

34. Phillips O'Brien, *The Second Most Powerful Man in the World: The Life of Admiral William D Leahy, Roosevelt's Chief of Staff* (New York, Dutton, 2019).

35. Roberts, *Masters and Commanders,* 377–8; Ismay, *Memoirs*, 300–1.

36. Ismay, *Memoirs*, 300.

37. Churchill, *Hinge of Fate*, 729.

38. Astley, *Inner Circle,* 99.

39. Ben Macintyre, *Operation Mincemeat. The True Spy Story that Changed the Course of World War II* (London, Bloomsbury, 2010), 97.

40. Ewen Montagu, *The Man Who Never Was* (Staplehurst, Spellmount, 2007), vi.

41. Wingate, *Lord Ismay*, 96–7.

42. Montagu, *The Man*, Foreword (un-numbered page).

43. Denis Smyth, *Deathly Deception. The Real Story of Operation Mincemeat* (Oxford, Oxford University Press, 2011), 182–7 and 320 Note 160.

44. Brooke diary, 30 July 1943; Danchev, *War Diaries*, 434; Holmes diary, 29 July and 2 August 1943; 'Diary of Marian (née Holmes) Walker Spicer', 4.

45. Ismay, *Memoirs,* 318–19.

46. Ibid., 308.

47. Brooke, comments on diary entry for 7 August 1943, Danchev, *War Diaries*, 437; Mary Soames, *Clementine Churchill* (London, Cassell, 1979), 338.

48. Jacob diary, 10 August 1943, CAC, Jacob Papers, JACB 11/5/2.

49. Brooke, comments on diary entry for 15 August 1943, Danchev *War Diaries*, 442.

50. Brooke, comments on diary entry for 19 August 1943, Ibid., 445.

51. Jackson, *The Chiefs,* 247.

52. David Reynolds, 'The Diplomacy of the Grand Alliance', in RJB Bosworth and Joseph Maiolo (eds.), *The Cambridge History of the Second World War, vol. 2. Politics and Ideology* (Cambridge, Cambridge University Press, 2015), 306.

53. Jacob to Churchill, undated but almost certainly 16 August 1943, TNA, PREM 3/333/15.

54. Ibid.

55. Ismay to Newall, 28 January 1944, LHC, Ismay 5/14.

56. Astley, *Inner Circle*, 107.

57. Cadogan diary, 30 August 1943, Dilks, *Cadogan Diaries,* 557.

58. David Reynolds, *In Command of History. Churchill Fighting and Writing the Second World War* (London, Allen Lane, 2004), 384; Wingate, *Lord Ismay*, 100–1.

59. Mary Soames, *A Daughter's Tale: The Memoir of Winston Churchill's Youngest Child* (London, Doubleday, 2011), 363.

60. Ibid., 365.

61. Mary Churchill to Ismay, 26 September 1943, LHC, Ismay 2/2/5.

62. Ismay to Clark, 21 September 1943, LHC, Ismay 4/7/3.

63. Brooke diary, 4 January 1943, Danchev, *War Diaries*, 356.

64. Ismay to Clark, 28 July 1944, LHC, Ismay 4/7/1; Clark to Ismay, 28 August 1944, LHC, Ismay 4/7/2.

65. Lascelles to Ismay, 23 September 1943, LHC, Ismay 4/20/2.

66. 'Notes on Foreign Secretary's Conference – Moscow 1943', LHC, Ismay 3/5/1.

67. Eden to Churchill, 8 November 1943, CAC, Churchill Papers, CHAR 20/123/110; Harriman, *Special Envoy*, 238

68. Churchill to Ismay 29 October 1943, CAC, Churchill Papers, CHAR 20/122/88.

69. 'Notes on Foreign Secretaries Conference, Moscow 1943', LHC, Ismay 3/5/1.

70. Ismay to Clark, 7 January 1944, LHC, Ismay 4/7/6.

71. Ismay, *Memoirs*, 328.

72. To Dallas Brooks, Lockhart diary, 9 May 1941, Young, *Diaries*, 98.

73. Eden to Churchill, 8 November 1943, CAC, Churchill Papers, CHAR 20/123/110.

74. Roy Jenkins, *Churchill* (London, Pan Books, 2017), 718.

75. Holmes diary, 7 October 1943, 'Diary of Marian Walker Spicer', 5.

76. Brooke diary, 1 & 20 October & 1 November 1943, Danchev, *War Diaries*, 459, 461 and 466.

77. Ibid., 3 November 1943, Danchev, *War Diaries*, 466. Cunningham had succeeded Pound following the latter's resignation in September 1943 due to ill health. Pound died one month later.

78. Eden and Ismay returned via Cairo where they held meetings with Turkish representatives.

79. Burgis, CAC, Burgis Papers, BRGS 1/2.

80. Chester Wilmot, 'Notes of Conversation with General Lord Ismay 25 Apr 1949', Wilmot Papers, LHC, Liddell Hart Papers 15/15/1.

81. Ismay to Admiral Sir James Somerville, 20 December 1943, LHC, Ismay 4/30/4.

82. Stillwell diary, quoted in Alex Danchev, 'Being Friends. The Combined Chiefs of Staff and the Making of Allied Strategy in the Second World War', in Lawrence Freedman, Paul Hayes and Robert O'Neill (eds.), *War, Strategy and International Politics: Essays in Honour of Sir Michael Howard* (Oxford, Clarendon Press, 1992), 208.

83. Brooke diary, 26 November 1943, Danchev, *War Diaries*, 481.

84. Ismay to Somerville, 20 December 1943, LHC, Ismay 4/30/4.

85. Astley, *Inner Circle*, 122.

86. Ibid.

87. Ismay, *Memoirs*, 338.

88. Harriman, *Special Envoy*, 264.

89. Ismay, *Memoirs*, 338.

90. Mark Stoler, *Allies and Adversaries. The Joint Chiefs of Staff, the Grand Alliance and U.S. Strategy in World War II* (Chapel Hill, North Carolina Press, 2000), 167.

91. Bond, *Britain's Two World Wars*, 173.

92. Ismay, *Memoirs*, 339.

93. Ismay to Somerville, 20 December 1943, LHC, Ismay 4/30/4.

94. Ismay, *Memoirs*, 340–1.

95. Emphasis in original, Ismay to Somerville, 20 December 1943, LHC, Ismay 4/30/4.

96. Brooke diary, 3 and 4 December 1943, Danchev, *War Diaries*, 490–1.

97. Wilmot, 'Notes of Conversation with Ismay 25 April 1949', Wilmot Papers, LHC, Liddell Hart Papers 15/15/1.

98. Ismay, *Memoirs*, 342.

99. George Mallaby, *From My Level: Unwritten Minutes* (London, Hutchinson, 1965), 120.

100. Hollis, 'Random Reminiscences', IWM, Hollis Papers, IWM/2773, 73.

101. Alistair Vale and John Scadding, *Winston Churchill's Illnesses 1886-1965* (Barnsley, Frontline Books, 2020), 100–1.

102. John Colville, 'He Had No Use for Second Best', *Finest Hour. Journal of Winston Churchill and His Times* (International Churchill Society), No. 41 (Autumn 1983).

103. Eisenhower to Major General Thomas Handy, Operations Division chief in the Pentagon, October 1943, Stoler, *Allies and Adversaries,* 116.

9.   'THE YEAR OF DESTINY'

1. Ismay to Dewing, 2 January 1944, LHC, Ismay 4/10/5.

2. Lascelles diary, 7 January 1944, Hart-Davis, *King's Counsellor,* 193.

3. Brooke diary, 20 January 1944, Danchev, *War Diaries* 515.

4. Ibid.

5. Churchill to Moran, September 1944, Reynolds, *In Command*, 393. Suvla Bay: the disastrous landing at Gallipoli in August 1915.

6. Mountbatten to Ismay, 3 January 1944, Hartley, Mountbatten Papers, MB1/C146; 17 January and 3 February 1944, TNA, WO 203/2533.

7. Somerville to Ismay, 3 and 9 December 1943, and 19 January 1944, LHC, Ismay 4/30/2, 4/30/3 and 4/30/5.

8. Ismay to Somerville, 20 December 1943, LHC, Ismay, 4/30/4.

9. Pownall diary, 10 June 1944, Brian Bond, *Chief of Staff. The Diaries of Lieutenant General Sir Henry Pownall, vol. 2* (London, Leo Cooper, 1974), 175.

10. Ismay to Redman, 31 January 1944, LHC, Ismay 4/27/5.

11. Ismay, *Memoirs,* 343.

12. Roberts, *Masters and Commanders,* 468.

13. As Churchill was to say to Ismay, 'It will be an ill day for Britain if the war ends without our having made a stroke to regain these places', 24 June 1944, Martin Gilbert, *Winston S Churchill, vol. 7, Road to Victory, 1941-1945* (London, Heinemann, 1986), 133.

14. Roberts, *Walking with Destiny*, 814.

15. John Ehrman, *Grand Strategy, vol. 5, August 1943-September 1944* (London, HMSO, 1956), 448–9; Ismay, *Memoirs*, 400.

16. Brooke diary, 8 March 1944, Danchev, *War Diaries*, 530.

17. Reynolds, *In Command*, 406.

18. Brooke diary, 21 March 1944, Danchev, *War Diaries*, 533.

19. Ismay to Pownall, 27 May 1944, LHC, Ismay 4/26/4.

20. This much misquoted anecdote comes from the transcript of a letter (undated) from Joan Bright Astley, in the file, 'Alanbrooke Biography. Notes by Marion Long', LHC, Alanbrooke Papers, 11/9. A similar account is in Lockhart diary, 21 March 1946, Young, *Diaries*, 534.

21. Ismay to Pownall, 14 March 1944, LHC, Ismay 4/26/1.

22. Ibid.

23. CAC, Burgis Papers, BRGS 1/1, 53.

24. Wingate, *Lord Ismay*, 107–8.

25. This element of the plan was codenamed 'Fortitude South'.

26. Richard Overy, *Why the Allies Won* (London, Pimlico, 2006), 185.

27. Ismay to Churchill, 5 February 1944, TNA, CAB 120/769; Holt, *Deceivers*, 512; Wingate, *Lord Ismay*, 107–9.

28. See, for example the plans for Operation Royal Flush, Bevan to Ismay, 29 April 1944, TNA, WO 169/24923.

29. Noel Wild to Dudley Clarke, from Weekly Letter No 19, 26 April 1944, Plan Copperhead, TNA, WO 169/24923.

30. Meyrick Clifton James, *I Was Monty's Double* (London, Rider, 1954).

31. Churchill to Ismay, 4 January 1944, Gilbert, *The Churchill Documents, vol. 19, Fateful Questions, September 1943 to April 1944* (Hillsdale, Hillsdale College Press, 2011), 1331.

32. Ismay, *Memoirs*, 350.

33. Antony Beevor, *D-Day. The Battle for Normandy* (London, Viking, 2009), 15.

34. Ismay, *Memoirs*, 352.

35. John Wheeler-Bennett, *King George VI. His Life and Reign* (London, Macmillan, 1958), 604–5.

36. Winston Churchill, *The Second World War, vol. 5, Closing the Ring* (London, Cassell, 1951), 623–4.

37. Ismay, *Memoirs*, 353.

38. Ibid.

39. Ibid., 355.

40. Ismay to Joan Bright, 5 June (though dated 4 June) 1944, IWM, Bright Astley Papers.

41. Ismay to Brocas Burrows, 22 June 1942, LHC, Ismay 4/4/3; Ismay, *Memoirs*, 357.

42. Ismay to Douglas, 11 June 1944, LHC, Ismay 4/11/1. Douglas was US Minister for Shipping; became US ambassador in London 1947–50.

43. Ismay to Churchill, 23 May 1951, LHC, Ismay 2/3/278.

44. Jenkins, *Churchill*, 749.

45. Ibid., 750.
46. Brooke diary, 30 June 1944, Danchev, *War Diaries*, 565.
47. Lascelles diary, 5 July, 1944, Hart-Davis, *King's Counsellor*, 241.
48. Roberts, *Walking with Destiny*, 828.
49. Pogue, interview with Ismay, 20 December 1946, USAH&EC, Pogue Papers.
50. Accusations made to de Gaulle's emissary, Pierre Viénot. Beevor, *D-Day,* 21.
51. Warren Kimball, *Churchill and Roosevelt:The Complete Correspondence, vol. 3* (Princeton, Princeton University Press, 2015), 170, quoting Forrest Pogue, interview with Ismay, November 1946.
52. Ismay to Richard Casey, 13 June 1944, LHC, Ismay 4/6/4.
53. Spears to Ismay, 3 July 1944, LHC, Ismay 4/31/9.
54. Ismay to Spears, 11 July 1944, LHC, Ismay 4/31/10.
55. Lockhart diary, 25 August 1944,Young, *Diaries*, 348.
56. Brooke diary 3 July 1944, Danchev, *War Diaries*, 565.
57. Brooke diary, 6 July 1944, Danchev,*War Diaries*, 567.
58. Roberts, *Walking with Destiny*, 830.
59. Kennedy diary, 19 July 1944, Kennedy, *Business of War*, 336.
60. Gerald Pawle, *The War and Colonel Warden, Based on the Recollections of Commander CR Thompson CMG OBE RN (ret), Personal Assistant to the Prime Minister 1940-45* (London, Corgi Books, 1965), 338.
61. Cunningham diary, 9 August 1944, Michael Simpson (ed.), *The Cunningham Papers: vol. 2:The Triumph of Allied Sea Power 1942-1946* (Farnham, Ashgate, 2006), 321.
62. Brooke diary, 8 August 1944, Danchev, *War Diaries*, 579.
63. Simpson, *Cunningham Papers, vol. 2,* 321–2.
64. Lascelles diary, 17 August 1943, Hart-Davis, *King's Counsellor,* 250.
65. Churchill to Ismay, 29 August 1944, CAC, Churchill Papers, CHAR 20/180/79.
66. Ismay, *Memoirs*, 373.
67. Colville diary, 9 September 1044, Colville, *Fringes of Power,* 139.
68. Ibid.
69. Danchev, *War Diaries*, 588.
70. Cunningham diary, 8 September 1944, BL, Cunningham Papers, Add MSS 52577.
71. Ismay, *Memoirs,* 372.
72. Emphasis in original, Ismay to Darry, 9 September 1944, Ismay Family Papers, 'HLI's Letters to LKI'.
73. Brooke diary, 12 September 1944, Danchev, *War Diaries*, 591.
74. Colville diary, 13 September 1944, *Fringes of Power*, 514.
75. Green, IWM, Oral History 13029, Reel 3.
76. Brooke diary, 14 September 1944, Danchev, *War Diaries*, 592.
77. Ismay to Darry, 15 September 1944, HLI's Letters to LKI, Ismay Family Papers; also Wingate, *Lord Ismay*, 115.
78. Brooke diary, 15 September 1944, Danchev, *War Diaries*, 593.
79. Ismay to Darry, 18 September 1944, 'HLI's Letters to LKI', Ismay Family Papers.
80. Ismay to Eden, 7 January 1964, LHC, Ismay 4/3/16.
81. Brooke diary, 14 September 1944, Danchev, *War Diaries*, 593.

82. Colville diary, 20 September 1944, Colville, *Fringes of Power*, 517.

83. Ismay, *Memoirs*, 375.

84. Holmes diary, 24 September 1944, 'Diary of Marian Walker Spicer'.

85. Ismay, *Memoirs*, 377.

86. Ibid.

87. Astley, *Inner Circle*, 164.

88. Ismay, *Memoirs*, 379.

89. Ismay to Casey, 8 December 1944, LHC, Ismay 4/6/7.

90. Halifax to Churchill, 6 November 1944, CAC, Churchill Papers, CHAR 20/174/92; Roberts, *Masters and Commanders*, 530.

91. See Ismay to Attlee, 5 August 1945, TNA, CAB 120/58.

92. Roberts, *Masters and Commanders*, 530.

93. Ismay to Casey, 11 December 1944, LHC, Ismay 4/6/7.

94. Ibid.

95. Ibid.

96. Ismay, *Memoirs*, 359. Interestingly, Ismay makes no mention in his personal correspondence or in his memoirs of what became known as the 'Baby Blitz'— the Luftwaffe bombing campaign against London and the south of England from January to May 1944.

97. Ismay to Casey, 11 December 1944, LHC, Ismay 4/6/7.

98. Alfred Chandler (ed.), *The Papers of Dwight David Eisenhower, vol. 4* (Baltimore, The Johns Hopkins Press, 1970), 2350.

99. Ismay to Eisenhower, 13 December 1944, LHC, Ismay 4/12/11.

100. Eisenhower to Ismay, 16 December 1944, LHC, Ismay 4/12/12.

101. Ismay to Smith, 30 December 1944, LHC, Ismay 4/29/15.

102. Record of Meetings 1944, TNA, CAB 127/20.

10. FROM WAR TO PEACE

1. Sir Ian Jacob, interview, Nigel Hamilton, *Monty: The Field Marshal 1944-1976* (London, Hamish Hamilton, 1986), 450.

2. Wingate, *Lord Ismay*, 120.

3. Crosswell, *Beetle*, 861.

4. Jacob to Hamilton, 28 June 1984, Hamilton, *Monty: The Field Marshal,* 450.

5. Ismay, *Memoirs* 385.

6. Crosswell, *Beetle*, 862.

7. Roberts, *Masters and Commanders*, 541.

8. Ibid.

9. Ehrman, *Grand Strategy, vol. 6*, 93.

10. Cadogan diary, 4 February 1945, Dilks, *Cadogan Diaries*, 703.

11. Ismay, *Memoirs*, 386.

12. Ibid., 387.

13. Ismay to Darry, 8 February [no year given, but from 'The Crimea'], Ismay Family

Papers, 'HLI's Letters to LKI'. Ismay also fails to mention one important military discussion at Yalta: firm Soviet agreement to help in the war against Japan.

14. Ismay to Douglas, 21 March 1945, LHC, Ismay 4/11/7.
15. Ismay to Casey, 26 February 1945, LHC, Ismay 4/6/8.
16. Lascelles diary, 23 February 1945, Hart-Davis, *King's Counsellor*, 297.
17. Ismay, *Memoirs*, 390.
18. Ibid., 387.
19. Ismay to Mountbatten, 17 February 1945, Hartley, Mountbatten Papers, MB1/C146.
20. Ismay, *Memoirs*, 389.
21. Ismay to Casey, 26 February 1945, LHC, Ismay 4/6/8.
22. Roberts, *Walking with Destiny*, 854.
23. Churchill to Eisenhower, 9 March 1945, Winston Churchill, *The Second World War, vol. 6, Triumph and Tragedy* (London, Cassell, 1951), 407.
24. Ismay, *Memoirs*, 393.
25. Vincent Orange, *Tedder. Quietly in Command* (London, Frank Cass, 2004), 299.
26. Churchill to Ismay, 11 April 1945, TNA, CAB 127/46.
27. Brooke diary, 12 April 1945, Danchev, *War Diaries*, 683; 'tight': under the influence of alcohol.
28. Ismay to Churchill, 20 April 1945, TNA, CAB 127/46.
29. Reynolds, *In Command*, 475.
30. Ismay, *Memoirs*, 394.
31. Ibid., 395.
32. Ibid., 396.
33. Ismay to Eisenhower, 5 May 1945, Alfred Chandler (ed.), *The Papers of Dwight David Eisenhower, vol. 6* (Baltimore, Johns Hopkins University Press, 1970), 73.
34. Eisenhower to Ismay, May [no further details]1945, LHC, Ismay 4/12/14.
35. Smith to Ismay, 8 May 1945, LHC, Ismay 4/29/16.
36. Joint Planning Staff Report, 22 May 1945, TNA, CAB 120/691.
37. Brooke diary, 24 May 1945, Danchev, *Diaries*, 693.
38. David Reynolds, 'Churchill as International Statesman', in Packwood, *Cambridge Companion*, 311.
39. Report dated 8 June 1945, TNA, CAB 120/691.
40. Ismay to Churchill, 8 June 1945, TNA, CAB 120/691.
41. Churchill to Ismay and Chiefs of Staff, 10 June 1945, TNA, CAB 120/691.
42. Lockhart diary, 19 January 1946, Young, *Diaries*, 517–18.
43. Emphasis in original, Ismay to Smith, 2 June 1945, LHC 4/29/18.
44. Lockhart diary, 20 June 1945, Young, *Diaries*, 452.
45. Ismay to Bickersteth, 2 July 1945, LHC, Ismay 5/2.
46. Lockhart diary, 14 July 1945, Young, *Diaries*, 467–8.
47. Ismay, *Memoirs*, 402.
48. Ibid., 401.
49. Ibid., 253.
50. Ismay to Casey, 19 July 1945, LHC, Ismay 4/6/13.

51. Ismay, *Memoirs*, 403.
52. Ismay to Darry, 31 July 1945, 'HLI's letters to LKI, Ismay Family Papers'.
53. Ismay to Eden, 31 July 1945, LHC, Ismay 4/3/6
54. Lascelles diary, 7 August 1945, Hart-Davis, *Kings Counsellor*, 349.
55. Lockhart diary, 7 August 1945, Young, *Diaries*, 485.
56. Author interview with Mary Seymour, Kintbury, 30 January 2020.
57. Ismay to Wavell, 9 August 1945, LHC, Ismay 4/9/20.
58. Ibid.
59. Lascelles to Ismay, 29 May 1946, LHC, Ismay 4/20/8. Awards of the Royal Victorian Order are in the personal gift of the sovereign.
60. Ismay, *Memoirs*, 404.
61. Ibid., 405.
62. Ismay to Ian McEwan, 13 November 1945, courtesy of Philippa McEwan.
63. Addison's recollection of his grandfather's view of Attlee, *Road to 1945*, 281
64. Ismay to Wavell, 9 August 1945, LHC, Ismay 4/9/20.
65. Amery diary, 18 March 1942, Barnes and Nicholson (eds), *Empire at Bay*, 284.
66. 'Our Defence Organisation After the War', 1 May 1944, LHC, Alanbrooke Papers, 6/3/12.
67. Michael Howard, *The Central Organisation of Defence* (London, Royal United Services Institute, 1970), 8.
68. 'Our Defence Organisation After the War', 1 May 1944, TNA, CAB 127/38
69. Jacob note, TNA, CAB 127/38.
70. Lockhart diary, 21 August 1945, Young, *Diaries*, 494,
71. Ismay to Bridges, 23 August 1945, TNA, CAB 127/38.
72. Ismay and Bridges to Attlee, 29 November 1945, TNA, CAB 127/38.
73. Command Paper: Cmd 6743 (London, HMSO, 1946).
74. See, for example, Howard, *Central Organisation,* 7; Jackson, *The Chiefs*, 268.
75. Command Paper: Cmd 6743; Franklyn Johnson, *Defence by Ministry*, 67.
76. Cmd 6743.
77. Johnson, *Defence by Committee*, 315.
78. Larry Bland (ed.), *The Papers of George Catlett Marshall, vol. 4, Aggressive and Determined Leadership, June 1, 1943-December 31, 1944* (Baltimore, The Johns Hopkins University Press), 53.
79. Walter Millis (ed.), *The Forrestal Diaries. The Inner History of the Cold War* (London, Cassell, 1952), 187.
80. Emphasis in original. Ismay to Eisenhower, 29 December 1945, LHC, Ismay 4/12/18.
81. Lockhart diary, 17 December 1945, Young, *Diaries*, 512.
82. Emphasis in original, Ismay to Attlee, undated, LHC, Ismay 4/2/4; Attlee's acknowledgement to Ismay, 10 December 1945, LHC, Ismay 4/2/5.
83. Emphasis in original, Ismay to Eisenhower, 29 December 1945, LHC, Ismay 4/12/18.
84. Lockhart diary, 10 January 1946, Young, *Diaries*, 517–18.
85. Eisenhower to Ismay, 29 January 1946, LHC, Ismay 4/12/19.

86. Attlee to Ismay, 21 May 1946, LHC, Ismay 4/2/6.
87. Emphasis in original, Alanbrooke to Ismay, 24 June 1946, LHC, Ismay 4/1/3.
88. Strachan, *Politics*, 241.
89. George Mallaby, *Each in His Office. Studies of Men in Power* (London, Leo Cooper, 1972), 79.
90. Confidential Annex to COS Minutes, 23 August 1946, TNA, CAB 121/674.
91. Goodman, *Official History*, 242.
92. Ismay to COS, 2 September 1946, TNA, CAB 127/55.
93. Eisenhower, 'Memorandum for Admiral Nimitz', 29 June 1946, Chandler, *Eisenhower Papers, vol. 8*, 1157; Ismay to COS, 30 September 1946, TNA, CAB 127/55; Eisenhower to Ismay, 28 October 1946, and Notes 1 and 2, Chandler, *Eisenhower Papers, vol. 8*, 1344.
94. Martin Gilbert, *Churchill: A Life* (London, Heinemann, 1991), 871.
95. Ismay to Eisenhower, 4 July 1946, LHC, Ismay 4/12/21; Entry for 20 June 1946, CAC, The Other Club Papers, vol. 2.
96. Ismay, *Memoirs*, 157.
97. Churchill to Ismay, 4 November 1946, LHC, Ismay 2/3/11.
98. Ismay to Churchill, 4 December 1946, LHC, Ismay 2/3/26.
99. In his capacity as Minister of Defence.

11. ISMAY'S WAR

1. In his capacity as Minister of Defence.
2. Jacob, in Wheeler-Bennett, *Action This Day*, 162.
3. Ronald Lewin, *Churchill as Warlord* (London, Batsford, 1973), 32.
4. Burgis, CAC, Burgis Papers, BRGS 1/1.
5. Churchill to Ismay, 24 June 1940, Gilbert, *Never Surrender*, 403.
6 Ehrman, *Grand Strategy*, vol. 6, 328
7. Todman, *Into Battle*, 368.
8. Churchill, *Hinge of Fate*, 78.
9. Ismay to Alanbrooke, 25 June 1946, LHC, Ismay 4/1/4.
10. Ismay, *Memoirs*, 124.
11. Pogue, Interview with Ismay, 17 December 1946, USAH&EC, Pogue Papers.
12. Ibid.
13. Ismay to Kennedy, 14 July 1944, Kennedy, *Business of War*, 336.
14. See for example: Tommy Thompson, in Pawle, *War and Colonel Warden*, 348; Colville, *Fringes of Power*, 281; Grace Hamblin, Patrick Kinna, Cecily Gemmell quoted in Stelzer, *Working with Winston*, 27, 42, 77–8, 199; Clementine Churchill quoted in Gilbert, *Finest Hour*, 587–8.
15. Richard Toye, *Churchill's Empire. The World that Made Him and the World He Made* (London, Macmillan, 2010), 197.
16. Lockhart diary, 21 March 1946, Young, *Diaries*, 535.
17. Bracken to Ismay, 23 December 1957, LHC, Ismay 5/2.
18. Ismay to Bousfield, 15 November 1962, LHC, Ismay 4/24/84.

19. For example, German intentions in Russia, November 1942, Gilbert, *Road to Victory*, 255, Note 2.
20. Ibid., 1060.
21. Ismay, *Memoirs,* 318.
22. Marion Long, Notes on Interview with Ismay, March 1957, LHC, Alanbrooke Papers, 11/7.
23. Ismay, *Memoirs*, 316–17.
24. Ibid., 318.
25. Emphasis in original. Richards, *Portal*, 183.
26. Burgis, CAC, Burgis Papers, BRGS 1/1. See also Jacob in *Churchill by His Contemporaries,* 70.
27. Connell, *Auchinleck*, 266.
28. Hollis, 'Random Reminiscences', IWM, Hollis Papers, IWM/2773, 40.
29. Jacob, in Wheeler-Bennett, *Action This Day*, 197.
30. Mallaby, *From My Level*, 98.
31. Ibid., 101.
32. Lecture to IDC, 1946, LHC, Ismay 3/4/11.
33. Emphasis in original. Green, IWM Oral History, 13029, Reel 2.
34. Astley, *Inner Circle*, 59.
35. Martin to Ismay, 1 July 1945, LHC, Ismay 5/13.
36. Charles Lysaght, *Brendan Bracken* (London, Allen Lane, 1979), 181.
37. Lockhart diary, 26 March 1946, Young, *Diaries*, 536.
38. Lockhart diary, 22 August 1944, Ibid., 343.
39. Ismay, *Memoirs*, 173.
40. Lockhart diary, 26 October 1941, Young, *Diaries*, 127.
41. Lockhart diary, 26 March 1946, Ibid., 536; see also Nicolson diary, 7 August 1942, Nicolson, *Diaries and Letters 1939-1945*, 238.
42. Jack Fishman, *My Darling Clementine* (London, WH Allen, 1963), 130.
43. Ibid., 219.
44. Bracken to Ismay, 23 December 1957, LHC, Ismay 5/2.
45. Ibid., 201.
46. Sonia Purnell, 'The Influence of Clementine Churchill', in Packwood, *Cambridge Companion*, 360.
47. Lockhart diary, 26 March 1946, Young, *Diaries*, 535.
48. Goodman, *Official History*, 91.
49. Patrick Howarth, *Intelligence Chief Extraordinary. The Life of the Ninth Duke of Portland* (London, Bodley Head, 1986), 143.
50. Rowan in Wheeler-Bennett, *Action This Day*, 249.
51. Rowan did not join Churchill's staff until 1941.
52. Ismay, Lecture to IDC, 1949, LHC, Ismay 3/4/12; Ismay, *Memoirs*, 167.
53. Sangster, *Pug*, 69.
54. Colville in Wheeler-Bennett, *Action This Day*, 63; Amery diary, 30 May 1943, Barnes, *Empire at Bay,* 890; Jacob diary, 7 August 1943, CAC, Jacob Papers, JACB 11/5/2; Ismay to Bousfield, 15 November 1962, LHC, Ismay 4/24/84.

55. Elizabeth Nel, *Mr Churchill's Secretary* (London, Hodder and Stoughton, 1958), 62.

56. Stelzer, *Working with Winston*, 90; Kinna, CAC, CHOG, PKNN Tape 2, Side 3.

57. Ismay's paper, Quetta 1922, LHC, Ismay 3/2/109.

58. Ismay to General Sir Henry Jackson, 18 February 1959, LHC, Ismay 1/14/71.

59. Forrestal diary, 22 July 1946, Millis, *Forrestal Diaries*, 187.

60. Ismay to Ben Glazebrook, 6 May 1960, LHC, Ismay 1/11/17.

61. Dwight Eisenhower, *Crusade in Europe* (London, Johns Hopkins University Press, 1948), 446.

62. LHC, Ismay 4/12; and Chandler, *Eisenhower Papers*.

63. Ed Cray, *General of the Army. George C Marshall, Soldier and Statesman* (New York, Cooper Square Press, 2000), 545.

64. Interview with Ismay, 13 November 1956, Pogue, *Ordeal and Hope*, 311.

65. John Colville, *Winston Churchill and His Inner Circle* (New York, Simon and Schuster, 1981), 244. Moran would have claimed to be very much a full member of this inner circle but as Colville commented, 'Moran was seldom, if ever, present when history was made; but he was quite often invited to dinner afterwards'. Wheeler-Bennet, *Action This Day*, 110.

66. Wheeler-Bennett, *Action This Day*, 249.

67. Ibid.; Lockhart diary, 21 February 1947, Young, *Diaries*, 586.

68. Lord Moran, *Churchill at War 1940-45* (London, Constable & Robinson, 2002), 137.

69. Morton to Thompson, 20 July 1960, RV Thompson, *Churchill and Morton: The Quest for Insight in the Correspondence of Major Sir Desmond Morton and the Author* (London, Hodder and Stoughton, 1976), 54

70. Lockhart diary, 7 February 1946, Young, *Diaries*, 520.

71. Channon diary, 23 June 1943, Heffer (ed.), *Channon, vol.2*, 1033.

72. Grigg to Butler, 12 May 1954, TNA, CAB 140/83.

73. Kennedy diary, 12 April 1941, LHC, Kennedy Papers 4/2.

74. Hankey diary, 6 May 1941, Roskill, *Hankey, vol. 3*, 505.

75. Kennedy, *Business of War*, 239. Kennedy would not have been human if he had not been a touch of jealous of Ismay. They were both major generals in 1942 but whereas Ismay was promoted to lieutenant general in October 1943 and to full general in May 1944, Kennedy, though highly competent in a most demanding job, recieved no further promotion.

76. Dewing diary, 1 May 1940, 'Diary 1939–1941', LHC, Dewing Papers.

77. Elliot Cohen, *Supreme Command. Soldiers, Statesmen and Leadership in War* (London, Simon and Schuster, 2003), 110–54.

78. Ismay, *Memoirs*, 117.

79. Ismay to Chandos, 9 September 1958, LHC, Ismay 1/14/34.

80. Ismay, *Memoirs*, 270.

81. Ismay, Draft Memoirs, LHC, Ismay 1/15/5/5.

82. Ismay, *Memoirs*, 208.

83. Colville diary, 1 May 1945, Colville, *Fringes of Power*, 595.

84. Ismay, Draft Memoirs, un-numbered page, LHC, Ismay 1/15/1.

85. Ismay to Eisenhower, 11 October 1951, LHC, Ismay 4/12/84.

86. Ismay, Draft Memoirs, un-numbered page, LHC, Ismay 1/15/1.

87. Ismay to Auchinleck, 1 February 1942, JRL, Auchinleck Papers, AUC/679.

88. Ronald Lewin, 'Ismay', in Hew Strachan (ed.), *Military Lives* (Oxford, Oxford University Press, 2002), 234.

89. Ismay, *Memoirs*, Foreword.

90. Colville, *Winston Churchill*, 161.

91. Max Hastings, *Finest Years. Churchill as Warlord 1940-45* (London, Harper Press, 2009), 143.

92. Ehrman, *Grand Strategy, vol. 6, 327.*

12. PARTITION—MAKING THE PLAN

1. Wingate, *Lord Ismay*, 137. In his memoirs Ismay gives his retirement date as November 1946. Ismay, *Memoirs*, 406.

2. Ibid., 409–10.

3. Sangster, *Pug*, 118; Andrew Lownie, *The Mountbattens* (London, Blink Publishing, 2019), 191.

4. Not in *The Mountbattens*, but verbally to this author, 15 May 2023; Shahid Hamid, *Disastrous Twilight. A Personal Record of the Partition of India* (London, Leo Cooper, 1993), 146.

5. For example, Alex Von Tunzelmann warns that 'Hamid's memoirs have been widely disputed'. *Indian Summer. The Secret History of the End of an Empire* (London, Pocket Books, 2008), 171.

6. For examples, see TNA, CAB 127/24.

7. Emphasis in original. Ismay to Mountbatten, 14 May 1946, LHC, Ismay 4/24/4.

8. Ismay to Mountbatten, 6 July 1944, Philip Ziegler, *Mountbatten: The Official Biography* (London, Collins, 1985), 215.

9. See for examples: Ismay to Mountbatten, 9 December 1942, TNA, CAB 127/24; Mountbatten to Ismay, 11 November 1943, Ibid.; Mountbatten diary, 25 July 1945. Ziegler, *Personal Diary of Admiral the Lord Louis Mountbatten, Supreme Commander South-East Asia, 1943-1946* (London, Collins, 1988), 232.

10. Marion Long, Notes on Interview with Ismay, March 1957, LHC, Alanbrooke Papers, 11/7.

11. See for examples: Ismay to Mountbatten, 22 November 1943, Ibid.; 21 March 1945, Hartley, Mountbatten Papers, MB1/C146.

12. Mountbatten to Ismay, 11 November 1946, LHC, Ismay 4/24/5.

13. 'The obvious choice', *The Observer*, 22 June 1947.

14. Lascelles to Ismay, 5 January 1947, LHC, Ismay 3/7/2.

15. Andrew Roberts, *Eminent Churchillians* (London, Phoenix, 1995), 250.

16. Ziegler, *Mountbatten*, 404.

17. Daniel Marston, *The Indian Army and the End of the Raj* (Cambridge, Cambridge University Press, 2014), 47.

18. von Tunzelman, *Indian Summer*, 109.

19. Barney White-Spunner, *Partition. The Story of Indian Independence and the Creation of Pakistan in 1947* (London, Simon & Schuster, 2017), 47.

20. Ian Talbot and Gurharpal Singh, *The Partition of India* (Cambridge, Cambridge University Press, 2009), 35.

21. Wavell to Ismay, 8 February 1944, LHC, Ismay 4/9/16.

22. Ismay to Wavell, 7 March 1944, LHC, Ismay 4/9/17.

23. Emphasis in original. Ismay to Casey, 13 June 1944, LHC, Ismay 4/6/4.

24. White-Spunner, *Partition,* 51.

25. Talbot and Singh, *Partition,* 67.

26. White-Spunner, *Partition,* 9; Churchill to Lascelles, 18 February 1947, TNA, PREM 8/558.

27. Ronald Lewin, *The Chief. Field Marshal Lord Wavell. Commander-in-Chief and Viceroy 1939-1947* (London, Hutchinson, 1980), 238.

28. Nicholas Mansergh, *The Transfer of Power 1942-7, vol. 9* (London, HMSO, 1970), 382–3.

29. Hankey to Ismay, 1 January 1947, LHC, Ismay 4/16/11.

30. Violet Attlee to Ismay, 1 January 1947, LHC, Ismay 4/2/9.

31. Ismay to Mountbatten, 25 April 1957, Hartley, Mountbatten Papers, MB1/I 229.

32. Ismay to Cherwell, 10 December 1946 and 9 January 1947, Cherwell Papers, Nuffield College, Oxford, CSAC 80.4.81/K.161.

33. COS Minutes, 30 August 1946, Nicholas Mansergh, *The Transfer of Power 1942-7, vol. 8* (London, HMSO, 1970), 348–9.

34. Ismay to Attlee, 30 August 1946, Ibid., 349-50; Defence Committee Minutes, 2 October 1946, Ibid., 645–7.

35. RJ Moore, *Escape from Empire. The Attlee Government and the Indian Problem* (Oxford, Clarendon Press, 1983), 223–4.

36. Ismay, *Memoirs,* 415.

37. Ismay, Draft Memoirs, LHC, Ismay 1/15/5/2.

38. Wingate, *Lord Ismay,* 139.

39. Ziegler, *Mountbatten,* 355–6. See also Moore, *Escape from Empire,* 236; James, *Raj,* 612.

40. Mountbatten to Attlee, 11 February 1947, Mansergh, *Transfer, vol. 9,* 673; Ziegler, *Mountbatten,* 357.

41. Ismay, *Memoirs,* 417.

42. Moore, *Escape from Empire,* 231–2.

43. Meeting of Ministers, 18 March 1947, Mansergh, *Transfer, vol. 9,* 984.

44. 'A British cartoon character… pompous, irascible, jingoistic and stereotypically British', https://en.wikipedia.org/wiki/Colonel_Blimp accessed 30 March 2023.

45. Robert Anderson, 'Blackett in India: Thinking Strategically about New Conflicts', in Peter Hore, *Patrick Blackett: Sailor Scientist and Socialist* (London, Taylor and Francis, 2002), 234.

46. Ismay, *Memoirs,* 416.

47. Ibid.

48. Ismay to Darry, 25 March 1947, LHC, Ismay 3/8/1.

49. Ismay, *Memoirs*, 417.

50. Ibid.

51. Ziegler, *Mountbatten*, 371.

52. John Christie, *Morning Drum* (London, BACSA, 1983), 100.

53. Emphasis in original, Ismay, 'India 18 March–18 July 1947', undated but written 'in the air between Malta and Karachi', therefore 20 July 1947, LHC, Ismay 3/7/65.

54. Ismay to Darry, 28 March 1947, LHC, Ismay 3/8/3.

55. Mountbatten to Attlee, 31 March 1947, Nicholas Mansergh, *The Transfer of Power 1942 7, vol 10* (London, HMSO, 1970), 91.

56. Emphasis in original. Ismay to Darry, 2 April 1947, LIIC, Ismay, 3/8/4.

57. Ismay to Darry, 6 April 1947, LHC, Ismay 3/8/5.

58. Record of Discussion, Viceroy's Staff Meeting, 11 April 1945, Mansergh, *Transfer, vol. 10*, 190.

59. Ibid.

60. Between 1939 and 1946 the British element of the Indian Civil Service had fallen from 587 to 429. Moore, *Escape from Empire*, 22.

61. Ismay, 'A Personal Account of the Last Days of British Rule in India', undated, LHC, Ismay, 3/7/56.

62. Ismay, *Memoirs*, 417.

63. Ismay, 'Personal Account', LHC, Ismay 3/7/56.

64. Ismay to Darry, 6 April 1947, LHC, Ismay 3/8/5.

65. Savory diary, 2 March 1947, NAM, Savory Papers, NAM 7603–93.

66. Emphasis in original. Ismay to Auchinleck, 20 February 1947, LHC, Ismay 4/9/10.

67. Ismay to Darry, 25 March 1947, LHC, Ismay 3/8/1.

68. Minutes of Viceroy's staff meeting 28 March 1947, Mansergh, *Transfer, vol. 10*, 35.

69. Ibid.

70. Record of interview between the Viceroy and Auchinleck, 1 April 1947, Ibid., 74.

71. Record of Discussion, Viceroy's Staff Meeting, 10 April 1947, Ibid., 178.

72. Record of Discussion, Viceroy's Staff Meeting, 12 April 1947, Ibid., 207.

73. 23 February 1933, Ismay Family Papers; 31 July 1935, LHC, Ismay 1/1/28.

74. Minutes of Governors Conference, 15–16 April 1947, Mansergh, *Transfer, vol. 10*, 250 and 274.

75. Connell, *Auchinleck*, 880–1.

76. Campbell-Johnson diary, 24 April 1947, Alan Campbell-Johnson, *Mission With Mountbatten* (London, Robert Hale, 1951), 71. John Connell warns that 'Campbell-Johnson['s]… evidence must always be treated with a measure of reserve'. Connell, *Auchinleck,* 872, Note 2.

77. Emphasis in original. Ismay to Darry, 24 April 1947, LHC, Ismay 3/8/7.

78. Ismay to Mountbatten, 25 April 1947, Mansergh, *Transfer, vol. 10*, 438.

79. Miéville to Mountbatten, 30 April 1947, Ibid., 487.

80. Ibid., 488–9.

81. Minutes of the India and Burma Committee meeting, 5 May 1947, Mansergh, *Transfer, vol. 10,* 628–9.

82. Mountbatten to Ismay, 11 May 1947, Ibid., 776.

83. Miéville to Ismay, 12 May 1947, Ibid., 780.

84. Ismay to Miéville 12 May 1947, Ibid., 798.

85. Ismay, *Memoirs,* 421.

86. Record of Viceroy's Miscellaneous Meeting, 11 May 1947, Mansergh, *Transfer, vol. 10,* 762.

87. Menon was later to assert that he had 'always been opposed to the plan' which Ismay took back to London but that 'my protests and my views in the discussions with the Viceroy's advisers went in vain'. VP Menon, *The Transfer of Power in India* (London, Longmans, Green and Co., 1957), 357. Menon later claimed he 'did not see the draft at all' before Ismay took it back to London. Menon interviewed by Hodson, September 1964, BL, Sound Archives C940/8, part 2.

88. Note by George Abell, 26 March 1947, Mansergh, *Transfer, vol. 10,* 27.

89. Minutes of the India and Burma Committee, 19 May 1947, Ibid., 896–8.

90. Ibid., 917.

91. Cabinet Conclusions, 23 May 1947, Ibid., 966.

92. CAC, The Other Club Records, vol. 12.

93. Ismay, *Memoirs*, 422.

94. Ibid.

95. Viceroy's Conference Paper 63, Nicholas Mansergh, *The Transfer of Power 1942-7, vol. 11* (London, HMSO, 1970), 53

96. Mountbatten to Patricia Mountbatten, 11 June 1947, Ziegler, *Mountbatten*, 388.

97. Ismay, *Memoirs,* 422.

98. Ibid., 425.

99. Ismay to Darry, 2 June 1947, LHC, Ismay 3/8/8.

100. Y Krishan, 'Mountbatten and the Partition of India', *History,* 68/22 (1983), 22–38.

101. Mountbatten to Patricia Mountbatten, 2 May 1947, Ziegler, *Mountbatten*, 378.

102. Ziegler, *Mountbatten*, 219.

103. HV Hodson, *The Great Divide. Britain - India - Pakistan* (London, Hutchinson, 1969), 511 (Note).

13. PARTITION—IMPLEMENTATION AND OUTCOME

1.   Emphasis in original, Ismay to Darry, 8 June 1947, LHC, Ismay 3/8/9.

2.   Mountbatten to Patricia Mountbatten, 11 June 1947, Ziegler, *Mountbatten*, 388.

3.   Campbell-Johnson diary, 24 June 1947, *Mission with Mountbatten*, 122.

4.   Marston, *Indian Army*, 263.

5.   Ismay, *Memoirs*, 425.

6.   Ismay, 'India 18 March–18 July 1947', LHC, Ismay 3/7/65.

7.   Connell, *Auchinleck*, 839.

8.   Ismay, 'India 18 March–18 July 1947', LHC, Ismay 3/7/65.

9.   Ismay to Mountbatten, 20 June 1947, Mansergh, *Transfer, vol. 11*, 534.

10. Auchinleck to Ismay, 11 June 1947, JRL, Auchinleck Papers, AUC/1229.

11. Marston, *Indian Army,* 270.

12. The only airconditioned office was the Viceroy's study. White-Spunner, *Partition*, 110.

13. Introduction, Mansergh, *Transfer, vol. 10*, xi.

14. White-Spunner, *Partition*, 101.

15. Ismay to Darry, 14–19 June 1947, LHC, Ismay 3/8/10.

16. Ibid.

17. Ismay to Darry, 24 June 1947, LHC, Ismay 3/8/11.

18. Ismay, 'Personal Account', LHC. Ismay 3/7/65.

19. Ismay, *Memoirs*, 429.

20. Ismay, 'India 18 March–18 July 1947', LHC, Ismay 3/7/65.

21. Emphasis in original, Ismay to Bright, 2 July 1947, IWM, Bright Astley Papers.

22. Campbell-Johnson diary, 7 July 1947, *Mission with Mountbatten*, 131

23. Ismay, 'Personal Account', LHC, Ismay 3/7/56.

24. Ismay, 'India 18 March–18 July 1947', LHC, Ismay 3/7/65.

25. Ibid.

26. Campbell-Johnson diary, 8 July 1947, *Mission with Mountbatten*, 132.

27. Ismay, 'India 18 March–July 1947', LHC, Ismay 3/7/65.

28. Christie diary, 18 July 1947, BL, Christie Papers, MSS Eur D 718/3b.

29. Campbell-Johnson diary, 20 July 1947, *Mission with Mountbatten*, 136. Becher's Brook: the notoriously challenging fence jumped (twice) in the annual Grand National horse race at Aintree, Liverpool.

30. Ismay, 'India 18 March–18 July 1947', LHC, Ismay 3/7/65

31. Ibid.

32. Francis Tuker, *While Memory Serves* (London, Cassell, 1950), 349.

33. Connell, *Auchinleck*, 908.

34. Robin Jeffrey, 'The Punjab Boundary Force and the Problem of Order', August 1947, *Modern Asian Studies*, 8/4 (1974), 498.

35. White-Spunner, *Partition*, 215.

36. Mountbatten to Listowel, 4 July 1947, Mansergh, *Transfer, vol. 11*, 904.

37. Lionel Carter, *Mountbatten's Report on the Last Viceroyalty: 22 March – 15 August 1947* (New Delhi, Manohar, 2003), *Conclusions and Part D*, 283 and 190–1; 'Use of British Troops after 14 August 1947', 29 July 1947, Nicholas Mansergh, *The Transfer of Power 1942-7, vol. 12* (London, HMSO, 1970), 394–5; although according to Auchinleck's aide de camp, Captain Shahid Hamid, 'British troops have not been included in the Force [PBF] despite the Auk's recommendation'. Hamid diary, 24 July 1947, Hamid, *Disastrous Twilight*, 209.

38. Ismay to Mountbatten, 29 July 1947, Mansergh, *Transfer, vol. 12*, 394–5.

39. Yasmin Khan, *The Great Partition: The Making of India and Pakistan* (London, Yale University Press, 2017) 3.

40. Christie diary, 25 July 1947. BL, Christie Papers, MSS Eur D 718/3b.

41. 'Record of [Viceroy's] Interview with Mr Jinnah and Mr Liaquat', 15 July 1947; Mansergh, *Transfer, vol. 12*, 163–4.

42. Viceroy's Report, 18 July 1947, Ibid., 225.

43. Ismay to Darry, 7 August 1947, LHC, Ismay 3/8/13.

44. Ismay to Bright, 9 August 1947, IWM, Bright Astley Papers.

45. Viceroy's Report, 16 August 1947, Mansergh, *Transfer, vol. 12*, 760.

46. Abell to Abbott, 8 August 1947, Mansergh, *Transfer, vol. 12*, 579.

47. Christie diary, 9 August 1947. BL, Christie Papers, IOR: Mss Eur D718/3.

48   For example, Royle, *The Last Days of the Raj* (London, Michael Joseph, 1989), 166n; Hodson, *The Great Divide,* 354; Ziegler, *Mountbatten*, 422; Wingate, *Lord Ismay*, 164.

49. Christopher Beaumont, 'The Truth of the Partition of the Punjab in August 1947', unpublished paper, 1989, All Souls College Library, Oxford, Beaumont Papers.

50   Roberts, *Eminent Churchillians,* 91–101.

51. Emphasis in original. Mountbatten to Ismay, 2 April 1948, LHC, Ismay 3/7/24 and Ismay to Mountbatten, 13 Apr 1948, LHC, Ismay 3/7/28.

52. Edmund Heward, *The Great and the Good. A Life of Lord Radcliffe* (Chichester, Barry Rose, 1994), 51. In a follow-up book to his biography of Mountbatten, Ziegler accepted that Mountbatten had, after all, met with Radcliffe and 'urged him to bear certain considerations in mind when reaching his conclusions'. Philip Ziegler, *Mountbatten Revisited* (Austin, Texas, University of Texas, 1995), 16. Not all historians were convinced; see, for example, Narendra Singh Sarila, *The Shadow of the Great Game: The Untold Story of India's Partition* (London, Constable, 2006), 411.

53. Beaumont, 'The Truth', 4.

54. Ismay makes no mention of the controversy in his memoirs. Wingate merely comments that 'it was not difficult to refute [the] allegation' (Wingate, *Lord Ismay,* 164). Sangster mentions the issue in passing but does not address it (Sangster, *Pug*, 129).

55. Viceroy's interview, 12 June 1947, Mansergh, *Transfer, vol. 11*, 232.

56. Monckton, 'Note of interview with Lord Ismay', 10 August 1947, Balliol College, Library, Oxford, Monckton Papers, 39/122; Ziegler, *Mountbatten*, 412–3.

57. Ismay to Darry, 14 August 1947, LHC, Ismay 3/8/14.

58. Wingate, *Lord Ismay*, 164.

59. Ismay, *Memoirs*, 431.

60. Ismay to Darry, 23 August 1947, LHC, Ismay 3/8/5.

61. Emphasis in original. Ismay to Mountbatten, 25 August 1947, Hartley, Mountbatten Papers, MB1/E83.

62. Emphasis in original. Ismay to Bright, 30 August 1947, IWM, Bright Astley Papers.

63. Ismay, *Memoirs,* 433.

64. Wingate, *Lord Ismay*, 165.

65. Ismay, *Memoirs*, 434; Sarah Ismay to Ismay, undated, LHC, Ismay 3/8/28; author interview with Sarah Allendale, West Illsley, 11 January 2019.

66. Ismay, 'The Indian Situation. A personal Note. Jul–Oct 1947', LHC, Ismay 3/7/66/3.

67. Shone to Carter, 13 September 1947, Lionel Carter, *Partition Observed. British Official Reports from South East Asia, 14 August-31 December 1947* (New Delhi, Manohar, 2011), 216. (There were, of course, no gas chambers in Belsen concentration camp.)

68. Ismay, *Memoirs*, 438.

69. Shone to Addison, 27 September 1947, Carter, *Partition Observed*, 341.

70. Ismay to Cunningham, 30 September 1947, LHC, Ismay 3/7/67/40.

71. Shone to Carter, 11 September 1947, Carter, *Partition Observed*, 183.
72. Ismay to Cunningham, 30 September 1947, LHC, Ismay 3/7/67/40.
73. Ibid.
74. Ismay, *Memoirs*, 440.
75. Ibid., 440–1.
76. Ismay to Darry, 8–12 September 1947, LHC, Ismay 3/8/18.
77. Ismay to Darry, 16 September 1947, LHC, Ismay 3/8/20A.
78. Ismay to Bright, 20 September 1947, IWM, Bright Astley Papers.
79. Ismay to Mountbatten, undated (but almost certainly on or about 16 September 1947), LHC, Ismay 3/7/67/43.
80. Ziegler, *Mountbatten*, 463.
81. Mountbatten, Governor General's Personal Report Number 2, 11 September 1947, Hartley, Mountbatten Papers, MB1/D86; Mountbatten to Auchinleck, 26 September 1947, JRL, Auchinleck Papers, AUC/1260.
82. Ismay to Auchinleck, undated, LHC, Ismay 3/7/67/37.
83. Ismay to Sir George Cunningham, 30 September, 1947, LHC, Ismay 3/7/67/40.
84. Ismay to Churchill, 30 September 1947, LHC, Ismay 2/3/35.
85. Ismay to Mountbatten, 9 October 1947, Hartley, Mountbatten Papers, MB1/D197a.
86. Ibid.
87. COS Minutes, 8 October 1947, Carter, *Partition Observed,* 476.
88. Savory diary, 7 October 1947, NAM, Savory Papers.
89. Ibid.
90. Ibid.
91. Ismay, 'Note on the Situation in India, 30 November 1947', LHC, Ismay 3/7/66/6.
92. Ismay, Untitled account, November 1947, LHC, Ismay 3/7/66/5.
93. Ismay to Darry, 2 November 1947, LHC, Ismay 3/8/20E.
94. i.e., in his most haughty mood.
95. Ismay, Untitled, November 1947, LHC, Ismay 3/7/66/5.
96. Ismay to Darry, 2 November 1947, LHC, Ismay 3/8/20E.
97. Ismay Untitled account, November 1947, LHC, Ismay 3/7/66/4.
98. Ismay to Darry, 15 November 1947, LHC, Ismay 3/8/19.
99. Ismay to Darry, 11 November, LHC, Ismay 3/8/20H.
100. Shone to Carter, 19 November 1947, Carter, *Partition Observed*, 695–6.
101. Ismay, 'Note on the Situation in India on 30th November 1947', LHC, Ismay 3/7/66/6.
102. Campbell-Johnson diary, 11 December 1947, *Mission with Mountbatten*, 250.
103. Ziegler, *Mountbatten*, 437.
104. Ismay to Darry, 17 November 1947, LHC, Ismay 3/8/22; Estimates of the number of people killed during Partition vary between Mountbatten's eventual figure of 200,000 and a figure of two million, with Talbot and Singh describing one million as 'a median figure' (Talbot and Singh, *Partition*, 62). Ismay's estimate was 'over one million' (Roberts, *Eminent Churchillians*, 131).
105. Ismay to Darry, 24 November 1947, Ismay Family Papers, 'HLI's Letters to LKI'.

106. Ismay to Darry, 25 November 1947, LHC, Ismay 3/8/25.

107. Ismay to Wingate, date not known, Wingate, 'Indian Papers', Ismay Family Papers.

108. Ismay to Mountbatten, 2 December 1947, LHC, Ismay 3/7/9.

109. Ismay, *Memoirs*, 445.

110. Prominent among the few authors to reject the idea that the transfer was too rushed was the highly pro-Mountbatten historian, HV Hodson, who asserted that 'Lord Mountbatten's insistence on the utmost speed was fully justified [and that] the price that was paid in bloodshed and misery was paid not for any British decision but for the inflaming of communal emotions that had been proceeding for months and years past'. Hodson, *The Great Divide*, 535.

111. Ismay interviewed by HV Hodson, 23 January 1965, BL, Sound Archives X940/19. Although many historians have argued that delay in Partition would have resulted in fewer casualties, recent historians who disagree include von Tunzelman, *Indian Summer*, 255, and Fennell, *Fighting the People's War*, 695.

112. Ismay interviewed by HV Hodson, 23 January 1965, BL, Sound Archives X940/19 and in Hodson, *The Great Divide*, 534.

113. Ismay, 'The Situation in India on 30 November 1947', LHC, Ismay 3/7/66/6.

114. Speech to the Indian Cavalry Association dinner, 4 June 1948, LHC, Ismay 1/7/2.

115. Carter, *Mountbatten's Report*, 284; Ismay to Erskine Crum, 17 September 1948, LHC, Ismay 3/7/40.

116. Mountbatten, Governor General's Personal Report Number 2 (Paragraph 16), 11 September 1947, Hartley, Mountbatten Papers, MB1/D86; Ismay's view remains controversial. Some historians maintain that the discipline of the army remained intact and that, in the words of Daniel Marston, 'the incidents of subunits showing a lack of discipline… [were] amazingly few'. Marston, *Indian Army*, 350.

117. Leonard Mosley, *The Last Days of the British Raj* (London, Weidenfeld and Nicholson, 1961), 247.

118. Film *Viceroy's House*, 2017.

119. Christie diary, 14 May and 28 October 1947, BL, Christie Papers, IOR: Mss Eur D718/3.

120. Lockhart diary, 20 July 1948, Young, *Diaries*, 668.

121. Ronald Lewin, 'Ismay', in Hew Strachan (ed.), *Military Lives*, 235.

122. Speech to Indian Cavalry Dinner, London, 4 June 1948, LHC, Ismay 1/7/2.

123. Olaf Caroe, Draft of Memoirs, BL, Caroe Papers, MSS Eur F203/85.

124. Ibid.

125. Speech to Indian Cavalry Dinner, London, 4 June 1948, LHC, Ismay 1/7/2.

126. Addison to Attlee, 30 October 1947, Carter, *Partition Observed*, 576.

14. INTERLUDE

1.   Churchill to Ismay, 4 January 1948, LHC, Ismay 2/3/38/1.

2.   Ismay, *Memoirs*, 447.

3.   Ismay to Darry, 15 January 1948, LHC, Ismay 3/8/28.

4.   Ismay, *Memoirs*, 448.

5.   *Daily Telegraph*, 7 February 1948.

6.   Casey to Ismay 19 Apr 1948, LHC, Ismay 4/6/16; Ismay to Casey, 27 April 1948, LHC, Ismay 4/6/17.

7.   Auchinleck to Ismay, 30 January 1948, LHC, Ismay 4/9/12.

8.   Lecture to the IDC, October 1949, LHC, Ismay 3/4/12.

9.   Recalling the acrimonious feud between Admiral of the Fleet Sir David Beatty and Air Chief Marshal (later Marshal of the Royal Air Force) Sir Hugh Trenchard who overlapped in their appointments as First Sea Lord and Chief of the Air Staff between 1919 and 1927. Bond, *British Military Policy*, 379, Note 16.

10. Ismay, *Memoirs*, 448.

11. Fred M Leventhal, '"A Tonic to the Nation": The Festival of Britain, 1951', *Albion* 27/3 (Autumn 1995), 445–53.

12. Paul Wright, 'The Festival of Britain: Some Memories', *RSA Journal*, 143/5459 (May 1995), 53; Paul Turner, *Beacon for Change: How the Festival of Britain Helped to Shape a New Age* (London, Aurum, 2011), 108.

13. Emphasis in original. Mary Banham and Bevis Hillier (eds.), A *Tonic to the Nation. The Festival of Britain 1951* (London, Thames and Hudson, 1976), 16.

14. Reynolds, *In Command*, 364.

15. Ismay to Churchill 20 May 1946, LHC, Ismay 2/3/1–3; Churchill, *Their Finest Hour*, 40–6, 57–60, 96–100, 136–42, and 158–62.

16. Ismay to Deakin, 1 September 1948, LHC, Ismay 2/3/87 & Churchill, *Their Finest Hour*, 137.

17. Ismay to Churchill, 28 November 1946, LHC, Ismay 2/3/21.

18. Reynolds, *In Command*, 148.

19. Duly corrected in effusive terms: Churchill, *The Grand Alliance*, 686–7.

20. Reynolds, *In Command*, 286.

21. Francis de Guingand, *Operation Victory* (London, Hodder and Stoughton, 1947); Cyril Falls, *The Second World War. A Short History* (London, Methuen, 1948).

22. Churchill to Ismay, 23 March 1948, LHC, Ismay 2/3/44.

23. Ismay to Churchill, 25 May 1948, LHC, Ismay 2/3/57.

24. Churchill to Eden, 20 February 1941, Gilbert, *Finest Hour*, 1013.

25. Marion Long, interview with Grigg, (no date given), LHC, Alanbrooke Papers, 11/7; corroborated by Kennedy, *Business of War*, 92.

26. Eden to Churchill, 21 February 1941, LHC, Ismay 2/3/43.

27. Interview Chester Wilmot/Jacob, 31 March 1948, LHC, Liddell Hart Papers, 15/15/1.

28. Ismay to Churchill, 22 April 1948, LHC, Ismay 2/3/43.

29. Reynolds, *In Command*, 235.

30. Ibid., 234.

31. Ismay to Churchill, 19 March 1948, LHC, Ismay 2/3/42 & Churchill, *Their Finest Hour*, 16–17.

32. Reynolds, *In Command*, 149.

33. Ismay to Churchill, 7 September 1949, LHC, Ismay 2/3/171. Churchill softened

his criticism, now referring to the decision as 'a mistake and a misfortune'. Churchill, *The Grand Alliance*, 364.

34. Winston Churchill, *The SecondWorldWar, vol. 1.The Gathering Storm* (London, Penguin Books, 1985), 558; Ismay to Churchill, 7 September 1949, LHC, Ismay 2/3/171.

35. Ismay's recollection was not completely accurate: Halifax had written, 'I do not myself think it would do any good, but I do not want to give the French any excuse for complaining'. Halifax to Ismay, 14 September 1948, LHC, Ismay 2/3/96.

36. Emphasis in original, Ismay to Churchill, 17 September 1948, LHC, Ismay 2/3/100. Halifax to Ismay, 10 and 14 September 1948, LHC, Ismay 2/3/95 and 96.

37. *Sunday Times*, 22 November 1948; Ismay to Eisenhower, 22 November 1948, LHC, Ismay 4/12/29.

38. *Daily Telegraph*, 26 November 1948.

39. Lascelles to Ismay, 26 November 1948, LHC, Ismay 4/12/33.

40. Lascelles to Ismay, 2 December 1948, LHC, Ismay 4/12/39.

41. Alfred Chandler (ed.), *The Papers of Dwight David Eisenhower, vol. 10* (Baltimore, Johns Hopkins University Press, 1970), 323 & 341.

42. Ismay's Appointments Diary, 1949. LHC, Ismay 1/9/2.

43. Ismay to Pownall, 20 June 1948, LHC, Ismay 2/3/161.

44. Ismay to Mountbatten, 18 August 1949, LHC, Ismay 4/24/13.

45. Ibid.

46. Mountbatten to Ismay, 3 May 1948, LHC, Ismay 4/24/6.

47. Ismay to Mountbatten, 12 May 1948, LHC, 4/24/7.

48. Ismay to Mountbatten, 1 October 1948, LHC, Ismay 3/7/47.

49. Mountbatten to Ismay, 6 October 1948, LHC, Ismay 3/7/49.

50. Ismay to Attlee, 21 September 1948, LHC, Ismay 3/7/41.

51. Attlee to Ismay, 21 September 1948, LHC, Ismay 3/7/43.

52. 7 April 1948, *Hansard,* House of Lords, vol. 154, no. 57, cols 1188–90.

53. 6 July 1949, *Hansard*, House of Lords, vol. 163, no. 93, cols. 929–30.

54. Ismay to Harold Gibson, 27 February 1950, LHC, Ismay 5/7.

55. Ismay to Cherwell, 26 January 1950, LHC, Ismay 2/3/199.

56. Reynolds, *In Command*, 275.

57. Ismay to Eisenhower, 8 July 1948, LHC, Ismay 4/12/28.

58. 27 Jul 1950, *Hansard*, House of Lords, vol. 168, no. 51, cols. 832–35.

59. Ibid.

60. 13 September 1950, *Hansard*, House of Lords, vol. 168, no. 51, cols. 1037–40.

61. Reynolds, *In Command*, 348–9.

62. Ismay to Morrison, 6 December 1950, Ismay Family Papers.

63. Ismay to Salisbury, 10 December 1950, Ismay Family Papers.

64. Emphasis in original. Ismay to Douglas, 25 December 1950, LHC, Ismay 4/11/16.

65. Ismay to Attlee, 3 and 21 January 1951, Ismay Family Papers.

66. Lascelles to Ismay, 19 January 1951; Ismay to Morrison, 19 January; both in Ismay Family Papers.

67. *News Chronicle*, 23 Feburary 1951.

68. 22 February 1951, *Hansard*, House of Lords, vol. 170, no. 34, cols. 521–3; *News Chronicle* and *Daily Express*, 23 February 1951; *Sunday Despatch*, 25 February 1951.

69. 'Defence of the Free World', *Daily Telegraph,* 16 August 1951.

70. Becky Conekin, *The Autobiography of a Nation. The 1951 Festival of Britain* (Manchester, Manchester University Press, 2003), 226.

71. Ibid., quoting *Daily Telegraph* [no date given].

72. Paul Rennie, *Festival of Britain 1951* (Woodbridge, Antique Collectors Club, 2007), 15.

73. Ismay, *Memoirs*, 453.

74. Colville, *Fringes of Power*, 633.

75. Andrew Wheatcroft, *Churchill's Shadow. An Astonishing Life and a Dangerous Legacy* (London, The Bodley Head, 2021), 382.

76. Ismay to Spears, 19 November 1951, CAC, Spears Papers, SPRS 1/180.

77. Ismay, *Memoirs*, 453–4.

78. Mallaby, *From My Level,* 39.

79. Author interview with Mary Seymour, Kintbury, 30 January 2020.

80. Ismay, *Memoirs,* 458.

81. Ibid., 460.

82. Lester Pearson, *Mike: The Memoirs of the Rt Hon Lester B Pearson, vol. 2, 1948-1957* (Toronto, University of Toronto Press, 2018), 78.

83. Emphasis in original. Ismay to Darry, 22 February 1952, 'HLI's Letters to LKI', Ismay Family Papers.

84. Ismay, *Memoirs*, 460.

85. 'Memorandum of Telephone Conversations by the Special Assistant to the Secretary of State, 10 March 1952', *Foreign Relations of the United States, 1952-1954*, Western European Security, vol. 5, part 1, 740. 5/3-1052. https://history.state.gov/historicaldocuments/frus1952-54v05p1 accessed 2 May 2023.

86. Ismay, *Memoirs*, 461.

87. *Daily Telegraph*, 13 March 1952.

88. *The Times*, 13 March 1952; *Manchester Guardian*, 13 March 1952.

89. Eisenhower to Ismay, 13 March 1952, LHC, Ismay 4/12/86.

90. *Daily Telegraph*, 20 March 1952.

91. Ismay to Michael Wright, HM Ambassador, Oslo, 24 March 1952, LHC, Ismay 5/23.

92. Author interview with Mary Seymour, Kintbury, 30 January 2020.

93. Michael Dutfield, *A Marriage of Inconvenience: The Persecution of Ruth and Seretse Khama* (London, Unwin Hyman, 1990), 133.

94. Ismay, 31 March 1952, *Hansard*, House of Lords, vol. 175, no. 43, cols. 1131–5 and 1160.

95. Ismay, 'Memorandum on Bamangwato Affairs', 19 November 1951, TNA, CAB 129/48/21; Cabinet Conclusions, 22 November 1951, TNA, CAB 128/23/10.

96. Liesching, Briefing notes for incoming SofS, 12 November 1951, DO 35/4136.

97. Cabinet Minutes, 22 November 1951, TNA, CAB 128/23/19.

98. Salisbury to Churchill, 18 March 1947, TNA, PREM 11/1182.

99. Thomas Tlou, Neil Parsons, Willie Henderson, *Seretse Khama. 1921-1980* (Braamfontein, Macmillan Boleswa, 1995), 121; Record of Meeting at Commonwealth Relations Office, 26 March 1952, TNA, DO 121/151.

100. Cabinet Conclusions, 22 March 1947, TNA, CAB 128/24/34.

101. 31 March 1952, *Hansard*, House of Lords, vol. 175., no. 43, cols. 1131–5.

102. Seretse Khama was to become the first president of Botswana in 1966; he was knighted by Queen Elizabeth II, re-elected three times and served until his death in 1980.

15. SECRETARY GENERAL

1. *The Times*, 5 April 1952.

2. Hart-Davis, *King's Counsellor*, 406.

3. Robert Jordan, *Political Leadership in NATO: A Study in Multinational Diplomacy* (Boulder, Westview Press, 1979); Robert Jordan, *The NATO International Staff/ Secretariat, 1952-1957* (London, Oxford University Press, 1967).

4. Hastings Ismay, *NATO, The First Five Years: 1949-1954* (Amsterdam, Bosch-Utrecht, 1954).

5. Jordan, *NATO International,* 45.

6. Ibid., 150.

7. Ibid., 117.

8. Later, Lord Coleridge.

9. *Manchester Guardian,* 19 April 1952.

10. *The Times*, 19 April 1952.

11. March 1953, Pearson, *Memoirs,* 78.

12. Geoffrey Myers, *Daily Telegraph*, 10 May 1957.

13. Jordan, *NATO International,* 47 & 53.

14. Ismay to Spears, 26 July 1952, CAC, Spears Papers, SPRS 1/180.

15. Lady Ismay, '10 Villa Säid', Ismay Family Papers.

16. *The Times*, 16 May 1952.

17. Jordan, *NATO International*, 53.

18. Sir John Hodsoll to Sir William Elliot, 10 August 1970, LHC, Elliot Papers, 4/4/21.

19. Ryan Hendrickson, 'NATO's Secretaries-General', in Gulner Aybet, Rebecca Moore and Lawrence Freedman, *NATO in Search of a Vision* (Washington, DC, Georgetown University Press, 2010), 52–3.

20. Ismay, *NATO*, 58.

21. LHC, Ismay 4/12/78 and 4/12/80; Chandler, *Eisenhower Papers, vol. 12*, 216.

22. Sulzberger diary, 2 May 1952, Cyrus Sulzberger, *A Long Row of Candles. Memories and Diaries, 1934-1954* (New York, Macmillan, 1969), 746.

23. List of Speeches, Broadcasts and Articles, LHC, Ismay 3/13.

24. *Daily Telegraph*, 11 September 1952.

25. Ismay to Churchill, 23 September 1952, LHC, Ismay 2/1/16.

26. *The Times*, 20 October 1952.

27. John Milloy, *The North Atlantic Treaty Organization 1948-1957. Community or Alliance?* (Montreal, Ithaca: McGill-Queen's University Press, 2006), 103.

28. *Manchester Guardian*, 9 October 1952.

29. *The Times*, 27 October 1952.

30. Ismay to Spears, 20 June 1952, CAC, Spears Papers, SPRS 1/180.

31. Ismay, *NATO,* 97.

32. Alfred Chandler (ed.), *The Papers of Dwight David Eisenhower, vol. 14* (Baltimore, Johns Hopkins University Press, 1970), 516.

33. Jordan, *Political Leadership*, 45.

34. Ismay to Eisenhower, 14 March 1953, LHC, Ismay 4/12/107.

35. Timothy Sayle, *Enduring Alliance: A History of NATO and the Postwar Global Order* (New York; Ithaca: Cornell University Press, 2019), 23.

36. Milloy, *North Atlantic*, 111.

37. Ibid., 113.

38. Ismay, 'NATO. The Present Position', 25 June 1953, https://archives.nato.int/nato-present-position-memo-by-secretary-general accessed 14 February 2023.

39. Sulzberger diary, 15 April 1953, Sulzberger, *Long Row*, 861.

40. Gruenther to Ismay, 6 January 1954, LHC, Ismay 4/5/10; Gruenther to Ismay, 15 July 1955, LHC, Ismay 4/15/44.

41. Grace Gruenther to Darry Ismay, October 1955, LHC, Ismay 4/15/51.

42. 'Telegraphic Summary by the US Delegation of the Foreign Ministers Second Meeting, Subject: NATO', *Foreign Relations of the United States, 1952-1954*, Western European Security, vol. 5, part 2, 396.1/12–753; https://archives.nato.int/report-by-secretary-general-on-progress-during-period-17th-april-1953-to-3rd-december-1953 accessed 2 March 2023.

43. Sulzberger diary, 8 December 1953, Sulzberger, *Long Row,* 933.

44. 'Note by Lord Ismay', 8 December 1953, LHC, Ismay 3/22/6.

45. Ismay to Lascelles. 16 September 1953, LHC, Ismay 4/20/11.

46. Ismay interview with Jordan 28 May 1959, Jordan, *Political Leadership*, 80.

47. Dulles to Ismay, 17 December 1954, LHC, Ismay 5/4.

48. Author interview with Wentworth, 4th Viscount Allendale, London, 13 May 2022; Wingate, *Lord Ismay*, 200. OTAN: Organisation du Traité de l'Atlantique Nord.

49. 'Lady Ismay's Description of Important Events', Ismay Family Papers.

50. General the Lord Ismay, 'The North Atlantic Treaty Organisation', *Journal of the Royal United Services Institute,* 100/597 (February 1955).

51. Emphasis in original, Edwina Mountbatten to Ismay, 5 August 1954, LHC, Ismay 4/24/43.

52. Emphasis in original, Edwina Mountbatten to Ismay, 15 August 1954, LHC, Ismay 4/24/47.

53. Ismay to Cunningham, 18 October 1954, LHC, Ismay 4/24/46.

54. Cunningham to Ismay, 23 October 1954, LHC, Ismay 4/24/48.

55. Edwina Mountbatten to Ismay, 22 October 1954, LHC, Ismay 4/24/47; Mountbatten to Ismay 23 October 1947, LHC, Ismay 4/24/48.

56. Colville to Ismay, 9 December 1954, LHC, Ismay 5/3.

57. As provided for in Article 2 of the North Atlantic Treaty.
58. *The Times*, 20 February 1953.
59. Sulzberger diary, 1 April 1954, Sulzberger, *Long Row*, 986.
60. Milloy, *North Atlantic,* 134-5.
61. Jebb to Macmillan, 29 September 1955, LHC, Ismay 3/12/30.
62. Sale, *Enduring Alliance*, 31.
63. Jordan, *NATO International*, 178.
64. Quoted by Jordan, Ibid., 177.
65. Ismay to Churchill, 5 March 1956, CAC, Churchill Papers, CHUR 2/190/111.
66. Jordan, *Political Leadership*, 37.
67. Ismay to Churchill, 27 March 1956, CAC, Churchill Papers, CHUR 2/190/108.
68. *Daily Telegraph*, 4 May 1956.
69. *Daily Express*, 6 June 1956, LHC, Ismay 4/15/68.
70. Ismay to Churchill, 1 September 1956, CAC, Churchill Papers, CHUR 2/190/112.
71. Montgomery, 'The Panorama of Warfare in the Nuclear Age', *Journal of the Royal United Services Institute*, 101/604 (November, 1956), 519.
72. Jordan, *Political Leadership*, 46.
73. UKDEL Paris to Foreign Office, Telegram 18231 October 1956, TNA, FO 371/121783.
74. Wingate, *Lord Ismay,* 209.
75. Sangster, *Pug*, 155 and 191.
76. Wingate, *Lord Ismay*, 209.
77. Sayle, *Enduring Alliance*, 28, quoting 'Memorandum of telephone conversation between the President in Augusta, Georgia and the Sec of State in Key West Florida, Nov 27 1956, 9.25 a.m., FRUS: 1955-1957:XVI, d618'.
78. Ismay to Churchill, 23 December 1956, CAC, Churchill Papers, CHUR 2/190/116.
79. Sayle, *Enduring Alliance,* 37.
80. *Daily Telegraph*, 10 December 1956.
81. Sayle, *Enduring Alliance*, 34.
82. HQ NATO website, "Report of the Committee of Three", 1 September 2022, https://www.nato.int/cps/en/natohq/topics_65237.htm accessed 4 February 2023.
83. Ismay to HE Caetano, 12 December 1956, LHC, Ismay 3/24/14.
84. Minutes of Council Meeting, 14 December 1956, LHC, Ismay 3/24/2.
85. *Daily Telegraph*, 15 December 1956.
86. Ismay to HE B Pipinelis, 15 January 1957, LHC, Ismay 5/7.
87. Jordan, *Political Leadership*, 48–9.
88. Ismay to Gruenther, 31 March 1957, LHC, Ismay 4/15/80.
89. Wingate, *Lord Ismay*, 210–11.
90. Lady Ismay, 'Account of the Royal Visit', LHC, Ismay 1/1/56.
91. Author interview with Patricia Smyly, Little Buckland, 20 July 2020.
92. Ismay to Mountbatten, 25 April 1957, Hartley, Mountbatten Papers, MB1/I229.

93. Clementine Churchill to Ismay, 23 April 1957, CAC, Churchill Papers, CHUR 2/190/126.

94. Ismay, *Memoirs*, 464.

95. Wing Commander Sir John Hodsoll, *The Times*, 21 December 1965.

96. The other exception was Manlio Brosio, Secretary General 1964–71.

97. Jordan, *NATO International*, 292.

98. Ryan Hendrickson, *Diplomacy and War at NATO: The Secretary General and Military Action after the Cold War* (Columbia, University of Missouri Press, 2006), 17.

99. Jamie Shea in Aybet, *NATO*, 12.

100. Jordan, *NATO International*, 79–80; *The Times*, 5 June 1957.

101. Quoted by Geoffrey Myers, *Daily Telegraph*, 10 May 1957.

102. Ismay, 'The Political Aspects of NATO', speech to NATO Defence College, 9 September 1954, LHC, Ismay 3/17/1.

103. Ismay, 'Pax Atlantica', *Unilever Magazine*, Winter 1954, www.nato.int/docu/articles/1954/a54000a.htm accessed 28 January 2023.

104. Jordan, *NATO International*, 293.

105. Peter Hennessy, *Whitehall* (London, Martin Secker & Warburg, 1989), 412.

106. 'Speech to the Political Council of the Junior Carlton Club', 5 June 1956, LHC, Ismay 3/18/9.

16. SUNSET

1. *Daily Telegraph*, 25 June 1957; Ismay to Selwyn Lloyd, 6 August 1957, LHC, Ismay 4/8/9.

2. Ismay to Mountbatten, 18 August 1957, Hartley, Mountbatten Papers, MB1/I229; Brooke to Ismay, 29 Sep 57, LHC, Ismay 4/1/24.

3. Sedbergh—at the request of Bracken who had attended the school.

4. Ismay to Coote, 8 February 1957, LHC, Ismay 4/1/11.

5. As indeed he was. According to his secretary, Jane Portal (later Jane Williams), Alanbrooke sent a proof copy of the book to Churchill. She remembered its arrival: Churchill 'sat reading it, weeping—he wept so easily—and he said, "I had no idea that they hated me so much".' Author interview with Jane Williams, London, 18 September 2019.

6. Ismay to Coote, 8 February 1957, LHC, Ismay 4/1/11.

7. *Daily Telegraph*, 18 February 1957.

8. Ismay to Churchill, 26 February 1957, LHC, Ismay 4/1/18.

9. Ismay to Brooke, 14 March 1957, LHC, Ismay 4/1/19; Ismay to Bryant, 29 March 1957, LHC, Ismay 4/1/21.

10. Ismay to Mountbatten, 22 December 1958, LHC, Ismay 1/14/85.

11. Ismay to Spears, 21 December 1957, CAC, Spears Papers, SPRS 1/180.

12. Ismay to Selwyn Lloyd, 15 November 1955, LHC, Ismay 3/4/40.

13. *Defence. Outline of Future Policy*, Cmd 124 (London, HMSO, 1957).

14. Mountbatten to Ismay, 28 March 1958, LHC, Ismay 3/4/54.

15. Ismay to Mountbatten, 30 April 1958, LHC, Ismay 3/4/60.

16. Ismay to Slessor, 10 June 1958, TNA, AIR 75/40.

17. Ismay to Coote, 8 July 1958, LHC, Ismay 3/4/65.

18. Howard, *Central Organisation of Defence*, 8 and 55–6.

19. *The Central Organisation for Defence,* Cmd 476 (London, HMSO, 1958).

20. Ismay to Brook, 3 February 1959, LHC, Ismay 1/14/9.

21. Bernard Montgomery, *The Memoirs of Field Marshal the Viscount Montgomery of Alamein* (London, Collins, 1958).

22. Ismay to Eisenhower, 9 January 1959, LHC, Ismay 4/12/130.

23. Ismay to Eisenhower, 8 June 1959, LHC, Ismay 4/12/133.

24. Ismay to Eisenhower, 30 December 1959, Alfred Chandler (ed.), *The Papers of Dwight David Eisenhower, vol. 20* (Baltimore, Johns Hopkins University Press, 1970), 1792n.

25. Eisenhower to Ismay, 12 January 1960, LHC, Ismay 4/12/137.

26. Eisenhower to Douglas Black, Doubleday and Company, 9 November 1959, *Eisenhower Papers, vol. 20*, 1730. The reprint did not, however, contain a foreword by Ismay.

27. From *The Bible*, St Paul's Epistle to the Ephesians, chapter 5, verse 20; LHC, Ismay 1/15/1.

28. Arthur Bryant, *Triumph in the West 1943-1946* (London, Collins, 1959).

29. Ismay to Elliot, 28 October 1959, LHC, Elliot Papers 4/4/3.

30. Ismay to Milton Waldman, Collins Ltd, 14 October 1959, LHC, Ismay 4/1/25.

31. Alanbrooke to Ismay, 17 October 1959, LHC, Ismay 4/1/27.

32. Colin Coote, *Editorial. The Memoirs of Colin R Coote* (London, Eyre and Spottiswoode, 1965), 273.

33. *London Evening Standard*, 4 October 1960; *Time and Tide*, 8 October 1960.

34. *National Newsagent*, 24 September 1960.

35. *The Observer*, 25 September 1960; *The Guardian*, 26 September 1960; *The New York Herald Tribune*, 9 October 1960.

36. *Sunday Times,* 25 September 1960; *The Listener,* 6 October 1960; *Sunday Express,* 25 September 1960.

37. Colville diary, 1 September 1940, Colville, *Fringes of Power,* 237.

38. Ismay, *Memoirs*, 162.

39. As late as February 1945 Churchill was expressing confidence that Stalin was a man to be trusted and that although Chamberlain had been wrong about Hitler, "I don't think I'm wrong about Stalin." Reynolds, *From World War to Cold War,* 242.

40. Fennell, *Fighting the People's War*, 52 and 678. See also Toye, *Roar of the Lion*, 58, 227–30.

41. Quoted in Sonia Purnell, *First Lady. The Life and Wars of Clementine Churchill* (London, Aurum Press, 2015), 79–80.

42. Sangster, *Pug*, 67.

43. Savory diary, 7 October 1947, NAM, Savory Papers, 7603-93; Ismay to Darry, 17 November 1947, LHC, Ismay 3/8/22; Ismay to Auchinleck, 2 February 1944, LHC, Ismay 4/9/6.

44. Sulzberger diary, 11 December 1953, Sulzberger, *Long Row,* 936

45. Ismay to Jacob, 26 December 1960, CAC, Jacob Papers, JACB 11/1/6

46. Author interview with Mary Seymour, Kintbury, 30 January 2020.

47. Ismay to Redman, 14 February 1961, LHC, Ismay 4/27/9.

48. Diary of Victor Cazalet (liaison officer with General Sikorski), 22 October 1940, in Robert Rhodes James, *Victor Cazalet: A Portrait* (London, Hamilton, 1976), 242.

49. Polish Senior Officers Appeal letter (undated), LHC, Ismay 3/10/23.

50. Ismay, *Memoirs,* 306.

51. Bomber Command aircrew wartime losses were some 57,200 men killed (a 46% death rate), 8,400 wounded and 9,800 prisoners of war.

52. Ismay to Spears, 24 November 1965, CAC, Spears Papers, SPRS 1/180. It is perhaps surprising that Ismay appeared to underestimate the sensitivity surrounding the ethics of the bombing campaign as a factor in Churchill's reluctance to make the award. Wheatcroft, *Churchill's Shadow*, 428.

53. Author interview with Patricia Smyly, Little Buckland, 20 July 2020; author interview with John Evetts, Saintbury, 9 August 2022.

54. Ismay to Spears, 1 January 1962, CAC, Spears Papers, SPRS 1/180.

55. Michael Brecher, in *Pacific Affairs* 35/3 (Autumn, 1962), 295–7.

56. Brecher, *Pacific Affairs*, 97–8.

57. When, after Ismay's death, Darry informed Mountbatten that Wingate was writing a biography of Ismay but was keeping in touch with Hodson about Partition, Mountbatten replied, 'As long as he really is in close touch with Harry Hodson I am not in the least worried about his chapter on India because Hodson will make sure he gets it right but I was very glad when he said he would send me the chapter to look at before it went to the printers'. Mountbatten to Darry, 11 October 1968, Ismay Family Papers.

58. Ismay to Fleming, 31 October 1962, LHC, Ismay 4/5/27.

59. Ismay to Elliot, 28 December 1962, LHC, Elliot Papers 4/4/12.

60. What Mountbatten did not mention was that the three Service Chiefs were bitterly opposed to his proposals and had already jointly submitted their own counter-proposals. Service Chiefs to Thorneycroft, 21 December 1963, LHC, Ismay 3/4/120.

61. Telephone call and letter, Mountbatten to Ismay, 1 January 1963, LHC, Ismay 3/4/68.

62. Ismay to Macmillan, 28 February 1963, LHC, Ismay 3/4/26.

63. Ismay to Jacob, 16 January 1963, LHC, Ismay 3/4/76.

64. Ismay to Jacob, 4 February 1963, LHC, Ismay 3/4/84.

65. Jacob to Ismay, 18 January 1963, LHC, Ismay 3/4/78.

66. Draft of letter (unsent) from Pike to Secretary of State, 15 December 1962, TNA, AIR 8/2356.

67. 'The Higher Direction of Defence', TNA, DEFE 7/1898; Johnson, *Defence by Ministry,* 116.

68. Ibid.

69. Howard, *Central Organisation of Defence*, 16; 'The Higher Direction of Defence',

Cmd 2097 (London, HMSO, 1963). A notable exception was the 'general list' of senior officers.

70. John Sweetman, 'A Process of Evolution: Command and Control in Peacetime', in Sweetman, *Sword and Mace*, 33.

71. Ismay to O'Connor, 27 August 1962, LHC, Ismay 4/5/8.

72. For details of Ismay's correspondence about the project, see LHC, Ismay 4/5. It was not for a further fifty-eight years that a biography of Carton de Wiart was to be written: Alan Ogden's *The Life and Times of Lieutenant General Sir Adrian Carton de Wiart: Soldier and Diplomat* (London, Bloomsbury, 2022).

73. Author interview with James Evetts, Wormington, 21 June 2023.

74. Clementine Churchill to Ismay, 14 November 1963, LHC, Ismay 2/2/31.

75. Eisenhower to Ismay, 7 January 1962, LHC, Ismay 4/12/139.

76. Eisenhower to Ismay, 30 August 1963, LHC, Ismay 4/2/140.

77. Eisenhower to Ismay, 18 September 1963, LHC, Ismay 4/12/142.

78. Ismay to Glazebrook, 17 March 1964, LHC, Ismay 4/5/123.

79. Ismay to Eisenhower, 18 June 1964, Eisenhower Library, Abilene, Post-Presidential Papers, 1961–69, Box 40.

80. Ibid.

81. Emphasis in original. Ismay to Lascelles, 4 February 1965, CAC, Lascelles Papers, LASC 8/7/9.

82. Clementine Churchill to Ismay, 29 September 1949, LHC, Ismay 2/2/9.

83. Ismay to Clementine Churchill, 3 October 1949, LHC, Ismay 2/2/10.

84. Author interview with James Evetts, Wormington, 21 June 2023.

85. Author interview with John Evetts, Saintbury, 9 August 2022.

17. EPILOGUE

1. Quoted in Toye, *Churchill's Empire*, 188.

2. Ismay, *Memoirs*, 16; Ismay to Wavell, 7 March 1944, LHC, Ismay 4/9/17; Ismay's 'scrapbook' [commonplace book], LHC, Ismay 3/2/110.

3. Hollis to Mountbatten, 14 October 1948, TNA, CAB 127/25.

4. Carton de Wiart, *Happy Odyssey. The Memoirs of Lieutenant General Sir Adrian Carton de Wiart* (London, Cape, 1950), 49.

5. Campbell-Johnson diary, 7 July 1947, *Mission with Mountbatten*, 131.

6. *The Times,* 19 December 1965.

7. Astley, *Inner Circle*, 70.

8. John Colville, *Man of Valour: The Life of Field Marshal the Viscount Gort, VC, GCB, DSO, MVO, MC* (London, Collins, 1972), 138.

9. For example, between 10 May 1940 and 28 May 1945 the War Cabinet met 919 times (Roberts, *Walking With Destiny*, 608) and the Chiefs of Staff 2,425 times (Roberts, *Masters and Commanders*, 107).

10. Astley, *Inner Circle*, 70.

11. Ismay to McEwan, 15 August 1945, courtesy of Philippa McEwan.

12. Wallace to Ismay, 25 August 1946, LHC, Ismay 5/23/6.

13. Hill to Ismay, 2 January 1947, LHC, Ismay 5/16.

14. Nel, *Churchill's Secretary*, 66.

15. Astley, *Inner Circle*, 70.

16. Green, IWM Oral History, 13029, Reel 1.

17. Ibid.

18. Astley, *Inner Circle*, 70.

19. Jacob, quoted in Marion Long, Notes on 'Lt General Sir Hastings Ismay', LHC, Alanbrooke Papers, 11/32.

20. 'Summary of Lord Ismay's Letters to Lady Ismay', probably by Wingate, Ismay Family Papers (copy in author's possession).

21. Astley, *Inner Circle*, 99.

22. Ismay, 19 December 1946, LHC, Ismay 1/5/10.

23. Author interview with Mary Seymour, Kintbury, 30 January 2020.

24. Astley, *Inner Circle*, 223.

25. Ismay to Wavell, 7 March 1944, LHC, Ismay 4/9/17.

26. Astley, *Inner Circle*, 100.

27. Ibid., 70.

28. Green, IWM, Oral History 13029, Reel 3.

29. Astley, *Inner Circle*, 123.

30. Jacob, quoted in Marion Long, 'Notes on Lt General Sir Hastings Ismay', LHC, Alanbrooke Papers, 11/32.

31. Eisenhower, *Crusade in Europe*, 446.

32. Moore, *Margaret Thatcher*, 680; as quoted in the introduction to this book.

33. Ismay, Lecture to the IDC, November 1956, LHC, Ismay 3/4/15.

APPENDIX A

1. LHC, Ismay 1/1/22.

APPENDIX B

1. For example: Brian Loring Villa, *Unauthorised Action. Mountbatten and the Dieppe Raid* (Ontario, Oxford University Press, 1994); Brian Loring Villa, 'Mountbatten, the British Chiefs of Staff, and Approval for the Dieppe Raid', *The Journal of Military History*, 54/2 (April, 1990); Brian Loring Villa and Peter Henshaw, 'Notes and Comments: The Dieppe Raid Debate', *The Canadian Historical Review*, 79/2 (June, 1998); Peter Henshaw, 'The British Chiefs of Staff Committee and the Preparation of the Dieppe Raid, March–August 1942: Did Mountbatten Really Evade the Committee's Authority?', *War in History*, 1/2 (July, 1994); Reynolds, *In Command*, 503..

2. Churchill to Ismay, 5 June 1940, Gilbert, *Never Surrender*, 251.

3. General Officer Commanding South-Eastern Command.

4. Nigel Hamilton, *Monty. The Making of a General. 1887-1942.* 555.

5. Villa, *Unauthorised Action*, 47.

6.   Chiefs of Staff minutes, 6 July 1942, TNA, CAB 79/56/64, also Peter Henshaw, 'The British Chiefs of Staff', 203.

7.   Henshaw, 'The British Chiefs of Staff', 199.

8.   Ibid., 207.

9.   Villa, *Unauthorised Action,* 123. A copy of the plan is at TNA, AIR 16/746.

10. Villa, Ibid., 47; Indeed, 'It was not until 1 August that the brigade commanders learnt that the Dieppe raid was on again'. Patrick Bishop, *Operation Jubilee. Dieppe, 1942: The Folly and the Sacrifice* (London, Viking, 2021), 201.

11. COS Minutes, 23 December 1942, TNA, CAB 79/24/55.

12. Villa and Henshaw, 'Notes and Comments', *Canadian Historical Review*, 309.

13. Villa, 'Mountbatten', 217.

14. The 1ˢᵗ Battle of El Alamein.

15. *The Times*, 27 July 1942.

16. Roberts, *Walking With Destiny*, 747.

17. Max Hastings, *Operation Pedestal. The Fleet that Battled to Malta 1942* (London William Collins, 2021), xvii.

18. Ibid., 28. For the scholarly debate on the strategic importance of Malta see Ibid., 22–3.

19. Ismay to Churchill, 14 August 1950, LHC, Ismay 2/3/258.

20. Churchill to Ismay, 21 December 1942, TNA, PREM 3/256.

21. Emphasis in original, Ismay to Mountbatten, 22 December 1942, LHC, Ismay 2/3/251.

22. Ismay to Churchill, 29 December 1942, TNA, PREM 3/256

23. Villa, *Mountbatten,* 206 & 237.

24. David O'Keefe, *One Day in August: Ian Fleming, Enigma and the Deadly Raid on Dieppe* (London, Icon Books, 2020), 336.

25. Churchill to Pownall, 20 March 1950, LHC, Ismay 2/3/247; Villa, *Unauthorised Action*, 22.

26. Robin Neillands, *The Dieppe Raid. The Story of the Disastrous 1942 Expedition* (London, Aurum Press, 2005), 111.

27. Ismay to Churchill, 22 March 1950, LHC, Ismay 2/3/248; Villa, *Unauthorised Action*, 28.

28. Ismay to Allen, 21 July 1950, LHC, Ismay 2/3/251; Villa, *Unauthorised Action*, 29.

29. Churchill to Ismay, 2 August 1950, LHC, Ismay 2/3/252; Villa, *Unauthorised Action*, 29–30, quoting Ismay 2/2/252.

30. Ismay to Churchill, 14 August 1950, LHC, Ismay 2/3/258; Reynolds, *In Command*, 345.

31. Telegram contained in TNA, CAB 120/67.

32. Ismay to Churchill, 14 August 1942, LHC, Ismay 2/3/252; Churchill to Ismay, 15 August 1942, (Reflex 99) [received at Air Ministry 160306A] & Ismay to Churchill, 16 August 1942 (Tulip 145), TNA, CAB 120/66 and 120/69; Villa, *Mountbatten*, 208.

33. TNA, CAB 120/66 and 120/69.

34. Churchill to Ismay, 15 August 1942, Reflex 99, TNA, CAB 120/66.

35.   Gilbert, *Road to Victory*, 198.

36.   Churchill to Ismay, September 1950 (no exact date given), CAC, CHUR 4/280A-B/157, not mentioned by Villa, Henshaw or Reynolds.

37.   Ismay to Churchill, 4 September 1950, CAC, CHUR 4/280A-B/158.

38.   Reynolds, *In Command*, 347.

39.   Churchill, *Hinge of Fate*, 414.

40.   Philip Ziegler, *Mountbatten Revisited* (Austin, Texas, Harry Ransom Humanities Research Center, The University of Texas, 1995), 10–11.

41.   Reynolds, *In Command*, 503.

42.   Ismay to Auchinleck, 23 September 1942, JRL, Auchinleck Papers, AUC/1007 A copy of this letter is notable by its absence among Ismay's papers.

APPENDIX C

1.   Quoted in *The Times*, 5 June 1957. See also Jordan, *NATO International*, 79–80.

APPENDIX D

1.   Eisenhower to Ismay, 14 January 1959, LHC, Ismay 4/12/131.

BIBLIOGRAPHY

Unpublished Primary Sources

1. Official Documents

The National Archives of the United Kingdom, Kew

ADM 223: Naval Intelligence
AIR 2: Air Ministry Files
AIR 8: Chief of the Air Staff Personal Files
AIR 75: Papers of Sir John Slessor
CAB 2: Committee of Imperial Defence Minutes
CAB 4&5: Committee of Imperial Defence Memoranda
CAB 21: Cabinet Office Files (incl Appeasement 1936–38)
CAB 23: War Cabinet Minutes
CAB 53: Chiefs of Staff Minutes and Memoranda
CAB 55: Joint Planning Committee Minutes and Memoranda
CAB 65: War Cabinet Minutes and Confidential Annexes
CAB 66: War Cabinet Memoranda
CAB 79: Chiefs of Staff Committee Minutes
CAB 80: Chiefs of Staff Committee Memoranda
CAB 120: Telegrams Whitehall to/from Overseas Commanders
CAB 121: Special Secret Information Centre Files
CAB 127: Cabinet Office Private Papers (including Ismay's)
CAB 128: Post-War Cabinet Minutes
CAB 129: Post-War Cabinet Memoranda
CAB 140: War Cabinet and Cabinet Historical Section
CAB 154: Deception—London Controlling Section Papers
DEFE 7: Higher Organisation of Defence
DO 35: Seretse Khama
FO 371: UK Delegation to NATO Files
PREM 1&3: Prime Minister's Wartime Correspondence
WO 106: War Office Operations and Intelligence
WO 169: War Diaries, Middle East (including deception planning)
WO 203: South East Asia Command Papers

BIBLIOGRAPHY

The National Archives of the United States

Department of State, *Foreign Relations of the United States, 1952-1954*, Western European Security, vol. 5, part 1, https://history.state.gov/historicaldocuments/frus1952-54v05p1

War Department G-2/2657-234, 50, Records of the War Dept Gen and Special Staffs (Record Group 165)

2. Other Documents and Sound Recordings

All Souls College Library, University of Oxford

Papers of Christopher Beaumont

Balliol College Library, University of Oxford

Papers of Lord Monckton

Bodleian Library, University of Oxford

Papers of Colonel Charles William Walker

British Library, London

Papers of:
Olaf Caroe
John Christie
Admiral of the Fleet Lord Cunningham
Sound recordings:
Ismay interviewed by Henry Hodson, (Sound Archive C940/16)
VP Menon interviewed by Henry Hodson, (Sound Archive C940/8)
Ronald Wingate, *Thinking Soldier: Lord Ismay*, BBC Radio 4, 30 June 1970 (Sound Archive P526)
Other:
Review Report of the 21st Cavalry 1908-09, (IOR/L/MIL//7/17017)
Review Report of the 21st Cavalry 1913, (IOR/L/MIL/7/17022)

Cadbury Research Library, University of Birmingham

Papers of the Earl of Avon

Charterhouse School Archives

Records for Verites House, 1900–04

Churchill Archives Centre, Cambridge

Papers of:
Lawrence Burgis

BIBLIOGRAPHY

Sir Winston Churchill (CHAR & CHUR)
Randolph Churchill
Sir John Colville
Lord Hankey
Lieutenant General Sir Ian Jacob
Sir Alan Lascelles
Sir Edward Spears
The Other Club
Sound Recordings:
Patrick Kinna

Eisenhower Library, Abilene
Post-Presidential Papers of President Eisenhower

Hartley Library, University of Southampton
Papers of Admiral of the Fleet the Earl Mountbatten

Houghton Library, University of Harvard
Papers of Robert E Sherwood

Imperial War Museum, London
Papers of:
Joan Bright Astley
Brigadier Dudley Clarke
Lieutenant General Sir Leslie Hollis
Sound Recordings:
Betty Green, Oral History 13029
Other:
Nigel de Lee, 'History of the Cabinet War Rooms', LBY 86/2038

John Rylands Library, University of Manchester
Papers of Field Marshal Sir Claude Auchinleck

Liddell Hart Centre for Military Archives, King's College London
Papers of:
Field Marshal Lord Alanbrooke
Air Chief Marshal Sir Robert Brooke-Popham
Major General Richard Dewing
Air Chief Marshal Sir William Elliot
General Lord Ismay
Major General Sir John Kennedy
Captain Sir Basil Liddell Hart

BIBLIOGRAPHY

General Sir Richard O'Connor
Chester Wilmot

National Army Museum, London
Papers of Lieutenant General Sir Reginald Savory

NATO Archives
NATO Council Reports
Photographs of Lord Ismay
Speeches by Lord Ismay
Secretary General's Reports

Nuffield College Library, University of Oxford
Papers of Lord Cherwell

Royal Military Academy Sandhurst Archives
Records for 1904–05

US Army Heritage and Education Center, Carlisle, Pennsylvania
Papers of Forrest Pogue

Privately Held
Holmes, Marian, 'Diary of Marian (née Holmes) Walker Spicer' by Thomas Walker
Ismay Family Papers by Patricia Smyly

3. Dissertations and Theses
Bergstrom, George, 'Lord Willingdon in India 1932–1936. A Study of an Imperial Administrator', DPhil Thesis, University of Oxford, 1978
Harris, JP, 'The War Office and Rearmament 1935–39', PhD Thesis, King's College London, 1983
Welch, Howard, 'The Origins and Development of the Chiefs of Staff Sub-Committee of the Committee of Imperial Defence 1923–1939', PhD Thesis, University of London, 1973

4. Author Interviews
James Evetts, Wormington, 21 June 2023
John Evetts, Saintbury, 9 August 2022
Mary Seymour, Kintbury, 30 January 2020
Patricia Smyly, Little Buckland, 20 July 2020
Lord Wentworth, 4th Viscount Allendale, London, 13 May 2022
Sarah, Viscountess Allendale, West Illsley, 11 January 2019
Jane Williams, London, 18 September 2019

BIBLIOGRAPHY

Published Primary Sources

1. Government Publications

The London Gazette

Despatch of the Governor and CinC Somaliland Protectorate, *London Gazette*, No. 32107, 29 October 1920

Despatch of Group Captain R Gordon, Commander Z Force RAF, *London Gazette*, No. 32116, 8 November 1920

British Parliamentary Papers

Report of the Committee of Imperial Defence, Cmd 2029 (1923)

The Central Organisation of Defence, Cmd 6743 (1946)

Defence: Outline of Future Policy, Cmd 124 (1957)

The Central Organisation for Defence, Cmd 476 (1958)

2. Parliamentary Debates

Singapore, 25 March 1942, *Hansard,* House of Lords, vol. 122, cols. 441–7 and 463–7

Indian Service Pensions, 7 April 1948, *Hansard,* House of Lords, vol. 154, no. 57, cols 1188–90

Indian Service Pensions, 6 July 1949, *Hansard*, House of Lords, vol. 163, no. 93, cols. 929–30

Foreign Affairs and Defence, 27 Jul 1950, *Hansard*, House of Lords, vol. 168, no. 51, cols. 832–5

Defence, 13 September 1950, *Hansard*, House of Lords, vol. 168, no. 51, cols. 1037–40

The Washington Talks, 14 December 1950, *Hansard*, House of Lords vol. 168, no. 20, cols. 1033–5

National Defence, 22 February 1951, *Hansard*, House of Lords, vol. 170, no. 34, cols. 521–3

Chieftainship of the Bamangwato Tribe, 31 March 1952, *Hansard*, House of Lords, vol. 175., no. 43, cols. 1131–5 and 1160

3. Diaries and Memoirs

Barnes, John and Nicholson, David (eds.), *Empire at Bay. The Leo Amery Diaries, vol. 2, 1929-1945* (London, Hutchinson, 1988)

Bland, Larry (ed.), *The Papers of George Catlett Marshall, vol. 4, Aggressive and Determined Leadership, June 1, 1943-December 31, 1944* (Baltimore, The Johns Hopkins University Press, 1981)

Bond, Brian, *Chief of Staff. The Diaries of Lieutenant General Sir Henry Pownall, vol. 2* (London, Leo Cooper, 1974)

Bryant, Arthur, *The Turn of the Tide, 1939-1943, A Study Based on the Diaries and Autobiographical Notes of Field Marshal The Viscount Alanbrooke* (London, Collins, 1957)

————, Arthur, *Triumph in the West, 1943-1946* (London, Collins, 1959)

Campbell-Johnson, Alan, *Mission With Mountbatten* (London, Robert Hale, 1951)

Carton de Wiart, Adrian, *Happy Odyssey. The Memoirs of Lieutenant General Sir Adrian Carton de Wiart* (London, Cape, 1950)

Chandler, Alfred (ed.), *The Papers of Dwight David* Eisenhower, *vol. 2* (Baltimore, Johns Hopkins University Press, 1970)

————, Alfred (ed.), *The Papers of Dwight David Eisenhower, vol. 4* (Baltimore, Johns Hopkins University Press, 1970)

————, Alfred (ed.), *The Papers of Dwight David Eisenhower, vol. 6* (Baltimore, Johns Hopkins University Press, 1970)

————, Alfred (ed.), *The Papers of Dwight David Eisenhower, vol. 14* (Baltimore, Johns Hopkins University Press, 1970)

————, Alfred (ed.), *The Papers of Dwight David Eisenhower, vol. 20* (Baltimore, Johns Hopkins University Press, 1970)

Christie, John, *Morning Drum* (London, BACSA, 1983)

Churchill, Winston, *The Second World War, vol. 1. The Gathering Storm* (London, Penguin Books, 1985)

————, Winston, *The Second World War, vol. 2, Their Finest Hour* (London, Penguin Books, 2005)

————, Winston, *The Second World War, vol. 3, The Grand Alliance* (London, Cassell, 1950)

————, Winston, *The Second World War, vol. 4, The Hinge of Fate* (London, Cassell, 1951)

————, Winston, *The Second World War, vol. 5, Closing the Ring* (London, Cassell, 1951)

————, Winston, *The Second World War, vol. 6, Triumph and Tragedy* (London, Cassell, 1951)

Clifton James, Meyrick, *I Was Monty's Double* (London, Rider, 1954)

Colville, John, *The Fringes of Power: Downing Street Diaries 1939-1955* (London, Hodder and Stoughton, 1985)

Danchev, Alex, *Establishing the Anglo-American Alliance. The Second World War Diaries of Brigadier Vivian Dykes* (London, Brassey's, 1990)

Danchev, Alex and Todman, Daniel (eds.), *War Diaries, 1939-1945. Field Marshal Lord Alanbrooke* (London, Weidenfeld & Nicholson, 2002)

Dilks, David (ed.), *The Diaries of Sir Alexander Cadogan, 1938-1945* (London, Cassell, 1971)

Eisenhower, Dwight, *Crusade in Europe* (London, Johns Hopkins University Press, 1948)

Hart Davis, Duff (ed.), *King's Counsellor. Abdication and War: The Diaries of Sir Alan Lascelles* (London, Weidenfeld & Nicholson, 2006)

Hart-Davis, Rupert, *Halfway to Heaven. Concluding Memoirs of a Literary Life* (Stroud, Sutton, 1998)

Harvey, John (ed.), *The Diplomatic Diaries of Oliver Harvey, 1937-1940* (London, Collins, 1970)

————, John (ed.), *The War Diaries of Oliver Harvey, 1941-1945* (London, Collins, 1978)

Heffer, Simon (ed.), *Henry 'Chips' Channon. The Diaries, vol. 2, 1938-1943* (London, Hutchinson, 2021)

Hollis, Leslie, *One Marine's Tale* (London, Deutsch, 1956)

BIBLIOGRAPHY

Ismay, Hastings, *The Memoirs of General the Lord Ismay KG, PC, GCB, CH, DSO* (London, Heinemann, 1960),

Kennedy, John, *The Business of War; The War Narrative of Major-General Sir John Kennedy* (London, Hutchinson, 1957)

Leahy, William, *I Was There. The Personal Story of the Chief of Staff to Presidents Roosevelt and Truman, Based on his Notes and Diaries made at the Time* (London, V Gollancz, 1950)

Leasor, James, *War at the Top; based on the experiences of General Sir Leslie Hollis* (London, Michael Joseph, 1959)

Leutze, James, *The London Observer: The Journal of General Raymond E Lee, 1940-1941* (Boston, Little Brown, 1971)

Liddell Hart, Basil, *The Memoirs of Captain Liddell Hart, vol. 1* (London, Cassell, 1965)

Macmillan, Harold, *War Diaries, The Mediterranean 1943-1945* (London, Macmillan, 1984)

Mallaby, George, *From My Level: Unwritten Minutes* (London, Hutchinson, 1965)

Millis, Walter (ed.), *The Forrestal Diaries. The Inner History of the Cold War* (London, Cassell, 1952)

Montgomery, Bernard, *The Memoirs of Field Marshal the Viscount Montgomery of Alamein* (London, Collins, 1958)

Nel, Elizabeth, *Mr Churchill's Secretary* (London, Hodder and Stoughton, 1958)

Nicolson, Nigel (ed.), *Harold Nicolson. Diaries and Letters. 1930-1939* (London, Collins, 1966)

———, Nigel (ed.), *Harold Nicolson. Diaries and Letters. 1939-1945* (London, Collins, 1966)

Pawle, Gerald, *The War and Colonel Warden, Based on the Recollections of Commander CR Thompson CMG OBE RN (ret), Personal Assistant to the Prime Minister 1940-45* (London, Corgi Books, 1965)

Pearson, Lester, *Mike: The Memoirs of the Rt Hon Lester B Pearson, vol. 2, 1948-*1957 (Toronto, University of Toronto Press, 2018)

Peck, John, *Dublin From Downing Street* (Dublin, Gill and Macmillan, 1978)

Simpson, Michael (ed.), *The Cunningham Papers: vol. 2: The Triumph of Allied Sea Power 1942-1946* (Farnham, Ashgate, 2006)

Soames, Mary, *A Daughter's Tale: The Memoir of Winston Churchill's Youngest Child* (London, Doubleday, 2011)

Sulzberger, Cyrus, *A Long Row of Candles. Memories and Diaries, 1934-1954* (New York, Macmillan, 1969)

Tuker, Francis, *While Memory Serves* (London, Cassell, 1950)

Wedemeyer, Albert, *Wedemeyer Reports!* (New York, Holt, 1958)

Young, Kenneth (ed.), *The Diaries of Sir Robert Bruce Lockhart*, vol. 2, 1939-1965 (London, Macmillan, 1973)

Ziegler, Philip, *Personal Diary of Admiral the Lord Louis Mountbatten, Supreme Commander South-East Asia, 1943-1946* (London, Collins, 1988)

4. Newspapers and Magazines

Daily Express
Daily Telegraph
London Evening Standard
Manchester Guardian
New York Herald Tribune
News Chronicle
Sunday Despatch
Sunday Telegraph
Sunday Times
The Independent
The Listener
The Observer
The Times
Time and Tide

Secondary Sources

1. Articles and Chapters

Anderson, Robert, 'Blackett in India: Thinking Strategically about New Conflicts', in Peter Hore (ed.), *Patrick Blackett: Sailor, Scientist and Socialist* (London, Taylor and Francis, 2002), 217–66

Colville, John, 'John Colville', in John Wheeler-Bennett (ed.), *Action This Day. Working With Churchill* (London, Macmillan, 1968), 47–139

———, John, 'He Had No Use for Second Best', *Finest Hour. Journal of Winston Churchill and His Times*, 41 (Autumn 1983)

Danchev, Alex, 'The Central Direction of the War 1940–41', in John Sweetman (ed.), *Sword and Mace. Twentieth Century Civil-Military Relations in Britain* (London, Brassey's, 1986), 57–79

———, Alex, ' "Dilly-Dally", or Having the Last Word: Field Marshal Sir John Dill and Prime Minister Winston Churchill', *Journal of Contemporary History*, 22/1 (January 1987), 21–44

———, Alex, 'Being Friends. The Combined Chiefs of Staff and the Making of Allied Strategy in the Second World War', in Lawrence Freedman, Paul Hayes and Robert O'Neill (eds.), *War, Strategy and International Politics: Essays in Honour of Sir Michael Howard* (Oxford, Clarendon Press, 1992), 195–211

Dockter, Warren, 'Learning Lessons. Lieutenant Churchill and Miliary Intelligence', in Allen Packwood (ed.), The *Cambridge Companion to Winston Churchill* (Cambridge, Cambridge University Press, 2023), 49–73

Farquharson, Iain, '"The Staff College candidates are not right yet". The Importance of Nomination to British Army Staff College Entry, 1919–1939', *British Journal for Military History*, 8/3 (November 2022), 108–27

BIBLIOGRAPHY

Frost, Mark, 'The British and Indian Staff Colleges in the Interwar Years', in Douglas Delaney, Robert Engen and Meghan Fitzpatrick (eds.), *Military Education and the British Empire 1815-1949* (Vancouver, The University of British Columbia Press, 2018), 152–74

Hamblin, Grace in Cita Stelzer, *Working with Winston. The Unsung Women behind Britain's Greatest Statesman* (London, Head of Zeus, 2019), 15–47

Hendrickson, Ryan, 'NATO's Secretaries-General: Organizational Leadership in Shaping Alliance Strategy', in Gulner Aybet, Rebecca Moore and Lawrence Freedman, *NATO in Search of a Vision* (Washington, DC, Georgetown University Press, 2010), 51–75

Henshaw, Peter, 'The British Chiefs of Staff Committee and the Preparation of the Dieppe Raid, March–August 1942: Did Mountbatten Really Evade the Committee's Authority?', *War in History*, 1/2 (July 1994), 197–214

Ismay, Hastings, 'The Machinery of the Committee of Imperial Defence', *Journal of the Royal United Services Institute*, 84/534 (May, 1939) 241–57

———, Hastings, 'Pax Atlantica', *Unilever Magazine*, Winter 1954, www.nato.int/docu/articles/1954/a54000a.htm

———, Hastings, 'The North Atlantic Treaty Organisation', *Journal of the Royal United Services Institute,* 100/597 (February 1955), 1–10

Jacob, Ian, 'Churchill as War Leader', in [no author cited] *Churchill by His Contemporaries: An Observer Appreciation* (London, Hodder and Stoughton, 1965), 65–80

Jacob, Ian, 'His Finest Hour', *Atlantic Monthly*, 215/3 (March 1965), 81–8

———, Ian, 'Lieutenant General Sir Ian Jacob', in John Wheeler-Bennett (ed.), *Action This Day. Working With Churchill* (London, Macmillan, 1968), 158–218

Jeffrey, Robin, 'The Punjab Boundary Force and the Problem of Order', August 1947, *Modern Asian Studies*, 8/4 (1974), 491–521

Kinna, Patrick, in Cita Stelzer, *Working with Winston. The Unsung Women behind Britain's Greatest Statesman* (London, Head of Zeus, 2019), 65–95

Krishan, Y, 'Mountbatten and the Partition of India', *History,* 68/222 (1983), 22–38

Leventhal, Fred, '"A Tonic to the Nation": The Festival of Britain, 1951', *Albion 27/3* (Autumn 1995), 445–53

Lewin, Ronald, 'Ismay', in Hew Strachan (ed.), *Military Lives* (Oxford, Oxford University Press, 2002), 232–6

Mahnken, Thomas, 'US Grand Strategy, 1939–1945', in John Ferris and Evan Mawdsley, *The Cambridge History of the Second World War, vol. 1, Fighting the War* (Cambridge, Cambridge University Press, 2015), 189–212

Montgomery, Bernard, 'The Panorama of Warfare in a Nuclear Age', *Journal of the Royal United Services Institute*, 101/604 (1956), 503–20

Moore, Robin, 'Imperial India 1858–1914', in Andrew Porter (ed.), *The Oxford History of the British Empire, vol. 3. The Nineteenth Century* (Oxford, Oxford University Press, 1999), 422–46

Morgan, JA, '"The Grit of Our Forefathers". Invented Traditions, Propaganda and Imperialism', in John MacKenzie (ed.), *Imperialism and Popular Culture* (Manchester, Manchester University Press, 1986), 100–30

BIBLIOGRAPHY

Purnell, Sonia, 'The Influence of Clementine Churchill', in Allen Packwood (ed.), *The Cambridge Companion to Winston Churchill* (Cambridge, Cambridge University Press, 2023), 342–62

Reynolds, David, 'Churchill and the Decision to Fight on in 1940: Right Policy, Wrong Reasons', in FH Hinsley and Richard Langhorne (eds.), *Diplomacy and Intelligence During the Second World War* (Cambridge, Cambridge University Press, 1985), 147–67

———, David, 'The Diplomacy of the Grand Alliance', in RJB Bosworth and Joseph Maiolo, *The Cambridge History of the Second World War, vol. 2. Politics and Ideology* (Cambridge, Cambridge University Press, 2015), 301–23

Rowan, Leslie, 'Sir Leslie Rowan', in John Wheeler-Bennett (ed.), *Action This Day. Working With Churchill* (London, Macmillan, 1968), 241–67

Sinnreich, Richard Hart, 'The Influence of Culture on the Victorian British Army', in Peter Mansoor and Williamson Murray (eds.), *The Culture of Military Organizations* (Cambridge, Cambridge University Press, 2019), 155–84

Sweetman, John, 'A Process of Evolution: Command and Control in Peacetime', in John Sweetman, *Sword and Mace: Twentieth-Century Civil-Military Relations in Britain* (London, Brassey's, 1986), 19–56

Taylor, Victoria, 'Churchill and the Bombing Campaign', in Allen Packwood (ed.), *The Cambridge Companion to Winston Churchill* (Cambridge, Cambridge University Press, 2023), 316–41

Villa, Brian Loring, 'Mountbatten, the British Chiefs of Staff, and Approval for the Dieppe Raid', *The Journal of Military History*, 54/2 (April 1990), 201–27

———, Brian Loring and Henshaw, Peter, 'Notes and Comments: The Dieppe Raid Debate', *The Canadian Historical Review* 79/2 (June 1998), 304–329

Wright, Paul, 'The Festival of Britain: Some Memories', *RSA Journal*, 143/5459 (1995), 52–5

2. Books

Addison, Paul, *The Road to 1945. British Politics and the Second World War* (London, Jonathan Cape 1994)

Astley, Joan Bright, *The Inner Circle: A View of War at the Top* (London, Hutchinson, 1971)

Banham, Mary, and Hillier, Bevis (eds.), A *Tonic to the Nation. The Festival of Britain 1951* (London, Thames and Hudson, 1976)

Beachey, Ray, *The Warrior Mullah. The Horn Aflame 1892-1920* (London, Bellew Publishing, 1990)

Beevor, Antony, *D-Day. The Battle for Normandy* (London, Viking, 2009)

Bishop, Patrick, *Operation Jubilee. Dieppe, 1942: The Folly and the Sacrifice* (London, Viking, 2021)

Bond, Brian, *British Military Policy between the Two World Wars* (Oxford, Clarendon Press, 1980)

———, Brian, *Britain's Two World Wars Against Germany. Myth, Memory and the Distortion of Hindsight* (Cambridge, Cambridge University Press, 2014)

BIBLIOGRAPHY

Bouverie, Tim, *Appeasing Hitler. Chamberlain, Churchill and the Road to War* (London, Penguin Random House, 2019)

Bowman, Timothy, *The Military Papers of Field Marshal Sir Claude Auchinleck: vol. 1, 1940-42* (Woodbridge, Boydell Press, 2021)

Boyle, Andrew, *Trenchard* (London, Collins, 1962)

Carter, Lionel, *Mountbatten's Report on the Last Viceroyalty: 22 March–15 August 1947* (New Delhi, Manohar, 2003)

———, Lionel, *Partition Observed. British Official Reports from South East Asia, 14 August-31 December 1947* (New Delhi, Manohar, 2011)

Churchill, Winston, *The Story of the Malakand Field Force* (London, Thomas Nelson & Sons, 1916)

Cohen, Elliot, *Supreme Command. Soldiers, Statesmen and Leadership in War* (London, Simon and Schuster, 2003)

Colville, John, *Man of Valour: The Life of Field Marshal the Viscount Gort, VC, GCB, DSO, MVO, MC* (London, Collins, 1972)

———, John, *Winston Churchill and his Inner Circle* (New York, Simon and Schuster, 1981)

———, John, *Footprints in Time* (London, Century, 1985)

Connell, John, *Auchinleck. A Biography of Field Marshal Sir Claude Auchinleck* (London, Cassell, 1959)

Coote, Colin, *Editorial. The Memoirs of Colin R Coote* (London, Eyre and Spottiswoode, 1965)

Cosgrave, Patrick, *Churchill at War* (London, Collins, 1974)

Cray, Ed, *General of the Army. George C Marshall, Soldier and Statesman* (New York, Cooper Square Press, 2000)

Crosswell, Daniel, *Beetle: The Life of General Walter Bedell Smith* (Lexington, University Press of Kentucky, 2010)

Dewey, Clive, *Anglo-Indian Attitudes. The Mind of the Indian Civil Service* (London, The Hambledon Press, 1993)

Downing, Taylor, *1942. Britain at the Brink* (London, Little, Brown, 2022)

Dutfield, Michael, *A Marriage of Inconvenience: The Persecution of Ruth and Seretse Khama* (London, Unwin Hyman, 1990),

Edgerton, David, *Britain's War Machine* (London, Allen Lane, 2012)

Ehrman, John, *Grand Strategy, vol. 5, August 1943-September 1944* (London, HMSO, 1956)

———, John, *Grand Strategy, vol. 6, October 1944-August* 1945 (London, HMSO, 1956)

Farrell, Brian, *The Basis and Making of British Grand Strategy, 1940-1945: Was There a Plan?* (Lewiston, Lampeter, 1998)

Fennell, Jonathan, *Fighting the People's War. The British and Commonwealth Armies and the Second World War* (Cambridge, Cambridge University Press, 2019)

Fishman, Jack, *My Darling Clementine* (London, WH Allen, 1963)

Fraser, David, *Alanbrooke* (London, Collins, 1982)

French, David, *Deterrence, Coercion and Appeasement: British Grand Strategy, 1919-1940* (Oxford, Oxford University Press, 2022)

Gelb, Norman, *Ike and Monty: Generals at War* (London, Constable, 1994)

Gibbs, Norman, *Grand Strategy vol. 1, Rearmament Policy* (London HMSO, 1976)

BIBLIOGRAPHY

Gilbert, Martin, *Winston S Churchill, vol. 5, The Prophet of Truth, 1922-1939* (London, Heinemann, 1997)

————, Martin, *Winston S Churchill, vol. 6, Finest Hour, 1939-1941* (London, Heinemann, 1983)

————, Martin, *Winston S Churchill, vol. 7, Road to Victory, 1941-1945* (London, Heinemann, 1986)

————, Martin, *Churchill: A Life* (London, Heinemann, 1991),

————, Martin, *The Churchill Documents, vol. 15, Never Surrender, May-December 1940* (Hillsdale, Hillsdale College Press, 2011)

————, Martin, *The Churchill Documents, vol. 16, The Ever-Widening War, 1941* (Hillsdale, Hillsdale College Press, 2011)

————, Martin, *The Churchill Documents, vol. 19, Fateful Questions, September 1943 to April 1944* (Hillsdale, Hillsdale College Press, 2011)

Gilmour, David, *The Ruling Caste. Imperial Lives in the Victorian Raj* (London, Pimlico, 2007)

————, David, *The British in India. Three Centuries of Ambition and Experience* (London, Penguin Books, 2019)

Goodman, Michael, *The Official History of the Joint Intelligence Committee* (Abingdon, Routledge, 2014)

Greenberger, Allen, *The British Image of India: A Study in the Literature of Imperialism, 1880-1960* (Oxford, Oxford University Press, 1969)

Gwyer, JMA and Butler, JRM, *Grand Strategy, vol. 3, June 1941-August 1942* (London, HMSO, 1956)

Hamid, Shahid, *Disastrous Twilight. A Personal Record of the Partition of India* (London, Leo Cooper, 1993)

Hamilton, Nigel, *Monty: The Making of a General. 1887-1942* (London, Hamish Hamilton, 1981)

————, Nigel, *Monty: The Field Marshal 1944-1976* (London, Hamish Hamilton, 1986)

Harriman, Averell and Abel, Elie, *Special Envoy to Churchill and Stalin 1941-1946* (London, Hutchinson, 1976)

Hastings, Max, *Finest Years. Churchill as Warlord 1940-45* (London, Harper Press, 2009)

Hastings, Max, *Operation Pedestal. The Fleet that Battled to Malta 1942* (London, William Collins, 2021)

Hendrickson, Ryan, *Diplomacy and War at NATO: The Secretary General and Military Action after the Cold War* (Columbia, University of Missouri Press, 2006)

Hennessy, Peter, *Whitehall* (London, Martin Secker & Warburg, 1989)

Heward, Edmund, *The Great and the Good. A Life of Lord Radcliffe* (Chichester, Barry Rose, 1994)

Hodson, HV, *The Great Divide. Britain - India - Pakistan* (London, Hutchinson, 1969)

Holmes, Richard, *Churchill's Bunker. The Secret Headquarters at the Heart of Britain's Victory* (London, Profile Books, 2009)

Holt, Thaddeus, *The Deceivers: Allied Military Deception in the Second World War* (London, Weidenfeld & Nicholson, 2004)

BIBLIOGRAPHY

Howard, Michael, *The Central Organisation of Defence* (London, Royal United Services Institute, 1970)

———, Michael, *Grand Strategy, vol. 4, August 1941-September 1943* (London, HMSO, 1972)

———, Michael, *The Continental Commitment* (London, The Ashfield Press, 1989)

———, Michael, *Strategic Deception in the Second World War* (London, Pimlico, 1992)

Howarth, Patrick, *Intelligence Chief Extraordinary. The Life of the Ninth Duke of Portland* (London, Bodley Head, 1986)

Imlay, Talbot, *Facing the Second World War: Strategy, Politics, and Economics in Britain and France, 1938-1940* (Oxford, Oxford University Press, 2003)

Irons, Roy, *Churchill and the Mad Mullah of Somaliland. Betrayal and Redemption 1899-1921* (Barnsley, Pen & Sword, 2013)

Ismay, Hastings, *NATO, The First Five Years: 1949-1954* (Amsterdam, Bosch-Utrecht, 1954)

Jackson, WGF, and Bramall, Lord, *The Chiefs. The Story of the United Kingdom Chiefs of Staff* (London, Brassey's, 1992)

James, Lawrence, *Raj. The Making and Unmaking of British India* (London, Abacus, 1997)

Jardine, Douglas, *The Mad Mullah of Somaliland* (London, H Jenkins, 1923)

Jeffery, Keith, *MI6: The History of the Secret Intelligence Service 1909-1949* (London, Bloomsbury, 2010)

Jenkins, Roy, *Churchill* (London, Pan Books, 2017)

Johnson, Franklyn, *Defence by Committee: The British Committee of Imperial Defence, 1855-1959* (Oxford, Oxford, University Press, 1960)

———, Franklyn, *Defence by Ministry: The British Ministry of Defence, 1944-1974* (London, Duckworth, 1980)

Jordan, Robert, *The NATO International Staff / Secretariat, 1952-1957* (Oxford, Oxford University Press, 1967)

———, Robert, *Political Leadership in NATO: A Study in Multinational Diplomacy* (Boulder, Westview Press, 1979)

Kennedy, Greg, *Anglo-American Strategic Relations and the Far East 1933-1939: Imperial Crossroads* (London, Routledge, 2011)

Khan, Yasmin, *The Great Partition: The Making of India and Pakistan* (London, Yale University Press, 2017)

Kimball, Warren, *Churchill and Roosevelt: The Complete Correspondence, vol. 3* (Princeton, Princeton University Press, 2015)

Kiszely, John, *Anatomy of a Campaign: The British Fiasco in Norway, 1940* (Cambridge, Cambridge University Press, 2017)

Lewin, Ronald, *Churchill as Warlord* (London, Batsford, 1973)

———, Ronald, *The Chief. Field Marshal Lord Wavell. Commander-in-Chief and Viceroy 1939-1947* (London, Hutchinson, 1980)

Lownie, Andrew, *The Mountbattens* (London, Blink Publishing, 2019)

Lysaght, Charles, *Brendan Bracken* (London, Allen Lane, 1979

Macintyre, Ben, *Operation Mincemeat. The True Spy Story that Changed the Course of World War II* (London, Bloomsbury, 2010)

BIBLIOGRAPHY

MacKenzie, John, *Popular Imperialism and the Military, 1850-1950* (Manchester, Manchester University Press, 1992)

————, John, *A Cultural History of the British Empire* (New Haven, Yale University Press, 2022)

Macrae, Stuart, *Winston Churchill's Toyshop. The Inside Story of Military Intelligence (Research)* (Stroud, Amberley, 2012)

Mallaby, George, *Each in His Office. Studies of Men in Power* (London, Leo Cooper, 1972)

Mansergh, Nicholas, *The Transfer of Power 1942-7, vol. 9* (London, HMSO, 1970)

————, Nicholas, *The Transfer of Power 1942-7, vol. 10* (London, HMSO, 1970)

————, Nicholas, *The Transfer of Power 1942-7, vol. 11* (London, HMSO, 1970)

————, Nicholas, *The Transfer of Power 1942-7, vol. 12* (London, HMSO, 1970)

Marston, Daniel, *The Indian Army and the End of the Raj* (Cambridge, Cambridge University Press, 2014)

Mason, Philip, *A Matter of Honour: An Account of the Indian Army, its Officers and Men* (London, Jonathan Cape, 1974)

Menon, VP, *The Transfer of Power in India* (London, Longmans, Green and Co., 1957)

Milloy, John, *The North Atlantic Treaty Organization 1948-1957. Community or Alliance?* (Montreal, Ithaca: McGill-Queen's University Press, 2006)

Milton, Giles, *Churchill's Ministry of Ungentlemanly Warfare. The Mavericks Who Plotted Hitler's Defeat* (London, John Murray, 2017)

Montagu, Ewen, *The Man Who Never Was* (Staplehurst, Spellmount, 2007)

Moore, Charles, *Margaret Thatcher: The Authorised Biography, vol. 1: Not for Turning* (London, Allen Lane, 2013)

Moore, RJ, *Escape from Empire. The Attlee Government and the Indian Problem* (Oxford, Clarendon Press, 1983)

Moran, Lord, *Churchill at War 1940-45* (London, Constable & Robinson, 2002)

Mosley, Leonard, *The Last Days of the British Raj* (London, Weidenfeld and Nicholson, 1961)

Neillands, Robin, *The Dieppe Raid: The Story of the Disastrous 1942 Expedition* (London, Aurum Press, 2005)

No author cited, *Churchill by His Contemporaries: An Observer Appreciation* (London, Hodder and Stoughton, 1965)

O'Keefe, David, *One Day in August: Ian Fleming, Enigma and the Deadly Raid on Dieppe* (London, Icon Books, 2020)

Orange, Vincent, *Tedder. Quietly in Command* (London, Frank Cass, 2004)

Overy, Richard, *Why the Allies Won* (London, Pimlico, 2006)

————, Richard, *The Road to War* (London, Vintage Books, 2009)

————, Richard, *Blood and Ruins. The Great Imperial War 1931-1945* (London, Allen Lane, 2021)

Packwood, Allen, *How Churchill Waged War. The Most Challenging Decisions of the Second World War* (London, Frontline Books, 2019)

————, Allen (ed.), *The Cambridge Companion to Winston Churchill* (Cambridge, Cambridge University Press, 2023)

Page, Malcolm, *King's African Rifles. A History* (Barnsley, Pen & Sword, 2011)

BIBLIOGRAPHY

Peden, GC, *Churchill, Chamberlain and Appeasement* (Cambridge, Cambridge University Press, 2022),

Phillips, Adrian, *Fighting Churchill, Appeasing Hitler. How a British Civil Servant Helped Cause the Second World War* (London, Biteback, 2019)

Pogue, Forrest, *George C Marshall: Ordeal and Hope, 1939-1942* (New York, Viking Press, 1966)

Porter, Bernard, *The Absent-Minded Imperialists: Empire, Society and Culture in Britain* (Oxford, Oxford University Press, 2006)

Purnell, Sonia, *First Lady. The Life and Wars of Clementine Churchill* (London, Aurum Press, 2015)

Rennie, Paul, *Festival of Britain 1951* (Woodbridge, Antique Collectors Club, 2007)

Reynolds, David, *The Creation of the Anglo-American Alliance 1937-1941: A Study in Competitive Co-operation* (London, Europa Publications, 1981)

————, David, *In Command of History. Churchill Fighting and Writing the Second World* (London, Allen Lane, 2004)

————, David, *From World War to Cold War: Churchill, Roosevelt, and the International History of the 1940s* (Oxford, Oxford University Press, 2006)

Rhodes James, Robin, *Victor Cazalet: A Portrait* (London, Hamilton, 1976)

Richards, Denis, *Portal of Hungerford. The Life of Marshal of the Royal Air Force, Viscount Portal of Hungerford, KG, GCB, OM, DSO, MC* (London, Heinemann, 1977)

Roberts, Andrew, *Eminent Churchillians* (London, Phoenix, 1995)

————, Andrew, *Masters and Commanders. The Military Geniuses Who Led the West to Victory in World War II* (London, Penguin, 2009)

————, Andrew, *Churchill. Walking with Destiny* (London, Allen Lane, 2018)

Roskill, SW, *Hankey, Man of Secrets, vol. 2, 1919-1931* (London, Collins, 1974)

————, SW, *Hankey, Man of Secrets, vol. 3, 1931-1963* (London, Collins, 1974)

Royle, Trevor, *The Last Days of the Raj* (London, Michael Joseph, 1989)

Sangster, Andrew, *'Pug' - Churchill's Chief of Staff. The Life of General Hastings Ismay KG GCB DSO PC, 1887-1965* (Barnsley, Pen & Sword Military, 2023)

Sarila, Narendra Singh, *The Shadow of the Great Game: The Untold Story of India's Partition* (London, Constable, 2006)

Sayle, Timothy, *Enduring Alliance: A History of NATO and the Postwar Global Order* (New York; Ithaca: Cornell University Press, 2019)

Schoenfeld, Maxwell, *The War Ministry of Winston Churchill* (Iowa, Iowa State University Press, 1972)

Schofield, Victoria, *Wavell. Soldier and Statesman* (London, John Murray, 2006)

Shortal, John, *Code Name Arcadia: The First Wartime Conference of Churchill and Roosevelt* (College Station, Texas A&M University Press, 2021)

Smart, Nick, *British Strategy and Politics during the Phony War. Before the Balloon Went Up* (Westport, Praeger, 2003)

Smyth, Denis, *Deathly Deception. The Real Story of Operation Mincemeat* (Oxford, Oxford University Press, 2011)

Soames, Mary, *Clementine Churchill* (London, Cassell, 1979)

BIBLIOGRAPHY

Spears, Edward, *Assignment to Catastrophe, vol. 1, Prelude to Dunkirk, July 1939-May* 1940 (London, Heinemann, 1954)

———, Edward, *Assignment to Catastrophe, vol. 2, The Fall of France, June 1940* (London, Heinemann, 1954)

Stoler, Mark, *Allies and Adversaries. The Joint Chiefs of Staff, the Grand Alliance and U.S. Strategy in World War II* (Chapel Hill, North Carolina Press, 2000)

Strachan, Hew, *The Politics of the British Army* (Oxford, Clarendon, 1997)

Sweetman, John (ed.), *Sword and Mace. Twentieth-Century Civil-Military Relations in Britain* (London, Brassey's, 1986)

Talbot, Ian and Singh, Gurharpal, *The Partition of India* (Cambridge, Cambridge University Press, 2009)

Taylor, AJP, *English History 1914-1945* (Oxford, Clarendon Press, 1965)

Terraine, John, *The Life and Times of Lord Mountbatten* (London, Arrow Books, 1980)

Tharoor, Shashi, *Inglorious Empire. What the British Did to India* (London, Hurst Publishers, 2017)

Thompson, RV, *Churchill and Morton: The Quest for Insight in the Correspondence of Major Sir Desmond Morton and the Author* (London, Hodder and Stoughton, 1976)

Tlou, Thomas et al, *Seretse Khama. 1921-1980* (Braamfontein, Macmillan Boleswa, 1995)

Todman, Daniel, *Britain's War. Into Battle 1937-1941* (London, Penguin Books, 2017)

———, Daniel, *Britain's War. A New World, 1942-1947* (London, Penguin Books, 2021)

Toye, Richard, *Churchill's Empire. The World that Made Him and the World He Made* (London Macmillan, 2010)

———, Richard, *The Roar of the Lion. The Untold Story of Churchill's World War II Speeches* (Oxford, Oxford University Press, 2013)

Turner, Paul, *Beacon for Change: How the Festival of Britain Helped to Shape a New Age* (London, Aurum, 2011)

Vale, Alistair and Scadding, John, *Winston Churchill's Illnesses 1886-1965* (Barnsley, Frontline Books, 2020)

Villa, Brian Loring, *Unauthorised Action. Mountbatten and the Dieppe Raid* (Ontario, Oxford University Press, 1994)

Von Tunzelmann, Alex, *Indian Summer. The Secret History of the End of an Empire* (London, Pocket Books, 2008)

Wheatcroft, Andrew, *Churchill's Shadow. An Astonishing Life and a Dangerous Legacy* (London, The Bodley Head, 2021)

Wheatley, Dennis, *The Deception Planners: My Secret War* (London, Hutchinson, 1980)

Wheeler-Bennett, John, *King George VI. His Life and Reign* (London, Macmillan, 1958)

———, John (ed.), *Action This Day. Working With Churchill* (London, Macmillan, 1968)

White-Spunner, Barney, *Partition. The Story of Indian Independence and the Creation of Pakistan in 1947* (London, Simon & Schuster, 2017)

Wingate, Ronald, *Not in the Limelight* (London, Hutchinson, 1959)

———, Ronald, *Lord Ismay. A Biography* (London, Hutchinson, 1970)

Winterbotham, FW, *The Ultra Secret* (London, Weidenfeld and Nicholson, 1974)

Ziegler, Philip, *Mountbatten: The Official Biography* (London, Collins, 1985)

———, Philip, *Mountbatten Revisited* (Austin, Texas, University of Texas, 1995)

3. Websites

Hughes, Michael, 'Lockhart, Sir Robert Hamilton Bruce' (2004), Oxford *Dictionary of National Biography* (Oxford, Oxford University Press), accessed 3 May 2021

Naylor, John, 'Hankey, Maurice Pascal Alers, first Baron Hankey' (2004), *Oxford Dictionary of National Biography* (Oxford, Oxford University Press), accessed 21 January 2021

4. Film

Viceroy's House (Pathé, 2017)

INDEX

Note: Page numbers followed by '*n*' refer to notes.

Abell, George, 207, 228–9, 230, 233

Abyssinia, 43

Addison, Lord (Christopher), 244

Adeane, Sir Michael, 288

Aden, 13, 16

Alanbrooke, Lord, *see* Brooke, General Sir Alan

Alexander, General Sir Harold, 116, 117, 148, 260, 266, 301, 329

Algeria, 119

Algiers, 125, 126–7

Allen, Gordon, 178

Americans, 93–4, 108, 134, 192

Amery, Leo, 86–7, 98, 172

Anderson, General Sir Kenneth, 118

Andover, RAF Staff College, 30–1

Anglo-Afghan War II, (1878–80), 6

Anglo-Afghan War III (1919), 28

ANZUS Pacific Pact, 282

Arnold, General Henry 'Hap', 169

Arts Council of Great Britain, 248

Ashanti Goldfields, 293

Athens, 250, 158, 163

Atlantic Charter, 96

Attlee, Clement, 69, 101, 142, 149, 168–9, 199, 251, 314
  Festival of Britain, 247, 257
  India, 204, 207–8, 211, 217–8, 236, 240, 244, 245, 254
  relationship with Ismay, 171–2, 176, 178–9, 197, 199, 207–8, 217–8, 224, 225, 235, 247, 254, 257
  Wavell, replacement as Viceroy, 205

Attlee, Violet, 206

Auchinleck, General Sir Claude, 117, 226
  dismissal as CinC Middle East, 115–6, 322
  dismissal as CinC India, 234
  Montgomery's disparagement of, 223, 236
  relationship with Churchill, 91, 92, 93, 105–7, 114, 251, 321
  relationship with Ismay, 29, 92, 105, 106–7, 114, 115–6, 196, 209, 214, 222, 234–5, 246
  relationship with Mountbatten, 214, 223, 234–5

Australia, 199, 205, 246, 282

Austria, 49, 148

Auxiliary Air Force, 49

Aylwen, Sir George, 248

Ayrshire, 272

Backhouse, Admiral Sir Roger, 51

Baldwin, Stanley, 33, 41, 45

Balliol College Oxford, 263

Bamangwato affairs, 263, 264

Bannu, 26

Barbados, 297, 298

Barry, Gerald, 248–9, 258

Battersea Gardens, 257
Battle of Omdurman (1898), 64
Battle of the Atlantic (1939–45), 90
Battle of the Somme (1916), 17–18, 129
BBC, 47, 101, 282, 306
Beaumont, Christopher, 227–9
Beaumont, Wentworth ('Wenty'),
    231–2, 246
Beaumont-Nesbitt, Brigadier Frederick,
    86
Beaverbrook, Lord (Max),
    antipathy to Mountbatten, 302
    Beaverbrook/Harriman mission to
        Moscow (1941), 97–8, 132
    opinion of Dill, 100
    relationship with Churchill, 60, 72,
        75, 78
    relationship with Ismay, 97, 188–9
Beaverbrook press, 189, 249, 253
Bechuanaland Protectorate, 263–4
Beda Fomm, 88, 250
Belgium, 61
Belgrave Square, 267
Bengal, 1, 203–4, 203, 215, 218
Berbera, 13
Berlin, 161, 168
Bermuda, 277, 278, 279
Bevan, Lieutenant Colonel Johnny, 111,
    128, 144, 147–8
Bevin, Ernest, 169, 172
Bickersteth, Burgon, 168
Bihar, 205, 210, 211
Blackett, Patrick, 208–9
Blitz, 81, 157, 249
Bombay (Mumbai), 12, 14, 38, 204,
    211, 239, 240
Bond, Brian, 46, 51, 247
Boundary Commission, 221, 227
Bouverie, Tim, 45, 50, 339n9
Bracken, Brendan, 75, 82, 184, 185,
    188, 189
Brammall, Edwin, 129

Briare, 70
Bridges, Sir Edward, 73, 166, 207,295
    future organization of defence, 173
    Military Coordination Committee,
        establishment of, 57
    relationship with Ismay, 187–8,
        250–1
    succession to Hankey, 48,49
    War Cabinet, establishment of, 53,
        54
Bright, Joan, 74, 99, 143, 224, 228,
    231, 233, 312
    conference administrator, 134, 162
    opinion of Ismay, 188, 310, 313–5
    relationship with Ismay, 127, 146–7
    Special Information Centre, 93, 127
British Expeditionary Force, 68, 183
British Legion, 288, 294
British Military Mission (Paris), 68
Brook, Norman, 260, 296, 297
Brooke, General Sir Alan, xviii, 100–1,
    104, 111, 113, 116, 119, 124, 131
    comments on Eisenhower, 117,
        161
    disdain for Mountbatten, 107, 201
    Ismay's comments on, 185, 294–5
    relationship with Ismay, 134, 139,
        143, 153, 176, 183, 193, 152,
        298
    relationship with American Chiefs
        of Staff, 123, 134, 161
    relationship with Churchill, 112,
        114, 117, 126, 128, 129, 133,
        139, 142, 143, 149–50, 152,
        153, 165, 167, 294
Brooke-Popham, Air Chief Marshal Sir
    Robert, 104
Brussels, Treaty of, 255, 279
Bryant, Sir Arthur, 294–5, 298
Buckingham Palace, 36, 97, 145, 166,
    171, 206, 225, 252
Burao, 15–16, 17, 18–9

Burgis, Lawrence, 35, 36, 46, 47, 48, 54, 144, 181–2
Burma, 104, 120, 122, 141, 157
Business of War, The (Kennedy), 295
Butcher, Captain Harry, 119, 176
Byng, General Sir Julian, 28

Cadogan, Sir Alexander, 72, 162
Cairo, 99, 115, 116, 250, 314. 323, 324
Cairo Conferences
    November 1943, 133–4
    December 1943, 135–6
Calcutta (Kolkata), 205, 210, 211, 226, 232
Camel Corps, 12, 14, 15–7, 19–22, 310
Campbell-Johnson, Alan, 215, 221, 224–5, 238, 310
Canada, 260, 276, 283, 286
Carabiniers, 5
Carezza, 252
Caroe, Sir Olaf, 211, 244
Carton de Wiart, Lieutenant General Sir Adrian, 14–15, 17, 18, 305
    comment on Ismay, 310
    Ismay plans biography of, 304
    Somaliland, 14, 15
Casablanca Conference, 121–6
Casey, Sir Richard, 149, 155, 157, 164, 169, 204, 246
Cavendish-Bentinck, Victor, 189
Chamberlain, Neville, 45–6, 52, 61, 65
    appointment of Ismay as CID secretary, 48
    appointment of Ismay as member of Chiefs of Staff Committee, 60
    establishment of War Cabinet, 53
    influence of Sir Horace Wilson, 55
    Ismay's advice pre-Munich meeting, 49–50
    replacement of Inskip by Chatfield, 59

visit to France with Ismay, 56
Chance, Neville, 110
Chance, Patricia, 288
Chandos, Lord, *see* Lyttleton, Oliver
Chaney, Major General James, 95, 97
Charterhouse School, 3–4, 30, 293
Chartwell, 110, 178, 206, 225, 283, 306, 307
Chatfield, Admiral of the Fleet, Lord (Ernle), 52, 56, 59. 109, 206
Cheltenham, 215, 231
Cheltenham Ladies College, 293
Chequers, 78, 79, 81, 86, 89, 90, 96, 101, 125, 193, 278, 280, 312
Cherwell, Lord, *see* Lindemann
Chetwode, Field Marshal Sir Philip, 37
Chiang Kai-Shek, 133, 136
Chiefs of Staff Committee, 35, 107, 119, 159, 235, 247, 296
    disputes with Churchill, 60, 85–6, 87–8, 90, 92–3, 100–1, 105, 114, 117, 129, 139, 141–2, 149–51, 152, 153, 165, 167, 182, 184
    formation of, 32
    Ismay's membership and role, 60, 64, 75, 167
    organisation of, 172, 182
China, 43, 157, 256
Christie, John, 224, 227
    comments on Ismay, 225
    comments on Mountbatten, 211, 228–9, 243
Churchill, Clementine, 101, 129–30, 154, 189, 252, 288, 305, 306–7
Churchill, Mary, 130–1, 189
Churchill, Winston, xviii, 20, 60, 68–9, 107, 120, 122–4, 136, 141–2, 166, 181, 196, 203, 247, 250–1, 256, 309
    Chiefs of Staff Committee, disputes with, 60, 85–6, 87–8, 90, 92–3,

100–1, 105, 114, 117, 129, 139, 141–2, 149–51, 152, 153, 165, 167, 182, 184
cronies/'secret circle', 73, 75, 188
Dieppe Raid, 249, 319–26
Greece, deployment to (1941), 87–8, 249–50
House of Commons, 65, 105, 114, 115, 131
India, 64, 203, 225, 235, 245
memoirs, 178, 206, 249, 252, 254–5
relationship with:
    Auchinleck, 91–2, 105, 114, 115, 251, 321–2
    Brooke, 100, 105, 112, 114, 129, 133, 139, 143, 150, 153, 165, 294–5
    Dill, 85–90, 100–1, 250
    Eisenhower 126, 136, 146, 150, 157–8, 164–5
    Ismay
        pre-war, 20, 33, 44–5, 57–8, 59–61
        wartime, 57–8, 59–61, 63–72, 73–4, 76–8, 81–3, 103–4, 106, 110, 111, 114, 115, 116, 125, 129, 136, 144, 145, 146–8, 150, 151–4, 155, 156, 167, 168, 170, 178, 181–97
        post-war, 218, 235, 249–51, 252, 259, 262, 266, 267, 273, 278, 280, 282, 283, 294–5, 298, 311
    Roosevelt, 96, 113, 124, 134–5, 148
    Stalin, 115, 134–5, 154
    Wavell, 86, 90–1, 249–50
Singapore (1942), 103–4
Soviet threat, 166–7, 177

CID. *See* Committee of Imperial Defence
Clark, General Mark, 131, 132
Clarke, Colonel Dudley, 98–9, 111
Clegg, Beatrice, 1–2, 38
Clegg, Henry, 26
Cohen, Eliot, 194
Coleridge, Captain Richard, 269
Collins, General Joe, 246
Colville, John (Jock), 55, 76, 83, 92, 282, 295
    comments on Churchill, 63, 66, 152, 259–60
    comments on Ismay, 196, 299, 311
    comment on Moran, 364n65
Combined Chief of Staff Committee, 174–5
    background to and establishment of, 95, 102
    heated disagreements in meetings, 112, 114, 123, 125–6, 129–30, 134, 136, 161–2, 321
Commercial Union Assurance, 293
Committee of Imperial Defence, 31–3, 43–5, 52–3, 104, 316, 338n31
Commonwealth Relations Office, 259, 260, 264, 268
Congress Party, 38, 202–3, 210, 213, 215, 216, 217, 221, 240–1
Connell, John, 87, 90, 186, 222
Conservative Party, 230, 249, 256, 258, 259
Coote, Colin, 294
Corbett, Major General Thomas, 116
Corfield, Richard, 14
Cray, Ed, 192
Crimea, 161
Cripps, Sir Stafford, 204, 203, 206, 255
Cubitt, Lieutenant Colonel Thomas Astley, 14–16, 17, 18, 25
Cunningham, Admiral Sir Andrew, 133, 161

relationship with Churchill, 142,
150, 152
relationship with Ismay, 57, 272,
301
relationship with Mountbatten,
253, 281
Cunningham, Sir George, 232, 235
Cunningham, Admiral Sir John, 161,
177, 253
Cyprus, 284, 289
Czech crisis (1938), 50–2
Czechoslovakia, 49, 52

Dakar, 83
Daly, Lieutenant Henry, 6
Danchev, Alex, 64, 76, 88, 95, 100
Dardanelles, 300
de Boisgelin, Gilles, 268
de Gaulle, Charles, 70, 148–9
de Guingand, Major General Sir
Francis, 249
Deakin, William, 178, 206, 252
Defence and Overseas Policy
Committee, 304
Defence Committee, 44, 92, 107, 108,
111, 116, 117, 142, 149–50, 173,
206, 304, 319
Delhi, 26, 27, 37, 38, 208, 209, 210,
212, 214, 216, 223, 224, 230,
231–2, 233, 237, 238, 239, 241
Denmark, 57–8
Desert Army, 100, 105, 114
Dewing, Major General Richard, 194
Dieppe Raid (1942), 114, 116, 120,
197, 249, 310, 319–26
Dill, General Sir John, 65, 69, 98
British intervention in Greece
(1941), 250
criticism of Ismay, 193
death, 156
head of Joint Staff Mission,
Washington, 102, 123, 130

Ismay's superior at the War Office,
40
relationship with Churchill, 85–6,
87–8, 90,
replacement of as CIGS by Brooke,
100
Dollis Hill, 82–3
Douglas, Lewis, 147, 166, 246, 257
Dulles, John Foster, 280, 286
Dunkirk, 68–70, 129
Dykes, Brigadier Vivian, 100

Eden, Anthony, 55, 101, 142, 146, 149,
153, 168
appointment of Ismay as NATO
Secretary General, 262
British invasion of Greece (1941),
250
foreign policy towards Italy (1937),
46
Ismay accompanies to Moscow
(1943), 131–133
meeting with Ismay reference Suez
crisis, 285
NATO council meeting, Lisbon
(1952), 260–1
reappraisal of higher defence
management, 296
resignation threat as Secretary for
War (1940), 86
Edgerton, David, 345n45
Egypt, 88, 89–90, 131, 285
Ehrman, John, 197
Eisenhower, General Dwight, 115–6,
128, 136, 144, 165, 176, 177,
195–6, 283, 285
Bermuda summit, 278–9
British criticism of, 118, 161,
297
Gruenther, opinion of, 305
Ismay acts in support of, 118–9,
158, 252

Ismay's friendship with, 113, 118, 157–8, 166, 174–5, 176, 192, 246, 262–3, 272, 276, 300
Ismay's visits to, 125, 126, 146, 150, 151, 164, 276
Ismay contacts reference Suez crisis, 286
Macmillan, opinion of, 305
Montgomery, opinions of, 287, 329
seeks Ismay's advice before visit to India (1960), 298
Stalin, message to, 164–5
support for US/UK relationship, 137
tributes to Ismay, 192, 305–6, 315
El Alamein, 114, 117, 120, 321
Elizabeth, Princess, 247
Elliot, Air Chief Marshal Sir William, 31, 53, 298, 302
Endow Pass, 19
English Speaking Union, 293
Erskine Crum, Lieutenant Colonel Vernon, 211, 223
European Defence Community (EDC), 275–9
Evetts, James, 305
Evetts, John, 307
Evetts, Mike, 254
Exercise Mainbrace, 274

Falls, Cyril, 249
Fennell, Jonathan, 299–300, 372n111
Ferozepur (Firozpur), 228–9
Festival of Britain, 247–253, 256–9
Finns, 57
Fisher, Sir Warren, 48–9
Fleming, Ian, 93, 74
Fleming, Peter, 302, 304
Foreign Office, 57, 94, 114, 146, 155, 177, 340n22
Forrestal, James, 174, 246

France, 13, 149, 156
declaration of war on Germany, 54
European Defence Community, 275–9
member of NATO's 'Big Three', 272, 283
planning for deployment of an expeditionary force to, 44, 46, 51
planning for Anglo-American invasion of, 132, 135
Suez crisis, 284–6
the fall of (1940), 55–6, 65–72
Frankfurt, 167
Franks, Sir Oliver, 262
Fraser, David, 64
Freeman, Air Marshal Sir Wilfred, 93

Game, Air Vice Marshal Philip, 30
Gamelin, General Maurice, 52, 66, 68
Gandhi, Mohandas, 38, 203, 212, 239
'Garden Suburb', 61, 73, 182
Gardone, 252
Geneva, 283
Genoa, 70
George VI, (King), 97, 108, 125, 145, 147, 166, 170–1, 176, 201, 206, 225, 252, 258
George V, (King), 2
Germany, 44, 52, 54, 57, 95, 114, 251
armistice with France, 72
invasion of Norway and Denmark, 67
invasion of Netherlands and Belgium, 61
invasion of Russia, 96
Ismay's assessment of (1938), 49–50
possible compromise with, 65
rearmament programme, 43
Germany, Federal Republic of, 279, 284

Ghormley, Rear Admiral Robert, 95, 97
Gibraltar, 174
Gilmour, David, 2
Gloucestershire, 26, 294
Gneisenau, 105, 120
Gordon, Group Captain Robert, 23
Gort, Field Marshal Lord (John), 51, 56, 69, 133
    Ismay's opinion of as CIGS, 75
    warning of Singapore's vulnerability, 104
Great Calcutta Killings, 205
Great Depression, 40
Great Exhibition (1851), 247–9
Great War. *See* World War I
Greece, 157, 158
    British deployment to (1941), 87–8, 90, 249–50
    Ismay's attempts to reconcile Turkey with, 284
Green, Betty, 152–3, 268, 313, 315
Grigg, Sir Percy ('PJ'), 193, 250
Gruenther, General Al, 278, 285, 305
Gurkhas, 226

Haldane, Lord (Richard Burdon), 33
Halifax, Lord (Edward), 156, 251
Hall, Read Admiral Reginald, 17
Hamid, Shahid, 200
Hamilton, Nigel, 11
Hankey, Sir Maurice, 31, 32–3, 35, 37, 41, 51, 53, 56, 58, 104, 109
    after retirement appointed Cabinet minister, 55
    antipathy to Churchill, 44, 109
    Ismay's increasing differences of opinion with, 44–7
    recommends Ismay (when an assistant secretary) for awards, 36
    recommends Ismay as his successor, 48

    proposal that he and Ismay share job, 54–5,
    support for appeasement policy, 45
    tribute to Ismay, 206
Harriman, Averell, 82, 109, 246
    acts on Ismay's warning at Teheran conference, 135
    recommends Ismay as NATO Secretary General, 262
    with Ismay at Chequers, 96
    with Ismay at Moscow conferences (1941 & 1944), 97–8, 154
Harvey, Oliver, 68, 114
Hassan, Mullah Muhammad Abdullah, 12–24, 336n42
    background, 13–14
    Camel Corps attack on, 20–2
    defeat of, 22–3
    Ismay's comments on, 22
Hastings, Max, 197
Heinemann, 298
Hendrickson, Ryan, 289
Hennessy, Peter, 291
Hitler, Adolf, 54, 71, 81, 148, 296, 303
    annexation of Austria, 44
    declaration of War on United States, 101
    reoccupation of the Rhineland, 43
HMS *Hood,* 90
Hodson, HV, 302, 372n111
Holland, 61
Holland-Martin, Ruby, 48–9
Hollis, Brigadier Leslie, 79, 80, 125, 183, 251, 295, 310
    comments on Ismay, 186, 312
    deputy to Ismay, 74, 77
    Ismay's breakdown (1943), 136
    Ismay's intention to parachute into France, 69
    Operation Jubilee, alleged role in cover-up, 321

pre-war role, 48, 52, 53
successor to Ismay, 179
Holmes, Marian, 154
Hong Kong, 101, 119–20
Hopkins, Harry, 95–6, 114, 118, 192, 321
Horne, Alistair, 304
Hoskins, Major General Arthur, 19
House of Lords, 109, 179, 206, 246, 264
   Clementine Churchill's introduction to (1965), 306
   defence debate (1950), 255
   Indian Civil Service pensions debates (1948 and 1949), 254
   international security debate (1951), 258
   Seretse Khama debate (1952), 265
Howard, Michael, 46, 118–19, 296, 302–4
Hugh Molyneux, 304
Hull, Cordell, 131
Humphrey, Hubert, 283
Hungary, 285, 286
Hurlingham Polo Club, 36
Hyderabad, 202, 230, 253–4

Imperial Defence College, 47, 76, 247
India and Burma Committee, 216, 218
India, 5–15, 27–31, 37–40, 309
India, Partition of, 199–224, 230, 238, 242, 243, 253, 300, 301–2, 311
   announcement of date of, 218–9
   Cabinet Mission Plan, 204, 215
   Dominion status, 203, 215, 217–8, 224–5,
   Ismay's retrospective analysis of, 240–2
   Kashmir crisis, see Kashmir
   Partition Bill, 226–7
   Partition Council, 226
   Plan Balkan, 215, 217, 240, 310

Plan Union, 215
   Punjab crisis, see Punjab
Indian Army, 6–7, 34, 213–4, 222, 231, 243
Indian Civil Service, 2, 6–7, 207, 212–3, 242, 254, 309
Indian Navy, 204
Inner Temple, 263
Inskip, Sir Thomas, 45, 52
Ireland, 226
Ironside, General Sir Edmund, 56, 75
Ismay, General Lord (Hastings) Ismay,
   family
      aunt and cousins, 3
      children, 29, 31, 36, 37, 40, 110, 170, 209, 230, 231–2, 254, 261, 263, 314
      grandchildren, 288, 305, 307, 314
      grandparents, 1–2, 37,
      parents, 2–4, 18, 23, 39, 40
      parents-in-law, 26, 27, 29, 31, 37, 40
      wife, see Ismay, Kathleen (Darry)
   finances, 4, 8, 26, 40–1, 311–2
   health, 10, 24, 26, 36, 39, 116–7, 125, 154, 185–6, 252, 276, 277–8, 283, 286, 287, 293, 297, 301, 302, 305, 306, 310, 313, 314, 326
   interests and activities
      bridge, 313
      farming, 230, 254, 313
      horse racing, 280
      polo, 8, 10, 11, 26, 27, 29, 30, 40, 215, 231, 313, 314
      reading, 10, 12, 44, 286, 317
      riding, 8, 10, 29, 286, 317
      socialising, 29, 65, 94, 110, 277, 313,
      tennis, 25, 30, 36, 313

personality/characteristics
  equanimity, 87, 185–6, 187,
    310
  intelligence, 3–4, 309–310,
    317
  inter-personal skills, 11, 188,
    189, 192, 270, 271, 310,
    312–313, 317
  integrity, 178, 266, 311, 317
  judgment, 67, 69, 92, 102, 148,
    153, 183, 190, 257, 259,
    298, 310, 317
  loyalty, 188, 190, 200, 222,
    240, 298, 309, 311, 317,
    326
  modesty, xviii, 3–4, 26, 33,
    262, 270, 290, 313, 316
  moral courage, 26–7, 39, 92,
    109, 183, 204, 305
  naivety, 163, 170, 266, 310–1
  patience, 39, 164, 186, 195,
    262, 287, 291, 315
  sense of duty, 63, 159, 171,
    176, 186, 221, 242, 254,
    303, 306, 309, 311, 316
  sense of humour, 31, 78, 187,
    188, 194, 270, 288, 291,
    305, 310, 313, 317
  tact and diplomacy, 39, 75, 108,
    112, 135, 149, 153, 165,
    197, 262, 270, 275, 290,
    299, 300, 312, 317
relationship with
  Attlee, 171–2, 176, 178–9,
    197, 199, 207–8, 217–8,
    224, 225, 235, 247, 254,
    257
  Auchinleck, 29, 91, 92, 105,
    106–7, 114, 115–6, 116,
    196, 209, 214, 222, 234–5,
    246
  Bridges, 187–8, 250–1

Beaverbrook, 97–8, 188–9
Bright, 127, 146–7, 188,
  250–1, 310, 313–5
Brooke, 134, 139, 143, 153,
  176, 183, 185, 193, 252,
  294–5, 298
Chamberlain, 48–50, 55, 56
Churchill,
  pre-war, 20, 33, 44–5,
    57–8, 59–61
  wartime, 57–8, 59–61, 63–
    72, 73–4, 76–8, 81–3,
    103–4, 106, 110, 111,
    114, 115, 116, 125, 129,
    136, 144, 145, 146–8,
    150, 151–4, 155, 156,
    167, 168, 170, 178,
    181–97,
  post-war, 218, 235, 249–51,
    252, 259, 262, 266, 267,
    273, 278, 280, 282, 283,
    294–5, 298, 311
Clark, Mark, 131, 132
Colville, 83, 196, 282, 295,
  299, 311
Cunningham, Andrew, 57, 272,
  301
Dill, 40, 86, 90, 193
Eden, 131–33, 260–1, 262, 285
Eisenhower, 113, 118, 125, 126,
  146, 150, 151, 157–8, 164,
  166, 174–5, 176, 192, 246,
  262–3, 272, 276, 286, 298,
  300, 305–6
Gruenther, 278, 285, 305
Hankey, 36, 44–7, 48, 54–5,
  206,
Harriman, 96, 97–8, 135, 154,
  262,
Hollis, 136, 186, 312
Hopkins, 95–6, 114, 118, 192,
  321

Jacob, 75, 181, 186, 310, 313, 315

Jinnah, 212, 222, 224, 233, 235, 236–7

Kennedy, 89–90, 101, 110, 193, 364n75

Lindemann, 188, 206, 255

Marshal, 112, 156, 192, 300

Montgomery, 223, 297, 306

Mountbatten, Louis, 107–8, 122, 200, 207, 214–5, 218, 219, 223, 224, 227, 231, 234, 236, 237, 238–9, 253, 300, 302, 319–326

Mountbatten, Edwina, 224, 227, 231, 237, 281

Nehru, 212, 223, 298

Pound, 185

Slessor, 30–1, 59, 123, 296

Smith, 114–5, 122, 140, 146–7, 158, 166, 305

Spears, 69, 113, 117, 123–4, 149, 260, 270, 275, 295

Stalin, 97, 134–5, 154

Wedemeyer, 108–9, 112, 246

Ismay, Kathleen 'Darry', 38, 54, 80, 94, 165, 258, 259, 267, 287–8, 297, 301, 307, 313–4, 315

career advice to Ismay, 48, 200, 286

family, 26, 27, 29, 30, 31, 36, 37, 38, 40, 41, 54, 55, 110, 169, 171, 199, 209, 259, 261

first meeting with Ismay, 25–6

health, 26, 27, 30, 37, 41

hosting guests in Paris, 270–1, 280

inheritance, 40, 311

Ismay's letters to, from overseas conferences, 152–3, 163, 169, 184, 245, 261

Ismay's letters to, from India (1947), 210, 211, 212, 214, 215, 221, 223, 227, 230

Ismay's tribute to, 314

reproaches Ismay over Munich Agreement (1938), 50

Ismay, Mary, 36, 40, 170, 209, 261, 263, 314

Ismay, Sarah, 40, 36, 209, 231–2, 246, 314

Ismay, Stanley, 1–2

Ismay, Susan, 26, 31, 36, 40, 110, 209, 230, 254

Israel, 285

Italy, 13, 46, 43, 87, 151, 251, 252, 286

Jackson, William, 129

Jacob, General Sir Claud, 74

Jacob, Colonel Ian, 76, 77, 85, 129, 183, 295

comments on Chatfield, 59

comments on Ismay, 75, 181, 186, 310, 313, 315

doubts about deployment to Greece (1941), 250

Ismay's assumptions about security of Singapore, 103–4

work with Ismay on higher organisation of defence, 172–3, 302–4

Jamaica, 265

Japan, 102

Jardine, Douglas, 13

Jebb, Gladwyn, 283

Jefferis, Brigadier Millis, 74–5

Jenkins, Sir Evan, 211, 226, 228

Jhelum (Punjab), 10

Jid Ali, 16

Jinnah, Muhammad Ali, 204, 205, 215, 216, 218, 234, 235

division of the Army, 222

governor-generalship of Pakistan, 224

Ismay's comments on, 212

Ismay's efforts to influence, 222, 233

Kashmir crisis, 236–7

Jockey Club, 280

Johnson, Franklyn, 51, 339n9

Joint Defence Council, 222, 226

Joint Staff Mission, 95, 102, 269

Jordan, Robert S, 268, 283, 287

Assessment of Ismay as Secretary General, 290–1

Junior Carlton Club, 291

Karachi, 204–5, 233

Kashmir, 11, 223, 230, 298

crisis and accession of, 225, 236–8, 245

Maharajah of, 215, 231, 236

Kelly, Dennis, 255, 304

Kennedy, Brigadier John, 87, 101, 110, 150, 295

clash with Churchill at Chequers, 89–90

criticism of Ismay, 193

Kennedy, Joseph, 95

Keyes, Admiral of the Fleet Sir Roger, 76

Ismay's comments on, 190, 251

Khama, Seretse, 263–6, 311

Khan, Dildar, 9

Khan, Liaquat Ali, 222, 238

Khan, Yasmin, 226–7

Khyber Pass, 5

King, Admiral Ernest, 112, 134, 154, 161, 169

Kinna, Patrick, 191

Kipling, Rudyard, 10, 309

Korean War, 255, 256, 258

Krishan, Yuvraj, 219

Labour Party, 179, 203, 247, 259

Lahore, 236–8

Lake Garda, 252

Lascelles, Sir Alan, 140, 151, 252, 257, 267, 280, 306

Churchill's proposed D-Day trip, 145

Governor Generalship of Canada, 131

Ismay's report of Roosevelt's state of health, 163

King's proposal to award Ismay a GCVO, 170–1

opinion of Mountbatten, 201

pressure of work on Ismay, 139

Lascelles, John, 209

Leahy, Admiral William, comments on Ismay, 126

Leathers, Lord, 260

Lee, Brigadier General Raymond, 80, 90, 94–5

Lend-Lease programme, 96

Lewin, Ronald, 181, 243

Lewis, Bryan, 305

Libya, 91, 100

Liesching, Sir Percivale, 264–5

Lindemann, Professor Frederick, 60, 75, 78, 182, 255, 260

Ismay's comments on, 188

relationship with Ismay, 206, 255

Lisbon, 260, 264, 267–8, 275, 277

Lloyd George, David, 52, 53–4, 60–1

Lloyd, Selwyn, 296

Local Defence Volunteers, 79

Lockhart, Robert Bruce, 38–9, 91, 149, 175, 184, 188–9, 192, 243, 339n60

Ismay confides being tired and sick, 170

comments on Ismay, 90, 168

London Controlling Section, 99–100, 110–11, 127–8, 144, 189

London County Council, 248

Lowndes Square, 77, 246, 259

Lowndes, Ellie, 25

Lownie, Andrew, 200
Lyttleton, Oliver, 60, 260

MacArthur, General Douglas, 140
Macmillan, Harold, 2, 122–3, 283, 296, 302, 305
Mad Mullah, *see* Hassan, Mullah Muhammad Abdullah
Mahnken, Thomas, 124
Maitland-Wilson, General Sir Henry, 156
Malakand Field Force, 64
Malaya, 101, 103–4, 141
Mallaby, George, 136, 186–7, 260
Malta, 133, 161, 322
Malta Conference, 161–2
Manchuria, 43
Marshall, General George, 108, 113, 126–7, 174, 246
    comments on Ismay, 192
    concern at hostility in US services towards Britain, 137
    heated discussions in CCS meetings, 114, 134, 161, 321
    Ismay's comments on, 112, 300
    suggests Ismay as successor to Dill, 156
Marston, Daniel, 372n116
Martin, John, 188
Mason, Philip, 7
McEwan, Lieutenant Commander Ian, 312
McMahon Act, 279
Mecca, 13
Mediterranean, 88–9, 122–4, 322
Menon, VP, 215, 217, 240, 243, 368n87
Menzies, Sir Stuart, 83
Mers-el-Kébir, 188
Mesopotamia, 17
Middle East, 40, 89, 97, 28, 116, 177
Miéville, Eric, 207–9, 216–17, 224, 233

Military Coordination Committee, 56, 59–60, 64
Military formations and units
    4th Indian Division, 226
    Corps of Guides, 11
    Gloucestershire Regiment, 5
    Punjab Frontier Force (Piffers), 6, 8
    Royal Scots Fusiliers, 254
    Somaliland Camel Corps, 14–16, 18–19, 20–2
    33rd Cavalry, 17
    21st Cavalry, 6, 8, 10, 19
Military Intelligence, 40, 65, 177
Milloy, John, 277
Ministry of Supply, 35, 51–2
Mohmand Expedition (1908), 9, 311
Mohmand tribe, 8–10, 64
Molotov, Vyacheslav, 131–2, 154–5
Molyneux, Hugh, 304
Monckton, Sir Walter, 230
Montagu, Ewen, 128
Monte Carlo, 287
Monte Cassino, 141
Montgomery, General Sir Bernard, 11, 116, 117, 144–5, 146, 158, 164, 252,
    comments on Auchinleck, 234, 236,
    Dieppe raid, 320, 322
    dislike of Tedder, 177
    Eisenhower's comments on, 329–30
    Ismay's comments on, 223, 297, 306
    use of nuclear weapons, 285
Montmorency Falls, 130
Moon, Penderel, 302
Moorehead, Alan, 302
Moran, Lord, 192, 260, 364n65
Morocco, 119, 121, 139
Morrison, Herbert, 248, 256–7
Morton, Desmond, 45, 60, 182
    attempt to bypass Ismay, 75
    comments on Ismay, 192–3

Moscow, 53, 96–7, 132–3, 154

Moslem refugees, 232–3

Mosley, Leonard, 242, 301–2

Mountbatten, Admiral of the Fleet,
  Lord (Louis), 107–8, 140, 199–
  201, 205, 221–33, 212, 222, 224,
  227, 243, 253, 288, 296–7, 302–4,
  381n57
  Dieppe Raid, 319–326
  dominion status, 215, 224–5
  Princely States, 214, 230,
  post-Partition violence, 226–7,
    231–33, 235, 236, 238, 241
  Radcliffe Report, 228–9
  relationship with Chiefs of Staff,
    107–8, 119, 303, 320
  relationship with Ismay, 107–8,
    122, 200, 207, 214–5, 218,
    219, 223, 224, 227, 231, 234,
    236, 237, 238–9, 253, 300,
    302, 319–326
  timing of transfer of power in India,
    211, 217, 218–9, 240–1
  work ethic, 210, 219–20, 223

Mountbatten, Lady Edwina, 210, 224,
  227, 231, 237, 281

Mullaly, Herbert, 3

Mullaly, Mabel, 3

Munich, 49–50

Muslim League, 202–3, 213, 221–2,
  232

Mussolini, Benito, 43, 46, 251

Mysore (Mysuru), 11

Nainital, 2

Narvik, 57, 58, 67

Nasser, Gamal Abdel, 284

National Film Institute, 248

National Film Theatre, 259

National Institute for the Blind, 246

National Party, 263

National Theatre, 259

NATO, xvii–xix, 267–291, 312
  assessment of Ismay as Secretary
    General, 289–91
  'Committee of Three', 286–7, 280
  EDC, 275–9
  Ismay's initial action, 268–73
  Ismay's departure, 288–9
  'purpose of NATO', 291
  'Rules for the Conduct of NATO',
    327–8
  'spirit of Geneva', 255
  Standing Group ('The Big Three'),
    272, 274, 276, 277, 283

NATO, The First Five Years: 1949–1954
  (Ismay), 268, 252

Nehru, Jawaharlal, 203. 205, 213, 218,
  227, 235, 239
  Hyderabad, 230, 253–4
  Ismay's comments on, 212, 223,
    298
  Kashmir crisis and accession,
    236–238,
  offer of Governor-Generalship to
    Mountbatten, 224
  pressure on Mountbatten, 219, 223,
    229, 230, 234
  rejection of Partition plan, 216–7

Nel, Elizabeth, 190–1, 312–13

New York, 112, 130, 171, 245–6, 269

New Zealand, 199, 205, 282

Newall, Air Chief Marshal Sir Cyril, 51,
  56, 58, 88, 124, 130

Nicolson, Harold, 115

Noel-Baker, Philip, 245

North Africa, 112, 115, 120, 136, 322

North Atlantic Council, 260–1, 268,
  284

North Atlantic Treaty, 255, 277, 328

North Korea, 255

Northern Ireland, 174

North-West Frontier, 5–6, 10, 26, 41,
  64, 225, 232

Norway, 57–8, 65, 67, 92, 117, 250, 286

Nye, Lieutenant General Sir Archibald, 100

O'Connor, General Sir Richard, 304

Oberkommando der Wehrmacht (Supreme Command of the Armed Forces), 296, 303

Onslow, Milo, 5–6, 17

Ootacamund (Ooty), 11

Operation
  Anvil, 148, 150
  Battleaxe, 90–1
  Bodyguard, 144
  Crusader, 251
  Husky, 126, 127–8
  Jubilee, 319–26
  Madhouse, 205
  Mincemeat, 127
  Overlord, 129–30, 132, 135, 141
  Tiger, 89
  Torch, 115, 116, 118
  Unthinkable, 167, 170

Organisation for European Economic Cooperation, 269

Orly airport, 289

Ottawa, 276

Overy, Richard, 50

Packwood, Allen, 80

Pakistan, 215, 232, 233, 235, 297–8
  division of Indian Army, 222
  Governor-generalship of, 224–6
  Kashmir crisis and accession of, 236–8, 245
  Radcliffe award, 228–9

Palais de Chaillot, 268, 271, 288

Paris, 65–6, 156, 262, 270, 276, 280, 283, 287–8, 315
  Ismay's arrival as Secretary General, 267–8

Ismay's departure as Secretary General, 288–9

Ismay's visits with Churchill, 68, 69, 156

Paris, Treaty of, 275

Pas de Calais, 144–5, 147–8

Pearl Harbor, 101–2

Pearson, Lester, 270, 261

Peck, John, 110

Peshawar, 239

Philip, Prince, 237, 287

Pike, Air Chief Marshal Sir Thomas, 303

Placentia Bay (Newfoundland), 96

Po Valley, 148

Pogue, Forrest, 108, 192

Poland, 40, 54, 143, 155, 164, 166–7, 301

Potsdam Conference, 168–70

Pound, Admiral of the Fleet Sir Dudley, 56, 75, 88
  Brooke's comments on, 116, 124
  disdain for Mountbatten, 107
  Ismay's comments on, 185

Pownall, General Sir Henry, 48, 143, 178, 183, 206, 252, 323

Principal Supply Officers' Committee, 34

Prinz Eugen, 105

Punjab Boundary Force, 226, 232, 241–2

Punjab Unionist Party, 203

Punjab, 5, 10, 215, 218, 228, 235
  escalating violence in, 210, 211–2, 231–2

Quebec, 130

Quebec Conference (1943), 128–32

Quebec Conference (1944), 151–4, 184, 185–6, 298

Queen Elizabeth Hall, 259

Quetta (Staff College), 24, 25, 27–9, 191, 221, 317

INDEX

'Quit India' (campaign), 203

Radcliffe, Sir Cyril, 227, 243
Radcliffe Award/Report, 227, 228–9, 243, 253, 310
RAF, 20, 22–3, 30, 56, 94, 204, 319
Rahman, Abdur, 209, 237
Rawalpindi Club, 27, 29, 38, 311
Rawalpindi, 26–7, 239
Raymond, John, 299
Read, Hastings, 1
Read, James, 1
Redman, Brigadier Harold, 140
Rees, Major General Pete, 226
Reith, Sir John, 47
Rennie, Paul, 259
Reynolds, David, 65, 95, 142, 167, 249, 324, 325
Rhineland, 43
Richards, Denis, 93
Richmond Terrace, 54, 83
Ridgway, General Matthew, 272–3, 277–8
Roberts, Andrew, 71, 100, 112, 121, 141, 148, 156, 164, 229
Robertson, Field Marshal Sir William, 191
Rome, 274
Rome-Berlin Axis, 46
Romilly, Esmond, 101
Rommel, General Erwin, 105, 118, 321
Roosevelt, Franklin D, 96–7, 102, 126, 174,
   acrimonious correspondence with Churchill, 148
   announcement of unconditional surrender policy, 124
   approval of Operation Torch, 115
   Ismay's comments on, 135, 163
   offer of help after fall of Tobruk, 113
   relationship with Stalin, 134–5
Roskill, Stephen, 46, 339n9
Rowan, Leslie, 190, 192
Royal Festival Hall, 248, 251, 258
Royal Military College (Sandhurst), 4
Royal National Institute for the Blind, 293
Royal Navy, 44, 56, 95, 253, 269, 319, 322
Royal Society of Arts, 247
Royal United Services Institute, 51
Russia, 40, 43, 167, 177, 242–3, 277–8
   Finns war against, 57
   relations between Western Allies and, 96
Russians, 97–8, 131–2, 136, 143, 155, 165, 170, 257, 291

Salisbury, Lord, 257–8, 265–6, 288
Sandys, Duncan, 182, 296–7
Sangster, Andrew, xiii, 190, 200, 286
Sardinia, 124, 127
Sargent, Sir Orme, 176
Savory, Lieutenant General Sir Reginald, 214, 235–6
Scandinavia, 57
Scharnhorst, 105, 120
Scotland, 53
Scott, Peter, 268
Sedbergh School, 293
Sefton, Earl of, see Molyneux Hugh
Sevastapol, 162
Shakespeare Memorial Theatre, 293–4
Shea, Jamie, 289
Shimberberris, 15–16
Shone, Sir Terence, 232, 238
Sicily, 124–5, 127, 137
Simla (Shimla), 29, 223, 231
Sinclair, Sir Archibald, 93
Sinclair, Sir Hugh, 49
Singapore, 103–4, 119–20, 141, 203
Singh, Baldev, 218

INDEX

Singh, Gurharpal, 205
Singh, Maharajah Hari
  Kashmir, accession of, 230–6
Slessor, Group Captain John (Jack),
  30–1, 59, 123, 296
Smith, General Walter Bedell, 114–15,
  122, 140, 146–7, 158, 305
  misunderstanding with Ismay,
    167–8
Somaliland, 12–24, 304, 309–10, 311
Somerville, Admiral Sir James, 133,
  135–6, 140
South Africa, 263–4
South Bank Centre, 259
South Bank Exhibition, 257
South Bank, 248, 259
South Carolina, 113, 151
South Korea, 255–6, 258
Southampton, 146
Soviet Army, 285
Soviet military, 163
Soviet Union, 178, 256, 274, 277
Spaak, Paul-Henri, 282, 287
Spaatz, General Carl, 246
Spain, 43
Spears, Major General Sir Edward, 69,
  70–1, 72, 149, 260, 275, 293, 301
  Anglo-French liaison, 68
  Ismay's comments to, 113,117,
    123–4, 149, 260, 270, 275, 295
Special Information Centre, 93, 127,
  313
Special Operations Executive, 173
Srinagar, 11, 230–1
Stalin, Joseph, 96–7, 115, 134–5, 274,
  299
  death and successors, 276–7
  Eisenhower's message to, 165
  Ismay's briefing to, 97
  Ismay's comments on, 97, 134–5
  proposes Ismay's health, 154
Stanley, Oliver, 99, 110–11

Stark, Admiral Harold, 246
Steel, Sir Christopher, 285
Stilwell, Lieutenant General Joseph,
  134
Stoler, Mark, 137
Stratford-upon-Avon, 294
Sturdee, Jo, 295
Suez Canal Company, 48
Suez crisis, 284, 285–6, 310, 314–15
Sulzberger, Cyrus, 272–3, 278–9, 282
Sumatra, 141
Supreme Allied Commander Europe,
  272, 285, 288
Supreme War Council, 52, 69

Talbot, Ian, 205
Tedder, Air Chief Marshal Sir Arthur,
  93, 165, 177
Teheran Conference (1943), 133–6,
  184
Thomas, Admiral of the Fleet Sir James,
  281
Thompson, Commander Charles
  (Tommy), 150
Thorneycroft, Peter, 302–4
Tobruk, 100, 105, 113
Todman, Daniel, 88
Toye, Richard, 184
Tree, Ronald, 297
Trenchard, Air Chief Marshal Sir Hugh,
  20, 22–3
Trevor-Roper, Hugh, 299
Trieste, 148
Trondheim, 58
Truman, Harry S., 168–9, 256
Tuker, Lieutenant General Sir Francis,
  226
Tunis, 127, 136
Tunzelmann, Alex von, 203, 365n5,
  372n111
Turin, 70
Turkey, 284

INDEX

Twenty Committee, 128

United Nations Organization, 162
United Nations, 245, 255, 269
United Service Corps, 294
United Services Club, 77
United States Navy, 95
United States, 174, 203, 272, 277,
    283
    establishment of trans-Atlantic
        alliance, 93–6
    Ismay's visits to, 111–3, 124–6,
        130, 171–2, 245, 260, 276
    National Emergency (1950), 255–6
    Suez Crisis, 285–6
University of Cambridge, 293

Vasilevsky, General Aleksandr, 132
Vaughan, Major General Louis, 27–8,
    191, 221
Victor, Albert (Prince), 6
Victoria (Queen), 202, 215
Villa Säid, 280, 288
Vorontzov Palace, 162
Voroshilov, General Kliment, 132

Walker, Colonel Charles, 31, 33
Wallace, Captain Wendy, 312
War Emergency Legislation
    Committee, 32–3
Washington Conference (1942),
    111–3
Washington Conference (1943), 125–6
Washington, 94–5, 102, 130, 171, 174,
    246, 276
Wavell, General Sir Archibald, 99, 111,
    127, 205
    Ismay's comments on, 91, 190
    relationship with Churchill, 86–88

requests Ismay's support for Bengal
    famine relief, 203–4
transfer of forces to Greece (1941),
    250
vulnerability of Singapore, 103
Wedemeyer, General Al, 108–9, 112,
    246
West Germany, 274–5, 279–81
West Indies, 297
Western Desert, 87, 117, 223, 249
Western European Union, 280, 281
Western Front, 16–17, 28, 64, 157–8,
    164
Western Union, 255
Weygand, General Maxime, 68, 70–1
Wheatley, Dennis, 111
Whitehall Gardens, 31–2
Williams, Ruth, 263–5
Williamsburg, 126
Willingdon, Lord, 37–9
Willis-O'Connor, Colonel Henry, 131
Wilson, Charles, see Moran, Lord
Wingate, Ronald, 99, 128, 207, 286
Wood, Sir Kingsley, 52
Woodham-Smith, Cecil, 302
Woolton, Lord, 260
World War I, 3, 24, 32, 197
World War II, 191, 196, 242
Wormington, 26, 27, 31, 37, 38, 40,
    78, 109–10, 136, 167, 188, 245,
    254, 276, 278, 280, 285, 303, 307,
    315
Wright, Paul, 247

Yalta Conference, 162–4, 301
Young, Desmond, 302

Zamoyski, Count Stefan, 301
Ziegler, Philip, 207, 230